PELICAN BOOKS

THE PELICAN GUIDE TO ENGLISH LITERATURE

4

FROM DRYDEN TO JOHNSON

THE EDITOR

Boris Ford read English at Cambridge before the war. He then spent six years in the Army Education Corps, being finally in command of a residential School of Artistic Studies. On leaving the Army, he joined the staff of the newly formed Bureau of Current Affairs and graduated to be its Chief Editor and in the end its Director. When the Bureau closed down at the end of 1951, he joined the Secretariat of the United Nations in New York and Geneva. On returning to England in the autumn of 1953, he was appointed Secretary of a national inquiry into the problem of providing a humane liberal education for people undergoing technical and professional training.

Boris Ford then became Editor of the *Journal of Education*, until it ceased publication in 1958, and also the first Head of School Broadcasting with independent television. From 1958 he was Education Secretary at the Cambridge University Press, and then in 1960 he became Professor of Education and Director of the Institute of Education at Sheffield University. In 1963 he became Professor of Education and Dean of the School of Educational Studies at the University of Sussex. He is editor of *Universities Quarterly*.

From Dryden to Johnson

VOLUME

4

THE PELICAN GUIDE TO ENGLISH LITERATURE

★

EDITED BY BORIS FORD

PENGUIN BOOKS

Penguin Books Ltd, Harmondsworth, Middlesex, England
Penguin Books Inc., 7110 Ambassador Road, Baltimore, Maryland 21207, U.S.A.
Penguin Books Australia Ltd, Ringwood, Victoria, Australia

—

First published 1957
Reprinted 1960
Reprinted with revisions 1963
Reprinted, with revisions to Part IV, 1965
Reprinted 1966
Reprinted, with revisions to Part IV, 1968
Reprinted 1970

—

Made and printed in Great Britain
by Hazell Watson & Viney Ltd,
Aylesbury, Bucks
Set in Monotype Bembo

CONTENTS

CONTENTS

PART IV

COMPILED BY C. J. HORNE

Appendix

GENERAL INTRODUCTION

In introducing this *Guide to English Literature*, it as well to remember that this is the age of the Digest and the Headline, of the Comic and the Tabloid, of the Bestseller and the Month's Masterpiece: an age when a 'deep-seated spiritual vulgarity ... lies at the heart of our civilization', in the words of the novelist L. H. Myers. Perhaps in response to this, the twentieth century has also been a period of unusually lively criticism, a time when a small number of writers and critics have made a determined effort to elicit from literature what is of living value to us today; to re-establish, that is, a sense of literary tradition and to define the high standards that this tradition implies. At the same time it is also important that this feeling for a *living* literature and for the values it embodies should be given as wide a currency as possible, and that literature – both today's literature and yesterday's – should have a real and not merely a nominal existence among a comparatively large number of general readers.

It is to meet this second need that the *Guide* has been planned and produced; and it is the general state of letters and reading today which has determined the shape that it has taken. For this *Guide* has been expressly designed for those thousands of people who might be described as something less than advanced and specialist students of literature, but who accept with genuine respect what is known as 'our literary heritage'. For many of them this amounts, in memory, to an unattractive amalgam of set texts and school prizes, and as a result they have come to read only current books – fiction and biography and travel. Though they are probably familiar with such names as Pope, George Eliot, Langland, Marvell, Yeats, Dr Johnson, Hopkins, D. H. Lawrence, they might hesitate to describe their work intimately, or to fit them into any larger pattern of growth and achievement. If this account is a fair one it seems probable that very many people would be glad of guidance that would help them respond to what is living and contemporary in literature, for, like the other arts, it has the power to enrich the imagination and to clarify thought and feeling. Not that one is offering literature as a substitute religion or as providing a philosophy for life. Its satisfactions are of their own kind, though they are satisfactions intimately bound up with the life of each

7

individual reader, and therefore not without their bearing on his attitude to life.

At any rate, it is in this spirit that the *Guide* is offered to the general reader. For this reason it does not set out to compete with the standard Histories of Literature, which inevitably tend to have a take-it-or-leave-it attitude about them. This is not a *Bradshaw* or a *Whitaker's Almanack* of English literature. Nor is it a digest or potted-version, nor again a portrait-gallery of the Great. Works such as these already abound and there is no need to add to the number. What this work sets out to offer is, by contrast, a guide to the history and traditions of English literature, a contour-map of the literary scene. It attempts, that is, to draw up an ordered account of literature that is concerned, first and foremost, with value for the present, and this as a direct encouragement to people to read widely in an informed way.

The *Guide* consists of seven volumes, as follows:

1. *The Age of Chaucer*
2. *The Age of Shakespeare*
3. *From Donne to Marvell*
4. *From Dryden to Johnson*
5. *From Blake to Byron*
6. *From Dickens to Hardy*
7. *The Modern Age*

The boundaries between the separate volumes cannot be sharply drawn, and in some instances there is an overlap. Far from being a disadvantage, however, this should help to make the *Guide* a single work rather than seven distinct works. Each separate volume, with the exception of the last, has been named after those writers who dominate or stand conveniently at either end of the period, and who also indicate between them the strength of the age in literature.

Though the *Guide* has been designed as a single work, in the sense that it attempts to provide a coherent and developing account of the tradition of English literature, each separate volume exists in its own right. Thus each volume sets out to provide the reader with four kinds of related material:

(i) An account of the social context of literature in each period, attempting to answer such questions as 'Why did the literature of this period deal with *this* rather than *that* kind of problem?', 'What factors tended to encourage the play rather than the novel, prose rather than verse, in this period?', 'What was the relationship between writer and public?', 'What was the reading public like in its tastes and make-up?' This section of each volume provides an account of contemporary society at its points of contact with literature.

(ii) A literary survey of the period, describing the general characteristics of the period's literature in such a way as to enable the reader to trace its growth and to keep his bearings. The aim of this section is to answer such questions as 'What *kind* of literature was written in this period?', 'Which authors matter most?' 'Where does the strength of the period lie?'

(iii) Detailed studies of some of the chief writers and works in the period. Coming after the general surveys, the aim of this section is to convey a sense of what it means to read closely and with perception, and also to suggest how the literature of a given period is most profitably read, i.e. with what assumptions and with what kind of attention. This section also includes an account of whichever one of the other arts particularly flourished at the time, as perhaps throwing a helpful if indirect light on the literature itself. In the case of this volume, *From Dryden to Johnson*, there are essays on Hogarth and on architecture.

(iv) An appendix of essential facts for reference purposes, such as authors' biographies (in miniature), bibliographies, books for further study, and so on.

Thus each volume of the *Guide* has been planned as a whole, and the contributors have been chosen as people whose approach to literature is based on common assumptions; for it was essential that the *Guide* should have cohesion and should reveal some collaborative agreements (though inevitably, and quite rightly, it reveals disagreements as well). They agree on the need for rigorous standards, and thus they have felt it essential to take no reputations for granted, but rather to examine once again, and often in close detail, the strength and weakness of our literary heritage.

BORIS FORD

NOTES

Notes designated by an asterisk, etc., are given at the foot of each page. Numbered notes are given at the end of each chapter.

PART
I

THE SOCIAL SETTING

A. R. HUMPHREYS

Professor of English, the University of Leicester

To give a clear account, in a single chapter, of a period as long, even though as straightforward, as the Augustan★ is anything but simple. The difficulty is not lessened by the fact that the age is often misrepresented by two prejudices – the one that it was decorative and elegant, a hundred years of costume drama; the other that it was unadventurous and dull, commendable but unimaginative, an age of prose and reason. Some limitations were certainly necessary for the consolidation of its very constructive achievement, but the intention of this chapter is to stress how interesting were its activity in the normal ways of life and its determination to make an enlightened best of human existence. This aim was a worldly one, but the term is not used in any bad sense, for the worldliness was guided by such qualities as imagination, zest, and the devotion of moral and religious responsibility. It is the first age in which we recognize the ordinary man as the norm, but the ordinary man here is not that dreary abstraction the statistically average citizen, but a variety of living persons – the merchant energetic in business, the divine addressing his fellow Christians with faithful good sense, the politician busy with elections and votes, the traveller observing life at home and abroad, the country gentleman directing his farms and estates, the engineer designing his roads, canals, and bridges, the lady in her social calls, the doctor, lawyer, soldier, sailor, shopkeeper, servant, and labourer in their occupations, and the writer comprehending all these as his public. None of these classes or activities of course was new; what was new was that the whole of life in its ordinary aspects became a source of interest and generally of comedy. Whether the record of this life seems prosaic or not depends partly on the writer and partly

---

★ 'Augustan', a term deriving from the prestige of Latin literature in the age of Augustus, and 'applied to the period of highest refinement of any national literature' (*Oxford English Dictionary*), normally refers in England to the years from about 1680 to 1750. It is here stretched from 1660 to 1780 in so far as the outlook of the central period is evident.

on the reader; the writer may fail in vigour or perceptiveness, and
the reader may fail in his sympathy for normal men and women.
But a good deal of Augustan writing does not fail in vigour or perceptiveness and there will always, one may hope, be a sufficiency of
readers ready for a while to forgo the headier passions in favour of
an imaginative sense of the normal. It is necessary first to examine the
conditions under which the normal came to be expressed.

Not the least important subject in literary history is the writer's
sense of his public.[1] What social conditions bore mainly on the
writer's mind? And why did those conditions produce a literature
so predominantly of social record? Apart from the drama, pre-
Augustan writing does little to call to mind any extensive public.
Sidney's *Arcadia*, Spenser's *Faerie Queene*, Bacon's *Advancement of
Learning*, Donne's *Songs and Sonets*, Herbert's *The Temple*, Browne's
Urne Buriall, and Milton's *Paradise Lost* appear to be written partly
for their own sakes and partly for the reader as a single person, a
private auditor, not as one of a wide community. On the other hand
Restoration comedy, the satires and prefaces of Dryden, the prose of
pamphleteers, essayists, and novelists, the addresses of philosophers
and divines, and the verses of almost all Augustan poets call up an
inescapable notion of an extended public, though not always the
same public. They are addressed rather to general than to individual
reception – though their immediate recipient may be a patron, as
representative of cultured taste – and their writers are choosing subjects which will strike readers as a record of what they themselves
know. Why the ordinary reader was interested in the normal rather
than the abnormal will be discussed shortly: the present point is that
a considerable public was coming into view.

The process was gradual and the Augustan period covers its
essential phases. In the last decades of the seventeenth and the first
decades of the eighteenth centuries, the writer wishing to profit by
his writing generally fixed his eye on a patron; he hoped less to make
his living professionally by his books than to recommend himself to
someone eminent in Church or State who would support him directly
or appoint him to civil or ecclesiastical office. This system had its
drawbacks. The writer sometimes humiliated himself (Johnson's
refusal to be humiliated led to his famous letter to Lord Chesterfield,
in February 1755, declaring his independence of patronage): the

patron was sometimes – like Pope's 'Bufo' (Halifax-*cum*-Dodington) – 'fed with soft dedication all day long'.[2] But it did also mix the worlds of letters and society intimately together, and this intimacy is appropriately reflected in Kneller's Kit-cat Club portraits in the National Portrait Gallery. The debt was not all from writer to patron: Godolphin begged Addison to write *The Campaign* (supporting, and dedicated to, Marlborough) for the Whigs, and Bolingbroke was glad to entertain John Philips, the author of the rival Tory eulogy *Blenheim*. The poet Prior entertained the politician Lord Harley; so did Pope the Prince of Wales. Halifax first, then Harley and Bolingbroke, sought the friendship of Swift; and Bolingbroke, Lyttelton, Peterborough, Chesterfield, Burlington, and Bathurst were as favoured by Pope's esteem as he by theirs. Under this system the interests and aims of art and letters were largely those current in the patron's circle, though since he was probably himself interested in politics, economics, philosophy, the Church, or the arts, those aims were not themselves narrow. The general public was in the background; taste was established in circles where social distinction, political importance, and classical reading predominated, and Dryden counted it one of the disadvantages of his Elizabethan predecessors that 'Greatness was not then so easy of access, nor conversation so free, as it now is'.

There were still patrons through much of the eighteenth century, from Queen Charlotte downwards (she took an interest in divines and philosophers like Berkeley, Butler, Sherlock, and Whiston, and also helped some struggling writers like Richard Savage and Stephen Duck, 'the thresher poet'). But in 1709 a Copyright Act had secured to authors certain rights in the publication of their works and so given them an improved chance of bargaining with the booksellers (the counterparts of modern publishers). At the same time the first signs of a wide popular market began to show themselves in a large sale for the more flamboyant sermons and pamphlets of Queen Anne's reign, and the circulation of the early periodicals. There were soon more writers than the market could stand, and these early and middle decades of the eighteenth century are the years of 'Grub Street', of those 'caves of poverty and poetry' Pope describes in *The Dunciad*, and of the hand-to-mouth hack-writing Fielding displays in *The Author's Farce* and in the story of Mr Wilson in *Joseph Andrews*.

Thomas Amory's curious novel *John Buncle* relates how Edmund Curll the bookseller had his hacks sleeping in relays, three in a bed; Johnson in the *Life of Savage* and elsewhere gives a first-hand account of literary poverty in sombre and moving terms.

But slowly the profession established itself. From the late seventeenth century certain kinds of writing proved lucrative; on Archbishop Tillotson's death (1694) his unpublished sermons brought in 2,500 guineas, and early in the eighteenth century the more popular sermons and plays could gain their authors £100, a sum which, in the case of plays, benefit nights might raise to £1,000. In 1712 Addison and Steele sold half their rights in the collected *Spectator* for nearly £600; in 1716, according to Johnson's *Life*, Prior's *Poems* reaped him 4,000 guineas, which the younger Lord Harley doubled. Circulations increased, and periodicals like *The Spectator* both fostered and benefited from wider circles of readers. Addison in particular took seriously his task of educating the public in morality and criticism, as well as amusing it by satire and portraiture. The fact that he could run eighteen *Spectator* papers on Milton and eleven on 'The Pleasures of the Imagination' is a sign of some literary maturity common to a considerable public. The trade began to have its publishing successes, the most famous of which were Pope's translations of the *Iliad* (1715–20) and *Odyssey* (1725–6). These translations were dedicated – it is a sign of the times – not to a noble patron but to Congreve, a fellow-writer, and their popularity was such as to make them the most notable landmarks on the way to professional success, bringing Pope money enough to give him independence and being recognized as striking evidence of the support which, in favourable circumstances, literature could mobilize.

Gradually the taste for reading, and the ability to read, spread with the spread of charitable foundations, Sunday schools, dissenting academies, and the Methodist movement, and circulating libraries and better roads made the procuring of books much easier, even in the country. From the founding of *The Gentleman's Magazine* in 1731 onwards there were periodicals reviewing and popularizing current literature. Johnson commented in the seventh *Idler*, in 1758, that 'the knowledge of the common people of England is greater than that of any other vulgar' (a fact which visiting foreigners corroborated), and in the *Life of Addison* that 'the knowledge which now

[1779] circulates in common talk was in his [Addison's] time rarely to be found'. The public in view during the Restoration decades had been a special and sophisticated circle, with the important exception, however, of the many who bought works of devotion – a large number of titles in the publishers' Term Catalogues are religious and theological.[3] In the late Stuart years it extended to include merchants and the better-off citizens, mainly of London, and under the Hanoverian kings stretched widely, until from the 1740s onwards the heady influences of popular enthusiasm could spread literary reputations with unprecedented contagion. Richardson's success with *Pamela* and *Clarissa*, Sterne's with *Tristram Shandy* and *A Sentimental Journey*, and Macpherson's with the Gaelic romanticism of *Ossian* were portents of an age of popular taste.

This period, then, sees the author facing a radical change in his public and prospects. But this would not in itself make his work what in fact it preponderantly was, a social record; it would merely incite him to provide what his public wanted. The question remains, then, why the public of the time was so interested in its own doings, why it asked less for substitutes for real life than for the recognizable facts of its own existence, not only in the greater part of its literature but in most of its art too. In the best Augustan work social fact is being not only described but felt with a particular reality; its substance, variety, and interest are perpetually being recorded, and social behaviour is both recorded and corrected in the interests of good sense. Indeed, the essence of Augustan literature is that it is integrated with social life, and treats, in their natural idiom, the interests of men in society. In so far as the idiom is modified by some other fashion – for classical or Miltonic diction, for Spenserian or Shakespearian imitation – and in so far as its substance is not the interested acknowledgement of social life, it is the less Augustan.

Why was society so interested in itself and so disposed towards the everyday stuff and proportion of life? Why were its dominant literary forms those of the essay, novel, and social poetry? Why, of the classical poets, was it the civilized sensible Horace whom it most read, re-read, translated, and re-translated? The answers lie in historical circumstances: political, economic, and intellectual conditions were favourable to a practical humanism. English society had crossed a watershed in the middle seventeenth century; dynamic and explosive conceptions of religion and politics, and complex but unstable fashions in prose and poetry, had, experience proved, to be abandoned in favour of modes which would unite rather than divide men, and unity would come most obviously on that common ground where men overlap rather than on the frontiers of individualism where they differ. Englishmen had suffered so much from intellectual fission that they wanted amalgamation. Their sentiments were expressed by Burke when, in the *Reflections on the French Revolution*, he defended England's mistrust of novelty:

> We are afraid to put men to live and trade each on his own private stock of reason; because we suspect that this stock in each man is small, and that the individuals would do better to avail themselves of the general bank and capital of nations and of ages.

The Civil War, and subsequent tragedies like the persecution of Dissenters after Monmouth's futile rebellion in 1685, provoked a wish for harmony. Moreover, economic expansion in town and country was encouraging confidence and co-operation; and in philosophy what Hume calls 'the science of man' was emerging as the focus of attention. As the convalescent invalid (or, say, Cowper recovering from his religious frenzies) sees the very ordinariness of life as blessed, so, one feels, the Augustans received the steady processes of social order almost as a revelation. In normality lay novelty. They were often satirical, since they contrasted the enlightenment men might well achieve with the folly they in fact commit; there are no more scathing comments on unreason than in Rochester's *Satyr Against Mankind* or Swift's greater satires. But what they satirized was departures from the 'general bank and capital' of reason, of decent responsible humanity. This, though it restricted originality, was in the circumstances a source of strength.

If, of many possible strands, we follow first the economic, it is not in deference to current fashion but because economic progress entered deeply into the national consciousness. Defoe's *Tour Thro' the Whole Island of Great Britain* (1724–7) mentions the difficulty of recording this progress adequately, 'from the abundance of matter, the growing buildings, and the new discoveries made in every part of the country'. The medieval and Elizabethan idea of organic harmony

between the parts of the body politic was reinforced and rein-
terpreted in terms of economic interdependence. Much was still
said about the hierarchy of superior and inferior ranks, but more
began to be heard about that 'secret concatenation of society which
links together the great and the mean, the illustrious and the obscure'
(*The Adventurer*, No. 67, 1753). 'The grand affair of business', in
Defoe's phrase, was not only, as it always must be, the main occupation of life: it came prominently to the forefront of conscious attention, largely because the old conventions of limited enterprise were
increasingly dislocated by new opportunities which technical developments and the expansion of trade afforded. 'Not sufficiency to
the needs of daily life', it has been said, 'but limitless expansion
became the goal of the Christian's efforts'.[4] The start of this process
cannot of course be dated; trade and industry have always been a
social concern and doubtless some men have always wanted as much
wealth as possible. Certainly the Middle Ages and the Tudor and
Caroline periods have their usurers and monopolists. Yet the degree
to which economic life was respected was something new. From
about 1660 the nation's conscious concern was the organization of
its practical affairs. Following Bacon, Locke desired man to be

> well-skilled in knowledge of material causes and effects of
> things in his power; directing his thought to the improve-
> ment of such arts and inventions, engines and utensils, as
> might best contribute to his continuance with conveniency
> and delight.

Robert Boyle, one of the founders of the scientific Royal Society
(1662), wrote to a friend in Paris, François Marcombe, about the
practical aims of

> natural philosophy, the mechanics and husbandry, according
> to the principles of the new philosophical college, which values
> no knowledge but as it has a tendency to use.

Important elements of business organization too came into being –
the Bank of England (1694), insurance and trading companies including Lloyd's coffee-house from which sprang the great shipping
agency, and the 'Society for the Encouragement of Arts, Manufac-

tures and Commerce' which has now (1954) celebrated its bicentenary. Encyclopedias of the arts and sciences began to appear, and periodicals ran columns of useful projects. On to this busy stage stepped the man of business, in the role of public benefactor – in literature Defoe's traders and merchants, and characters in periodicals and plays like Sir Andrew Freeport (*The Spectator*), Mr Charwell (*The Guardian*), Mr Sealand (Steele's *Conscious Lovers*), and Mr Thorowgood (Lillo's *London Merchant*), in life the bankers, industrialists, and agricultural improvers.[5] No longer an uncouth money-grubber to be wittily cheated by impudent rakes (which is his role in Restoration comedy), the merchant becomes a figure of honour evincing the 'indefatigable industry, strong reason, and great experience' of a Sir Andrew Freeport, who defends trade as a liberal pursuit. Far from being incompatible with gentlemanliness, Defoe contends in *The Complete English Tradesman*, the wealth of business sustains high place and distinction. 'In this great commercial country', Boswell remarks, 'it is natural that a situation which produces much wealth should be considered as very respectable'. This is the strongest assertion of the middle class, and it profoundly colours the age; that class's emergence has been called an outcome of the Puritan spirit in its energy of self-justification, and works like *The Tradesman's Calling* (1684) by Richard Steele (a nonconformist divine, not the essayist),[6] Defoe's novels and pamphlets, and Benjamin Franklin's *Autobiography* (written 1771–90) have indeed the true Dissenting flavour. Yet it was characteristic not only of Dissent but of the whole nature of the time: men of all sects and creeds were, in fact, taking to business as to a philosophy of life.

The economic and cultural heart of England was London, whose predominance is a commonplace of social history. This predominance, as will be suggested later, was not absolute, yet no reader of Augustan literature can overlook how much London meant in the literary world. Its growth during the eighteenth century, from 500,000 to 900,000, was thought extraordinary; even the ebullient Defoe found it 'a great and monstrous thing', sprawling seven miles from Limehouse to the Earl of Peterborough's mansion at the western end of Westminster. Between 1660 and 1780 London was transformed from a late medieval into an early modern city, not only by the fire of 1666 but by the steady replacement of medieval brick and timber by neoclassic brick and Portland stone, which translated a city in touch with Ben Jonson into one in touch with Thackeray.[7] Yet despite the speed of its change and growth it remained a healthy centre for literature because, while large enough to provide the desirable social and intellectual opportunities, its scale and character were still comprehensible and, in a way, intimate. Journalists, poets, and novelists dealt with this world of coffee-house and tavern, of church, theatre, and club, of book- and print-shop, of street-market, pleasure-garden, and residential square, until no territory seems more familiar; here, and in many a personal record like the *Journeys* of Celia Fiennes, Boswell's *London Journal* and *Life of Johnson*, Horace Walpole's letters, and William Hickey's *Memoirs*, is the portrayed personality of an amply felt place. Such works deal less with individualistic glimpses of life than with communal knowledge, with a participated spirit.

London's special significance was as the symbol of national life; the popular pulse beat strongest there, in the turbulence of mobs, the enterprises of trade, the schemes of politics, the curiosity of intellect, the pursuit of amusement. Celia Fiennes's *Journeys* has pages of lively description which are worth referring to, but the indispensable guide is Defoe's *Tour*. As a government propagandist he was out to make the best possible showing for the existing state of things, and one learns somewhat to discount his superlatives, yet the enthusiasm for the great city rising with its churches, mansions, and commercial houses is much more captivating than any cooler account could be. London was for him, as two centuries before for Dunbar, the flower of cities all – 'the most glorious sight, without exception, that the whole world at present can show'. His eulogies were not unsupported: Marvell had written, in his *Last Instructions to a Painter* (1667), of the multiplying ships which –

> Unloaded here the birth of either Pole:
> Furs from the *North*, and silver from the *West*,
> From the *South* perfumes, Spices from the *East*,
> From *Gambo* Gold, and from the *Ganges* Gems.

A succession of writers recited praises not less eager, and Smollett, prefacing his *Continuation of the History of England* (1761), signalized a high tide in the nation's affairs – 'such a fortunate assemblage of objects as never occurred in any other era of English history'.

Commercial prosperity, then, centring on London and extending its activities thence throughout the world, inspired confidence only slightly chequered with qualms about luxury and indulgence, and we may glance at the interest in practical life it afforded the Augustans. Here was the evidence that Britannia had emerged on to the world stage, that she was likely, in war and peace, to rule the waves, as James Thomson's patriotic poem urged her to do. Thomson, the poetic epitome of the time, elsewhere (in *Liberty*, 1736) expressed the mood of enterprise:

> For Britons, chief,
> It was reserv'd, with star-directed prow,
> To dare the middle Deep, and drive assur'd
> To distant nations thro' the pathless realm.

Augustan horizons were wider and more exotic than we sometimes remember. In Pope's *Rape of the Lock*, Belinda's dressing-table, with 'all Arabia' breathing from perfume-boxes, tortoise-shell and ivory uniting in combs, 'the various off'rings of the world' assembled for her adornment, reflects the enrichment of commercial ventures just as, in its ornate pattern of luxurious products from all the continents, does Addison's *Spectator* paper (No. 69) on the Royal Exchange. The interest in remote lands, of which Defoe's novels are a symptom and Swift's *Gulliver's Travels* a satiric reflection, was greatly heightened by Captain William Dampier's *New Voyage Round the World* (1697, dedicated to Lord Montague as President of the Royal Society), followed by his *Voyages and Descriptions* (1699) and the *Voyage to New Holland* (1703). Throughout the eighteenth century interest in the East was keen: the South Sea Company was launched in 1711 (and the South Sea Bubble burst in 1720): Commodore Anson circumnavigated the globe in 1740–4, Byron's grandfather, Commodore John Byron, in 1764–6, and Captain Wallis in 1766–8, and Captain Cook made his great expeditions in 1768–71, 1772–5, and 1776–9. Eastern trade was a small part only of economic life; the American was far greater (Burke's speeches refer admiringly to its extent and the rapidity of its increase), and the European far greater still. But the imaginative effect of the Orient's luxuries and of its reported wisdom and virtue was much more influential than its actual economic importance; trade was the channel for a wave of Oriental interest which overflowed Europe, bringing (it seemed) fascinating and unusual aesthetics, and a more enlightened morality (whether of the wise Chinese or of the paradisally-innocent Tahitians) than Europe could show outside the works of the ancient philosophers. But that is a digression.

When the Englishman looked around at home he was not less gratified; for most of the century rural England seemed busy and prosperous. It is the sense of local vigour that to some extent counterbalances the dominance of London, and gives Augustan culture a healthily wide basis. Again it is the practical Defoe who in his *Tour* gives the richest sense of the countryside's occupations. Much of the land, it is true, was still unimproved; an estimate of 1696 reckoned one-quarter of it to be barren. It is not wildness that Defoe likes: upland Derbyshire he finds 'a howling wilderness', the Lakeland hills are 'most barren and frightful', and the Pennines, with an 'inhospitable horror', lack not only pleasant valleys but even lead-mines and coal-pits, and so have no attraction for him whatever. But in better circumstances Defoe exuberates; he celebrates the great houses which were the economic and cultural centres of local life, and a whole series of country towns, with particular praise for their social advantages. His particular forte is agricultural prosperity – Kent flourishing with hops, pastures, and 'abundance of large bullocks'; the South Downs covered with sheep; Leominster, Lincoln, the Midlands famous for wool; 'innumerable droves and flocks of sheep' at Boston and on the Yorkshire wolds; 'the land rich, the grass fine and good, and the cattle numberless' along the East Anglian rivers; rich Cheshire pastures, Evesham fruit-orchards, and everywhere 'most fertile rich country'. Defoe's statistics rarely stand analysis, but the important point is the spirit, the belief, of his writing, and it is a spirit which rises also from many other quarters, from Thomson's *Seasons*, Gay's *Rural Sports*, Dyer's *Fleece*, and many an essayist, novelist, and diarist. At the end of the century the quizzical and sophisticated Horace Walpole was as pleased as the serious and plebeian Defoe had been at its beginning; in a letter of 1793 he writes to his cousin, George Montagu, of 'the felicity of my countrymen' and of –

such a scene of happiness and affluence in every village and amongst the lowest of the people. ... New streets, new towns, are rising every day and everywhere; the earth is covered with gardens and crops of grain.

This picture, it may be admitted, was a partial one, drawn at harvest-time in a good summer. Goldsmith's *Deserted Village* (1770) mourns the lost happy peasantry of his youth (a lament partly, but only partly, justified); Crabbe's early poems like *The Village* (1783) are revelations of rural poverty; and economists like Arthur Young were not lacking to point out, as Goldsmith did, the misery caused by the enclosure system, by which the old communally farmed open fields were being replaced by enclosed private estates, and a great many labourers dispossessed, to become an urban proletariat. The major results, however, were happier; farming stock and methods greatly improved, and many a dreary landscape was transformed into fertility and prosperity. The result was to consolidate the pattern of landed aristocracy, well-to-do squirearchy, and substantial yeomanry which forms the bucolic background to much Augustan literature (and later to Jane Austen and Trollope),[8] to produce that scenic change from large featureless fields to the detailed beauty of enclosed meadows and hedgerows, accompanied by an enthusiasm for landscape-gardening and rural beautifying which was perhaps the most fruitful of all aesthetic fashions in England, and finally to improve the countryside with the seemliness of new manors, parsonages, and farms, and with the palatial beauty of great houses which still in their hundreds dominate, with classical porticoes and far-spreading symmetrical wings, the serene beauties of their undulating park-lands.

All this is not so remote from economic life or from literature as it may appear. The development of the countryside was a great eighteenth-century interest; the skill which devised new industrial processes and the development of commerce went also into the draining and fertilizing of land, its organization into efficient units, and the improvement of livestock: the eighteenth century is one of practical adventure, not the less adventurous for being practical. As Mr Christopher Morris observes in his introduction to Celia Fiennes's *Journeys* (1949), there was widespread interest in development:

It must be remembered that a new discovery of England was in progress. Aristocratic house-parties would sometimes go to watch a river being made more navigable or a fen being drained. Treatises were written on Stonehenge and poems on 'the wonders of the Peak'. A new edition of Camden's *Britannia*, brought up to date by Bishop Gibson, seems to have lain on the parlour tables of most well-to-do people. ... Ogilby's wonderful road-book had appeared in 1675, and there were also surveys, comparable with modern directories and gazetteers.

A comparison of Adam Smith's *Wealth of Nations* (1776) with a modern economic treatise throws this sense of man into relief. Everything in Adam Smith is personal activity; the 'nations' whose wealth is his subject are gatherings of men and women. Economics, he knows, can get out of human control; indeed, behind the façade of what man proposes he sees the 'invisible hand' of a disposing God, contriving a result superior to anything intended by shortsighted humanity. But there is no alarm in this, no sense that an economic juggernaut is overwhelming the individual. In the eighteenth-century world of farming, small business, and a merely embryonic stock-market (though there were already some City magnates, mostly Whigs, in the chartered companies), we are still amidst the personal efforts of the single man making his livelihood. Indeed, though Adam Smith's style is more urbane, his world is still that of Defoe, and of all English writers it is Defoe who best gives the human side of economic life, interested as he is in the economic side of human life. His characters keep themselves alive: if women, they exploit their sex, and after each spell as mistress or wife they count gains and losses ('As for me', says Moll Flanders of one inamorato, 'my Business was with his Money, and what I could make of him'); if men, they sail the world, outward-bound with bays and druggets, inward with silks and spices. It is this Defoe world, of traders abroad or citizens and farmers at home, that Adam Smith welds into economic philosophy. His main doctrine, at the end of his fourth book, leaves trade (as he feels God meant it to be left) to 'the industry of private people'. The fatal flaw in this is the non-existence of any wise 'invisible hand', but the point is that this outlook preserved the traditional scale of man in society while allying it with the opportunities of an expanding economy and with traditional notions (reinforced by science) of providential harmony. In its economic as well as its moral philosophy the age was eager to unite 'self-love and social'. Its practical emphasis differed (to generalize with dangerous brevity) from the medieval theological reading of life, the Elizabethans' heroic passion, and pre-Commonwealth religion-and-royalism, but was by no means a mere dehumanized materialism. If literature dealt so much with normal activities, it was because these seemed to take on a new air of constructive vigour and compulsion.

Before economic themes are finally left there is something more to be said on country life (even though its bearing is not strictly economic: a mixed subject cannot be completely disentangled), since an interest in its prosperity was widespread, and since the Augustans are sometimes thought to have limited their horizons to town, and even to London. Country life provided them with bucolic pleasures and occasionally (though rarely) with some approach to 'the divinization of Nature'. Even in Restoration comedy, indeed, the town is not allowed to have everything its own way; Bellamy, in Shadwell's *Bury Fair*, is an admirable supporter of country life. And later, Swift writes to Stella of his willows at Laracor, and the beauty of cherry-blossom and fine days; Steele, in the 118th *Spectator*, speaks of a fine scene as inspiring 'a certain transport which raises us above ordinary life, and yet not ... inconsistent with tranquillity'; Mr Ironside, the pseudonymous author of *The Guardian*, prefers bird-song to the best Italian singers, and likes 'to rise with the sun, and wander through the fields'; Pope evokes the pleasures of rural Twickenham in the 425th *Spectator*; and Sophie von la Roche, a visiting German lady, writes in 1786 of how –

> Nature and man both enjoy noble freedom; the landscape over which hundreds and hundreds of fertile hills extend is set with splendid country houses of the great, and charming well-built farms.

Such pleasures the Augustans were by no means too urbanized to feel. More deeply, however, country life was an assertion of stability, and Augustan literature is that of a pre-industrial society. Many of its concerns are admittedly, as Gay observes, those of the town –

Where news and politics divide mankind,
And schemes of state involve th' uneasy mind,
Faction embroils the world, and every tongue
Is mov'd with flattery, or with scandal hung.

But the slow steadiness of a country economy may be felt behind many a praise of rural retirement, deriving ultimately perhaps from Horace and Martial but felt to be corroborated in contemporary circumstances – in Cowley's *The Wish*, Pomfret's *The Choice*, Lady Winchilsea's *Petition for an Absolute Retreat*, Matthew Green's *The Spleen*, Goldsmith's *Deserted Village*, in Shenstone's and Cowper's letters, in Cowper's poetry, in the patient naturalism of Thomson's *The Seasons*, Dyer's *The Fleece*, and (more sensitive and skilful) in Gilbert White's *Natural History of Selborne*, and in many a country diary like those of William Cole of Bletchley or the more famous James Woodforde. The Augustans had extricated themselves from theological and political fears, and they were not yet seriously under the shadow of industrial or international fears. They inherited a social order (agriculture supported four Englishmen out of five) which linked them as firmly to the past as their spirit of enterprise led them to the future. On this firm agricultural foundation (despite passing dearths and gluts) they might instinctively sense that nothing fundamentally would go wrong.

A comparable, and more conscious, double sense of progress and order arises from the Augustan philosophy of politics. 'Great Britain', the 1708 edition of Edward Chamberlayne's *Magnae Britanniae Notitia* observes, 'is of all countries the most proper for trade, as well from its situation as an island as from the freedom and excellency of its constitution'. That freedom and excellency, consequent on the Revolution of 1688, were a fundamental of post-revolutionary faith[9]; their spirit is that for which the astute statesman Halifax pleads in his *Character of a Trimmer* (1688) – impartial law, latitude in faith, and a middle way between absolute monarchy and mob-republicanism. James II's Roman Catholicism and exercise of royal authority over universities, judiciary, and the Church had threatened constitutional tradition: 'our great Restorer', as Locke called William III, appeared to rescue that tradition and safeguard it for the future. The 1689 Convention Parliament settled the political system on what Burke describes as 'that ancient constitution formed by the original contract of the British state' – that is, the balanced powers of the realm. By its initiative in restoring that tradition, however, Parliament had asserted its own supremacy, and the Court-centred society which (except during the Commonwealth) prevailed up to 1688 yielded to that Parliamentary predominance by which membership of either House bestowed peculiar prestige and privilege.

The new system, indeed, evolved amid violence. There was Titus Oates's anti-Catholic 'Popish Plot' (1678); there were subsequent attempts to block James II's succession (during which the nicknames of Whig and Tory emerged), and explosive episodes like Shaftesbury's manoeuvres against James which Dryden counter-attacked in *Absalom and Achitophel* and *The Medall* (1681–2); there were the executions of Algernon Sidney and Lord William Russell (1683), and Monmouth's revolt (1685) and its suppression. Even when the century turned, the Tory Occasional Conformity Bill (1702) led to anti-Dissenter riots, violent sermons from High Church fanatics, and Defoe's parody of this fury *The Shortest Way with the Dissenters* (1702) which brought him to the pillory. There was a bitter Tory campaign against Marlborough, in which Swift's *Conduct of the Allies* (1711) contributed to the idol's fall in a single month; there were party intrigues, on the verge of civil war, leading to the Whig replacement of the Stuart line by the Hanoverian in 1714; there were the Jacobite invasions of 1715 and 1745; there were strong personal animosities during Walpole's long prime ministership (1721–42), and again over John Wilkes's disputed election to Parliament (1763), and over the American War of Independence and the French Revolution. Yet against this the concern for social order was strong enough to avert disaster. Of many moderating voices there might be said what Johnson said of Addison's *Spectators*, that 'to minds heated with political contest they supplied cooler and more inoffensive reflections'. If a ruling Augustan interest is political understanding, the reason lies in seventeenth-century experience of disaster. The politics of the age could be bitter – bitterest perhaps in the years closely (though partisanly) documented in Swift's *Examiner* papers (1710–11) and *The Four Last Years of the Queen* (written 1713), the years first of the Whigs and Marlborough's triumphs, then of the Tories and Marlborough's fall. But though the invitation to George of Hanover might have precipitated civil war, it did not do so; a peaceful succession inaugurated the long stability of the Hanoverians. Weaknesses abounded in eighteenth-century politics – hostility to reform, electoral violence and corruption, the spoils system, ignorant high-handed justices – but they were weaknesses within a general accep-tance of the rule of law and the autonomy of judges. By a happy circumstance, Locke's political philosophy, which had been long maturing in antithesis to the absolutism of Hobbes's *Leviathan* (1651), culminated in the second of his *Treatises of Civil Government* (1690), a work which so well expounds the balance of constitutional power and the maintenance of the subject's rights that it has become a classic.[10] If political philosophy, even in such opposed writers as Godwin and Burke at the end of the eighteenth century, breathes confident enlightenment, if the great claims made for the normal man in the American and French revolutions are now the dogmas of Western thought, the reason largely is the way Locke's treatise crystallized a long, sensible tradition.

Since the theme of this chapter is the Augustan ethos of normal life, and since the political thought of the age is characteristically concerned with the needs of the normal man (as that useful fiction is envisaged in Britain), Burke (1729–97) earns a place alongside, and in amendment of, Locke.[11] He earns it too in a literary study not only because his ample and animated style is a great accomplishment in prose, but also because he represents an evolution of ideas closely re-flected in literature; the evolution from the prestige of reason to that of feeling is exemplified in the way Burke supplements Locke. For Locke (to compress a complex matter ruthlessly) considered man as predominantly a reasoning creature, and both in political and moral philosophy the Augustans came to find this view not so much wrong as incomplete. Burke's is the most compelling voice speaking for the political importance of instinct, and for the sentiment of history which was becoming immeasurably powerful. In his later works he often seems an oracle of reaction, distrusting any reform, even of admitted wrong. But that is not the central Burke; the central Burke studies the organic growth of political institutions, wants equally to preserve and develop ('a disposition to preserve, and an ability to improve', he asserts, 'would be my standard of a statesman'), and studies human behaviour in the nexus of its place and time. His great speeches on American affairs (1774–5) and his attack on the oppression of India are true historical understanding, whereas his profound antipathy to revolution, rather than evolution, leads him to neglect the causes of the French Revolution in horror at its excesses. But despite this late inflexibility Burke is of all English political thinkers the one most sensitive to growth and adaptation, to a richly organic conception of society. The Burke who, in his *Enquiry into the Origin of our Ideas of the Sublime and the Beautiful* (1757), analysed the emotional effects of grandeur, darkness, and mystery, and so enriched the modes of aesthetic analysis, deepened in politics that psychology of emotion which was to be the spirit of Romanticism.

The politics of the period were not, of course, mainly philosophical. They must figure in accounts of social life because they interested so many men so much. From 1660 to 1800 few notable writers were not actively concerned; to run through the roll-call from Samuel Butler and Dryden to Tom Paine, Godwin, and Burke would be to recite nearly all the major and minor names. They attended on the whole less to philosophical principles than to current political prac- tice, particularly when religion and politics intermingled. Party business, election contests, foreign policy, Church and State, Church and Dissent, the prevalence of corruption – such topics were the perpetual agitation of news-sheets and pamphlets. But under the surface froth the current was steady and assured; Britain was free both negatively (from absolutism) and positively (to exert herself and enjoy the fruits of exertion). This was the liberty rooted (so the belief went) in tradition, and bearing fruit in art and knowledge; Richard Savage celebrated its past and present triumphs in his *Epistle to Sir Robert Walpole*:

> From Liberty each nobler science sprung,
> A Bacon brighten'd, and a Spenser sung;
> A Clarke and Locke new tracts of truth explore,
> And Newton reaches heights unknown before.

It was liberty with a divine sanction: ordered freedom was what God ordained for man. Its guardian was Parliament, the nation's focus ('to be out of Parliament is to be out of the world', said Admiral Rodney), with its nobility-gentry-professional membership not split by any great division of interests.[12] All in all, political affairs were a typical function of Augustan life, with their practical bent, their basic assurance, and their reference to the normal man's frame of mind, reflected incidentally in the numerous (though seldom good) patriotic verses in any collection like Johnson's *Poets*.

There was, then, much in the Augustan background that gave a sense of freedom and harmony. A sociologist, no doubt, could easily deny that Augustan society was free and harmonious; indeed, as the eighteenth century advanced and for various reasons (including the ministrations of the Methodists) the actual circumstances of the poor came to light, complacency began to evaporate. The conditions that hackwriters knew, that are glimpsed in Johnson's life, that Hogarth drew in many of his cartoons, and that his friend Fielding saw as a magistrate and revealed in his sociological pamphlets and *Amelia*, began to press more strongly on the world of letters, though with nothing like the force they were to exert in Dickens and Mrs Gaskell. But our concern here is less with social fact than with what writers from Dryden to Johnson felt about their world, and generally they considered that the standards of the well-to-do were the natural codes of literature, the expressions of sense and civilization, provided that a perpetual corrective of satiric criticism was played upon them. This was on the whole a reasonable and not a snobbish attitude; the Augustans were not foolish enough to equate human worth with social station, and some of their most stinging criticism (the satires of Dryden, Swift, Pope, and Churchill) was directed against those unworthy of the responsibilities of place and privilege. But it was on society's upper levels that economic, political, and intellectual circumstances seemed to have liberated energy for partnership in a sane world, building bulwarks of good sense against tyrants, pedants, and fanatics. Here were most observable what the distinguished French exile Saint-Évremond, whom Restoration society so warmly received, calls 'that natural cheerfulness ... that readiness of wit and freedom of fancy, which are required towards a polite conversation', and that knowledge of philosophy, politics, and polite learning which, he assures us, 'particularly deserve the care of Gentlemen'.

Indeed, gentlemen began, in their well-bred way, to become rather prominent in the Augustan scheme of things.[13] If their attributes are displayed in Addison's *Spectators*, and embodied in Richardson's Sir Charles Grandison, with too much unction they were at least a creditable discipline in behaviour, the more so in that much actual social conduct was boorish and heartless. Gentlemanliness was not mere outward decorum or the show of courtesy; it included all the qualities, including religious faith, moral and physical courage, and mental and physical energy, which make up the force of social life, as well as the culture and considerateness which give it grace. The gentleman, we are informed in the 34th *Guardian*, is 'the *most uncommon* of all the great characters of life', 'a Man completely qualified as well for the Service and Good, as for the Ornament and Delight, of Society'. It was to such a person, insofar as an imperfect world could produce him, that the Latitudinarian divines preached, and journalists, poets, and philosophers directed their works. He was the recipient of Locke's religious *Letters on Toleration*, his political *Treatises of Civil Government*, and his psychological *Essay Concerning Human Understanding*, which seem to be merely the enlightened social man making those practical adjustments to faith, politics, and his own mind which men of sense approve. Locke's pupil, Shaftesbury, the third Earl (1671–1713), took an airier flight; his *Characteristicks of Men, Manners, Opinions, Times* (1711) was the main source of that fashionable refinement in art and morals which became an Augustan code. Yet patrician though his tone, Shaftesbury's aim was to encourage in his fellows the companionable disposition and enlightenment which are 'natural' to man. And Hume's felicitous considerate style equally clarifies his own mind and engages the reader's by its admirable tone: it is the style of the gentleman.

Gentlemanliness, even when the word has a responsible rather than a merely refined connotation, is doubtless an inadequate ideal; in any case it would hardly cover such Augustan figures as Swift, Defoe, and Johnson (though it would Fielding). But it recognized the value of social decency, and in literature it imposed its discipline. An essential element in its art of expression was consideration for the reader, together with such harmony of phrase and effectiveness of image (misleadingly referred to as 'polish' and therefore wrongly seeming superficial) as would best recommend the meaning. The writer's sense of his public has already been discussed, and even as the circles of that public widened its core still remained as his court of appeal – the reliable minority of experienced persons, active and shrewd in the affairs of the world, of sound social standing, and fairly seasoned in classical literature.

To enter on the related theme of education would be to broach too large a subject here. What may briefly be said is that in all its reaches beyond the elementary it served and strengthened the same ideals by instilling a reasonable knowledge of Latin authors and probably some modest skill in Latin composition. Its canons of careful metrics, chosen phrasing, and orderly structure, and its sense of writing as a craft and of the reader as a judge of craftsmanship, bore markedly on the ways the Augustans wrote English. The results were bracing in some ways and enervating in others.[14] Gentlemanliness and a classical training conduced to good prose; their influence on poetry was less happy, though (in view of Dryden, Pope, Johnson, and Gray) not so unhappy as is sometimes supposed. In a kindred spirit the Augustans did much of their reading; they went to the major authors of antiquity (in original or translation) and to those of the Renaissance who best understood human nature (Chaucer, Shakespeare, Cervantes, Rabelais, Molière) or moral truth (Milton). Much else they ignored, and so avoided (at the price of a limited range) the confusions of omnivorous cosmopolitanism. They took their good where it suited them, and they simplified their search by going to the most likely places. If their reading was restricted ('All ancient authors, Sir, all manly', Johnson said of his own education), it did at least reinforce their responsible sense of life and their care for an enlightened coherent civilization. This is the education of humanism; it selects its tradition to produce social man according to the canons of the past's enlightened best: it adopts as models those who have shown how to live well in the world.[15]

The pursuit of social and literary amenity, of classical reading, of agreeable style and 'polite conversation', looks from the outside like dilettantism. The suspicion is not baseless; many of the Augustans have no adequate defence against those accusations of shallowness which it is almost a routine to bring against them. On the other hand there is another routine charge, that of didacticism, which points to a very different quality, and that didacticism, though often tedious, reflects something far removed from dilettantism. For basically the hold of moral and religious faith was still very strong; even the ideal gentleman was incomplete without his Anglican orthodoxy, and lower down in society there were religious impulses cruder but more fervent, where 'enthusiasm' survived from the seventeenth century and Methodism caught hold earliest, where sects splintered apart and zealots saw by an inner light. At many levels religion still provoked intellectual though no longer physical combat; indeed, the second quarter of the eighteenth century has been declared more vigorously controversial than any equal period in English history. What is more important is that (except in some fashionable circles angrily spotlighted by the devout) religion was a continuing concern of life, deeply represented in the work not only of the divines like Archbishop Tillotson, William Law, Bishop Berkeley, and Bishop Butler, but also of laymen like Dryden, Swift, Addison, Johnson, Burke, Cowper, and many others, respectfully deferred to (with few exceptions) by scientists and philosophers, and served with an architectural passion by Wren, Hawksmoor, Gibbs, and their fellows.

'In the last analysis, it is the ultimate picture which an age forms of the nature of its world that is its most fundamental possession.'[16] That ultimate picture depends not only on what an age makes explicit about itself but also, more deeply, on what lies implicit. The Augustan age is not one of metaphysical distinction (except in Hobbes, Berkeley, and Hume), yet a metaphysical fact – its belief in a moral and intellectual Absolute, which it is simplest to call God, establishing moral laws and requiring man to discover and obey them, by revelation or reason or both – is the deepest thing in the Augustan intellectual world. In this the Augustans were continuous with the Middle Ages and deeply divided from the twentieth century: they were, even when deistically inclined, believers.[17] For believers, God has embodied in man that spiritual being which is the supreme fact of life, making him the crowning phenomenon of the created (or evolved) universe, its florescence into spirituality. Juxtapose with this belief, which both Christians and humanists would endorse (and *a fortiori* a Christian-humanist ethos such as the Augustans inherited from the Renaissance), such a statement of the modern 'ultimate picture' as Bertrand Russell once provided in *A Free Man's Worship*, and the difference is seen to be fundamental:

> That man is the product of causes which had no prevision of the end they were achieving; that his origin, his hopes and fears, his loves and his beliefs, are but the outcome of accidental collocations of atoms; that no fire, no heroism, no intensity of thought and feeling, can preserve an individual life

beyond the grave; that all the labours of the ages, all the devotion, all the inspiration, all the noonday brightness of human genius, are destined to extinction in the vast death of the solar system, and that the whole temple of Man's achievement must inevitably be buried beneath the debris of a universe in ruins – all these things, if not quite beyond dispute, are yet so nearly certain that no philosophy which rejects them can hope to stand. Only within the scaffolding of these truths, only on the firm foundation of unyielding despair, can the soul's habitations henceforth be safely built.

However Russell's formulation may be disputed, a world view maintaining an impersonal universe, the merely relative nature of 'truth', and a general meaninglessness of existence (in any sense involving a spiritual end) is the characteristic, though not the universal, modern philosophy. The notion of man as created to obey a divine moral reality through his free will is, though widely accepted, apt to seem rather a mirage in a desert of materialism than a certain truth.

The Augustans were not unaffected by the modern earthquake; they had the materialism and virtual atheism of Hobbes's *Leviathan* to contend against. But they did contend against it, as so blind an error that its refutation could be a matter only of time and energy; there was an absolute truth of things against it. It is easy to quarrel with them for their conformity, for not pursuing their inquiries with more sceptical rigour, for reasserting the old moral and critical commonplaces. But this was not laziness; it reflected the prestige that accepted 'truths' gained by being 'demonstrable', in the sense that heterodoxy, far from being laudable, was as eccentric a divergence from tried experience as if a man denied that the three angles of a triangle make two right angles. This should not be put too sweepingly, no doubt; there is mental independence among the Augustans, and anything but enervation in the way orthodoxy is accepted. Englishmen, and Protestants, were proud of their opinions; Dryden, Locke, Swift, Addison, Berkeley, Shaftesbury, Law, Butler, Johnson, and Burke were not diffident about offering intellectual leadership. But even when, as with the Deists, the conclusions were unorthodox, they generally included a supreme moral authority: the Mosaic laws might be suspect, but those of Nature and Reason would, it was felt, produce a sound and right philosophy of life and were, moreover, demonstrably sanctioned by the existence of God.[18]

Moreover, 'natural laws' were the evidence of God's beneficence. They were not merely statements of verifiable phenomena, such as that bodies fall at fixed speeds, that the heavenly bodies move by predictable courses, or that certain economic causes will produce certain economic results. They were laws in seeming not only to impose such speeds, courses, and results, but also to bear the imprint both of intelligent direction and good will, to be the means by which a benevolent God directed his universe towards the best ends. The notion of cosmic laws as designed for the best ends occurs in the thought of the time with significant frequency, and Augustan literature draws a deep moral assurance from its certainty as to a fundamental spiritual goodness, accessible to man through his conscience and intelligence as well as through Revelation. The point may be illustrated from Colin Maclaurin's *Account of Sir Isaac Newton's Discoveries* (1748), which was efficient and popular (1,300 copies of a large quarto edition were subscribed for). This declares that 'natural philosophy' is to be 'subservient to purposes of a higher kind' (as a 'sure foundation for natural religion and moral philosophy'), and is to lead 'in the most satisfactory manner' to the knowledge of God:

> Our views of Nature, however imperfect, serve to represent to us, in the most sensible manner, the mighty power which prevails throughout, acting with a force and efficacy that appears to suffer no diminution from the greatest distances of space or intervals of time; and that wisdom which we see equally displayed in the exquisite structure and just motions of the greatest and subtlest parts. These, with the perfect goodness by which they are evidently directed, constitute the supreme object of the speculations of a philosopher; who, while he contemplates and admires so excellent a system, cannot but be himself excited and animated to correspond with the general harmony of Nature.

There (and similar quotations offer themselves from scores of writers after about 1650) is the new, confident, natural philosophy reasserting the medieval belief in omniscient, infinitely wise, divine superintendence. In a sense the Augustans had all the advantages; with traditional confidence in God's purposes they could enjoy a new intellectual technique of enquiry (science) which seemed progressively to reveal those purposes as more convincingly admirable.

But why, if the Augustan bases were so traditional, did they provide a foursquare assurance more evident than before the Restoration? There is indeed no more metaphysical certainty in Locke and Berkeley than in St Thomas Aquinas and Dante, no more confidence in natural law than there had been in stoic philosophy or in Hooker's *Lawes of Ecclesiastical Politie* (1594), no more theory of an ordered universe than the Elizabethan world-picture had afforded. In Dante or St Thomas there is a complex structure of faith, for the formulation of which reason has been intensively mobilized and tradition deeply drawn upon. In Shakespeare and Milton there is a poetic sense of life in its context of moral order and disorder. The Elizabethan universe was one of cosmic law. But these systems, it came to be felt, were unsatisfactory because not based on demonstrable fact: they were symbolic inventions of man's mind, myths elaborated to provide life with purpose and relationships but essentially matters of theory, and, moreover, of theory encrusted with superstition. 'Natural philosophy' seemed to make impressively for clarification and rational conviction based on fact. Whatever the technical complexities of Newtonian physics or of biological science (with all the wonders of the microscope), a wilderness of apparently miscellaneous phenomena seemed to be rectified by the co-ordinating power of 'laws' objectively and demonstrably 'true'. These were far more comprehensible, trustworthy, and indeed astonishing than the methods of Aristotelian science (which Joseph Glanvill's *Vanity of Dogmatizing* (1661) calls 'inept for new discoveries'), or of medieval theology, or of pre-Restoration pseudo-science. The old philosophies had left so much, so enormously much, obscure; life had remained, despite all arguments of divine wisdom, so extraordinarily mysterious and incomprehensible that irrationality and superstition could flourish in the absence of evident criteria by which they could be refuted. The new sense of things is expressed in Mulgrave's *Essay on Poetry* (1682):

> While in dark ignorance we lay, afraid
> Of fancies, ghosts, and every empty shade,
> Great Hobbes appear'd, and by plain reason's light
> Put such fantastic forms to shameful flight.

Hobbes's 'atheism' was repellent to the Augustans; his cool analytical reason was not. Under the new dispensation much was still mysterious: the Augustans were not so immodest as to suppose the human mind capable of omniscience. But what was discovered – in particular, gravitation, the nature of light, and the beauties of microscopic biology – seemed to prove a universe so intelligent in cause and effect as to be admirable and reassuring. The scholastic philosophers, it may be said, were as certain of this as the Augustans; God's laws, directing each thing according to its nature, were a supreme witness to divine order. But the novelty lay in the proofs of experiment rather than those of scholastic logic; the metaphors of dawn, of enlightenment breaking on darkness, often applied to this process both then and now are justified. The process was perhaps less revolutionary than it seemed at the time: the 'New Philosophy' would still agree with the tenor of St Thomas Aquinas's pronouncement that –

> The first [stage of God's schooling] is the enlightening of intellect by faith, and this is the most excellent lesson. It is a greater thing that a man have a modicum of faith than that he should know everything that all the philosophers have discovered about the universe.
>
> (*Sermon on the Feast of St Martin*)

But faith seemed progressively to be a matter less of taking the universe on trust than of understanding it. The Augustan enlightenment was no more rational, no more convinced of divine goodness and wisdom, than medieval or Elizabethan cosmogony, but it still broke like a flood of light across a confused sky because the cherished faith in that goodness and wisdom seemed confirmed by such evidence, macroscopic and microscopic, as no man with eyes could fail to see and accept. This was what faith seemed to have been waiting for.

Faith, of course, came not only through the new science but also through religious tradition. To speak of an Augustan tradition in religion may seem perverse, since what first strikes the eye is either apathy or sectarian dissension. The faith of the time is quiet compared with that of the century before or after, but this is not because the tide has ebbed away to nothing but because it runs with a steadier current.[19] It would be a complicated business to describe the structure of religion, with the mutual relations of Church and Dissent, or the divisions of these each within itself; in the briefest compass it may be said that Anglicanism, which had a High Church phase under the Stuart kings (persisting after 1688 with Non-jurors loyal to the divine right of the exiled line), became thereafter Low Church and latitudinarian in the spirit of rationalism, and preached a reasonable faith and the social virtues instead of dogma, or the conviction of sin, or ecclesiastical privilege. Though inspired by Christian charity, its characteristic flavour is ethical: 'our business here', Locke asserted, 'is not to know all things but those which concern our conduct.' Being unfanatical and comprehensive it is apt to seem dull, and above all it feared 'enthusiasm', that ardent sense of divine stimulus which had fired the sects of the seventeenth century. But in its own circumstances it was a sign of maturity and understanding, an honourable attempt to unite rather than divide the Christian faith, and it engaged the assent of the majority of divines and laymen, who had, on the whole, no less serious a sense of their moral responsibilities than their predecessors and successors.

Yet it came to need the force of a new spirit, and it found it (without entirely liking it) in Methodism, the one great movement of Hanoverian religion, originating inside the Church and only reluctantly parting from it. Influenced by their father's High Church devotion, and by the passion of William Law's *Serious Call to a Devout and Holy Life* (1728: one of the century's great books), John and Charles Wesley instilled into their followers in England and the American colonies an urgent sense of religious experience, a sense which shocked more sedate believers by manifestations of frenzy and physical convulsions. Since the Church had subsided into plain sense and reason, and since Dissent now tempered with sobriety its former righteous and godly zeal, there was indeed a psychological need for Methodism and for certain other similar evangelical movements, just as the whole social-reasonable temper of the time was coming to need the deeper emotions of the nineteenth century. Methodism broke like a sudden storm across the placid sky of Anglicanism, reminding men of fundamental power, and of sin and salvation. One side of it was Calvinistic, and worked through dread (this, unfortunately, was the side of Evangelicalism which afflicted Cowper), but the Wesleys' own message was Arminian, the doctrine of salvation for all, bringing a sense of sin but in the very process a simultaneous sense of divine mercy.

The religion of the age is relevant to literature in various ways: firstly, because its conviction of moral truth and moral law, to be found by faith and good sense, was a source of assurance; secondly, because its latitudinarian charity had much to do with the eighteenth century's social sympathies; thirdly, because more than any other subject it deepened the writing of men like Law, Berkeley, Johnson, and Cowper; and fourthly, because the insurgency of Methodism was a sign of something profoundly evolving in the temper of the time, the passing of the phase of reason and judgement in favour of that of passion and 'possession'. To call the Methodist and kindred movements parallels to Romanticism is to beg some large questions but is not really untrue. Hanoverian religion had many faults – an episcopate wedded to politics, an impoverished lower clergy, dull orthodoxy and Dissent, a sceptical world of fashion, and an hysterical evangelical resurgence. Yet with all its faults it contributed much more valuably to the outlook of the time than has been customarily allowed; it inspired much scholarly and pastoral devotion, and much in the way of Christian apologetics. Sermons and theological works abounded, and many of the most popular and impressive hymns date from the period from Bishop Ken to William Cowper.

It remains, finally, to trace an aspect of mental evolution already touched on, under which many miscellaneous phenomena can be, and indeed must be, subsumed – that is, the transition from the dominant prestige of reason to that of feeling. It is true that no sensible Augustan at any time doubted that man is actuated by his feelings – there had been throughout the seventeenth century, and there were throughout the eighteenth, treatises analysing the symptoms of 'the passions'. Yet the triumphs of science, and the clear advantages of being reasonable rather than fanatical in the discussion of religion and politics, invested reason with a high renown. This involved a fresh investigation, on the lines inaugurated by Bacon, of the mind's powers, and as in politics and religious thought the stage was set by Locke, in his *Essay Concerning Human Understanding* (1690). He analyses human capacities in a way dictated by his own thoughtful and practical temperament and by his subject, which is, avowedly, 'understanding', the function not mainly of imagination but of reason.[20] It is the rational mind which receives most of Locke's attention: he is alert for sources of intellectual confusion; he elevates judgement (which analyses and distinguishes ideas) over 'wit' (which unites them by their resemblances, as in a wider sense does what we now call imagination); he is concerned for the clear definition of words and ideas so that the mind can work properly, and his pleas for a more exact use of language were reinforced by the scientists and the admirers of French criticism.

One important result was to produce a basic Augustan style of exemplary clarity, and a confidence that in any context the words mean what at first sight they appear to mean. This is not precisely to say that the Augustan grasp of verbal meanings is supremely accurate; no writers have used words more exactly than Shakespeare or Donne, Wordsworth or Hopkins. But while in these cases the exactness is complex and perhaps inexhaustible, the Augustan exactness is that of clear equivalence of word to thing or notion, an exactness by limitation of range. It may still, as in Swift and Pope, have subtle implications, but that is not frequent; normally it works as Locke recommended, lucidly and without mystifying aura.[21] 'Reason', then, is a powerful talisman in the Augustan understanding of the world, in the critical establishing of clear expression, and in the control of ideas and feelings which might otherwise be extravagant. The characteristic Augustan mode of discussion (Dryden's *Essay of Dramatic Poesy* is a signal example) is much better than the characteristic Elizabethan or Caroline, its ideas being pruned of excess, its tone steadier, and its prose much more persuasive. Bacon, Donne, Milton, Browne, and Jeremy Taylor are magnificent prose artists but as advocates leave much to be desired, not because they were less anxious than the Augustans to sway by the pen, but because the whole apparatus of reasonable argument – a sceptical disposition, a civilized attitude to the opponent, a sense of the audience, an appropriate prose, and the very conception of language itself – needed half a century of development.

If Locke, for his particular purposes, gave reason his predominant attention, he did at least also stimulate psychological analysis, and 'the science of man' is a leading topic of Augustan philosophy. Wherever one looks, there are discourses on human nature – in *The Spectator* and other periodicals, in the *Essay on Man* and other poems, and in scores of moral treatises. What is remarkable, particularly as time passes, is the recognition increasingly given to feeling – in Steele's *Christian Hero* (1701), which upholds the generous emotions; in Shaftesbury's *Characteristicks* (1711), which puts 'our passions and affections' in the centre of attention; in Addison's 'Pleasures of the Imagination' *Spectators* (Nos. 411–21); in the Shaftesburyan portions of Thomson's *Seasons* (1726–30); and in the moral philosophy of Francis Hutcheson, Hume, Burke, and Adam Smith. In critical theory, too, whereas the fashion of Hobbes and Locke is to apply standards of intellectual judgement, the fashion of Dryden and Dennis, of Addison, Shaftesbury, and Welsted, is to transcend 'rules' and rational criteria for the 'grace beyond the reach of art', which only instinct can achieve or appreciate.[22]

In other words, Augustan criticism knows, as well as does moral philosophy, that we react to letters as to life by intuition, instinct, and impulse rather than by reason. And Augustan literature, whose allegiances in the Restoration had been predominantly intellectual (not in a palely logical sense of the word, but one strong and vigorous, whether heartlessly witty or severely thoughtful), became after 1740 predominantly a matter of sentiment (as in Richardson and Sterne, and indeed in Fielding too; and as in Gray, or Goldsmith, or Cowper), exaggerated at times into a luxuriant indulgence of sentimentality, which Henry Mackenzie exploited in *The Man of Feeling* (1771), and Goldsmith, Sheridan, and Jane Austen satirized. It is time to put the rationalism of the Augustans into its place, as a discipline, a process indispensable in the evolution of English civilization, but only subsidiary to the motivating passions of life. If the Augustans sang the praises of reason, it is partly because of reason's intellectual triumphs, and partly because their feelings were strong enough to require control.

Within that general evolution from the prestige of reason to that of feeling there were many related aspects of social morals and literary taste. In social morals the main relevant phenomenon is the Augustans' growing humanitarianism: in literary taste it is their increasing admission of emotions and interests which turn their backs on sense and reason. In respect of the former, the eighteenth-century's characteristic philosophy is 'utilitarianism', whose famous principle is 'the greatest happiness for the greatest number'. The rights of 'life, liberty, and the pursuit of happiness', written into the American Declaration of Independence, were man's due expectations, as Locke had defined them: they might be, and often were, pursued in the spirit of selfishness, but they were often seen also to involve help to others – the attainment of social good on earth was a preliminary to eternal happiness earned by virtue and charity. Since the great concern of Augustan moral philosophy was the individual's relations with his fellows, the major theme was that of general well-being and interdependence:

> Heav'n forming each on other to depend,
> A master, or a servant, or a friend,
> Bids each on other for assistance call,
> Till one Man's weakness grows the strength of all.
>
> (POPE: *Essay on Man*, ii, 249–52)

A social conscience, propagated through poems, periodicals, novels, sermons, and philosophy, bore fruit in works of welfare – the foundation of charity schools, of dispensaries providing medicine for the poor, and of bodies like the Marine Society (1756: for two centuries it has prepared poor boys for a seafaring life) and the Royal Humane Society (1777); the investigation of prison conditions (the devoted life-work of John Howard); the assistance of debtors (the great name here is that of James Oglethorpe, the founder of the colony of Georgia where debtors might make a new start); the rescuing of poor children and particularly of chimney-sweeps. The humanitarian philosophy with its concern for personality involved, too, a growing respect for women (Steele distinguished himself in this respect). As the years passed, women played an increasingly important part in social life, which improved markedly in moral tone and politeness, and in the constitution of the reading public. The later eighteenth century is noted for the expression of feminine taste through the Blue-stocking salons of ladies like Mrs Vesey, Mrs Boscawen, and the famous Mrs Montagu, and the literary activities of others like Elizabeth Carter (who translated Epictetus to general admiration), Mrs Thrale (Dr Johnson's hostess and friend), and Fanny Burney. The long road that female emancipation had still to travel is the theme of Mary Wollstonecraft's revolutionary *Vindication of the Rights of Woman* (1792) where, perhaps for the first time, eighty-seven years before *A Doll's House*, we perceive the lineaments of the Modern Woman, demanding in the spirit of Ibsen and Shaw a full share of civic and domestic rights and duties. Still, social consideration and intellectual respect had advanced as much since the Restoration as libertinism and grossness had declined; literary society of 1800 was in all respects, sexual and sociological, more humane than that of 1700.

The last word must be for that other aspect of the century's emotional evolution, its growing sensitiveness to those moods which lie on the periphery of rationalism. An increasing pleasure in natural landscape, after the geometrical French and Dutch gardens of the late seventeenth century; a reviving interest in Gothic architecture, given a distressing modishness from 1747 onwards in Horace Walpole's Strawberry Hill; sensitiveness to the moods and atmosphere, over and above the human activities, of the country, of which the first landmark is Thomson's *Winter* (1726); a fashion of twilight or graveyard poetry; a taste for pre-Restoration styles, like the Spenserianism of Thomson's *Castle of Indolence* (1748) and Shenstone's *Schoolmistress* (1737–42), or the pseudo-medievalism of the 'Rowley' poems by the precocious Chatterton (1752–70) and the heavily edited balladry of Thomas Percy's *Reliques of Ancient English Poetry* (1765); a prepossession for the primitive, such as Gray showed in *The Bard* and his interest in Celtic and Norse verse, and the public at large in the sensational Ossianic poems foisted on it by James Macpherson in the 1760s and '70s; a cultivation of solitary pleasures, as reflected in Akenside's *Pleasures of Imagination* (1744), and of picturesque scenes, as George Morland's paintings show and William Gilpin's travel-books describe them; a curiosity about exotic and particularly Eastern cultures, and a general responsiveness to those aesthetics of gloom, sublimity, and mystery of which Burke's thesis on *The Sublime and the Beautiful* (1757) is an interesting example – all such things chequer what might otherwise be the too-simple pattern of Augustan sense and assurance, and witness to the complexity of human moods. 'Romantic' curiosities which in the progressive confidence of early Augustanism were scarcely admitted, like an interest in medieval art and letters, became respectable, even the rage; and that tide which set away from unvaried daylight and reason carried the English, and the European, mind towards the social and cultural turbulence of the nineteenth century.

After so miscellaneous a survey it is not easy to sum up. Augustan life is so unspecialized that every social movement may impinge on literature, and, indeed, it is hard to name a single aspect of it which literature ignores. The erudite learning of the seventeenth century had gone and the nineteenth century's specializations had not yet arrived: economics, politics, religion, philosophy, criticism, the arts, and social and natural science were available as the natural interests of the normal intelligent man, to be discussed in the confident vocabulary of sound sense. Inevitably this state of affairs could not long persist; knowledge accumulates and the standards of expertness rise. But in the lively participation of normal minds in the interdependent intellectual life of the age, and in the interaction of self- and social-love which still enabled men to feel their society as an organism of humane proportions, there lies an integration of literature and society so thorough that one responds to Augustan idiom as to the active speech of social life rather than as dream or introversion, and looks upon Augustan letters in the healthy terms of a useful rather than a fine art.

NOTES

I should like to express my gratitude to Messrs Methuen & Co. Ltd for allowing me to use in abbreviated form, in this and other essays in this volume, material on social, political, philosophical, and architectural history more fully presented in my book *The Augustan World*, of which they are the publishers; to Messrs Allen & Unwin Ltd for permission to quote from Bertrand Russell's *Mysticism and Logic*; and to the Cresset Press for the passage from Mr Christopher Morris's introduction to *The Journeys of Celia Fiennes*.

1. For treatment of the reading public, see particularly Q. D. Leavis, *Fiction and the Reading Public* (1932), pp. 118–50; also A. S. Collins, *Authorship in the Days of Johnson* (1928); F. A. Mumby, *Publishing and Bookselling* (1930); A. Beljame, *The Public and Men of Letters in the Eighteenth Century* (1948); and R. W. Chapman, 'Authors and Booksellers', in *Johnson's England* (1933), ed. A. S. Turberville.

2. See *Epistle to Arbuthnot*, lines 231–48, for the sham virtuoso.

3. J. L. Lowes, *Of Reading Books* (1930), pp. 8–10.

4. R. H. Tawney, *Religion and the Rise of Capitalism* (edition of 1933), p. 248.

5. For the 'vertical mobility' of eighteenth-century society, see T. S. Ashton, *The Industrial Revolution* (1948), p. 17, and A. R. Humphreys, *The Augustan World* (1954), chapter ii.

6. For Richard Steele, see Tawney, *Religion and the Rise of Capitalism*, chapter iv, 'The Puritan Movement'.

7. See J. Summerson, *Georgian London* (1945), for building developments.

8. See H. J. Habakkuk, 'English Landownership 1680–1740', *Economic History Review*, x, No. i; G. M. Trevelyan, *English Social History* (1944), pp. 267–9, 273–82, 298–302, 306–10.

9. See G. M. Trevelyan, *The English Revolution 1688–9* (1938), *passim*.

10. For Locke, see H. Laski, *Political Thought from Locke to Bentham* (1920), C. H. Driver, 'Locke', in *Social and Political Ideas of Some English Thinkers of the Augustan Age*, ed. F. J. C. Hearnshaw (1928); *The Second Treatise of Civil Government*, ed. J. W. Gough (1946); B. Willey, *The Seventeenth-Century Background* (1943), pp. 246 ff.

11. For Burke, see B. Willey, *The Eighteenth-Century Background* (1940), pp. 240–52; P. Magnus, *Edmund Burke* (1939); J. Morley, *Burke* (1882).

12. The best studies of eighteenth-century politics are L. B. Namier, *The Structure of Politics at the Accession of George III* (1929); R. Walcott, *English Politics in the Early 18th Century* (1956). See also G. N. Clark, 'The Augustan Age', in *Social and Political Ideas of … the Augustan Age*, ed. Hearnshaw; R. Lodge, *Political History of England 1660–1720* (1910); I. S. Leadam, *Political History of England 1720–60* (1912); W. Hunt, *Political History of England 1760–1801* (1905). There are some pleasant contemporary pages by the visiting Moritz, *Travels in England* (1924), pp. 52–65, 219–20.

13. See F. R. Leavis, *The Common Pursuit* (1952), pp. 103–4; J. R. Sutherland, *Preface to Eighteenth-Century Poetry* (1948), pp. 65 ff.

14. For the influence of Latin verse composition, see A. R. Humphreys, 'A Classical Education and Eighteenth-Century Poetry', *Scrutiny*, viii, 2 (1939), and for general classical background, Sutherland, *Preface*, pp. 51 ff.

15. For the prestige of moral philosophy, see W. J. Bate, *From Classic to Romantic* (1946), pp. 2 ff.

16. See E. A. Burtt, *The Metaphysical Foundations of Modern Physical Science* (1924), p. 3.

17. For continuity of cultural tradition and faith, see C. S. Lewis, *De Descriptione Temporum* (1955).

18. See C. Becker, *The Heavenly City of the Eighteenth-Century Philosophers* (New Haven, 1932), pp. 7 ff., 21 ff., 45 ff., 62 ff. For moral uniformity, see Bate, *From Classic to Romantic*, pp. 13 ff.

19. For Augustan religious life and its relationship to literature, see A. R. Humphreys, *The Augustan World* (1954), chapter iv.

20. See Willey, *The Seventeenth-Century Background* (1934), pp. 290–5.

21. Though it may have overtones and allusions; see Sutherland, *Preface*, pp. 61–2.

22. See J. E. Spingarn, *Critical Essays of the Seventeenth Century* (1908), I, pp. xcii–ci; Atkins, *English Literary Criticism: 17th and 18th Centuries* (1951), pp. 146–85; Bate, *From Classic to Romantic*, pp. 44–8.

PART
II

THE LITERARY SCENE

A. R. HUMPHREYS

The Critical Background

THE vigour and variety of Augustan literature are commonly under-rated. Often supposed to be uniform over a century and a half, it in fact reflects the enormous process by which the late Renaissance becomes the onset of nineteenth-century modernity, a psychology of reason and the conscious mind turns into one of subtle intuitions, a cosmos of stable revealed truth changes to subjectivity and agnosticism, and verbal habits sharing the experimenting exuberance of Jacobean speech moderate into the sensible, well-directed idiom of the Hanoverians. Far from reflecting an unadventurous worldliness, it is the utterance of intelligent men concerned to make the most of human nature, and facing always new problems which compel continual evolution of idea.

Basically, the critical injunction which gained the widest, indeed almost universal, acceptance was the call to 'follow Nature'. This call the Augustans did not invent; the classical stoics had expressed through it man's duty of following moral law as the central cosmic reality, and Renaissance critics had repeated it, in a variety of senses, according as they interpreted 'Nature' as the normal course of the world or as ideal truth by which art should be guided. In Augustan criticism there are almost as many interpretations as there are critics, but beneath them the common sense has been defined as 'the universe conceived of as governed by law, with general human nature as the microcosm of this mechanical order'[1] – in other words, the notion (reinforced by science) that there is a divinely appointed 'right' way for the universe to work and, with respect to man, there is a permanent (as opposed to local or temporary) 'truth' of human behaviour and also a principle (of reason) which man should obey. 'Follow Nature' might mean 'portray the world as you see it' – in that sense Restoration comedy followed Nature and was true to life. It might mean 'show the permanent truths underlying the individual varieties of man' – in that sense Homer and Shakespeare, Chaucer and Molière, were poets of Nature. It might mean 'obey reason; seek order and harmony in life and art' – in that sense the higher forms of philosophy, art, or science (the classical philosophers, the great Renaissance painters, and such moderns as Milton and Newton) had followed Nature, and in accordance with it Rymer claimed that poetry should express the 'constant order, harmony, and beauty of Providence' and Dennis desired the arts to 'restore the decays that happened to human nature by the Fall, by restoring Order'. Clearly an injunction that sets up as a goal the ordinary realism of life, the permanent truth of humanity, and the mind's achievement of transcendent order, is anything but precise; nevertheless, in all senses it directs the study of mankind to man. Following Nature becomes following life, and following life means recording it as one's good sense and wide knowledge tell one that men in general experience it. 'The manners of men' is how Hobbes defines the subject of poetry, and even critics less swayed by the Renaissance prestige of epic agree. According to Pope, 'the best employment of human wit' is to present human nature interestingly. Such concepts as universality (what has always, of all men, been true), reason as being a guide to 'Nature' and 'common to all people' (Rymer), and the 'art' of writing as being the accomplished technique whereby the mind most clearly and pleasantly communicates its ideas, are the signs of Augustan humanism. Properly to write in this way a large equipment is needed (though the untaught genius like Shakespeare may manage without), of classical scholarship, history, general reading, and critical principles[2]: new writing should be supported (though not smothered) by the lessons of inherited experience. Yet its substance should be the first-hand knowledge of life. Denham summed up the ideal in praising Cowley – 'To him no author was unknown, But what he writ was all his own.' Following Nature – understanding life, and expressing the lasting truth about it in accomplished and convincing words – was a highly responsible ideal.

Literature, then, was a responsible art. The *Essay on Poetry* by Lord Mulgrave, later the Duke of Buckinghamshire, reflects this responsibility; it came naturally, even to a fashionable dilettante in letters, to express such ideas –

> Of all those arts in which the wise excel,
> Nature's chief masterpiece is writing well;
> No writing lifts exalted man so high

> As sacred and soul-breathing Poesy.
> No kind of work requires so nice a touch,
> And, if well finished, nothing shines so much.

With prestige of that kind, deriving from classical and Renaissance tradition, literature must be perpetually criticized, just as social habits must be perpetually satirized, and so the theory and practice of criticism, as of satire, become unusually important. Prefacing his *Sullen Lovers* (1668), Shadwell speaks of 'this very critical age, when every man pretends [i.e. claims] to be a judge': Swift's *Battle of the Books* (1704) calls criticism a 'malignant Deity': the 12th *Guardian* (1713), by Pope, assumes that any new poem will be severely scrutinized since 'most men, at some time of their lives', set up for critics. This criticism was often mere angry pedantry, or pedestrian common sense, or personal spite – 'a man seldom sets up for a poet', *The Spectator* (No. 253) declares, 'without attacking the reputation of all his brothers in the art'. But basically it was rooted in a sense of literature as 'Nature's chief masterpiece', man's greatest intellectual achievement, the treasury of his creative power, the standard of his civilization.

The desire for order, then, was a prepossession to which the Augustans were moved both by the disorder, the eccentricity, and the extravagance of preceding literature, and by the belief that it had a divine sanction, that, as Dennis asserts, 'there is nothing in Nature that is great and beautiful without rule and order'. Yet order was even then recognized to be secondary, particularly in poetry, to the energy of creative genius. The most important classical influence on Augustan criticism after (perhaps even before) that of Horace was that of Longinus's treatise *On the Sublime*, which praises passion and ecstasy. The terms in which Pope extols Homer, in the preface to *The Iliad*, are typical; only 'common critics', lacking inspiration, will prefer 'a judicious and methodical genius to a great and fruitful one'. 'Invention [that is, imaginative creation] is the very foundation of poetry.' In this, Homer is unrivalled; his 'unequalled fire and rapture' make his epic 'a wild paradise', in which everything is animated. Shakespeare and Milton, too, though not so supremely, share 'this poetical fire, this *vivida vis animi*'. Dryden's praise of Shakespeare in the *Essay of Dramatic Poesy* (1668) had already stressed the same quality; it strikingly admits that Shakespeare has 'the largest and most comprehensive soul' of all modern and perhaps of all ancient poets, and presents his images so vigorously as to affect the reader like the very experience of life itself. Other critics were no less definite about the prime requirement of creative force. Mulgrave demands 'e'en something of divine, and more than wit'; Edward Phillips in his *Theatrum Poetarum* (1674) prefers energy to 'wit, ingenuity, and learning in verse, even elegancy itself'; Thomas Sprat praises the 'masculine' qualities in Cowley; and Roscommon's *Essay on Translated Verse* (1684) elevates 'the sterling bullion of an English line' over the elegant gilding of the French. One may sometimes feel that the Augustans used the snaffle and the curb too much, yet there was undoubtedly meant to be a horse – Pegasus they would call it – beneath the harness. The very experience of writing proved, if common sense did not, that rule and order must be the rule and order of something energetically alive.

That being axiomatic, the critical aim was to express this grasp of living reality as well as possible. This is where 'wit', in its most important Augustan meaning, came in. The basic, though not the only, Augustan concern was to understand things and express them plainly. 'We love plain truth', said Saint-Évremond, 'good sense has gained ground upon the illusions of fancy, and nothing satisfies us nowadays [about 1690] but solid Reason'. Away with the conceits of metaphysical poetry, the freaks of Caroline sermon-style, the 'fantastic fairy-land' of romance which Cowley rejects from English epic (*To Sir William Davenant*), the 'monstrous, singular fancy' which Rymer deplores, the 'gigantic forms and monstrous births' which Lansdowne condemns in his *Essay upon Unnatural Flights in Poetry* (1701; it is based on Bouhours' significantly-named *Manière de bien penser*). These must yield before the true function of 'wit', which is 'to copy out ideas in the mind' (Lansdowne) with an exact correspondence. The ideas themselves are to be objectively 'true' to life. Cowley's *Ode to Wit* (1663) protests against the stylistic acrobatics of puns, quibbles, and encrusted imagery; true style is the power of expressing a truth with the clarity which serves it well, instead of the showiness which degrades it. Dryden defines wit as 'deep thoughts in common language', and Robert Wolseley as 'a true and lively expression of Nature' (*Preface to Valentinian*, 1685). 'Wit' has other meanings, certainly, some damagingly near to irresponsible fancy, some like the 'occult resemblances in things apparently unlike' that Johnson found overdone in metaphysical poetry, some like our own sense of piquant surprise. But that the Augustans should so often have linked it with perspicuity ('a propriety of words and thoughts adapted to the subject '– Dryden) indicates their desire to define life well and express enduringly the truth about it. Incidentally, Pope's definition of wit as 'what oft was thought but ne'er so well expressed' is criticized by Johnson for reducing wit from strength of thought to happiness of language; Johnson prefers to describe wit as –

> that which is at once natural and new, and that which though not obvious is upon its first production acknowledged to be just; ... that which he that never found it wondered how he missed it.

Wit is the clear and fresh comprehension and expression of representative truth.[3]

Augustan criticism praises the general, the familiar, the traditional, because the 'truth' of human nature (the basic quest of literature) lies not in idiosyncrasies but in common humanity. 'Human nature is ever the same': so, Pope argues in the 12th *Guardian*, the moderns are bound to describe life much as the ancients had done. Hurd's *Discourse Concerning Poetical Imitation* (1751) describes the passions as 'constant in their effects', and for Hume the aim of history is 'to discern the constant and universal principles of human nature' (*Essays*, 1767). Basically this goes back to Aristotle and Horace but it suits the Augustans so well as to seem their own property. Yet wit does not merely recite the familiar truths; it finds fresh ways of impressing them and it also discovers new truths. Johnson condemns Gray's *Eton College*, because it contains nothing that every reader does not already realize: he praises Gray's *Elegy* because it 'abounds with images which find a mirror in every mind'. He is not being inconsistent: the former, he feels, does not bring the familiar to life while the latter does – a difference which is a common experience in reading, though often hard to account for. With its fresh perceptions wit may indeed go further than the familiar, especially with non-human subjects, and discover unprecedented methods and subjects. Denham admires Cowley for novelty; Rochester praises Etherege as 'a sheer Original'; Swift's *Proposal for Correcting the English Tongue* (1712) speaks of the genius as being 'one who is able to open new scenes and to discover a vein of true and noble thinking'; and Johnson commends Savage for being individual in style and Denham for inventing 'local poetry' with *Cooper's Hill*, and so earning 'the rank and dignity of an original author'. The idea that originality is anathema to the Augustans is quite false – but originality is not endorsed unless it extends our sphere of 'true' experience, either by revivifying the old or by profitably widening our view of life.

John Hughes's essay *Of Style* (1698) defines the Augustan aims – 'propriety, perspicuity, elegance, and cadence.'[4] These seem superficial until their purpose is remembered; their value lies in the intelligent, ordered, and appropriate expression of what has been clearly grasped. Horace's *Ars Poetica* and Boileau's *L'Art poétique*, with their counsels of critical care and the adjustment of means to ends, were written gospels, but not less effective was the influence of good conversation and good manners, which Swift describes as 'the Art of making those people easy with whom we converse' (*A Treatise on Good-Manners and Good-Breeding*). The ideal was that 'gracious and dignified simplicity … the mean between ostentation and rusticity' which the preface to Pope's *Iliad* prescribes, the 'strength and grace united' which Goldsmith's *Account of the Augustan Age in England* sees accomplished in the days of Queen Anne. Literature kept, on the whole, to those emotions which could be expressed in public; it considered its reader's convenience and echoed Sprat's approval of 'a natural easiness and unaffected grace, where nothing seems to be studied yet everything is extraordinary' [i.e. unusually well-expressed]. Dryden's *Defence of the Epilogue* (1672) thinks Restoration styles better than Elizabethan because of 'the last and greatest advantage of our writing, which proceeds from *conversation*'. There was general, though not universal, agreement that the language was less faulty than ever before and more suitable to be the medium of literature, and that what Pope calls 'the present purity of writing' was born from the stylistic needs of the new philosophy and from the happy alliance of literature and polite society.[5] Clarity, coherence, polite idiom, a gentlemanly and sociable tone were the ideals appropriate to the effective expression of 'truth', though actual discourse and manners often failed to realize them.

The influences forming the new styles were mostly, and most deeply, English, yet they were given extra authority by classical and

French precedent to a degree which at times, though not in general, suggests subservience. Even for this there was some excuse; as Voltaire was to say, those who love the arts are fellows of one commonwealth. Ancient Rome, Louis XIV's France, and Augustan England embodied the ideals of civilization, expressing in manly good sense and urbanity the 'best' elements of human nature. The French contribution, for reasons of space and because it goes less deep than the Latin, must be treated tersely[6]: it amounted, especially during the first half of the Augustan era, to a strong influence of Corneille on Dryden (the explanatory *Discours* and *Examens* prefixed to Corneille's plays beget Dryden's critical prefaces), and to a general admiration for Boileau and a more transient one for other critics. Sir William Soames's *Art of Poetry* (1683) translates, and Mulgrave's *Essay upon Poetry* (1682) adapts, Boileau; Rymer translates Rapin's *Reflexions sur la Poétique d'Aristote* the year it appears (1674) and Dryden's *Apology for Heroic Poetry* (1677) couples Rapin and Boileau as 'the greatest of this age'. A lot of this criticism – on the dramatic unities, for example, or the nature of dramatic characterization, or 'rules' of various kinds – has lost its interest, but the general importance of French thought was to encourage sceptical instead of dogmatic discussion and to strengthen the ideals of energy and clarity. On this point Addison's tribute to Bouhours and Boileau is worth quoting, since every phrase has the hallmark of its age:

> Bouhours, whom I look upon to be the most penetrating of the French critics, has taken pains to show, that it is impossible for any thought to be beautiful which is not just and has not its foundation in the nature of things; that the basis of all wit is truth; and that no thought can be valuable of which good sense is not the groundwork. Boileau has endeavoured to inculcate the same notion. ... This is that natural way of writing, that beautiful simplicity, which we so much admire in the compositions of the ancients; and which nobody deviates from but those who want strength of genius to make a thought shine in its own natural beauties.
>
> (*Spectator* 62)

The French pioneered the way the English wished to go; their mistakes could be avoided, their successes could be a model for the new styles. They were allies rather than masters.

The masters, though by no means the tyrants, were the ancients. To resemble them was not only desirable – it was, since they had so expressed the civilized mind, almost inevitable. This had its drawbacks; some kinds of writing, Cowley remarks in the *Preface* to his poems (1656), could only be '*Cold-meats* of the *Antients*, new-heated', and charges of plagiarism were easy to bring. Pope faces this situation in the 12th *Guardian*, and also in prefacing his poems in 1717; voluntary or involuntary borrowing is inevitable, but the classically versed reader's enjoyment will be increased rather than diminished by his remembrance of an original. Over and above its clarity and definiteness Augustan language often had its enriching echoes, and Augustan literature could gain in confidence by a family resemblance to the classics. 'Those who say our thoughts are not our own because they resemble the Ancients', Pope observes, 'may as well say our Faces are not our own because they are like our Fathers'.' Devotion to the classics fostered some faults, such as an 'external' conception of literary graces, some loss of linguistic subtlety, an obtrusion of unassimilated Latin diction, and (in poetry) a heavy or artfully deliberate composition. But then each age has its own reasons for writing badly. On the credit side it encouraged a vigorous grasp of social themes, a concern (which could be strengthening) for discipline and verbal skill, and a range of literary 'kinds' (epic, Pindaric or Horatian ode, epistle, epigram, and so on) into which the order-seeking Augustan mind liked to fit.[7] They provided too the perspective of a successful and honoured tradition.

It is easy to overstress the Augustans' debt to the past. They lived their own lives, thought their own thoughts, and developed their own styles. Yet a respect for the way things had been done before, by those who had done them well, was part of their sense of responsibility, no more to be deplored than their addiction to classical architecture. They felt themselves part of a majestic ideal of humanity, emulating and striving to surpass but not rejecting 'the masters'. 'Those great men' (Dryden quotes Longinus, in the Preface to *Troilus and Cressida*, 1679) –

> whom we propose to ourselves as patterns of our imitation, serve us as a torch which is lifted up before us, to enlighten our passage, and often elevate our thoughts as high as the conception we have of our author's genius.

In terms as little obsequious do Reynolds's *Discourses* recommend antique and Renaissance models (though at times these might result in tedious academicism – Blake was to reject Reynolds's doctrines outright, and Constable to complain of ' "high-minded members" who stickle for the "elevated and noble" walks of art'). The intention was to benefit from the past, to discipline but not subdue individuality, and to capture either in ideal or real terms that human nature which Pope pronounces 'the most useful object of human reason'. The ancients were, says the 86th *Guardian*, 'fountains of good sense and eloquence': familiarity with them was considered the source of 'that good and manly taste which distinguishes so many English writers' (the phrase is that of a German visitor, Friedrich August Wendeborn), and Burke's *Letter to a Member of the National Assembly* (1791) credits England's disdain of Rousseauistic anarchy to her reverence for 'sound antiquity'.

Not all this reverence was first-hand; translations abounded and so, more significantly, did adaptations, classical originals adjusted to the latitude of London with a sense of kinship. Yet whatever may have been the readers' case, writers were well-grounded in Latin; indeed, as Leslie Stephen remarks, since they held most earlier English literature to be obsolete, where else could they find sustenance? A classical allegiance had its faults; Eachard's witty *Contempt of the Clergy* (1670) deplores the neglect of English studies, and there was a cant of classicism which Johnson, stalwart classic as he was, rejected.[8] Yet the ancients provided so much that the moderns needed – the discipline of central style, the stimulus of models, the fire of Homer, dignity of Virgil, energy of Juvenal, eloquence of Cicero, pith of Seneca, and urbanity of Horace, Terence, and Petronius–that no influence could better have co-operated with the concrete and vigorous native styles to produce the sense of living civilization.

Yet there remains an important critical question. Augustan intellectual habits had revolutionary effects on poetry and prose, hailed enthusiastically then but with cooler feelings ever since. Much Augustan prose, by being plain and reasonable, much Augustan verse by being trim and disciplined, is dull. The problem is, How far do Augustan styles still live for us?

A current commonplace is that they lack the intimate life which animated the rich 'metaphysical' technique of language, and that the prestige of judgement and reason killed something which, until the death of Cowley (1667), had been alive and imaginative. This commonplace has gained its fame from Mr T. S. Eliot's diagnosis of a 'dissociation of sensibility', the loss of that power which could feel a thought as immediately as the odour of a rose, and whose literary expression was 'the direct sensuous apprehension of thought, or a recreation of thought into feeling, which is exactly what we find in Donne'.[9] If language before 1660 could, and afterwards could not, express this 'sensuous apprehension', something perhaps invaluable had been lost. What, in fact, is the case?

One might answer, as Professor Bonamy Dobrée has done – 'Is it really better to write like Sir Thomas Browne than to write like Swift, or to write like Nashe than to write like Defoe?' One might further note (Mr F. W. Bateson has done so) that not only other scholars but indeed Mr Eliot himself in his later criticism found the theory, in any simple form, not at all satisfactory. Restoration and Hanoverian styles show a plainer mental process than some (but not all) Jacobean styles, arising from a world of ideas more familiar to us and from what seems a more straightforward organization of mind. But any split between thought and feeling is slow to operate, and the best post-Restoration writing does not at all suggest schizophrenia. Dryden, Swift, and Pope are obvious examples; in Sterne a fantastic complexity emerges again, based on self-consciousness, wit, and immediate connexions between intellect and sense. Hardly less is this the case with Horace Walpole. Even when complexity is not evident, there can be an absolutely firm impact of language, as in Fielding and Johnson, which shows the full integration of personality.

The fact that styles were simplified is obvious, the more so since such a simplification is stated repeatedly as a critical aim and a need of the time. Yet that still leaves Augustan styles with a great fund of strength, which critical reiteration of 'polish' and 'elegance' tends to obscure. The 'higher' imagination may be suspect, but the imagination which grasps the material of life and embodies it in concrete images and a vigorous speech drawing on the vernacular is there in abundance. To write Pope's *Epistle to Arbuthnot* requires as much imagination as to write Wordsworth's *Tintern Abbey*, though of a different kind. The reason the dissociation-of-sensibility theory seems misleading (despite the arguments based on the Augustan divorce of wit-imagination from judgement) is that the best Augustan writing is strongly personal and is, if any writing be so, 'thinking in images', images which strike the mind as the projections of other minds in immediate contact with social realities. Augustan literature gives us fact, variously patterned and ordered, but fact none the less. And this fact is conveyed in a vigorous vernacular which expresses its reality. The impact of Restoration comedy, for instance, comes largely from the graphic force with which deportment, gesture, expression, and social habit are seized: even the cosmopolitan Saint-Évremond preferred its grasp of manners and its satirical social force to the mere gallantries of the Spanish and French. It derives from Ben Jonson and the 'character' tradition and, though far less vital than the comedy of Jonson, is still alive with keen curiosity and vehemence. The signs are its concrete imagery, vigorous metaphor, and picturesque phrases; Shadwell, Etherege, Wycherley, Congreve, Vanbrugh, and Farquhar abound in them. So, in general, do the novelists. Semantic vitality and metaphoric invention overflow in Aphra Behn (for instance, in the elaborate-fantastic portrait of the fop, in *The Fair Jilt*, 1688); even a minor writer like Mrs Manley (in *The New Atalantis*, 1709) has a vivid and full natural idiom which is clearly her uninhibited whole personality. Defoe writes with all his practical nature, with a speaking voice and the energy of gossip; much the same is true of Smollett, and Sterne's feeling, thought, and style are all one. Nor is Swift's sensibility noticeably dissociated in the *Journal to Stella* (1710–13): flaccid idiom he scarifies in his *Genteel and Ingenious Conversation* (as the comic playwrights often do also), but he is himself idiomatic and personal. Lady Mary Wortley Montagu's *Letters* (1709–62) give the very pulse both of herself and of the thrusting social scene she describes; so, in their own ways, do Boswell's personal papers. As for verse, Butler's tumbling octosyllabics in *Hudibras* (1663–78), Oldham's ferocious *Satires upon the Jesuits* (1681: provoked by the 'Popish Plot' of 1678 and gaining him the title of 'English Juvenal'), and supremely Dryden's satires, whose brilliance is that of bold wit working through the concrete vigour of contemporary vernacular – these have no split personality; thought in them cannot be distinguished from feeling. Nor, indeed, can it in Defoe's *True-Born Englishman* (1701), vehement with rough witticism, or in Ned Ward's anti-Defoe-and-Dissenter *Hudibras Redivivus* (1707), or in

Swift's *Death of Dr Swift* (1731), or in Johnson's *London* (1738) or Goldsmith's *Deserted Village* (1770) or much of Crabbe. To say that they feel their thought as immediately as the odour of a rose would be to introduce an analogy from a realm of experience other than that most Augustan writers work in, but they *do* feel their thought immediately. In Pope this is clear. 'Vivid *and* abstract', Mr Bateson has called *The Dunciad*, since it unites concreteness and thought, components which in one sense – but with violence to the poem – might be dissociated but in another and truer completely coincide. A similar conclusion arises from Maynard Mack's Twickenham edition of the *Essay on Man* (1950)[10]; far from this poem's being a speciously-felt versification of borrowed ideas, it fuses into a passion-ately-apprehended whole a tradition-charged philosophy; thought in it is indistinguishable from feeling – each prompts and reflects the other. As for the *Epistle to Arbuthnot*, no more 'un-dissociated' poem exists; fluctuating moods, varying tones, shifting stress and speed, attitudes from venomous to pathetic – these are only the most obvious of the vitalities which make the *Epistle* both completely social (in its references, communicative skill, and demeanour) and completely personal (in its 'dramatic' expression of one man's thought-and-feeling). While not precisely in the 'metaphysical' mode, Pope is in that which makes a man write in the full context of all his interests, with the 'literary' undivided from the non-literary sides of life. Imaginative daring is less prominent in the eighteenth century than in that before or after, and on the whole poetry suffers. But the notion that even the better Augustan writing is merely a well-bred art suffering from a split personality is as mischievous as it is common.

One argument that might be added to refute it is that of verbal vitality. This is widespread until Addison spreads his ideals of urban-ity, and even then it survives for a while. Congreve is a virtuoso of the vivid word and surprising simile. 'He was once given to scram-bling with his hands and sprawling in his sleep', Mellefont says of Sir Paul Pliant in *The Old Bachelor* (1693), 'and ever since she [Lady Pliant] has had him swaddled up in blankets, and his hands and feet swathed down, and so put to bed, and there he lies with a great beard like a Russian bear upon a drift of snow.' 'An she should [frown]', Sir Wilful declares of Lady Wishfort in *The Way of the World* (1700), 'her forehead would wrinkle like the coat of a cream-cheese.' Proper discussion of comedy-styles would take too much space; one can only state summarily that Congreve's image-finding and graphic phrase has its kinship with Shakespearian comedy, that Etherege has the precise sharp flavour of vernacular, and that Wycherley's close-wrought language with its mordant Jonsonian strength has a peculiarly sensory life – 'the canonical smirk, and the filthy clammy palm of a chaplain', 'this toad, this ugly, greasy, dirty sloven', 'Well madam, now have I dressed you and set you out with so many ornaments and spent upon you ounces of essence and pulvilio; and all this for no other purpose but as people adorn and perfume a corpse for a stinking second-hand grave' (*The Country Wife*, 1675). There is something of Webster in Wycherley, something of Wycherley in Swift. Non-dramatic prose, also, shows this sensory quality; Shadwell writes of 'rejected authors, who will strut, and huff it out, and laugh at the ignorance of the age', and Vanbrugh of hypocritical 'saints – your thorough-paced ones, I mean, with skrewed faces and wry mouths'. Eachard's *Contempt of the Clergy* (1670) has an Elizabethan nut-cracking virtuosity in satirical extravagance. Sir Roger L'Estrange's *Observator* papers (1681–7) – 'the chief manager of all those angry writings', he is called in Gilbert Burnet's *History of his Own Time* – and a great deal of miscellaneous political and critical polemic have the hammering colloquial scorn which was the idiom of controversy until well into the eighteenth century and which invigorated if it did not refine the written language. The greatness of Dryden in prose is partly that he so well unites the raciness of such writing (going back to the Elizabethans – Oldham's grotesque *Character of an Ugly Old Priest*, c. 1680, is akin to Nashe) with the new ideal of clarity and coherence. Both in verse and prose Dryden is, though immeasurably more civilized than Oldham or Butler, rooted in image-making vernacular inventiveness and immediacy, and so, strikingly, is Swift. There is a passage in *A Tale of a Tub*, sec. ix (pub. 1704) beginning –

> When a Man's Fancy gets astride on his Reason, when Imagination is at Cuffs with the Senses, and common Understanding, as well as Common Sense, is Kickt out of Doors; the first Proselyte he makes is Himself.

If with this one compares Johnson's own meditation in *Rasselas*

(1759) on 'The Dangerous Prevalence of the Imagination', it is clear what prose has sacrificed to gain greater decorum. The hey-day of racy invention is over by about 1720, though much remains in Defoe. The politer work of the Hanoverians rejects it, as it rejects the 'Senecan' (pithy) kind of sentence for the 'Ciceronian', or at least the Addisonian, with its easy sequences.[11] Much verse becomes too insipid or too Miltonic, much prose too suave or (sometimes with Johnson or Gibbon) too grandiose. Yet though squibs and explosions may cease, there is health in the later Augustans – in epistolary vigour (Lady Mary Wortley Montagu, John Byrom, Gray, Cowper, and Walpole), unadorned cogency (Smollett, Captain Cook's *Voyages*), bold firm discipline (Fielding), flexibility and immediacy (Sterne), precision and order (Berkeley and Hume), and a considerate gravity (Gray's *Elegy*, Johnson). 'Art' gradually gains on vivacity, but when the results include Hume's philosophy, Goldsmith's verse, Gibbon's history, and Johnson's criticism the losses are well compensated.

Finally, there is the formal side of Augustan style, which the modern reader does not always find interesting. The concern for verse- and prose-form, for literary species and kinds, was, however, reasonable and sound; an obvious need, in the early years, was for technical skill. The Sedleys and Dorsets, Pope's 'mob of gentlemen who wrote with ease', were often careless; popular anthologies like *The Covent-Garden Drollery* (1672) show that tone and technique have coarsened since Elizabethan and 'metaphysical' days. Shadwell's plays, Rochester noted, show 'great mastery with little care'. Marvell's and Oldham's satires are rough, and though Dryden admires the vigour of Butler's thought he finds his helter-skelter verse and double rhymes unsatisfactory – 'we are pleased ungratefully'. Improved technique is a corollary of an ordered language and civilized ideals. It is not formal for formality's sake; Augustan patterns – heroic couplets, octosyllabics, anapaests, *Elegy*-quatrain, and prose-balances – are not mere docility to rule (though complaints were heard even then of over-discipline); they aim at effective transmission of sense. The rhymes in Dryden's satires are both the bases of sound-pattern and the bearers of the satiric barb; no form but the couplet, enlivened with alliterations, functionally varied pauses, and paragraph continuity, would serve the purpose so well. But the couplet had other resources; Oldham and Defoe tore into it with straightforward colloquial syntax, rough rhythms and rhymes, and demagogic vocabulary. Pope is quite different – his brilliant calculation of effect adjusts sound and movement to a more complex correspondence with sense than anyone else in his century achieved, and his couplets are the frame which by its limiting edges and gleam of gilding sets off the lively tonal relationships within the picture. For Gay again the couplet is different, is richly coloured, and mockingly grandiloquent within the fortifying expected rhythm; a burlesque elegy on a drowned pippin-seller is to be –

> Soft as the breath of distant flutes, at hours
> When silent evening closes up the flow'rs;
> Lulling as falling water's hollow noise,
> Indulging grief, like *Philomela's* voice.

(Trivia)

Lady Mary Wortley Montagu's pastoral parody *Town Eclogues* (1716) has, less skilfully, a similar light mockery and the couplet tune. Johnson is slow and momentous, with Dryden's weight and his own darkness of mood; Goldsmith and Cowper can shade the couplet with a dying fall conveying the poignancy of loss; and Crabbe, by subtly sensory language, regulation of pause, and careful placing of image, evolves again another character from the same form. In all this, however, the couplet retains its power to shape its content into symmetry, definition, and controlled progression. Octosyllabics were freer, lighter-footed in social verse, more of a holiday (Congreve's *An Impossible Thing*, Swift's *Death of Dr Swift*, Green's *The Spleen*, Gay's and Cowper's *Fables*, and Thomas Warton's comic stories), or else galloping-grotesque following *Hudibras* (Mandeville's *Grumbling Hive*, Ward's *Hudibras Redivivus*, Hughes's *Hudibras Imitated*, Mallet's *Tyburn*, and Churchill's *The Ghost*). The triple rhythm of anapaests served for badinage or easy sentiment, the irregular Pindaric ode for the higher raptures (generally a calamitous failure), and blank verse unhappily imitating Milton for discursive meditation. In prose, symmetries patterned the sense into phases the mind could methodically grasp. Augustan order was not really a superficiality; it came as fugue- or sonata-form comes to the musician, not without practice but bringing the reward of craftsmanship in the effective display of its material. Technical command is no more over-polish than the brilliance of Augustan visual arts is over-refinement; it includes the functional formlessness of Swift's doggerel verse and Defoe's or Richardson's prose as well as the formality of Johnson, with many 'middle' styles between. To display life widely and well, to command general acceptance in forms which symbolize the high morality of order, was the philosophy of Augustan letters.

Literary Outlines: Prose

The Restoration's prose ambition was to ally traditional vivacity with emergent discipline and evolve a medium for reasonable discourse. Its realization was a fight against ingrained habits of colour and passion, and for a long time the older modes fought a rearguard action. Puritans and their like, for instance, still recorded their struggles in a characteristic idiom of Biblical phrase crossed with the speech of the market-place – Bunyan is full of it, and so are Baxter's vigorous *Life and Times* (1696) and George Fox's formless but vivid *Journal* (1694). Much Anglican oratory was not very different; Glanvill's *Essay Concerning Preaching* (1678) objects equally to erudite incomprehensible divines and to emotional popular preachers with their 'Roll upon Christ, close with Christ, get into Christ'. Picturesque oratory passed by slowly; when Jeremy Taylor died in 1667 Robert South, Prebendary of Westminster, wittily contrasted his elaborate style with the apostles' simplicity. Yet South himself, if not as convoluted as his predecessors, is still surprising; he likes fantastic, grotesque, or homely detail (wherefore Fielding is sarcastic about him in the *Voyage to Lisbon*), is eloquent, alert, and dramatically varied in tone. Isaac Barrow, his graver contemporary, is more logical and coherent but still has the Caroline weight, and so, outside the pulpit, has Clarendon's great *History of the Rebellion* (written 1646–71). After Clarendon the most impressive of these writers of the older styles is Thomas Burnet, in his *Sacred Theory of the Earth* (1684), a long-breathed majestic argument explaining the Deluge, sombrely passionate in its contemplation of the ruined world. Burnet responds to his vast matter with vast grandeur; themes of Eternity, the beauty of Paradise, the tragedy of the subsequent cataclysm, and the changes of the earth throughout millennia stir in him a rich sense of mystery and a heightened tone consonant with his majestic topics. Great and theological matters can still arouse sublimity.

If darker themes are still resonant, the lighter can still be opulent. In *Oroonoko* and *The Fair Jilt* (both pub. 1688), Mrs Aphra Behn tilts a shapeless style towards the heroic-romantic and achieves a huddle of vivid detail, an exuberant and exotic life. She has the good sense of the Augustans brightened with a happy credulity in romantic wonders and an enriched manner; *The Fair Jilt*, though its theme is the crimes of an impassioned courtesan, conveys by its imagery of wealth a valid stateliness and splendour of living. This one might call Stuart literature in its florid worldliness, its bold colour and feeling for the heroic.

But soberer fashions were encroaching. The later *Essays* (1668) of Cowley, though mildly intoxicated with wit, show this: they are landmarks in alert discourse, with a Montaigne-like self-analysis in neat short rhythms, though still here and there ingeniously pointed. The great virtues of Dryden (1631–1700) in this respect have already been mentioned; in this as in other forms without precisely innovating he knew how to make the best of current modes, and his critical essays (the best are *Of Dramatic Poesy*, 1668, and the *Preface to the Fables*, 1700) have a ranging personal manner, encouraged by Montaigne and Corneille, and a racy sense of phrase typical of his century from Bacon and the character-writers downwards. His style is the more satisfactory in that he shares it with others – for instance, with Halifax (1633–95), whose *Character of a Trimmer* (1688) is witty political persuasion, or with Richard Bentley (1662–1742), whose *Boyle Lectures* (1692) and preface to his *Epistles of Phalaris* (1697–9) are trenchant and firm polemic, not unlike Swift. Swift himself, Bentley's mocker in *The Battle of the Books* (1704), makes the style his own, and with Arbuthnot and Mandeville provides the early decades of the eighteenth century with much of its most searching and enviable prose. It is prose addressed, though not to the erudite, yet to men of wit and knowledge, who do not need the easy manner and predigested substance which Addison and his fellow-journalists necessarily devised for their wider circle, and who enjoy strong idiom rather than undue refinement. In this same phase of style, incidentally, Peter Motteux completed Sir Thomas Urquhart's translation of Rabelais, in 1693–4, in a style adequate to his vigorous Commonwealth precursor.

But still plainer prose was on the way, encouraged both by the

scientists and their supporters like Locke, and by the religious seriousness of this supposedly cynical age. Discussions of pulpit oratory,
such as Glanvill's *Essay Concerning Preaching*, insisted earnestly on the
forging of a style fit for those great purposes of faith which are above
ornament or ostentation. Religion even more than science had truths
to announce too sincere for tinsel, and the clearest Restoration writing comes from the Latitudinarian divines, and eminently from
Archbishop Tillotson (1630–94), whom Gilbert Burnet praises as 'a
man of a clear head and a sweet temper', with 'the brightest thoughts
and the most correct style of all our divines'. Tillotson's prose now
seems to lack flavour, yet without any spectacular qualities it is free
from affectation and in a restrained way is equal to its themes of
charity and reason. Goldsmith's praise in *The Bee* (24 November
1759) shows how exactly it served Augustan ideals of expression:

> There is nothing peculiar to the language of Archbishop
> Tillotson, but his manner of writing is inimitable: for one who
> reads him wonders why he himself did not think and speak
> in that very manner.

Dryden, Addison, Steele, Johnson, and many others praised him, and
rightly found impressive his lucid dignity and his fortifying alliance
of reason and religion. Gilbert Burnet (1643–1715), also a Whig
Latitudinarian, follows the same road; his account of *Some Passages
in the Life and Death of John, Earl of Rochester* (1680) has a grave
charm, in prose clear but not cold. As for the philosophers, the style
of Locke, though steady and methodical, is all that is meant by
prosaic – his matter is much more impressive than his manner – but
both Berkeley (1685–1753) and Hume (1711–76) are masters of as
much civilized skill as is to be found in English.

By the time of Addison (1672–1719) the new prose was completely
naturalized, and was getting used to its wider public. The periodical
essay not only benefited from, it was created by, the new manner.
A kind of writing which in Cowley's essays had been a private
meditation enlivened with wit developed into a generalized medium
of social commentary, eagerly sought by middle-class readers and
moderated in style to the highest common denominator of taste. The
smoothing-out which went with the social motive reduces the present
interest of most Augustan essays; a century after Addison, Alexander

Chalmers, prefacing *The Spectator* in his series of *British Essayists* (1817), admitted a general triteness, though he excused it on the grounds that the essays had been too much imitated and in their own time had been valuably popular. This popularity was indeed important; it broadcast the civilizing influences of literature, philosophy, and the arts, engaged men's thoughts not towards the separatist tendencies of sects and individualism but towards a harmonious corporate life, and provided a mild but effective current of criticism. At first a vehicle for news, the periodical developed a commentary on social life – the first, and popular, steps were taken in John Dunton's *Athenian Mercury* (1690 onwards, soon imitated by other *Mercuries*) – and Defoe's *Review* (1704–13) contained 'a weekly history of Nonsense, Impertinence, Vice, and Debauchery'. The essay gradually relegated the news to a minor role, and because it so well cultivated the general body of readers it was largely responsible for evolving the characteristic eighteenth-century style.[12] Restoration prose is lively but often moves jerkily by galvanic impulses; Shaftesbury the philosopher (1671–1713) declared that his age had 'scarce the idea of any other model' than the epigrammatic 'Senecan'. Addison distinguished between two essay-methods, that of spontaneous sallies and that of careful order, and while the former was more animated he preferred the latter as being easier to follow. His great achievement, accomplished in *The Tatler* (1709–11) and *The Spectator* (1711–14), was to simplify prose, even at the expense of dilution, so that the reader need never retrace his steps or query an unfamiliar word, to organize his ideas and to carry them forward on sentence-rhythms with an onward undulation instead of momentary sparkles, and never to vary from the tone of good manners. 'Propriety, perspicuity, elegance, cadence' are here attained infallibly. In an age of uneasy technique and of strong animosities his style and matter were healthy, the more influential in that he was widely admired for himself; Swift speaks of his pleasant conversation, and Lady Mary Wortley Montagu thought him, of all contemporary wits, the best companion. Garth, Tickell, Young, and Pope (despite the Atticus satire in the *Epistle to Arbuthnot*) admired him, and Steele told Congreve that a night in his company was like 'conversing with an intimate acquaintance of Terence and Catullus', who had 'all their Wit and Nature heightened with Humour more exquisite and delightful than any other man ever possessed' (Prefatory letter to Addison's *Drummer*). Frequently republished in book form, *The Spectator* essays (largely though not wholly Addison's) did as much as any literary work to shape the Augustan ethos.[13]

Of many kinds of wide appeal the periodical essay chose that which best combined amenity and responsibility, and it mediated between the common reader and the best thought of the day. The other important papers of the century are *The Guardian* (1713: the best essays are from Steele, Addison, and Berkeley), Steele's *The Englishman* (1713–14), Addison's *Freeholder* (1715–16), Fielding's *Champion* (1740) and *Covent-Garden Journal* (1752), Johnson's *Rambler* (1750–2) and his 'Idler' essays in *The Universal Chronicle* (1758–60), Moore's *World* (1753–6: the liveliest of mid-century papers), Colman and Thornton's *Connoisseur* (1754–6), Goldsmith's *Bee* (1759), and his 'Citizen of the World' essays in *The Public Ledger* (1760–1). In all these there is much that is trivial or repetitive, but there is much too that is a true focus of Augustan thought, both light and serious.

Making the easy transition from essayists to 'occasional' writers, one observes Swift (1667–1745) as the most powerful, and his friend Arbuthnot (1667–1735) as one of the most interesting – 'the most universal genius', Johnson thought him, of Queen Anne's reign. With Pope, Gay, and Parnell (and the approval of Congreve, Addison, and Lord Oxford), they constituted the Scriblerus Club (1713), intending, Pope said, 'to have ridiculed all false tastes in learning'. Its monuments are Pope's own *Dunciad* and Arbuthnot's *Memoirs of the Extraordinary Life, Works and Discoveries of Martinus Scriblerus* (written *c.* 1714; comprehensively satirical on educational, philosophical, and scientific theories), which forms a link in the chain of the learned wit popularized by Rabelais and continued by Sterne. Arbuthnot's grave manner and vigorous dialogue resemble Swift's, but the eccentric theories by which 'Martin's' father educates him are rooted in the extravagances of Renaissance polymaths. Arbuthnot's other main works, the *John Bull* pamphlets (1712) and *The Art of Political Lying* (1712: Swift's 15th *Examiner* paper in 1710 has the same subject), have much of Swift's sardonic power, and *The Humble Petition of the Colliers* is a Swiftian absurdity against the scientists. This kind of writing is among the Augustan best – firm in rhythm, assured in tone, in vital but not vulgarizing contact with current idiom, and satirical with a controlled extravagance. Its supreme exponent is, of course, Swift himself. *The Battle of the Books* and *A Tale of a Tub* (pub. 1704) show his genius in image-making on the scale of allegory. Each is a concrete fiction of an abstract situation – a literary dispute, and the prevalence of fanaticism. His 'sensuous apprehension of thought' works in images which are not only metaphors as the passing mintage of imagination but also whole symbolic situations. His favourite tone is ironic, and his favourite intellectual exercise is the ingenious protraction of the link between idea and image; his wit lies less in the initial conception than in the inimitable follow-through, so that Johnson was merely obtuse in complaining, of *Gulliver's Travels*, that anyone might think of big and little men. Swift's mind moves among 'real' things and promptly embodies abstractions; his fable is metaphor at its most vital. In a long series of satires and political pamphlets – *An Argument Against Abolishing Christianity* (1708), *The Examiner* papers (1710–11: a Tory weekly), *The Conduct of the Allies* (1711), *The Public Spirit of the Whigs* (1714), a momentous succession of Irish pamphlets (especially *The Drapier's Letters*, 1724, the *Short View of the Present State of Ireland*, 1728, and *A Modest Proposal*, 1729), and *Gulliver's Travels* (1726) – he wielded a prose unequalled for pungent short rhythms, lively images and analogies, and the subversive deceptions of its honest-citizen reasonableness. In a not-dissimilar kind is the series of essay-commentaries which Bernard de Mandeville (1670–1733) appended to his satirical poem *The Grumbling Hive* under the title of *The Fable of the Bees* (1714); Mandeville's prose is clear, forceful, and sardonic, and his matter – a realistic appraisal of social behaviour – is meant to shock the idealists. 'Shavian', one might call its methods.

After 'occasional' prose, the personal: diaries, memoirs, letters, travels, biography, and autobiography. These were peculiarly congenial to the Augustan mind, and from being previously a minor interest took on a major importance. Social life was being fertilized by wealth and leisure, by better transport (Horace Walpole carried on one of his longest correspondences with Sir Horace Mann, as far away as Naples), and also, no doubt, by the satisfaction of using an easy and civilized prose style; there is a sensuous and intellectual pleasure in the very form of good Augustan writing, regardless of its content.

Diaries and journals are not always intended as communication, and art is often less prominent in them than spontaneity. Foremost in any enumeration must be the name of Pepys (1633–1703), whose diaries are so famous that any comment is superfluous except, perhaps, a reference to their almost hallucinatory vividness and their maturity and intelligence. They are supreme in an absorbing but diverse species. This embraces also the devotion of religious enthusiasts (Fox's *Journal*, Bunyan's *Grace Abounding*, Thomas Ellwood's *History of His Life*, and John Wesley's *Journal*), the quieter Anglican character emerging variously in the records of James Woodforde and William Cole, and White's *Natural History of Selborne*. The Augustan temperament is characteristically reflected in the ironic gravity and formality of Gibbon's *Autobiography*, and the Augustan variety of character in the miscellaneous interest of John Evelyn's *Diary*, Colley Cibber's *Apology*, John Byng's *Torrington Diaries*, William Hickey's *Memoirs*, Fanny Burney's *Diary and Letters*, and, with effusive self-display, in Boswell's various journals (the *Tour to Corsica*, 1768, *Tour to the Hebrides*, 1785, and the frankly revelatory *London Journal 1762-3*, and *Boswell in Holland 1763-4*, and others). Even in so rapid a survey the comic-pathetic intimacy and persistence of Boswell's interest in others and in himself would lay claim to more room than can be allowed, were it not that the current publication of the Boswell papers is turning as much publicity on him as even he himself would have wished. In the circumstances he can take care of himself.

The transition from journals to letters is a small one; indeed, Swift's *Journal to Stella*, a commentary in his most personal idiom from the centre of affairs in the years of his greatest power (1710–13), is in fact a series of letters to Stella and Mrs Dingley. Unlike Swift in scope and intensity, but still deeply coloured by the Augustan world, are two correspondents in differing spheres of life, Lady Mary Wortley Montagu (1689–1762) and John Byrom (1691–1763). Alike in their dates, they are not unlike in lively, economical styles, close to the realities of persons and places. Byrom translates his family motto – 'Frustra per plura' – as 'the less ado the better', and the phrase would suit either Lady Mary or himself. When the former's letters appeared in 1763, *The Critical Review* spoke of 'the sprightliness of her wit, the solidity of her judgement, the elegance [i.e.

critical intelligence] of her taste, and the excellence of her real character'. Her honest mind and vigorous phrase are refreshing after Addisonian amenity; in some ways they suggest Jane Austen's strong wit, a control of head over heart which is not coldness but a frank judgement of the world. Her interests are intelligent; she maintains her style without lapses. Like Lord Byron she responds to romantic scenes (the most interesting of her letters are those about her expedition to Turkey), but unlike him she sees them not as an orchestration of her own personality but for their own strangeness and interest. As for Byrom's *Journals and Papers*, they have recently been re-edited (1950, by Henri Talon) and revealed as a good record of London and provincial life. The stamp of the period shows in the plain vocabulary, the accurate manner, the clear grasp of subject. Vigorous in the normal events of life, Byrom is as sound as a bell on a harder occasion; his letters on his daughter Ellen's death (November 1729) are models of firm but not unfeeling sense.

Other letter-writers, perhaps better-known, must be briefly recorded. Shenstone (1714–63), writing to country clergy, comfortable gentry, and literary amateurs, luminaries of the fourth rather than the first magnitude, recounts his landscape gardening, reading, small dissatisfactions, and pleasures, in a sensitive manner which reflects the tastes of the time the better for lacking the force, prominent in Horace Walpole, necessary to transform them. Cowper (1731–1800) does still better than Shenstone the things Shenstone does well; his 'enjoyment of country air and retirement' comes through a style quietly perfect in tone, lucid, and not a whit insipid; the subdued but real vivacities which gleam in his verse appear also in the prose. As for Horace Walpole (1717–97), his vivacities are anything but subdued; his world seems to have existed in order to be written about. His phrases move quickly, and their subjects are caught not motionless but in those moments of amusing self-expression which suggest a successful mime. He exaggerates, sometimes subtly, sometimes flagrantly, is malicious, is sentimental, but always intent, and vivid. For their vitality, agility, and brilliant social panorama Walpole's letters are unrivalled in English; in deeper qualities – scholarship, poetic sensitiveness, and subtle humour – they are surpassed in their own time by those of Gray (1716–71), which have, if any English letters have, the true note of friendship. Page after page, rich in comment on literature, history, art, building, and landscape (which he sees not in raptures but in full and careful detail), Gray reveals a personality whose depth and variety not even the *Elegy* quite prepares us for.

Lastly, as 'personal' prose, there is biography, with Walton's *Hooker* and *Sanderson* (1670, 1678), Aubrey's *Lives* (written by 1697), Sprat's *Cowley* (1668), and Burnet's *Rochester* (1680), and then waiting for its next triumph in Johnson's *Life of Savage* (1744), a small masterpiece which, though possibly too lenient to an obstinate Bohemian and certainly too generous to his verse, is an example not of exculpation so much as of sympathy and charity, careful in its 'placing' of both Savage and his acquaintances, and finally dignified in exorcising any condescension to the dead man. The later *Lives of the English Poets* (1779–81) have an abundance of human interest, and much of their century's most stimulating criticism. But, of course, the supreme biographical achievement of the age, and the language, is Boswell's *Life of Samuel Johnson* (1791), unprecedented in scope and detail, and unequalled in recording the substance of life. Here, as with Pepys's *Diary*, comment is superfluous; the *Life* is an unimpeachable triumph.

Biography is a form of history, and history is a growing Augustan passion. The great pre-Hanoverian records are Clarendon's *History of the Rebellion* (written 1646–71, published 1702–4), penetrating in character-study, judicious in analysis and carried on a strong-shouldered prose, and Gilbert Burnet's *History of His Own Time* (written before 1715, published 1723–34), expounding a Whig interpretation of history. As for minor history, it is the more abundant as the Augustans the more closely examine their society; Swift's pamphlets on *The Conduct of the Allies, The Barrier Treaty*, and *The Four Last Years of the Queen* have even more than Swift's usual serried marshalling of fact and argument, though their aim (to vindicate Tory policy) has lost its interest. The same eclipse has overtaken the miscellaneous Whiggism of Defoe and Steele, the Toryism of Johnson, and Bolingbroke's above-party *Idea of a Patriot King* (1749), but emphatically not Burke's American and Indian speeches and the *Reflections on the Revolution in France* (1790). History proper was among the most widespread of serious literary interests in the age of Johnson; Hume, Smollett, and William Robertson made once-popular though now outmoded contributions to it, but the supreme monument of Augustan historiography is Gibbon's *Decline and Fall of the Roman Empire* (1776–88), whose patterned style allots to every fact in an intimidating multitude its due shape and relationship, as a great civilization dwindles into anarchy. The major part of Gibbon's life went into the gathering and ordering of his material and the evolution of his ample manner, and the result is a panorama of majestic and melancholy magnitude. Besides history in large perspective the Augustans provide also history as men lived it, not often better recorded than in Defoe's and Arthur Young's tours (social history, these), Horace Walpole's *Memoirs* (of the reigns of George II and George III), and Nathaniel Wraxall's *Memoirs of My Own Time*.

The particular new continent conquered for literature by Augustan prose is, however, the novel. By comparison the development of the essay is the cultivation of a garden plot, slight when contrasted with the energy by which wide stretches of life were subdued to ordered narrative – an exertion comparable in significance with the development of Elizabethan drama or of seventeenth-century spiritual poetry.

Fiction was anything but a new invention. Even if legend and myth be omitted (since their religious or symbolic bearing differs from that of ordinary narrative) and the enquiry be confined to invented prose stories, abundance of them is to be found in the Middle Ages. The Renaissance has its classical translations, pastoral-Arcadian romances, allegories, character-studies, and records of rascality. Yet then the main creative channels ran elsewhere; fiction's relation to life was peripheral, as idealization or moral doctrine or satire. For the central current to carry it, certain conditions were required – a reliable prose, sufficient readers ready to follow the long evolutions of an organized rendering of life, and, above all, a belief that prose fiction was artistically and intellectually worthy of major talent. Abroad it had been proved so, with Rabelais and Cervantes and, as an influential but passing fashion, with French heroic romances and (more lastingly) Scarron's realistic *Roman comique* (1651). The novel might clearly be important, though in England its growth was less a matter of Continental discipleship than apparent accident – Bunyan spontaneously inspired to *The Pilgrim's Progress* (1678), Defoe transforming travel narrative or artless biography, Richardson stumbling from model letters into the epistolary story, Fielding reacting from Richardson's prudential morality. The Augustan achievement was the use, on a large coherent plan, of 'real' social material, amplified and varied by following a longer or shorter period of the hero's life story, and by allowing a good deal of coincidence and digression. Its important technical innovation was its understanding of character and of plot – not as mere episodes (though in all the novelists these still abound, and in Defoe and Smollett predominate), but as cause and effect artistically unifying a particular phase of life. Such a conception is not, in itself, realism; life is generally casual, not organized to a particular end, and Defoe's and Smollett's haphazard progress is, strictly, more realistic than the organized sequence of Richardson or Fielding. Yet in general the mind prefers the order of plot to the disorder of episode: man's significance is heightened when his experiences have a shape.

Bunyan's work, great as it is, belongs to an older mode than the Augustan. Aphra Behn has been mentioned already; she hardly survives save for the remarkable and moving *Oroonoko*, the story of a Noble Savage enslaved by white tyrants. There is a miscellany of fiction before Defoe – Congreve's *Incognita* (1692) is piquant and pert, as we should hope from him – but it is only with Defoe (1660–1731) that the novel becomes something more than a minor accomplishment. He raises the adventure story to greatness, seemingly by a mere desire to exploit the commercial possibilities of travellers' tales and picaresque realism. 'Adventure' here has its double meaning; the episodes occur by chance, and their substance is self-preservation in danger. For his characters, as for Defoe himself, to live is to struggle for survival. He was nearly sixty when, apparently casually, *Robinson Crusoe* appeared (1719). Prolific pamphleteering and journalism (mercantile, political, religious, and social) had preceded it, and this with its originating commercial and political experience had established his points of reference as the material and practical conditions of life. *Robinson Crusoe* and the other novels – *Captain Singleton* (1720), *Moll Flanders* (1722), *Colonel Jack* (1722), *A Journal of the Plague Year* (1722), and *Roxana* (1724) – are as much the spirit of their age as are Pope's satires, though in a different way. They seem less works of literature than products of sheer unminded natural process, the rough reality of the time expressing itself. While Pope's interests are those of 'polite' society (though not snobbishly so),

Defoe's are those of economic man. The main characters are un-protected by social advantages – Colonel Jack the waif, living like a small animal on his wits, yet feeling things as a child; Moll Flanders, Newgate-born, orphan-reared, living by intermittent matrimony; Crusoe on his island. Life is chance, though with elements of coïnci-dence which can be interpreted (as the characters themselves point out) as destiny and retribution. Chance is the main thing; 'my ill Fate push'd me on now with an obstinacy that nothing could resist', Crusoe remarks, 'I hurried on and obeyed blindly the Dictates of my Fancy, rather than my Reason'. It is by their exertions in this state of life that we know the characters; they represent the struggle to live. Consequently the best of the novels have a symbolic power and an extraordinarily broad significance. Superficially bound to their time and place, they have (*Robinson Crusoe* above all) a universality beyond any other Augustan work. 'Defoe's excellence it is', Coleridge observes, 'to make me forget my specific class, character and circum-stances, and to raise me, while I read him, into the universal man.'

With the *Pamela* (1740) and *Clarissa* (1747) of Richardson (1689–1761) the full experience of plot-compulsion seized the public; the sexual dangers which Moll Flanders and Roxana had taken as the inevitable conditions of survival were immensely concentrated and made matters of life and (in Clarissa's case) death. To us the novels are far too long, and they were so even to some of his leisured con-temporaries, like Shenstone. Yet to others the length was not a deterrent, and the reason for the length (the protraction of suspense) was hypnotically magnetic. The same may be said of the epistolary method; often improbable, it can be startlingly immediate – it comes directly from those engaged and almost in the very moment of engagement. Any way of conveying material without loss is justified, and for many Augustan readers that is what the urgent voluble letters of Richardson's heroines (considerably less of his heroes) did. He experimented, from limited comedy of victorious virtue (*Pamela*) to extended tragedy of seduction (*Clarissa*) and extended comedy of social ethics (*Sir Charles Grandison*, 1753). His intensity (he is both intense and prolix) comes from his exploiting of the strongest natural feelings – the pressure of family influence, the magnetism of filial ties, pity for helpless innocence, the fear of outrage. His emotional world rose out of sexual peril or (in *Grandison*) sentimental beneficence, it is true, but this all the more invites the reader's apprehensive or admiring participation, heightened by Richardson's instinct (a partial foreshadowing of Sterne) for the minuter expressiveness of behaviour, each look and phrase telling. There is a deep and novel significance in this unprecedented interplay of personal tempers. Elizabethan drama has wars of nerves as intense, but they are briefer, are shared (by the playgoer) in a communal response, and invite nothing like so sentimental an indulgence. Richardson's achievement is a large one, even though its length and sentimental basis make it on the whole a historical landmark rather than a surviving pleasure; he had an electrical sensitiveness to the inner world of impulse which philosophy and psychology also were exploring.

The achievement of Fielding (1707–54), as all critics have remarked, is different. His novels are a kind of parallel-in-inverse to Richardson's: *Joseph Andrews* (1742), vivacious itinerant comedy, follows *Pamela* which it sketchily parodies; *Tom Jones* (1749), full-length comedy of unvirtuous man, follows *Clarissa*, full-length tragedy of virtuous woman; and *Amelia* (1751), near-tragedy of virtuous woman, precedes *Grandison*, sentimental comedy of virtuous man. Richardson puts one at the heart of a situation to feel its emotional luxury; Fielding derives his method from the tradition of mock-heroic whose essential quality is that the narrator preserves his separate status as dramatic presenter and manipulates his material for comic effect. Besides the novels there are *Jonathan Wild* (1743), a sardonic portrayal of flourishing villainy, and the *Journal of a Voyage to Lisbon* (published 1755), which despite his ill health (he died shortly after reaching Portugal) has all his flavouring of human comedy.

Smollett (1721–71) is, in a sense, more elementary than his great contemporaries in that until *Humphry Clinker* (1771) he deals in episodes rather than plots; there is, again until *Humphry Clinker*, least evidence of intellectual control or, save for a strong infusion of satire, any purpose superior to the primal impulse to tell a story. *Roderick Random* (1748), partly autobiography, is, like *Peregrine Pickle* (1751) and *Ferdinand Count Fathom* (1753), one of the century's tough novels (its toughness is amply paralleled in real life); it has the shape, to some extent, of Smollett's own life, and its hero, though less markedly than the later two, is unappealing. *Sir Launcelot*

Greaves (1760) is mellower – Smollett was influenced by Cervantes – and *Humphry Clinker* shows his extending humanity; the characters are presented, with lively illuminations of humour, for themselves and not as projections of their author's self-assertion. Smollett here presents his material in letter-form, and since the correspondents comment on events from complementary points of view the resulting synoptic view of life and scene makes this the novel in which the later eighteenth century most abundantly embodies itself.

Sterne (1713–68) is among the most disputed of novelists. The controversy centres on whether or not the experience of reading him is a rewarding one. In both *Tristram Shandy* (1760–7) and *A Sentimental Journey* (1768) he is often repellently self-indulgent, with his frequent prurience, his smirking and impudence, and his 'dear Sensibility! source inexhausted of all that's precious in our joys, or costly in our sorrows!' On the other hand, he provides an extraordinary complex of speech, thought, and action, in prose often reduced to a syntactic minimum with startling vagaries of punctuation, which sometimes serves for laughter alone, but sometimes, more functionally, suggests the quick slipping of thought from subject to subject (he made play with Locke's theory of the association of ideas). His allegiances are to something older and less rational than the Augustan vogue – to Cervantes as master of the noble-minded absurd, to Elizabethan satirists, to the great prose extravagants of the seventeenth century like Browne and Burton (though since he had also absorbed Tillotson and Swift there is a plainer manner in the *Sermons of Yorick*, 1760–9), and to Rabelais as the liberator in morals and style, the celebrant of Nature's joyful proliferations as against narrowness and sterility. Yet for the future too he had his significance, in showing new possibilities by which the novel might become not a simple mirror held up to Nature but a complex of nuances, associations, and apparent irrelevances. Fielding has the typical *ordonnance* of his time: Sterne's structure is that of a world where the fringes of the mind encroach on its central clarities.

It would be wrong to suggest that from Defoe to Sterne the novel was solely in the hands of five major practitioners. There were many others who, their works being dead, have no memorial, a few who are still just readable, and two or three who are persistently read. In the second category come that ominous portent of Gothic sensations,

Walpole's *Castle of Otranto* (1764), Henry Mackenzie's ultra-senti-
mental *Man of Feeling* (1771), an exercise in the well-meant pathetic
which reflects the ravages of 'sensibility', and Richard Graves's more
satisfactory fun with Methodism, *The Spiritual Quixote* (1772). In
the third category there are Johnson's *Rasselas* (1759), discussed in a
later chapter, Goldsmith's *Vicar of Wakefield* (1766), with its mellow
style and sympathetic comedy, Fanny Burney's *Evelina* (1778), a
narrative with the liveliness of youth, which Johnson praised un-
reservedly and which Reynolds and Burke read in a night and
Gibbon in a day, and finally Bickford's *Vathek* (1786), a fantastic
result of the eighteenth century's interest in Eastern story. Some of
these works, Goldsmith's particularly, deserve far more comment than
a phrase or two, but their reputations are safe and they may be left
for 'the common reader' to take his pleasure in.

Verse

As for verse, its general evolution is similar; first, disentanglement
from complexity (though still with wit and force); then the main
Augustan manner; then, or concurrently, new or revived modes of
feeling. In general the 'life and sharpness' that Ben Jonson liked, and
the eccentricities of metaphysical conceits, were moderated to a manner which sought (as Gray said of his own aims) 'extreme conciseness
of expression, yet pure, perspicuous, and musical'. Here, as in prose,
'wit' became not fantastic surprise but the cutting edge of reason,
surprising only by the fresh clarity with which it carved out true
perceptions. Poets and painters alike, Lansdowne's *Essay Upon Unnatural Flights* (1701) informs us, copy what is really 'in' Nature, in
its due proportions. Poetry is truth, and poetic 'figures' are admissible
only to 'grace, illustrate, and adorn', metaphors only to clarify:

> As veils transparent cover, but not hide,
> Such metaphors appear, when right apply'd,
> When thro' the phrase we plainly see the sense.

Allied thus to the intellectual revolution, poetry observes the 'real'
world, its social intercourse, its ethics, and its temper.

The Augustan stock is now lowest, perhaps, in lyric. The standards
of comparison are the supreme ones of the flanking pre-Restoration
and Romantic periods. Yet the Augustan lyric should be more es-

teemed than it is, for there is much to be said for poetry's being widely welcome in social life. This wide welcome included (though it spread far beyond) lyric, the more so that the lyrics of the time were easy to read and not hard to write. In brief and often pleasant verses poets expressed little perhaps of poignancy or rapture (good manners forbade the intensities) but much civilized compliment, morality, and even fun, the quantity of which in Augustan verse is surprising and not at all to its discredit.

The Restoration lyric has indeed been praised, though with a natural regret for lost pre-Restoration felicities. Briefly, it is remarkable for its poised movement, its 'private' content conveyed in 'public' expression as though (as was indeed the case) the personal thought was being adduced for the pleasure of a lively and sophisticated circle. The mode derives ultimately, though with decreasing power, from Jonson and his Cavalier followers like Carew and Lovelace, and predominantly from verse like that of Waller (1606–87). His *Go, lovely Rose* is in a straight syntax carrying a straight plea, with a beautifully 'hanging' rhyme which gratifies the ear and distracts attention from some banality of phrase ('How sweet and fair she seems to be'; 'In deserts where no men abide'). The sway of movement comes through sensitive alternation of longer and shorter lines, and the same qualities of trim form and movement characterize his lines *On a Girdle*. With Dorset's *To all you ladies now at land* we are in the Restoration world; the tone is gay, the language that of badinage, the syntax neat, and the persons (revealingly) plural. In other words, the social mode is here. In it there cannot be much artistic seriousness, and in comparison with the pre-Restoration lyric there is a blunted feeling, a loss of imaginative and intellectual power. 'The last and greatest advantage of our writing which proceeds from conversation' was not always an advantage. Still, the conversational self-possession behind many Restoration lyrics is not without appeal; it remains on the surface but it shows how integrally verse with spirit and point was a part of social life. Characteristically, many lyrics were written for plays, and have the gallantry or artful poignancy of their setting, just as many Hanoverian lyrics were written for (or appear in) periodicals or middle-class miscellanies and so have a more domestic air.

In the best Restoration work, however, the note is more serious and the rhythmic poise finer – in Cowley (though he belongs rather to the declining mode), Rochester (1647–80), and Dryden particularly. Rochester's *Love and Life* has a fine movement, an ostensibly insouciant argument, a hyperbole of light cynicism, yet its sense of transience is haunting and colours the professed inconstancy. The sense is more striking still in *Absent from Thee*, where the lilt and the decisive phrasing bear an overtone of world weariness that anticipates Byron. It is not surprising that Burnet commented on Rochester's 'strange vivacity of thought' and his 'subtility and sublimity both, that were scarce imitable'. Dryden's lyrics are among the Restoration's most impressive: thought moves in them (as in so much of his best work) without intricacy but with beautiful management and haunting gravity. *I feed a flame within*, from *Secret Love* (1668), has a grave movement with a yielding regret in the breaking-away of double rhymes, the emotion contained and not extravagant, the imagery subdued save for one perfect tremulous moment:

> Not a sigh, not a tear, my pain discloses,
> But they fall silently, like dew on roses.

The wonderful *Farewell, ungrateful Traitor*, from *The Spanish Friar* (1681), is a dramatic lyric from the woman betrayed; it carries its thought on a firm rhythm with falling rhymes in plangent succession. The best lyrics of Sedley (1639–1701) are almost as good in careful thought and earnest phrase – *To Cloris, Constancy, Ah Cloris that I now could sit, Love still has something of the sea*, and the exquisite *Not Celia that I juster am.*

Of other Restoration qualities there is room only for two – for the moral lyric deriving through Jonson from Horace (Waller's *When we for age could neither read nor write* is a famous example), and for bravura-fancy deriving from an older magic, like Aphra Behn's *Love in fantastique Triumph sate*, from *Abdelazar* (1677), with bleeding hearts, love's 'strange tyrannic power', and a paradoxical idea (woman providing love's weapons, man his passive yearning). The Restoration liked its Elizabethan drama, after all, and witnessed the last years of the 'last' Elizabethan (Shirley, 1596–1666) and of Carolines like Vaughan, Cowley, and Traherne. A fine and late example of the richer fashion is Congreve's *On Mrs Arabella Hunt, Singing* (1692).

The eighteenth century lowers the lyric to the level of prose sense, and draws its style from conversation, from Dryden's disciplined grace, and from the spareness of the moral lyric (as in Dryden's exequy for the Restoration years, *Diana's Hunting-song*, or Pope's *Happy the Man*, both 1700). But if less piquant the species still ranges widely, as an art-form co-extensive with social life: there are ballad-opera verses (wedded, often, to folk-tunes), like those in Gay's *Beggar's Opera* or *Acis and Galatea*; there are patriotic songs – *The National Anthem*, *The British Grenadiers*, Thomson's *Rule, Britannia*, Garrick's *Hearts of Oak*, or Cowper's *Loss of the Royal George*; there are bucolics – *A-hunting we will go*, *The Roast Beef of Old England*; there are ballad-imitations – Carey's *Sally in our Alley*, Goldsmith's *Elegy on a Mad Dog*, and Cowper's *John Gilpin*; there are mock-heroics, social chitchat, domestic vignettes, compliments, satires – light like *The Vicar of Bray*, or severe in Swift, and in Johnson's *Short Song of Congratulation*; and there is controlled meditation like Dodington's *Love thy Country, wish it well*, Johnson's *Death of Dr Levet*, and (its climax) Cowper's *Castaway*, which combines terror and economy in one of the century's great poems. The Augustan lyric amply covers normal experience; in Prior (1664–1721) it has a virtuoso in the easy and witty vernacular of the fashionable world, in that truly Augustan social use of the living language, and in Cowper (1731–1800) it has, outside the moments of tragedy, a modest master of domesticity, amusing or poignant.

The Augustan verse a modern reader usually hears about first, unfortunately, is satire, which eludes him in proportion as it came home to its contemporaries. Still, satire's vogue was to the age's credit, since it was the ally of civilization; as Mulgrave wrote:

> Of all the ways that wisest men could find
> To mend the age, and mortify mankind,
> Satire, well-writ, has most successful prov'd.

Its first triumphs were political, particularly in Butler's *Hudibras* (1663–78), and Dryden's *Absalom* (1681–2), *MacFlecknoe* (1682), and *The Medall* (1678–82). Butler's art is the satiric grotesque with much strength of idea, in hurtling and humorous octosyllabics to which the later Augustans looked back as a change from the discipline of more respectable forms. But whereas Butler is a stimulating curiosity, Dryden is a great poet, for the reason that makes great poets great –

a genius for verse-rhythm and an exceptional expressiveness of language. With the satires go the discourse-poems *Religio Laici* (1682) and *The Hind and the Panther* (1687), where satire is incidental. The ruling qualities are decisive wit, good-tempered scorn, and vernacular energy. The poems are public utterance, emphasized by assonance and alliteration, varied in speed and pause, impudently reminiscent of such dignified precedents as the Bible and Milton, and tightly managed in thought.

Yet there are degrees of greatness, and Dryden, though often more easily enjoyable than Pope (1688–1744), cannot really contest the supremacy of his successor, whose range of interest and vitality of expression are much greater than his own. Pope is the greater poet in virtue not of immediate accessibility (one must grow into much of his work in a way unnecessary with Dryden) but of his crystallization of the Augustan world in a style not less animated by vernacular but more subtle in its complex of sense-and-feeling. *The Rape of the Lock* (1712–14) not only recounts a social frivolity but acts the scenes and emotions, conveys colour and texture of materials, light and warmth of summer, airy substance of sylphs, sheen and whisper of their wings, pride and passion of the outraged lady – and all this by multiple activity of words in which sound, meaning, movement, sensory qualities, and feelings are evoked simultaneously, the total situation being given immediately, as very rarely elsewhere in poetry. The same is true of the other great poems – the best *Moral Essays* (1731–5), the *Epistle to Augustus* (1737), *The Epilogue to the Satires* (1738), parts of *The Dunciad* (1728–43), and, best of all, the *Epistles to Arbuthnot* (1735), that clear and complex poem in which the poetasters can be seen, felt and heard, their tempers high and desperate, their voices strident, their scribbling frenzies symbolized by a madman's charcoal squeaking on his whitewashed cell.

Not all Pope's work is satire, yet to include the rest of it here is convenient. There are delicate *Pastorals* (1709), whence Handel composed 'Where'er you walk'; the ingenious discourse-poems the *Essay on Criticism* (1711) and *Essay on Man* (1733–4); the *Elegy to the Memory of an Unfortunate Lady* (1717), where strains of metaphysical wit link up with heroic rant on one side and on the other with purity foreshadowing Collins and dignity foreshadowing Gray; simulated passion in *Eloisa to Abelard* (1717 – his venture into medieval-picturesque); pleasant *Epistles – To a Young Lady on her Leaving Town*, *To Robert Earl of Oxford*, *To James Craggs*, *To Mr Jervas*, and *To Miss Blount*; and finally the *Imitations of Horace* (1733–8), in which Pope adapts to Augustan England his predecessor's commentary on Augustan Rome. One deterrent to the modern reader is Pope's dependence on contemporary references; another is the worldliness of his interests (save, he might properly protest, in the *Essay on Man*, where the theme of human life related to God and society is as highly conceived as possible). Experienced readers often admire him profoundly, but to others he must be introduced with a care unnecessary in the case of the greater nineteenth-century poets. Indeed, argument about his poetic status started almost with his death (to neglect the personal enemies who questioned it even earlier): deeper veins were available in the always-admired Shakespeare and the increasingly-admired Milton, and as early as 1726 James Thomson's preface to *Winter* (2nd edition) called for poetry's rescue from social satire, by the choice of 'great and serious subjects' such as arise in 'wild romantic country'. Pope's greatness lies elsewhere, in a deeply responsible concern for taste, intelligence, and humanity, expressed with an artistic intensity and personal passion which fuse into vividness, and sometimes beauty, the raw material of Hanoverian life.

Pope does not monopolize satire and social verse; other poets have their own voices. Swift can be racy in doggerel (*Mrs Harris's Petition*) journalistic in songs and ballads, tart, friendly, angry, or disgusting in squibs and narratives. The best of him is in the verses *On the Death of Dr Swift* (1731), a sardonic apologia as much in the idiom of Augustanism as any poem could be. Swift never quits reality an inch; he recites the substance of life. Gay's is another personal voice: *The Fan* (1714) is interesting mainly as showing how inimitable is *The Rape of the Lock* from which it derives; still, its melody is lithe and continuous, and its imagery has Gay's heightened gleam. *Trivia* (1716) is intimate comedy of town life; in the dignity of heroic couplets it maintains an affectionate mockery and sometimes attains a beauty which transforms the commonplace. The town reappears in Johnson's *London* (1738), vigorous and severe, full of epigrams in that mode by which epigram is the moral passion of a deeply-experiencing mind. The same, more decidedly, is true of *The Vanity of Human Wishes* (1749), imitating Juvenal's tenth satire as *London* the third, evoking a crowded scene not of the ambitiously futile insect-nuisances of the *Epistle to Arbuthnot*, bound to Grub Street in place and time, but more symbolic of general human life with its named and nameless figures pressing towards fatedly elusive or unattainable goals. Of succeeding satirists (*The Vanity* is satire not as ridicule but as moral rectification) the major names are those of Churchill (1731–64) and Crabbe (1754–1832). The former is too attached to his time now to be much read, yet his energy reminds us that force was a prized Augustan quality and his bite of phrase is not entirely outdone by Dryden or Byron. Crabbe's best poems (*The Parish Register*, 1807, and later works) fall outside this volume, but even the early *Inebriety* (1775) and *The Village* (1783) have exact observation and bold attack, later modulated to subtle correspondences with sense and psychological skill in realistic narrative. *The Village*, a hit at Goldsmith's pastoral sentiment, records his Suffolk scene with severe accuracy, and uses its couplets to sharpen detail and determine closely the reader's response.

A mode as characteristic of the Augustans as satire was the discourse, the reflection of personal interests and observations. In its aspect as a dream of country retirement it goes back to Martial and Horace; Cowley translated Martial in that poem praising moderate life which he includes in the essay *Of Myself*: he wrote *The Wish*, in verse, and *The Garden*, in prose, in the same mode. As for Horace, translating him was an Augustan pastime; he appealed through his praise of the golden mean, his sober morality of human life, his desire for his Sabine farm, and his enjoyment of friendship; he encouraged that praise of gentry-pleasures which the Augustans made their own. Swift began to translate the sixth satire of his second book –

> I've often wished that I had clear
> For life, six hundred pounds a year,
> A handsome House to lodge a Friend,
> A River at my Garden's end –

and Pope finished it (*Imitations of Horace*). Pomfret's *The Choice* (1700) is an alert significant poem in the same manner; so, in parts, are Lady Winchilsea's *Petition for an Absolute Retreat* (1713) and Matthew Green's witty and sensible *The Spleen* (1737). This cheerful mode in which the Augustans unbuttoned is in Cowper, though he transforms it as much as Goldsmith's *Deserted Village* transforms the pastoral. His leisurely blank verse in *The Task* (1785), and many of his letters, record the quiet pleasures of his retirement. Their placidity does not entirely conceal the religious torments from which he sought refuge; his observation of friends, pets, village life, and the country-side is the escape of a man who has looked into hell: its concealed frame of reference is anything but mere Horatian amenity.

In another sense *The Task* is more than the ripe fruit of gentry-contentment; it is a long meditation on life, perambulating agree-ably through quiet landscapes and personal reflections. James Thomson's *The Seasons* (1726-30) had been the first triumph in this genre, elaborated in successive editions and gradually losing its early fresh flavour, but long remaining a much-loved poem. It is important in revealing the possibilities, pictorial and emotional, of landscape; with absorbed though laborious care it observes its subject. Some-times it is grandiosely effective, sometimes sensitively true. But an age which inherits Wordsworth, Keats, Tennyson, and Arnold does not benefit much from Thomson's heavy embroidery and often dense style. Except to the professed student, one mentions *The Seasons* without special commendations; the true life of Augustanism runs in less congested channels. The same applies more strongly still to Akenside's *Pleasures of Imagination* (1744), even though it fore-shadows Wordsworth; to Somerville's *Chace* (1735 – source of the phrase 'the sport of kings'), though it has the charm of sporting prints; and to Dyer's *Fleece* (1757), though it sings the wool-trade with honest observation and amiably rotund diction. Dyer's *Grongar Hill* (1726), however, is an agreeable landscape-poem which will survive, as will the amusing Spenserian imitations of Shenstone's *Schoolmistress* (1737-42) and Thomson's *Castle of Indolence* (1748), signs of a more indulgent literary taste.

Goldsmith, Gray, Smart, and Collins are the other poetic orna-ments of Johnson's age. Goldsmith's *Traveller* (1764) is a true and thoughtful poem; *The Deserted Village* (1770) is much more. Gold-smith's gift is a pure style, not at all aseptic, but lucid and gently effulgent; his feelings are simple but haunting, for the lost years of youth and the vanished 'innocence and ease' of country life, banished by oppressors. To them the reader easily and rightly yields unless he is too distrustful of the thin partitions dividing sentiment from sentimentality. About Gray's *Elegy* (1751) there is not even that qualification to make; it is rich in effect, harmonious in mood and substance. The richness comes from the ranging of the theme (the simple country burial ground) through perspectives of literary reminiscence, historical greatness, 'the boast of heraldry, the pomp of power', Nature's laws which ordain that gems shall be hidden in ocean-depths and flowers in deserts, and finally time's inevitability which parts man from the loved familiarities of life. Round the humble theme Gray amasses a large potency, but balances it so that nothing of strain or melodrama enters; this is that troubling and familiar commonplace of mortality given the steadiness of acceptance, the fortifying breadth of universal relevance, and the music of phrases evolving with grave decorum. Each line, less decently handled, might touch off sentimentality, but Gray carries a full tide of feeling without letting it overflow. The best of his other work is the *Odes* (1747–57) – *On the Spring*, *Eton College*, *The Progress of Poesy*, *The Bard*, and *The Pleasure Arising from Vicissitude*. It is remarkable among Augustan odes for the rhythmical impetus which bears it along, and for phrase after phrase that dwells in the mind with a happy finality; yet it remains at a distance, rhetorically splendid but personal neither to the reader nor on the whole, it would seem, to the writer. Into the *Elegy* went the ordering, the literary memories, the thoughtful though conventional moralizing, the generalized but communicative phrasing, the modulated sound and movement which the *Odes* abound in, and for once they were transformed from the 'cumbrous splendour' that Johnson deprecates there into perfect thought and phrase.

As for Smart (1722–71), he lives virtually by one poem, the *Song to David* (1763). He is often spoken of as a poetic oddity, a kind of 'sport' in inappropriate surroundings. The only odd thing, critically speaking, is his brilliance and passion, for he has behind him a long tradition, by no means dead in the eighteenth century, of Biblical inspiration, and the shorter but powerful one of hymnody. Augustanism was not restricted to drawing-rooms and coffee-houses, and its churches and chapels were not always prosaic. Line by line in shining and urgent phrases the poem sings David's virtues and through them creation's manifold duties of praise. It ranges the world partly with the enriching imagery of the Bible to express the urge of religious adoration, but partly also with a strong independent vision of living things in their beauty and power. This would be an astonishing poem at any time; it is not really the more astonishing for being written when it was.

To end this survey of Augustan poets with Collins (1721–59) is not to climax them (indeed, they are too varied to submit to any single figure), but is certainly to leave them with one whose quality outshines nearly all of them and whose best work, though minute in bulk, is major poetry. Often coupled with Gray, Collins has a different, indeed finer, imagination: where Gray is dignified and haunting but not precisely *inward* in sensing his subject, Collins penetrates it by what seems sheer intuition. A good deal of his work was put carefully together of the approved Miltonic echoes and allegorical personifications, but those few poems which are his best – *How sleep the brave*, the *Dirge in Cymbeline*, and the odes *To Simplicity*, *The Passions*, *On the Death of Thomson*, *On the Popular Superstitions of the Highlands*, and above all, *To Evening* – have a purity and delicacy which sound Shakespearian even behind the Miltonic reminiscence. That Collins shares certain new interests – crepuscular landscape, ghosts, fays, and Highland mythology – is significant, but not so significant as the fact that he has a shifting grace of phrase, a fragility almost, which in delicacy and imaginativeness has no equal in his century.

Drama

For the brevity of this section the excuse must be that Augustan drama is less important than prose or poetry, and that it lends itself less to reading. Both serious and comic plays were, of course, mainly opportunities for acting, for the delivery of animated speech, the playing of strong situations, and the creation of a direct relationship with an audience. Much that in print is awkward (elaborated wit, elementary psychology, open ironies and asides, crowded plots, and stilted 'refined' dialogue) is useful material for the stage, and to apply standards other than stage-effectiveness is to miss the main point. Dramatic conditions gave the actor pre-eminence. Audiences and players knew each other well: a close relationship was further encouraged by prologues, epilogues, and the apron-stage (though the latter was fore-shortened in the eighteenth century as the auditorium was enlarged); type-casting encouraged expert acting in expected roles; and resounding tragic bombast or comic repartee was meant to dominate unruly pits and galleries.

The main Restoration forms are heroic drama (sometimes rhymed), 'humour' comedy, and comedy of manners. In his essay *Of Heroic Plays* (1672) Dryden derives heroic drama particularly from Davenant's *Siege of Rhodes* (1656), defends rhyme as exalting the tone, and claims that his own tragedies are modelled on epic as the most noble, the most pleasant, and the most instructive way of writing in verse, 'the highest pattern of human life'. The heroic drama's superhuman love and honour came to be satirized in Buckingham's *Rehearsal* (1672), robustly but more crudely in Fielding's *Tom Thumb* (1730), and sketchily in Carey's *Chrononhotonthologos* (1734). Yet heroic plays were an assertion of human splendour made, not altogether incongruously, by a court circle whose libertinism did not exclude flamboyant devotion and courage. Roger Boyle (1621–79) and Sir Robert Howard (1626–98) really set them going, Settle (1648–1724), Lee (1653–92), and Otway (1652–85) developed them, but their best exponent is Dryden in *Tyrannic Love* (1669, with the heaven-defying Maximin), *The Conquest of Granada* (1670, with the astonishing Almanzor and Lyndaraxa), and *Aurungzebe* (1676, his last rhymed play). It is outside the heroic fashion, however, that the best Restoration tragedy lies, in Dryden's well-modelled *All for Love* (1678), Otway's pathetic domestic tragedy *The Orphan* (1680) and vigorous *Venice Preserved* (1682), Southerne's *Oroonoko* (1696), and Rowe's *Fair Penitent* (1703) and *Jane Shore* (1714). The psychological climate of the eighteenth century was not favourable to the poetic force required to generate real tragedy, though it brought forward high-minded 'literary' drama like Addison's 'classical' and sententious *Cato* (1713), which died quickly after a brief *succès d'estime*, and Johnson's *Irene* (1749), which died even more quickly after even briefer success. It was favourable also to melodrama and pathos, such as gave Lillo's *London Merchant* (1731) and Edward Moore's *The Gamester* (1753) a long-continued hold on the stage; both these plays are vehemently histrionic, with strong villains and weak victims, effective for their age but certainly not for all time. But at least they remind us that the eighteenth century was, in its own way, almost naïvely susceptible to emotion.

'Humour' comedy and comedy of manners are not always separable; most playwrights indulge themselves in a fool or two drawn after Jonson's formula of 'one particular quality', and they all display social behaviour though not always in that witty fashion that 'comedy of manners' implies. Shadwell (1642–92) is the best 'humorist', in the old sense of caricaturist, owing debts to Molière and to Jonson, 'whom I think all dramatic poets ought to imitate' (*The Sullen Lovers*, preface). In speech often strong and picturesque he ranges from cheerful farce to coarse verisimilitude: in *The Sullen Lovers* (1668), *Epsom Wells* (1673), *The Squire of Alsatia* (1688) with its urban turbulence, and *Bury Fair* (1689) with its country pleasures, his prosaic but vigorous mind plants the reader in Restoration life more faithfully than does the wit and intrigue-comedy of Dryden, Etherege, and Congreve.

About wit-comedy, the Restoration's speciality, opinions differ. Condemned as immoral, vindicated as amoral, or praised as moral (since it satirizes folly), it has been found cheaply cynical or brilliantly gay, sparkling with wit, or factitious and dull. Its pedigree is from Beaumont, Fletcher, and Shirley, through Dryden's early comedy to Etherege (1634–91). After his unremarkable *Love in a Tub* (1664), the latter came nearer to comedy of manners in *She Wou'd if She Cou'd* (1668) and achieved it in *The Man of Mode* (1676), with the debonair cynicism of Dorimant (drawn from Rochester), the affectation of Sir Fopling Flutter, and amatory intrigue presented in repartee and witty extravagance. Such close recording of sophisticated society was considered a new style; it was, he claimed, 'the modern way of writing', and a contemporary remarked that 'What he writes is but translation/From Dog-and-Partridge conversation' (i.e. fashionable tavern-talk). The master of light comedy was Congreve (1670–1729) in *The Old Bachelor* (1693), *The Double Dealer* (1694), *Love for Love* (1695), and, most famous, *The Way of the World* (1700).

The flavour of Wycherley (1640–1716) is different. His contemporaries admired his mordant satire; 'in my friend', wrote Lansdowne, 'every syllable, every thought, is masculine', and his nickname of 'Manly' was not merely a nominal transfer from the hero of *The Plain Dealer*. His plays are *Love in a Wood* (1672), *The Gentleman Dancing-Master* (1673), *The Country Wife* (1675), and *The Plain*

Dealer (1673): the two latter in particular make a formidable impact, since a complex intrigue is carried on (as already mentioned) in language with a strong sensory charge and a flurry of satiric violences. The ferocity of Wycherley's moral judgements belongs to the Jonsonian tradition of corrective comedy; prefacing *The State of Innocence* (1677), Dryden wrote that *The Plain Dealer* was 'one of the most bold, most general, and most useful satires' ever shown on the stage.

Morally speaking, the general heartlessness of all the plays mentioned (except *The Way of the World*) and the triviality of what is so elaborately displayed are innutrient. But they stand or fall not on such grounds but on their virtuosity as stage entertainments, by characters which for stage-purposes are bold and actable, and by speech which, if often tedious to close scrutiny, electrifies the ear with unexpected simile, realistic imagery, and pungent vernacular.

Succeeding comedies must be enumerated cursorily. Vanbrugh (1664-1726) wrote *The Relapse* (1697), *The Provok'd Wife* (1697), *The Confederacy* (1705), and the lively fragment *A Journey to London* which Colley Cibber completed as *The Provok'd Husband* (1728); he provides clear plots, good cues, easy cynicism and sentiment, and energy rising to strong satire in *The Provok'd Wife*'s Sir John Brute. Farquhar (1678-1707) produced genial comedy of provincial humour in *The Recruiting Officer* (1706) and *The Beaux' Stratagem* (1707). To venture into the comedy of Cibber, Mrs Centlivre and Steele is to descend too far into the second-rate; it is more necessary to note how Restoration wit-cynicism modulated, through a more extended and sober taste, into virtue and didacticism (Cibber made a small and Steele a larger contribution here), and by the 1750s into sentimentality, against which Goldsmith's comedies of humour – *The Good-Natured Man* (1768) and *She Stoops to Conquer* (1773) – are reactions, and Sheridan's *School for Scandal* an anti-hypocrisy satire. Of all the dramatists mentioned, Sheridan (1751-1816) is doubtless the best-known; to name *The Rivals* (1775), *St Patrick's Day* (1775), *The School for Scandal* (1777), and *The Critic* (1779) is to recall clear plot, excellent cueing, captivating stage-situations managed with deceptive ease, and agile wit and fun. The 1770s, which contain these plays as well as *She Stoops to Conquer*, are a most fruitful decade in comedy.

Nearly all writers attempted a play or two, and Gay's *Beggar's*

Opera (1728), Colman's *The Jealous Wife* (1761, indebted to *Tom Jones*), and Colman and Garrick's *The Clandestine Marriage* (1766) have proved their vitality in modern revivals. Moreover, the eighteenth century is rich in dramatic ephemera – farces, ballad-operas, and entertainments – which are not literature but serve as a reminder that the theatre is not primarily a literary medium. The stage was a centre of attraction in London (the platform for a succession of famous players – Cibber, Quin, Macklin, Garrick, Mrs Oldfield, Kitty Clive, Mrs Siddons, and others) and a provincial pleasure too (Garrick organized a celebrated Jubilee at Stratford in 1769). It reflects the evolution from satire to sentiment, and the increasing appeal of Shakespeare; but except for Goldsmith and Sheridan its original works lack the final vitality.

NOTES

1. See Spingarn, *Critical Essays of the Seventeenth Century* (1908), I, p. lxviii. For the whole idea of following nature, see Spingarn, pp. lxvii ff.; Willey, *Eighteenth-Century Background* (1940), *passim*.

2. For intellectual equipment, see Sutherland, *Preface* (1948), pp. 58–9.

3. For 'wit' see Atkins, *English Literary Criticism: 17th and 18th Centuries* (1951), pp. 40–1, 56, 63, 99, 163; W. Empson, *The Structure of Complex Words* (1952), pp. 84–100; Spingarn, *Critical Essays*, pp. xxix–xxxi.

4. For comment on these aims, see F. W. Bateson, *English Poetry and the English Language* (1934), pp. 47–58; Spingarn, *Critical Essays*, pp. xxxii ff.; Sutherland, *Preface*, chapters v and vi; J. Lannering, *Studies in the Prose Style of Joseph Addison* (Uppsala, 1951), pp. 131–2.

5. See Bateson, *English Poetry and the English Language* (1934), pp. 47 ff.

6. For French influence, see Spingarn, *Critical Essays*, introduction, *passim*; W. P. Ker, *Essays of John Dryden* (1900), introduction, sections i–vi.

7. On the kinds, see Sutherland, *Preface*, pp. 121–30.

8. See *Johnsonian Miscellanies*, ed. G. B. Hill (1897), I, pp. 201–2 fns.

9. See T. S. Eliot, *Selected Prose* (1953), 'The Metaphysical Poets', and Willey, *Seventeenth-Century Background*, p. 87; *Essays in Criticism* (ed. F. W. Bateson), July 1951, April 1952: F. Kermode, *Romantic Image* (1957), ch. viii.

10. See the introduction to this edition, and especially pp. xlvii–lxxx.

11. For the differences between pre- and post-Addisonian prose, see Lannering, *Studies in the Prose Style of Joseph Addison*, pp. 85–94.

12. For details of the periodicals, see Beljame, *The Public and Men of Letters* (1948), pp. 248 ff.

13. For Addison's personal influence, see Beljame, *The Public and Men of Letters*, pp. 275–300.

PART
III

JOHN DRYDEN

F. N. LEES

Senior Lecturer in English, the University of Manchester

In 1649, while still at school, Dryden wrote a poem for a collection of elegies on the death of Lord Hastings, a collection to which Marvell, Herrick, and Denham also contributed. This was his first published work.

> Must noble Hastings immaturely die,
> The honour of his ancient family,
> Beauty and learning thus together meet,
> To bring a *winding* for a *wedding* sheet?*

it begins, and very typical it *looks*. Here are the decasyllabic couplets – a form which he was to develop as his own favourite and establish as that of a whole age; and here is the 'public' theme – no less prophetic of Charles II's Poet Laureate and a writer who was to be a *professional*[1] in quite a new degree. But as one really reads the lines it becomes evident that these are *not* the couplets of the mature Dryden, not, in fact, post-Waller, Restoration couplets at all.

> Must Virtue prove Death's harbinger? must she,
> With him expiring, feel mortality?

it continues;

> Is death, sin's wages, grace's now? shall art
> Make us more learned only to depart?
> If merit be disease; if virtue death;
> To be good, not to be; who'd then bequeath
> Himself to discipline? Who'd not esteem
> Labour a crime? study self-murther deem?

These are couplets reminiscent of those of Donne, with the poet struggling to bend the form to the shape of the dramatic blank verse of the age just passed – and the couplet has, as it were, grown strong enough to put up a fight. The result is unfortunate; cumbrous throughout, at times ('Is death, sin's wages, grace's now?') a positive

* Original italics. Other italics by present author, except where indicated.

feat of awkwardness; and it shows plainly Dryden's metrical relationship with the poetry of the century. The hint of a late 'metaphysi-
cality' in the wit of 'To bring a *winding* for a *wedding* sheet' is only
too fully confirmed in the conceits of some forty lines farther on:

> Was there no milder way than the small pox,
> The very filth'ness of Pandora's box? ...
> Blisters with pride swell'd, which thro' 's flesh did sprout,
> Like rosebuds, stuck i' th' lily skin about.
> Each little pimple had a tear in it,
> To wail the fault its rising did commit. ...

(note the tight squeeze of 'thro' 's' and 'i' th' '); and in the lines,
near the end:

> But thou, O *virgin-widow** left alone, ...
> With greater than Platonic love, O wed
> His soul, tho' not his body, to thy bed:
> Let that make thee a mother; bring thou forth
> Th' *ideas* of his virtue, knowledge, worth. ...

This is writing of the metaphysical decadence, what Dryden himself
would later call Clevelandism, the kind of 'wit' that was to arouse
Dr Johnson's disapproval in his Life of Cowley. To see it attempted
so conscientiously by the young Dryden not only fixes his point of
contact with the poetry of his time, but throws into relief the qualities
of his later work. As here, for example, from *To the Memory of
Mr Oldham* (1684):

> Farewell, too little, and too lately known,
> Whom I began to think and call my own:
> For sure our souls were near allied, and thine
> Cast in the same poetic mould with mine. ...
> O early ripe! to thy abundant store
> What could advancing age have added more? ...

with its easy, yet firm, verse-movement, and its natural simplicity of
expression, combining in a due solemnity of tone which is sincere
and moving. This time the natural quality, the spontaneity, of speech –
the speech movement, is caught by working *with* the couplet and its
pause, not against it. In the lines on Hastings there is, it is true, some

---

* Hastings's betrothed. Original italics in this passage.

promise of a characteristic conciseness and decisiveness of expression,
as in

> His Native soil was the four parts o' th' earth;
> *All Europe was too narrow for his birth,*

but it is to show what Dryden grew from, grew out of, that the poem
is worth quoting here.

Not that Dryden's later elegiac touch is always as in the *Oldham*
lines. He could in 1685 produce the superficial ornateness of the ode
To the Pious Memory of the accomplish'd young lady, Mrs Anne Killigrew,
grandiose in idea and form (that of the loose 'Pindaric' ode made
fashionable by Cowley – though, interestingly, a great part of it
consists of heroic couplets), artificial in a damaging sense, not much
less exaggerated in its hyperbole than the lines on Hastings but without the concentration of idea and conceit, the 'metaphysical' energy:

> Thy brother-angels at thy birth
>> Strung each his lyre, and tun'd it high,
>> That all the people of the sky
> Might know a poetess was born on earth.
>> And then, if ever, mortal ears
>> Had heard the music of the spheres!

– and showing the persistence in Dryden of a certain coarseness of
taste and insensitivity, with its melodramatic and intrusive

> O gracious God! how far have we
> Profan'd thy heav'nly gift of poesy! ...
> O wretched we! why were we hurried down
>> This lubric and adult'rous age,
>> (Nay, added fat pollutions of our own,) ...

and its almost comic closing stanza:

> When in mid-air the golden trump shall sound,
> To raise the nations underground ...
>> When rattling bones together fly
>> From the four corners of the sky:
> When sinews o'er the skeletons are spread,
> Those cloth'd with flesh, and life inspires the dead;
> The sacred poets first shall hear the sound,
>> And foremost from the tomb shall bound,
>> For they are cover'd with the lightest ground.

And the *Oldham* lines, of course, give no idea of the interests and vitality of his mature work as a whole.

Dryden himself at a late date in his life wrote in a letter to the Earl of Abingdon (prefaced to *Eleonora*, 1692): 'They say my talent is satire'; and few today would disagree with that judgement. 'If it be so', he continued, ''tis a fruitful age, and there is an extraordinary crop to gather.' These remarks lead straight to the part of Dryden's voluminous work that most compels attention today – and first to the poem written, it seems pretty certain, at the request of Charles II, to turn opinion against Shaftesbury and the Whigs, *Absalom and Achitophel* (1681). His couplets had taken most of their true shape as early as 1660, as his piece on 'the Happy Restoration', *Astraea Redux*,* or *To my honour'd friend Sir Robert Howard*, both of that year, will show; and before 1681 he was to exercise his versification strenuously in the heroic drama, and in his numerous prologues and epilogues – these latter bringing into play also his turn for the pithily mocking. He came, then, to his first considerable undertaking in non-dramatic poetry since *Annus Mirabilis* (1667) with a highly developed technique.

The poem begins with a swing, a good-humoured satiric irony accompanying the placing of Charles II (David) within the Old Dispensation:

> In pious times, ere priestcraft did begin,
> Before polygamy was made a sin:
> When man on many multiplied his kind,
> Ere one to one was cursedly confined, ...
> Then Israel's monarch after Heaven's own heart,
> His vigorous warmth did variously impart
> To wives and slaves; and, wide as his command,
> Scatter'd his Maker's image thro' the land,

the verse moving with conversational ease while the interest is engaged by the series of preparatory clauses in the paragraph, alliteration working to promote significant emphasis, the diction plain yet with body, and the metre really *used* in the expression. One notices how the repeated 'v' gives point to 'variously', and how the rhythmic plunge into 'Scatter'd' animates the word and thence the line, and strengthens the end of the paragraph. Or again:

* That is, 'Astraea – virgin goddess of Justice – brought back'.

> The Jews,* a headstrong, moody, murm'ring race,
> As ever tried th'extent and stretch of grace;
> God's pamper'd people, whom, debauch'd with ease,
> No king could govern, nor no God could please;
> (Gods they had tried of every shape and size,
> That god-smiths could produce, or priests devise:) ...

the first line of which shows a control of and freedom within the couplet which should disprove any idea that variety is in the keeping of a single caesural pause. Dryden's vibrant language and gift for expressing assured contempt shows already, and something of the power of narration which was to make his adaptations of Boccaccio in the *Fables* (1700) so attractive to Keats. But the poem has not a genuine 'action', and it is in the individual character-sketches that Dryden achieves most. First, of Shaftesbury himself:

> Of these the false Achitophel was first;
> A name to all succeeding ages curst:
> For close designs and crooked counsels fit;
> Sagacious, bold, and turbulent of wit;
> Restless, unfix'd in principles and place:
> In pow'r unpleas'd, impatient of disgrace:
> A fiery soul, which, working out its way,
> Fretted the pigmy body to decay,
> And o'er-informed the tenement† of clay,

in which a figure simply described in moral terms is created concrete, positive, enough to survive as a character in the poem by the sheer precision of the language, the energy, the capability of the words. Without such positive emergence, satiric comment on actual persons will rapidly fade to something of interest only as a record, hardly to be revivified by even the fullest explanatory footnote. Giving this terse sketch added life and increased value is its acknowledgement of the powers of Shaftesbury, an admiration for them, and, even so early in the portrait, the beginnings of a distinct personal feeling of regret at the perversion and waste of talents; particularly when they are turned to the upsetting of that 'common quiet' which, as he says in *Religio Laici*, is 'mankind's concern'. The humanizing sense of regret gets plain statement soon after:

* The English.   † That is, the body.

> O, had he been content to serve the crown,
> With virtues only proper to the gown.*
> Or had the rankness of the soil been freed
> From cockle, that oppress'd the noble seed;
> David for him his tuneful harp had strung. ...

Dryden's attitude varies from character to character, of course, and with it his methods of presentation. Zimri (Buckingham) receives a much tarter treatment:

> A man so various, that he seem'd to be
> Not one, but all mankind's epitome:
> Stiff in opinions, always in the wrong;
> Was everything by starts, and nothing long;
> But, in the course of one revolving moon,
> Was chymist, fiddler, statesman, and buffoon:
> Then all for women, painting, rhyming, drinking,
> Besides ten thousand freaks that died in thinking. ...

'Nothing long' though '*always* in the wrong'; the insinuation in 'revolving moon'; the juxtaposing of 'chymist', 'fiddler', 'statesman', and so on: there is not much respect here, but there is a trace of pity. For Shimei (Bethel, Sheriff of London), a very fourth-rate personage is created by a brilliant comic use of a kind of bathos:

> Shimei, whose youth did early promise bring
> Of zeal to God and *hatred* to his king,
> Did wisely from *expensive* sins refrain,
> And never broke the Sabbath, but for gain; ...
> The city, to reward his pious *hate*
> Against his *master*, chose him magistrate.
> His hand a vare† of justice did uphold;
> His neck was loaded with a chain of gold.

(It is remarkable how 'loaded' is given both physical and moral weight.)

> During his office, treason was no crime;
> The sons of Belial had a glorious time;
> For ...

and he relentlessly resumes the account,

---

* Shaftesbury was a judge.   † Wand or staff.

> For Shimei, tho' not prodigal of pelf,
> Yet lov'd his *wicked* neighbour as himself. ...

In the depiction of Corah (Titus Oates), to aid in the effect of sheer contemptibility, he employs a direct insulting language – though wittily embodied in a play of word and idea – and finally drops to rough physical description (in lines which provide one of his strikingly few reminders of Chaucer):

> Yet, Corah, thou shalt from oblivion pass:
> Erect thyself, thou monumental *brass*,
> High as the *serpent** of thy metal made. ...
> Ours was a Levite, and as times went then,
> His tribe were God Almighty's gentlemen.
> Sunk were his eyes, his voice was harsh and loud,
> Sure signs he neither choleric was nor proud. ...

– and what in contrast with the other sketches is not far from mere abuse takes on something of a positive character. His share in the sequel, *The Second Part of Absalom and Achitophel* (1682) (mostly by Nahum Tate), and his own piece *The Medal* (1682), offer nothing of the same positive moral creation as does *Absalom and Achitophel*, Part I, but they show again his command of expression and his power of caricature. In *The Medal*, for instance, we have Shaftesbury:

> Bart'ring his venal wit for sums of gold,
> He cast himself into the saintlike mold;
> Groan'd, sigh'd, and pray'd, while godliness was gain,
> The loudest bagpipe of the squeaking train ...;

in *The Second Part of Absalom and Achitophel* there is Shadwell:

> Round as a globe, and liquor'd ev'ry chink,
> Goodly and great he sails behind his link.
> With all his bulk there's nothing lost in Og,
> For ev'ry inch that is not fool is rogue:
> A monstrous mass of foul, corrupted matter,
> As all the devils had spew'd to make the batter ...
> But tho' Heav'n made him poor, (with rev'rence speaking,)
> He never was a poet of God's making.

---

* The serpent of brass made and set up by Moses to save the Israelites from the fiery serpents. See Numbers xxi, 6–9.

The midwife laid her hand on his thick skull,
With this prophetic blessing: *Be thou dull* ...*

Mac Flecknoe, published first in 1682, but now accepted as written
in 1678, though a highly entertaining lampoon on Shadwell, with
passages of fine comic description, is light in weight and too often
merely topically allusive; but its mock-heroic framing, which suggested Pope's *Dunciad*, is skilful. *Absalom and Achitophel* is, of course,
genuinely 'heroic' (it is entitled 'a Poem', not, as *The Medal*, 'a Satire'),
and in it Dryden is at bottom making another attempt at what his
age so desired, epic poetry, as a form of which he and others had
been cultivating the fantastic 'heroic play'. The confident, unfaltering
zest of the poem surely owes much to the concurrence of his long
developing weariness with the theatre, and his sense of a waiting
public, thirsty for the political literature that the licensing authority
denied them, with the pressure of this deep-rooted urge to produce
an epic. The reminiscences of *Paradise Lost*, then, are not without
significance – the reference to Adam and the Temptation in the
preface, and such phrases as 'Him staggering so when hell's dire agent
found' or 'Some had in courts been great, and thrown from thence,
Like fiends were harden'd in impenitence.' The poem is witty, but
not at all in a 'metaphysical' manner now – the power behind the
'conceitedness' has been schooled into one of clear analysis and
epigrammatic expression; yet it is the same intelligence in the anti-
climaxes of the Shimei portrait as in the 'metaphysical' notion of:

How shall I then begin, or where conclude,
    To draw a fame so truly circular?
For in a round what order can be shew'd
    Where all the parts so equal-perfect are?

from the *Heroic Stanzas* of 1658. His previous attempt at a heroic
poem, *Annus Mirabilis* (1667), achieves nothing of the order of
Absalom and Achitophel, though it contains in an assortment of styles
a good deal of promise and some passages of distinct quality. Its
quatrains (copied from Davenant's *Gondibert*) are monotonous, its
actions (sea-fights with the Dutch, the Great Fire of London) are
insufficiently interesting in themselves, are incapable of the moral
development of the later poem.

* Original italics.

In *Absalom and Achitophel* there is much evidence of the author's
gift and liking for clear, summing statement, for telling exposition;
and we should not be surprised, therefore, to find that his two other
major *original* poems, *Religio Laici; or, a Layman's Faith* (1682) and
The Hind and the Panther (1687), are works very largely of exposition
and argument, and that he translated – and impressively – parts of
Lucretius. The preface to the former, written before he (in 1685)
became a Roman Catholic, concludes with remarks on style which
well suggest the judicious, workmanlike approach of Dryden and
the 'age of Reason' then beginning: 'The expression of a poem
design'd purely for instruction ought to be plain and natural, and
yet majestic. ... The florid, elevated, and figurative way is for the
passions. ... A man is to be cheated into passion but to be reason'd
into truth.' There is a sense of calculation, of concoction, in reference
to the 'passionate', and a separation of it from the 'truthful', which
it is hard to imagine in Shakespeare or Donne or, in general, their
contemporaries. And Hobbes's philosopher's distrust of metaphorical
language in argument has evidently become a commonplace. All the
more seriously, then, must we take the purport of the imagery in the
rather surprising opening lines of the poem:

> Dim as the borrow'd beams of moon and stars
> To lonely, weary, wand'ring travellers,
> Is Reason to the soul; and, as on high
> Those rolling fires discover but the sky,
> Not light us here, so Reason's glimmering ray
> Was lent, not to assure our doubtful way,
> But guide us upward to a better day.
> And as those nightly tapers disappear,
> When day's bright lord ascends our hemisphere;
> So pale grows Reason at Religion's sight;
> So dies, and so dissolves in supernatural light.

Some feeling emerges from the imaginative expression here, enough
to draw attention to Dryden's restriction of the authority of Reason
in an increasingly rationalistic age – (which is not incompatible with
the truly Cartesian Adam of *The State of Innocence* (1673–4), his
rhymed dramatization of *Paradise Lost*, who rises, 'as newly created',
with: 'What am I? or from whence? For that I am I know because
I think ...').[2] Yet, of course, the imagery is 'plain' enough, 'natural',

and, to use Dryden's word in the preface to *The Hind and the Panther*, 'perspicuous': neatly analogous and explanatory above all. The perspicuity elsewhere in the poem may be testified to by continuing a little our quotation:

> Some few, whose lamp shone brighter, have been led
> From cause to cause, to nature's secret head;*
> And found that one first principle must be:
> But what, or who, that UNIVERSAL HE;
> Whether some soul incompassing this ball,
> Unmade, unmov'd; yet making, moving all; ...

The brevity, conciseness, and exactness in the sixth line, its precision of tone and rhythm, make a piece of perfect expression, and show not merely a satisfactory versification of ideas, but verse functioning positively to create lucidity.

The Hind and the Panther is a very differently constituted work. It is of great, indeed excessive, length, and sets out to express the now Catholic Dryden's altered views by means of a beast fable, the 'milk-white Hind, immortal and unchang'd' standing for Dryden's new Church, 'the Panther, sure the noblest, next the Hind' for his old one. Other beasts represent various sects – 'The bloody Bear, an *Independent* beast ...', 'Among the timorous kind the *Quaking* Hare ...', 'Next her the *buffoon* Ape ...', 'The bristled *Baptist*† boar, impure as he, (But whiten'd with the foam of sanctity,) ...'; but they are given no parts to play in the action, or, truer, there is no action for them to have parts in. The poem soon develops into a disputation between the Hind and the Panther, enlivened by occasional satirical characterizing touches, and couched in Dryden's most accomplished eloquence; but the allegory does little more than set the scene for the conversation piece and give opportunity meanwhile for a little satire on the other animals which is not susceptible of development in relation to their human parallels. The cautionary tale of the Martlets, presented with some narrative brilliance, is obscure in its point, and that of the Doves and the Chickens, though vividly told, has only the final interest of the contemporary allusion it makes. The poem is very deficient in narrative interest, but in eloquence, ease, and command

* Source.   † Original italics in these quotations.

of expression it is unsurpassed in his works. An autobiographical passage may be quoted here as a rarity:

> My thoughtless youth was wing'd with vain desires,
> My manhood, long misled by wand'ring fires,
> Follow'd false lights; and, when their glimpse was gone,
> My pride struck out new sparkles of her own.
> Such was I, such by nature still I am;
> Be thine the glory, and be mine the shame.
> Good life be now my task: my doubts are done:
> (What more could fright my faith, than three in one?)

– and how much less individually, less sharply, is this expressed than where he is not concerned with himself! The repetition in 'misled by wand'ring fires' and 'Follow'd false lights', the weakness of meaning in 'thoughtless' and 'new', the stock adjective-noun pairs that the couplet form encouraged, are all involved in this comparative debility of effect, all indicative of uncertainty with the intimately personal, all contributory to the unexpected tinge of emotionalism.

His adaptations of Boccaccio and Chaucer in the *Fables* should be mentioned. They have a narrative interest he never created in his original poems. Of the former Wordsworth wrote to Sir Walter Scott, 'I think his translations from Boccaccio are the best, at least the most poetical, of his poems' – but it will be well to recall Wordsworth's Romanticism and to note that he has just previously said that 'Whenever Dryden's *language* is poetically impassioned, it is mostly upon unpleasing subjects, such as the follies, vices, and crimes of classes of men, or of individuals.' He rightly observes that Dryden has coarsened Boccaccio considerably, a coarsening which appears too in his adaptation of Chaucer. Of the odes *Alexander's Feast* (1697) and *A Song for St Cecilia's Day* (1687) and his many songs, one can admire the complete assurance and ease of execution, but it is in much inferior modes. The verse is unsubtle; the substance, the thought and feeling, in the odes is trivial yet portentous, and in the songs is of a now happily outmoded archness and, often, a clever, superficial indecency typical of the Restoration drama from which they mostly come. One finds a refreshing quality in a very early song from *The Indian Emperor* (1665), written before the hardness and the smartness of the Restoration had set in:

Ah fading joy, how quickly art thou past!
　　Yet we thy ruin haste.
As if the cares of human life were few,
　　We seek out new:
And follow fate, which would too fast pursue.

See how on every bough the birds express
　　In their sweet notes their happiness.
　　They all enjoy, and nothing spare;
But on their mother Nature lay their care:
Why then should man, the lord of all below,
　　Such troubles choose to know,
As none of all his subjects undergo? ...

– where with all the slightness there is a modesty of manner befitting that slightness, a delicacy and point in the rhythm, not to be found in his later lyric verse: the curious melodic reminders of Marvell's *Garden* certainly do not recur. Dryden was not a lyric poet, has nothing to offer in the way of illuminating or moving states of mind. His attention is directed outward and it is rather on states of things, on events and the people in them, that he brings his strong and mobile intelligence to bear, his wit, his feeling for language, and his highly trained verse-technique.

Our greatest debt to his years of work in the theatre is for no play or part of a play of his, but for what they did to develop this verse-technique. It was in the 'heroic' play that the couplet took 'possession of the stage', to use Dryden's own words in the preface to that arch-example, *The Conquest of Granada* (1670). The dramatic blank verse of the Elizabethans and Jacobeans, by the time of the closing of the theatres in 1642, had arrived at a slack and poetically empty facility, which would hardly do for a genre of 'greatness and majesty' whose laws, Dryden suggests in the same place, demand the 'drawing all things as far above the ordinary proportions of the stage, as that is beyond the common words and actions of human life ...'. The couplet succeeds in these plays in conferring something of ceremony, an invitation to elocution, to declamation, which suggests a certain grandeur; but they are not endowed with any sufficient quality of feeling and imagination, and their poetry is negligible, even, surely, the passage on life in *Aureng-Zebe* (1675) – in the prologue to which

Dryden declares that he 'grows weary of his long-loved mistress, Rhyme' and 'would quit the stage':

> When I consider Life, 'tis all a cheat;
> Yet, fool'd with hope, men favour the deceit;
> Trust on, and think tomorrow will repay:
> Tomorrow's falser than the former day;
> Lies worse; and, while it says, we shall be blest
> With some new joys, cuts off what we possest.
> Strange cozenage! None would live past years again,
> Yet all hope pleasure in what yet remain;
> And, from the dregs of Life, think to receive,
> What the first sprightly running could not give.
> I'm tir'd with waiting for this chymic gold,*
> Which fools us young, and beggars us when old.

A commonplace sentiment issuing in language which is characteristically clear and fluent, and given apt metrical movement, yes – but hardly entitled to the considerable amount of praise that it has received. Its meaning is thin, yet it strikes an attitude, gives itself unwarranted airs. Dryden's habit of easy intelligibility, his taste for and knack of philosophizing in verse in these plays is clearly enough suggested here. *All for Love*, however, his treatment of the story of Antony and Cleopatra, with which he made a return to the drama in 1677, is his only serious play which has much claim upon modern attention, and in this, as in later plays, he uses blank verse, coming back to the verse-form as well as the material of Shakespeare, and thereby to a closer concern with reality. To have laid aside so completely the heroic couplet and to have produced such eloquent blank verse is a considerable achievement, but the poetry rarely rises above eloquence, and then never far above it. Consider, for instance, Antony's

> How I loved,
> Witness, ye days and nights, and all ye hours,
> That danced away with down upon your feet,
> As all your bus'ness were to count my passion.
> One day passed by, and nothing saw but love;
> Another came, and still 'twas only love;
> The suns were weari'd out with looking on,
> And I untir'd with loving.

* Refers to the never-ending quest of the alchemists.

Pretty in its way certainly, but merely fanciful, and in meaning tenuous in the extreme. Or his:

> ... my eyes
> Are open to her falsehood: my whole life
> Has been a golden dream of love and friendship;
> But now I wake, I'm like a merchant, roused
> From soft repose, to see his vessel sinking,
> And all his wealth cast o'er. Ingrateful woman!
> Who follow'd me, but as the swallow summer,
> Hatching her young ones in my kindly beams,
> Singing her flatt'ries to my morning wake;
> But now my winter comes, she spreads her wings,
> And seeks the spring of Caesar ...,

where one gets a little set piece of 'delightful' imagery which fails of any immediacy of expression because of the presumably decorative repetitious extensions of idea. 'But now I wake' is elaborated with the merchant simile, there are 'young ones' 'hatched', and so on. Neither Antony nor Cleopatra attains much stature; and such things as Antony's

> 'Tis time the world
> Should have a lord, and know whom to obey.
> We two have kept its homage in suspense,
> And bent the globe, on whose each side we trod,
> Till it was dinted inwards,

certainly do not increase it for him; while Cleopatra's

> Nature meant me
> A wife, a silly, harmless, household dove,
> Fond without art; and kind without deceit ...

merely softens the sentiment and makes Cleopatra an unconvincing mixture. It is an Antony that can say to the downright Ventidius, on receiving a gift sent by Cleopatra:

> What, to refuse her bracelet! On my soul,
> When I lie pensive in my tent alone,
> 'Twill pass the wakeful hours of winter nights,
> To tell these pretty beads upon my arm,
> To count for every one a soft embrace,
> A melting kiss at such and such a time ...

(*To Alexas, her messenger*)

    ... We soldiers are so awkward – help me tie it.

The neo-classic Unities of Time and Place are closely observed, and this further impedes the creation of anything like the sense of power and grandeur which heightens the tension and increases the significance of Shakespeare's play. The result is a talented but unconvincing treatment of these 'famous patterns of unlawful love' whose 'end accordingly was unfortunate'; and it is both impossible and, surely, pointless not to bring into blasting comparison that *Antony and Cleopatra* which it confessedly imitates.[3]

Clarity, ease, intelligibility are obviously present in a high degree in the passages quoted here, after the very earliest, and with them there is vigour and variety. These are features of his prose, too; and it is as a prose writer with these qualities that Dryden's genius has never been questioned – not even by Matthew Arnold, whose description of him, however, as a 'classic of our prose' had reference to his verse.[4] In his discussions of drama, heroic poetry, translation, satire, and other topics Dryden shows a seldom flagging interest in often strenuously detailed consideration of literary principles, techniques, examples; and the clearness of his exposition, the vivacity of his style, render surprisingly palatable discussions on matters of intrinsically little interest to the general reader of today; matters, too, which, although he was rightly distinguished by Johnson as 'the father of English criticism', are of some remoteness, as they stand, from the concerns of modern critics. They have an historically important and permanently refreshing freedom of judgement, a generous responsiveness (except in the niggling and patronizing *Defence of the Epilogue*), and an infectious zest. Historically, of course, they are most informative, not least the *Defence* just mentioned.[5] The *Essay of Dramatic Poesy* (1668) and the Preface to the *Fables* (1700) are justly his most celebrated essays, the one discussing in dialogue form the main dramaturgic questions of the day, the other containing his tribute to Chaucer: quotation here, however, will be of passages from the *Dedication* of *The Spanish Friar* (1681) which show his characteristic easy free manner present in both a vivid expression of feelings towards a particular play and a lucid statement of principle:

But these false beauties of the stage are no more lasting than a rainbow; when the actor ceases to shine upon them, when he gilds them no longer with his reflection, they vanish in a twinkling. I have sometimes wondered, in the reading, what was become of those glaring colours which amazed me in *Bussy D'Amboys* upon the theatre; but when I had taken up what I supposed a fallen star, I found I had been cozened with a jelly; nothing but a cold, dull mass, which glittered no longer than it was shooting; a dwarfish thought, dressed up in gigantic words, repetition in abundance, looseness of expression, and gross hyperboles; the sense of one line expanded prodigiously into ten; and, to sum up all, uncorrect English, and a hideous mingle of false poetry, and true nonsense; or, at best, a scantling of wit, which lay gasping for life, and groaning beneath a heap of rubbish ...

... as 'tis my interest to please my audience, so 'tis my ambition to be read: that I am sure is the more lasting and the nobler design: for the propriety of thoughts and words, which are the hidden beauties of a play, are but confusedly judged in the vehemence of action: all things are there beheld as in a hasty motion, where the objects only glide before the eye and disappear. The most discerning critic can judge no more of these silent graces in the action than he who rides post through an unknown country can distinguish the situation of places, and the nature of the soil. The purity of phrase, the clearness of conception and expression, the boldness maintained to majesty, the significancy and sound of words, not strained into bombast, but justly elevated; in short, those very words and thoughts, which cannot be changed, but for the worse, must of necessity escape our transient view upon the theatre; and yet without all this a play may take. For if either the story move us, or the actor help the lameness of it with his performance, or now and then a glittering beam of wit or passion strike through the obscurity of the poem, any of these are sufficient to effect a present liking, but not to fix a lasting admiration; for nothing but the truth can long continue; and time is the surest judge of truth.

There is interest, too, in the verdict upon Chapman, and the terms in which 'hidden beauties' and 'silent graces' are defined; and the figurative language is typical in its neat, sufficient, illustrative quality, and its accession of immediacy and expressiveness when, in the 'cozened with a jelly' sentence, his satiric humour is touched. The looser articulation of the sentences, the disappearance of a strong sense of Latin construction or vocabulary, the easier, more relaxed, good-humoured, more conversational tone – these are the marks of his prose; and it is from the loosening of structural habits derived from the Latin and the incursion of ways of informal talk that Dryden's variety comes, and in them his modernity resides.

A writer, too, of comedies, of a Life of Plutarch, a great translator of Virgil,[6] Juvenal and others, Dryden was a professional man of letters of rare versatility. Not surprisingly, much of his work has come to be of only specialist interest; but at its best, in both verse and prose, there is a completeness of expression, a feeling for language and a sureness of technique, which any reader should find exhilarating and educative.

NOTES

1. For a full treatment of this point, see *Men of Letters and the English Public in the XVIIIth Century, 1660–1744* (1948), by Alexandre Beljame, translated from the French by E. O. Lorimer and edited by Bonamy Dobrée.

2. For discussion of the intellectual background to Dryden's work, see L. I. Bredvold, *The Intellectual Milieu of John Dryden* (1934), and Basil Willey, *The Seventeenth-Century Background* (1934).

3. A higher opinion of *All for Love* is expressed in *Restoration Tragedy* (1930) by Bonamy Dobrée; from which F. R. Leavis dissents vigorously in '*Antony and Cleopatra* and *All for Love*', in *Scrutiny* v (1936), pp. 158 ff.

4. For Arnold's views on Dryden, see 'The Study of Poetry' and 'Thomas Gray' in his *Essays in Criticism: Second series*.

5. A full discussion of Dryden's critical views will be found in the Introduction to *The Essays of John Dryden*, edited by W. P. Ker (1900). See also Barbara M. H. Strang, 'Dryden's Innovations in Critical Vocabulary', *Durham University Journal*, LI (1959).

6. See L. Proudfoot, *Dryden's 'Aeneid' and its Seventeenth-Century Predecessors* (1960).

SAMUEL BUTLER AND 'HUDIBRAS'

IAN JACK

Lecturer in English, the University of Cambridge

> Nor is the world so well understood by observation of the little Good that is in it, as the Prodigious variety of Wickednes Folly and Madnes with which it is Possest.

(BUTLER: *Characters and Passages from Note-books*, p. 344)

BUTLER took the name of his hero from Spenser, and his great comedy cannot be understood without glancing back to *The Faerie Queene*. In Book II, which is concerned with Temperaunce, Sir Guyon reaches a castle inhabited by three sisters. The youngest loves pleasure, the second moderation, while the third is a sour hater of all delights. Sir Hudibras, who is contrasted with Sans-loy, the wooer of the younger sister, makes his suit to the eldest. In a stanza which throws a great deal of light on *Hudibras*, he is described as 'an hardy man',

> Yet not so good of deedes, as great of name,
> Which he by many rash aduentures wan,
> Since errant armes to sew he first began;
> More huge in strength, then wise in workes he was,
> And reason with foole-hardize ouer ran;
> Sterne melancholy did his courage pas,
> And was for terrour more, all armd in shyning bras.
>
> (II, ii, st. 17.)

Butler's Hudibras resembles Spenser's in being more famous than he deserves, in having more strength than wisdom, and in being inspired less by true courage than by 'melancholy' (in this context, madness). But by giving his hero this name Butler does not only indicate the main traits of his character: he also states his own attitude to the civil wars and the discontents which led up to them. The suggestion is that the Royalists, or the more extreme among them, bear an affinity to the youngest daughter Perissa and her lover Sans-loy; that the Parliamentary Party may be similarly compared to the eldest daughter and her wooer Hudibras; while the poet himself, and all moderate men, support the 'great rule of Temp'raunce'.

The title is not the only thing about *Hudibras* which reminds one of *The Faerie Queene*. In its whole conception and organization Butler's poem has affinities with Spenser's. The parallel between the adventures of Sir Hudibras and those of the hero of each of the Books of *The Faerie Queene* must have been deliberate. Like one of Spenser's knights, Butler's hero is involved in continual disputes and adventures, and woos a lady. But in all his endeavours he is an un-Spenserian failure.

The fact that Butler was familiar with the Renaissance doctrine of the heroic poem has a bearing on *Hudibras* which is frequently over-looked. Butler knew as well as Spenser or Milton that an allegorical meaning was expected in any long poem, and in fact *Hudibras* has something of the same complexity as *The Faerie Queene*. The strong element of the *roman à clef* has always been recognized; and there is no doubt that the poem was intended to embody a complicated allegory. As each of Spenser's knights represents one of the cardinal virtues, or the striving for that virtue, so Sir Hudibras represents one of the basic vices. John Dennis suggested that *Hudibras* is a satire on hypocrisy. Sir Hudibras is Hypocrisy embodied. Near the beginning of the poem the reader is told that 'Hipocrisie and Non-sence' are in control of Sir Hudibras's conscience; hypocrisy is satirized with particular intensity throughout; and in the brilliant passage, parodying the confessional dialogues and self-communings of the Dissenters, in which Ralpho scares Hudibras into thinking him a supernatural 'Voice', he asks him point-blank:

> Why didst thou chuse that cursed Sin,
> Hypocrisie, to set up in?

To which the knight replies, without demur:

> Because it is the thriving'st Calling,
> The onely Saints-Bell that rings all in.
>
> (III, i, 1221-4.)

Throughout *Hudibras* great emphasis is laid on the difference between profession and performance, outer seeming and inner reality. It would hardly be an exaggeration to say that in this poem every species of human folly and crime is represented as a species of hypocrisy.

Although political satire is the most obvious 'end' of *Hudibras*, therefore, Hazlitt was right when he remarked that Butler 'could not, in spite of himself,

> narrow his mind
> And to party give up what was meant for mankind'.

There are many passages where Butler makes no pretence to be limiting his satire to a political party, but attacks lawyers, women, the Royal Society, and pedantry of every kind. If *Hudibras* had been completed it seems likely that every type represented in Butler's prose 'Characters' would have found its niche in a comprehensive 'Anatomy of Melancholy'.

In giving his satire this wide scope Butler was following the tradition of such books as Barclay's *Ship of Fools* and the *Encomium Moriae* of Erasmus. Another writer whose work may have encouraged Butler to widen the scope of his satire was Jonson, for whom he had a great admiration. As in *Volpone* and *The Alchemist*, Jonson's main satire against greed is accompanied and enriched by incidental attacks on other species of folly and sin, so in *Hudibras* hypocrisy is only the principal target. Butler 'in general ridicules not persons, but things', said Hazlitt, 'not a party, but their principles, which may belong, as time and occasion serve, to one set of solemn pretenders or another'. Because Butler was a man of genius, what began as a political burlesque ended as what Dennis truly called a very just satire.

No passage in *Hudibras* is more familiar than that in which Butler ridicules his hero's addiction to rhetoric:

> For *Rhetorick* he could not ope
> His mouth, but out there flew a Trope:
> And when he hapned to break off
> I' th' middle of his speech, or cough,
> H' had hard words, ready to shew why,
> And tell what Rules he did it by.
>
> (I, i, 81–6.)

Such satire was thoroughly conventional: one has only to turn to Erasmus to find all the charges that Butler brings against rhetorical pedantry brilliantly deployed by the greatest of all the humanists. What is satirized is not rhetoric itself but the pedantic affectation of rhetoric, fine words and elaborate figures out of season. It would be a serious mistake to suppose that Butler is here rebelling against old attitudes; and it would be equally false to imagine, from his satire on rhetoric, that he himself had no use for it. What Butler wrote of Sprat – 'The Historian of Gresham Colledge, Indevors to Cry down Oratory and Declamation, while He uses nothing else' (*Characters*, p. 424) – is equally true of himself. The point is important because the modern reader, knowing little of decorum and the accepted 'kinds', has a natural tendency to regard *Hudibras* as inspired doggerel and its author as a literary jester who knew no other way of writing. Nothing could be farther from the truth. Butler's other works make it clear that Sir William Temple's description of Rabelais as 'a Man of Excellent and Universal Learning as well at Wit' is no less applicable to him.

It follows that Butler's choice of verse and style was deliberate. The limited value of metrical notations appears in the fact that the same name must be given to the metre of *Hudibras* as to that of Marvell's *To his Coy Mistress* and *The Garden*, as well as many parts of *L'Allegro* and *Il Penseroso*. Like the iambic pentameter, the tetrameter is endlessly adaptable: it is the use that Butler makes of it, the tune that he plays on it, that is significant. What is particularly remarkable is the rushing vigour of *Hudibras*, the unfailing energy of the verse.

Butler's metre cannot usefully be considered in isolation from the other aspects of his idiom, for there is a perfect partnership between his versification and his diction. Even if the verse itself were what is misleadingly termed 'heroic' (iambic pentameters rhyming in pairs), any serious attempt at the 'harmonious numbers' appropriate to heroic verse in the full sense would be ludicrously out of place as an accompaniment to the prosaic diction which is Butler's chosen medium. For this reason Dryden's censure of the metre of *Hudibras* (quoted in part on p. 118) must be read rather as a reflection of his own choice of a suitable metre for satire than as impartial literary criticism.

The characteristic mode of satire in *Hudibras* is that of describing everything in the most undignified manner possible. Satire and the sympathetic feelings are absolutely incompatible. Butler's aim is to kill any sympathy which the reader may feel for the subject of his satire, moving him instead to amusement and contempt. There is nothing indirect in the working of the satire. The method is that of straightforward 'diminution': the reader is told that the quarrels which led to the civil war were of no more account than a brawl for a whore, and his acceptance of this view is made inevitable (at least temporarily) by the fact that the whole affair is described in an idiom which ridicules everything it touches. Butler's subject is as different as possible from that of the romantic epic poet. Instead of Ariosto's

> Le donne, i cavallier, l'arme, gli amori,
> Le cortesie, l'audaci imprese,

he is concerned with light wenches and prudish viragos, coster-mongers and fanatics, rudeness in every sense and of every kind. And his style is equally remote from that of heroic verse. The elementary principle on which he works is that while many people might sympathize with a *crowd*, no one cares to take sides with a *rout*. The essence of low satire could not be more simple.

All has not been said of what Johnson called the 'original and peculiar' diction of *Hudibras* when it has been assigned to the category of low style. It is remarkably varied. The second paragraph of the poem, for example, introduces a new element, that of parody:

> A *Wight* he was, whose very sight wou'd
> Entitle him *Mirror of Knighthood*;
> That never bent *his stubborn knee*
> To any thing but *Chivalry*.
>
> (I, i, 15–18 – my italics.)

This element of literary satire demands modifications of style which enhance the variety of the poem.

The critical attitude which inspires the parodies in *Hudibras* is precisely that which one would expect of Butler, an Augustan conservatism looking back to classical models and suspicious of innovation. The principal targets are such writers of 'romantic' epics as Ariosto, Spenser, and Davenant. Other unclassical genres which are parodied include the ballad, the metrical romance of the Middle Ages, which survived among humble readers during the seventeenth century, and the prose heroic romances so popular in France and England during Butler's lifetime. Although Butler has his fling at modern translators, the great classical epics themselves are parodied comparatively seldom.

The literary satire which finds expression in perpetual 'allusions' throughout *Hudibras* is only one aspect of a comprehensive critique of the uses and abuses of the English language. No less than Rabelais or James Joyce, Butler was a fascinated student of language. Odd words interested him as much as odd ideas. It would not be hard to imagine him spending an evening with Robert Burton listening to the swearing of the bargees at Folly Bridge. It may be that he had no need to go out of his way to find freaks of language. If there is any truth in the tradition that he was at one time secretary to Sir Samuel Luke, he must have had every opportunity of hearing the latest in cant terms. Perhaps he used some of his numerous notebooks for recording the words he heard. With an intense satiric mastery he culled the language of sectarians and pedants of every sort. *Hudibras* became the receptacle of this wealth of strange words; as a result it has a greater variety of idiom than any other poem in the language.

Yet it would be quite wrong to think of Butler simply as an enthusiast for odd words. He lived in an age of linguistic flux when the native genius of 'the finest of the vernacular tongues' seemed to many good judges to be in peril. Sprat complained that the language had 'receiv'd many fantastical terms, which were introduced by our *Religious Sects* ... and *Translators*' (*History of the Royal Society*, p. 42). Dryden returned to this subject time and time again. 'I have endeavoured to write English', he wrote in his first considerable critical essay, which appeared in the same year as the Second Part of *Hudibras*, 'as near as I could distinguish it from the tongue of pedants, and that of affected travellers. Only I am sorry, that (speaking so noble a language as we do) we have not a more certain measure of it, as they have in France.' In this revival of the Renaissance zeal for ennobling the vernacular, Butler played his own part. 'That Barbarous Canting which those use who do not understand the sense and Propriety of a Language' is continually a target of his satire.

'This Canting runs through all Professions and Sorts of men', Butler added, 'from the Judge on the Bench to the Beggar in the Stocks' (*Characters* ..., p. 312); and he laid all these sources under contribution for his great satire. His use of the special vocabularies of trades and professions may be regarded as a satirical footnote to the dispute about 'terms of art' which raged so fiercely from the early Renaissance onwards. 'The Tearms of all Arts are generally Nonsense',

he wrote, 'that signify nothing, or very improperly what they are
Meant to do, and are more Difficult to be learn'd then the things they
are designed to teach' (*Characters* ..., p. 445). The cant of lawyers
he found even more objectionable than that of astrologers; it is
satirized in the language of the practitioner whom Sir Hudibras
consults about his complicated affairs. He says that he can find his
client plenty of 'Knights of the Post', ne'er-do-wells who live

> [By] letting out to hire, their Ears,
> To Affidavit-Customers:
> At inconsiderable values,
> To serve for Jury-men, or Tales,*
> Although retain'd in th' hardest matters,
> Of Trustees, and Administrators.
>
> (III, iii, 729–34.)

The affectation of legal terms by the half-educated so common
among the Roundheads is unsparingly parodied in the speeches of
Sir Hudibras, who delights to give authority to his pronouncements
by a judicious smattering of the 'Barbarous French' and Latin of the
law. His verbal habits are precisely those which John Eachard censured when he described 'a sort of Divines, who, if they but happen
of an unlucky hard word all the week, ... think themselves not careful
of their flock, if they lay it not up till Sunday, and bestow it amongst
them, in their next preachment' (*The Grounds, & Occasions of the
Contempt of the Clergy and Religion Enquired into*, in Arber's *English
Garner*, vii (1883), p. 268). Like Eachard's preacher, the Knight
disdains words 'such as the constable uses' as much as matter 'such
as comes to the common market'.

While the diction of *Hudibras* is remarkably varied, it is the astonishing profusion of witty images that distinguishes it most sharply from
the common run of burlesques. It is clear from the 'character' of *A
Small Poet* and from numerous prose jottings that Butler was keenly
interested in the analogical uses of language. Like Bacon's, indeed,
his was 'a mind keenly sensitive to all analogies and affinities ...
spreading as it were tentacles on all sides in quest of chance prey'.
If ever a man was haunted by 'the demon of analogy', it was he.

As one would expect, a very large number of the images in

* 'Tales' is a legal term.

Hudibras are of the 'diminishing' sort characteristic of direct satire. The realistic bent of Butler's mind led him to fill his satire with imagery from the most commonplace objects of daily use, 'Out-of-fashion'd Cloaths', bowls, watches that go 'sometime too fast, sometime too slow', 'a Candle in the Socket', and beer 'by Thunder turn'd to Vineger'. He takes his choice from the familiar things of the farmyard and kitchen-hearth, children's games and men's employments. Images from animals are particularly common. Mahomet

> Had Lights where better Eyes were blind,
> As Pigs are said to see the Wind.
>
> (III, ii, 1107–8.)

The Rump Parliament

> With new Reversions of nine Lives,
> Starts up, and, like a Cat, revives.
>
> (III, ii, 1629–30.)

We Dissenters – says one of them – have friends who

> Are only Tools to our Intrigues,
> And sit like Geese to hatch our Eggs.
>
> (III, ii, 895–6.)

Again,

> ... All Religions flock together,
> Like Tame, and Wild-Fowl of a Feather.
>
> (III, ii, 1455–6.)

These are only a few of the animal-images from a single canto: to quote more would be tedious. What is remarkable is the effect that Butler achieves. By crowding his poem with similes from animals of 'low' associations like dogs, cats, pigs, and mice he gains an effect of homely caricature. The reader feels that no more is needed to demonstrate the folly of Butler's targets than reference to the store of common sense summed up in the nation's proverbs and homely sayings.

In creating this profusion of imagery Butler was again adapting to the purposes of his own satire a common practice of the Dissenters, who were accused, with justice, of being 'indiscreet and horrid Metaphor-mongers'. 'As for the common sort of people that are addicted to this sort of expression in their discourses', Eachard complained in 1670, 'away presently to both the Indies! rake heaven and earth! down to the bottom of the sea! then tumble over all Arts and Sciences! ransack all shops and warehouses! spare neither camp nor city, but that they will have them!' Sir Hudibras's proud principle, never to speak 'to Man or Beast, In notions vulgarly exprest' (II, i, 157–8), inspires the speeches of many of Butler's characters: in nothing is its meaning more clearly illustrated than in their imagery.

As might be expected, it is not only the Dissenters whose verbal habits are parodied in the imagery of *Hudibras*. A connoisseur of folly in all its forms, Butler was equally amused by the extravagances of the poets of his day, and satirized their commonplace images:

> Some with *Arabian Spices* strive
> To embalm her cruelly alive;
> Or *season* her, as *French* Cooks use
> Their *Haut-gusts*, *Buollies*, or *Ragusts*;
> Use her so barbarously ill,
> To grind her Lips upon a *Mill*,
> Until the *Facet Doublet* doth
> Fit their *Rhimes* rather than her mouth;
> Her mouth compar'd t' an *Oyster's*, with
> A row of *Pearl* in't, stead of *Teeth*.
>
> (II, i, 595–604.)

Of the prevalent fashions none interested Butler more than the different varieties of the Metaphysical idiom, now (in spite of numerous late appearances) past its hey-day. As he turned the pages of such poets as Donne and Cowley and of his friends Davenant and Cleveland, there was nothing that drew his attention more frequently than their bold juxtapositions of ideas. His own relation to the Metaphysical poets is never more evident than in some of his images:

> His Body, that stupendious Frame,
> Of all the World the Anagram,
> Is of two equal parts compact
> In Shape and Symmetry exact.
> Of which the Left and Female side
> Is to the Manly Right a Bride.
>
> (III, i, 771–6.)

Butler was the first comic poet to invade the territory of Metaphysical verse and use with genius the spoils that he found there.

More brilliantly than any previous poet, he used 'wit' for the purposes of low satire. As a result he occupies a distinctive place in the evolution of the idioms of English poetry in the later seventeenth century. *Hudibras* was one of the principal channels by which the 'wit' of the earlier part of the century was transmitted to the greatest of the Augustans.

Yet it would be a mistake to think of Butler too narrowly as a satirist. Dennis found 'a vivacity and purity in his Language, *wherever it was fit it should be pure*, that could proceed from nothing but from a generous Education, and from a happy Nature' (my italics). Such a passage as this illustrates what Dennis meant:

> For though out-number'd, overthrown,
> And by the Fate of War run down;
> Their Duty never was defeated,
> Nor from their Oaths and Faith retreated.
> *For Loyalty is still the same,*
> *Whether it win or lose the Game;*
> *True as a Dial to the Sun,*
> *Although it be not shin'd upon.*
>
> (III, ii, 169–76.)

This is not 'high style', which would be out of place; but there are no cant terms in these lines, the diction is pure, and the image is handled with a remarkable felicity. The same is true of the *Heroical Epistle of Hudibras to his Lady*, which is not the work of a man completely unskilled in the mode of writing which it parodies. Indeed, *Hudibras* contains a number of passages that would lend distinction to any lyric of the age:

> For as we see th' eclipsed Sun
> By mortals is more gaz'd upon,
> Than when adorn'd with all his light
> He shines in Serene Sky most bright:
> So Valor in a low estate
> Is most admir'd and wonder'd at.
>
> (I, iii, 1051–6.)

No 'Caroline lyrist' could do better than this:

> To bid me not to *love*,
> Is to forbid my *Pulse* to move,
>
> (II, i, 343–4.)

or excel this image, perhaps the finest of all:

> Like *Indian*-Widows, gone to Bed
> In Flaming Curtains to the Dead.
>
> (III, i, 639–40.)

Such a simile reminds one for a moment that Butler was a younger contemporary of Henry King. Occasionally in reading him one hears the rhythms of the Caroline lyric resonant beneath the surface of the verse. A gift for epigram was not the only thing he had in common with Andrew Marvell.

In spite of the 'kinds' there was in the seventeenth century no such hard-and-fast distinction between 'poetry' (conceived of as a serious and, indeed, solemn thing) and 'light verse' as became a commonplace in the nineteenth century. As many of the love-poems of the time make clear, verse was a much subtler instrument then than it was later to become. A poet could modulate from one level of seriousness to another in a couplet, or within a single line. Satire and elegy, burlesque and 'the lyric note' were not always mutually exclusive. The best Augustan poetry retains something of this subtlety of tone.

Butler's distinction is twofold. He took over a traditional manner of 'low' writing and used it with a brilliance and variety of effect which were new things, and which led Dennis to call him 'a whole Species of Poets in one'. And, secondly, he differed from earlier burlesque writers in using this amazing idiom 'with a just design, which was to expose Hypocrisie'. So doing, Butler was true to his own ideal of satire: 'A Satyr', he wrote, 'is a kinde of Knight Errant that goe's upon Adventures, to Relieve the Distressed Damsel Virtue, and Redeeme Honour out of Inchanted Castles, And opprest Truth, and Reason out of the Captivity of Gyants or Magitians' (*Characters*, p. 469). By adapting burlesque to the fundamental requirement of decorum, a worthy and unifying 'end', Butler was able to write one of the greatest comic poems in the language.

ACKNOWLEDGEMENT

This essay is an abbreviated version of chapter ii of the author's book, *Augustan Satire: Intention and Idiom in English Poetry 1660–1750* (1952). It is reproduced by permission of the Delegates of the Clarendon Press.

LANGUAGE 1660-1784

A. S. COLLINS

THE development of the English language in the period from
Dryden to Johnson inevitably harmonized very closely with that
of the literature and ideas of the age. When men desired stability in
politics and society, they advocated stability in language. Since
correctness and elegance became the ideals in literature, words and
their usage had to be submitted to the same criteria. Order and harmony in life and thought must be reflected in the clear and graceful
structure and cadence of sentences. The good breeding of a gentleman was impossible without well-bred speech free from affectation,
pedantry, rusticity, and crudeness. As both the upper and professional
classes and the growing mercantile middle class became increasingly
conscious that material prosperity was a prime ideal to be pursued,
language was required to be primarily useful, a clear, easy, precise
means of communication. Science too demanded direct, unelaborate
expression. The expanding journalism of newspapers and periodicals
likewise favoured an easy, but dignified, use of words. The coffee-
houses of Dryden's and Addison's days put English to a refining
conversational schooling whereby Dryden's Prefaces and the
Spectator papers could be entertainingly discussed. As women helped
to swell the numbers of the reading public, authors kept their books
freer from 'hard' words. The new literary form, the novel, called for
a good central English to attract the general reader. In fact, the English
language from Dryden's day through the eighteenth century
developed steadily away from the rich individual freedom and variety
of the earlier seventeenth century, with its licence, excess, obscurity,
and crudity, until it became an instrument fully adapted to the needs
of a broad-based society which valued, above all, order, discipline,
good manners, common sense, prosperity, and a comfortable ease of
communication. Probably in no other period in our history has
English been so well written in the middle manner by all ranks of
society, even in the diaries and letters of the least literary.

From about 1660 there gradually developed a conscious anxiety about the stability of the language and a sense of the need both to reform it and fix it. If the language could not be rendered stable, then modern poets would in their turn become as hard to read as was Chaucer with his then obsolete English, which justified Dryden, as he declared in the Preface to his *Fables* in 1700, in presenting Chaucer in a modern version despite the protests of such as held there was 'a veneration due to his old language'. What could arrest such change? How could a standard of correctness be attained and enforced? How could the vocabulary be pruned of the undesirable excesses which for many years had been entering it by borrowings, adaptations, and coinages from foreign sources and from the jargon of political and religious fanatics of the Commonwealth era? For half a century it seemed to many that the answer lay in the setting up of an Academy on the model of the several Italian Academies and of the French Academy, which had been founded in 1635. Dryden in his Dedication to *The Rival Ladies* in 1664 wrote: 'I am sorry, that (speaking so noble a language as we do) we have not a more certain measure of it, as they have in France, where they have an Academy erected for the purpose.' In the same year Dryden was a member of a small committee set up by the recently founded Royal Society to consider means 'for improving the English language'. The committee met only a few times and nothing resulted, but the idea remained in Dryden's mind. Roscommon thought similarly. An Academy was one of the proposals in Defoe's *Essay upon Projects* in 1697. In 1712 Swift addressed to Harley, the Tory Lord Treasurer, the last notable plea for an Academy in *A Proposal for Correcting, Improving and Ascertaining* (i.e. fixing) *the English Tongue*, but whatever prospects lay in his powerful advocacy were ruined no doubt by the collapse of the Tories in 1714. Sir Robert Walpole was not the man to spend good public money on an Academy.

That the idea of an Academy failed to take shape was due to various factors. For one thing, an Academy with any real authority over the language hardly seems a natural institution to grow in the soil of that practical, common-sense, and individualistic age, even though that age exalted the virtues of order and correctness. It was natural enough for an Academy to be advocated by Dryden, who was something of a literary dictator, by Defoe, whose bent was for planning, and by Swift, a dictator at heart, but one may well imagine that to most of the Augustans the answer lay in common-sense efforts by all who were concerned for the well-being of the language and the future of literature. That, at any rate, was how the reform of the language was largely achieved. From many quarters came the plea for 'correctness', for easy, direct, and perspicuous communication of meaning. Sprat in his *History of the Royal Society* (1667), while himself strongly in favour of an Academy ('such a project is now seasonable to be set on foot, and may make a great reformation in the manner of our speaking and writing'), told how the Royal Society was already doing its utmost to reform the writing of English by exacting 'from all their members, a close, naked, natural way of speaking; positive expressions; clear senses; a native easiness; bringing all things as near the Mathematical plainness, as they can: and preferring the language of Artizans, Countrymen, and Merchants, before that of Wits, or Scholars'. In the schools Locke's earnest plea, in *Some Thoughts Concerning Education* (1693), for the exercising of children in English must have encouraged a better attention to the task in the following generation and have helped to lay a sound foundation: his book was steadily reprinted. And Locke further declared that 'whatever foreign languages a young man meddles with (and the more he knows the better), that which he should critically study, and labour to get a facility, clearness, and elegancy to express himself in, should be his own, and to this purpose he should daily be exercised in it'. Dryden was influential not only by what he said about good writing in Prefaces, and surely in Will's coffee-house, but by the contagious example of all he wrote. Addison too preached good English by the very success of his own style, and no doubt orally too to his 'little senate'. Swift by example and precept taught that good style was no more and no less than 'proper words in proper places'.

Reference, however, to lesser rather than major writers perhaps conveys best how the campaign for a reformed English was fought and won. One such was John Hughes, who in 1698 wrote an essay, *Of Style*, at the request of a friend whose 'enquiry seems more particularly concerning the language'. Hughes therefore spoke mainly of prose style 'as being that which is most necessary'. Summing up all the qualities of a good style in Propriety, Perspicuity, Elegance, and Cadence, he recommended to his friend as 'the best direction ... a diligent and careful perusal of the most correct writers of the language in their various kinds, with the conversation of people of fashion, that speak well and without affectation. The most correct writers that I know are Sir William Temple, Dr Sprat, and Dr Tillotson for prose, and Mr Waller for verse.' His friend must consider that for purity of language 'the rule ... is modern use'. Formal rules Hughes did not favour, especially for writing letters and essays; rules there must be, but his friend should furnish himself with rules deduced from the example of correct writers. Thus those who took the advice of a man like Hughes and were influenced too by the leading writers of the day, went a long way towards achieving a reformed English without the help of an Academy. Chesterfield, writing to his son in 1749, still spoke with contempt of his countrymen for not studying their language as carefully as the Italians and French studied theirs ('Witness their respective academies and dictionaries, for improving and fixing their languages'), but in urging the lad to 'make [him]self a pure and elegant English style' he admitted 'it requires nothing but application'. So, indeed, experience was proving that an Academy was unnecessary, and Dr Johnson in his Preface to his Dictionary (1755) went further, declaring such an institution un-English. The English in fact now turned to dictionaries and grammars as the best way of advancing that reform of the language which had already gone far, and the idea of fixing the language was generally given up. Johnson held that the inevitable mutability of language evidenced by history could be stopped neither by dictionaries nor by academies.

But before discussing dictionaries and grammars it is necessary to say something more of the Augustan vocabulary, and particularly of the 'poetic diction' which often comes between the Augustan poets and the modern reader, though rarely in the best poems. Gray remarked in a letter to his friend West in 1742 that 'the language of the age is never the language of poetry', and it was a view generally held, but the kind of language used by the poets depended largely on the kind of poem to be written. In satire the poet could and often did keep to the simplest language of everyday use: a scribbler 'at his dirty work again', 'pride that licks the dust', the soul that 'sits at squat, and peeps not from its hole', the 'painted child of dirt that stinks and stings' – for such themes Pope used the most direct vernacular. But as epic, pastoral, and ode were different in 'kind', and the Augus-

tans were convinced of the virtue of observing difference of literary
'kind', a different poetic vocabulary was considered necessary for
them. Pope remarked in the Preface to his *Homer*: 'To throw the
language more out of prose, Homer seems to have affected the com-
pound-epithets. This was a sort of composition peculiarly proper to
poetry, not only as it heightened the diction, but as it assisted and
filled the numbers with greater sound and pomp, and likewise conduced in some measure to thicken the images.' Similarly, when
attempting themes epical or of high seriousness or the loftier lyric,
the Augustans sought 'to throw the language more out of prose' by
a special vocabulary to which a study of Virgil and Milton contributed much. In this kind of diction Dryden, a close student of the
Latin poets and of Milton, led the way; Pope brought it to perfection
in his translation of Homer, and then it became for many years the
normal diction of the average serious poet. Hence arose such Latinisms as the constantly used *purple* in the sense bright, and *horrid* as
rough, *gelid*, *mellifluous*, *turgent*, *irriguous*, *concoctive*, *diffusive* (view),
protended (spear), *ovarious* (food). Thomson's *Seasons* is full of such
words, though he could often be simplicity itself: indeed, the contrasts jostle oddly, as in his description of a stag-hunt, where we read
of the huntsmen 'adhesive to the track', while of the stag he writes
simply 'the big round tears run down his dappled face'. The more
ordinary or utilitarian the subject, the more needful the poet generally felt it to avoid the prosaic word at which his sophisticated readers
might laugh. So Dyer in his *Fleece* may let his sheep 'with busy
mouths ... scoop white turnips', but he quickly changes the vulgar
turnip to 'the watery juices of the bossy root'. Poetry indeed stood
on its dignity when it could not on its inspiration. Cowper, very
capable of simple English, felt still that the tobacco in a woodman's
pipe required dignifying as 'the fragrant charge of a short tube that
fumes beneath his nose'. Such efforts may to us seem verging on
parody, but they were in part due to fear of the Augustan parodists
to whom the natural often appealed as the ridiculous.

What perhaps particularly offends the modern reader is the constant use in Augustan poetry of terms like 'the feather'd choir', 'the
wingy swarm', 'the finny tribe', 'our fleecy wealth', and 'the foodful
brine'. Yet they had the merit often of being both precise and concise,
and they came into existence for that end, carrying normally a fuller

meaning than superficial reading detects. Thus 'feather'd choir' was not merely an evasion of 'birds' but a semi-scientific statement that these particular singers were birds, and 'fleecy wealth' conveys at once the physical and economic with verbal thrift. Moreover, this use of language harmonized with the Augustan belief in generalization, which Johnson famously expressed in *Rasselas*, where it is laid down that 'the business of the poet is to examine, not the individual, but the species: to remark general properties and large appearances'. It was an attitude to poetry which appealed to and sprang from the eighteenth-century's love of order and its desire for intellectual clarity, and from this pursuit of the abstract and generalized idea there followed naturally two other characteristics, the constant use of certain 'poetic' words and of personification. The stock of poetic words and phrases included *gales*, which commonly *blow*, *vales* often *verdant*, *train* perhaps *glittering*, *swain* and *nymph*, *lawn*, *azure main*, *tender tears*, *melt* ('pity melts the eyes'), *smiling* (land), *blooming*, *genial*, *frantic*, *solemn hour*. The list could be a long one. Many of these words – for example, *gale*, *blow*, and *swain* – were, by virtue of their long vowels, especially useful for rhymes, but on the whole the significance of this choice of certain words in preference to many others available lies in their general nature. *Gales* are merely the air in movement, *vales* a broadly conceived aspect of landscape. Formal epithets like *smiling* or *solemn*, *verdant* or *azure*, with 'decent' grace supported the generalization. It was all Propriety, conforming to the now established tradition of the reformed and refined language, which, as Johnson said, had been transformed from brick to marble. Similarly, personification was a 'decent', but rarely successful, attempt to give animation to the marble of the abstract nouns with which eighteenth-century verse was inevitably overladen. Partly following Milton's example, it was as near as the Augustans generally felt justified in approaching concrete treatment of ideas. For them it was vivid enough to conceive 'Youth at the prow and Pleasure at the helm'.

Poetic diction also favoured compound adjectives. Homer, as Pope said, showed the example, and so did Milton. Welsted in *A Dissertation Concerning the Perfection of the English Language, the State of Poetry, &c.* (1724) considered one virtue of English to be 'that it is capable of finely compounding the words often times, like the Greek'. Hence came such compounds as Gray's '*rosy-bosomed Hours*' and 'incense-breathing morn'. Outside his Homer, Pope hardly used them at all, but Thomson in the Seasons made free use of them, often agreeably – blood-happy hounds, romp-loving miss, lovely-shining leopard, and thick-nibbling sheep are typical instances. Adjectives in -y also became prolific in the poetic language. This suffix had, from the earliest stages of the language, been of the greatest use, and Elizabethans had used such words as paly and steepy, but with the Augustans the use and coinage of such adjectives became monotonous, partly for the value of the extra syllable, partly for poetic elevation and for conciseness. So, in addition to such favourites as plumy, wingy, finny, gloomy, dewy, balmy, there occur everywhere such formations as spiry, stenchy, sleeky, lawny, and brooky. Downy could apply to snowflakes, fleece, or even an orchard, such was the virtue of its typical lack of definition. Then, too, there were the Spenserian words. Earlier the imitation was deliberately humorous. Ween, wight, mickle, perdie, withouten, participles like y-covered and infinitives like grieven were an amusing colouring. A later Spenserian like Thomas Warton with his paynim, orison, besprent, and emprise was quite serious. In between, Thomson in The Castle of Indolence, truest Spenserian poem of the century, both smiled and worshipped as he used words like replevy, swink, and bedight.

The prose of this period invites less detailed comment. As in the poetry, a limitation of vocabulary was exercised. In the long run the general tendency was towards greater formality, as can be seen in the passage from the easy conversational style of Dryden to the balance and dignity of Johnson. As the aristocratic supremacy in life and letters of the Restoration period yielded to the middle class in the next century, the language naturally conformed to the change. The colloquial and easy, as well as the coarse, were avoided for fear of being 'low'. The free sparkling wit of Restoration drama was not to the taste of the later audiences who were addicts of the genteel sentimental drama; they might let Goldsmith and Sheridan laugh at their taste, but those dramatists had to observe greater propriety of speech than Wycherley and Congreve. A sense of literary 'kinds' was felt in prose too, though with less force. Thus No. 25 of the Guardian (1713) declared an historian's 'style must be majestic and grave, as well as simple and unaffected; his narrative should be animated, short, and clear, so as even to outrun the impatience of the reader, if possible. This can only be done by being very sparing and choice in words' – a remark followed by disapproval of Bacon's style in his *Henry VII*, for Bacon 'lived in an age wherein chaste and correct writing was not in fashion'. Hughes, similarly, in *Of Style*, held Philosophy to require a grave style, while Morality and Divinity 'were capable of all the ornaments of Wit and Fancy' and History 'is content with a plainer dress'. Probably the novel exercised the strongest levelling influence on the prose vocabulary. Richardson's middle-class sense of what was decent and suitable to be read especially by women reinforced the example of Addison's essays for women. Fielding had Eton and the Classics behind him, but a wider and less educated public to win. Smollett, ex-naval surgeon and prolific hack writer, employed a broad average vocabulary. All the novelists indeed, Sterne excepted, in their different ways kept to the middle kind of English, avoiding affectation and pedantry. Moreover, it should be remembered that the institution of circulating libraries dates from 1740.

On the whole, the eighteenth century soon became satisfied with the current state of English. Welsted in his *Dissertation* claims that English has reached 'the Perfection, which denominates a Classical Age'. After our having 'trafficked with every country for the enriching of it', he holds 'we have laid aside all our harsh antique words and retained only those of good sound and energy; the most beautiful polish is at length given to our tongue and its Teutonic rust quite worn away'. The time for extensive 'trafficking' had certainly passed. The foreign language that continued to contribute most to English was French, but even in the Restoration period, though there was a fashion of using French words in conversation and in plays, the number of French words that were adopted into English was not large. They include *ballet*, *nom-de-plume*, *group*, *tableau*, *champagne*, and *reservoir*, and in *envoy*, *aide-de-camp*, and *commandant* successors to military terms like *dragoon*, *platoon*, and *brigade* borrowed before 1640. Military terms indeed continued to come in during Marlborough's campaigns, and Addison in No. 165 of the *Spectator* mocked at the 'modish' use of such 'modern military eloquence' as *gens d'armes*, *corps de reserve*, *carte blanche*, and *cartel*, and wondered whether 'superintendents of our language' were not required to prevent the entry of foreign, and especially French, words. *Enfilade, bivouac,* and *corps,* however, entered in Queen Anne's reign, and there was a trickle of French words throughout the century, increasing slightly at the French Revolution. Among these were *envelope, salon, bureau, canteen, roulette, connoisseur, coterie, glacier, chenille,* and words of cooking and social life, such as *casserole, croquette, picnic, etiquette, sangfroid,* and *gauche.*

In fact, the process of borrowing was now limited to taking a few words belonging to the arts or sciences or describing special things. Thus from Italian in the later seventeenth century came the architectural terms *dado* and *rotunda,* the musical *sonata, solo, spinet,* and *vivace,* and the artistic *mezzotint, cartoon, caricatura,* and *chiaroscuro,* and these were followed in the eighteenth century by *colonnade, arcade,* and *loggia, soprano, trombone, pianoforte, cantata, oratorio, libretto, adagio,* and similar terms, and by *picturesque, portfolio,* and *dilettante,* together with *malaria, influenza, lava,* and *bronze, conversazione* and *alfresco, poplin,* and the word *firm* for a trading company. Many a country indeed throughout this period made a small contribution through the medium of trade and travel books. Of such were *vanilla, caramel, cigar,* and *quadrille* from Spanish, *verandah* from Portuguese India, *shawl* and *carboy* from Persian, *albatross* and *candy* from Arabic, *mongoose, bungalow,* and *shampoo* from India, *mammoth* and *knout* from Russian, and from China *tea* itself, together with *pekoe, hyson, souchong,* and *ketchup* and *kaolin.* From nearer home came Scandinavian *to run the gauntlet, cosy,* and *muggy,* and the old terms *saga* and *skald,* the High German *cobalt, shale, quartz,* and *iceberg,* the Dutch *smuggle, schooner,* and *Geneva* (shortened to *gin* in 1714), the Irish *Tory* and *banshee,* and the Scotch *whisky, pibroch,* and *claymore.* Latin, not so long before a prolific source, now contributed only a few words, including *pendulum, nebula, fulcrum,* and *calculus* before 1700, and *nucleus, propaganda, ultimatum,* and *insomnia* later, while the Greek contribution was smaller still, as with *botany* (1696) and *bathos* (1727). Of all such borrowings the foreign origin is generally clear enough at sight, except for such words from Germanic languages as *smuggle* and *muggy,* but all borrowings quickly received an English pronunciation, and one may note that even foreign personal names were anglicized as in a rhyme like that of *Racine* with *line.*

But if, with Welsted, satisfaction could be felt about the language itself, there was a growing realization that the use of the English language left much to be desired. There was often uncertainty about the correct meaning of words, and spelling, pronunciation, and grammar were all subject to variation according to the class and education of the writer or speaker. Hence arose the work of lexicographers and grammarians. The former were much concerned to register the correct spelling, and some dictionaries, such as J.K's *A New English Dictionary* (1702) and Dyche's *Spelling Dictionary* of a little later date, made that their principal aim. Nathaniel Bailey advanced further with his *Universal Etymological English Dictionary* (1721), which went into several editions and was recommended by Mrs Western in *Tom Jones* as the book to consult in order to learn 'a proper use of words'. Bailey was the first lexicographer to aim at including all English words. But there was still no authoritative dictionary in existence when Johnson issued his Plan in 1747, and when his Dictionary itself appeared in 1755 his achievement was considered, as indeed it was, prodigious. He aimed to include all good English words, excluding only technical or vulgar words, though he did admit many scientific words, particularly medical and botanical, and in respect of learned words his scope was too wide, for he gave many such words as *cynegeticks* ('the art of hunting'), *enubilate*, *favillous*, and *geoponical*. Some words he allowed in only with a warning, such as 'a cant word' (*fiddlefaddle*) or 'an old word' (*gim* = neat). Above all, he sought to fix the meaning or meanings of words, and to this end he added illustrative quotations ranging forward from Sir Philip Sidney. Each word, where possible, was provided with an etymology, and though many of his etymologies are even absurd in the light of modern philological studies, Johnson did make good use of the growing work of Anglo-Saxon scholars. Further, one of his aims was, of course, to fix the spelling, for, though spelling had largely been stabilized by 1660 by the efforts of the printers, a standard authority was still desirable: here Johnson tended to be conservative. Of giving pronunciation Johnson fought shy, holding that there existed such variations even among good speakers that it was impossible to indicate more than the accentuation of words – which he did. Not that accentuation was without its variations still (in 1721 Isaac Watts had printed a list of words differently accented by different educated speakers), but Johnson felt more scope for his authoritative verdict in that matter. And, the tendency running by 1780 strongly in favour of authority, in that year Thomas Sheridan, father of the dramatist, in his *Complete Dictionary of the English Language* ventured beyond Johnson in laying down the pronunciation too.

The grammarians especially yielded to the growing temptation to impose order. Apart from the eighteenth-century's desire for uniformity in language as in society, the utilitarian middle-class order of the day increasingly justified it, for, as men of trade and commerce made themselves more prosperous, they felt it essential that their children should live up to their rising social position. Their sons particularly, but their wives and daughters too, must speak and write genteelly and not betray themselves by vulgarisms of grammar. One of the earliest grammarians was the scholarly John Wallis, a founder of the Royal Society, with his *Grammatica Linguae Anglicanae* in 1653, but it was not till after 1700 that the attempt began to be made to teach English grammar, and then not in the grammar schools, which kept to Latin, but in the Dissenting academies and private schools. Locke was a pioneer in advocating the teaching of English grammar. 'It will be matter of wonder', he declared in 1693, 'why young gentlemen are forced to learn the grammars of foreign and dead languages, and are never once told of the grammar of their own tongues: they do not so much as know there is any such thing, much less is it made their business to be instructed in it.' A gentleman, he held, 'ought to study grammar amongst the other helps of speaking well ... since the want of propriety and grammatical exactness is thought very misbecoming one of that rank, and usually draws on one guilty of such faults the censure of having had a lower breeding and worse company than suits with his quality'. Soon, largely from such motives of class distinction and from that of business success, the task was undertaken. In 1700 a schoolmaster called Lane wrote a grammar under the title, *A Key to the Art of Letters*; in 1711 John Brightland produced *A Grammar of the English Tongue* and James Greenwood *An Essay Towards a Practical English Grammar*; in 1721 Isaac Watts, the hymn-writer, published his *Art of Reading and Writing English*. There were others, and Johnson prefaced his Dictionary with a brief grammar.

From the beginning a problem which faced the grammarians was whether the rules of English grammar were deducible from good current usage, or whether there was a grammatical absolute ('according to the unalterable rules of right reason', as Lane declared). Wallis had based his grammar on the study of good usage. Locke believed that good grammar was the usage of good writers and speakers. We have noted the dislike by Hughes of rules for writing in general. Dr Johnson, in the matter of language as a whole, as witness in particular his attitude on pronunciation, favoured usage rather than rule; indeed, his treatment of syntax in his grammatical preface was almost contemptuous – 'our language has so little inflection or variety of terminations that its construction neither requires nor admits rules'. But other grammarians favoured rule above usage, and, worse still, in contempt of the quite different nature of the English language, they sought to force English grammar into the mould of Latin grammar. For rule there undoubtedly was a case, for, whereas an aristocrat could speak confidently in the assurance of his breeding, the new middle class would be happier if safeguarded by a grammarian's rule. For the assimilation to Latin grammar the schoolmasters were largely responsible. Locke had asserted, 'I know not why any one should waste his time and beat his head about the Latin grammar, who does not intend to be a critic, or make speeches and write despatches in it', but in this freedom of view he was not followed, and it was not unnatural that, when it was thought desirable to teach children English grammar, the drill book for that exercise should be as close as possible to the Latin. Moreover, schoolmasters, then at any rate, were lovers of rule, and so it was on the side of grammatical logic and of rule as against custom, idiom, and variety, of a Latin formalism as against English freedom that this period ended. Nor should it be forgotten that the historical study of the English language had not yet proceeded far enough to influence the grammarians of whom we are speaking, so that they worked in a real ignorance of the true nature and principles of the language they were presuming to formalize and 'correct'.

As late as 1761 Joseph Priestley, the scientist, still kept an open mind on the question of custom and use versus rule, and indeed favoured practice, for he held 'the general prevailing custom … the only standard for the time that it prevails'. But in 1762 Robert Lowth, later Bishop of London, came out definitely on the side of logical 'correctness' as against practice, and his *English Grammar* was very influential. Lowth employed the method of giving examples of wrong usage in order to inculcate the 'correct', and, to him, even such writers as Addison and Pope were guilty of incorrectness. From about this time, in fact, the grammarians came forth as lawgivers, claiming to decide all questions of doubtful usage and giving their verdicts in favour of a neat and logical uniformity. Lindley Murray's *English Grammar* of 1795 followed Lowth's example, and it achieved such pre-eminence with its repeated editions that the victory for formal rules was won for a century. *It is me*, *you was*, *who did you meet*, *these sort of*, *I object to him coming*, double negatives, a plural verb with a collective subject, a singular verb with a double subject, superlatives like *perfectest*, preterites as past participles as in *An Elegy Wrote in a Country Churchyard* – such idiomatic usages and anomalies were to be no more, though they had been common in the practice of some of the best eighteenth-century authors. The rules for the correct use of *shall* and *will* were laid down. Murray, who wrote his grammar for a Quaker girls' school at York, included in it exercises in parsing as well as in correction of all kinds of errors. So far had 'the teaching of English' advanced in the course of the eighteenth century.

But it is time to consider the sounds of the spoken language. Our vowel sounds, which had undergone in the fifteenth century the great shift by which Modern English is mainly differentiated from Middle English, had by the first half of the seventeenth century approximately reached those of today. But, as is immediately noticeable from the rhymes of the poets, there were some important differences between the pronunciation of Dryden and Pope and our own. Thus we find Pope rhyming *speak* and *take* and Lady Winchilsea rhyming *day* and *tea*. Here, while present-day English has the same vowel sound in *take* and *day*, the sound commonly spelt *ee* has replaced the earlier sound represented by *ea*. In the early eighteenth century it would seem that the sound common to these three types of word (*speak*, *take*, *day*) was a long front vowel (slack, or more probably tense *e*) which was developing towards the diphthong now heard in *fate* and *day*. That the same sound is not heard now in words like *speak* indicates that a different development replaced that responsible for the long tense *e* in such eighteenth-century rhymes. This modern *ee* sound had clearly been developed in some areas by Elizabethan days, for Spenser could rhyme *stream* with *seem*. What happened was that gradually the speech of those who pronounced *ea* words with the sound represented by *ee* replaced in the standard speech the regularly developed long tense *e*. Pope could use either type (he also rhymes *seat* and *fleet*); by Johnson's time most words with *ea* were pronounced with the present-day *ee* sound. Again, there is the difference indicated by the frequent occurrence of such a rhyme as *line* with *join*. Here, too, one sound (that in *line*) had not quite reached the present-day stage, and the other has been replaced by a different sound from that of its normal development – modern dialect pronunciations like *bile* for *boil* show what the regular development would have been. Cowley, Dryden, Swift, and Pope readily illustrate this kind of rhyme. The stage at which these sounds rhymed in this period was that of a diphthong of which the first element was the sound in the modern *but* and the second short *i*: the first element was later retracted to give the present-day sound, but the words in which the sound was represented by the spelling *oi* gradually came to be pronounced as their spelling was considered to indicate, a process accomplished by 1800. This influence of spelling upon pronunciation grew only too rapidly with the growth of education from print.

Other differences of pronunciation revealed by the rhymes of poets include those arising from the shortening of long vowels. At least as late as the middle of the eighteenth century there existed a good deal of variety in pronunciation among good speakers and it was often possible to use a long or a short vowel. This is particularly noticeable in words containing the vowel spelt *oo*. Dryden, for instance, rhymes *food*, *blood*; and *wood*. Here each word contained in Middle English a long tense *o*, which was raised to the present-day sound in *food* in the fifteenth century: our sound in *blood* is due to an early shortening, and that in *wood* to a later one, but certainly until 1700 no one type of pronunciation had become received standard – indeed, by some good speakers *soot* was pronounced with the vowel in *but* as late as 1900. Again, when Dryden rhymes *great* and *yet*, and Pope *beat* (as past participle) with *set*, we see that words with the long vowel spelt *ea* could also be pronounced with the vowel shortened. In addition, there were many variants which have since been levelled out, but which are all regular developments of certain linguistic tendencies. Thus the rhyme of *Rome* with *doom* found as late as

Collins, those of *God* with *road* and with *unawed* by Pope, Dryden's *sense* with *prince* and *lost* with *boast*, and the rhyming of *have* with words like *crave* and *wave* by many poets are only a few examples of pronunciations which had full historical justification. It should indeed be taken as a general rule that the rhymes of the poets of this period represent pronunciations both genuine and linguistically explicable as variants naturally persisting in a time when a received standard was still far from being as fixed as it is today.

Many other details deserve mention. Everyone knows the fashionable *obleege* of Pope's day, aping the French pronunciation, and the ousting of the regularly developed *sarmon*, etc., by our *sermon*, partly perhaps as being nearer the French but chiefly from the influence of the spelling. Here it must suffice to state the general truth that in pronunciation, as in all the other aspects of language, this period was characterized by a steady approach to uniformity. Invaluable guides to the sounds of the period, in addition to the rhymes of the poets, are books like the *Practical Phonography* (1701) of John Jones which attempted to describe current pronunciation, and, most important perhaps of all, collections of letters and documents like the *Verney Memoirs*, covering 1639–96, and the *Wentworth Papers*, covering 1705–39, in which the writers often spelt words as they spoke them and not according to the conventional spelling fixed by printers, which was often remote from the writer's own speech. From such evidence it is clear that, well into the eighteenth century, these people spoke their sounds as they had developed on the lips of their forebears and not as teachers or print would prescribe. The difference in the treatment of vowels in unaccented positions is striking: *ow* in words like *narrow* was normally pronounced *er*; *fortune* was *fortin* and *picture* was *pikter* (even the scholarly Gray rhymes *venture* with *enter*); *value* and *nephew* were *valy* and *nevy*. Consonants too were treated with disrespect to the spelling: thus Jones in his book of 1701 lists *neglect*, *strict*, *corrupt* and many such words as being pronounced without the final *t*, and *beyond*, *scaffold* and a large number of similar words without the final *d*. Pope rhymed *neglects* with *sex*. *Ridin* not *riding* was the normal pronunciation of words with final *ing*, and Swift shows this frequently in rhyme. In the eighteenth century *Lunnon* was the usual pronunciation of *London*. Gradually, however, just as the formal grammarians put themselves forward as lawgivers, so those who wrote of pronunciation began to declare what the pronunciation *ought* to be. A good example was John Walker, author of a popular *Rhetorical Grammar* (1785), who, after abandoning the stage, lectured on elocution from about 1770. Such instructors were in general in favour of pronunciation close to the spelling, and, where words had two pronunciations, a careful one of formal speech and a slurred one of easy conversation, they insisted on the careful one. Since neither they nor those who required their teaching were of the higher class, the tendency naturally was towards a conscious refinement. In fact, we see again the joint effect of the eighteenth-century's desire for correctness, elegance, and uniformity and that of the middle class to be genteel. By the end of our period laxity in pronunciation was generally deprecated.

Even if such an important aspect of language as, among many others, change in the meaning of words has to be omitted in this brief survey (as, for instance, *sensible* was to lose such an ordinary eighteenth-century meaning as that of being capable of sensory or emotional reactions, and *awful* was to degenerate from its meanings of feeling or inspiring awe), the dawn of Anglo-Saxon studies deserves a place. Much honour is due to a small group of scholars at Oxford. The Dutchman Francis Junius, who printed the so-called Cædmon MS. in 1655, spent several years at Oxford. Somner published the first Anglo-Saxon dictionary in 1659, and George Hickes the first Anglo-Saxon grammar in 1689. Wanley made an invaluable catalogue of Anglo-Saxon manuscripts, published as part II of the famous *Thesaurus* of Hickes. Thomas Hearne, the antiquary, printed the *Battle of Maldon* in 1726, five years before the manuscript was destroyed in the fire of the Cottonian library. And there was the remarkable young woman, Elizabeth Elstob, who in 1715 produced the first Anglo-Saxon grammar written in English, for that of Hickes was in Latin. She too began an edition of Ælfric's Homilies. With the death of Hickes in 1715 Anglo-Saxon studies ceased to advance and failed to reach a wide audience, but an enduring foundation had been laid, on which nineteenth-century scholars proceeded to build, so that with our fuller knowledge of our language we can see it in a truer perspective than could the eighteenth-century grammarians.

In conclusion, it is well to remember that the language of any age was always heard more upon the lips than it was set upon paper.

Therefore, though we must rely for our evidence mainly upon the written word, upon which the eighteenth-century's tendency to formalism had its fullest effect, we must not exaggerate the extent to which that formalism permeated all classes and restrained all individuals. There surely survived that freedom which Sterne suggests by his phrase 'the sportability of chitchat'. Again, there were the diarists and letter-writers too much at ease to be formal – even like Gray from whose letters his friend Mason felt it necessary to prune the slang before he published them.

JOHN WILMOT, EARL OF ROCHESTER

V. DE S. PINTO

Emeritus Professor of English, the University of Nottingham

THE last English court which can fairly be described as a centre of intellectual and artistic culture was the court of Charles II. The Whig and Puritan tradition, as embodied for example in Macaulay's *History of England*,[1] gave wide currency to the belief that the Restoration courtiers were all corrupt and cynical pleasure-seekers. Many of them certainly deserve this reputation, but modern research has shown that the Whig view is an over-simplification. J. H. Wilson in his admirable study, *The Court Wits of the Restoration* (Princeton, 1948), proves that a number of the more sensational stories which have gone to build up the legend of the Wicked Restoration Courtier are apocryphal: 'About them', he writes, 'has grown up a considerable body of lurid tradition, nourished by the gossip-mongers of the eighteenth century, and by the errors and credulities of modern biographers.' The young men of the Restoration Court certainly drank hard, indulged in a good deal of sexual promiscuity, made bawdy jokes, and wrote bawdy verses, but their sins seem to have been simply those common to idle young people belonging to a privileged class with money in their pockets in all periods when moral codes have been loosened through the disintegration of traditional beliefs. Many of the courtiers were undoubtedly men of wide culture and creative ability, and there is plenty of evidence of their reading and their interest in literature and the theatre. Dryden's tributes to the civilized quality of their conversation in *An Essay of Dramatic Poesy* (1668) and in the Epistle Dedicatory to *The Assignation* (1673) are of great significance and should be used as a corrective to the Victorian tradition of the men with 'foreheads of bronze, hearts like the nether mill-stone, and tongues set on fire of hell'.[2]

Soon after the restoration of Charles II in 1660 a group of literary courtiers, called by Andrew Marvell the 'merry gang', became prominent. They included George Villiers, Duke of Buckingham, Charles Sackville, Lord Buckhurst (afterwards Earl of Dorset), John Sheffield, Earl of Mulgrave (afterwards Duke of Buckinghamshire),

Sir Charles Sedley, and others. A little later they were joined by Sir George Etherege, John Wilmot, Earl of Rochester, William Wycherley, and Henry Savile. These were Pope's 'mob of gentlemen who wrote with ease', the last English courtier poets, inheritors of a tradition which went back to Sir Thomas Wyatt and his friends at the court of Henry VIII. Their immediate predecessors were Carew, Suckling, and Lovelace, the poets of the mid-seventeenth century, but something had been lost which was never quite regained. Dr F. R. Leavis has indicated the nature of this loss with his usual acuteness:

> Charles II was a highly intelligent man of liberal interests, and his mob of gentlemen cultivated conversation and the Muses. But that the old fine order, ... the 'Court culture', did not survive the period of disruption, exile and 'travels' is apparent even in the best things of Etherege, Sedley, Rochester and the rest: their finest specimens of the tenderly or cynically gallant or polite lack the positive fineness, the implicit subtlety ... in Carew. The cheaper things remind us forcibly that to indicate the background of Restoration poetry we must couple with the Court, not as earlier the country house, but the coffee-house, and that the coffee-house is on intimate terms with the Green-Room.[3]

There is, perhaps, some slight exaggeration or overstatement here. Some part of the 'old fine order' remained, and there was still an intimate connexion between the court and the country house, as well as between the Court and the coffee-house, but it is perfectly true that the richness and subtlety of the courtly culture which produced men like Sir Henry Wotton, George Herbert, and Thomas Carew did not survive the Civil War.

The new courtiers were a 'post-war generation' in some ways rather like the post-war generation of the nineteen-twenties, consciously reacting against the idealisms both of the Puritans and of the old Cavaliers. Clarendon was shocked by what seemed to him to be their heartlessness.[4] Their favourite philosopher was Thomas Hobbes of Malmesbury, author of *Leviathan*, who was a frequent visitor at Whitehall in the years immediately following the Restoration. We are told that 'order was given that he should have free accesse to his majesty, who was always much delighted in his witt and smart repartees'.[5] Hobbes's thorough-going materialism and his rejection of the 'kingdom of darkness' (superstition and priestcraft) seemed to free his young disciples from all the inhibitions which were part of the religiosity that hung like a cloud over their early years. The ideal of the 'merry gang' was the perfect Man of Wit and Fashion, the aesthetic hero, or witty, aristocratic rake already sketched before the Civil War by Fletcher in his comedy *The Wild Goose Chase* and by Sir John Suckling in real life. Sir George Etherege, a prominent member of the group and certainly the most gifted dramatist among them, painted a finished portrait of this character in his most successful play *Sir Fopling Flutter or the Man of Mode* (1676). His hero Dorimant is the ancestor of a long line of witty, attractive rakes in English comedy, which extends from Congreve's Mirabel to Wilde's Lord Goring. Lamb's description of the world of the Comedy of Manners can well be applied to his way of life. It is 'the Utopia of gallantry, where pleasure is duty, and the manners perfect freedom'.[6] Dorimant gets rid of an inconvenient mistress with the grace and poise with which he would change his cravat, and he leads on the absurd Sir Fopling Flutter to display his affectations with the fine touch of a comic artist.

The man on whom the character of Dorimant was said to be based was John Wilmot, second Earl of Rochester, the son of one of the most able Cavalier generals and a pious lady belonging to a famous Puritan family. He seems to have inherited a good share of his father's audacity and some part of his mother's sense of spiritual reality. Educated at Wadham College, Oxford, one of the chief centres of the new scientific movement which led to the establishment of the Royal Society, he was enabled by a generous grant from the King to travel on the Continent for several years and to spend some time studying at the University of Padua. He appeared at Court at Christmas 1664 and at once became the most prominent figure in 'the merry gang'. 'The Court', we are told by Anthony à Wood, 'not only debauched him; but made him an absolute Hobbist.' Hobbes's *Treatise of Human Nature* had appeared in 1651 when Rochester was a child of three, and his more famous work *Leviathan* in the following year. Rochester probably met the old philosopher, who, as we have seen, was often to be found at Court in the early years of the reign of Charles II. He appears to have accepted Hobbes's doctrines wholeheartedly. '*Pleasure*, therefore, or *delight*', wrote the philosopher in the First Book of *Leviathan*, 'is the appearence, or sense of good; and *molestation* or *displeasure*, the appearence, or sense of evil. ... Of pleasures or delights, some arise from the sense of an object present; and those may be called *pleasures of sense*, the word *sensual*, as it is used by those only that condemn them, having no place till there be laws.'[7] In other words, the only criterion of good and evil is the presence or absence of sensuous pleasure, and the condemnation of sensuality is a purely artificial inhibition which has no place in nature. To the modern reader Hobbes's philosophy does not seem very favourable to poetry; the universe which it reveals consists of colourless, tasteless, soundless atoms perpetually moving in accordance with mathematical laws. But this was not the aspect of it that appealed to his young disciples of the Restoration Court. They were attracted by its boldness and freshness. It seemed to liberate them from the traditional inhibitions of priestcraft (the 'kingdom of darkness') and to offer a 'scientific' justification for sensuality.

Rochester's mind was essentially serious. He plunged into the experiment of living the complete life of pleasure with the same ardour as that with which Boyle and the *virtuosi* of the Royal Society devoted themselves to the investigation of nature and John Bunyan and George Fox to living according to the Word of God. His extant writings consist of lyrics, satires, a few verse translations, some dramatic fragments, including an unfinished rehandling of Fletcher's tragedy *Valentinian*, an amusing prose lampoon, and a number of letters. His poems are difficult to date, but the earliest, apart from some complimentary verses said to have been written when he was an undergraduate, are probably his lyrics and love poems. These include a handful of love songs which, as Dr Leavis has said, are 'peculiarly individual utterances, with no such relation to convention or tradition as is represented by Carew and Marvell'.[8] Their characteristics are a purity and intensity that only Sedley among his contemporaries approaches in a few lines (never in a complete poem), though he never quite achieves the peculiar lightness and transparency of Rochester's best songs, which, as Sir Herbert Grierson has said, 'might have been written by Burns with some difference'.[9]

A fine poem, almost certainly addressed to his wife, is the expression of a complex mood in which the poet at once regrets his infidelities

and also values them, not for themselves, but as a contrast to the only
love which brings him happiness.

> Absent from thee I languish still,
>   Then ask me not, when I return?
> The straying Fool 'twill plainly kill,
>   To wish all Day, all Night to Mourn.
>
> *Dear*; from thine Arms then let me flie,
>   That my Fantastick Mind may prove,
> The Torments it deserves to try,
>   That tears my fixt Heart from my Love.
>
> When wearied with a world of Woe
>   To thy safe Bosom I retire
> Where Love, and Peace, and Truth does flow,
>   May I contented there expire.
>
> Lest once more wand'ring from that Heav'n,
>   I fall on some base heart unblest;
> Faithless to thee, False, unforgiv'n,
>   And lose my Everlasting Rest.[10]

This is not the voice of a selfish sensualist but of a tortured realist who
has learned from bitter experience that the 'pleasures' of the 'merry
gang' soon become 'Torments' and a 'World of Woe'. Such a man
is well on the road to a renunciation of Hobbes's utilitarian ethics.
Alone among the Restoration Court lyrists, Rochester constantly
breaks through the convention of courtly compliment and writes
poetry that is dialectical and personal.

The lampoon in verse (usually scurrilous and obscene) was a well-
established form of sport at the Court of Charles II,[11] and Rochester
was known to his contemporaries chiefly as a writer of 'libels'. His
best satires, however, are as different from the verse squibs produced
by the other Court wits as his best lyrics are from their songs to
Chloe and Phyllis. They are no mere denunciations of individuals,
but embody a serious and devastating criticism of all the values of the
life of pleasure and fashion into which he had plunged so recklessly.
The criticism is all the more effective because it comes from one who
is within the society which is criticized and who possesses its virtues
of easy sureness of tone and diction and poise of gesture and rhythm.

The aesthetic hero, or purely selfish ideal bearing no relation to truth (Etherege's Dorimant), now gives way to the ethical hero, the disillusioned, keen-sighted observer, whose relation to truth is real but entirely negative. In an ironic monologue worthy of Browning and justly praised by Charles Whibley as 'a masterpiece of heroic irony',[12] this observer shows us *The Maim'd Debauchee* in the likeness of a brave old admiral 'Depriv'd of Force, but prest with Courage still'. This product of a life of gentlemanly pleasure-seeking foresees his impotent old age when he will have to content himself with urging on younger men to the vices which have wrecked his own constitution:

> So when my days of Impotence approach,
>   And I'me by Love and Wine's unlucky chance,
> Driv'n from the pleasing Billows of Debauch,
>   On the dull shore of lazy Temperance.
>
> My pains at last some respite shall afford,
>   While I behold the Battels you maintain:
> When Fleets of Glasses sail around the Board,
>   From whose Broad-Sides Volleys of Wit shall rain.[13]

In his social satires Rochester shows us the obverse of Dorimant's Utopia of gallantry. He has now come to see that the heaven of the lusty courtier is precariously constructed over an underworld of ugliness, cruelty, and filth. The horror of the life of the poor prostitute in Restoration London is etched with the remorseless power of a Hogarth in *A Letter from Artemisa in the Town to Cloe in the Country*:

> That wretched thing *Corinna*, who has run
> Through all the sev'ral ways of being undone:
> Cozen'd at first by Love, and living then
> By turning the too-dear-bought cheat on Men:
> Gay were the Hours, and wing'd with joy they flew,
> When first the Town her early Beauties knew:
> Courted, admir'd, and lov'd, with Presents fed;
> Youth in her Looks, and Pleasure in her Bed:
> Till Fate, or her ill Angel, thought it fit
> To make her doat upon a man of Wit:
> Who found 'twas dull to love above a day;
> Made his ill-natur'd jeast, and went away.
> Now scorn'd of all, forsaken, and opprest,

She's a *Memento Mori* to the rest:
Diseas'd, decay'd, to take up half a Crown
Must Mortgage her Long Scarf, and Manto Gown;
Poor Creature, who, unheard of, as a Flie,
In some dark Hole must all the Winter lye:
And want, and dirt, endure a whole half year,
That, for one month, she Tawdry may appear. ...[14]

There is a substance and a grain in these couplets which express perfectly the vision of Rochester's searching and sceptical mind and give the reader a kind of satisfaction which can rarely be obtained from seventeenth-century poetry.

The most memorable of Rochester's satires is the poem which can be fairly described as marking the culmination of his revolt against the values of contemporary English and European society and, indeed, an extension of that revolt to an attack on humanity as a whole. This poem, entitled in the most reliable editions *A Satyr against Mankind*,[15] is suggested by the Eighth Satire of Boileau, reinforced by many suggestions from the essays of Montaigne and particularly from the *Apologie de Raimond Sebond* and from the *Maximes* of La Roche-foucauld.[16] Nevertheless, it is a thoroughly original work stamped with the peculiar strength of Rochester's personality in every line and expressing with an almost terrifying intensity his mood of indignation and disillusionment.

The poem opens with a denunciation of the folly of humanity in preferring 'Reason, an *Ignis fatuus*, in the *Mind*' to sense, the 'light of Nature' (or, as D. H. Lawrence would have said, the 'Intellect' to the 'Blood'). Rochester never created a happier image than his picture of mankind as the lost Traveller who

Stumbling from thought to thought, falls head-long down
Into doubt's boundless Sea, where, like to drown,
Books bear him up awhile, and make him try
To swim with Bladders of *Philosophy*;
In hopes still t' o'retake the escaping light,
The *Vapour* dances in his dazled Sight,
Till spent, it leaves him to eternal Night.
Then Old Age, and experience, hand in hand,
Lead him to death, and make him understand,
After a search so painful, and so long,

> That all his Life he has been in the wrong.
> Hudled in Dirt, this reas'ning *Engine* lyes,
> Who was so proud, so witty, and so wise. ...

Nowhere in the English literature of the seventeenth century has the central dilemma of the age been expressed with such force and precision. In the new mechanico-materialistic universe of Descartes, Hobbes, and the scientists, man is only a 'reas'ning *Engine*' (the phrase is probably suggested by an expression of Robert Boyle).[17] Yet the pitiful creature is, in his own opinion at any rate, proud and witty and wise, and even has the presumption to seek an explanation of a universe which is no longer the divinely planned cosmos of Greek and Christian tradition, but a place where man seems to be little better than an irrelevant accident.

Like most of Rochester's best work the *Satyr against Mankind* is dialectical, dramatic, and witty. It is a dialogue in which the satirist is answered by 'a formal Band and Beard' – in other words, a conventional clergyman, who is pleased enough with his rejection of the 'gibing, gingling knack call'd *Wit*', but shocked by his 'grand indiscretion' in railing at 'Reason and Mankind', which he answers by rather pompous praise of

> Blest glorious *Man*! to whom alone kind *Heav'n*
> An everlasting *Soul* hath freely giv'n; ...

The reply of the satirist is devastating, and expressed with a combination of seriousness and fantastic humour which recalls some of Donne's best work. 'Reason', so far from being the light of Heaven, is simply the plaything of idle busybodies. It is a

> busie, puzling stirrer up of doubt,
> That frames deep *Mysteries*, then finds 'em out,
> Filling with frantick Crowds of thinking *Fools*,
> Those rev'rend *Bedlams*, *Colledges*, and *Schools*,
> Borne on whose Wings, each heavy *Sot* can pierce
> The limits of the boundless Universe.
> So charming Oyntments make an Old *Witch* flie,
> And bear a Crippled Carkass through the Skie.

'Right Reason' is something very different. It co-operates with the body instead of condemning it, and

> bounds desires, with a reforming Will,
> To keep 'em more in vigour, not to kill.

If 'Right Reason' can be defended, mankind as a whole is indefensible. The central passage of the poem, a comparison between man and the beasts, is one of the most searching pieces of moral realism in English poetry. It owes much to Montaigne and probably influenced Swift considerably.[18] Rochester is now fighting on another front; it is not the conventional religiosity of the 'formal Band and Beard' which he is attacking now but his own class, the ruling class of Europe, with its obsolete ideal of the predatory warrior:

> Be Judge your self, I'll bring it to the test,
> Which is the basest *Creature*, *Man*, or *Beast*:
> *Birds* feed on *Birds*, *Beasts* on each other prey;
> But Savage *Man* alone does *Man* betray.
> Prest by necessity, they Kill for Food;
> *Man* undoes *Man*, to do himself no good.
> With Teeth and Claws by Nature arm'd, they hunt
> Nature's allowances, to supply their want:
> But *Man* with smiles, embraces, Friendships, praise,
> Unhumanely his Fellow's life betrays:
> With voluntary pains works his distress;
> Not through necessity, but wantonness.
> For hunger, or for Love they bite or tear
> While wretched *Man* is still in Arms for fear:
> For fear he armes, and is of Armes afraid;
> From fear to fear successively betray'd.
> Base fear, the source whence his best passions came,
> His boasted Honor, and his dear bought Fame:
> The lust of Pow'r, to which he's such a *Slave*
> And for the which alone he dares be brave:
> To which his various Projects are design'd,
> Which makes him gen'rous, affable, and kind.
> For which he takes such pains to be thought wise
> And screws his actions, in a forc'd disguise:
> Leading a tedious life, in Misery,
> Under laborious, mean *Hypocrisie*. ...

There is little doubt that it is a passage like this, quite as much as the alleged 'licentiousness' of his poetry, which gave Rochester his traditional evil reputation. He is penetrating the defences of his aristocratic readers and showing the primitive man behind the age-old inhabitions of 'Honour' and 'Fame'.

The nihilism of the *Satyr against Mankind* is slightly mitigated in a curious epilogue appended to it in some editions and possibly added by Rochester as a rejoinder to the Answer to the poem ascribed to a certain 'Reverend Mr Griffith', which appeared shortly after the publication of the broadside edition of the *Satyr* in the summer of 1679.[19] Here it is suggested that, if a man of real integrity ('In *Court*, a just Man, yet unknown to me') could be found, he would be willing to 'recant his paradox'. The description of this ideal, that of the ethical hero, is mainly in negatives and is not very inspiring. The interest of the Epilogue, however, is psychological rather than literary. It shows that Rochester was conscious of the lack of a positive element in his satire and that he was looking for an affirmative answer to his 'obstinate questionings'.

A clue to the kind of experience for which he was striving is to be found in a fragment of a letter to his wife which is, perhaps, the most self-revealing statement in his extant correspondence. In this fragment, he speaks of the 'disproportion 'twixt our desires & what is ordained to content them' and of those who are 'soe intirely satisfyed with theire shares in this world that theire wishes nor theire thoughts have not a farther prospect of felicity & glory'.[20] It was not a system of ethics that Rochester was looking for, but the 'felicity and glory' which he had vainly sought in sensuality and aesthetic experience.

The last act of the drama of Rochester's short life was the famous episode of his conversion.[21] The author of *A Satyr against Mankind*, like the author of *The Waste Land*, was bound ultimately to turn to religion. Rochester had, in Dr. Johnson's words, 'blazed out his youth and health in lavish voluptuousness', and his health, which was never robust and which appears to have been undermined by venereal disease early in his career, was failing in the last years of the second decade after the Restoration. Early in 1679 he seems to have been searching for a religious position which he could accept without compromising his intellectual integrity. He consulted the deist Charles Blount, but found little satisfaction in the arid and abstract 'religion of nature' which the seventeenth-century deists (following Lord Herbert of Cherbury) professed. A more fruitful contact was with Gilbert Burnet, afterwards Bishop of Salisbury but then a young Scottish clergyman, who had won a reputation at Court for his frankness, unconventionality, and eloquent preaching. Rochester made his acquaintance in the autumn of 1679 after he had read the first volume of his *History of the Reformation*, which appeared in the spring of that year. In him he found a parson of a kind that he had not met before, a man with a keen and fearless intellect, not a mere conventional mouthpiece of traditional pietism. It must have seemed that he had at last met the sort of hero that he had sketched in the Epilogue to *A Satyr against Mankind*:

> A *Church-Man* who on *God* relyes?
> Whose Life, his Faith, and Doctrine Justifies?

All through the winter of 1679–80 this strangely assorted pair had a series of conversations on religion and ethics which Burnet recorded with admirable fidelity in the short memoir of Rochester which he published soon after the poet's death. At the end of their conversation in the spring of 1680 he seems to have been rationally convinced by Burnet's exposition of Christian ethics, though he had not, in Burnet's words, 'arrived at a full persuasion of Christianity'. It was not till June, when he was lying mortally ill at the Ranger's Lodge at Woodstock, that he found in religion that 'felicity and glory' which he had been seeking for so long.

Like W. B. Yeats in 1914, Rochester had now reached a stage of spiritual development when the life of aesthetic and sensuous pleasure was a 'Fool's coat' (Yeats uses the same image in his poem 'A Coat')[22] and nothing but the naked spirit could satisfy him. Unfortunately, he only lived for five weeks after this experience. We know from the sermon preached by Robert Parsons at his funeral that before his death he was planning to write 'Divine Poetry' and also that he actually dictated in the last weeks of his life. It is probable that two poems printed in one of the early editions[23] of his works are attempts made in the last weeks of his life to express his new conception of the religious hero. Both of them appear to be closely related to the figure of the Suffering Servant in the fi'ty-third chapter of Isaiah. In one 'Plain Dealing' is shown as a poor country girl driven out of the town and forced to return to the country, where even the rustics

refuse to have anything to do with her when they know that she
will bring poverty in her train:

> Long time plain dealing in the Hauty Town,
> Wandring about, though in a thread-bare Gown,
> At last unanimously was cry'd down.
>
> When almost starv'd, she to the Countrey fled,
> In hopes, though meanly, she shou'd there be fed,
> And tumble Nightly on a Pea-straw Bed.
>
> But Knav'ry knowing her intent, took post,
> And Rumour'd her approach through every Coast,
> Vowing his Ruin that shou'd be her host.
>
> Frighted at this, each *Rustick* shut his door,
> Bid her begone, and trouble him no more,
> For he that entertain'd her must be poor.
>
> At this grief seiz'd her, grief too great to tell,
> When weeping, sighing, fainting down she fell,
> Whil's Knavery, Laughing, Rung her passing Bell.[24]

Voltaire rightly called Rochester 'homme de génie et grand poète'.
He is not a great poet in the sense that the word can be applied to
the professional masters, Milton, Dryden, Pope, and Wordsworth.
Judged as works of art, his achievements are those of a brilliant
amateur, a handful of exquisite lyrics, and the satires, which, as
Dr R. F. Leavis has pointed out, have a distinguished place in the
'line of wit' that leads from Donne to Pope. Rochester, however, is
one of those poets who are important as daring and original explorers
of reality, and his place is with the restless spiritual adventurers such
as Marlowe, Blake, Byron, Wilfred Owen, and D. H. Lawrence.
Like Byron and Lawrence, he was denounced as licentious because
he was a disturbing and outspoken critic of conventional ethics. His
poetry expresses individual experience in a way that no other
English poetry does between Donne and Blake; it makes us feel what
it was like to live in a world which had been suddenly transformed
by the new science into a vast machine governed by mathematical
laws, where God has become a remote First Cause and man an
insignificant 'reas'ning *Engine*'. In his time the great Augustan

attempt to found a new orthodoxy based on the Cartesian-Newtonian world picture was beginning. The Anglo-French civilization of the eighteenth century, the civilization of Voltaire and Diderot, of Addison, Johnson, and Gibbon, came near to achieving the civilized city of good sense, good taste, reason, and common sense, which was the objective of the new orthodoxy. Rochester's glory was that he rejected the new orthodoxy at the very outset, and perceived, as Swift was to perceive after him, that the civilized city of the Augustans, though it might be a resting-place for the human spirit, could very easily become a prison. In the history of English poetic thought his work is an event of major importance. Much of it remains alive in the twentieth century, not for its craftsmanship, but as what D. H. Lawrence called the 'unrestful, ungraspable poetry of the sheer present ... the soul and the mind and body surging at once, nothing left out'.[25]

NOTES

1. See Macaulay's *History of England*, chapter II. A. Beljame's monumental work, *The Public and English Men of Letters in the Eighteenth Century* (1881), is coloured by the traditional Whig view, but this is corrected to some extent by the notes of Professor Bonamy Dobrée to the English translation by E. O. Lorimer (1948).

2. Macaulay, *Essay on the Comic Dramatists of the Restoration*. It is true that Macaulay is referring to the characters in the comedies of the period, but part of his argument is that these characters are realistic in the sense that they reflected the ideals of the audience.

3. F. R. Leavis, *Revaluation* (1936), p. 34.

4. Clarendon, *Life* (1857), I, p. 307.

5. Aubrey's *Brief Lives*, ed. Clark, I, p. 340.

6. Lamb, 'On the Artificial Comedy of Last Century' in *Essays of Elia*.

7. Hobbes, *Leviathan* I, vi. Cf. also the statement in I, xiii, that 'the desires, and other passions of man, are in themselves no sin'.

8. Leavis, *Revaluation*, p. 35.

9. H. J. C. Grierson, *Metaphysical Lyrics and Poems of the Seventeenth Century* (1921), Introduction, p. xxxviii.

10. *Poems by John Wilmot, Earl of Rochester*, ed. V. de S. Pinto (1964), p. 18.

11. For the typical Restoration lampoons, see the various collections of *Poems on Affairs of State* (1689, 1697, 1703, etc.).

12. *The Cambridge History of English Literature*, VIII, p. 215.

13. Rochester's *Poems*, ed. Pinto, p. 75.

14. Rochester's *Poems*, ed. Pinto, p. 85.

15. Rochester's *Poems*, ed. Pinto, pp. 118–24.

16. See the important study of the background of the poem by S. F. Crocker in *West Virginia University Studies* III, *Philological Papers*, vol. 2, May 1937.

17. Boyle called men 'engines endowed with wills'. See E. A. Burtt, *The Metaphysical Foundations of Modern Science* (1925), p. 176.

18. Cf. particularly Chapter IV of 'A Voyage to the Country of the Houyhnhnms' in *Gulliver's Travels*.

19. According to Anthony à Wood, Griffith's answer to *A Satyr against Mankind* was published a month after Rochester's poem, in the summer of 1679. It is reprinted in Tonson's edition of Rochester's *Work* (1714).

20. See Pinto, *Enthusiast in Wit* (1962), p. 141.

21. For a complete account of this episode, see Burnet, *Some Passages in the Life and Death of John, Earl of Rochester* (1680), reprinted in *English Biographies of the Seventeenth Century*, ed. V. de. S. Pinto (1951), and Pinto, *Rochester, Portrait of a Restoration Poet*, pp. 184–258.

22. See W. B. Yeats, *Collected Poems* (1950), p. 142.

23. *Poems On Several Occasions Written by a late Person of Honour. London, Printed for A. Thorncome, 1685* (Br. Mus. 11623, a. 37).

24. Rochester's *Poems*, ed. Pinto, p. 125.

25. D. H. Lawrence, 'Preface to American Edition of New Poems', reprinted in *Selected Essays* (Penguin Books), p. 288.

RESTORATION COMEDY

P. A. W. COLLINS

Senior Lecturer in English, the University of Leicester

... The stage but echoes back the public voice;
The drama's laws the drama's patrons give,
For we that live to please, must please to live.

(JOHNSON)

OF all literary forms, the drama is the most dependent upon and sensitive to its immediate audience. Shakespeare's achievement was born
of a happy cross-fertilization between the man and the moment;
such moments, like such men, occur perhaps only once in a nation's
dramatic literature. English drama since then has been a poor thing.
Restoration drama sparkles by comparison with the virtual nullity
which followed it, but it is clearly inferior, in range and depth,
to the Elizabethan. The course and causes of the deterioration of
drama during the seventeenth century show the extent to which the
individual talent is dependent upon the external forces of environment and tradition. Of course, like most ages, the Restoration could
see gain rather than loss when it compared its life and literature with
those of 'the last age'; the Elizabethans seemed 'barbarous' or
'Gothic' compared with 'our refined age'. The Restoration age was
highly self-conscious, particularly about those social practices which
distinguished it from pre-Commonwealth England, and Restoration
comedy provided the main literary expression for this self-consciousness. A new form of comedy – later called the 'Comedy of Manners'[1]
– was evolved in response to these new habits and values. No such
forces and convictions supported the tragedy of the age, and that is
one reason why so little of it survives. For most readers, a sufficient
sample of its heroics can be found in the 'tragic' plots of such tragi-
comedies as Dryden's *Spanish Friar*, but the more serious student of
Restoration culture should read and ponder more of the Heroic
tragedies, remembering that the same audiences enjoyed these ridiculous displays of incredible loyalty and undying passion as applauded
Restoration comedy, with its very different ethos and conventions.

The tragedies reflect the sentimentality of cynicism: the comedies reflect the cynicism itself. Bishop Burnet remarked of Charles II that 'His private opinion of people was very odd. He thought no man sincere, nor woman honest, out of principle; but that whenever they proved so, humour or vanity was at the bottom of it'. Charles's love-life, wrote another contemporary, Halifax, manifested 'the effects of health and a good constitution, with as little mixture of the seraphic part as ever a man had'. Charles notoriously differed from his entourage rather in the scope than in the nature of his private activities, and as the most illustrious and one of the most assiduous of the drama's patrons he was not without influence on the drama. 'During the forty years that followed the Restoration, English literature, English culture was "upper-class" to an extent that it had never been before. ...'[2] On the re-opening of the theatres in 1660, two companies, sometimes only one, sufficed for London, though the smaller Elizabethan London supported six. The tendency of the drama to appeal less generally, and more specifically to the Court, had been noticeable before 1642[3]; by the Restoration period, the audience had become much more limited and homogeneous than the Elizabethan. This audience prided itself on being critical, and certainly there was a good deal of discussion about dramatic theory among the readers, as well as the creators, of drama; but the taste of the audience was not nice, and least of all was this audience critical of itself. That the comic dramatists depicted this society without attempting to disturb its self-complacency aroused, of course, much protest at the time (Collier's famous attack, *A Short View of the Immorality and Profaneness of the English Stage*, 1698, was the most comprehensive and influential[4]), and many later critics have been equally scandalized. Macaulay's emphatic essay is well-known; Leslie Stephen echoes him in saying that this is a comedy 'written by blackguards for blackguards'; Dr Johnson gives to this common attack on 'the wits of Charles' his usual weight and finality of phrasing:

> Themselves they studied, as they felt they writ;
> Intrigue was plot, obscenity was wit.
> Vice always found a sympathetic friend;
> They pleas'd their age, and did not aim to mend.
>
> (*Prologue spoken ... at Drury Lane*, 1747)

Some did 'aim to mend'. Wycherley's attitude was ambiguous, and Dryden was unhappy with both the ethos and the form of current drama; but, as a professional, Dryden had to comply with popular taste, so he contrived his 'mechanical obscenities' and continued writing in the loose dramatic form inherited from the Elizabethans, though he could not believe in it himself. Similarly, Shadwell, another professional, began his career with protests against the bawdy and repartee so popular in the comedy, as in the life, of the period, but he soon succumbed to the pressure of the times, and provided the conventional characters, situations, dialogues, and attitudes. The authority of the social mode is apparent when we find Dryden assuming that repartee is 'the very soul of conversation', and Steele asserting that 'the chief qualification' of a dramatist is 'to be a very well-bred man'.

These professionals, Dryden (1631–1700) and Shadwell (?1640–92), wrote copiously (twenty-eight and seventeen plays respectively). They have generally, and rightly, been considered inferior to the Big Five of Restoration comedy – Sir George Etherege (?1634–?91), William Wycherley (1640–1716), William Congreve (1670–1729), Sir John Vanbrugh (1664–1726), and George Farquhar (1677–1707). Of these, only Farquhar was a professional, and he only intermittently; in his short life he produced seven plays. The others wrote only three or four original comedies apiece, and those when they were fairly young. They belonged by birth to at least the fringes of the society they depicted. Etherege and Wycherley wrote themselves into the inmost circle of Court wits; Dryden, Shadwell, and Congreve acknowledged in various Dedications the help they had received from enjoying the conversation of noble gentlemen. They knew the world they reproduced with such vividness; the world of their plays was not the 'Utopia of gallantry' which Lamb professed to find it, but a heightened version of contemporary life. (It was the Heroic drama, rather than the comedy, which presented an Utopia; as Evelyn's wife innocently wrote of Dryden's *Conquest of Granada*, '... love is made so pure and valour so nice, that one would imagine it designed for an Utopia rather than our stage'.) The most common setting for these comedies was London (Shadwell and Farquhar provide notable exceptions, and it is worth noting that both 'gloried' in acknowledging Jonson as master), and the action was generally seen through the eyes of the Metropolitan wit, who was the hero. Commonly, the hero was a projection of the dramatist himself, who accepted the assumptions that the Countryman was a boor, the Puritan a hypocrite, and the Citizen the husband of a wife who might be tempted. The presence of the upper-class Wit – impoverished though he often was – at the centre of the comic action marked off Restoration comedy from its predecessors. Traditionally, comedy dealt with lower-class persons, and one of the limitations which the Restoration found in Elizabethan comedy was its poor showing in 'gentlemen'. Dryden complains that the Elizabethan dramatists' wit 'was not the wit of gentlemen'.

Nevertheless, it was from Elizabethan comedy that Restoration comedy derived.[5] Not from Shakespeare, for, like Jonson, the Restoration looked askance at his romantic comedy; but rather from the more realistic comedy of Jonson (the descriptive surnames for the characters remind us of him), and above all from Beaumont and Fletcher. Dryden noted in 1668 that they were more popular than the other Elizabethans:

> ... they understood and imitated the conversation of gentlemen much better; whose wild debaucheries, and quickness of wit in repartee, no poet before them could paint as they have done.

It was Fletcher, wrote Flecknoe four years before, who had introduced and popularized 'witty obscenity' in English drama. Their popularity is significant. A recent critic has said that their work 'indicates the collapse of a culture, an adult scheme is being broken up and replaced by adolescent intensities'.[6] This may, perhaps, suggest the central criticism of Restoration comedy: not only, or chiefly, that it is limited in the social class it portrays, but that its attitudes towards experience are immature. The preoccupation with love (in both tragedy and comedy), the stress on sex-antagonism, the common conventions that marriage is a bore and love primarily or exclusively a physical appetite – all these are as typically immature attitudes as is the complementary love-idealism of Restoration tragedy. Here, perhaps, may be suggested a critical approach to the 'immorality' of Restoration comedy. Henry James, in a famous passage, asserted 'the perfect dependence of the "moral" sense of a work of art on the amount of felt life concerned in producing it'. The amount of life *felt* by Restoration dramatists was severely limited, and the feeling too often at the level of *cliché*. One important limitation is suggested by Wordsworth's remark on Dryden (it applies to his contemporaries), that his language becomes impassioned 'mostly upon unpleasing subjects, such as the follies, vices, and crimes' of men, and that he rarely succeeds in 'the amiable, the ennobling, or the intense passions'. An instance from a minor dramatist, one therefore largely dependent upon the common stock of contemporary achievement, may be illuminating. Colley Cibber (1671-1757) amazed audiences in 1696 with *Love's Last Shift*, a comedy in which the rakish hero is strikingly reclaimed by his faithful wife. Cibber absorbed enough from his contemporaries to give pungency to the speeches of the unregenerate Loveless, but the speeches of the faithful Amanda and the repentant Loveless are preposterously unconvincing.

Restoration comedy, then, has conspicuous limitations, the extent of which may be seen by a comparison with Elizabethan comedy. But, inside this limited range, certain situations and character-types are seen sharply and amusingly; the dramatists' keen interest in the social achievements and follies of their extraordinary society is communicated down the ages. If, for example, sex-antagonism and physical appetite are not the whole of love, they are important phases of it, and the Restoration dramatists had the honesty, or the nonchalance, to display these manifestations more adequately than many subsequent ages have done. Similarly, one may disagree with Dryden, that repartee is 'the very soul of conversation' but acknowledge that it can be an agreeable ingredient. If the 'wit' of the Restoration quickly palls (one sees with Keats, the 'lover of fine phrases', that to strike off fine passages is not enough), still this wit often has the element of truth and perception one may expect of an epigram, and certainly it is stage-effective. Indeed, the most conspicuous quality of Restoration comedy is the witty exchange of words, and one of the best books on this comedy has traced its rise, fullness, and decline in the handling of the most frequent participants in these exchanges – the 'gay couples' of heroes and heroines.[7] Wit and repartee were, of course, highly prized qualities in the 'conversation of gentlemen'; verbal cleverness and intellectual agility of this kind were comparative novelties in English social life, and if like most novelties they were overrated, they still remain attractive elements in the comedies which reproduce them. No comedies, however, rely entirely on wit-exhibitions. Dryden most approved 'the mixed way of comedy; that which is neither all wit, nor all humour, but the result of both'; and though it is convenient to adopt the scholars' categories of Comedy of 'Manners', of 'Humour', and of 'Intrigue', most plays contain elements of all three, partly because they had to please all sections of the audience – the Wits of the Pit, the ladies of the Boxes, and the servants and wenches of the Gallery.[8]

Every dramatist mixed these and other elements in varying proportions, but a glance at early Restoration comedy shows clearly that the strength lies in the witty scenes; contemporary dramatists realized this, and there is a steady increase in and refinement of this 'Manners' element. The early plays of Dryden and Etherege are a hotchpotch of gay-couple adventures, low farcical intrigues and humours, and romantic-heroic love-and-honour plots in verse, but the vitality clearly belongs to the gay couples, Etherege's Sir Frederick Frolick and Widow Rich in *The Comical Revenge* (1664), Dryden's Loveby and Constance, Celadon and Florimel, Wildblood and Jacintha, in his *Wild Gallant* (1663), *Secret Love* (1667) and *An Evening's Love* (1668).* The recent introduction of actresses on to the English stage contributed, of course, to the success and popularity of these sharp encounters between the sexes. One prominent element in Dryden's plays was the 'Proviso-Scene', in which hero and heroine bargained about the conditions under which each might contemplate matrimony; Dryden's success with these scenes established them as a stereotype, and they were much imitated and burlesqued, the bargaining of Congreve's Mirabel and Millamant being the most brilliant of the series. Dryden's gay couples begin from such premises as these:

> *Florimel* (a Maid of Honour). But this marriage is such a bugbear to me! much might be if we could invent but any way to make it easy.
> *Celadon* (a Courtier). Some foolish people have made it uneasy by drawing the knot faster than they need; but we that are wiser will loosen it a little.
> (*Secret Love, or, The Maiden Queen*, V. i)

* Plays are dated in this essay by their first production, not by publication.

The couple traverse some familiar grounds for marital discord: Florimel hopes that Celadon may find 'marriage as good as wenching', if they are married, not into the damning titles of 'husband and wife', but 'by the more agreeable names of mistress and gallant'. This, like Dryden's fuller examination of *Marriage à la Mode* (1672), is bright and shrewd rather than penetrating; the premises about human nature, and about the satisfactions and frustrations of marriage, are too narrow. One cannot, for instance, imagine any set of 'provisos' that would make marriage 'easy' enough to be endurable to persons of such shallow character and roving disposition as the quartette in *Marriage à la Mode*: nor can one agree with Professor Dobrée that there is 'health and sanity in every phrase' of that play. Professor Dobrée maintains that Restoration comedy expressed 'not licentiousness, but a deep curiosity, and a desire to try new ways of living'; but experiments at this level of understanding are not very significant. *Marriage à la Mode* is successful at the level of light comedy, and Dryden acquired considerable expertise in this kind, uncongenial though he personally found it. His *Sir Martin Mar-All* (1667), based on Molière, is one of the gayest farces of the period, if one ignores the nauseous subplot which Dryden added to the French original. (It is noteworthy that Restoration adaptations of Molière were always made both more coarse and more complicated than their originals.)

Marriage à la Mode is a 'mixed' play, of a kind which Dryden continued to write all his life; scenes from a half-length love-and-honour verse play are interspersed with scenes from a half-length comedy. Sometimes, as in *The Spanish Friar* (1680), the two plots are mechanically interdependent, but they remained two plays 'tacked together ... for the pleasure of variety', and Dryden later admitted that it was 'an unnatural mingle', done to meet the audience's 'Gothic' taste. 'This critical age', indeed, was like Polonius: 'he's for a jig, or a tale of bawdry, or he sleeps.' The popular demand for multiplicity of plot – one Elizabethan habit which survived new fashions and theories – was a bane of Restoration drama. Although most comic dramatists abandoned the mixture of verse and prose, it is rarely that any unity of impression is achieved. Often, as in Dickens, there is 'rotten architecture, but wonderful gargoyles'.[9] Wycherley and Congreve are extreme in retaining melodramatic plots in *Love in a Wood* and *The Double Dealer*, but most plays have at least three plots of various kinds, connected in so bewildering a way that one too often asks, as Granville-Barker does of *Love in a Wood*: 'How could an audience both be clever enough to understand the story, and stupid enough to be interested by it when they did?'[10]

Etherege, in his second play, *She Wou'd if She Cou'd* (1668), and his third and last, *The Man of Mode, or, Sir Fopling Flutter* (1676), does not err in this respect: they were, as contemporaries remarked, 'two talking plays without one plot'. Etherege drops the romantic elements present in *The Comical Revenge*, though in *She Wou'd* he retains some rough humour and farcical situations: he now concentrates on witty persiflage. He has learned to catch the atmosphere of his times, to 'shoot folly as it flies, And catch the manners living as they rise'. This is the 'modern way of writing' which he proclaims in the Prologue of his first play, and now refines. The heroines of *She Wou'd*, Ariana and Gatty, are an admirably high-spirited and witty pair (their first encounter with their partners in II. i is a delight), and, in Lady Cockwood, Etherege gives impetus to a character-type which became excessively familiar on the Restoration stage – the superannuated amorous lady, usually in love with the hero. (This type survives in Gilbert and Sullivan, and in the Pantomime Dame.[11]) In *The Man of Mode*, Etherege attains a unity of tone, by excluding plots and situations of discordant kind, and was thus credited with having written 'the pattern of genteel comedy'. The plot is slight; it concerns the amorous adventures of Dorimant, who is simultaneously casting off one mistress (his '*pis-aller*', or 'convenient'), seducing another, and courting a third. The diverting fop who provides the title has little part in this plot, and indeed first appears in Act III; he is in part a glorious sideshow, and in part a contrast to the hero. Dorimant is a credible, memorable, and highly disagreeable figure; one recalls Professor Krutch's remark that Restoration fine gentlemen 'were gentlemen in everything – except essentials'. But Dennis's *Defense of Sir Fopling Flutter* (1722) against such aspersions innocently reveals the temporary degradation of the chivalric ideal, by asking:

> What indeed can any one mean, when he speaks of a fine gentleman, but one who is qualified in conversation, to please the best company of either sex?

Some of Dorimant's affections are nicely undermined by his witty Lady Harriet (his 'grave bows', for instance), and her rejoinder, when he declines to look foolish by paying unsuccessful court to her in public, is shrewd:

> When your love's grown strong enough to make you bear
> being laughed at, I'll give you leave to trouble me with it: till
> then, pray forbear, sir.

> (IV, i.)

Harriet admirably justifies Dorimant's description of her – 'wild, witty, lovesome, beautiful, and young' (as in the excellent scene when she and the pleasant Young Bellair parody the conventional love-birds of the period), and she has the sense not to expect too much from Dorimant's promises of reformation. Yet, despite all the evidence of his faithlessness and 'ill-nature', she clearly regards him – and Etherege seems to intend us to share her view – as a desirable mate: the crucial criticisms of him have been left unsaid, or have been made by jealous, angry, or foolish characters (one might contrast Henry James's placing of the charming, but heartless, Gilbert Osmond in *Portrait of a Lady*). For Etherege, as John Palmer has written, 'there was form: and there was bad form. The whole duty of man was to find the one, and to eschew the other.' Etherege's insight and values are restricted; there is an emotional inadequacy which corresponds to the hardness of the surface and the mechanical quality of the polished witty dialogue. Yet there are suggestions of a delicacy and tenderness which are never made central in the fable or the dialogue: as in the often-quoted final speeches of Harriet, when she warns Dorimant that he must leave London to find her in

> ... a great rambling lone house, that looks as it were not in-
> habited, the family's so small; there you'll find my Mother,
> an old lame Aunt, and myself, Sir, perched up on chairs at a
> distance in a large parlour; sitting moping like three or four
> melancholy birds in a spacious vollary. Does not this stagger
> your resolution?

One recalls that Dryden thought Etherege 'the undoubted best author' of prose in English. This charming and imaginative vision remains peripheral, however: Etherege in general suffers (actually or by modish affectation) from emotional constipation.

By the time Etherege wrote his last play, Restoration comedy had its favourite character-types and situations. There were, of course, individual modifications of the pattern. Marriage remains a joke, but Vanbrugh and Farquhar see how bad a joke it can be; country remains a stock butt, though again Vanbrugh and Farquhar are less shy of it, less arrogantly Metropolitan; the rake-Heroes persist, until they are gradually ousted by Virtue and Sense after 1700, though Farquhar again produces an interesting variant, a warmer-hearted rip, belonging to that 'School of Good Intentions' which holds that 'a good heart will cover a multitude of sins'.[12] The similarities, however, are as striking as the divergencies; Congreve's *Way of the World*, commonly considered the finest of Restoration comedies, is also their quintessence, hardly an incident or character or dialogue being original. Congreve perfects the common mode, adding to it a nicety of feeling and phrasing. His main contemporaries are individual in their divergencies from the mode.

Shadwell is uneven; he aspired to a Jonsonian breadth and seriousness, but was easily deflected by need or whim. He is gaily bawdy in *Epsom-Wells* (1672), virtuously didactic in *Bury Fair* (1689); his *True Widow* (1678) has some amusing satire, and his *Squire of Alsatia* (1688) is a lively play, providing a vivid evocation of London's underworld, but ballasted with some well-meant discussions on the theory of education. Shadwell is not always the dullard his fame would suggest; his better plays are at least as worth reading as the lesser plays of his greater contemporaries, and, if his high Jonsonian ideal remained only an aspiration, at least his admiration for Jonson led him to explore social classes which his contemporaries ignored.

Vanbrugh's plays are an unsatisfactory mixture of a personal gaiety, some conventional adultery and intrigue, and a persistent but inconclusive interest in two human plights – the unhappy marriage, and the penurious younger son of good family.[13] Vanbrugh was a dilettante in the drama: this is clear in the uneven quality of the dialogue and in the construction of his plays – none is satisfactory as a whole, except *The Confederacy* (1705), an adaptation from the French, though all contain good scenes and successful stage-characters. He lacked the power or the will to organize the materials he gathered or the ideas he started. In *The Relapse* (1696), the treatment of the marriage-theme is half-sentimental, half-realistic (or, as the Mermaid editor solemnly pronounces, 'Some very noble sentiments' and characters largely 'redeem ... whatever may be considered immoral in the piece'); but Vanbrugh becomes more interested in the quite irrelevant sub-plot concerning Lord Foppington, the most finished and reflective of fops. Vanbrugh is more interested in the unhappy marriage of the Brutes in *The Provok'd Wife* (1697), he treats infidelity farcically in *The Confederacy*, and his fragment *A Journey to London* contains the most serious and convincing sketch of a marriage between incompatibles.

Farquhar perhaps derives from Vanbrugh his similar presentation of the Sullens' unhappy marriage in his last and best play, *The Beaux' Stratagem*: certainly, although fortified by a reading and rehash of Milton's Divorce-pamphlets, he uses a Vanbrugh device for evading the logic of the situation, by having the unhappy wife's seduction by a lover fortunately, if accidentally, prevented by an interruption. This play ends with an amusing anti-Proviso-Scene, in which the Sullens at least agree with one another – to separate. But marriage is not a main theme for Farquhar. His brief career is more varied than the others'. He starts with high-spirited and morally incurious plays, *Love and a Bottle* (1699) and *The Constant Couple* (1699); moved, perhaps, by the Collier controversy, he moralizes ingenuously if intermittently in *Sir Harry Wildair* (1701), and in *The Twin-Rivals* (1703) writes moral melodrama. Finally, in *The Recruiting Officer* (1706) and *The Beaux' Stratagem* (1707) he moves his scene from London to the provinces, and presents convincingly and without being patronizing sets of characters more varied in type and origin than was usual. He is less self-consciously moral here (though he spoils the end of *The Beaux' Stratagem* by the implausible and sentimental confession of Aimwell); his heroes and heroines are good-natured, 'natural', and lively, rather than cynical, sophisticated, and brilliant, or tearfully good. If these plays lack the nicer insights of Congreve and the mordancy of Wycherley, they are more generously human than theirs, and are the most attractive (as they were long among the most popular) of Restoration comedies.

Wycherley is unmistakably the most individual of Restoration dramatists. He impresses by the sheer vehemence of his language and the energy of his characterization – the manifestations of a moral passion which even made Collier acknowledge him 'an author of

good sense'. But this he certainly is not: he is too narrow and confused in his apprehension of moral issues. He satirizes the stock butts
of Restoration comedy – fops, lawyers, country-folk, the over-
forties – but his distinctive gifts only appear when he can exercise
his indignation against 'that heinous, and worst of women's crimes,
hypocrisy'. His first play, *Love in a Wood* (1671), is a confused mixture
of various stock situations and characters; the strength lies in the
scenes involving the hypocritical Alderman Gripe and Lady Flippant.
His second, *The Gentleman Dancing Master* (1672), does not engage his
major talent. It is an amusing, if trivial, farce, and is characteristic of
Wycherley only in its main fault – that of iteration. Here it is a joke,
not a moral or a hatred, that is repeated and made over-obvious, but
Wycherley never learned discretion or economy in dramatic projection. The lengthy asides which occur so implausibly and undramati-
cally in all his plays are one sign of this unwillingness to leave anything
to the audience's imagination, this inability to subsume into the fable
and dialogue the full significance which he wishes to express. In his
two next, and final, plays Wycherley finds himself: *The Country
Wife* and *The Plain Dealer*[14] have a force, a bitterness and scorn unique
in Restoration comedy. One can understand, if not fully share, the
enthusiasm Dryden felt for 'the satire, strength, and wit of Manly
Wycherley', who, in his *Plain Dealer*, had 'obliged all honest and virtuous men by one of the most bold, most general, and most useful
satires which have ever been presented on the English theatre'.

Wycherley's dramatic talents are deployed best in *The Country
Wife*; the characterization is assured, the dialogue incisive, and the
management of situation (as in the 'china' scene, and the finale)
masterly. The play has a theme, too, which gives it force and something approaching unity: the hypocrisy which underlies female
'honour'. The best scenes are those which expose the frailty and dis-
honesty of the ladies; but, beyond this, the moral scheme of the play
is chaotic. Horner should perhaps be accepted as the almost impersonal
assumption of the play, its means of providing a test-situation for
female honour; certainly the play invites no judgement upon him –
rather admiration for the audacity, ingenuity, and unashamed zest
with which he satisfies his insanely omnivorous appetite for fornica-
tion. Conscious deceit, such as Horner practises on the husbands, is
accepted, while the less self-aware hypocrisy of the ladies is derided.

Similarly, Wycherley fails to focus the contrasts between the hypocritical 'honour' of Horner's victims and the true but fatuous honour of Alithea, and between Pinchwife's brutal jealousy and Sparkish's foolish superiority to jealousy. Wycherley, complained Pope, was 'always studying for antitheses'. The opening remarks of this play exhibit this well, and the trick of style is paralleled by the patterning of the play; and, in both style and pattern, there is something mechanical and ill-considered in Wycherley's grab at the half-truth.

The strengths and weaknesses of *The Country Wife* recur in exaggeration in *The Plain Dealer*. Again, the opening lines show Wycherley's energy, and his lack of control over it:

> *Enter Manly, surlily, Lord Plausible following him.*
> *Manly.* Tell not me, my good Lord Plausible, of your decorums, supercilious forms, and slavish ceremonies! your little tricks, which you, the spaniels of the world, do daily over and over, for and to one another, not out of love or duty, but your servile fear.
> *Lord Plausible.* Nay, i'faith, i'faith, you are too passionate ...

Indeed, Manly is too passionate, but it is only the tainted witnesses – Lord Plausible, Olivia, Freeman, and Novel – who say so. Wycherley is indulgent towards Manly: we need not look at his Dedication (signed 'The Plain Dealer'), or recall how the cognomen stuck to him, to realize how thoroughly he identifies himself with this naïvely and brutally 'honest' hero. (A profitable comparison can be made with D. H. Lawrence's treatment of his misanthropic hero Somers, in *Kangaroo*. Somers is largely a projection of Lawrence himself, but Lawrence makes the reader, and even sometimes Somers, see the elements of self-indulgence, subjectivity, and sheer folly in his 'diabolic' misanthropy.) There is some validity in both Manly's and Somers's violent rejection of their worlds; but the worth of Manly's criticism of life is impaired by the self-centred and adolescent quality of his splenetic contempt for social forms. 'Is railing satire?' Manly asks Novel. The question should have been asked of Manly and his creator, who both too obviously enjoy railing; they have an obsessed attraction towards the subjects on which they may exercise their verbal aggression.

'Since the *Plain-Dealer*'s Scenes of Manly Rage', wrote Congreve, 'Not one has dar'd to lash this Crying Age.' Congreve – 'friendly Congreve, unreproachful man', as Gay called him – did not try to. *The Old Bachelor* (1693), his first play, is like Wycherley's first, a medley, of unequal interest; the opening dialogue, however, suggests where his talent lies. *The Double Dealer* (1693) is a mixture of different, and more discordant, kind – of melodrama with romance and light comedy; but again Congreve shows his individual talents, his 'prodigious sense of human absurdity'[15] in Lady Plyant, and an uncommon tenderness and sensitivity in the love-scenes between Mellefont and Cynthia. Congreve's most popular comedy was *Love for Love* (1695), and it has justly remained a perennial stage-favourite. Even the minor characters have moments of dramatic life; they belong to familiar types, but are vivified and individualized by the excellence of dialogue which Congreve gives to them as well as to his Wits. The Nurse, for instance, replying to Angelica's playfully monstrous accusations about her relations with old Foresight:

> Marry Heav'n defend – I at midnight practices – O Lord, what's here to do? – I in unlawful doings with my Master's Worship – Why, did you ever hear the like now – Sir, did ever I do anything of your midnight concerns – but warm your bed, and tuck you up, and set the candle and your tobacco-box, and your urinal by you, and now and then rub the soles of your feet? – O Lord, I ! –
>
> (II, iii.)

Valentine's 'mad' speeches, if not the 'pure poetry' some assert, are an admirable artefact. Angelica is delightful, though she remains a 'riddle' to the audience as well as to Valentine, whom she urges –

> Never let us know one another better; for the pleasure of a Masquerade is done when we come to shew our faces.
>
> (IV, xx.)

Perhaps Professor Dobrée is right in finding here and elsewhere in Congreve 'a strong element of wistfulness, ... a constant fear of disillusion'; perhaps it is merely the case that Congreve, like his fellow-dramatists, is unable fully to imagine and present, without sentimentality, a permanent affection or relationship.

The Way of the World (1700) was not, and has not proved, so success-

ful a stage-piece, though it contains some of the best scenes and acting
roles in Restoration comedy, even the severest critics of which have
been charmed by Millamant. Actresses, from Mrs Bracegirdle in the
first performance to Dame Edith Evans and Miss Pamela Brown in
our day, have excelled themselves in portraying this mixture of
gaiety, mockery, and genuine affection. As a contemporary critic
said of a recent production, justice must be done to the quality of
Congreve's dialogue, and he rightly criticized the Lady Wishfort of
that production for failing to project with exactness the phrases given
to her: 'Comic business is not enough here.' Congreve's phrasing is
nice, often surprising: indeed, this strength is too consistently and
exclusively exploited. He delights the style-fanciers, such as Hazlitt,
but he works too much in terms of the fine phrase, the dazzling or
more robustly amusing scene. This play, like his others, lacks
coherence; the parts are more important than the whole. There
is, in fact, no whole of any importance: the plot is intricate, but
meaningless. Congreve has a sharp eye for certain situations – the
gross self-deception of Lady Wishfort, the back-biting of Witwoud,
the inability of Millamant, who loves Mirabel 'violently', to say
more to his face than that she 'might by degrees dwindle into a wife',
or the love that Mirabel feels for her:

> ... for I like her with all her faults; nay, like her for her
> faults. Her follies are so natural, or so artful, that they become
> her; and those affectations which in another woman would
> be odious, serve but to make her more agreeable.
>
> (I, iii.)

But Congreve's perceptions are not extensive; they remain the perceptions of a dramatist who abandoned the stage at the age of thirty,
and whose primary inspiration was literary. Dr Johnson noted this
of his first play, and it is true of his last. He answers to the description
commonly given of Jane Austen, as the amusing but superficial
observer of a superficial and restricted society: 'Miss Austen is only
shrewd and observant', said Charlotte Brontë. But Jane Austen is, as
Virginia Woolf has remarked, 'mistress of much deeper emotion than
appears on the surface'. Congreve sometimes has these depths of im-
plication (Millamant's love is the best example), but he lacks the understanding of and concern for human values which make Jane Austen a
major, while he remains a minor, writer.

'Congreve quitted the stage in disdain, and Comedy left it with him', wrote Dennis in 1717. 'What plays! What wit!' wrote Byron a century later. '*Hélas!* Congreve and Vanbrugh are your only comedy. Our society is too insipid now for the like copy.' The best period of Restoration drama, as of Elizabethan, was brief: the plays which followed, though informed by higher moral intentions, were dull, un-lifelike, fundamentally insincere (Steele's are the typical example). Byron's instinct was right: the strengths of Restoration comedy, like its weaknesses and limitations, were to a great extent dependent upon a particular social situation. No equally adequate dramatic form was discovered when Sense, and later Sensibility, joined and replaced Wit as the social ideal.

NOTES

1. On the meaning and evolution of this term, see F. W. Bateson's note in *Essays in Criticism*, I, 1, pp. 90–3.

2. See L. C. Knights, 'Restoration Comedy: the Reality and the Myth', in *Explorations* (London, 1946). Contemporary reports of and rumours about the Court will be found in the *Diaries* of Pepys and Evelyn, *The Memoirs of Grammont*, and Bishop Burnet's *History of His Own Time* (abridged edition in the Everyman Series). See also John Harold Wilson, *The Court Wits of the Restoration* (Princeton, 1948), and Harold Wendell Smith, 'Nature, Correctness and Decorum', in *Scrutiny*, XVIII, 4 (1952).

3. See Alfred Harbage, *Cavalier Drama: An Historical and Critical Supplement to the Study of the Elizabethan and Restoration Stage* (New York, 1936), and Leslie Hotson, *The Commonwealth and Restoration Stage* (Harvard, 1928).

4. See J. W. Krutch, *Comedy and Conscience after the Restoration* (New York, 2nd ed., 1949), and extracts from Collier in *Critical Essays of the Seventeenth Century*, III, pp. 253–91, ed. J. E. Spingarn (1908). Alexandre Beljame's *Men of Letters and the English Public in the Eighteenth Century, 1660–1744* (English translation, 1948) amasses a formidable amount of evidence of the 'immorality' complained of.

5. The contention that Restoration comedy owed anything substantial to French comedy has now been discredited; see, e.g., John Wilcox, *The Relation of Molière to Restoration Comedy* (New York, 1938).

6. John F. Danby, 'Beaumont and Fletcher: Jacobean Absolutists', in *Poets on Fortune's Hill* (1952), p. 165. See also John Harold Wilson, *The Influence of Beaumont and Fletcher on Restoration Comedy* (Ohio, 1928). Useful comments on the transition from Elizabethan to Restoration Comedy will also be found in Leslie Stephen's 'Massinger', in *Hours in a Library* (1892), II, pp. 141–76; Kathleen M. Lynch, *The Social Mode of Restoration Comedy*, II–V (New York, 1926); Bonamy Dobrée, *Restoration Comedy*, IV (London, 1924).

7. See J. H. Smith, *The Gay Couple in Restoration Comedy* (Harvard, 1948).

8. See Clifford Leech, 'Restoration Drama: the Earlier Phase', in *Essays in Criticism*, I, 2 (Oxford, 1951), and George Farquhar, *Discourse upon Comedy* (1702), in *Critical Essays of the Eighteenth Century*, ed. W. H. Durham (Yale, 1915).

9. The likeness to Dickens is not accidental, nor the comparison unilluminating: see R. C. Churchill, 'Dickens, Drama and Tradition', in *Scrutiny*, x, 4 (1942).

10. See his stimulating attack on Restoration drama, *On Dramatic Method*, IV (London, 1931).

11. Sir Arthur Quiller-Couch's essay on W. S. Gilbert, in *Studies in Literature: Third Series* (Cambridge, 1929), can usefully be read in relation to Restoration comedy.

12. F. W. Bateson, *English Comic Drama, 1700–1750* (London, 1929), p. 93: a useful introduction to this later period.

13. See Paul Muesche and Jeanette Fleisher, 'A Re-Valuation of Vanbrugh', in *P.M.L.A.*, xlix (1934), pp. 848–89.

14. Published 1675 and 1677, and probably first performed in 1673 and 1676 respectively. But the dates, and the order of composition, are disputed; for a summary of the evidence, see pp. xv–xxvii of the Introduction, by George C. Churchill, to his excellent Belles-Lettres Series edition of these two plays.

15. Virginia Woolf, 'Congreve's Comedies', in *The Moment, and other Essays* (London, 1947), p. 36.

LITERARY THEORY AND LITERARY
CRITICISM

P. A. W. COLLINS

'TILL of late years', wrote Thomas Rymer in 1674, 'England was as free from critics as it is from wolves.' Rymer was exaggerating, but during this period criticism does increase in bulk and quality. In formal treatises and (more often) in essays and prefaces to new poems and plays and to reprints of old ones, ideas on the principles of writing were set forth, defined, and clarified, and a determined effort was made to assess both current literature and the inheritance from the past; for England now had a literature which could stand comparison with the other great modern literatures, Italian and French, and even (some claimed) with the Ancient. Shakespeare was the writer most generally considered our champion against the masters of other literatures, and the present essay will take most of its examples from Shakespeare-criticism from Dryden to Johnson. When a large subject is to be discussed in a short space, some drastic selection is necessary, and Shakespeare is (as Pope wrote) 'of all English poets ... the fairest and fullest subject for criticism'. All the major critics discuss him, and their critical principles and methods are exemplified in and may be inferred from what they say of him. And it is during this period that Shakespeare was first systematically criticized and accorded the rank he has since retained. By 1765, Johnson could claim for him 'the dignity of an ancient'; veneration for him was, as another critic wrote in the same year, part of the national religion. A century before, Dryden was being adventurous in asserting that Shakespeare 'of all modern, and perhaps ancient poets, had the largest and most comprehensive soul', and at his best towered 'high above the rest of poets'.

Dryden's *Essay on Dramatic Poesy* (1668), where this remark appears, was not an academic exercise: Dryden wrote dramas besides criticizing them, and his judgement of Shakespeare had implications for his practice as a dramatist. The theatres had reopened in 1660, after nearly twenty years, and during this time a good deal of theorizing about the drama and its 'Rules' had been produced in France. As Pope wrote later, in 1711,

> ... Critic-learning flourish'd most in France.
> The rules a nation, born to serve, obeys ...
> But we, brave Britons, foreign laws despis'd ...
> (*Essay on Criticism*, 712–15)

The political analogy used here was often invoked, and the chauvinism which Pope displays makes his praise, a few lines later, for 'the sounder few [who] here restor'd Wit's fundamental laws' sound half-hearted. These 'Rules' had been known, but little regarded, in Shakespeare's England; by 1660, however, Corneille had shown that they worked, and his success, together with the prestige of France as the centre of European civilization, presented a challenge to the English native dramatic tradition. The most prominent Rule of drama was that the 'three Unities' should be observed: the plot should develop one action, with no irrelevancies or sub-plots, and this action should be completed in one day and one place. This Rule was not so arbitrary and pedantic as many Englishmen then, and since, have thought it, though a scrupulous and unimaginative 'working to rule' could be, in drama then as in Trade Unions now, awkward rather than effective. But, properly understood, the discipline of the Unities was a wholesome reaction against laxity and incoherence of construction, and could help a Racine to economy of means and concentration of effect.[1]

This notion of having 'Rules' for writers is alien to us now, and so is another practice of the time – looking to the literature of the past for 'models'. Some explanation may be helpful. To Dryden, as to his fellows, it seemed self-evident, that 'if nature is to be imitated [and this was the aim of drama], then there is a rule for imitating nature rightly; otherwise there may be an end, and no means conducing to it'. Ancient Greek and Latin literature was still the common standard of reference for modern Europe; to emulate it, and the civilization which produced it, was the height of achievement. Not implausibly, many critics recommended more or less direct imitation of the Ancients. Horace, in his *Ars Poetica*, an influential document at this time, had advised the ancient Romans to imitate the Greeks, and Virgil's success had shown what could be done by following in

Homer's footsteps. But the poet need not confine himself to imitating particular writers or works, which inevitably had some faults: he could follow the 'Rules', a set of which existed for every form or 'Kind' (e.g. epic, tragedy, comedy, ode, pastoral, satire). The Rules were formulae abstracted by critics from a study of the admitted successes of the past, perhaps supplemented by an 'exercise of right reason'. This process of formulating Rules is analogous to the scientist's generalizing after observing many particular instances, and indeed it owed something of its prestige to science. It had been one of the preoccupations of seventeenth-century philosophers, such as Bacon and Descartes, to find and formulate a correct 'method' of investigation, the use of which would make the discovery of truth an easier, and almost a mechanical, task. No literary critics denied that poets needed 'Nature' (inborn abilities) as well as Art (which included a knowledge of the Rules), but they thought that in poetry as in science 'well begun is half done'.

In drama, there was little direct imitation of the Ancients; the modern stage and audience, it was agreed, made this impossible. But drama had its Rules which, according to the common account, were derived ultimately from Aristotle's *Poetics*, which, in its turn, had been derived from Aristotle's 'observation of those things in which Euripides, Sophocles, and Aeschylus pleased' (as Dryden asserted). Now, Shakespeare had notoriously broken all the Rules: he lived in 'a barbarous age', and either did not know them or had been forced by his barbarous audience to ignore them. And not only his dramatic structure, but also his language, versification, and often his subject-matter offended against the critical principles developing in the 1660s. The critics had, then, to decide whether respect for these new principles of writing should modify or destroy their respect for Shakespeare, or *vice versa*; or whether the Shakespearian mode of writing, and the one now favoured, should both be recognized as valid. In fact, all three things happened, and often in the mind of the same critic. Critics differed as to the balance between Shakespeare's 'beauties' and 'faults', the tendency being for the faults to seem less important to each succeeding generation and eventually to be adjudged not faults at all. In the earlier stages of this discussion, a favourable judgement upon Shakespeare was often justified by an appeal to the authority of Longinus, whose *On the Sublime* had recently been translated from the Greek and popularized. Longinus' criticism was enthusiastic rather than judicial. He did not go fault-finding, but 'surveyed the Whole' (the words are Pope's, who is paraphrasing Longinus) and warmly praised those poems which, even though faulty, displayed great genius and 'transported' the reader. His example was important for the eighteenth century, and was 'method-ized' by those critics who referred literary judgements to their 'taste' – the emotional impact which a poem made on them – rather than to formal principles. By this test, Shakespeare succeeded with all but the most prejudiced: for as Addison said,

> Our inimitable Shakespeare is a stumbling-block to the whole tribe of these rigid critics. Who would not rather read one of his plays, where there is not a single rule of the stage observed, than any production of a modern critic, where there is not one of them violated!
>
> (*Spectator* 592)

The walls of the critical Jericho did not fall at once, however, and there was some justice in the critics' continuing to recommend obedience to the Rules rather than imitation of Shakespeare's form. Shakespeare is 'inimitable' in a stricter sense than Addison intends: if great writers are to be regarded, as they were then, as potential 'models', few are more disastrous than Shakespeare. The poetical-dramatic unity of his plays is not obvious or easily defined; for most imitators, his freedom of time and place, his double-plots and mixture of tragedy and comedy, only gave authority for a chaos that was euphemistically called 'variety'. Even those critics who defended Shakespeare's mode of construction thought him a bad precedent.[2] Critics were in a similar dilemma over Spenser and Milton, who by early in the eighteenth century had been recognized as our greatest poets after Shakespeare. Neither of them conformed to current ideals of vocabulary and versification; Spenser's form, too, offended against the epic Rules. Both of them did prove, in fact, bad models, and again critics were torn between admiration for their sublime and imagina-tive qualities (of a kind rare in the first half of our period) and dislike of their faults and their imitators.

Shakespeare, Spenser, and Milton were alike, too, in 'going beyond Nature', in the sense that they did not confine themselves to the naturalistic reproduction of ordinary human experience. It was a critical commonplace that

> it is impossible for any thought to be beautiful which is not just, and has not its foundation in the nature of things; that the basis of all wit is truth; and that no thought can be valuable, of which good sense is not the ground-work.
>
> (ADDISON: *Spectator* 62)

One agrees that poetry, to be significant, must be 'truthful', in some sense of the word; but 'truth' could be very narrowly conceived. The works of Rymer (1641–1713), one of the most discussed and influential critics of his time, are a good example of what may happen then (translation of Rapin 1674, *Tragedies of the Last Age* 1678, *Short View of Tragedy* 1692). Spenser had great genius but, in *The Fairie Queene*, 'all is fanciful and chimerical, without any uniformity, without any foundation in truth; his poem is perfect Fairy-land'; *Paradise Lost* is only what 'some are pleased to call a poem'; and Shakespeare fares no better. Rymer examines the tragedies of the last age 'by the Practice of the Ancients and by the Common Sense of All Ages'; but he does not often invoke the Rules, for 'there is no talking of Beauties when there wants Essentials'. Learning is superfluous, even 'women-judges' can detect the faults of the Elizabethans: 'common sense suffices.' Rymer's very literal and prosaic common sense demonstrates that 'the tragical part [of *Orhello* is] plainly none other than a Bloody Farce, without salt or savour'. Shakespeare's language was as Bedlam-like as his plots: 'In a play one should speak like a man of business.' Not that Rymer wanted photographic realism in drama; he quotes with approval Aristotle's claim (*Poetics*, 1451) that the poet, by limiting himself to the typical and essential, is 'more philosophical' than the historian, who must record also the exceptional and accidental in human affairs. Thus, soldiers have for centuries been notoriously 'open-hearted, frank, plain-dealing': yet Shakespeare has offended against the 'decorum' for this type in creating his Iago –

> ... to entertain the audience with something new and surprising, against common sense and Nature, he would pass upon us a close, dissembling, false, insinuating rascal.
>
> (*Short View of Tragedy*)

Rymer invented and popularized the phrase 'poetical justice'; in life, the wicked may sometimes flourish like the bay-tree, but this is not typical, and the unfortunate exception to the rule is not a properly instructive spectacle for the stage.

The rationalism represented by Rymer was an important ingredient in the criticism of the period. It was, of course, a literary manifestation of the dominant philosophy; well might Boileau complain that 'Descartes had cut the throat of poetry'.[3] For Rymer, as for others, 'enthusiasm', whether poetical or religious, was suspect. 'Reason' should control poetical Fancy and religious faith: 'Those who object against reason are the Fanatics of poetry, are never to be saved by their good works.' Rymer was an able and intelligent man, but it was clear even to most of his admirers that his critical equipment was inadequate. Nevertheless, even a century later he was still being referred to as a prominent adversary of Shakespeare. At least, as Spingarn notes, Rymer inaugurated the detailed study of literary texts, and thus aided the movement away from general to concrete criticism.

Despite Rymer, Shakespeare became recognized as the greatest of English, and perhaps of all, dramatists. In 1660 Jonson was commonly regarded as greater, and Beaumont and Fletcher were more popular, but Dryden decisively asserted Shakespeare's superiority.[4] Jonson was 'the more correct poet ... I admire him, but I love Shakespeare'. Dryden's *Essay* was written 'chiefly to vindicate the honour of our English writers, from the censure of those who unjustly prefer the French before them', and quotations have already been made from his famous passage on Shakespeare, which Johnson later called 'a perpetual model of encomiastic criticism': to write it in 1668 was a major critical achievement. The *Essay* is the best critical piece of its generation. It traverses most of the current controversies over drama: the relative merits of the Ancient, the French and the Elizabethan plays, of Shakespeare, Jonson, and Fletcher, of blank verse and rhyme, the validity of the Rules and of Imitation, the necessity of verisimilitude. Dryden adulates Shakespeare and the other Elizabethans, though he declines to imitate them, chiefly because they cannot be equalled on their own ground; but in other essays (for Dryden's criticism is almost all occasional, and fluctuates) he sometimes patronizes them. They lived in a barbarous age, and lack the wit, polish, and refined language now demanded of dramatists; but still –

> Theirs was the Giant Race before the Flood ...
> Our Age was cultivated thus at length,
> But what we gain'd in skill we lost in strength.
>
> (*To Mr Congreve*)

This assessment of the relation between his and 'the last age' came the more easily to Dryden and his fellows, because similar comparisons had long been made between the Golden and Silver Ages, between Homer, the earlier and 'the greater genius', and Virgil, 'more correct' but inferior. Only occasionally is this idea modified or supplanted by literary analogies with scientific 'progress', and then most commonly it is only asserted that progress has been made in limited respects, of 'skill', 'wit', and versification, not of total greatness.

A more serious limitation in Dryden's criticism, which he shared with his contemporaries and successors, is suggested by such remarks as that he agrees with Jonson's (apocryphal?) horror at 'some bombast speeches of Macbeth, which are not to be understood', and that Shakespeare's 'whole style is so pestered with figurative expressions, that it is as affected as it is obscure'. He admits elsewhere that 'it is almost a miracle that much of [Shakespeare's] language remains so pure'; but a man and an age which cannot understand, let alone approve, Shakespeare's use of language are clearly prevented from anything approaching a full appreciation of him. Dryden's complaint is repeated by all the major critics for a century.[5] Shakespeare's earlier poetry was most congenial. Dryden, to 'do justice to that divine poet', quotes him at his best in *Richard II*. Pope makes the illuminating remark that the style of *Two Gentlemen of Verona* 'is less figurative, and more natural and unaffected, than the greater part of this author's [plays] though supposed to be one of the first he wrote'. Gray illustrates his famous assertion that 'Shakespeare's language is one of his principal beauties ... Every word in him is a picture' by quoting *Richard III*. The effectiveness of Shakespeare's poetry was often *felt*, and the striking passages, or 'beauties', were distinguished in some eighteenth-century editions, and collected into anthologies. Dr Johnson, while criticizing the 'mean words' which provoked his 'risibility' in Lady Macbeth's 'Come, thick night!' speech, recognizes that here 'is exerted all the force of poetry, that force which calls new powers into being, which embodies sentiment, and animates matter': but 'perhaps scarce any man now peruses it without some disturbance of his attention from the counteraction of the words and the ideas' (*Rambler* 168). No eighteenth-century critics could read Shakespeare – any more than they could read Donne[6] – without experiencing this counteraction; the new ideals of correctness, smooth versification, clear expression, and simple imagery were too potent. One of the few points of agreement for all four participants in Dryden's dialogue on *Dramatic Poesy* is that 'the sweetness of English verse was never understood or practised by our fathers'; only recently had English poets learned 'to mould their thoughts into easy and significant words; to retrench the superfluities of expression', and to master rhyme. Waller and Denham were usually credited with this achievement; Denham's *Cooper's Hill*, said Dryden, 'is, and ever will be, the exact standard of good writing'. Shakespeare's versification was as licentious, by this standard, as his imagery was imperfect by Johnson's definition of the perfect simile: it 'must both illustrate and ennoble the subject; must show it to the understanding in a clearer view, and display it to the fancy with greater dignity'. Shakespeare's plays were generally acted in 'adapted' versions during this period: not only is the structure often simplified and 'regularized', but so is the verse, to the point of emasculation.[7]

The great eighteenth-century exemplar of correctness in verse is, of course, Pope, and the neatness of his couplets in the *Essay on Criticism* contributes much to its tone and implies something of its critical attitude. The *Essay* is not original in its ideas, as Addison noted with approval in *Spectator* 253. It is well-phrased and typical rather than profound, and typical not least in its muddled eclecticism, its rejection of any one orthodoxy. Thus, the Rules are at one point an inference from the practice of the Ancients, at another they existed before the Ancients wrote and the Ancients grandly broke them, at another they were delivered to the hitherto 'un-confin'd' poets by Aristotle. Modern writers should 'beware' of breaking the Rules, but modern critics should not judge mechanically by them. Pope variously advises the poet to imitate the Ancients, obey the Rules, and 'follow Nature'; these three prescriptions are reconciled by the identification – a commonplace of the time – of Nature and the Rules (which are 'Nature methodized') and Nature and the Ancients ('To copy Nature is to copy them', 'Nature and Homer were, he [Virgil] found, the same'). Again, Pope fluctuates between recommending the reserve of the man of sense ('For fools admire, but men of sense approve'*), and acclaiming 'the generous pleasure to be charm'd with Wit' when 'rapture warms the mind'. Pope does not clarify this when he says that the ideal critic is 'Blest with a taste exact, yet unconfin'd'. These inconsistencies, though they are signs of the weakness of Pope's critical position, are at least also evidence of his wish to tolerate and enjoy literature of various sorts.

This allowance for 'rapture', and for the 'grace beyond the reach of art', and the recognition that 'Applause, in spite of trivial faults, is due', owe something to Longinus, and Pope's *Preface* to his *Iliad* (1715) is an excellent example of criticism inspired by the Longinian spirit and style. Pope praises Homer, as elsewhere he praises Spenser and Shakespeare, for that 'unequalled fire and rapture', which can 'over-power criticism, and make us admire even while we disapprove', and he shrewdly remarks that

> perhaps the reason why most critics are inclined to prefer a judicious and methodical genius to a great and fruitful one, is because they find it easier for themselves to pursue their observations through an uniform and bounded walk of Art, than to comprehend the vast and various extent of Nature.

Actually, the major critics did not, in general, reject or depreciate the 'great and fruitful' geniuses. Dryden had written admirably of Chaucer, who was not, by the standards of the day, 'judicious and methodical', and Shakespeare and Spenser were generally extolled. The critics did fail, however, to give a satisfactory account of the kind of poetic unity which the works of the immethodical geniuses possessed. 'To judge of Shakespeare by Aristotle's rules', said Pope, 'is like trying a man by the laws of one country, who acted under those of another.' This historical approach sounds promising, and was to be a useful development in the criticism of Shakespeare and other by-

* 'Admire' is here used in the Latin sense of 'to feel astonishment' (cf. Horace's 'nil admirari'), and 'approve' means 'put to the test'.

gone writers, during the course of the century; but here it is inadequate. As Professor Butt has remarked, 'Pope does not take the further step of discovering what the rules of Shakespeare's country were'. Pope does hazard an analogical justification for Shakespeare's plan: his plays resemble a Gothic cathedral as more regular plays resemble a 'neat modern building'.

> The latter is more elegant and glaring, but the former is more strong and more solemn. ... [The Gothic] has much the greater variety, and much the nobler apartments; though we are often conducted to them by dark, odd and uncouth passages. Nor does the whole fail to strike us with greater reverence, though many of the parts are childish, ill-placed, and unequal to its grandeur.
>
> (*Preface to Shakespeare*)

This Gothic analogy had already been used by Hughes, and was later to be used by Hurd, with reference to Spenser; but not until Coleridge wrote (and again used it) do we find the beginning of a full understanding of the Shakespearian form. Pope is still at the stage of finding too 'many of the parts' faulty.

Long before Coleridge's time, however, Shakespeare was generally exonerated from breaking the Unities: Johnson, in his *Rambler* 156 (1751) and his Shakespeare *Preface* (1765), had made the final statement of his century's case for Shakespeare, in this respect. Johnson rightly insists that the Unities are not an essential in drama, though the arguments he uses are not altogether convincing. There is no reason why the scene should not be altered in a play, he urges: for 'the spectators are always in their senses, ... and where is the absurdity of allowing that place to represent first Athens, and then Sicily, which was always known to be neither Sicily nor Athens, but a modern theatre?' This is an inadequate account of stage-illusion, and does not grapple with the cases for and against changes of scene in plays of various kinds. When it comes to the point, Johnson cannot find 'any art of connexion or care of disposition' in *Antony and Cleopatra*. Similarly, Johnson's defence of tragi-comedy is inadequate. 'When Shakespeare's plan is understood, most of the criticisms of Rymer and Voltaire vanish away' – but an understanding of 'Shakespeare's plan' is not much furthered by suggestions that these plays exhibit 'the real state of sublunary nature, which partakes of good and evil, joy and sorrow', that they are doubly instructive because they may 'convey all the instruction of tragedy or comedy', and that anyway 'all pleasure consists in variety' – and least of all by the assertion that Shakespeare's 'disposition ... led him to comedy. ... In tragedy he is always struggling after some occasion to be comic.' Shakespeare's 'variety', both in his whole canon and within each play, Johnson appreciated; but neither he, nor any of his contemporaries, understood the unity-in-complexity of either his plotting or his poetry, let alone the interrelation between his plotting, his poetry and his characterization.

If neither Shakespeare's poetry nor his 'plan' could be understood or heartily approved, inevitably he was praised chiefly for his characterization (rather as Chaucer, today, is rarely praised for any specifically poetic qualities, but for his 'warm humanity'). Thus Dryden claims that 'no man ever drew so many characters, or generally distinguished 'em better, excepting only Jonson'; Pope asserts that Shakespeare is 'not so much an imitator, as an instrument, of Nature ... he seems to have known the world by Intuition, to have looked through human nature at one glance'. Such general praises of Shakespeare's characterization abounded, and were followed in the second half of the eighteenth century by a number of detailed studies of particular characters in Shakespeare, of which Morgann's *Dramatic Character of Falstaff* (1777) is the most elaborate.[8] So for Johnson, 'the praise of Shakespeare is that his drama is the mirror of life', it contains 'human sentiments in human language'. Johnson is, as Mr T. S. Eliot has said, 'a mature if limited critic', and the strength of his Shakespeare-criticism is that he judges Shakespeare by his mature and profound sense of the human situation. Shakespeare, he insists, shows us, not the phantoms and impossible heroes so common in literature, but *men*: and Shakespeare's men are not so particular and unique, such 'individuals', that we can learn little from their conduct, but are 'the genuine progeny of common humanity, such as the world will always supply, and observation will always find'. Shakespeare's picture of life is just, and his observation both wide and subtle. Johnson continually points to the 'strokes of nature' in Shakespeare: Lady Macbeth's arguments are those of any wicked wife to any husband, the difference between the effects of grief on Leonato in *Much Ado* and Constance in *King John* shows Shakespeare's 'knowledge of the passions'. This knowledge and wisdom Shakespeare sometimes makes explicit in 'practical axioms and domestic wisdom' which, if collected, would form 'a system of civil and economical prudence'; but it is for the picture, not for the wise saws and modern instances, that he is most to be valued.

Shakespeare has, however, his faults, which Johnson will not ignore; for the business of a critic, he said, is not (as Addison and other Longinian critics had asserted) to 'point out beauties rather than faults' – nor was it the opposite: rather, 'to hold out the light of reason, whatever it may discover' (*Rambler* 93). Moreover, it was expedient as well as honest to 'confess the faults of our favourite, to gain credit to our praise of his excellencies'. There is justice in some of Johnson's criticisms: Shakespeare's plotting and climaxes are sometimes loose and careless, some of his bawdry and word-play is tedious and otiose. But some of the 'faults' are rather Johnson's than Shakespeare's.

> He sacrifices virtue to convenience, and is so much more careful to please than to instruct, that he seems to write without any moral purpose.

While one agrees with Johnson's claim – and it is part of his strength as a critic that he insists on it – that 'he that thinks reasonably must think morally', one is forced to recognize, as Dr F. R. Leavis puts it in an excellent essay on Johnson, that 'he cannot appreciate the ways in which not only Shakespeare's drama but all works of art *act* their moral judgements. For Johnson a thing is stated, or it isn't there.' Nor can Johnson see how truth may be stated in myth or symbol, how *The Tempest* and *Winter's Tale*, for instance, are more than pleasant romantic pieces: significantly, he says of the latter that 'with all its absurdities, it is very entertaining', but praises specifically only 'the character of Autolycus, ... very naturally conceived, and strongly represented'.

Johnson's Shakespeare-criticism shows the strengths and the weaknesses of his sensibility, and of the critical tradition he had inherited. This tradition he did not accept inertly, as an authoritative substitute for independent judgement: for him, 'Reason wants not Horace to support it', 'there is always an appeal open from criticism to nature', and no respect is due to those who 'draw their principles of judgement rather from books than from reason'. Johnson was independent about the letter of his tradition but not rebellious against its spirit. Mrs Thrale noted 'his extreme distance from those notions which the world has agreed, I know not very well why, to call romantic'. Johnson, she explained, admires Shakespeare for his 'just representation of human manners', but the romantic critics expatiate rather on his 'creative powers and vivid imagination'. The second half of the eighteenth century had critics, as well as poets, who have later been described as 'Romantic precursors': the most interesting are the brothers Warton, both minor poets too, and Bishop Hurd (Joseph Warton, 1722–1800, *Adventurer* papers on Shakespeare 1753–4, *Essay on the Genius and Writings of Pope*, volume I, 1756, volume II, 1782; Thomas Warton, 1728–90, *Observations on the Fairy Queen* 1754, *History of English Poetry* 1774–81, *Preface* to Milton's *Minor Poems* 1785; Richard Hurd, 1720–1808, *Letters on Chivalry and Romance* 1762).[9] These critics were all dissatisfied with the poetry of Pope and the like, who seemed to them to lack the 'nobler' qualities of our earlier masters. They suggested that poetry had declined in force and depth because the climate of opinion was uncongenial: science and philosophy had impoverished the imagination, and poets had languished under a literary-critical reign of terror. 'The Sublime and the Pathetic', Joseph Warton asserted, 'are the two chief nerves of genuine poesy. [Warton's archaism is symptomatic.] What is there transcendently sublime or pathetic in Pope?'* 'Sublimity', like 'Imagination', was becoming an important critical notion by now; in the same year as Volume I of Warton's *Essay on Pope*, there appeared Burke's *Philosophical Enquiry into the Origin of our Ideas of the Sublime and the Beautiful*, the best of a series of such enquiries beginning with Addison's *Spectator* papers (411–21) on the Pleasures of the Imagination. The 'sublime' – a term taken from Longinus, but expanded beyond his meaning – was often used to describe those great effects that could not be accounted for in terms of Rules and correctness. But this new 'cant of criticism' could be as limiting as the old. If the cant of correctness and regularity had led to an overestimation of Waller and Denham and their inheritors, and an injustice to Shake-

---

* *Pathetic* in the eighteenth century sometimes means simply *moving*: it is significant that, just about the mid-century, it begins to take on its later, more specialized meaning – conducive to *sorrowful or pitiful* emotion.

speare, the cant of sublimity and imagination too often justified an indulgence, fundamentally frivolous, in poetic fancies and fairylands, and in manifestations of emotion, however chaotic or factitious. Thus, Joseph Warton was too readily impressed by *Otranto* and *Udolpho*, and the 'sublime' poetry of Young, Akenside, and Gray.

Here Johnson is sounder. His *Lives of the Poets* (1779–81) are his finest work, and the finest piece of criticism in our period. On Cowley and Milton, two of the earliest poets discussed there, he betrays some of the limitations which affected his Shakespeare-criticism, the same inability to appreciate uses of language outside his tradition, and indirect or symbolical ways of conveying truths. But in his discussions of the poets nearer his own time, his limitations are less exposed: Joseph Warton's swans, for instance, he rightly sees are half goose. Warton had enthused over Gray's *Odes* ('the most exquisite pieces of *pure poetry* in our language') and particularly his *Bard* ('truly sublime'). Johnson sees through this notion of 'pure poetry': his insistence that poetry, in Arnold's phrase, 'is at bottom a criticism of life' is more responsible and rewarding. 'I do not see that *The Bard* promotes any truth, moral or political' – this, as Dr Leavis remarks, is Johnson's way 'of saying that for a mature, accomplished, and cultivated mind such as Gray's to be playing this kind of game and exhibiting itself in these postures is ridiculous'. None of the 'Romantic precursor' critics had this strength and seriousness of approach, and we should beware, in literary as in political history, of what Professor Butterfield has called 'the Whig interpretation' – of valuing, say, the Wartons because they 'anticipated' later critical developments, such as those of Wordsworth and Coleridge, which we esteem: in fact, these Romantics were little helped by, or respectful of, their 'precursors', and it was the weaknesses rather than the strengths of Romantic aesthetic and criticism that were 'anticipated'. They are, for the most part, interesting historically, as straws in the wind, rather than intrinsically. Johnson, as an unfriendly contemporary, Thomas Twining, admitted, with all his faults 'is always entertaining, never dull or trite ... he has his originalities of thought, and making you see things. ... There is in him no echo.' For this reason, if for no other, Johnson still deserves the praise given him by his eminent friend and follower, Sir Joshua Reynolds,[10] that he has 'the faculty of teaching inferior minds the art of thinking'.

NOTES

1. See W. P. Ker's discussion of the Unities in his *Essays of John Dryden*, I, pp. xxxix–xlix (Oxford, 1900).

2. See W. P. Ker, *op. cit.*, pp. 176–7; *Taste and Criticism in the 18th Century*, ed. H. A. Needham (London, 1952); and Johnson, *Rambler* 156.

3. Basil Willey's *Seventeenth Century Background* (London, 1934) is useful on this point; see especially pp. 86–92, 205–40, 290–5.

4. See W. P. Ker, *op. cit.*, pp. 79–82; and G. E. Bentley, *Shakespeare and Jonson: Their Reputations in the 17th Century Compared* (Chicago, 1945). Suggestions about the significance of the great popularity of Beaumont and Fletcher will be found in T. S. Eliot's *Selected Essays* (2nd ed., 1934), pp. 155, 194, 211, and in L. C. Knights's *Drama and Society in the Age of Jonson* (London, 1937), pp. 292–300.

5. See, e.g., W. P. Ker, *op. cit.*, pp. 167–72, 201, 202–4, 224–6; *Shakespeare Criticism: a Selection (1623–1840)*, ed. D. Nichol Smith (World's Classics, 1916), pp. 28, 58, 60; *Johnson on Shakespeare*, ed. Walter Raleigh (London, 1925); and *Spectator*, 39, 285.

6. On the rejection of Metaphysical 'wit', see *Spectator* 58–63, Pope's *Essay on Criticism* ll. 289–304, and Johnson's *Life of Cowley*. Cf. Pope's *Satires of Dr Donne versified* (1733).

7. See examples in Montagu Summers's selected *Shakespeare Adaptations* (Boston, 1922), and F. R. Leavis's comparison between *Antony and Cleopatra* and Dryden's *All for Love* in *Scrutiny*, V (1936).

8. D. Nichol Smith, *op. cit.*, pp. 173–214; see also pp. 143–72, and L. C. Knights's notes on the development of Shakespeare-criticism in his 'How Many Children Had Lady Macbeth?', in *Explorations* (London, 1946).

9. Selections from some of these works can be found in *English Critical Essays, 16th–18th Centuries*, ed. E. D. Jones (World's Classics, 1922), pp. 365–80, 451–60; D. Nichol Smith, *op. cit.*, pp. 60–79; and H. A. Needham, *op. cit.*, pp. 112–17, 144–9.

10. See Blake's marginalia (c. 1808) on Reynolds's *Discourses* (1769–90) for a stimulating criticism of assumptions which Reynolds shared with Johnson: Nonesuch *Blake* (1939 ed.), pp. 770–812.

LITERATURE AND SCIENCE

C. J. HORNE

Jury Professor of English Language and Literature, Adelaide University

LITERATURE written after 1660 is markedly more modern in style and spirit than much that was written only a few years earlier. This modernity, as also a depression of the poetic imagination that went with it, is to be explained in part by the remarkable advance of science in the seventeenth century and the dominance of the scientific attitude throughout the eighteenth. The change in literature reflects that larger shift in thought which raised the seventeenth century as the frontier between the modern world and all the preceding ages. That probing of the physical world by sensory observation and experiment, by mathematical measurement and inductive reasoning, the process that we now shortly label as science, had been effectively established by the bold activities of men like Galileo the astronomer and Kepler the mathematician. This first eager age of science culminated in England in the work of Sir Isaac Newton (1642–1727) with his demonstration of the laws of gravitation and motion by which the planets move in their orderly courses.

These early achievements in science were not the work of specialists alone; they were, moreover, intelligible to most educated men and philosophical thought generally was soon involved with the new materialist view of the universe. The clear legal mind of Francis Bacon (1561–1626) promulgated the method of inductive reasoning, and the versatile Frenchman Descartes (1596–1650) applied it to metaphysics in an attempt to prove the existence of God and the soul. The schism between science and traditional Christian humanism, a gulf so wide open in our own day, was for much of this period still capable of being bridged by men whose education fitted them to reconcile the old learning and the new. The revolutionary new branch of knowledge was still known as 'philosophy', or more specifically, 'natural philosophy', one part of the integrated discipline of all learning.

There were, of course, big changes in the attitude to older beliefs. Without rejecting the Christian faith or the refinements of classical culture, these men broke finally with the authority of Aristotle and medieval Scholasticism, subjecting all beliefs and all knowledge to a rational examination based on the evidence of fact as supplied by the senses. For Galileo, Descartes, Hobbes, the only real truth was that discoverable by inductive and mathematical methods. On this view the universe appeared as a great machine and the principles on which it worked were taken as a demonstration of the ultimate rationality of creation; all was capable of explanation.

There were obvious advantages in the new attitude. A great burden of fear and superstition was lifted off the minds of men. Hobbes, it was justly claimed, had put 'Fancies, Ghosts, and every empty Shade' to shameful flight. Men had now more confidence in their own unaided and unrestricted intellect, and with increased understanding of the ways of Nature felt better able to control and dominate their environment; though some, it is equally true, felt that man's importance lessened when measured against the newly-discovered systems of Nature, so vast and intricate after the comfortably delimited Ptolemaic cosmogony and the macrocosm of older thought. On the whole, however, self-confidence, eagerness about the world of wonders opened up before them, and a belief in human progress, now thought to be nearing a splendid culmination, were the predominant effects of scientific thought throughout the eighteenth century. Its upholders worked in a plain daylight world of fact and reason, and anything lurking in the shadows, too insubstantial to be snared by observation and dragged out into the light by rational processes, was derided and dismissed as fanciful.

It was a climate unfavourable to religion and poetry. Bacon, Locke, and Newton, while wishing to preserve religion (though inevitably it was trimmed to natural theology and deism), had no use and little respect for poetry. Poetry, said Newton, 'was a kind of ingenious nonsense'; at the best it was a pleasing cheat, supplying 'pleasant pictures and agreeable visions', as Locke admitted without intending greatly to praise it. The imagination was distrusted and its value depreciated, an attitude reinforced by the disgust with zeal and enthusiasm that the religious disputes of the seventeenth century had provoked. From such disquiets the eighteenth century was thankful to have escaped. The effect on prose was salutary, forcing order and distinctness upon it and extending its usefulness as a medium both of common intercourse and learned discussion. Poetry, on the other hand, was circumscribed and poets were on probation. Strangeness, mystery, 'metaphysical' exuberance, were dropped, and the poet often fell into line with the prose writer as a sensible instructor who, though perhaps less reliable, could temper his instruction with pleasing adornments. At the same time it was not a bad thing that poetry had to take on a new precision and apply it in the study of man. A new and often rigid distinction between thought and feeling, reason and imagination, fact and fiction, prevailed throughout the eighteenth century and it was more favourable to prose than to poetry.

The early history of the Royal Society of London for the Improving of Natural Knowledge illustrates the inclusiveness of the new philosophy. Beginning in Oxford in the middle of the seventeenth century as an informal association of like-minded individuals, the Society received public recognition with its royal charter in 1662 and became at once the centre for scientific studies. The first members were men of diverse talents and interests, but all united by the common bond of a classical education and an implicit acceptance of humanist culture, as much as by their interest in the new enquiries. They included, besides many dilettanti noblemen, persons as distinguished as the Honourable Robert Boyle, John Evelyn, Samuel Pepys, Sir William Petty, John Ray, and Christopher Wren. One of the first books issued with the support of the Society was Evelyn's *Sylva* (1664), an elegant and charming discourse on forestry. Along with his other writings on horticulture, it was designed for 'the benefit and diversion of gentlemen and persons of quality', who had throughout the century shown an increasingly practical interest in the arts of planting and gardening. There were poets in the Society too, notably Denham, Dryden, and Waller; and Cowley, the most admired of poets in his time, hastened on the Society's schemes with his *Proposition for the Advancement of Experimental Philosophy* in 1661, and honoured it with an ode.

The Society was careful not to give any countenance to the atheistical tendencies of the new philosophy, and at first tried even to maintain a distinction between its own predilection for experimental science and the mechanistic philosophy of Descartes. For this reason Hobbes was kept out of the Society, and clergymen and bishops enrolled among its Fellows without any scruples of conscience. Its first History (1667) was, in fact, written by a future Bishop of Rochester, Thomas Sprat. His view, and it was fairly representative, was that this 'learned and inquisitive age' could move forward most freely in its pursuit of true knowledge by not attempting to meddle with the spiritual and supernatural part of Christianity. Instead, the Society would direct men's energies away from futile religious disputes to the fruitful enquiries of natural philosophy. Reason, after all, was the best support religion could have.

Sprat also gives us more distinctly than any other writer of the time the new attitude to literature. Poetry could be of no assistance in scientific enquiries; on the contrary, its deceitful fables, apt enough for primitive ages, must now be banished with the fairies. Poetry was commanded to cease its correspondence with the slavish passions and, in style, to retrench 'this abundance of Phrase, this trick of Metaphors, this volubility of Tongue'. Reason must be its rule, and science could supply it with better matter and imagery than the outworn lore of the Ancients.

With poetry, however, promoters of the new learning like Sprat were not much concerned. Prose was their instrument and they were early determined to discipline it for their needs. They required a clear and unequivocal instrument of expression, and to this end the Society set up a committee in 1664–5 to examine and 'improve' the English language. At a time when the vernacular prose had undergone a century of exuberant development, it was trimmed and redirected by these new demands and given a new importance in intellectual commerce by the decision of the Royal Society to make full use of their native English for recording their experiments and conclusions, matters that had previously been as often expressed in Latin, the international language of learning. Already in 1663, it was reported,[1] French scholars were learning English in their eagerness to read the scientific works of Boyle before the Latin translations were ready. Thus science was in some measure paying back the debt that England owed to French culture after the Restoration.

In this new prose no flourish was to be permitted to obscure reason and plain sense. The Society, therefore, to quote from Sprat, was most rigorous in applying the only remedy for past extravagances:

... and that has been, a constant Resolution, to reject all the amplifications, digressions, and swellings of style: to return back to the primitive purity, and shortness, when men deliver'd so many *things*, almost in an equal number of *words*. They have extracted from all their members, a close, naked, natural way of speaking; positive expressions; clear senses; a native easiness; bringing all things as near the Mathematical plainness, as they can: and preferring the language of Artizans, Countrymen, and Merchants, before that of Wits, or Scholars.

(*History of the Royal Society*, p. 113)

The decision was not entirely novel; the plainer new prose had been maturing throughout the century and its seeds are to be found earlier in Bacon, Jonson, and Hobbes. Science, of course, was not the only influence shaping it, though it has been demonstrated that the prose of writers such as Joseph Glanvill and Abraham Cowley, and many of the preachers, changed markedly as they became more interested in the new science.[2] The style of Dryden, the master of Restoration prose, harmonized with the new requirements from the start, his *Essay of Dramatic Poesy* (1667) appearing in the same year as Sprat's *History*, having been written even earlier. That individuality was not abolished along with 'the luxury and redundance of speech' is evidenced by the vigour of Dryden's prose. It reads like the distinguished and easy talk of a clear, independent, and inquisitive mind, sensitive to the tastes and prejudices of his audience, whose judgement he directs without dictation.

The most eminent of English scientists in this period before Newton was the Honourable Robert Boyle (1627–91). Recognized in his day as 'one of the Deepest and Most indefatigable searchers of Nature',[3] he provides the most representative view of the accommodation at this time between the old thought and the new. A devout theologian and an eager scientist, he seemed quite unaware of any possible clash between Christian tenets and the mechanistic philosophy. Likewise, as a tireless experimenter and a creative thinker in science, he was 'the sceptical chymist' who demolished the lingering medieval belief in the four elements of earth, air, fire, and water, and the three principles of salt, sulphur, and mercury; and yet he was also a professed alchemist, clinging to a belief in the possibility of the transmutation of matter. In rejecting the vague theories of 'the hermetick Philosophers' and the Schoolmen he appealed for lucid expressions and factual arguments, even if in his own prose the wish to divert and recreate his readers as well as excite them was defeated by his wearisome manner. Though he aims, like Dryden, to write as a cultured man would talk, his style is hurried and careless, and his sentences rattle on without form or elegance.

The excitement that we miss in the prose of Dryden almost as much as in Boyle is to be found in Thomas Burnet's *Theory of the Earth* (1684–90), written first in Latin and then in English. Addison compared Burnet with Cicero for eloquence, and it is in the magnificently sonorous prose of an older generation that he presents his imaginative view of the earth as an awesome ruin. The methods of science are used to justify the older theology. In his travels Burnet had been startled by the Alps, 'those wild, vast and undigested heaps of stones and earth', and became convinced that Nature was in chaos. This he attributes to man's sin, and with an almost Miltonic cast of imagination unfolds his striking quasi-scientific explanations of the processes by which God's anger has wrought catastrophic changes in an originally smooth and perfect globe.

Burnet's prose remains something of a curiosity for this period, though affinities may perhaps be traced later in William Law and Edmund Burke. The main trend in style was otherwise. Clear statements and settled sentence forms with a simple vocabulary (though more extensive in its simplicity than formerly) became the rule. Thereby English was at last provided with a plain, direct, and workaday prose that offered the right tools for writers so different in their trade as Defoe, Addison, Swift, and Goldsmith, in addition to all the host of lesser men who wanted to write clearly and correctly without aiming at literary distinction.

Newton's *Philosophiae Naturalis Principia Mathematica* was published in 1687 and immediately put science in the top ranks of learning. John Locke's *Essay concerning Human Understanding* followed in 1690 and applied the scientific method to the empirical study of the human mind, suggesting that mind is a form of matter, that human knowledge is strictly limited, and that knowledge comes initially only through the senses, innate ideas being an impossibility. Together, Newton and Locke were to dominate eighteenth-century thought and find their echo, often indistinctly, in much of the literature of the period. Newton was praised almost without exception.[4] Addison and Thomson were whole-hearted in their admiration of both the man and his discoveries. To Addison he was 'the Miracle of the present Age', and it was Addison who, in the popular homilies of the *Spectator*, gave the lead to a succession of popularizers of science in filtering the ideas of Newton and Locke for the understanding of an inquisitive public, insisting always on the wisdom and piety to be gathered from them. On Newton's death in 1727 Pope devised for his tomb in Westminster Abbey the witty epitaph:

> Nature and Nature's Laws lay hid in Night:
> God said, *Let Newton be!* and all was Light.

But that is not the whole story. During these same years at the opening of the eighteenth century a sharp and scornful challenge to the new science came from men of letters. In some part the objection arose from a fear of the irreligious tendency of the modern philosophy, an attitude complicated by the eagerness with which the Puritans and Dissenters had taken up these studies and sought to impose them as a reform upon the Universities.[5] A conflict with religion was not, however, in England as distinct from France, the most serious issue in this period, partly because of the impeccable piety of men like Boyle and Newton, and even more because of the conviction with which the teaching of 'physico-theology' was received. Initiated in part by the Cambridge Platonists, this hybrid study was established mainly by John Ray (1627–1705), the greatest of English naturalists, in *The Wisdom of God Manifested in the Works of Creation* (1691) and was carried on in the Boyle Lectures for 1713 by the Reverend William Derham (1657–1735). Ray's book was a serious and informed survey of scientific knowledge, often making original contributions, and in it he laid down the foundations of all future biological studies (botany and zoology having hitherto lagged behind the physical sciences), thus preparing the ground for the work of eighteenth-century naturalists such as Gilbert White. Derham's published lectures were a more popular compendium. In vindicating and stimulating scientific enquiry, both writers were concerned above all to provide through science a 'Demonstration of the *Being* and *Attributes* of an infinitely wise and powerful Creator',[6] who had not, as Burnet contended, given Nature over to the corruption of sin but still worked actively through 'some intelligent *plastick Nature*' to maintain his perfect design and purpose. The views of the physico-theologists happily suited the ordinary needs of the age and stilled much of the religious doubt that science was suggesting. They were commended, and their teaching promulgated even beyond the end of the century, by clergymen and moralists as diverse as Addison, Wesley, Johnson, and Paley.

More effective opposition to science in the first half of this period came from those wits and scholars who found much of the work of the Royal Society intellectually contemptible and culturally subversive. In an age much given to ridicule it provided a fertile subject for burlesque and satire. In the first place the virtuosi, or gentlemen scientists, were derided for pedantry and lack of practical usefulness in their studies. Their self-regarding seriousness seemed grotesquely disproportionate to the trivial and vulgar objects of some of their enquiries, 'useless experiments upon Flies, Maggots, Eels in Vinegar, and the Blue upon Plumbs', as Shadwell described them in his play *The Virtuoso* (1676). These were unusual subjects for learned study, and those who embraced them were marked down as gullible triflers and enemies of true learning. This was the attitude taken up by Samuel Butler in *The Elephant in the Moon*, and it recurs in the essays of Addison and Steele, and in the elaborate burlesques written by Dr William King, *The Transactioneer* (1700) and *Useful Transactions in Philosophy* (1709). These last may have provided some suggestions for the papers of the Scriblerus Club (1713), in which Swift, Arbuthnot, Pope, and a few others joined in their leisure hours to make fun of the excesses of the new learning. King may even have provided the suggestion for Swift's Academy of Lagado in *Gulliver's Travels*, where the author's disgust with many of the projects of the virtuosi culminates in that wild nightmare of ridicule. Several of Swift's works demonstrate how closely he had read many of the scientific writings of his day, and *Gulliver's Travels* is shot through and through with allusions to them. The technological benefits of science were slow in appearing, and it was Swift again who summed up a very general attitude about the apparent uselessness of scientific enquiry when he applauded the Brobdingnagians because with them the study of mathematics 'is wholly applied to what may be useful in Life; to the

Improvement of Agriculture and all mechanical Arts; so that', he comments, 'among us it would be little esteemed'.

These men of letters, moreover, were perturbed by the way many scientists were using the English language. On the whole, the style of the *Philosophical Transactions* of the Royal Society in the eighteenth century was a poor return for the hopes Sprat had entertained when he wrote his manifesto. In attempting a factual plainness and conciseness, many writers had avoided the old sins of eloquence only to fall into the opposite errors of a stilted bareness, a conventional phraseology, and a low poverty of expression. The jargon of science was already proliferating and men of taste found it entirely disgusting.

It was in such matters that the rift between science and the humanities first openly appeared. Behind it all was something more than an itch for carping or the exhilaration of a witty burlesque. Men educated in the older tradition of learning were genuinely repelled by the growing pedantry of the times ('dulhness' was their comprehensive term for it), and Pope's *Dunciad* is the greatest literary monument to their concern. In that poem, it may be recalled, the lesser breed of scientists, 'A tribe, with weeds and shells fantastic crown'd',[7] find their dishonourable niche. The rejection of the complacent claims of the natural philosophers and their optimistic belief in human progress gave an urgent interest to the controversy about the comparative merits of Ancients and Moderns, set going in England by Sir William Temple's essay, *On Ancient and Modern Learning* (1690). The deeper extension of the contest is seen in the work of Swift and Pope when they seek to expose the pretensions of scientific optimism by making a rational study of the nature of man and recalling attention to the science of morality; for a science Locke claimed it to be, more exact than natural philosophy and more proper to mankind.[8] Pope's own philosophy in *An Essay on Man* (1733–4), half-baked as it may be, was a restatement of traditional concepts to harmonize with the Newtonian evidence for a rational and orderly universe. If that leads him to the glib deism of his *Universal Prayer* and the belief that 'Whatever is, is RIGHT', he also makes it a cause for rebuking the pride that man's new sense of his own importance has generated. Though in the 'Vast chain of Being' man is immeasurably raised above the lowest creatures now revealed by the microscope, he is still, Pope duly reminds him, infinitely below the wisdom and goodness of God.

It is ironical that Newton, who had himself so little regard for poetry, was the one scientist whose work the poets appropriated with delight and admiration. The reason is obvious. In an age when inner revelation (as necessary to poetry as to religion) was generally distrusted, it was some relief for poets to be able to turn to the physical evidence of God in Nature. Newton's revelation of a limitless but systematic universe, where God in Nature appeared by all the evidence the greatest of artists, gave a much needed stimulus to the repressed poetic imagination by providing poets with something vast and sublime to contemplate. In their response to Newtonian theory, eighteenth-century poets were unconsciously striving to fill the gap in the creative imagination left by the exhaustion of classical and Christian mythology. In similar manner the prevalence of personification in eighteenth-century poetry may be explained as a less successful attempt to keep up some human warmth among the depersonalizing forces of science: Thomson's handling of Newton's theories frequently suggests that he imagined the natural elements as having a conscious will and purpose in performing their part in the great scheme of universal Nature. Furthermore, it was Newton's *Opticks* (1704) that helped to bring descriptive power back to English poetry by giving a new fascination to the play of light and colour in the landscape and a metaphysical interest in what has been called a 'symbolism of the spectrum'.* Description was added to moral and philosophical discourse in poetry, though the intention remained didactic rather than a joyous surrender to the purely aesthetic delight of the natural world.

In this attempted rehabilitation of the imagination Addison once more gave the lead with his notable series of essays on 'The Pleasures of the Imagination' (1712) in the *Spectator* (Nos. 411–21), and again his argument is a popular blend of Newton and Locke. Sight was regarded as the most important of the senses, the one to which all the discoveries of philosophy, or science, were due, and sight, Addison begins his discourse, is the 'Sense which furnishes the Imagination with its Ideas'. But when we read on, it is difficult not to be disappointed by the limited conception of imagination that he holds. It is no more than the awareness of visible objects, present or absent, along with the secondary ideas that they call up in the mind, and the whole argument is applied to show that Art is inferior to Nature, and the imagination limited and defective because on an empirical view it is inadequate to follow where Reason and the understanding lead. This is by no means the view of Francis Hutcheson in his *Inquiry concerning Beauty, Order, etc.* (1725), where he insists that the poet has a finer perception of the objects of natural beauty than the man of science; but Addison's is the more representative view for his age.

How closely Newton and the astronomers were read, how eagerly accepted, is apparent from the poetry of Blackmore, Thomson, Mallet, Young, Savage, Akenside, and others. All of them make interesting adaptations of Newton's theories and, missing the Miltonic sublimity at which in some measure they aim, fall back on grandiose invocations of divine glory and goodness, and admonitions to man to conform to the dictates of natural piety and reason. At the same time they exhibit in varying degrees a new awareness of the beauty of Nature made manifest in light and colour. Akenside, a medical man, besides giving a blank-verse account of *The Pleasures of Imagination* (1744), wrote also a *Hymn to Science*; but of all these poets James Thomson (1700–48) was the most responsive to the advance of science. He had a good layman knowledge of its findings, and the scientific matter which permeates his poetry was carefully brought up to date in successive revisions of *The Seasons*. The philosophy of Nature, so learnedly documented in his poetry, leads him back to a rosy and even indolent view of life, in which the beauty of Creation and the beneficence of the great Creator are seen as one harmonious whole.

The advance in scientific knowledge went on steadily during the remainder of the eighteenth century, with new discoveries about the nature of gases, the separation of the component elements of matter, experiments with electricity, and the introduction of a system of classification in botany and zoology. None of these advances was as spectacular as the earlier discoveries in astronomy, so that the mental climate of the age was much less sharply affected by them. The effects were to be seen rather in a widening of the public interest in science and in technological improvements in industry. It was still possible for the amateur to make useful contributions in all fields. Public lectures accompanied by scientific demonstrations were a favourite diversion of the time, the Lunar Society was founded at

Birmingham in 1766, and though the Royal Society became less the workshop of science than a comfortable club, less distinguished bodies of enthusiasts founded Philosophical Societies in several provincial centres. While the number of popular compendiums of science multiplied and science subjects were given an important place in the curriculum of the Dissenting Academies, the most active educational institutions of the day, the two Universities, were still apathetic, and that partly explains the declining enthusiasm for the new discoveries among creative writers. They were, of course, interested. Dr Johnson intermittently carried out minor chemical experiments (though he valued them only as an enchanting way 'to fill the day with petty business'), and John Wesley studied the effects of electricity on the human body. But writers were no longer excited by new prospects, and in Rasselas (1759) Johnson made a further assault on the optimistic view of human happiness that materialistic philosophies had encouraged. The increasingly cautious attitude was expressed by Joseph Priestley (1733–1804), the Unitarian minister and political philosopher, himself the discoverer of oxygen in 1774 and a notable writer on science, when he declared that 'a taste for science, pleasing and even honourable as it is, is not one of the highest passions of our nature, that the pleasures it furnishes are even but one degree above those of sense'.

The effects of scientific activity are to be observed in other ways, often less directly, in the later writers of the period. The sharpened powers of social observation in the novelists may be taken as one instance. More obviously the influence is reflected in vocabulary and imagery. A large number of technical and scientific words are recorded in Johnson's Dictionary (1755), and many of them, especially colour words, were finding a wider currency.[10] Johnson's writings are diversified with similes drawn from chemistry, optics, scientific instruments, and animal life, and Gibbon records of himself that courses in anatomy and chemistry, together with a taste for books on natural history, contributed to the ideas and images in his Decline and Fall of the Roman Empire (1776–88). Scientific commonplaces are to be found also in the poetry of Cowper (1731–1800), but it is only in Christopher Smart (1722–71) that prosaic objects of science, the air pump and capillary tubes, are mingled with the beauties of Nature in a lyrical adoration of Nature's God. Elsewhere the combination with science, for reasons we have noted, had usually resulted in the subjection of the poetic imagination.

The prevalence of stock poetic diction can, in this connexion, be explained as a mistaken attempt to provide for poetry a set vocabulary, as exact and appropriate as that used in scientific writings.[11] Dryden had early abandoned the attempt to employ correct technical terms for description in poetry, though the scientific images remained, as when he drew an analogy between the nature of tragedy and the laws of motion. Others, Pope and Thomson most importantly, tried to substitute more poetic equivalents for scientific jargon, stilted phrases like 'scaly breed' and 'feathered race' being in their day a novel method of designating the particular class of creature by characterizing it with a precisely descriptive epithet. It was a procedure significantly akin to the binominal system of classification that was being developed during the same period in natural history.

The result of the scientific study of Nature had been, after all, to lead poetry away from particular experience and individual insight into abstractions and accepted generalizations. All knowledge is useful to a poet, says Johnson's Imlac in *Rasselas*, but, he continues,

> The business of a poet ... is to examine, not the individual, but the species; to remark general properties and large appearances. He does not number the streaks of the tulip, or describe the different shades in the verdure of the forest ...

Such a view, and it was prevalent, reflects in literature the overriding concern of eighteenth-century science with those universal laws in which can be comprehended all the diversity of individual phenomena.

The pleasing novelties of descriptive detail that we should expect from scientific observation are more often met with in the prose than in the poetry. This is notable in the travel books. Some of them are accounts of voyages undertaken, like those of Captain James Cook between 1768 and 1779, with a scientific purpose, others being records of tours in the homeland by such naturalists as Thomas Pennant (1726–98), who, as Johnson said, 'observes more things than anyone else does'. It was likewise the enthusiasm of field naturalists in the eighteenth century that nurtured the belief in the recuperating joys and interest of the English countryside and pointed the way to the intenser harmony between man and Nature in the Romantic poets. There is more delightful description and a finer natural sensibility in the correspondence of Gray (1716–71), who was a keen botanist, than in his poetry, and prior to Wordsworth and Coleridge the most truly poetic response to the life of the plant and animal world is to be found in Gilbert White's *Natural History and Antiquities of Selborne* (1789).

The revolt of the Romantics at the end of the century, though for Blake it entailed the anathema of Bacon, Descartes, Locke, and Newton, was not a rejection of scientific knowledge but a recovery of the sense of mystery and spirituality in Nature. In the Romantics the philosophy of the five senses was overturned by the recovery of a sixth sense that transcended all, the creative imagination, and that ended the dominance of the rational attitude so far as literature was concerned.

NOTES

1. By Henry Oldenburg in 'The Publisher to the Reader', prefaced to Boyle's *Experiments and Considerations Touching Colours* (1664).

2. See R. F. Jones, 'Science and English Prose Style in the Third Quarter of the Seventeenth Century', in *Publications of the Modern Language Association of America*, XLV (1930), pp. 977–1009; and Joan Bennett, 'An Aspect of the Evolution of Seventeenth Century Prose', in *The Review of English Studies*, XVII (1941), pp. 281–97.

3. Oldenburg, *loc. cit.*

4. The chief exception is Swift, who in addition to his contempt for mathematicians in general had a political prejudice against Newton.

5. When the Puritans came to power in the middle of the seventeenth century, they not only appointed experimental scientists to important posts in the universities but proposed to reform the universities by introducing the new sciences in place of the traditional studies as more conducive to 'the general good and benefit of mankind'. There was even a proposal to turn Christ Church into a scientific institute; which partly explains why that college became the centre of opposition to the new science. See further, R. F. Jones, 'The Background of the Attack on Science in the Age of Pope', in *Pope and His Contemporaries* (1949), ed. J. L. Clifford and L. A. Landa.

6. W. Derham, *Physico-Theology: or, A Demonstration of the Being and Attributes of God, from His Works of Creation*, fifth edition (1720), p. 3.

7. *The Dunciad* (1742), iv, l. 398.

8. John Locke, *Essay concerning Human Understanding* (1690), IV, iii, 18, 26; IV, xii, 10–11. Mathematics, he held, was the most exact science, and morality could be classed with mathematics 'among the sciences capable of demonstration'.

9. For a study of the effect of the *Opticks* on poetry, see Marjorie Hope Nicolson, *Newton Demands the Muse. Newton's 'Opticks' and the Eighteenth Century Poets* (1946). The distinction Miss Nicolson makes between the equation of colour with beauty, and light with sublimity, is disputed.

10. See A. D. Atkinson, 'Dr Johnson and Newton's "Opticks"', in *The Review of English Studies*, New Series, II (1951), pp. 226–37; C. S. Emden, 'Dr Johnson and Imagery', in *R.E.S.*, New Series, I (1950), p. 30; and W. K. Wimsatt, *Philosophic Words: A Study of Style and Meaning in the 'Rambler' and 'Dictionary' of Samuel Johnson* (1948). Wimsatt traces the growth of scientific vocabulary from Bacon to Johnson and studies its effect on prose style. He demonstrates that Johnson collected specimens for his *Dictionary* from all the major scientific writers.

11. This attempt began as early as Sylvester's translation of Du Bartas (1592–9). See J. Arthos, *The Language of Natural Description in Eighteenth Century Poetry* (1949).

DEFOE AS NOVELIST

IAN WATT

Professor of English, Stanford University

DEFOE was nearly sixty when his first novel, *Robinson Crusoe*, appeared. He had been known to his contemporaries as a journalist and pamphleteer, however, long before he took overtly to fiction. The first work which brought him fame was *The True-Born English-man* (1701), probably the most influential verse satire in English after Dryden's *Absalom and Achitophel*. It was a defence of William III against those who thought that it was intolerable for a Dutch king to govern 'true-born Englishmen'. Defoe retorted that there was no such thing:

> We have been Europe's sink, the jakes where she
> Voids all her offal outcast progeny.

He was no poet, although his crude vigour was undeniable. It is further evidenced in such couplets as:

> But English gratitude is always such
> To hate the hand which doth oblige too much,

and the famous opening:

> Wherever God erects a house of prayer,
> The devil always builds a chapel there:
> And 'twill be found upon examination,
> The latter has the largest congregation.

Defoe knew his poetic limitations full well. He wrote in poetic form because that, since Dryden, was the favoured mode for public polemic; but Defoe's real aim was not literary greatness, but imme-diate effect. So in his Preface he anticipated the critics very jocularly: 'Without being taken for a conjuror, I may venture to foretell, that I shall be cavilled at about my mean style, rough verse, and incorrect language, things I indeed might have taken more care in. But the book is printed; and though I see some faults, it is too late to mend them. And this is all I think needful to say. ...'

He could be cavalier because his main audience cared little for such niceties; they were not the cultivated patrons to whom so much of previous literature had been primarily addressed, but plain middle-class folk, who constituted an important new force in the reading public, and were strongly asserting their independence, cultural as well as political. They felt, and Defoe agreed, that

> Fate has but small distinction set
> Betwixt the counter and the coronet,

and that the tastes of those who worked behind the counter must also be served.

So if the great Augustans, Swift and Pope, sneered at him as an outsider, Defoe took little notice. He had more than his share of the truculent self-reliance of the trading classes and he was less an artist than a literary tradesman himself, producing, in a career that was as much devoted to business and politics as to literature, some four hundred separate works, as well as a vast amount of journalism, including the whole of his thrice-weekly newspaper, *The Review*, which ran for nine years from 1704 to 1713.

His novels – which are certainly the works that interest us most today – were among the greatest concessions he made to the tastes of the reading public. His own literary preference seems to have been for something more factual – for the political, economic, social, and moral improvement of his countrymen. But he had learned as editor of *The Review* that his readers often needed to be 'wheedled ... in to the knowledge of the world'; and, to 'carry out this honest cheat and bring people to read with delight', he had made an important journalistic innovation. To the usual contents of his paper, an essay-like editorial on a political topic, he had added a lighter section, 'Advice from the Scandalous Club', which dealt humorously with controversial aspects of the social life of the day. This innovation was very successful, and paved the way to *The Tatler*'s more polished presentation of similar matter; it also taught Defoe much about this side of the public's interests and gave him practice in catering to them.

In any case, he was a professional writer, and always ready to supply whatever the printing press could use. Pope might attack what he called Grub Street and the Dunces that wrote for it; but

Defoe saw Grub Street as merely an application of commercial principles to the manufacture of literary goods. As he wrote in a letter signed 'Anti-Pope', published in the popular *Applebee's Journal* in 1725: 'Writing, you know, Mr Applebee, is become a very considerable Branch of the English Commerce. ... The Booksellers are the Master Manufacturers or Employers. The several Writers, Authors, Copyers, Sub-writers, and all other Operators with pen and Ink are the workmen employed by the said Master Manufacturers.' He was true to his understanding of his proper role, then, in writing fiction, whatever his personal inclinations.

He was also true to himself in imposing on what he wrote so much of his own personality and outlook that it became something quite different from anything that the world had seen before; and thus almost accidentally created a form of prose narrative which, if it was not quite the novel in our sense, undoubtedly led to the rise of the novel proper. It is, incidentally, highly appropriate that the rise of the novel – then regarded as a sub-literary form – should begin with a sub-literary figure like Defoe, responsive to the greatly enlarged reading public and independent of patronage and the critical standards of the *literati*.

* * *

Defoe's most important innovation in fiction was his unprecedentedly complete narrative realism. There is little doubt that it springs directly out of his long practice of journalism. Leslie Stephen has described[1] how his early pamphlet, the famous *A True Relation of the Apparition of one Mrs. Veal, the next day after her death, to one Mrs. Bargrave at Canterbury, the 8th of September, 1705*, contains all the hallmarks of Defoe's later narrative style, including 'the manufacturing of corroborative evidence' and the deflection of attention from weak links in the chain of evidence. Stephen thought that it was a work of fiction, but it has since been discovered that Defoe was merely reporting a popular news item of the day in his own characteristic manner. He was to use exactly the same technique when he came to write fiction, and even there we are never quite sure how much is pure invention. *Robinson Crusoe* itself was widely regarded as authentic at the time of publication, and it is still not certain to what extent some of Defoe's works, such as the *Memoirs of a Cavalier* and the *Carleton Memoirs*, are fictitious or genuine.

It was certainly Defoe's overriding intention that readers should be gulled into thinking his fictions true. If he did not know already that the illusion of authenticity was his forte, he could have learned it from one of his journalist rivals who wrote in 1718 of 'the little art he is truly master of, of forging a story, and imposing it on the world for truth'. Defoe never admitted that he wrote fiction; and typically prefaced his greatest success, *Robinson Crusoe*, published the next year, with the statement that he, writing merely as 'Editor', 'believes the thing to be a just history of fact; neither is there any appearance of fiction in it'.

This, of course, is not literally true. For, although Defoe had read about Alexander Selkirk and other castaways, the story and the character are very largely of Defoe's invention. But they are described with so much circumstantial detail, whose only justification would seem to be that things actually happened in just that way, that we do not think of the book as fiction but accord it at least a semi-historical status. Consider for example the way in which the famous finding of the green barley sprouts is told:

> In the middle of all my labours it happened, that rummaging my things, I found a little bag, which, as I hinted before, had been filled with corn for the feeding of poultry, not for this voyage, but before, as I suppose, when the ship came from Lisbon. What little remainder of the corn had been in the bag was all devoured with the rats, and I saw nothing in the bag but husks and dust; and being willing to have the bag for some other use, I think it was to put powder in, when I divided it for fear of the lightning, or some such use, I shook the husks of corn out of it on one side of my fortification, under the rock. It was a little before the great rains, just now mentioned, that I threw this stuff away, taking no notice of anything, and not so much as remembering that I had thrown anything there; when, about a month after, or thereabout, I saw some few stalks of something green shooting out of the ground, which I fancied might be some plant I had not seen; but I was surprised, and perfectly astonished, when, after a little longer time, I saw about ten or twelve ears come out, which were perfect green barley of the same kind as our European, nay, as our English barley.

The main aim of the writing is clearly to keep as close as possible to the consciousness of the narrator as he struggles to make the situation clear to himself and to us. Nothing but the exclusive pursuit of this aim, we feel, would have brought about such abrupt dislocations of rhythm and syntax as are found in the first sentence; no other reason could explain the repetitions, the parentheses, the stumblings. And the upshot is that the little bag takes its place with all the other objects of Crusoe's life that have fastened themselves on our imaginations – the first clay pot, the climatically inept fur garments, the umbrella, the boat, the grindstone.

For Defoe's style obeys more fully than ever before the purpose of language as Locke redefined it: 'to convey knowledge of things'. Defoe concentrates his description on the primary qualities of objects as Locke saw them: especially solidity, extension, and number; and he gives them in the simplest language – Defoe's prose contains a higher percentage of words of Anglo-Saxon origin than that of any other well-known writer, except Bunyan. His sentences, it is true, are often very long and rambling, but he somehow makes this a part of his air of authenticity. The lack of strong pauses within the sentence gives his style an urgent, immediate, breathless quality; at the same time, his units of meaning are so small, and their relatedness is made so clear by frequent repetition and recapitulation, that he nevertheless gives the impression of perfectly simple lucidity.

Defoe had been exposed to all the influences which were making prose more prosaic in the seventeenth century: to the Lockian conception of language; to the Royal Society's wish for a language which would help its scientific and technological aims by keeping close to the speech of 'artisans, countrymen, and merchants': and to the plain unadorned style of later seventeenth-century preaching which obtained its effects by repetition rather than by imagery or structural elaboration. Most important of all, his twenty years of journalism had taught him that it was impossible to be too explicit for the audience of 'honest meaning ignorant persons' he kept continually in mind. As a result, his natural prose style is not only an admirable narrative vehicle in itself: it is also much closer to the vernacular of the ordinary person than any previous writer's, and thus admirably adapted to the tongues of Robinson Crusoe, Moll Flanders, and his other characters.

But the effect of the passage quoted does not depend only on its style: there is behind it Defoe's emphatic pressure forcing us to attend to the matter. Every relevant detail of the occurrence is made explicit: and after Crusoe has evidenced his scrupulous honesty by admitting that he cannot be absolutely certain about all of them – when the bag had originally been filled with corn, or what he had wanted the bag for later – we are in no mood to take seriously the objection that, as Crusoe admits, 'the climate ... was not proper for corn': for fiction has long before been accepted as established fact. So, wholly convinced, we rejoice with Crusoe at this miracle of divine Providence.

The Puritans saw the whole world, and every incident of their experience, as alive with secret indications of divine intervention or intention; and Crusoe follows the tradition in looking for signs of Grace or Reprobation in this, and in all else that happens to him. *Robinson Crusoe* is not just a travel story; it is also, in intention at least, one of Defoe's 'honest cheats', a sincere attempt to convert a godless form of literature to the purposes of religion and morality: Crusoe's story is supposed to demonstrate how God's Providence saves an outcast who has sinned against the divine will by leaving his family and forgetting his religious training, out of a 'secret burning lust of ambition for great things'.

Defoe wrote two continuations of the book we know, *The Life and Strange Surprising Adventures of Robinson Crusoe*; they were called the *Further Adventures*, and the *Serious Reflections of Robinson Crusoe*,[2] and were written mainly to cash in on the first volume's phenomenal success. In the latter he repeats the moral and religious aim he had avowed earlier; his book 'is calculated for, and dedicated to, the improvement and instruction of mankind in the ways of virtue and piety, by representing the various circumstances to which mankind is exposed, and encouraging such as fall into ordinary or extra-ordinary casualties of life, how to work through difficulties with unwearied diligence and application, and look up to Providence for success.'

We look at Defoe's work rather differently today. His was a much secularized puritanism, which put its emphasis on 'unwearied diligence and application' rather than on faith. Defoe's heroes tend to act on the assumption that the more you keep your powder dry the less you will need to rely on the imponderable effects of your trust in God. We do not find Crusoe's religious ruminations very convincing: they are, like bouts of benign malaria, easily shaken off, and indicating no organic spiritual change. As soon as he remembers that previously he had 'shook a bag of chicken's meat out in that place ...' his wonder ceases; and, as a result, he confesses that '.... my religious thankfulness to God's Providence began to abate too, upon the discovering that all this was nothing but what was common'. The same primacy of non-religious considerations is evident in the book as a whole. For, of course, Crusoe is well rewarded for his sins: without them he would hardly have risen above the 'middle station of low life' to which he had been born, and become a wealthy merchant, plantation owner, slave trader, and colonizer.

If today we are sceptical about the book's religious significance, we see much else in it which was no part of Defoe's intention. We see Robinson Crusoe as the symbol of economic man,[3] who, by recapitulating on his island all the basic productive processes, provides the economists with their favourite example. We see him too as the empire builder, leaving a crowded homeland for the wide-open places, establishing a little city in a tropical forest and converting the heathen. We may notice too that, just as economic individualism in general stands in the way of harmonious personal and social relations, so Crusoe's radical egocentricity leads him to sell the Moorish boy Xury, who has saved his life, to the Portuguese trader for sixty pieces of silver, and later to treat Friday in the manner of a benevolent slave owner rather than in that of a friend. Defoe, it seems certain, was not conscious of the prophetic nature of his tale; but he had experienced the crucial social and economic processes of his time more fully and deeply than anyone, and, as an honest reporter, he reflected their effects on human behaviour with absolute fidelity.

Not that he was wholly blind to the symbolic quality of Crusoe's experience. In the preface to the *Serious Reflections* he hints that the story is an allegory of his own life: and though this assertion is mainly an afterthought to defend himself against the critics who had charged that *Robinson Crusoe* was fiction, his plea has a certain essential truth. Defoe tends to identify himself with all his protagonists and most fully perhaps with Crusoe; his own life, too, had been one of solitary and heroic achievement against great odds. In an eloquent chapter,

'Of Solitude', which begins the *Serious Reflections*, he converts Crusoe's island existence into an image of the perpetual aloneness of man which springs from his basic egocentricity: '... it seems to me that life in general is, or ought to be, but one universal act of solitude. Everything revolves in our minds by innumerable circular motions, all centering in ourselves ... we love, we hate, we covet, we enjoy, all in privacy and solitude.'

It seems then that *Robinson Crusoe*, one of the myths of modern civilization, does not celebrate only the material triumphs of its society, and the strength of its rational will to conquer the environment: it also prefigures some of the spiritual loneliness and social alienation which this civilization has brought with it.

Some of this loneliness is itself a reflection of a force which did much to build modern civilization – Puritan individualism. The Puritans saw the activities of the world as a diversion from man's proper spiritual purpose, which is the scrutiny of his conscience for signs of his probable destiny in the divine plot of redemption and damnation. So Defoe makes Crusoe write in his *Serious Reflections*: 'It is the soul's being entangled by outward objects that interrupts its contemplation of divine objects'; and he concludes that 'the business is to get a retired soul', which can be done anywhere: 'so I can affirm that I enjoy much more solitude in the middle of the greatest collection of mankind in the world, I mean, at London, while I am writing this, than ever I could say I enjoyed in eight and twenty years' confinement to a desolate island.'

We must not underestimate Defoe's dissenting background. If he is not as serious as Bunyan, he has many of his qualities; if he does not convince us that considerations of piety are really the controlling factors in his stories, at least they are there, and their presence gives Defoe's novels a real moral dimension which had been as largely absent as narrative realism in previous prose fiction.

Indirectly, Puritanism is also partly responsible for Defoe's literary realism. Defoe shared its hatred of fiction, as he tells us in the *Serious Reflections*: 'This supplying a story by invention is certainly a most scandalous crime, and yet very little regarded in that part.* It is a sort of lying that makes a great hole in the heart, at which by degrees a habit of lying enters in.' Pressure of circumstances led him to write

* 'in that light' as we would say.

novels: but one feels that, with a curious obliquity, he resolved to make his lies as like truth as possible so that his scandalous crime would escape detection.

* * *

If Defoe's Puritan forebears need not have turned too often in their graves at *Robinson Crusoe*, their slumbers must have been seriously incommoded by the major works of fiction which succeeded it. Their protagonists were not merely successful sinners, like Crusoe, but successful criminals, whores, and pirates. The best of these later works are probably *Moll Flanders* (1722), *Colonel Jack* (1722), and *The Fortunate Mistress* (1724), usually called *Roxana*; all three are closer to being novels than *Robinson Crusoe*, which is too little concerned with personal relationships and has too restricted an emotional range. But all Defoe's other narratives are worth reading, especially *Captain Singleton* (1720) and *A Journal of the Plague Year* (1722), which are closer to the quasi-historical mode of *Robinson Crusoe*.

The earlier pages of *Colonel Jack* are perhaps Defoe's finest piece of writing; they have all his characteristically vivid reporting, his penetrating sociological understanding of the conditions which make children into criminals, and they also have an insight into the whole moral world of a young waif which he hardly equalled elsewhere. The final scenes of *Roxana* have a powerful dramatic interest unique in Defoe: the desperate expedients of the heroine to avoid discovery by the daughter she has abandoned have great psychological and narrative tension; they also – and this is rare in Defoe – embody in the action the story's moral theme – the terrible price exacted by Roxana's life of prostitution in forcing her to deny the claims of motherly love.

But *Moll Flanders* has, at least since the praise of E. M. Forster[4] and Virginia Woolf,[5] been generally accepted as the best of Defoe's novels. It is richer in feeling than *Robinson Crusoe*; it is full of Defoe's best-written episodes; the heroine is perhaps Defoe's most successful piece of portraiture; the theme is concerned, not with a fight against Nature, but with something more typical of the novel, the individual's struggle against society; and the plot, though rambling and confused, is based on a pattern of personal relationships which is finally rounded out with a degree of unity by the restoration of Moll to her husband and her son, and a final curtain closing on a peaceful old age of penitence and prosperity.

Much of *Moll Flanders* is concerned with plain reporting of the heroine's loves and larcenies, often brilliantly done in a narrative manner very similar to that in *Robinson Crusoe* (except that some unregenerate spirits may find the subject-matter inherently more interesting). This narrative mastery is already much: no novelist can succeed unless he is a good reporter, and there is a long and honourable tradition in the novel which makes the depiction of social reality its main aim. But there is more than this in *Moll Flanders* – much humour and drama, and some genuinely novelistic presentation of personal relations.

The humour is often of a blunt cockney variety, as when Robin quiets his sister who opposes his marriage with the penniless orphan Moll: 'Prithee, child, beauty's a portion, and good humour with it is a double portion; I wish thou hadst half her stock of both for thy portion.' And Moll adds: 'So there was her mouth stopped'. But we also get more complex effects, sometimes ironical in their psychological point: as when Moll, having robbed a child, reflects that she had 'given the parents a just reproof for their negligence, in leaving the poor lamb to come home by itself, and it would teach them to take more care another time'; or when, giving her son a gold watch '... I desired he would now and then kiss it for my sake. I did not, indeed, tell him that I stole it from a gentlewoman's side at a meeting house in London. That's by the way.' There are also examples of a more polished wit that recalls Addison or Swift: Moll comments of her first lover, the elder brother, that 'though he had levity enough to do an ill-natured thing, yet had too much judgement of things to pay too dear for his pleasures'.

Moll Flanders has more conscious literary craftsmanship than *Robinson Crusoe*, and its orientation to the social and emotional world brings it much closer to the novel. The account of the first seduction and many of the episodes with the Lancashire husband combine vivid reporting with a command of character and emotion that foreshadow the later triumphs of the novel form. Such a scene occurs when, after a long absence, Moll Flanders is reunited with her Lancashire husband:

He turned pale, and stood speechless, like one thunder-struck, and, not able to conquer the surprise, said no more but this, 'Let me sit down'; and sitting down by a table, he laid his elbow on the table, and leaning his head on his hand, fixed his eyes on the ground as one stupid. I cried so vehemently, on the other hand, that it was a good while ere I could speak any more; but after I had given some vent to my passion by tears, I repeated the same words, 'My dear, do you not know me?' At which he answered, 'Yes', and said no more a good while.

This passage, and a few others, have a supremely evocative quality; they show how powerful Defoe's narrative manner could be when focused on human feeling. But such passages are rare. Selected quotations normally give us a much more favourable opinion of Defoe than reading the whole work would; and *Moll Flanders* is no exception. Its pages contain a great deal of uninspired filling-in; and this is one reason for believing that Defoe's stature as a novelist has tended to be overestimated of late.

His central defect is a lack of serious order or design, a lack which is manifested, not only in the development of the story, but in the psychological and moral aspects of his work. What narrative unity there is comes from the fact that it is Moll Flanders who is the chief character throughout; but this is lost by a somewhat undiscriminating attempt to tell all that happened in a busy and eventful life, so that the movement of the novel is very episodic.

The moral disunity of the work is even more striking. The purported moral does not tally with the plot. Defoe says in his preface that 'there is not a wicked action in any part of it, but is first or last rendered unhappy'; but actually the heroine does not have to disgorge her ill-gotten gains, and they are the basis of her final prosperity. Even if Defoe had avoided this contradiction, the quality of his moral would have little to commend it, since it amounts to little more than telling the reader to look to his silver and be on his guard against pickpockets. The actual moral which emerges is even worse: if honesty, the story suggests, will not maintain you genteelly without your being driven to ply your needle, then crime may prove more rewarding – you can always settle your spiritual accounts later on. This crassly material nature of Defoe's outlook is well shown in the moral reformation scene which occurs when Moll brings home to her husband all the wealth from her mother's plantation, '... the horses, hogs and cows, and other stores for our plantation; all which added to his surprise, and filled his heart with thankfulness; and from this time forward I believe he was as sincere a penitent and as thoroughly a reformed man as ever God's goodness bought back from being a profligate, a highwayman, and a robber'.

Reformation by cows and hogs. The book is indeed an example of 'mercantile morality that Defoe has apparently neglected to measure'.[6] So much so that many have been tempted to regard the whole moral aspect of the book ironically, although certainly against Defoe's intention.

The psychological defects of the book are less obvious to the eye and could not be demonstrated without lengthy analysis. It can only be suggested, therefore, that Moll Flanders is not seen objectively by Defoe as a character in the round; like many other of his characters, she is at times indistinguishable from her author, despite the various feminine traits she is given, particularly in her first love-affair with the elder brother, and in her regular concern for genteel lodgings, clean linens, and the creature comforts of her males. But the autobiographical form, which Defoe always uses in his fiction, makes it particularly difficult for him not to identify himself with the heroine; it certainly makes it difficult for his picture of her to have much depth, since we do not know what other characters think of her, and can only see her through her own eyes. It is certainly suspicious that nearly all the other characters are shown treating her with adoring and selfless devotion, whereas she is always less than completely honest with everyone. If we try to get deeper, and ask whether she or her author are aware of her duplicity, we find that Defoe has not told us enough of the relevant facts for an opinion to be possible. It seems that Defoe did not ask such questions himself, or conceive that his readers would. His heroine's moral and emotional life were not within his terms of reference. Defoe keeps us informed, as no other novelist does, of his heroine's holdings in cash and personal effects: he does not bother to make clear her emotional development, or to take stock of her real character.

Nor, apparently, does he consider the nature of her personal relationships any more seriously. We are told nothing about most of her lovers or her children: it appears she had a dozen or so of each, but it is impossible to be sure, because most of them are treated very cursorily. She is suitably maternal on being reunited with one son, Humphry, in Virginia; but what of the remaining seven children whose deaths have not been indicated? The answer is surely that all these are items mentioned merely as items of realistic detail, and that then Defoe does not give them another thought, and does not intend the reader to; we are certainly not meant to draw the conclusion that she is a heartless mother, nor, indeed, any conclusion, but only to forget as easily as she does. Everything that is told is real, but much of it has no existence once it is off-stage: convincing the reader of the reality of the story is for Defoe not only the means, but the end. There is no developing personality in Moll to be observed, no moral or psychological pattern to the loosely-strung-out network of personal relations. Defoe is too intent on getting away with the reality of his characters to be able to get into them.

* * *

Defoe's forte, then, is the brilliant episode. His imagination creates events and characters, and sets them solidly in their background; in this his narrative is much in advance of anything that fiction had seen; and in many respects it has not been surpassed since. But in the larger units of composition his shaping imagination is much less in evidence. The novel as a literary form could be considered established only when realistic narrative was organized into a plot which, while retaining Defoe's lifelikeness, also had a genuine unity of development; when the novelist's eye was focused on character and personal relationships as essential elements of the continuity of the novel and not as incidental matter to be used in furthering the verisimilitude of the actions described; and when all these things were related to a unifying theme, a controlling intention. Defoe had begun the process, but it was left to Richardson and Fielding to take these further steps.

However, now that later novelists have gone so much further than they did, we tend to read Richardson and Fielding in the perspective of the novel tradition as a whole, and they may suffer in comparison. Defoe, on the other hand, does not really compete, and this perhaps lends his artless veracity an adventitious charm: we rejoice to see a writer so innocently unaware of how novels are supposed to be written, and are tempted to find irony and moral sophistication because we cannot credit that so remarkable a writer and so amazing a man could as a novelist be genuinely innocent. That, at least, is the main critical problem he seems to pose.

NOTES

1. In his excellent essay, 'De Foe's Novels', in *Hours in a Library*, 1 (London, 1874).

2. This is difficult to obtain; it is most easily available in *Romances and Narratives*, ed. G. A. Aitken (London, 1902).

3. See my '*Robinson Crusoe* as a Myth', in *Essays in Criticism*, 1 (Oxford, 1950), for a treatment of this aspect of the book.

4. See E. A. Levett, 'Daniel Defoe', in *The Social and Political Ideas of the Augustan Age*, ed. F. J. C. Hearnshaw (London, 1928).

5. See Virginia Woolf's essays on Defoe in *The Common Reader, First Series* (London, 1925), and on *Robinson Crusoe* in the *Second Series* (London, 1932).

6. See Mark Schorer's Introduction to *Moll Flanders* in the Modern Library College Edition, Random House (New York, 1950), for an excellent critical appraisal of the novel. A fuller treatment of *Robinson Crusoe* and *Moll Flanders* may be found in my *Rise of the Novel: Studies in Defoe, Richardson and Fielding* (London, 1957). The latter book's interpretation of these works has been challenged in many quarters. That of *Robinson Crusoe* by, among others, Maximilian E. Novak, *Economics and the Fiction of Daniel Defoe* (Berkeley and Los Angeles, 1962).

My interpretation of *Moll Flanders* has been attacked by Arnold Kettle, 'In Defence of *Moll Flanders*', *Of Books and Humankind: Essays and Poems Presented to Bonamy Dobrée*, ed. John Butt, London, 1964. Among the other contributions to the controversy the following may be cited: Robert R. Columbus, 'Conscious Artistry in *Moll Flanders*', *Studies in English Literature*, III (1963), 415–32; Howard L. Koonce, 'Moll's Muddle: Defoe's Use of Irony in *Moll Flanders*', *English Literary History*, XXX (1963), 377–94; Maximilian Novak, 'Conscious Irony in *Moll Flanders*: Facts and Problems', *College English*, XXVI (1964), 198–204; and George A. Starr, *Defoe and Spiritual Autobiography* (Princeton, 1965), which also shows the importance of spiritual autobiography in *Robinson Crusoe*.

THE PERIODICAL ESSAYISTS

JANE H. JACK

IT is not often that the appearance of a new literary form can be dated as precisely as that of the periodical essay, which was virtually invented by Steele in April 1709. 'The world has been obliged to an author of distinguished merit, now living, for having been the inventor of a manner of writing no less entertaining than any which had been established by the practice of the most celebrated ancients', Sir Richard Blackmore remarked a few years later in the preface to a 'sequel to the *Spectators*' called *The Lay Monk*, and Boswell, writing towards the end of the hey-day of the form, was no less certain of the modernity than of the merit of 'one of the happiest inventions of modern times'. 'A periodical paper of instruction and entertainment is truly of British origin', he remarked in the first number of his 'Hypochondriack' essays (1777). 'It first appeared in London; and from the great lustre with which it was produced to the world by the constellation of wits in Queen Anne's reign, it would at any rate have for a time had eminence and imitators. ... But from the long esteem and public favour with which a periodical paper has been attended, and the several successful works of that kind; nay, the many unsuccessful attempts of which there might be a large catalogue given, we must be convinced that this mode of writing has intrinsic excellence, and that mankind are fully sensible of its value.'

It will be convenient to take our cue from Blackmore and Boswell and to leave aside what might be termed the prehistory of the periodical essay. What concerns us is the remarkable proliferation of this type of essay in the years following the first number of *The Tatler*. At least in the first half of the eighteenth century it might well be said to be the 'dominant form', if that term were not a trifle pretentious for a mode of writing which belongs essentially to the minor key. It is evidence of the adaptability of the periodical essay that it presented itself as an eligible medium to men of the most varied talents. Writers as different as Steele, Johnson, and Goldsmith wrote some of their finest work in it. It may be said to be the only literary form used by every major author of the century: it would not be easy to name many writers of the first or second rank who never used it at all. From the days of Queen Anne – who had *The Spectator* taken in with her breakfast – to the time of the French Revolution and beyond, periodical essays on the lines laid down by Steele and Addison flooded the country and met the eye in every bookseller's shop and coffee-house. If they had the slightest merit they found a ready public. It follows that a modern reader who wishes to breathe the atmosphere of the eighteenth century can hardly do better than spend a few hours with *The Tatler*, *The Spectator*, *The Connoisseur*, and *The Citizen of the World*. He will not find in them the spiritual peaks or abysses of the age, the scarifying satire of *A Tale of a Tub* or the eloquent political insight of Burke; but he will find a faithful and well-composed portrait of the age.

The first numbers of *The Tatler* (which originally came out on Tuesdays, Thursdays, and Saturdays, the days on which the post left London) are particularly interesting because in them one sees the new form shaking off the trammels of its origins. From the first, news was not the primary concern of the paper, and padding was particularly disclaimed: 'we shall not upon a dearth of news, present you with much foreign edicts, or dull proclamations.' Yet in the first few issues 'St James's Coffee-House' (from which Steele proclaimed his intention of dating foreign and domestic news) makes numerous appearances. Several reasons soon combined drastically to limit the space given to political news, however. The first was the fact that the culminating victory of Malplaquet presaged the end of Marlborough's long compaigning. In his first contribution Addison ironically commiserates the writers of news-sheets. 'There is another sort of gentleman whom I am much more concerned for', he comments, after mentioning the plight of discharged soldiers, 'and that is the ingenious fraternity of which I have the honour to be an unworthy member; I mean the news-writers of Great Britain. ... The case of these gentlemen is ... more hard than that of the soldiers, considering that they have taken more towns, and fought more battles. ... Where Prince Eugène has slain his thousands, Boyer* has slain his ten thousands. ... It is impossible for this ingenious sort

---

* Abel Boyer issued *The Postboy*, *The Political State of Great Britain*, and other similar publications.

of men to subsist after a peace: every one remembers the shifts they were driven to in the reign of King Charles the Second, when they could not furnish out a single paper of news without lighting up a comet in Germany, or a fire in Moscow.' He goes on to suggest that apartments in Chelsea Hospital should be set aside 'for the relief of such decayed news-writers as have served their country in the wars', and points out that he is not thinking of himself. 'I cannot be thought to speak this out of an eye to any private interest; for as my chief scenes of action are coffee-houses, play-houses, and my own apartment, I am in no need of camps, fortifications, and fields of battle to support me; I don't call out for heroes and generals to my assistance. Though the officers are broken [discharged], and the armies disbanded, I shall still be safe as long as there are men or women, or politicians, or lovers, or poets, or nymphs, or swains, or cits, or courtiers in being' (No. 18).

While the refusal of the House of Commons to renew the Licensing Act in 1695 led to the increase in journalism of which *The Tatler* was a by-product, politics – as Steele was shortly to discover – was still not a safe subject for writers. Addison, who was less interested in politics than Steele and less impulsive, saw that it would be more profitable as well as safer to exclude the subject from the new periodical altogether. So it happened that within six months of its first appearance *The Tatler* was almost wholly devoid of political news and comment. It soon became common form with the essayists to disparage the appetite for news. 'Is it not much better to be let into the knowledge of one's self, than to hear what passes in Muscovy or Poland', Addison asks in the tenth number of *The Spectator,* 'and to amuse ourselves with such writings as tend to the wearing out of ignorance, passion, and prejudice, than such as naturally conduce to inflame hatreds, and make enmities irreconcileable?'

News being excluded, what was to be the scope of the essayists? They might have replied, with Fielding in *Tom Jones,* 'The provision then which we have made is no other than HUMAN NATURE' (Bk. I, introd.). 'The general purpose of this paper', Steele wrote in the dedication which accompanied the first volume of *The Tatler* when it was published as a book, 'is to expose the false arts of life, to pull off the disguises of cunning, vanity, and affectation, and to recommend a general simplicity in our dress, our discourse, and our behaviour.' The essentially moral intention of the essayists obtains equal emphasis in the tenth number of *The Spectator*, where Addison echoes Cicero's description of the mission of Socrates: 'It was said of Socrates, that he brought philosophy down from heaven to inhabit among men; and I shall be ambitious to have it said of me that I have brought philosophy out of closets and libraries, schools and colleges, to dwell in clubs and assemblies, at tea-tables and in coffee-houses.'

The exclusion of political news was not only safer: it also made for a larger circulation. When Pope was first coming into prominence, Addison gave him a piece of advice which shows how conscious he himself had been of this consideration. He advised Pope 'not to be content with the applause of half the nation'. What he meant was that Pope should refrain from throwing in his lot with either the Whigs or the Tories. 'There cannot a greater judgement befall a country', he had written in *The Spectator*, No. 125, 'than such a dreadful spirit of division as rends a government into two distinct peoples and makes them greater strangers and more averse to one another than if they were actually two different nations. The effects of such a division are pernicious to the last degree. ... This influence is very fatal both to men's morals and their understandings; it sinks the virtue of a nation, and ... destroys even common sense.' After emphasizing the particular harm this spirit does in literary matters (in a passage with which Matthew Arnold would have been in decisive agreement), Addison goes on: 'For my own part, I could heartily wish that all honest men would enter into an association, for the support of one another against the endeavours of those whom they ought to look upon as their common enemies, whatsoever side they may belong to. Were there such an honest body of neutral forces, we should never see the worst of men in great figures of life [positions in life], because they are useful to a party; nor the best unregarded because they are above practising those methods which would be grateful to their faction.'

In the preface already quoted, Blackmore lays particular stress on Steele's 'invention' of 'introducing a set of persons of different humours and characters, acting on some imaginary occasion, which might draw out a variety of incidents and discourses'. The significance of the club which appears in *The Spectator* and many of its imitators should now be clear. The invention of the characters of Sir Roger de Coverley, Captain Sentry, Sir Andrew Freeport, and the rest was at once a rhetorical or literary device, a symbol for the English people as it struggled to coalesce, and a flattering portrait of the reading public that the writers had as their aim. The Spectator Club forms an appropriate introduction to the literature of the eighteenth century – the century in which Parliament (the 'talking-shop') was rejoicing in its new powers, the great century of talk and talkers. Discussion had brought about the 'Glorious Revolution' and shown itself more useful than the blows of civil war. In the *History of the Royal Society* Sprat had rejoiced in the fact that scientific discussion, being now 'admitted into our Exchange, our Church, our palaces, and our Court', had begun to keep 'the best company'. It was time that encouragement should also be given to discussion of the great common question of how to live. To promote this was the chief object of the periodical essayists.

One of the main trends in the eighteenth century – it had begun much earlier – was a trend towards secularization. Although the Church remained much more powerful than it is today, it had retreated a long way from the position of predominance which it had occupied in the early seventeenth century. One cannot read far in the periodical essayists without realizing that they were taking over many of the functions earlier fulfilled by the Church. In this Addison made a suitable leader, a sort of lay Archbishop of Good Taste. Indeed, his quasi-episcopal characteristics were noticed by everyone, not only by the philosopher, Bernard Mandeville, with his sneer about a 'parson in a tye-wig', but also by Tonson the publisher. 'Old Jacob Tonson did not like Mr Addison', Pope once told Spence. 'He had a quarrel with him: and ... used frequently to say of him: "One day or other, you'll see that man a bishop! I'm sure he looks that way; and indeed I ever thought him a priest in his heart." ' It is certain that Addison did at one time think of seeking high position in the Church. He wrote a work called *The Evidences of the Christian Religion*. And although he did not take the final step of seeking Orders, it might be said that the 'discourses against Atheism and Infidelity, and in defence of the Christian Revelation' contained in this book received stronger support from his periodical essays than they could have received from any sermons he could have written. In fact, many of the *Tatlers* and *Spectators* are very close to sermons. Avoiding alike the rigorous dialectic of Lancelot Andrewes and the argument from terror of John Donne, Addison's style of lay-preaching derives rather from the well-bred apologetics of men like Tillotson (from whom Dryden said that he learned to write English prose). His message is summed up in the motto to *The Spectator*, No. 112: 'Honour the gods according to the established modes.' His approach is readily suggested by the title of a widely read book of the time, *Christianity Not Mysterious*. What he wanted to promote was not wild and ungovernable religious feeling, 'enthusiasm' of the sort that had led to so much trouble in the previous century, but rather a cheerful and 'rational' faith. Addison would have agreed with many of his contemporaries that too much argument about religion was dangerous; but he would not have approved of the practice of some later essayists in excluding religion as well as politics from their pages. 'To say truth', Edward Moore wrote in the first issue of *The World*, 'I have serious reasons for avoiding the first of these subjects. A weak advocate may ruin a good cause. And if religion can be defended by no better arguments than some I have lately seen in the public papers and magazines, the wisest way is to say nothing about it.' To avoid religion altogether in this way would not have been acceptable to Addison, who wished to 'recommend' Christianity. This he did by discussing the subject 'in a clear and lively manner, without unseasonable passions' (as he once said in commendation of a piece by Swift). He excelled in suggesting that not to be a Christian was slightly ridiculous, a breach of good manners. This set the tone in which most of the essayists (with the notable exception of Johnson) were to deal with religion.

What Addison and Steele and their successors were doing was to carry on at a much higher and more intelligent level the work of the people to whom Steele referred as 'my friends and fellow labourers, the Reformers of Manners'. Perhaps there was an absurd side to their work: in some ways they point forward to the strained 'gentility' of the Victorian age. But one has only to read the letters and memoirs of the time to see that some reformation of manners was highly desirable. There is a revealing passage in one of the notebooks of Mrs Thrale: 'How great a change has been wrought in female manners within these few years in England!', she wrote. 'I was reading the letter in the third volume of the *Spectator* [No. 217] where the man complains of his indelicate mistress: I read it aloud to my little daughters of 11 and 12 years old, and even the maid who was dressing my hair burst out o' laughing.' This was written towards the end of the century by a woman who had put up with the manners of Samuel Johnson, which would horrify most people today. It suggests that a revolution of manners did really take place in the course of the century, and helps to make intelligible Jane Austen's objection to the 'coarse' language of *The Spectator* (*Emma*, chapter iv). Clearly there was room for reform at the beginning of the eighteenth century.

The strength of Steel and Addison lay in their ability to take a middle course, and they refused to go to the lengths advocated by many members of the Society for the Reformation of Manners, whose spiritual ancestors were the Puritans of the previous century. They gave strong and effectual support to the campaign against heavy gambling and duelling, but they did not share the distrust of plays which was still widespread in the middle and lower classes of society. Among Steele's earliest literary ventures were plays in which he tried to meet the objections levelled by Jeremy Collier against the moral effect of the drama. Steele would have been pleased with Parson Adams's remark that there were passages in his plays 'almost good enough for a sermon': it was his contention that 'a good play acted before a well-bred audience must raise very proper incitements to good behaviour, and be the most quick and most prevailing method of giving young people a turn of sense and breeding'. Nothing illustrates more clearly the reconciliatory course steered by Addison and Steele than their attitude to the drama. It gives definition to their famous objectives 'to enliven morality with wit, and to temper wit with morality'. They were always mindful of the cleavage in the English mind which had most recently and most dramatically been demonstrated in the Great Rebellion, but which went back farther and did not simply correspond to the two sides in that strange conflict. Behind Addison's phrase lies the whole history of the Reformation. Was 'wit', and perhaps art itself, dangerous to morality? Was not the Bible alone literature enough to teach a man to lead a good life? Attacks on 'wit' abounded in the seventeenth century, and they had more justification than is often admitted now. The great work of *The Tatler* and its successor was a work of civilization through conciliation. It is not surprising that the highest standards in literature and morality and religion too were sometimes compromised. It was the price that had to be paid for keeping Free-port, de Coverley, and Wimble together in one club.

If it had been necessary to placate also a Mrs Wimble and a Lady de Coverley, the difficulties would have been much greater; but one has only to play with the idea to realize that the society represented by the Spectator Club is essentially a masculine society. The fact that no woman is a member is a true reflection of the position of women in English society at the beginning of the century. A little later, the 'blue-stockings' were to attract attention and raise the question of the status of women; but at the point when *The Tatler* began to appear, the prevalent literary attitudes to women were not flattering. The accession of a woman to the throne made the time propitious for a change of attitude, however, and Steele – who had always stood out stoutly against the 'wenching' attitude which lingered on as a legacy from the Restoration – was the man to seize this opportunity. It became an important part of the *Tatler* and *Spectator* 'platform' to stress that the authors were writing for women as well as men, and to emphasize that women must play a large part in the process of civilizing which they were striving to promote. 'There are none to whom this paper will be more useful than to the female world', Addison wrote in the tenth number of *The Spectator*. 'I have often thought there has not been sufficient pains taken in finding out proper employments and diversions for the fair ones. Their amusements seem rather contrived for them as they are women, than as they are reasonable creatures; and are more adapted to the sex than to the species.' Most people now agree with Swift, who found the tone in which Addison 'fair-sexed it' intolerably condescending. But it is clear that few women shared this feeling, for they made up a large proportion of his readers from the first: this general (though not universal) absence of irritation speaks volumes on the position of women before this time. Attention to the interests of 'the fair sex' became one of the invariable conventions of the periodical essay, and there can be little doubt that the essayists did much to improve the status and education of women. Within forty years it had become possible for Johnson to comment that 'whatever might be the state of female literature [literacy, education] in the last century, there is now no longer any danger lest the scholar should want [lack] an adequate audience at the tea-table' (*The Rambler*, No. 173).

It should have become clear by now that one principal reason for the success of Addison and Steele was the fact that they kept the tastes and requirements of their readers, male and female, constantly in mind. Not the least of the attractions of their new form was its brevity. The seventeenth century had been the century of long books. A seventeenth-century reader seems to have been able to read anything. The only brief forms with any literary pretensions were stiff with 'wit'. The increasing 'reading public' of the eighteenth century brought a demand for easier reading. As Blackmore pointed out in the Preface to his *Essays*, 'The disrelish of ... diffusive pieces in these times is ... carried so far, that great books are looked on as oppressive ..., while those in which the principal end, as well as the sentiment of the author, are contracted into a narrower compass, if well writ, meet with general approbation.' It may seem paradoxical to claim that the century of *Clarissa* and *Tom Jones*, Boswell's *Life of Johnson* and Gibbon's *Decline and Fall of the Roman Empire* was a period of short books; but so it was, by comparison with the preceding century. It was a time when writers paid more attention to the human frailty of their readers, and treated them with greater consideration. As in the format of books folios with double columns in small print were dying out and reputable publishers were paying more attention to clear type, so more care was devoted to presentation and style in the manner of writing. The periodical writers prided themselves on being 'nearer in our styles to that of common talk than any other writers' (*Tatler*, No. 204), and there can be little doubt that the ubiquity of these essays had a good effect on the prose style of the century as a whole. A writer who had undergone the discipline of writing a few periodical essays was the less likely to have recourse to unnecessary pomposity or meaningless jargon in his other writings. The influence of the periodical essay made for clarity, simplicity, and literary good manners.

In nothing is this more evident than in the essays in literary criticism which were from the first a feature of the periodicals. It is as true today as it was in 1780 that the word 'critic' is 'a name which the present generation is scarcely willing to allow [Addison]'. But as Johnson pointed out in his *Life of Addison*, 'his instructions were such as the character of his readers made proper. That general knowledge which now circulates in common talk, was in his time rarely to be found. Men not professing learning were not ashamed of ignorance; and, in the female world, any acquaintance with books was distinguished only to be censured.' It followed that 'an instructor like Addison was now wanting, whose remarks being superficial might be easily understood, and being just might prepare the mind for greater attainments'. His two series of essays on *Paradise Lost* and on the imagination are favourable examples of high-class popularization, and he wrote essays which deserve attention on such subjects as stage-comedy, the ballad of *Chevy Chase*, verse-epistles, and the style proper to tragedy. To explore any of the periodicals of the century is to come on numerous essays of this sort: they are brief, unpretentious, and sometimes surprisingly good (not least when they deal with some minor subject such as letter-writing or the composition of songs). One of the essayists was a great critic. Johnson used the form for some of his finest criticism, such as the essays in *The Rambler* on biography, the dramatic unities, and 'low' words in poetry (Nos. 60, 156, and 168). But the sovereign merit of Johnson's best criticism quite apart, the fact that the essayists habitually devoted a proportion of their work to literary topics had important results. It made it clear that knowledge of a few great writers was not a matter for professional scholars only, but a part of general culture, almost of good manners. The same is true of the papers devoted to the English language, to points of style that concern anyone who tries to speak or write correctly. A critical interest in the spoken language is a mark of literary maturity: it may still be found in France, but since the eighteenth century it has not been an outstanding characteristic of our own country.

In spite of the excellent literary criticism which it contains, Johnson's *Rambler* did not sell at all well in periodical form. It is said that only the number written by Samuel Richardson sold more than 500 copies. In volume form, however, it came to rival every other series of essays except *The Spectator*. It was not Johnson's instructional purpose (pronounced as that was) that was an innovation, but his refusal to insinuate his instruction in an agreeable and easy form.

There will always be a few readers who agree with the talented Anna Seward in becoming easily bored with Addison's 'water-gruel style' – 'nothing wearies me like [his] prosing about and about the good cardinal virtues in their old robes' – and preferring 'the bright armour of Johnsonian eloquence'. But the average reader of the periodical essay found Johnson stiff going. Johnson's choice of subjects may be indicated by quoting some of the titles appended to the essays in the collected editions: 'Happiness not Local'; 'The Miseries of an infirm Constitution'; 'The Voyage of Life'; 'The frequent Contemplation of Death necessary to moderate the Passions'; 'Religion and Superstition, A Vision'; 'The Luxury of vain Imagination'. The staple topics of *The Rambler* are those which form the warp and woof of *Rasselas*: the inevitability of disappointments in human life, the dangers of excessive leisure, all the difficulties attending 'the choice of life'. The Prince of Abyssinia who travels about the world to see the manners and ways of many men is an image of Johnson's own ambition: perhaps this is one reason for his choice of 'The Rambler' as a title. His periodical essays form one of the principal repositories of his reflections on 'the various conditions of humanity'. It is noticeable that not only do moral subjects preponderate: even subjects which might seem to belong to the domain of manners, and would have been treated by Addison or Steele with a light touch, tend to be treated by Johnson in the same way as papers on fundamental moral duties. There are flashes of humour here and there; but were it not for *The Idler*, which (like Boswell's *Hypochondriack*) was a 'column' in a larger periodical and not an independent publication, the reader might conclude that Johnson was devoid of humour. These briefer and more amusing papers also show a dramatic power which might have remained unsuspected. Instead of the characters in *The Rambler*, derived too obviously (with their ponderous Latin names) from classical models and the 'characters' of the seventeenth century, we find Dick Minim and a number of other characters in *The Idler* who are described with a much lighter touch. On the whole, however, the merits of *The Rambler* and *The Idler* are less those proper to the periodical essay as a form than those characteristic of all Johnson's writing. Every paper exhibits the sovereign merit of Johnson's work as a whole: he closes with his subject and grapples with it with all his strength, bringing to bear all his experience of human life.

The Rambler and *The Idler* form a storehouse of mature reflections on human life and perceptive literary judgements.

The sixth decade of the century, which saw the appearance of Johnson's periodical essays, was the decade also of *The Adventurer*, *The World*, *The Connoisseur*, and Goldsmith's delightful *Citizen of the World*. This was the second great period of the periodical essay. Not that there was any notable diminution in the flood after 1760. Essayists consoled themselves with the reflection of Fielding in *The Champion*, that 'there is a sort of craft attending vice and absurdity; and when hunted out of society in one shape, they seldom want address to reinsinuate themselves in another: hence the modes of licence vary almost as often as those of dress, and consequently require continual observation to detect and explode them anew'. It is particularly noticeable that periodical essays tended to appear in other centres where there was an approximation to the conditions of London at the beginning of the century. The Edinburgh *Mirror* (1779–80) and *Lounger* (1785–6) were among the best examples of these: less important periodicals appeared in Dublin, Newcastle, and other provincial towns. But it is not surprising that the periodical essay began to exhibit the characteristics of a decadent form. The same conventions were repeated with less and less effect. Writers mistook the externals for the essence. The remorseless literary law of diminishing returns made itself felt. Then, as now, the essay attracted people who were anxious to 'commence author', but had nothing new to say. If Theobald had lived about the middle of the century he would have had more reason for the complaint he had made near the beginning: 'This period may well be called the Age of Counsellors, when every blockhead who could write his own name attempted to inform and amuse the public.'

The form was wearing out, with the society which had sustained it. The peculiar blend of seriousness and lightness of touch which was (in spite of Johnson) the essence of the periodical essay did not sort with the new age, and has never been possible since. That sureness of tone which characterizes so much of the literature of the eighteenth century was to go under in the Romantic flood. The Romantic essayists learned a good deal from their predecessors, indeed: Coleridge's *Friend* has many of the characteristics of the old kind. But two influences were incompatible with the old tradition: the tendency to

228

autobiography and to the 'putting over' of the essayist's own idiosyncrasies which marks Romantic essay-writing and Romantic
literature as a whole; and political events on a scale which made it
impossible to live any longer in this temperate zone of literature.
By a strange chance the inventor of the form made a remark about
the situation in 1713 which was undoubtedly true in the years following the French Revolution. 'It is not now a time to improve the taste
of men by the reflections and railleries of poets and philosophers',
Steele had written in the first number of *The Englishman*, 'but to
awaken their understanding by laying before them the present state
of the world like a man of experience and a patriot. It is a jest to
throw away our care in providing for the palate when the whole
body is in danger of death, and to talk of amending the mien and air
of a cripple that has lost his legs and arms.' After the French Revolution a writer who wrote in the old form was being as consciously
archaic as a man who wore a full-bottomed wig; the periodical
essay passed away with the world into which it had been born.

AN APPROACH TO SWIFT

D. W. JEFFERSON

Senior Lecturer in English Literature, the University of Leeds

TOO much emphasis, perhaps, has been laid on the simplicity of
Swift's prose style. It is to this virtue in particular that Sir Herbert
Read draws attention in his remarks on Swift in *English Prose Style*:
'however widely his vision might extend, however deep his insight,
his mode of expression remained simple, and single, and clearly
comprehensible'.[1] And it was to this virtue that Swift himself drew
attention in various places; for example, in his remarks on preaching
in the *Letter to a Young Gentleman*, where he refers to 'that Simplicity,
without which no human Performance can arrive to any great
Perfection'. Yet the habit, in critics and teachers, of referring to it
as the first and foremost of his qualities needs to be resisted. Swift's
remarks on prose style, though of great interest, bear very little on
the secret of his own greatness in that medium. The student, influenced by the emphasis on simplicity, is liable to get a limited impression of Swift's powers. It is a case of association of ideas. Simplicity
of style suggests plain statement and a straightforward approach;
qualities which, as it happens, are found together – or so it seems –
in some frequently quoted passages of Swift; for example, in the
description of Gulliver's arrival on the shore of Lilliput, so often
produced as a classroom illustration by lecturers on the advantages
of plain prose. But what ought to be said, whenever it is so used, is
that the author has a special ironical motive here for cultivating the
matter-of-fact narrative style of contemporary books of travel. It is
essential to the effectiveness of *Gulliver's Travels* that its hero should
seem to be a plain man telling a plain tale, and it is what Swift
achieves under cover of this assumed manner that is interesting.
The early pages of each of the four books, where a brief account is
given of the commonplace circumstances leading to the strange
adventures, are written in a dry and pedestrian manner which
borders on parody. In the many roles which Swift adopts as a writer
it sometimes suits his purpose to deal plainly and straightforwardly
with this subject, but often he only appears to do so or does so only in

230

part. His simplicity in syntax and diction is liable to be a camouflage for insidious intentions.

To emphasize his simplicity is to emphasize the differences between his art and that of the early seventeenth-century writers, and hence to deflect attention from the qualities which he shares with them. Both the differences and the affinities need to be recognized, but literary historians have been far too much preoccupied with the former. The demand for a simpler prose is historically related to the requirements of the new science and philosophy and the rejection of the old, fanciful type of speculation associated with Sir Thomas Browne; and Swift's style tends to be regarded, in some imperfectly defined way, as expressive of the new intellectual virtues; as the style of one who followed what Professor Basil Willey refers to as 'the plain path of Nature and Reason'.[2] This is not the place for a discussion of his attitudes to contemporary philosophical developments, but it may be suggested that in stressing his indebtedness to the intellectual habits of the earlier period we should do more justice to the richness and variety of his art. In his brilliant play with the old modes of learned speculation, his imaginative fertility in developing concretely an absurd pseudo-scientific conception, his dialectical resourcefulness and effrontery, Swift is of the world of Rabelais, Donne, and Ben Jonson. There are two clear reasons for giving priority to this aspect of him. First, the imagination is by nature conservative; it flourishes most when it has old forms and techniques and procedures at its disposal, and it is by adapting and modifying these rather than by discovering new ones that even the most original artist meets the demands of the contemporary world. The immediate contemporary influences upon a writer, though in one sense the most important, are in another sense secondary, because they can operate only on an inherited equipment, and will operate feebly if the equipment is inadequate. The Augustan economy of Swift's prose is not a quality to be isolated. It must be studied in relation to the arts which he inherited from earlier periods, which it modifies and which modify it. Secondly, the earlier period is the greater period, and by realizing his link with it we acquire a more generous sense of his greatness. Plainness and simplicity in themselves are not sufficiently interesting qualities to be given first place in our account of such an artist.

It is in the earlier works, such as *A Tale of a Tub*, that the more exuberant side of his art is most apparent. There are some delectable examples here of his ability to play with learned ideas, exploiting them ingeniously to build up a comic conception. One of his masters in this art was Rabelais, the English translation of whose work was completed in the 1690s, not long before Swift wrote these satires. A pleasant example, in the third book of Rabelais, is Panurge's celebrated defence of his own improvidence (he has just run through three years' income in a fortnight) in which arguments are drawn from astronomy, physiology, and other branches of learning to prove that borrowing and lending are the basic principles governing the universe. A witty misapplication of learned ideas in support of an audacious conclusion was one of the arts of the metaphysical poets. We should not expect such effects to occur in literature long after the seventeenth century, for they involve a parody of the pre-scientific methods of speculation which were discredited by the new scientists; and parody demands a certain nearness to the thing parodied. But Swift is not the last writer to make lavish use of them. They are abundantly present in Sterne's *Tristram Shandy*.

It is not enough to say that Swift is ridiculing the old ideas and intellectual procedures. To make such superb comic use of them he had to be imaginatively at home with them. The ideas he uses are *his* ideas, so far as his art is concerned.

One of his arts, much in evidence in the early works, consists in inventing a theory based on learned or pseudo-learned ideas in order to explain the phenomenon which is the object of his satire; for example, the fanaticism or 'enthusiasm' of the nonconformist sects. He begins with a suave, apparently innocuous, statement of the theory, and then proceeds to develop a series of grotesque images showing the theory in action. In *A Tale of a Tub* (Ch. viii) this treatment is applied elaborately to a sect called the Aeolists, the believers in direct inspiration:

> The Learned *Aeolists* maintain the Original Cause of all Things to be *Wind*. ...

For two paragraphs he dwells solemnly on the different names for wind (*spiritus, animus, afflatus, anima*) and on learned theories concerning the various kinds of wind with which man is endowed. Apparently there are four kinds, but man brings with him into the world:

> ... a peculiar Portion or Grain of Wind, which may be called a *Quinta essentia*, extracted from the other four. This *Quintessence* is of a Catholic Use upon all Emergencies of Life, is improveable into all Arts and Sciences, and may be wonderfully refined, as well as enlarged, by certain Methods in Education. This, when *blown* up to its full Perfection, ought not to be covetously hoarded up, stifled, or hid under a Bushel, but freely communicated to Mankind. Upon these reasons, and others of equal Weight, the wise *Aeolists* affirm the gift of BELCHING to be the noblest Act of a Rational Creature. To cultivate which Art, and render it more serviceable to Mankind, they made use of several Methods. At certain Seasons of the Year, you might behold the Priests amongst them, in vast Numbers, with their *Mouths gaping wide against a Storm*.

He then goes on to describe how a crowd of the faithful would blow each other up, and

> ... when, by these and the like Performances, they were grown sufficiently replete, they would immediately depart and disembogue, for the Publick Good, a plentiful Share of their Acquirements, into their Disciples' Chaps.

The Aeolists apply this principle to learning. 'Learning puffeth men up', and there is a syllogism to support this: 'Words are but wind; and learning is nothing but words; *ergo*, learning is nothing but wind'; hence, the philosophers of this school deliver all their teachings by eructation.

In the Introduction to *A Tale of a Tub*, Swift discusses the desirability of an elevated position for an orator, if he is to secure the attention of the public. Again, as in the passage about the Aeolists, he puts forward a learned theory and then a grotesque concrete demonstration of it:

> The deepest Account, and the most fairly digested of any I have yet met with, is this, That Air being a heavy Body, and therefore (according to the System of *Epicurus*) continually descending, must needs be more so, when loaden and press'd down with Words, which are also bodies of much Weight and Gravity, as it is manifest from those deep *Impressions* they make and leave upon us; and therefore must be delivered from

a due Altitude, or else they will neither carry a good Aim, nor fall down with a sufficient Force. ...

And I am the readier to favour this Conjecture, from a common Observation; that in the several Assemblies of these Orators, Nature herself hath instructed the Hearers to stand with their Mouths open, and erected parallel to the Horizon, so that they may be intersected by a perpendicular Line from the Zenith to the Center of the Earth. In which Position, if the Audience be well compact, every one carries home a Share, and little or nothing is lost.

I confess there is something yet more refined, in the Contrivance and Structure of our Modern Theatres. For, First; the Pit is sunk below the Stage, with due regard to the Institution above-deduced; that, whatever *weighty* Matter shall be delivered thence (whether it be *Lead* or *Gold*) may fall plum into the Jaws of certain *Criticks* (as I think they are called) which stand ready open to devour them. Then, the Boxes are built round, and raised to a Level with the Scene, in deference to the Ladies; because, That large Portion of Wit, laid out in raising Pruriences and Protuberances, is observ'd to run much upon a Line, and ever in a Circle. The whining Passions, and little starved Conceits, are gently wafted up, by their own extreme Levity, to the middle Region, and there fix and are frozen by the frigid Understandings of the Inhabitants. Bombast and Buffoonry, by Nature lofty and light, soar highest of all, and would be lost in the Roof, if the prudent Architect had not, with much Foresight, contrived for them a fourth Place, called *the twelve-peny Gallery*, and there planted a suitable Colony, who greedily intercept them in their Passage.

In another early work, *The Mechanical Operation of the Spirit*, Swift pretends to examine scientifically the physiological means whereby preachers produce a spiritual response in their congregations. The following passage is concerned with the part played by the members of the assembly:

The Methods of this *Arcanum* is as follows: – They violently strain their Eye balls inward, half closing the Lids; Then, as they sit, they are in a perpetual Motion of *See-saw*, making long Hums at proper Periods, and continuing the Sound at equal Height, choosing their Time in those Intermissions while the Preacher is at Ebb.

He then adds that this trick with the eyes is a secret of the Indian Yogis and accounts for their visions, and he makes learned comments of a similar kind on the origin of the other part of the performance. A concrete scene follows:

> Now it is usual for a Knot of *Irish*, Men and Women, to abstract themselves from Matter, bind up all their Senses, grow visionary and spiritual, by Influence of a short Pipe of tobacco, handed round the Company, each preserving the Smoak in his Mouth, till it comes again to his Turn to take it in fresh: At the same Time there is a Consort of a continued gentle Hum, repeated and renewed by Instinct, as Occasion requires, and they move their Bodies up and Down, to a Degree, that sometimes their Heads and Points lie parallel to the Horizon. Mean while, you may observe their Eyes turn'd up, in the Posture of one who endeavours to keep himself awake; by which, and many other Symptoms among them, it manifestly appears that the Reasoning Faculties are all suspended and superseded, that Imagination hath usurped the Seat, scattering a thousand Deliriums over the Brain.

What is notable in all these passages is the imaginative play between the idea and the concrete detail, the one always enhancing the other. Here and there the illusion is created that the fantastic posturings embody something significant, like ritual. The absurdities take on a mysterious piquancy, and at the same time a mathematical sharpness. The ability to give a pointedness to the concrete particulars of a description, to achieve a certain flavour by the ordering of them in relation to an extraordinary intellectual pattern, is one of the characteristic arts of Ben Jonson, while the assimilation of image to idea is especially associated with the Metaphysical poets. Swift is in their tradition. An admirable example of the metaphysical art of 'arguing through images' occurs in *The Battle of the Books*, where the quarrel between the Bee and the Spider serves, by a nice manipulation of terms, as the embodiment of the dispute between Ancients and Moderns. The difference between the two intellectual types is stated by the Spider, who intends the comparison to favour himself, but achieves the opposite effect:

> Your Livelihood is a universal Plunder upon Nature; a Freebooter over Fields and Gardens; and, for the sake of

Stealing, will rob a Nettle as readily as a Violet. Whereas I
am a domestick Animal, furnisht with a Native Stock within
myself. This large Castle (to shew my Improvements in the
Mathematicks) is all built with my Own Hands, and the
Materials extracted altogether out of my own Person.

A play of idea and image may seem not to be characteristic of
Swift's work in his later period. The fantastic exploitation of learned
materials was, for the most part, abandoned, and his subjects were
often such as called for a more-or-less straightforward factual treatment. But Swift never lost his power of charging concrete details
with a peculiar intensity, of using them to give an unexpected force
and nuance to an argument. His art, in pamphlets like the *Drapier's
Letters*, of marshalling squads of particulars into menacing patterns
of monstrosity, so that the idea he is illustrating (Wood's halfpence,★
for instance) takes on an appalling proliferation of life, should be
recognized as akin to the art of *A Tale of a Tub*.

If there is less play with learned ideas after this earlier period, there
is no diminution but rather an intensification in his use of the arts
of argument. The witty use of these techniques in literature belongs
historically to the age when dialectic was still important in education,
when the ability to dispute on either side of a question was an
accepted accomplishment in schools and universities. The English
masters of ratiocinative wit, of the art of developing a plausibly
outrageous argument, are Donne, Dryden, and Swift, of whom the
latter is, surely, the most astonishing. But dialectical dexterity declined in importance, the new philosophers and scientists of the
seventeenth century having no use for the traditional logic, and
English writers after this period show much less skill in these arts.

An analysis of Swift's dialectical technique in one of the more
wonderful pamphlets would be a formidable and lengthy task. His
capacity to see all the possibilities for wit in a situation, and to achieve
a series of surprises as he moves from position to position exploiting
each possibility, can be illustrated adequately neither by a summary
nor by selection, but we must make the best of these means. His

★ Swift, writing in the character of a Dublin draper, published a series of
letters denouncing the project to provide Ireland with copper coins, the
patent for which was held by an Englishman, William Wood. Largely as a
result of his efforts the scheme was abandoned.

basic strategy in a number of works is to write in the character of someone from whose standpoint the facts he is satirizing can be stated with disconcerting freedom. This freedom depends on the ignoring of certain considerations, but trouble is in store for anyone who insists on them. The imaginary reader who is the victim of the manoeuvre is so placed that protest only leads to further embarrassment. Thus, in *A Modest Proposal* – perhaps the most tremendous pamphlet ever written – the horror of the proposal, which is that the children of the poor should be sold as food for the tables of the rich, can be stated with impunity in all its shocking details; for it is no more than commensurate with the horror actually existing and permitted by the social group which Swift's readers, roughly speaking, represent. His technique is to develop the one by continual reference to the other, so that every statement is double-edged:

> I have already computed the Charge of nursing a Beggars Child (in which list I reckon all *Cottagers, Labourers*, and four fifths of the *Farmers*) to be about two shillings *per Annum*, Rags included, and I believe no Gentleman would repine to give Ten shillings for the *Carcass of a good fat Child*. ...

The horrors are all the more effective in that they are not presented as such. They are just introduced casually as part of the evidence for, or in illustration of, his project. The tone of most of the pamphlet is easy and matter-of-fact; the appeal is to the reader's practical reasonableness, any attempt to excite pity or indignation being excluded. It is only towards the end that he finds a pretext for a change of tone and an overwhelming frontal attack. Replying to the timid objection, that under this scheme 'the Number of People will be thereby much lessened in the Kingdom', he admits that,

> ... it was indeed one Principal design in offering it to the world. I desire the Reader will observe, that I calculate my Remedy *for this one individual Kingdom of IRELAND, and for no other that ever was, is, or, I think, ever can be upon Earth. Therefore let no Man talk to me of other Expedients: Of taxing our Absentees at five Shillings a pound: Of using neither Cloaths, nor household Furniture, except what is of our own Growth and Manufacture: Of utterly rejecting the Materials and Instruments that promote Foreign Luxury: Of curing the Expenciveness of Pride, Vanity, Idleness,*

and Gaming in our Women: Of introducing a Vein of Parcimony,
Prudence and Temperance: Of learning to Love our Country,
wherein we differ even from LAPLANDERS, and the inhabitants
of TOPINAMBOO. ...

In the *Abolishing of Christianity* pamphlet, which is more elaborate,
the fictitious assumption is that there is a general unanimity in
favour of abolition, and he writes in the character of one who
thinks, but is conscious of his temerity in so doing, that the step may
be 'attended with some inconveniences'. From the opening page
or two we are led to expect an attack only upon the irreligious, but
he turns the tables on the conventional Christians among his readers
by announcing that it is only 'Nominal Christianity' that he proposes
to defend:

> I hope no Reader imagines me so weak to stand up in the
> Defence of Real Christianity, such as used in Primitive Times
> (if we may believe the Authors of those Ages) to have an
> Influence upon Mens Belief and Actions: To offer at the
> restoring of That would indeed be a wild Project; it would
> be to dig up Foundations, to destroy at one Blow all the
> Wit, and half the Learning of the Kingdom; to break the
> entire Frame and Constitution of Things, to ruin Trade,
> Extinguish Arts and Sciences with the Professors of them;
> In short, to turn our Courts, Exchanges, and shops into
> Deserts....

As in *A Modest Proposal*, the imaginary victim is caught. Faced with
the alternative of defending 'real' Christianity, he is in no position
to protest. 'Nominal' Christianity proves a fruitful idea for exploitation from a variety of angles. It seems that its observances, considered as obstacles to business and pleasure, are hardly worth the fuss
of abolishing; for example, church-going:

> I readily own there hath been an old Custom time out of
> mind, for People to assemble in the Churches every *Sunday,*
> and that shops are still frequently shut, in order as it is con-
> ceived, to preserve the Memory of that antient Practice; but
> how this can prove a hindrance to Business or Pleasure, is
> hard to imagine. What if the Men of Pleasure are forced one
> Day in the Week to Game at Home instead of the *Chocolate-*

House. Are not the *Taverns* and *Coffee-Houses* open ? Can there be a more convenient Season for taking a Dose of Physick ? Are fewer Claps got upon *Sundays* than other Days ?

As for the objection that religion endangers freedom of thought, the truth is that people are free to scoff and blaspheme to their hearts' content, and it is a good thing that they should have a religion to scoff at:

> Great Wits love to be free with the highest Objects, and if they cannot be allowed a God to revile or renounce; they will speak Evil of Dignities, abuse the Government, and reflect upon the Ministry, which I am sure few will deny to be of much more pernicious Consequence....

Confining himself to the humbler advantages of established Christianity he makes surprisingly effective use of them as a stick to beat the world of fashion and free-thinking:

> It is likewise urged, that there are by Computation in this Kingdom above Ten Thousand Parsons, whose Revenues added to those of my Lords the Bishops, would suffice to maintain at least Two hundred Young Gentlemen of Wit and Pleasure, and Free-thinking, Enemies to Priest-craft, narrow Principles, Pedantry, and Prejudices, who might be an Ornament to the Court and Town: And then, again, so great a Number of able (bodied) Divines might be a Recruit to our Fleet and Armies. This indeed appears to be a Consideration of some Weight: But then on the other side, several Things deserve to be considered like-wise: As, First, Whether it may not be thought necessary that in certain Tracts of Country, like what we call Parishes, there should be one Man at least, of Abilities to Read and Write. Then it seems a wrong Computation, that the Revenues of the Church throughout this Island would be enough to maintain Two Hundred Young Gentlemen, or even half that Number, after the present refined way of Living, that is, to allow each of them such a Rent, as in the modern Form of Speech, would make them Easy. But still there is in this Project a greater Mischief behind; And we ought to beware of the Woman's Folly, who killed the Hen that every Morning laid her a Golden Egg. For, pray what would become of the Race of Men in the next Age, if we had nothing to trust to besides

the Scrophulous consumptive Productions furnished by our Men of Wit and Pleasure, when having squandred away their Vigor, Health and Estates, they are forced by some disagreeable Marriage to piece up their broken Fortunes, and entail Rottenness and Politeness on their Posterity. Now, here are Ten Thousand Persons reduced by the wise Regulations of *Henry* the Eighth, to the necessity of a low Dyet, and moderate Exercise, who are the only great Restorers of our Breed, without which the Nation would in an Age or two become but one great Hospital.

This is a paragraph to marvel at as an example of Swift's extraordinary fertility and vigour in argument. But perhaps the most withering stroke of irony occurs in the following passage, where he has shifted to an entirely different position and is aiming at a different target:

Nor do I think it wholly groundless, or my Fears altogether imaginary, that the abolishing of Christianity may perhaps bring the Church in Danger, or at least put the Senate to the Trouble of another Securing Vote. I desire I may not be mistaken; I am far from presuming to affirm or think that the Church is in Danger at present, or as Things now stand, but we know not how soon it may be so when the Christian Religion is repealed.

Swift's virtuosity in works like this transcends anything that a mere textbook of rhetoric or dialectic could have taught him on the subject of 'invention', the traditional name for the art of opening up a topic and finding all there was to be said about it; but a tradition of formal training is to be reckoned with if we are to account for the existence of this quality in him and in other writers like Rabelais, as compared with writers of later periods. Although there is no trace in his work of pedantic methodicalness, such as Rabelais delighted in parodying, one feels that Swift's capacity to seize every advantage that a situation offered has behind it something of the old discipline. When he has done, to quote Dryden on Juvenal, 'the wit of man can carry it no further'.

The effect of his manoeuvrings, of the general strategy of his pamphlets, depends very largely on certain uses of language. Swift's habit of writing in the character of a fictitious person allows him freedoms in the choice of idiom from which he is always ready to profit. The *Drapier's Letters*, for example, are written in the character of a plain-spoken citizen, who expresses his indignation in round terms, and illustrates his point with common-sense arithmetic. That is the fiction, but under cover of it Swift writes with a studied baldness and an ominous mathematical explicitness, the effect of which is far different from that of plain, homely exposition. The idiom appropriate to the assumed character is manipulated as an artistic medium and applied with an intense deliberateness. In *A Modest Proposal*, the scientific approach, the easy tone with which the problem is reduced to one of agricultural economics, permits him occasionally to use an appalling phrase:

> It is true a Child, *just dropt from its Dam*, may be supported by her Milk, for a Solar year with little other Nourishment, at most not above the Value of two Shillings....

And the fact that, in the *Abolishing of Christianity* pamphlet, no higher principle than political expediency is invoked, gives him a pretext for expressions like, 'if the Gospel should be repealed'. Significant variations in tone and diction often occur within the same work, sometimes within the same sentence. Of these the long paragraph from the *Abolishing of Christianity* quoted above is quite rich in examples. Swift was a master of destructive juxtapositions of words: 'Young Gentlemen of Wit and Pleasure, and Free-thinking, Enemies to Priest-craft, narrow Principles, Pedantry, and Prejudices'. From these ironical phrases at the beginning of the paragraph he moves to the openly ruthless 'Rottenness and Politeness' of the later part. The double-edged phrase 'able-bodied Divines' echoes a callously secular view of the usefulness of the clergy, but is unexpectedly applied to their advantage. It is a typical stroke on Swift's part that they should be proved indispensable without reference to the things for which they primarily exist. 'Certain Tracts of Country, like what we call Parishes' conveys, beneath the innocently 'helpful' tone, the suggestion that the reader's familiarity with the elementary organization of Christianity is not beyond the need of a reminder. More drastic variations than these, involving sudden violence after suavity and polite detachment, are favourite devices of Swift, occurring more frequently in the earlier works.

It is generally admitted that the earlier works abound in imagery, but the view that the other works are altogether deficient in this respect is not quite just. He occasionally uses a destructive image to enhance an argument, as in this passage from the *Abolishing of Christianity* pamphlet:

> If the Quiet of a State can be bought by only flinging Men a few Ceremonies to devour, it is a purchase no Wise Man Would refuse. Let the Mastiffs amuse themselves about a Sheepskin stufft with Hay, provided it will keep them from Worrying the Flock.

Wood's halfpence provided endless stimulus to Swift's imagination, perhaps the most piquant example being the comparison between himself and David fighting Goliath. Goliath is Wood, he is wearing five thousand shekels of brass (Wood's halfpence), 'and he defied the Armies of the Living God'. A very pleasing sequence of images appears in a work of which Swift's authorship has recently been queried by Dr Herbert Davis: *A Letter to a Young Poet*.[3] This is not the place for an examination of the evidence, but if the paragraph below is not by Swift, historians of literature are going to have an extremely brilliant anonymous satirist on their hands. The development of the idea in physical terms is, surely, very close to Swift's technique in *A Tale of a Tub*. The subject is the literary life of Dublin:

> Seriously then, I have many Years lamented the want of a *Grub-street* in this our large and polite *City*, unless the whole may be called *one*. And this I have accounted an unpardonable Defect in our Constitution, ever since I had any Opinions I could call my own. Every one knows, *Grub-street* is a Market for *Small-Ware* in WIT, and as necessary considering the usual Purgings of *Human Brain*, as the *Nose* is upon a Man's *Face*. . . . And truly this Defect has been attended with unspeakable Inconveniences; for not to mention the Prejudice done to the Common-wealth of *Letters*, I am of opinion we suffer in our Health by it: I believe our corrupted Air, and frequent thick *Fogs* are in a great measure owing to the common exposal of our *Wit*, and that with good Management, our Poetical *Vapours* might be carried off in a *Common Drain*, and fall into one Quarter of the Town, without infecting the whole, as the Case is at present, to the great Offence of our *Nobility*, and *Gentry*, and *Others* of nice *Noses*.

One becomes so accustomed to piquancies and *nuances* of phrasing in Swift that the habit of looking for them is liable to be carried over into the reading of works like *The Conduct of the Allies*, where he is arguing a straight case and such subtleties would seem not to be called for. In such writings he sometimes succeeds in conveying the impression, which adds much to the effect, that he is acting a part, and that it is trying his patience a little; that he is stating mere facts, and trying only to place them in the clearest light, but that behind this restraint, which is a matter of expediency, is a consuming exasperation. In his sermons, which are not among his greater works, he really writes 'straight'. He would have scorned to use a sermon as an opportunity for virtuosity or for the indulgence of temperament. The role of preacher is not one in which he is especially happy; he has no remarkable insight into religion, and is unable to state his convictions feelingly; but there is an impressiveness in the rigid integrity with which he abides within his sometimes rather disconcerting limits. But if we turn to another piece of straight writing, *On the Death of Mrs Johnson*, we find restraint without the inadequacy of the sermons; through the perfect decorum of the style he gives the right public expression to his great regard for a woman towards whom his private feelings must very largely remain a mystery.

That Swift uses a number of styles, varying according to his theme and purpose, is one of the facts that deserve to be emphasized. Some of the works not discussed in this essay, like *Directions to Servants*, present further variations, and in a complete survey it would be necessary to consider also his parodies, such as *A Meditation upon a Broomstick* and the specimens of vapid social talk in *A Compleat Collection of Genteel and Ingenious Conversation*. Swift was a connoisseur of the different uses of language. If it is true that throughout all, or most, of these variations, the virtues of simplicity and conciseness remain as constants, is this the point which deserves priority, the aspect of his art most likely to lure a beginner on to enjoy the prodigies of wit that await him?

There is no work by Swift over which such revealing and significant differences of opinion occur as the last book of *Gulliver's Travels*. To the kind of reader who inclines towards the 'Augustan' view of him, this book is a straight attack on the filthy degradation of the human species in the name of 'Nature and Reason'; and, in so far as

Gulliver (who is Swift) rejects humanity, it is the work of a misan-thropist. 'Jonathan Swift aimed at mankind the most venomous arrow that scorn has ever yet let loose', writes Mr Carl van Doren, whose very readable biography is marred by the excessive promin-ence given to the misanthropic and tormented side of his nature. But if we see Swift first and foremost as a wit, skilled in the elaboration of ideas which do not directly represent his own beliefs, we may arrive not only at a more satisfactory interpretation of this book, but also at a more acceptable view of its author.

In this book a piquant situation is presented to us, which may be stated as follows: 'In the real world the gift of reason is bestowed upon human beings and withheld from animals. In the land of the Houyhnhnms reason has been given to horses and withheld from —.' Here we naturally pause, but we are intended to continue: '... withheld from human beings.' The Yahoos are human beings, with-out the gift of reason. Into this world comes Gulliver, different from both in that he is a human being with reason. An important factor is that everything is seen and judged from the Houyhnhnms' angle: it is their country and their point of view imposes itself. Gulliver is alone and unique. Anxious to make his hosts understand that he is not a Yahoo, he must abide the test of the physical evidence, which is against him, and here Swift, by a peculiarly inhuman detachment in his use of detail, makes us see him as the Houyhnhnms see him:

> ... he then stroked my Body very gently and looked round me several Times, after which he said it was plain I must be a perfect *Yahoo*; but that I differed very much from the rest of my Species, in the softness and whiteness and smoothness of my Skin, my want of Hair in several parts of my Body, the Shape and Shortness of my Claws behind and before, and my Affectation of walking continually on my two hinder Feet.
>
> (Ch. III.)

Gulliver's superiority in the matter of reason is, however, recog-nized; but this leads to graver embarrassment. He is obliged to give an account of the uses to which reason is put in those lands where human beings dominate. Swift takes advantage of the fact that the Houyhnhnms know nothing of wickedness, so that everything has to be explained in detail. This device, of presenting the facts as they would have to be presented to an uninitiated listener, must be regarded as one of the modes of artistic distortion. It enables Swift to order his details in an ominous way, to secure heightening and emphasis. What purports to be a cold, purely matter-of-fact statement becomes a fearful concentration of images:

> What you have told me (said my Master) upon the Subject of War, does indeed discover most admirably the Effects of that Reason you pretend to: However, it is happy that the *Shame* is greater than the *Danger*; and that Nature hath left you utterly incapable of doing much Mischief: For your Mouths lying flat with your Faces, you can hardly bite each other to any Purpose, unless by Consent. Then as to the Claws upon your Feet before and behind, they are so short and tender, that one of our *Yahoos* would drive a Dozen of yours before him. And therefore in recounting the Numbers of those who have been killed in Battle, I cannot but think that you have *said the Thing which is not.*
>
> I could not forbear shaking my Head and smiling a little at his ignorance. And, being no Stranger to the Art of War, I gave him a Description of Cannons, Culverins, Muskets, Carabines, Pistols, Bullets, Powder, Swords, Bayonets, Battles, Sieges, Retreats, Attacks, Undermines, Countermines, Bombardments, Sea-fights; Ships sunk with a Thousand Men; twenty Thousand killed on each Side; dying Groans, Limbs flying in the Air: Smoak, Noise, Confusion, trampling to Death under Horses' Feet; Flight, Pursuit, Victory; Fields strewed with Carcases left for Food to Dogs and Wolves, and Birds of Prey; Plundering, Stripping, Ravishing, Burning, and Destroying. And to set forth the Valour of my own dear Countrymen, I assured him that I had seen them blow up a Hundred Enemies at once in a Siege, and as many in a Ship, and beheld the dead Bodies come down in Pieces from the Clouds, to the great Diversion of the Spectators.
>
> (Ch. V.)

Human beings are superior to Yahoos, then, mainly in their capacity for mischief. We are obliged to consider the Yahoos in a new light. They are more primitive than human beings, more openly filthy; but are not human beings, with their complicated diseases, capable of even worse physical nastiness? Swift presents us with a number of descriptions of Yahoo behaviour, provokingly reminiscent of human behaviour but cruder; more contemptible in one sense, and yet more harmless. For example, Yahoo avarice:

> ... in some Fields of his Country, there are certain shining *Stones* of several Colours, whereof the *Yahoos* are violently fond; and when part of these *Stones* are fixed in the Earth, as it sometimes happeneth, they will dig with their claws for whole Days to get them out, and carry them away, and hide them by Heaps in their Kennels; but still looking round with great Caution, for fear their Comrades should find out their Treasure. My Master said, he could never discover the Reason of this unnatural Appetite, or how these *Stones* could be of any Use to a *Yahoo*; but now he believed it might proceed from the same Principle of *Avarice*, which I had ascribed to Mankind; that, he had once, by way of Experiment, privately removed a Heap of these *Stones* from the Place where one of his *Yahoos* had buried it: whereupon, the sordid Animal missing the Treasure, by his loud lamenting brought the whole Herd to the Place, there miserably howled, then fell to biting and tearing the rest; began to pine away, would neither eat nor sleep, nor work, until he ordered a Servant privately to convey the *Stones* into the same Hole, and hide them as before; which when his *Yahoo* had found, he presently recovered his Spirits and good Humour; but took Care to remove them to a better hiding Place; and hath ever since been a very serviceable Brute.

> (Ch. VII.)

There are similar pictures of the Yahoo treatment of a fallen favourite and a Yahoo female sexually excited. It is the human equivalent that we are continually confronted with in these descriptions. The Yahoo is a mirror in which human nature must see itself. Swift's technique here may be regarded as an extended example of the device of 'arguing through images'. The Yahoo is the image of man, but distorted: man with a difference. Each picture of the Yahoo reminds us of the odious resemblance, but if we try to escape from it by insisting on the difference we come up against another set of images, of human behaviour, which show us what the difference really amounts to. Between the two sets of images we are caught, much as

Swift's imaginary victim is caught in the two pamphlets discussed earlier.

The conclusion which Swift has forced us to entertain – that man is virtually a Yahoo or worse – is impossible and outrageous. Clearly some trick of logic has been practised upon us, and we must try to find out what it is. Where has Swift deviated from a true view of human nature to achieve this distortion? What is the relevant fact about man which he has succeeded in misrepresenting or suppressing? The answer will vary according to whether we resort to Christian orthodoxy or not. To a Christian, which Swift was, the relevant facts would be man's moral weakness owing to the Fall and the need for Christian charity in judging him. A modern, non-theological answer might be that man, in his development from primitive forms of life, has achieved only a limited rationality and morality, so that a measure of failure in all human beings must be expected.

Swift's strategy is to cause man to be judged by creatures who are unequipped to understand him sympathetically. The Houyhnhnms, living the placid life of reason, neither troubled nor inspired by irrational forces, know nothing of the indignity or the glory of the human state. They are on a different metaphysical level from man: there is no equivalent to the Fall in their history. But, as we have seen, it is their sense of values which imposes itself. The great mistake, surely, is to suppose that Swift seriously intended the Houyhnhnm standard to be applied to man. The Houyhnhnms are a device for embarrassing mankind. That Gulliver, the plain man who seems to represent average human nature, should be converted to the Houyhnhnms' standpoint is simply a part of Swift's strategy. It is also part of the strategy that Gulliver, in giving an account of the human race, should omit important truths which would have explained the more disgraceful side of the picture.

What do the Houyhnhnms represent? They may perhaps remind us of the impossible and inhuman standard of perfection which people sometimes apply to their fellow-men when they are feeling unreasonable. It is part of Swift's witty purpose here to be unreasonable. Can they represent his ideal of moral perfection? To say so is to bring his sense of values seriously into question, for the Houyhnhnms are in several respects unsympathetic, even repellent. They feel no sorrow at the death of their relatives; they marry according to the wishes of parents and friends, knowing nothing of love and courtship; and they seem depressingly deficient in urges and enthusiasms such as make life exciting, if less orderly, for human beings. As Dr Leavis wittily expresses it, 'they may have all the reason, but the Yahoos have all the life. ... The clean skin of the Houyhnhnms, in short, is stretched over a void.'[4] He identifies them with, 'Reason, Truth and Nature, the Augustan positives', but claims that, 'it was in deadly earnest that Swift appealed to these'. This would imply that Swift's art is at fault, that he fails to make his point with us because his positives are thinner and less satisfying than he realizes. But is there not some injustice here? To a sensibility as much outraged by disorder and dirt as Swift's, mere order and cleanliness must have had an appeal, but this does not mean that they were his 'positives', any more than incidental, even frequent, exasperation at human behaviour is to be labelled 'misanthropy'. One has to distinguish here between the beliefs and attitudes to which the author, as a responsible moral being, commits himself, and those very different, sometimes livelier, reactions which are a matter of temperament, and which often lend themselves irresistibly to artistic treatment. It was easier in Swift's period than later for the author to step down from one level of attitude to the other, and it is the healthier state of affairs that this should be natural. The need to distinguish between the two levels is very important for readers of Swift, and the failure to do so is a frequent occasion for misunderstanding. The Houyhn-hnms were an idea to be played with, offering scope for the indulgence of temperamental animus, but not to be taken too seriously. Is there not a slight humorous awareness in the suavity with which he dwells on their solemn simplicity and innocence?

Some modern critics think that the Houyhnhnms embody the self-sufficient ethics of contemporary Deist or neo-Stoic thinkers, to which Swift was hostile. Miss Kathleen M. Williams, in an interesting paper,[5] suggests that they represent 'an inadequate and inhuman rationalism', and that 'the negativeness of their blameless life is part of Swift's intention'. This view, whether we accept it or not, is certainly valuable as a corrective to the view that they represent Swift's ideal.

If the foregoing analysis of *Gulliver's Travels*, Book IV, is accepted, it reveals that Swift's techniques here are fundamentally similar to

those which were pointed out in the earlier works. There is an outrageous thesis to be proved, an ingenious exploitation of logic for
that purpose, and a translation of the ideas into concrete conceptions
('arguing through images'); and in the development of the concrete
elements there is a significant ordering of detail to produce a tenden-
tious distortion of the truth.

To critics who complain of Swift's negativeness, of his lack of
positives or of their inadequacy, part of the answer is that his capacity
to accommodate so much negativeness within an artistic pattern,
often transforming it into comedy, is the sign of an heroic digestion.
And an heroic digestion is what Swift, condemned to more than his
share of unpleasantness in life, most certainly had. The immense
freedom, which is also a consummate control, with which Swift
handles his material is evidence of a liberating experience for him
akin to that which it affords the reader. Perhaps we have become too
reluctant to admit to the satisfaction which satirical expression
provides. 'He gives me as much pleasure as I can bear', writes Dryden
of Juvenal. 'His spleen is raised and he raises mine.' Swift was, in
curious ways, inhibited about his positives, suffering perhaps from
certain forms of emotional impotence. This may be regarded
sympathetically as an infirmity, giving a strange aloofness, but also
a certain distinction, to the very real goodness in his nature. For an
expression of his attitude to the good life, reserved yet with more
feeling than was usual with him, the composition *On the Death of
Mrs Johnson* may again be cited. Sometimes he masked true benevolence beneath the cloak of curmudgeonliness, as in *A Letter to a
Very Young Lady*.

Both as man and as artist Swift gains by being studied in relation
to a tradition of wit which provided for a free play of fictitious attitudes. Too 'straight' a reading of certain works has led to an exaggeration of the grimmer sides to the man, and emphasis on the
element of frustration and tragedy in his life has deflected attention
from what must have been an immense delight in successful artistic
creation.

NOTES

1. Sir Herbert Read, *English Prose Style* (1928), p. 116.
2. Basil Willey, *The Eighteenth-Century Background* (1940), p. 103.

3. *The Prose Writings of Jonathan Swift*, ed. Herbert Davis (Oxford), volume IX, Introduction, pp. xxiv ff.

4. F. R. Leavis, *The Common Pursuit* (1952), p. 84.

5. 'Gulliver's Voyage to the Houyhnhnms', *A Journal of English Literary History* (December 1951).

ALEXANDER POPE

NORMAN CALLAN

Professor of English, University of London

POPE's first and most important claim to greatness is the fact that he is pre-eminently the poet of his age. As with the work of Chaucer and Shakespeare, his poetry 'dates' sharply and vividly: it crystallizes in memorable speech the emotional and intellectual attitudes of his day, and the reader who is going to receive the full effect of his poetry must be aware of him as speaking not solely for himself but for the age and society in which he lived.

If we sometimes fail to recognize this, one of the reasons is the relatively narrow appeal of Pope's culture when compared with that of Chaucer or Shakespeare. The culture of Chaucer's age, and even Shakespeare's, is more than half non-literary; it is made up of folktales, proverbs, ballads, and much else which belongs to oral tradition. When it is embedded in the literary art of a poet, the emotional overtones which go with the oral tradition persist, adding their strength to the effect of the poet's art. Thus Portia's words –

> How far that little candle throws his beams:
> So shines a good deed in a naughty world –

have fixed themselves in the memory of succeeding generations not simply because of the associations encircling the image of 'candle' on the one hand, or the exquisite modulation of phrase on the other: it is the inclusion within a single poetic statement of both a mature, sophisticated outlook and one which is traditional and unsceptical that gives the words their remarkable power. One senses that a harmony has been achieved between two different ways of looking at things, and the effect is therefore one of completeness.

Such an effect – surely one of the signs of great poetic utterance – is present in Pope's poetry too: but because the attitudes which are harmonized in, let us say, the opening lines of the *Epistle to Arbuthnot* –

> Shut, shut the door, good John, fatigued I said,
> Tie up the knocker, say I'm sick, I'm dead.
> The Dog Star rages, nay, 'tis past a doubt,
> All Bedlam, or Parnassus, is let out –

are less easily recognizable than those in Portia's words, the full effect of such a passage is often missed. By Pope's time, for good or ill, our culture had become pervasively literary; except for ridicule, poets had dismissed from their repertoire the vernacular phraseology which often makes the poetry of Shakespeare or the Authorized Version so telling; and critics, when they met it (particularly in the plays of Shakespeare), did not always recognize its effectiveness. Therefore, since Pope is a child of his time, we shall not find in his poetry that harmonizing of naïveté and self-consciousness which is so satisfying and so easily recognized in earlier writing. His harmonies are more subtle, their components more tenuous and less clearly contrasted.

The passage from the *Epistle to Arbuthnot* makes a good starting-point, for it illustrates an irony which is typical of much of Pope's later verse. A learned reference is being deliberately set off against a casual conversational tone. The 'dog star', which in Spenser would have suggested traditional astrology, is now a conscious reference to Horace, while the phrasing is effortlessly colloquial. Thus two attitudes are still combined, but both are sophisticated. In Portia's speech childlike acceptance and adult self-awareness are fused: in Pope both the component attitudes are adult and fully conscious.

A moment's reflection will show that the passage could never have been written, let alone written with such devastating assurance, without certain clearly recognized assumptions. First, it assumes a cultivated audience with a literary field of reference; secondly, an audience alive to subtle shades of manner and tone; and thirdly, an audience with whom the poet can safely be on friendly terms. In this case, of course, the 'audience' is Pope's close friend John Arbuthnot, himself a literary man; but the fact that a poem of this kind could be made public without incongruity emphasizes the nature of the readers for whom Pope was writing. They are in some measure a panel of experts, capable by training of appreciating, though not, of course, of emulating, virtuosity. This brings us face to face with two important considerations, the one relating to Pope's poetry itself, the other to our appreciation of it.

To succeed before a panel of experts demands not only innate genius but also the highest degree of acquired skill; and Pope was born with the one and acquired the other at a remarkably early age. The rigorousness of his artistic training is evident in everything he published: one is conscious of standards meditated first and then kept continually in mind. In this way it may be said that the stringency of contemporary criticism contributed somewhat to that exquisite poise of judgement which is the mark of all Pope's work. But in writing to satisfy a limited and homogeneous audience there is the risk of accepting their standards as the only possible ones. Because Pope is so much of his age, his limitations tend to be those of the culture of that age:

> Be sure yourself and your own reach to know,
> How far your genius, taste, and learning go;
> Launch not beyond your depth, but be discreet,
> And mark that point where sense and dullness meet.

By comparison with Shakespeare's *The heavens themselves, the planets and this centre*, or Milton's *Things unattempted yet in prose or rime*, these limitations may seem narrow. They were made so largely by social considerations, for literature in Pope's day was, above all, a social art, and those poets who overstepped the conventions of art overstepped the social conventions also. Such poets as Christopher Smart and William Blake are sometimes solitary voices speaking unearthly things to an unearthly audience. Pope is never that: he is a professional speaking to professionals. His achievement lies in the perfection of what his age called 'judgement' – a sense of fitness so exquisite that it transcends all mere calculation. It is from this that the excitement of Pope's poetry derives.

The second point to remember is that Pope's writing for a specialized audience in his own day presents something of a challenge for readers in ours. His awareness of his audience is important not solely, or even preponderantly, for historical reasons, but because it forms an outstanding characteristic of his poetry. In all he wrote, even in the early pastorals and 'heroic' poems, there is a sense of something shared. The nature and strength of this implied relationship varies from poem to poem. In the verse-letter to Teresa Blount 'On her Leaving the Town after the Coronation' we come as near to personal tenderness as Pope ever reached in a poem:

> In some fair ev'ning, on your elbow laid,
> You dream of triumphs in the rural shade:
> In pensive thought recall the fancied scene,
> See coronations rise on ev'ry green;

Before you pass the imaginary sights
Of lords, and earls, and dukes, and garter'd knights,
While the spread fan o'ershades your closing eyes;
Then give one flirt, and all the vision flies.
Thus vanish sceptres, coronets, and balls,
And leave you in lone woods, or empty walls!

In the epistles to Arbuthnot and Harley we are sensible of a dual relationship; the personal one between the poet and the recipient, and the wider one between the poet and an audience made up of people not unlike Arbuthnot and Harley. In *The Dunciad* and the *Essay on Man* Pope comes nearest at times to what may be called solitary utterance:

All nature is but art, unknown to thee;
All chance, direction, which thou canst not see;
All discord, harmony not understood;
All partial evil, universal good:
And, spite of pride, in erring reason's spite,
One truth is clear, Whatever is, is right.

Yet even in this passage from the *Essay on Man* he assumes sufficient understanding on the part of his audience to prevent them from taking his words as an outburst of personal complacency. That the words have been so often quoted as evidence of Pope's 'facile optimism' demonstrates clearly enough how lack of such understanding can destroy the effect of his poetry.

Pope, in fact, presents a remarkable example of the poet who is topical without being ephemeral, and it is the business of his readers therefore to make something of an imaginative leap, to put themselves in something of the frame of mind of Pope's contemporaries. The nature of this leap is easier to understand than to define. On the one hand, it is obvious that much of the detailed contemporary reference in a poem like *The Dunciad* has lost its immediacy; historical research, though very necessary for the scholar, will not bring it back. On the other hand, the reader who fails to recognize its literary, and especially its Homeric and Virgilian, background, will never come within range of its full effect. What is required is not primarily the ability to recognize echoes of earlier poetry: that is a valuable talent for those who have it, and for those who have it not there are always footnotes. Rather, it is the knack of recognizing and relishing what the Augustans called 'imitation', the art of re-creating *in strictly contemporary form* something that had been written by a poet of an earlier age.

That the Augustan age was the first to define imitation critically and practise it systematically is not surprising. Poets like Dryden and Pope are intensely aware of the traditions of European literature, and by imitating Horace or Juvenal or Donne they regard themselves as both preserving and continuing the tradition. Secondly, they and their readers are delighted to see something old and well known given a suddenly new significance by being placed in a new context. The advice which Horace gave about using words –

> dixeris egregie notum si callida verbum
> rediderit inctura novum –*

applies to poems as a whole. Almost all Pope's poems are 'imitations', and the ability to recognize at least some of the resemblances is necessary for an adequate response to his poetry. These imitations are not in any sense antiquarian efforts to write in the style of some earlier poet: that he would have regarded as mere pedantry. Rather, they are attempts to re-create the effect of a poem (or type of poem) as a whole in contemporary terms.

For the newcomer to eighteenth-century poetry the term 'imitation', with its suggestion of an intellectual *tour-de-force*, may prove something of a stumbling-block. In point of fact, the framework enabled Pope to organize within the context of a single poem a remarkable diversity of appeal. The following passage from the *Pastorals* (some of Pope's earliest published work) will show clearly what happens:

> Resound, ye hills, resound my mournful strain!
> Of perjur'd Doris, dying I complain.
> Here, where the mountains less'ning as they rise
> Lose the low vales, and steal into the skies:
> While lab'ring oxen, spent with toil and heat,
> In their loose traces from the field retreat:
> While curling smokes from village tops are seen,
> And the fleet shades glide o'er the dusky green. ...

* 'You will advance your reputation if, by skilful placing, you give an old word a new meaning.'

Pope is here imitating the Virgilian eclogue, and the skill with which he has suggested the atmosphere of the original without recourse to archaic vocabulary or syntax is remarkable. The sense of reverence and affection for Virgil and the Virgilian tradition which descends through Spenser, Milton, and Dryden forms, as it were, the ground-work on which the other levels of feeling lie. On further analysis the passage is seen as a texture of specific echoes, each carrying its own charge of emotion – the third line a direct borrowing from Virgil's ninth eclogue,[1] the fifth and sixth from Milton's *Comus* and (less directly) from *The Faerie Queene*, the last two from Dryden's trans-lation of the first eclogue:

> For see, yon sunny hill the shade extends,
> And curling smoke from cottages ascends.

Thus within a short passage Pope has managed delicately to hint the main line of English pastoral in a way which his readers will quickly recognize.

And when we turn from the literary aspects of the piece to its more obvious visual ones we meet this same combination of emotion and conscious allusion. Pope is quite clearly 'composing' a landscape. Here is a picture suggestive of the countryside in the Thames valley; but suggestive also of the paintings of Claude Lorraine (whom Pope, one feels, must have had in mind). Thus even the direct visual appeal is in some measure derivative, and one begins to wonder how the piece avoids frigidity. The answer is undoubtedly in the language which Pope uses, again with astonishing restraint. Regarded separ-ately the words 'less'ning ... rise ... lose ... steal ... curling ... fleet ... glide' are in no way remarkable: together they produce a subtle effect of mobility which keeps the lines stealthily alive and stirring. It would be absurd to load a fragment such as this with critical implications out of all proportion to the gravity of the poetic occasion: nevertheless, one may glimpse, even here, below the urbane and charming surface, forces at work which would not be suspected at first reading.

To tease out the strands of a poem will not, of course, explain its effect on the reader: but analysis of this kind is worth while partly because it may give the beginner with Pope some idea of the inter-weaving and counterpointing of strains of feeling to be found

almost everywhere in his poetry, and partly because it is only by some
such illustration that one can rebut the assertion that Pope's poetry
is unemotional – the product (as Matthew Arnold thought) of an
age of prose and reason. Let us, then, examine two more instances:
one a short extract from Pope's translation of the *Iliad* which has
come in for much ill-considered abuse since Coleridge cited it as an
example of pseudo-diction, the other a poem of some length,
Eloisa to Abelard, which raises in an acute form some difficulties connected with the approach to Pope's poetry.

First, then, the lines which close the eighth book of the *Iliad*:

> So many flames before proud Ilion blaze,
> And lighten glimm'ring Xanthus with their rays:
> The long reflections of the distant fires
> Gleam on the walls, and tremble on the spires.
> A thousand piles the dusky horrors gild,
> And shoot a shady lustre o'er the field.
> Full fifty guards each flaming pile attend,
> Whose umber'd arms, by fits, thick flashes send.
> Loud neigh the coursers o'er their heaps of corn,
> And ardent warriors wait the rising morn.

To anyone looking impartially at this passage, with its brilliant lights
and deep shadows, it will occur that Pope is thinking as much about
painting (and perhaps about Rembrandt's 'Night Watch' in particular)
as about Homer. It is, in fact, an essay in interpreting a certain style
of painting in terms of poetry. Again it is the language – 'glimmering
... umber'd arms ... thick flashes ...' – which reveals the excitement
underlying the more formal elements of the composition. Coleridge[2]
mistook the nature of the passage because he was thinking about
Homer more than about Pope; and certainly there is no strong tie
between the Greek and the English. But what matters is that a notable
passage in Homer has released in Pope this spring of imagination
which fuses the emotional associations of the original with feelings
closer to his own time.

Eloisa to Abelard is an imitation of the Ovidian heroic epistle. It is
a poem whose difficulties are more specifically those of the eighteenth
century than any other work of Pope: yet it cannot be ignored, since
it shows in a unique and vivid way certain important qualities of
Pope's mind. The theme of *Eloisa* is frustrated passion; and for an age

in which the novels of Richardson were best sellers, Pope's elaborate and explicit analysis of the feelings of a woman torn from her lover and forced to recant against her will had a strong appeal. That the poem is brilliantly executed there can be no doubt. Pope is master of the rhetoric of passion throughout its range, from –

> Still as the sea, ere winds were taught to blow,
> Or moving spirit bade the waters flow;
> Soft as the slumbers of a saint forgiven,
> And mild as opening gleams of promis'd heav'n ...

to –

> When from the censer clouds of fragrance roll,
> And swelling organs lift the rising soul,
> One thought of thee puts all the pomp to flight,
> Priests, tapers, temples, swim before my sight:
> In seas of flame my plunging soul is drown'd,
> While altars blaze, and angels tremble round ...

and his manipulation of the antithetic couplet is masterly in its sustained variety. Yet such considerations are only partly satisfying, and for two reasons. First, because it is difficult for us who live in an age in which the emotion of poetry is almost invariably private, to project ourselves into one in which it was almost invariably public. This is something about which one can do very little, and it is by no means an absolute obstacle to appreciating the poem. The second is more fundamental. It concerns the nature of the emotion in the poem. Usually both those who like *Eloisa* and those who do not assume that Pope's feeling (or lack of it) must focus on the central figure of the heroine. In fact, it focuses on Ovid – or rather the kind of poetry which Ovid first created.

Eloisa to Abelard is an astonishing evocation of an earlier poet's way of writing: an evocation which goes far beyond the copying of mannerisms, or the hinting of a manner. Ovid comes literally alive in eighteenth-century verse: to such an extent that for anyone who is well acquainted with Pope's poem it is impossible to read the *Heroïdes* without thinking of it. Pope responds to the 'story' of Eloisa by seeing her in terms of an Ovidian heroine. From the vividness and appositeness of this response arises the poem's intensity.

When we realize this we have in our hands a key to the emotional range of Pope's poetry. He responded to different kinds of theme with remarkable variousness, and both the excitement and the variety in his poetry derive from the perfect adjustment of style to feeling in such widely differing poems as *The Rape of the Lock* and *The Dunciad*, or *Eloisa* and the verse-letter to Teresa Blount quoted on p. 253.

It is, of course, true that all considerable poetry depends partly on the relationship between style and content; but poetry like Pope's is more dependent on our recognizing this relationship than, let us say, poetry like Wordsworth's. Moreover, there are two kinds of relationship possible: that in which the poet seems to gain his effect by triumphing over his material, and that in which he seems to suggest that no difficulties exist because the medium is so perfectly suited to the theme. Donne's poetry, Milton's, and perhaps Wordsworth's belongs to the first kind; Pope's to the second. Inevitably the first is more spectacular: it conveys a greater sense of power, if only because it calls attention to its own emotional urgency. The second calls for far greater perceptiveness on the part of the reader. If we fail to notice the exquisite judgement with which theme and tone are linked in 'To a Young Lady' or *The Rape of the Lock*, or the imaginative power with which the epic possibilities of the theme have been exploited in *The Dunciad*, we shall see little to attract us but technical virtuosity.

Moreover, unless we recognize in this term 'judgement' something more than an ability to know when to stop, we shall certainly miss most of the overtones in Pope's poetry. In Pope's case 'judgement' is rather the intuitive perception of the fitness of means for an end. It is from this perception and from the fusion of materials produced in its application that the emotional force arises.

It is axiomatic, then, that all Pope's poems have their roots in some original of an earlier period, and that this original is of greater importance in his poetry than in that of most English poets. It is, in fact, by the use of this original as a point of reference that associations, both emotional and intellectual, and shades of tone can be controlled. The method is economical and of a kind which one would expect from a poet who wrote his poems on the backs of his friends' letters: it is subtle, compressed, and allusive. It makes stringent demands on the reader's mental and emotional alertness.

The Rape of the Lock and *The Dunciad* are both mock-heroic poems, depending on the three great classical epics. As they are both satirical poems, however, the function of such reference is different from anything we have seen so far. Primarily it is to establish a scale of values whose extreme limits are epic sublimity and human pettiness, and whose point of equilibrium is the 'good sense' which conditions the outlook, social, moral, and artistic, of the period. It is as a philosophic rather than an emotional denominator that the 'original' is mainly employed.

As most people know, *The Rape of the Lock* is a poem ridiculing the fashionable world of Pope's day, its immediate aim being to laugh two families of his acquaintance into making up a quarrel over a somewhat trivial incident. This quarrel is presented in terms of the great epic contentions (Greeks and Trojans, God and Satan), and the effect of the poem, which for brilliance of conception and consistency of execution is unsurpassed in our literature, lies in the exquisite adjustment between the epic and mundane planes on which it moves. Nothing could better illustrate Pope's power of bearing in mind at one and the same time general design and particular detail. Everything is kept in proportion, from the comparative importance of the quarrels themselves to the physical measurements of armour and costume. Thus the gods, whose Olympian indifference to the human predicament so heightens the pathos of the *Iliad*, become, in Pope's poem, the sylphs and gnomes of Rosicrucian mythology[3] derived from a frivolous French romance. Even their names (Zephyretta, Momentilla) are suitably diminished. When the Homeric Zeus summons the assembly of the gods at the opening of the eighth book of the *Iliad* he threatens all who disobey with appropriately massive penalties:

> Back to the skies with shame he shall be driv'n,
> Gash'd with dishonest wounds, the scorn of Heav'n:
> Or far, oh far from steep Olympus thrown,
> Low in the dark Tartarean gulf shall groan;
> With burning chains fix'd to the brazen floors,
> And lock'd by Hell's inexorable doors; ...

The Miltonic echoes in this passage are suitably paralleled by echoes from *The Tempest* when Ariel summons an assembly to brief his subordinate sylphs in the second canto of *The Rape of the Lock*:

> Whatever spirit, careless of his charge,
> His post neglects, or leaves the fair at large,

> Shall feel sharp vengeance soon o'ertake his sins,
> Be stopp'd in vials, or transfix'd with pins;
> Or plunged in lakes of bitter washes lie,
> Or wedg'd whole ages in a bodkin's eye. ...

The bite of this mock-heroic comparison lies in the social criticism it achieves so adroitly. It is not simply a display of literary virtuosity, but a superb example of what Dryden called fine raillery, which tickles while it hurts. Pope's description of the passage as 'parody' must not be taken too strictly in our modern sense of the word, which implies that the entrenched past is being made to look ridiculous in terms of the enlightened present. Here it is the trivial present which is being mocked in the light of the past.

Other poets of Pope's day made effective use of this mock-heroic scale, but it is the measure of Pope's genius and of his superiority over his contemporaries that he alone never allows it to become rigid. By a continual adjustment of the two planes he is enabled to move without apparent effort from ridicule bordering on farce (as in the last passage) to something like direct moral comment (as in the one which follows):[4]

> Say, why are beauties prais'd and honour'd most,
> The wise man's passion, and the vain man's toast?
> Why deck'd with all that land and sea afford,
> Why angels call'd, and angel-like ador'd?
> Why round our coaches crowd the white-glov'd beaux,
> Why bows the side-box from its inmost rows?
> How vain are all these glories, all our pains,
> Unless good sense preserve what beauty gains:
> That men may say, when we the front-box grace:
> Behold the first in virtue, as in face ... &c. &c.

This derives from a *locus classicus* of the *Iliad*, the speech of Sarpedon to Glaucus in the twelfth book:

> Why boast we, Glaucus! our extended reign,
> Where Xanthus' streams enrich the Lycian plain;
> Our num'rous herds that range the fruitful field,
> And hills where vines their purple harvest yield,
> Our foaming bowls with purer nectar crown'd,
> Our feasts enhanc'd with music's sprightly sound?

Why on those shores are we with joy survey'd,
Admir'd as heroes, and as gods obey'd?
Unless great acts superior merit prove,
And vindicate the bounteous Pow'rs above.
'Tis ours, the dignity they give, to grace;
The first in valour as the first in place ... &c. &c.

It will be seen at once that whereas the parallels in the previous pair
of passages depend on outrageous fantasy, here they gain their effect
by a closer and more sober approximation. In this way the tone is
deepened without being distorted, and Pope is able, as he says, to
'open more clearly the moral of the poem'. The skill with which he
has succeeded will perhaps be more evident if we recall the violence
which Coleridge had to do to *The Ancient Mariner* when faced with a
similar problem.

The Dunciad is not so perfect artistically as *The Rape of the Lock*.[5]
It began as a 'brief sketch', which Swift may have saved from the fire
in 1726, and grew by a process of accretion until it reached its final
form as *The Dunciad in Four Books* in 1743. It lacks, therefore, the
precision of form to be found in *The Rape of the Lock* or in that other
formally exquisite poem *An Essay on Man*. But the fact is that the
accretive method of composition was the one which suited Pope, as
it has suited many other fine writers. *Clarissa*, for all its volubility, is a
more satisfying novel than the carefully planned *Charles Grandison*;
Pickwick Papers than *Little Dorritt*. And *The Dunciad*, though its
method of growth undoubtedly makes difficulty for the reader, has
always seemed to me most representative of Pope's poetic genius.[6]

The most obvious, though not the most troublesome, aspect of
the poem is its personalities. These were, perhaps, its starting-point,
and it is all too easy, if we take them out of relation to the rest, to
see *The Dunciad* as an arbitrary and ill-natured attack on those who,
whether living or dead, had offended Pope. In the final form of the
poem, however, they fall into place as symbols of moral and intellectual obtuseness, much as the personalities of the *Purgatorio* epitomize
particular aspects of sin, and not merely Dante's private enemies.

Of its kind, *The Dunciad* may fairly be called Pope's vision of
torment. From the laborious annotator –

There, dim in clouds, the poring scholiasts mark,
Wits, who, like owls, see only in the dark.

> A lumber-house of books in ev'ry head,
> For ever reading, never to be read. ...

to the vulgar spectacles of pantomime –

> All sudden, Gorgons hiss, and dragons glare,
> And ten-horn'd fiends and giants rush to war.
> Hell rises, heaven descends, and dance on earth:
> Gods, imps and monsters, music, rage and mirth,
> A fire, a jig, a battle and a ball,
> Till one wide conflagration swallows all. ...

Pope sees them all as part of a spiritual and intellectual decay which, in this long passage from the third book, he pictures as overwhelming England. Whether he was justified in taking this gloomy view is debatable. Today we accept as inevitable an appalling gulf between literature and other kinds of writing; and both worlds suffer because of it. Pope has not learned to make this dichotomy – indeed, it was just this he was fighting against – and one cannot fully appreciate the poem until one recognizes the genuine moral indignation behind it.

An index of this indignation is the way he uses the mock-heroic technique. In *The Rape of the Lock*, Belinda, the Baron, Sir Plume, and the rest are dwarfed, and so rendered harmless, by their epic counterparts: in *The Dunciad*, the Burnets, Oldmixons, and Cookes, themselves petty and contemptible, are inflated to epic proportions in the gargantuan caricatures of the first two books.

The use of the mock-heroic scale is thus the reverse of that in *The Rape of the Lock*, where Pope's vision of the pretty, if absurd, world of fashion has all the delicacy of a landscape seen through the wrong end of a telescope. In *The Dunciad*, meanness is magnified until it becomes as grotesque as a Daumier cartoon. This method makes it easier for Pope to move from the level of mockery to that of prophetic commination; and since the indictment of the poem is so much graver than that of *The Rape of the Lock*, such transitions are both more frequent and more moving. Pope's own favourite was the fourth book, but throughout the work, and especially in the third book where Dullness is generalized in terms of history, one meets passages where the poetry becomes the physical manifestation of desolation:

Lo! Rome herself, proud mistress now no more
Of arts, but thund'ring against heathen lore;
Her gray-hair'd synods damning books unread,
And Bacon trembling for his brazen head.
Padua, with sighs, beholds her Livy burn,
And ev'n th' Antipodes Virgilius mourn.
See, the Cirque falls, th' unpillar'd temple nods,
Streets paved with heroes, Tyber choak'd with gods:
Till Peter's keys some christen'd Jove adorn,
And Pan to Moses lends his pagan horn.

We have so far observed peculiarities of Pope's work as they are to be seen in particular poems. These, however, arise from something which is to be recognized in all his poetry – the remarkable integration of the world in which his imagination moves. The concept of unified (or dissociated) sensibility has been of great value to our understanding of seventeenth-century poetry. Unluckily, however, we have come to regard a unified sensibility as the perquisite of a small group of writers: we are too ready to say with Falstaff, 'Who hath it? He that died before 1660.' Pope's poetic universe is no less closely integrated than that of (say) George Herbert, as I hope will appear. But we must also beware of making another mistake by claiming that it is the *same* universe, and that the approach to the poetry of Pope is not essentially different from the approach to that of a seventeenth-century metaphysical. The terminal points of Herbert's universe or Donne's are God and Man: Pope's begins and ends with Man. But granted the limitation this imposes, there remains between that beginning and end the almost infinite scope of human activity. And it is the way his poetry expresses one aspect of this multifariousness in terms of another that makes it ultimately so satisfying. Pope does not, like Homer's steeds, leap from heaven to earth in one bound; but he can move from Augustan to Aztec civilization without apparent effort, or from the exploration of literature to the exploration of the Sahara and back again without seeming to stir:

One simile, that solitary shines
In the dry desert of a thousand lines ...

and it is difficult to say which seems more vivid – thought or image. He may not see a world in a grain of sand, but the ceaseless industry of the insect and of the scribbler become inseparable:

> Who shames a scribbler? Break one cobweb through,
> He spins the slight, self-pleasing thread anew;
> Destroy his fib, or sophistry; in vain,
> The creature's at his dirty work again,
> Throned in the centre of his thin designs,
> Proud of a vast extent of flimsy lines. ...

In all such passages – and Pope's poetry is crammed with them – it is possible to see, when we pause to notice it, an exquisite sense of equivalence between thought and image. We are not at one moment talking about scribblers and the next about spiders; we are speaking about both at once.

If we fail to recognize the unified sensibility inherent in Pope's poetry it is probably for two reasons. The first is the astonishing ease and speed with which the identification of thought and image is reached:

> Something, whose truth convinced at sight we find.
> That gives us back the image of our mind. ...

This second couplet of Pope's definition of wit in general admirably describes the process of his own. It is a process different altogether from, let us say, an image of Donne:

> While thus to ballast Love I thought,
> And so more steadily to have gone,
> With wares that would sink admiration,
> I saw I had Love's pinnace overfraught,
> Every thy hair for Love to work upon
> Is much too much, some fitter must be sought. ...

In this passage from *Aire and Angels*, Donne enumerates all the details of his image, not because he has a laborious mind but because the details are all important. Like many of his images, this is a developing one: and it is the development quite as much as the total image that is significant. Now take a couplet from Pope's *Epistle to Augustus*:

> Authors, like coins, grow dear as they grow old;
> It is the rust we value, not the gold. ...

The identification has been achieved 'at sight': the 'image' has been given back to the thought without any perceptible interval. We do not dwell on the nature of old coins and writers, because Pope does not require us to do so. He has made his point with economy and restraint; with the result that he leaves us meditating the thought itself rather than the image which has driven it home.

The object of such comparison is not to belittle one poet at the expense of another – a fruitless, though popular, form of criticism. Donne's image is aimed at making apprehensible a metaphysical experience, Pope's at rendering vivid and active 'a known truth that has been suffered to lie neglected'. Both aims are important and both are difficult. Donne moved from *a* to *b* and from *b* to *c* because the process by which he reaches the conclusion is as important as the conclusion itself. With Pope it is the terminals which matter: the greater the speed of the spark between them, the greater the shock administered to the reader.

The second reason why we tend to neglect the fine qualities of Pope's imagery is that the distance to be travelled, as it were, between thought and image is seldom so great as to give the reader pause. Even if it is considerable, as when we are whisked from the emendations of scholars preserved in a poet's text to fossils preserved in amber –

> Pretty! in amber to observe the forms
> Of hairs, or straws, or dirt, or grubs, or worms!
> The things, we know, are neither rich nor rare,
> But wonder how the devil they got there –

we are not asked to go beyond the range of human observation. Pedants and desiccated bugs are both part of the social world; both odd, and both equally worthless. However he may develop an image, as, for instance, in the following lines:

> A little learning is a dangerous thing;
> Drink deep, or taste not the Pierian spring:
> There shallow drafts intoxicate the brain,
> And drinking largely sobers us again –

the same holds good. Here the activities of the expert poet and expert drinker meet on the level of social experience and without derogation to either term of the equation. And that they are able to do so is due to the integration of the world of Pope's poetry: the refinements of the mind are not things apart from daily existence, they are a means of enjoying the existence more fully.

The *Essay on Criticism* from which these lines are taken is a poem that has been somewhat spoiled by attempts to use it as a text illustrating the critical opinions of the period. Most of the material derives from the great critics of former ages – Aristotle, Horace, Quintilian, Boileau – but it is material which had been handled by almost every critic of the day, and of which all educated readers would have been aware. What we miss (and Pope's contemporaries assuredly did not) by treating the poem in this way is the life which informs the aridities of literary criticism:

> First follow Nature, and your judgement frame
> By her just standard, which is still the same:
> Unerring Nature, still divinely bright,
> One clear, unchang'd, and universal light,
> Life, force, and beauty must to all impart,
> At once the source, and end, and test of art.
> Art from that fund each just supply provides,
> Works without show, and without pomp presides:
> In some fair body thus th' informing soul
> With spirits feeds, with vigour fills the whole,
> Each motion guides, and every nerve sustains;
> Itself unseen, but in th' effects remains. ...

The ultimate derivation of this is probably Aristotle's assertion that a work of art must be a living organism; but if we can ignore the critical dicta we see that a passage which sets out to instruct us in how to form our literary judgements develops into something of much wider significance. From abstract assertion we move to an unobtrusive but telling political image, and from the body politic to the body human in the last four lines. The *Essay on Criticism* is early work; in fact, it is the first poem of any length which Pope published. Thus, as we should expect, the fusion between thought and image is less instantaneous and less complete than in a passage such as the following from the first of the *Moral Essays*, published more than twenty years later:

> Nor will life's stream for observation stay,
> It hurries all too fast to mark their way:
> In vain sedate reflections we would make,
> When half our knowledge we must snatch, not take.
> Oft, in the passion's wild rotation tost,
> Our spring of action to ourselves is lost:

Tir'd, not determin'd, to the last we yield,
And what comes then is master of the field.
As the last image of that troubl'd heap
When sense subsides, and fancy sports in sleep,
(Though past the recollection of the thought)
Becomes the stuff of which our dream is wrought:
Something as dim to our internal view
Is thus, perhaps, the cause of most we do. ...

Here material from Horace, Shakespeare, and Hobbes is so closely interwoven with the imagery that it is scarcely distinguishable. But in the *Essay on Criticism* we see what Coleridge called the esemplastic power of a poet's imagination beginning to function, fusing, though not quite perfectly, such disparate things as literary criticism, the human microcosm, and the administration of public money.

If we can rid our minds of the preconception that Pope's poetry is 'intellectual', the strongest impression we shall gain is that of a constant interchange between various sorts of human activity and experience. It is a restless effect, like that of sunlight on disturbed water, and one cannot fix one's eyes on it for too long. One is not, of course, meant to. It is on the central clue of thought that the reader is asked to concentrate, allowing the flash and interplay of image and allusion around him to act as a stimulus to sharper perception. Nevertheless, if for a while we allow ourselves to forget the conceptual element of the poetry and watch, as it were, the medium in which it is suspended, we find ourselves in a world as unexpected and varied as a kaleidoscope, never knowing quite what form the pattern will take next or what pieces will compose the pattern; yet recognizing certain general shapes as belonging distinctively to Pope's poetry. To call this medium Pope's 'illustration' or Pope's 'wit' and to distinguish it from his thought would be entirely misleading. In a passage such as this (from the first of the *Moral Essays*) –

Know, God and Nature only are the same:
In man, the judgement shoots at flying game,
A bird of passage! gone as soon as found,
Now in the moon, perhaps, now underground. ...

the imagery, which embraces partridge shooting, natural history, and *Orlando Furioso, is* the thought – or perhaps one might better say 'is the way Pope has this kind of thought'. Or again, take a simpler passage from the *Essay on Man* –

> What nothing earthly gives, or can destroy,
> The soul's calm sunshine, and the heart-felt joy
> Is virtue's prize. A better would you fix?
> Then give humility a coach and six,
> Justice a conqueror's sword, or truth a gown,
> Or public spirit its great cure, a crown.

Once more the passage is fascinating as a reflection of the poet's mind, not primarily as a philosophic aphorism.

The fact is that in the first couplet of his definition –

> True wit is Nature to advantage dress'd;
> What oft was thought, but ne'er so well express'd –

Pope is far from just to Pope: it suggests, as Johnson indicated, the mere verbal elaboration of an accepted commonplace. Had he said 'what oft was thought, but ne'er so well thought', English literature would have wanted one immortal couplet, but Pope would have come nearer to describing his own poetic processes. The Augustan age delighted in the great simplifications of philosophy and science, because it seemed to them that the universe itself was simple. It is Pope's distinction that in his poetry these commonplaces emerge not as abstractions relevant only to the rarefied atmosphere of science or philosophy, but as operative in the concrete and highly detailed day-to-day life of his age.

NOTES

1. The reader of Augustan poetry should not be unduly daunted by the field of classical reference. In Pope's time most of the major poems of classical literature had been rendered into English: the *Iliad* and *Odyssey* by Chapman (and, of course, by Pope himself); the whole of Virgil by Dryden; Ovid (in part) by George Sandys, and by a host of occasional translators (among them Dryden and Pope). These versions formed as much part of the Augustan literary background as the original poems, and the reader who will take the trouble to study them will be well equipped for eighteenth-century literature.

Horace was (and still is) an insuperable problem. A passable verse translation appeared in 1747 (republished by Unit Books with the Latin text in 1902). But the best reference for the hesitant Latinist is the Loeb edition of Horace's works with a prose translation by Fairclough.

2. *Biographia Literaria* (London, 1894), p. 19 (footnote). Coleridge misquotes the passage from Pope.

3. The first version of *The Rape of the Lock* (1712) contained no reference to the sylphs and gnomes, which were added in the final version (1714). For the two versions and a valuable introduction, see the edition by Geoffrey Tillotson (1940).

4. This point has already been made by John Butt in his essay 'The Inspiration of Pope's Poetry' (*Essays Presented to David Nichol Smith*, 1945).

5. For the growth of the poem, and an indispensable introduction, see the edition by James Sutherland (1943). I should like to take the opportunity of acknowledging the debt this chapter owes to the assistance of Professor Sutherland.

6. See Ian Jack, *Augustan Satire* (1952). Dr Jack dissents from this view.

POETRY IN THE EIGHTEENTH CENTURY[1]

T. S. ELIOT

THERE is an essay to be written on the quotations which Sir Walter Scott used for the chapter headings of his novels, to illustrate the wide reading and critical good taste of that novelist. It is a great many years ago – about thirty years ago[*] – that I was struck by a quotation of four lines; I cannot now remember at what chapter of which of Scott's novels it is placed:

> His fall was destin'd to a barren strand,
> A petty fortress, and a dubious hand;
> He left the name, at which the world grew pale,
> To point a moral, or adorn a tale.

It was not for a good many years after, that I read *The Vanity of Human Wishes*, but the impression which the whole poem made upon me was only a confirmation of the impression which the four lines had made upon me long before. These lines, especially the first two, with their just inevitable sequence of *barren*, *petty*, and *dubious*, still seem to me among the finest that have ever been written in that particular idiom.

It is dangerous to generalize about the poetry of the eighteenth century as about that of any other age; for it was, like any other age, an age of transition. We are accustomed to make a rough tripartite division between the poetry of the age of Pope, the poetry of sentimental philosophizing – Thomson, Young, Cowper – and the early Romantic movement. What really happened is that after Pope there was no one who thought and felt nearly enough like Pope to be able to use his language quite successfully; but a good many second-rate writers tried to write something like it, unaware of the fact that the change of sensibility demanded a change of idiom. Sensibility alters from generation to generation in everybody, whether we will or no; but expression is only altered by a man of genius. A great many second-rate poets, in fact, are second-rate just for this reason, that they have not the sensitiveness and consciousness

* Thirty years before 1930, when this essay was written.

271

to perceive that they feel differently from the preceding generation, and therefore must use words differently. In the eighteenth century there are a good many second-rate poets: and mostly they are second-rate because they were incompetent to find a style of writing for themselves, suited to the matter they wanted to talk about and the way in which they apprehended this matter.

In such a period the poets who are still worth reading may be of two kinds: those who, however imperfectly, attempted innovations in idiom, and those who were just conservative enough in sensibility to be able to devise an interesting variation on the old idiom. The originality of Gray and Collins consists in their adaptation of an Augustan style to an eighteenth-century sensibility. The originality of Goldsmith consists in his having the old and the new in such just proportion that there is no conflict; he is Augustan and also sentimental and rural without discordance. Of all the eighteenth-century poets, Johnson is the nearest to a die-hard. And of all the eighteenth-century poets, Goldsmith and Johnson deserve fame because they used the form of Pope beautifully, without ever being mere imitators. And from the point of view of the artisan of verse, their kind of originality is as remarkable as any other: indeed, to be original with the *minimum* of alteration is sometimes more distinguished than to be original with the *maximum* of alteration.

Certain qualities are to be expected of any type of good verse at any time; we may say the qualities which good verse shares with good prose. Hardly any good poet in English has written *bad* prose; and some English poets have been among the greatest of English prose writers. The finest prose writer of Shakespeare's time was, I think, Shakespeare himself; Milton and Dryden were among the greatest prose writers of their times. Wordsworth and Coleridge may be cited, and Keats; and Shelley – not I think in his correspondence, but certainly in his *Defence of Poetry*. This is not a sign of versatility but of unity. For there are qualities essential to good prose which are essential to good verse as well; and we may say positively with Mr Ezra Pound, that verse must be at least as well written as prose. We may even say that the originality of some poets has consisted in their finding a way of saying in verse what no one else has been able to say except in prose written or spoken. Such is the originality of Donne, who, though employing an elaborate metric and an uncommon vocabulary, yet manages to maintain a tone of direct informal address. The talent of Dryden is exactly the same: the difference is only that the speech which he uses is that of a more formal age. Donne makes poetry out of a learned but colloquial dialogue speech, Dryden out of the prose of political oratory; and Pope out of the most polished drawing-room manner. And of Goldsmith and Johnson we can say the same; their verse is poetry partly because it has the virtues of good prose.

Those who condemn or ignore *en bloc* the poetry of the eighteenth century on the ground that it is 'prosaic' are stumbling over an uncertainty of meaning of the word 'prosaic' to arrive at exactly the wrong conclusion. One does not need to examine a great deal of the inferior verse of the eighteenth century to realize that the trouble with it is that it is not prosaic enough. We are inclined to use 'prosaic' as meaning not only 'like prose', but as 'lacking poetic beauty' – and the Oxford and every other dictionary give us warrant for such use. Only, we ought to distinguish between poetry which is like *good* prose, and poetry which is like *bad* prose. And even so, I believe more prose is bad because it is like bad poetry, than poetry is bad because it is like bad prose. And to have the virtues of good prose is the first and minimum requirement of good poetry.

If you look at the bad verse of any age, you will find most of it lacking in the virtues of prose. When there is a period of good verse, it has often been preceded by a period in which verse was bad because it was too poetic, too artificial; and it is very commonly followed by such another period. The development of blank verse in the hands of Shakespeare and some of his contemporaries was the work of adapting a medium which to begin with was almost in-tractably poetic, so that it could carry the burdens and exhibit the subtleties of prose; and they accomplished this before prose was highly developed. The work of Donne, in a lesser form, was the same. It has prose virtues, and the heavy toil of his minor imitators was wholly to degrade the idiom of Donne into a lifeless verse con-vention. Speech meanwhile was changing, and Dryden appeared to cleanse the language of verse and once more bring it back to the prose order. For this reason he is a great poet.

The idiom of the Augustan age could not last, for the age itself could not last. But so positive was the culture of that age, that for many years the ablest writers were still naturally in sympathy with it; and it crushed a number of smaller men who felt differently but did not dare to face the fact, and who poured their new wine – always thin, but sometimes of good flavour – into the old bottles. Yet the influence of Dryden and Pope over the middle of the eighteenth century is by no means so great, or so noxious, as has been supposed. A good part of the dreariest verse of the time is written under the shadow of Milton.

> Far in the watery waste, where his broad wave
> From world to world the vast Atlantic rolls,
> On from the piny shores of Labrador
> To frozen Thule east, her airy height
> Aloft to heaven remotest Kilda lifts.
>
> (MALLET: *Amyntor and Theodora*)

> Thus far of beauty and the pleasing forms
> Which man's untutored fancy, from the scenes
> Imperfect of this ever changing world
> Creates; and views, enamoured.
>
> (AKENSIDE: *Pleasures of the Imagination*)

But besides this Miltonic stuff, which is respectable only because Cowper, Thomson, and Young made this line the vehicle for reflection and for observation of nature which prepared the way for Wordsworth; and besides the innumerable Odes, of which none but Gray's and Collins's are remembered, there was a considerable output of five-foot couplets of which one can only say that this form of verse is hardly more unsuitable for what the man had to say than any other would have been. Of such is the *Botanic Garden* and its competitors.

> Who that beholds the summer's glistening swarms,
> Ten thousand thousand gaily gilded forms,
> In violet dance of mixed rotation play,
> Bask in the beam, and beautify the day....
>
> (BROOKE: *Universal Beauty*)

This is decadence. The eighteenth century in English verse is not, after Pope, Swift, Prior, and Gay, an age of courtly verse. It seems more like an age of retired country clergymen and schoolmasters.

It is cursed with a Pastoral convention – Collins's Eclogues are bad enough, and those of Shenstone consummately dull – and a ruminative mind. And it is intolerably poetic. Instead of working out the proper form for its matter, when it has any, and informing verse with prose virtues, it merely applies the magniloquence of Milton or the neatness of Pope to matter which is wholly unprepared for it; so that what the writers have to say always appears surprised at the way in which they choose to say it.

In this rural, pastoral, meditative age Johnson is the most alien figure. Goldsmith is more a poet of his time, with his melting sentiment just saved by the precision of his language. But Johnson remains a townsman, if certainly not a courtier; a student of mankind not of natural history; a great prose writer; with no tolerance of swains and milkmaids. He has more in common in spirit with Crabbe than with any of his contemporaries; at the same time he is the last Augustan. He is in no way an imitator of Dryden or Pope; very close to them in idiom, he gives his verse a wholly personal stamp.

The two Satires [which follow] are Johnson's only exercises in this genre. *London* appeared in 1738; *The Vanity of Human Wishes* in 1749. To my mind the latter is the finer poem; but both of them seem to me to be among the greatest verse Satires of the English or any other language; and, so far as comparison is justifiable, I do not think that Juvenal, his model, is any better. They are *purer* satire than anything of Dryden or Pope, nearer in spirit to the Latin. For the satirist is in theory a stern moralist castigating the vices of his time or place; and Johnson has a better claim to this seriousness than either Pope or Dryden. In the hands of Dryden the satire becomes almost the lampoon; and Dryden had a special gift for farce. Pope also is more personal than the true satirist. In one way, Johnson goes back to an earlier tradition; however inferior as satires Marston's or even Hall's may be to Johnson's, they are surely much nearer to the spirit and intention of Juvenal than are those of Dryden or Pope. Dryden is, in the modern sense, humorous and witty; Pope is in the modern sense witty though not humorous; Johnson, neither humorous nor witty in this sense, has yet 'the proper wit of poetry' as the seventeenth century and the Augustan age had it also. I can better expose this by a few quotations than by a definition.

There mark what ills the scholar's life assail,
Toil, envy, want, the patron, and the jail.

Condemned a needy supplicant to wait,
While ladies interpose, and slaves debate.

Fate never wounds more deep the generous heart,
Than when a blockhead's insult points the dart.

Some fiery fop, with new commission vain,
Who sleeps on brambles till he kills his man;
Some frolick drunkard, reeling from a feast,
Provokes a broil, and stabs you for a jest.

The precision of such verse gives, I think, an immense satisfaction to the reader: he has said what he wanted to say, with that urbanity which contemporary verse would do well to study; and the satisfaction I get from such lines is what I call the *minimal* quality of poetry. There is much greater poetry than Johnson's; but after all, how little, how very little, good poetry there is anyway. And the kind of satisfaction these lines give me is something that I must have, at least, from any poetry in order to like it. It is the certainty, the ease with which he hits the bull's-eye every time, that makes Johnson a poet. The blundering assaults of his contemporary Churchill – a man of by no means poor abilities – do not make poetry; Churchill gives us an occasional right line, but never a right poem.

And the verse of Johnson has the good qualities of his own best prose, and of the best prose of his time. Bolingbroke, for instance, at his best, has some of the same merit.

Those who demand of poetry a day dream, or a metamorphosis of their own feeble desires and lusts, or what they believe to be 'intensity' of passion, will not find much in Johnson. He is like Pope and Dryden, Crabbe and Landor, a poet for those who want poetry and not something else, some stay for their own vanity. I sometimes think that our own time, with its elaborate equipment of science and psychological analysis, is even less fitted than the Victorian age to appreciate poetry as poetry. But if lines 189–220 of *The Vanity of Human Wishes* are not poetry, I do not know what is.

NOTE

1. This essay first appeared, under the title 'Johnson's *London* and *The Vanity of Human Wishes*', as the Introduction to the Haslewood Books edition, 1930. It is reprinted in *English Critical Essays, Twentieth Century*, selected by Phyllis M. Jones (The World's Classics, Oxford University Press, 1933), and is reproduced here by kind permission of Mr Eliot and the publishers.

WILLIAM HOGARTH

V. DE S. PINTO

THE place of William Hogarth is certainly with the great English Augustan writers, Defoe, Swift, Pope, Gay, and Fielding, rather than with the elegant eighteenth-century portrait painters such as Reynolds and his successors. More clearly perhaps than any other Englishman of his period Hogarth saw that his age needed a new kind of art to express the spirit of a new kind of civilization. About a hundred years after the beginning of Hogarth's career as an artist William Blake wrote

> May God us keep
> From Single vision & Newton's sleep![1]

'Single vision' for Blake was the vision of the 'Enlightenment' produced by the scientific thinkers of the seventeenth century, a 'universe of death' consisting of abstract, colourless, soundless, tasteless atoms obeying rigid mathematical laws. Blake himself aspired to the 'fourfold vision' of the prophet or seer. The English artistic heritage was, however, saved by the men of the Augustan age who explored with fearless energy the world revealed by the 'twofold vision' of the common sensuous observer illuminated by occasional flashes of the 'threefold vision' of the poet. These men re-created the English artistic tradition after the dissolution of the old Court culture in the reigns of the last Stuart kings, and produced new forms such as the realistic painting, the novel and the ballad opera, which embodied the lusty, vigorous, social and intellectual life of the young 'bourgeois' civilization of which England was now the chief representative in Europe. In this work William Hogarth, painter, draughtsman, engraver, and dramatic, realistic, and comic artist, played a decisive part.

The history of pictorial art in England has been very different from that of literature. English literature has a continuous history since the Middle Ages, but in the history of English pictorial art there is a great gap extending for about two hundred years from the beginning of the sixteenth till the beginning of the eighteenth century. Medieval English craftsmen had a European reputation.[2] Their art was anonymous like the medieval lyrics and ballads, and it seems to have been the product of the great religious houses.[3] When they were dissolved at the Reformation, the tradition came abruptly to an end. From the time of Henry VIII to that of William III, pictorial art in England was mainly an upper-class luxury purveyed to wealthy patrons by foreign artists such as Holbein and Zuccaro in the sixteenth century and Rubens and Van Dyck in the seventeenth, as well as numerous lesser men such as the admirable Czech engraver Wenceslas Hollar, who has provided us with our most vivid pictorial records of the England of Cromwell and Charles II.[4] Of course, there was some English painting in these two centuries. There were the delicate Elizabethan miniature portraits of Nicholas Hillyard and Isaac Oliver[5] and the works of Van Dyck's English pupils such as Dobson and Cooper in the seventeenth century, and at the other end of the social scale the rough but sometimes spirited and vigorous woodcuts found in many of the broadsides and chap-books. Taken as a whole, however, it can be said that there was no real English tradition of pictorial art in this period. English noblemen, following the example of Charles I, bought Italian, Spanish, Dutch, Flemish, and French pictures, and there grew up the cult of the Old Masters, the snobbish, dilettante adoration of everything in art that was old and foreign and covered with dirt and brown varnish. The whole of Hogarth's career was a protest against this sort of culture-snobbery. In a letter printed in *The St James's Post* in June 1737, he attacked the picture-dealers who 'depreciate every English work, as hurtful to their trade, of continually importing shiploads of dead Christs, holy families, Madonnas, and other dismal dark subjects, neither entertaining nor ornamental; on which they score the terrible cramp names of some Italian masters, and fix on us poor Englishmen the character of *universal dupes*. If a man, naturally a judge of Painting, not bigoted to those empirics, should cast his eye on one of their sham virtuoso-pieces, he would be very apt to say, "Mr Bubbleman, that grand Venus (as you are pleased to call it) has not beauty enough for the character of an English cook-maid".'[6] Hogarth was more interested in English cook-maids than Italian Venuses and he learnt to paint not in Italy but in London. He delivered English painting from the dilettanti and turned it into a living, popular art, using it to express the abounding vitality and bursting energy of the England of his day and also to expose its folly, its hypocrisy, and its cruelty with a satiric force not inferior to that of his great contemporaries Swift, Pope, and Fielding.

The son of a poor schoolmaster and literary hack from Westmorland, William Hogarth was born in London in 1697, when Dryden still had three years to live, Pope was a boy of nine, Swift in his thirtieth year and still unknown, and Defoe a man of thirty-six, who had already published several pamphlets, failed in business, and held a minor government post. Like William Blake about seventy years later, Hogarth left school when he was still a boy and was apprenticed to an engraver. He appears to have taught himself drawing in the first instance and to have deliberately trained his visual memory. At first he designed and engraved shop bills and coats of arms, then he passed to the drawing and engraving of illustrations to books (including a notable set for *Hudibras*), and original satiric designs.

It was in the third decade of the eighteenth century that Hogarth really began his career as a great popular artist re-establishing in England the tradition of popular satiric and moralizing art: it was the tradition that goes back to the marginal illustrations in medieval manuscripts, grotesque ornamental features in Gothic architecture, and the satirical carvings on misericord seats.[7]

A good example of the early satiric work of Hogarth is the print called *Masquerades and Operas* (1724), a vigorous attack on the bad taste of his day and especially on that of the aristocracy. This plate, though it does not show the profound knowledge of life and insight into the human comedy of Hogarth's later pictures, is nevertheless the starting-point for much of his subsequent satire. It is a kind of pictorial parallel to *A Tale of a Tub* and *The Dunciad*. We see in it crowds of people flocking to the Italian Opera, a Pantomime of Doctor Faustus and Heidegger's Masquerades, while the neglected volumes of Shakespeare, Otway, Dryden, and Congreve are wheeled away to be pulped. On a show-cloth hung from the Opera, the Earl of Peterborough is seen on his knees before Francesca Cuzzini (Ambrose Philips's 'Little Siren of the Stage'[8]), while in the background rises the façade of Burlington House, the mansion of the Earl of Burlington, the famous aristocratic dilettante and collector of Italian pictures. It is labelled 'Academy of Arts' (a curious prophetic stroke, for it actually became the headquarters of the Royal Academy later on) and is surmounted by an effigy of William Kent, a showy, conceited English painter (but an architect of some merit) who had been trained in Italy and was a favourite of Lord Burlington. It was probably Hogarth's attack on Kent that recommended him to the notice of Kent's mortal enemy Sir James Thornhill (1678-1734), a painter of considerable ability, not an empty-headed imitator of Continental fashions, but an intelligent student of the baroque style of contemporary Italy, which he adapted with some success in his mural paintings at St Paul's Cathedral, Greenwich Hospital, and elsewhere. He is also notable for starting the first regular school of painting in England since the dissolution of the monasteries. Hogarth attended this school and learnt much from Thornhill, particularly in the way of composition, grouping, and the painting of interiors. Thus he was now in a position to unite the popular, satiric realistic tradition descending from Bosch, Breughel, Callot, and the Dutch engravers with the grace and distinction of the aristocratic baroque tradition, transmitted by Thornhill and Thornhill's Italian masters. As a painter in oils Hogarth first made his reputation by his 'conversation pieces', little paintings of figures in natural attitudes and group-ings either in rooms or in the open air.[9] They correspond to the periodical essays of Steele, Addison, and their successors, and have the same virtues of urbanity, informality, and civilized ease. Hogarth's genius, however, was too strong and exuberant to be confined for long in such narrow limits. His kinship was to the authors of *A Tale of a Tub*, *The Dunciad*, *Moll Flanders*, and *Jonathan Wild*, not to those of the *Tatler*, the *Spectator*, and *The Guardian*.

* * *

From satiric prints and conversation pieces in oils Hogarth passed to that peculiar type of realistic, satiric, and moralizing painting which made him the most famous English artist of his day and gave him a European reputation.[10] The most memorable part of this work is to be found in the four great series of pictures which David Garrick in his Epitaph on Hogarth called his 'pictur'd Morals'.[11] They are *A Harlot's Progress* (1731), *A Rake's Progress* (1735), *Marriage à la Mode* (1745), and *Industry and Idleness* (1747). With them can be classed also the shorter sequences, such as *The Four Stages of Cruelty* and *The Four Times of the Day* (1738), *Beer Street* and *Gin Lane* (1751), and the *Election* series (1754–66), as well as a number of single pictures of a similar character such as *A Modern Midnight Conversation* (1733), *The Distressed Poet* (before 1736), and *Taste à la Mode* (1742). In these works Hogarth invents a new kind of popular pictorial art very closely analogous to the English realistic, moralizing novel of the early eighteenth century, which was certainly profoundly influenced by his example. It is highly significant that the second of the two decades in which Hogarth's four great 'pictur'd Morals' appeared also saw the publication of the four major novels of Richardson and Fielding: *Pamela* (1740), *Joseph Andrews* (1742), *Clarissa* (1748), *Tom Jones* (1749).

Hogarth's 'pictur'd Morals' are a remarkable anticipation of the modern art of the film: the telling of a dramatic story in a series of pictures. The difference between the Hogarthian picture-sequence and the modern popular film is that, unlike the directors of Hollywood dramas, Hogarth does not aim primarily either at thrills or wish-fulfilment but at unflinching realism combined with a penetrating criticism of moral and social conditions. He described his aims in a famous passage:

> I therefore turned my thoughts to a still more novel mode, *viz.* painting and engraving modern moral subjects, a field not broken up in any country or any age. ... I wished to compose pictures on canvas, similar to representations on the stage; and further hope they will be tried by the same test, and criticized by the same criterion.... I have endeavoured to treat my subjects as a dramatic writer; my picture is my stage, and men and women are my players. ... This I found was most likely to answer my purpose, provided I could strike the passions, and by small sums from many, by the sale of prints I could engrave from my own pictures, thus secure the property to myself.[12]

This important statement was actually made by Hogarth when he was petitioning for an Act of Parliament to protect his copyrights. It shows that Hogarth regarded himself as a popular dramatist who taught by 'striking the passions', and that he aimed at reaching a wide audience by making engravings from his own paintings to be sold at a low price. This was a revolutionary aim in an age when painters usually depended on aristocratic patrons. Hogarth certainly achieved it. Engravings of these famous sets of pictures (often pirated in spite of the Act of Parliament) very soon found their way all over England and became as familiar to Englishmen and Englishwomen as *The Pilgrim's Progress*, *Robinson Crusoe*, and *Gulliver's Travels*. Probably they were more widely known than any of those books, because even the illiterate could read Hogarth's 'pictur'd Morals', if only in poor engravings hung on the walls of innumerable inns, coffee-houses, shops, schools, and private houses, and few middle-class households in the eighteenth and nineteenth centuries were without a copy of one of the many books containing them, from which a very large number of people, like the present writer, derived some of their earliest impressions of pictorial art.

This meant that Hogarth became widely known less as the great painter which he undoubtedly is than as a popular moralist. In 1768, four years after his death, the Rev. John Trusler with the help of Mrs Hogarth published a collection of engravings of his pictures called *Hogarth Moralized*. The letterpress of this collection consists of unctuous expositions of Puritan middle-class morality, which show Hogarth's picture sequences in the light of tracts inculcating the virtues of hard work, thrift, and prudence, and showing the terrible fates which overcome the idle, the profligate, and the improvident. Hogarth, of course, was a moralist, but his pictures have a much deeper meaning than the copybook lessons which lie on the surface and are so easily measured by Dr Trusler's little yardstick. Every picture in the famous sequences is at once a vivid portrayal of the lusty, vigorous life of contemporary England and a powerful exposure of the cruelty, the heartlessness, and the stupidity of a society in which all human and moral values are being threatened by the power of money. Hogarth's harlots and rakes are not shown as naturally evil; they are pathetic, helpless figures who seem to be caught up and mangled by a pitiless mechanism of commercialized greed and vice.

Marriage à la Mode is the finest of the 'pictur'd Morals'. It is a satiric commentary on contemporary society as powerful as that of Pope's *Moral Essays*. The marriage of the depraved young nobleman with the daughter of the rich citizen typifies the alliance between the aristocracy and the commercial magnates which was the keystone of the Augustan social and political system. This masterly sequence has many meanings: one certainly is that the new money power was fundamentally hostile to human values. The pretty doll-like countess and the corrupted boy earl are like spoilt children who drift to their ruin amid sinister figures like the Quack and the Procuress in Plate III. There is extraordinary pathos in the famous scene (Plate II)[13] in which the newly married pair sit yawning on opposite sides of the fireplace, their boredom and spiritual emptiness contrasted with the beauty and dignity of the noble eighteenth-century room where they are sitting.

The Four Stages of Cruelty is a great pictorial manifestation of humanitarianism. 'The prints,' Hogarth wrote, 'were engraved with the hope of, in some degree correcting that barbarous treatment of animals, the very sight of which renders the streets of our metropolis so distressing to every feeling mind.'[14] Here the story is a much simpler one, the 'progress' of Tom Nero, who starts by torturing dogs and horses, advances to rape and murder, and ends his career on the gallows, after which his corpse is dissected at Surgeons' Hall. Again we are confronted by something far bigger than a mere Cautionary Tale. The sequence is an outburst of bitter indignation against the brutality of the age. Hogarth, the lover of life, who delighted in children and animals, joins hands here with the Blake of Auguries of Innocence, whose burning lines may well have been inspired by these terrible prints:

> A dog starv'd at his Master's Gate
> Predicts the ruin of the State.
> A Horse misus'd upon the Road
> Calls to Heaven for Human blood.
> Each outcry of the hunted Hare
> A fibre from the Brain does tear.[15]

If the The Four Stages of Cruelty is the fiercest of the 'pictur'd Morals', The Four Times of the Day is the gentlest. Here there is no connecting thread of dramatic narrative, but simply four brilliant 'shots' of street scenes in Augustan London, full of delight in the comedy, the vitality, and ironic contrasts of contemporary English life. More typical of the Hogarthian spirit are the twin pictures Beer Street and Gin Lane. They were often used for temperance propaganda, but they have a much profounder significance than the truism that beer is a healthier drink than gin. Actually these two pictures are revelations of eighteenth-century slum life, a powerful comment on the condition of the proletariat in the early period of capitalism. In *Beer Street* the atmosphere is one of fuddle and fatuous cheerfulness: in *Gin Lane*, perhaps Hogarth's most penetrating social satire, it is sordid, hopeless misery. Here Hogarth is certainly not preaching a sermon against drink. He is showing that, in a world dominated by the power of money, the poor are left to rot in the gutter and drink themselves to death. Dickens in his comment on this picture puts his finger on its true meaning: 'I think it a remarkable trait in Hogarth's picture [Gin Lane], that, while it exhibits drunkenness in its most appalling forms, it also forces on attention a most neglected wretched neighbourhood, and unwholesome, indecent, abject condition of life. ... There is no evidence that any of the actors in the dreary scene have ever been much better than we see them there. The best are pawning the commonest necessaries, and tools of their trade; and the worst are homeless vagrants, who give us no clue as to their having been otherwise in bygone days. All are living and dying miserably. Nobody is interfering for prevention or for cure in the generation going out before us, or the generation coming in. ... The church is indeed very prominent and handsome; but ... quite passive in the picture as it coldly surveys these things in progress beneath its tower.'[16] Dickens is right; this is a picture of a world in which the Church has forgotten its duty towards the poor and the helpless, and the State has not yet learnt to take care of them. It is the beginning of the great age of *laissez-faire* and 'free enterprise', which reached its culmination in the time of Dickens. Again Hogarth is prophetic of Blake, the poet who wrote:

> The Harlot's cry from Street to Street
> Shall weave old England's winding Sheet.
> The Winner's Shout, the Loser's Curse,
> Dance before dead England's Hearse.[17]

* * *

Hogarth is by no means always a moralist or satirist of social conditions. The *March to Finchley* (1750), one of his most popular prints, is simply a piece of comic realism, which is also, incidentally, good-humoured deflation of heroics. The *Strolling Actresses Dressing in a Barn* (1738) has no satiric or moral intention at all; it is as Horace Walpole said,[18] 'a work of wit and imagination without any other end', a splendid and exuberant impression of the lawless, bohemian element of the population of eighteenth-century England, not the hopeless misery of *Gin Lane* or the 'High Life' of *Marriage à la Mode* or the *bourgeois* respectability of Frank Goodchild, but the world of the folk who lived by their wits on the fringe of society and snapped their fingers at convention and decorum. These strolling players (the predecessors of Vincent Crummles and his troupe), drinking, declaiming, dressing, and preparing for a performance of a farce called *The Devil to Pay in Heaven*, are portrayed with a breadth, a gusto, and an Aristophanic gaiety that recalls the only other great eighteenth-century work of art which deals effectively with the same world of vagrants, Burns's *The Jolly Beggars*:

> What is title, what is treasure,
> What is reputation's care?
> If we lead a life of pleasure,
> 'Tis no matter how or where!
>
> With the ready trick and fable
> Round we wander all the day,
> And at night in barn or stable
> Hug our doxies on the hay.

Coleridge is reported by Charles Lamb to have said of Hogarth that in his work 'the satirist never extinguished that love of beauty which belonged to him as a poet'.[19] Hogarth's poetry is to be found throughout his works, in the delicate childlike head of the petulant girl countess in the second plate of *Marriage à la Mode*, in the saturnalia of the third plate of *A Rake's Progress*, and many other places in the famous sequences. The purest manifestations of it, however, are to be found in his portraits and figure studies such as the gay and brilliant picture of Mrs Elizabeth Salter in a yellow silk dress that sets off her dashing figure and pure complexion so admirably. Above all, it is to be found in that miracle of light, colour, and fresh sensuous girlhood, the sketch of *The Shrimp Girl*, the most lyrical of all Hogarth's paintings, which has the spontaneous, birdlike quality of a Shakespearian song.[20]

Hogarth went on painting and engraving till his death in 1764.

He lived long enough to design some vigorous illustrations for *Tristram Shandy* and to produce a splendid satiric portrait of Jack Wilkes.

In his last years he seems to have been haunted by the idea of Time. The figure of Time as a kind of humorous, old winged God is seen in the strange print 'Time smoking a picture',[21] a humorous lamentation of an ageing painting and a comment on the snob-worship of dark, smoky, heavily varnished 'Old Masters'. It is also a painter-poet's conception of Mortality. The same figure of the old winged Time-god appears in Hogarth's strangest and most enigmatic production *The Bathos or Finis* (1764).[22] This print was designed as a tail-piece for a collection of his pictures. In it the great realist, the painter of the solid three-dimensional eighteenth-century world governed by the laws of Newtonian physics, shows us a prophetic vision of that world in ruins. Here Time is seen lying propped on a broken column with his broken scythe under his arm. The sign of the inn called 'The World's End' is collapsing on one side of the picture while smoke pours out of a ruined town on the other. In the foreground are various broken objects, including a cracked hourglass, and in the background a landscape with a corpse on a gallows lit by a lurid sky where Apollo, the Sungod, lies dead in his chariot. The title of the picture could be the words of Hotspur in *Henry IV*, Part I, 'Time ... must have a stop', and it might be called Hogarth's surrealist master-piece. Here for once he has transcended realism, by creating a world of vision, a haunting vision of ruin and madness like that which Pope shows us at the end of *The Dunciad*. *The Bathos or Finis* is the epilogue to the Augustan age, the pictorial parallel to the madness of Collins and Smart, the work of an artist who remained sane but saw in a prophetic flash an image of the terror which sent poets to the madhouse and their graves in the mid-eighteenth century. When Hogarth engraved this picture, Blake was a child of six. His art began where Hogarth's left off. For a moment at the end of his career, Hogarth had a glimpse of the Fourfold Vision, the region in which Blake was to live and move and have his being.

*   *   *

Hogarth is a literary artist, not in the sense that he borrowed many of his themes from literature like the pre-Raphaelites, but in the sense that his aims were similar to those of the chief contemporary English writers and that his influence on literature was quite as important as his influence on painting.[23] When he was young the English literary scene was dominated by the famous group of Queen Anne wits, Swift, Pope, Gay, Addison, and Steele. Hogarth seems to have had little personal connexion with this group. He certainly knew Pope's work and Gay's *The Beggar's Opera* and was probably considerably influenced by both these writers. Swift does not seem to have heard of Hogarth till he was an elderly man in Dublin in the seventeen-thirties. Probably he enjoyed the prints of *A Harlot's Progress* (1732) and *A Rake's Progress* (1735); he certainly recognized in Hogarth a kindred spirit, for, in that terrific denunciation of human stupidity and depravity, *The Legion Club* (1736), he actually envisages a collaboration between himself and the painter:

> How I want thee, humorous *Hogart*?
> Thou I hear, a pleasant Rogue art;
> Were but you and I acquainted,
> Every Monster should be painted;
> You should try your graving Tools
> On this odious Group of Fools;
> Draw the Beasts as I describe 'em,
> Form their Features, while I gibe them;
> Draw them like, for I assure you,
> You will need no *Car'catura*;
> Draw them so, that we may trace
> All the Soul in every Face.[24]

Hogarth's most significant literary relationships were, however, as I have already suggested, with the new art of the English novel as it developed in the fourth and fifth decades of the eighteenth century. He was personally acquainted with both the great pioneers of this art, Samuel Richardson and Henry Fielding. The prim, fastidious, puritanical Richardson with his hatred of anything 'low' and his narrow *bourgeois* morality seems at first glance to have very little in common with the painter of *A Modern Midnight Conversation* and *Strolling Actresses Dressing in a Barn*. Yet we know from Boswell[25] that Hogarth was on intimate terms with Richardson, and R. E. Moore has shown convincingly that *Familiar Letters* (1741), the book on which Richardson was at work when he conceived the plan of

Pamela, is full of reminiscences of *A Harlot's Progress* and *A Rake's Progress*.[26] *Pamela* itself has none of the broad humour and full-blooded exuberance of Hogarth, but it certainly owes much to his pictures. Mrs Jewkes, the wicked old tool of Mr B— in Richardson's novel, bears a strong resemblance to Hogarth's procuress in Plate I of *A Harlot's Progress*, and the description of Colbrand, Mr B—'s Swiss valet, is extremely Hogarthian.[27] This vivid, realistic word-painting is found both in Richardson and Fielding, and it was something new in prose fiction. Even Defoe does not often give clear visual impressions of his scenes and characters, and much of the difficulty which a modern reader finds in getting through the stories of Aphra Behn and, still worse, the 'heroic' romances of the seventeenth century is due to the fact that those writers are incapable of visualizing, and when we read their books we seem to be moving through a world of formless and colourless abstractions. One of Hogarth's great services to English prose fiction was that he made our novelists use their eyes.

Hogarth's relationship to Henry Fielding, Richardson's rival, was certainly very close indeed, and can be described without exaggeration as a collaboration between two artists of equal stature and ability. R. E. Moore has shown that Fielding's dramatic burlesques (1730-7) are considerably influenced by Hogarth's early satiric prints, and there is no doubt that Hogarth and Fielding were working in close co-operation at this time.[28] The pattern of Fielding's career closely resembles that of Hogarth's. His first successes, the dramatic satires of the seventeen-thirties, correspond closely to Hogarth's early, topical satiric prints. Like Hogarth he found his true strength when he turned to comic, realistic narrative, and Hogarth undoubtedly helped to show him the way to the new art of *Joseph Andrews*. By 1742, when Fielding published his first novel, Hogarth had already produced *A Harlot's Progress*, *A Rake's Progress*, *The Four Times of the Day*, and the *Strolling Actresses Dressing in a Barn*, as well as such minor masterpieces as *A Modern Midnight Conversation* and *The Laughing Audience*. Already in 1740 in his periodical *The Champion*, Fielding had praised 'the ingenious Mr Hogarth' as one of the most 'useful *Satyrists* that any Age hath produced'. Of course, all sorts of ingredients went to make the delicious compound of *Joseph Andrews*. The influence of Hogarth, however, was certainly one of the determining factors in Fielding's new art of fiction. It seems to have been Hogarth who taught him not, indeed, the critical commonplace that there was a difference between burlesque and comedy, but the inward meaning of that difference and the immeasurable superiority of comedy: 'Now what Caricatura is in painting, Burlesque is in writing; and in the same manner the comic writer and painter correlate to each other. ... He who should call the ingenious Hogarth a burlesque painter, would, in my opinion, do him very little honour; for sure it is much easier, much less the subject of admiration, to paint a man with a nose, or any other feature, of a preposterous size, or to expose him in some absurd or monstrous attitude, than to express the affections of men on canvas. It has been thought a vast commendation of a painter, to say his figures seem to breathe; but surely it is a much greater and nobler applause, that they appear to think!' These words from Fielding's Preface to *Joseph Andrews* are full of significance. He undoubtedly had a strong tendency to burlesque and caricature. It was the example of his friend Hogarth which taught him to restrain that tendency and create three-dimensional characters that not only 'breathe' but 'think', such as Joseph Andrews, Parson Adams, Mrs Slipslop, and the rest. Although there are few specific borrowings from Hogarth's pictures in *Joseph Andrews*, it is clear from references throughout the book that Fielding had them constantly in mind and pictures his scenes as they would have appeared to the painter. In the famous scene in which Joseph after being robbed is found naked by the stagecoach, the lady shrieks with horror, but nevertheless looks at the naked man through the sticks of her fan, comes straight from the last plate of *A Rake's Progress*, where she is seen ogling a naked Bedlamite through the sticks of a fan.

Tom Jones is, perhaps, even more indebted to Hogarth than *Joseph Andrews*. Three important characters, Mrs Bridget Allworthy, Partridge, and Square, are lifted (with generous acknowledgements) straight out of pictures by Hogarth. Again, throughout the story, we are constantly shown scenes and characters in terms of Hogarth's painting. 'O, Shakespeare! had I thy pen! O, Hogarth! had I thy pencil!'[29] Fielding exclaims, and then promptly, as it were, takes up Hogarth's 'pencil' and paints 'the pale countenance, staring eyes, chattering teeth, faltering tongue, and trembling lips' of the servant who comes to tell Squire Western of Sophia's disappearance. But Fielding's debt to Hogarth in *Tom Jones* is not merely to be found in detailed borrowings. The breadth, the vigour, the delight in every aspect of life, the crowded scenes, and the genial but unsentimental humour of *Tom Jones* are exactly the qualities of Hogarth's great picture. *Joseph Andrews* and *Tom Jones* are, in fact, Hogarthian 'progresses' in literary form. It would be a slight exaggeration to call them the 'books' of Hogarth's 'films', but to study them without reference to the 'pictur'd Morals' is like studying Shakespeare without reference to the Elizabethan theatre.

A writer in *The Times Literary Supplement*[30] has described the relationship between the great painter and the great novelist in words that can hardly be bettered: 'Hogarth and Fielding revelled in the human medley. There is such a temperamental and intellectual bond between them that it can be said that Hogarth's pictures give a more exact idea of Fielding's attitude to life than the novelist does in the theories propounded in the celebrated preface to *Joseph Andrews*.'

Hogarth was not only a major influence on the new English art of prose fiction; he was also the pregenitor of a great line of English cartoonists. F. D. Klingender has given an admirable description of his relationship to Rowlandson, Gillray, and their successors.[31] But Hogarth should not be studied merely as an 'influence'. An appreciation of his work is the best possible corrective to the still commonly held belief that the eighteenth century in England was a period of dry formalism and pedantic neo-classicism. Hogarth's pictures are the expression of the spirit of a great age of dynamic and revolutionary thought and imagination.

He is the one great popular English pictorial artist, the sensual, humorous, realistic, moralizing, poetic, illogical English genius expressing itself in colour, line, and form as it expresses itself in words in Chaucer, Ben Jonson, Fielding, and Dickens.

NOTES

1. *The Complete Writings of William Blake*, ed. G. Keynes (1957), p. 818.

2. See Joan Evans, *English Art, 1307–1361* (1949), pp. 102–4.

3. See R. H. Wilenski, *English Painting*, pp. 37–43, and, for more elaborate accounts, Talbot Rice, *English Art, 871–1100*, and Joan Evans, *English Art, 1307–1361*.

4. See Arthur M. Hind, *Wenceslaus Hollar* (1922).

5. See Wilenski, *op. cit.*, pp. 44–58; Carl Winter, *Elizabethan Miniatures* (King Penguin Books), and J. Pope Hennessy, *A Lecture on Nicholas Hilliard* (1949).

6. Austin Dobson, *William Hogarth* (1891), pp. 69, 70.

7. See F. D. Klingender, *Hogarth and English Caricature* (1944), pp. iv, 1, 6.

8. See *The Poems of Ambrose Philips*, ed. M. G. Segar (1937), pp. 107 and 179.

9. For examples, see R. B. Beckett, *Hogarth* (1949), pp. 22–4 and plates 19, 20, 24–30.

10. As early as 1746 Jean Rouquet, a French critic, published *Lettres de Monsieur XX à un de ses Amis à Paris, pour lui expliquer les Estampes de Monsieur Hogarth.*

11. Quoted by R. E. Moore in *Hogarth's Literary Relationships* (1948), p. 68.

12. Austin Dobson, *William Hogarth*, pp. 42, 43.

13. See the original painting in the National Gallery, London, reproduced in R. B. Beckett, *Hogarth*, plate 143.

14. John Ireland, *Hogarth Illustrated*, III, p. 355.

15. Blake, *Complete Writings, op. cit.*, p. 433.

16. See John Forster, *The Life of Charles Dickens*, II (1873), pp. 382, 383.

17. Blake, *Complete Writings, op. cit.*, p. 433.

18. H. Walpole, *Anecdotes of Painting*, IV (1827), p. 133.

19. *The Works of Charles and Mary Lamb*, ed. E. V. Lucas, I, p. 91.

20. Both the pictures mentioned in this paragraph are reproduced in R. B. Beckett's *William Hogarth*. The original paintings of both are in the National Gallery, London.

21. Austin Dobson, *William Hogarth*, pp. 160, 161.

22. *The Works of William Hogarth*, II (1833), p. 278. The original drawing is reproduced in *The Drawings of William Hogarth*, ed. A. P. Oppé (1948), plate 91.

23. See R. E. Moore, *Hogarth's Literary Relationships*, pp. 107–95.

24. *Swift's Poems*, ed. H. Williams, p. 839. Further evidence for Swift's admiration of Hogarth is given in a note by A. Dobson, *William Hogarth*, p. 53.

25. Boswell's *Life of Johnson*, ed. Powell (1934), I, pp. 145, 146.

26. R. E. Moore, *Hogarth's Literary Relationships*, pp. 187, 188.

27. See the quotations from *Pamela* on p. 296 of this volume.

28. See R. E. Moore, *Hogarth's Literary Relationships*, pp. 77–102.

29. H. Fielding, *Tom Jones*, Book X, chapter viii.

30. *The Times Literary Supplement*, 4 November 1949 (review of R. E. Moore's *Hogarth's Literary Relationships*).

31. See F. D. Klingender, Introduction to *Hogarth and English Caricature* (1944).

SAMUEL RICHARDSON

FRANK BRADBROOK

Lecturer in English, the University College of North Wales, Bangor

THE novels of Samuel Richardson present an almost impossible problem for the student of literature, who is not likely to have the time, interest, or stamina to read the nineteen bulky volumes of the standard edition. 'The father of the English novel' is curiously neglected. If read at all, he is usually dipped into in abridged versions. Yet it has been argued that Richardson was so exactly correct in his proportions that any attempt at abridgement must fail, and that it is therefore much better never to read *Clarissa* than to read it clipped. Certainly, it is better to read *Clarissa* in full than to read *Pamela*, *Clarissa*, and *Sir Charles Grandison* in snippets. For it is generally agreed that of Richardson's three novels *Clarissa* is the greatest, though not, perhaps, the most influential. The difficulty, however, is not only one of bulk. From this point of view, Richardson presents no greater obstacle than many of the Victorian novelists, the Russians, or Proust in *A la recherche du temps perdu*. Coleridge, in one of his brief and brilliant critical asides in *Anima Poetae*, described his response to the novels, and it is a fairly typical one: 'I confess that it has cost, and still costs, my philosophy some exertion not to be vexed that I must admire, aye, greatly admire, Richardson. His mind is so very vile, a mind so oozy, so hypocritical, praise-mad, canting, envious, concupiscent.' Richardson combines a daunting bulk, with extreme unevenness of quality, and several quite repellent characteristics. Coleridge's response to the novels, the mingled fascination and repulsion, is a common one. An entertaining anthology might be compiled recording the horror and disgust aroused by this most moral of writers.

It was in middle age and by accident that Richardson became a novelist, though his profession of master-printer made him naturally interested in books. Compared with Fielding, his great rival, however, Richardson was not a cultured man. He was incapable of writing a great 'comic epic in prose', such as *Tom Jones*, since he was without any deep first-hand knowledge of the classics and almost completely humourless. Yet he querulously criticized his contemporaries, while resenting any criticism of himself. Surrounding himself with syco-phantic women of second-rate intellect, he was treated by them as if he was the hero of one of his own novels. Despite all his limita-tions, however, this vulgar, complacent little bookseller gained a reputation in his own country and on the Continent second to none, and his influence is still to be seen in more recent times in the novels of Henry James, Mr E. M. Forster, and Proust. How was it done?

Richardson's first approach to fiction (though not a novel) was *The Familiar Letters on Important Occasions*. These letters were intended to show young ladies how to think and act justly and prudently in the common concerns of human life. The combination of the letter and the didactic moral intention was to be characteristic of Richardson's fiction. A voluminous correspondent himself, he lived in an age that regarded letter-writing as an art. One of the few foreign writers whom he recommended was Mme de Sévigné. She is praised in *Clarissa* for giving 'a faithful and chaste copy of real life and manners'. In the novel, the letter form heightens and sustains dramatic tension and introduces variety, subtlety, and complication, owing to the illusion it creates that the reader is sharing in the events described, and because of the variety of points of view that is given of each situation that arises. It is both more intimate and more objective than the ordinary narrative method, and lends itself to the creation of ironic effects. Henry James saw the advantages of this technique, and after recording in his notebook the possibility of writing 'a story told in letters written alternately by a mother and her daughter and giving totally different accounts of the same situation', he produced in less than a year *A Bundle of Letters*.[1] The complex interweaving of comments by different groups of people, the sense that the reader has of individuals working at cross-purposes and according to different standards, the sudden dramatic and ironic contrasts that occur, are typical of the novels of Henry James. They are equally characteristic of the apparently clumsy epistolary method of Richardson.

The transition from *The Familiar Letters* to Richardson's first novel *Pamela* was simple. He himself said in one of his letters 'I almost slid into the writing of *Pamela*'. But once having done so, the novel took him only three months to write. The first two volumes were published in 1740, and later two further volumes, *Pamela in her Exalted Condi-*

tion, were added. The aim of the novel was to show virtue rewarded, and it consisted (in the words of the title-page) of 'a series of Familiar Letters from a Beautiful Young Damsel to her parents. Now first published in order to cultivate the Principles of Virtue and Religion in the Minds of the Youth of Both Sexes.' The theme of the novel, the resistance of the virtuous servant to the attempts at seduction made by her master, was familiar in Puritan literature, and not one that was confined to prose. In the Elizabethan age it had been the subject of *Willobie His Avisa. Or, The True Picture of a modest Maid, and of a chaste and constant Wife*. This moral and allegorical poem was as popular in its time as Richardson's novel, and for the same reasons. In the words of one critic 'the heroine is precisely the sort to appeal to the bourgeoisie, then and now. Resisting all improper advances of noble suitors, she exemplifies Puritan virtue and provides a warning, patly stated, for other maids'.[2] The heading of Canto II of the poem, 'The first triall of Avisa, before she was married, by a Noble man: under which is represented a warning to all young maids of every degree, that they beware of the alluring intisements of great men', might serve as a motto for *Pamela*. Both works were the object of satire and parody. Avisa was described as a wanton minion, and Pamela, rechristened Shamela, was depicted as a feigned innocent against whom all gentlemen should be cautioned. It was even maintained that Richardson, under the pretence of cultivating the principles of virtue, had conveyed 'the most artful and alluring Ideas'. He certainly provided the inspiration for the early part of Fielding's burlesque *Joseph Andrews*, where the adventures of Pamela's brother are described.

The earlier part of *Pamela*, which is the most powerful, forms a complete contrast to the later volumes, which show a more placid and detached interest in the social scene. The atmosphere of these early volumes is unreal in the manner of a fairy-story. Pamela acts the role of the heroine locked in the castle of the villain Mr B— and threatened by his two ogre-like servants Mrs Jewkes and Monsieur Colbrand. Her enemies are described with a wealth of detail and have the reality of figures seen in a nightmare. These characters and the main part of the action are seen through the eyes of the heroine, and the picture that Pamela gives of Mrs Jewkes might have served as a model for one of Hogarth's paintings:

> She is a broad, squat, pursy, fat thing, quite ugly, if any-thing human can be so called; about forty years old. She has a huge hand, and an arm as thick as my waist, I believe. Her nose is fat and crooked, and her brows grown down over her eyes; a dead, spiteful, grey, goggling eye to be sure she has. And her face is flat and broad; and as to colour, looks like it had been pickled a month in saltpetre: I daresay she drinks. ...[3]

> (I, p. 119.)

The portrait of Monsieur Colbrand is equally macabre:

> He is a giant of a man for stature; taller by a good deal than Harry Mowbridge, in your neighbourhood, and large boned and scraggy; and has a hand! – I never saw such an one in my life. He has great staring eyes, like the bull's that frightened me so; vast jaw-bones sticking out; eye-brows hanging over his eyes; two great scars upon his forehead, and one on his left cheek; and two large whiskers, and a monstrous wide mouth; blubber lips; long yellow teeth, and a hideous grin. ...

> (I, p. 180.)

Such gusto and vivid detail are what one normally associates with Elizabethan prose rather than with Richardson, but if one compares such passages with a typical piece of, say, Nashe, one can, while noting resemblances, also recognize the subtler verbal ingenuity that has been lost:

> A bursten belly inkhorne orator called *Vanderhulke*, they pickt out to present him with an oration, one that had a sulpherous big swolne large face, like a Saracen, eyes lyke two kentish oysters, a mouth that opened as wide every time he spake, as one of those old knit trap doores, a beard as though it had been made of a birds neast pluckt in peeces, which consisteth of strawe, haire, and durt mixt together. He was apparelled in blacke leather new licourd, and a short gowne without anie gathering in the backe, faced before and behinde with a boistrous beare skin, and a red night-cap on his head.
> (*The Unfortunate Traveller*)

It was from Defoe that Richardson probably directly inherited his firm grasp of realistic detail. He had almost certainly read Defoe's

Robinson Crusoe and *The Family Instructor*, and in both writers the tendencies towards realism and didacticism naturally go together. But Richardson was much more interested in analysing feelings and mental processes than Defoe was. He brought to such analysis the same passion for precision that Defoe showed when describing external details, while his predecessor's influence was sufficiently strong to act as a restraining guard against his own particular weakness and vice, sentimentality.

In the company of the two vividly evoked henchmen and of the inevitable Mr B—, Pamela's virtue is tried. Many readers find both her character and the long-drawn-out tale of attempted seduction repulsive and tedious. Yet one cannot but admire the exactness and thoroughness with which her fluctuating feelings and states of mind are described, the psychological insight shown into the reactions of the frightened and fascinated victim. For Pamela, despite her protests (and some would say that she protests too much and does too little), is fascinated at the same time that she is frightened. She, herself, naïvely records her feelings:

> What is the matter, that with all his ill usage of me, I cannot hate him? ... I could not in my heart forbear from rejoicing at his safety; though his death would have ended my afflictions. ...
>
> (I, p. 194.)

After several attempts have been made to break down her resistance by force and intimidation, she is allowed to escape. Before reaching her home she receives a letter from Mr B— inviting her back. The description of her conflicting impulses that follows is all the more effective as self-revelation and confession because of its ingenuousness and apparent lack of subtlety:

> Oh my exulting heart! how it throbs in my bosom, as if it would reproach me for so lately upbraiding it for giving way to the love of so dear a gentleman! – But take care thou art not too credulous neither, oh fond believer! Things that we wish, are apt to gain a too ready credence with us. This sham marriage is not yet cleared up; Mrs Jewkes, the vile Mrs Jewkes! may yet instigate the mind of this master: his pride of heart, and pride of condition, may again take place: and

a man that could in so *little* a space, first love me, then hate, then banish me his house, and send me away disgracefully; and now send for me again, in such affectionate terms, may *still* waver, may *still* deceive thee. Therefore will I not acquit thee yet, oh credulous, fluttering, throbbing mischief! that art so ready to believe what thou wishest! and I charge thee to keep better guard than thou hast lately done, and lead me not to follow too implicitly thy flattering and desirable impulses. Thus foolishly dialogued I with my heart; and yet, all the time, this heart is Pamela.

(I, p. 276.)

Pamela's own lack of insight into her thoughts and feelings does not prevent her from presenting them clearly. The reader is encouraged to supply the extra comment and analysis that are needed. The moment when she recognizes her own feelings for what they are is more attractive for being artless and unaffected:

I know not *how* it came, nor *when* it began; but crept, crept it has, like a thief, upon me; and before I knew what was the matter, it looked like love.

(I, p. 272.)

After all the attempts of Mr B—, Pamela can still exclaim, as marriage draws nearer – 'Oh! what halcyon days are these', and record her final naïve confession:

I hope he loves me! – But whether he does or not, I am in for it now, over head and ears I doubt, and can't help loving him; 'tis folly to deny it.

(II, p. 42.)

Unfortunately, the character of Pamela does not create the impression of pure and injured innocence that Richardson intended. The weakness of Richardson as a moralist is that he appears to be unconscious of the implications of the situations that he describes. There are elements of hypocrisy and coarse-grained vulgarity in his heroine. What repels the reader is not merely the inconsistency of a supposedly chaste maiden 'whose dreams are filled with ideas of rape, but whose waking moments resound to prate about her honour',[4] nor the ridiculousness of a situation where, in the words of a French critic, 'une fille qu'on veut séduire, qui en est persuadée, se résout tranquillement à rester exposée: et quel important motif la détermine? Une veste à broder'.⁵ By some perverse obliquity of the writer the intended moral is reversed. Instead of showing virtue rewarded Richardson has written an apologia for a self-righteous equivalent of Roxana or Moll Flanders. And in describing how she defended her 'honour' Richardson dwells with a lingering relish on scenes that are supposed to be the prerogative in English literature of the more pornographic playwrights of the Restoration. D. H. Lawrence remarked that 'Boccaccio at his hottest seems to me less pornographical than *Pamela* or *Clarissa Harlowe*.'⁶ So far as *Pamela* is concerned, he erred on the side of understatement. For, like Swift's broom-stick, Richardson is 'sharing all the while in the very same pollutions he pretends to sweep away'.⁷ *Pamela* is sentimental and obscene: its obscenity is a direct result of its sentimentality.

The comments of Mr B— occasionally introduce a wholesome note of satire, which contrasts with what Pamela calls 'the naked sentiments of my heart'. For him she is 'an artful young baggage', 'a subtle artful gipsy' who 'has a lucky knack of falling into fits, when she pleases' and 'has wit at will, when she has a mind to display her own romantic innocence, at the price of other people's characters'. But Mr B— has exactly the same mixture of hypocrisy, vulgarity, and (strangely enough!) of innocence and unawareness as Pamela herself. After attempting for two volumes (and occasionally with success) to put his hand into her bosom, he can still, when they are reconciled and the marriage arranged, blithely refer to 'our innocent enjoyments', and express the wish to 'pour my whole soul into your bosom'. He, too, prates of honour as much as she does. The combination of triteness and indecency with pious professions is not limited to any one character, but pervades the whole novel. Pamela's father, to whom she has written constantly describing Mr B—'s conduct, has a dream after the alliance has been put on a nominally respectable basis. He sees 'nothing but Jacob's ladder, and angels ascending and descending to bless him and his daughter' (II, p. 53).

By this time Pamela's prison has become her palace and 'the dear, once naughty assailer of her innocence, by a blessed return of Providence, is become the kind, the generous protector and rewarder of it' (II, p. 105). As she herself remarks, 'sure nobody was ever so blessed as I!' She visits the summer-house again, where she had previously been assaulted, prays and thanks God, then 'whips out again, so that Mr B— hardly missed me'. At this point Mr B— discovers that she has a mind, and praises it. Later the marriage guests join in approval of her blasphemous rewriting of the one hundred and thirty-seventh Psalm to suit her own case while she was Mr B—'s prisoner. The clergyman, Mr Williams, himself lectures her on the right use of riches, quoting Proverbs: 'The liberal soul shall be made fat: and he that watereth, shall be watered himself' (II, p. 70). Unconscious irony could hardly go farther than this.

Where Richardson is most successful is in catching the tone and manner of Pamela's speech. Her talk, too, is full of proverbs and colloquialisms. She refers to 'God, whose graciousness to us we have so often experienced at a pinch'; she is so confounded at something that Mr B — says that 'you might have beat me down with a feather'; 'What I do, must be at a jerk, to be sure', she remarks. This habit was characteristic of Richardson himself, and the novels are full of a similar kind of moral aphorism: 'a man who has sons brings up chickens for his own table, whereas daughters are chickens brought up for the tables of other men'; 'those who will bear much, shall have much to bear'; 'the coyest maids make the fondest wives'. In the character of Pamela, Richardson was dealing with something that he knew and could cope with. Her language is his language, and her exchanges with Mrs Jewkes have a genuine dramatic liveliness:

> 'Pray, Mrs Jewkes,' said I, 'don't *madam* me so: I am but a silly poor girl, set up by the gambol of fortune, for a May-game; and now am to be something, and now nothing, just as that thinks fit to sport with me: And let you and me talk upon a foot together; for I am a servant inferior to you, and so much the more, as I am turned out of place.'
>
> (I, p. 114.)

It is when Richardson has to deal with characters from 'high life' that his touch fails. In the following conversation between Pamela, Mr B —, and Lady Davers, his sister, one notes how the style of the writing gradually degenerates into melodramatic fustian:

> Not considering anything, I ran out of the closet, and threw myself at my dear master's feet, as he held her hand, in order to lead her out; and I said, Dearest sir, let me beg, that no act of unkindness, for my sake, pass between so worthy

and so near relations. Dear, dear madam, said I, and clasped her knees, pardon and excuse the unhappy cause of all this evil; on my knees I beg your ladyship to receive me to your grace and favour, and you shall find me incapable of any triumph but in your ladyship's goodness to me.

Creature, said she, art *thou* to beg an excuse for me? Art *thou* to implore my forgiveness? Is it to *thee* I am to owe the favour, that I am not cast headlong from my brother's presence? Begone to thy corner, wench! begone I say, lest thy paramour kill me for trampling thee under my foot!

Rise, my dear Pamela, said my master; rise, dear life of my life; and expose not so much worthiness to the ungrateful scorn of so violent a spirit. And so he led me to my closet again, and there I sat and wept.

(II, p. 190.)

The crudeness of this needs no emphasizing. Yet it was such raw material that Jane Austen refined to create the scenes between Elizabeth Bennet, Mr Darcy, and Lady Catherine de Bourgh in *Pride and Prejudice*. Elizabeth Bennet is, of course, a gentleman's daughter, and aware of the fact. The nearest that Jane Austen ever got to depicting a Pamela was in the satirical portrait of Lucy Steele in *Sense and Sensibility*. She adopts the same tone of ignominious flattery towards Mrs Ferrars as Pamela does to Lady Davers. The description given of Lucy Steele's character is perhaps as good a summary of Pamela as one could hope to find: 'the active, contriving manager; uniting at once a desire of smart appearance with the utmost frugality, and ashamed to be suspected of half her economical practices; pursuing her own interest in every thought; courting the favour of Colonel Brandon, Mrs Jennings, and of every wealthy friend ... a most encouraging instance of what an earnest, an unceasing attention to self-interest, will do in securing every advantage of fortune, with no other sacrifice than that of time and conscience' (Chs. xlviii and l). By her gratitude for the unkindness she receives, Lucy Steele becomes necessary to Mrs Ferrars as Pamela does to Lady Davers. The interest in social distinctions, in manners and morals, is common to Richardson and Jane Austen, though the discriminations of the later novelist are so much more delicate as to make the efforts of the pioneer read like a burlesque. But the sentiments of Lady Davers are essentially those of Lady Catherine de Bourgh. The one says:

'Thou'rt almost got into a fool's paradise, I doubt! And wilt find thyself terribly mistaken in a little while, if thou thinkest my brother will disgrace his family to humour thy baby-face!'

(II, p. 146.)

Lady Catherine de Bourgh is equally violent:

'The upstart pretensions of a young woman without family, connections, or fortune. Is this to be endured? But it must not, shall not be. If you were sensible of your own good, you would not wish to quit the sphere, in which you have been brought up.'

(*Pride and Prejudice*, Ch. lvi.)

The reactions of Pamela and Elizabeth Bennet to the formidable challenge are, of course, completely different, the one passively retiring to her closet, the other, after utterly annihilating her enemy, politely escorting her to her carriage. The difference in response accords with the difference in social standing of the two characters, and this, in its turn, reflects the widely different interests of the two writers.

Despite the number of parodies of it that were made, *Pamela* won immediate popularity. In January 1741, two months after the publication of the book, *The Gentleman's Magazine* stated that it was 'judged in Town as great a Sign of Want of Curiosity not to have read *Pamela* as not to have seen the *French* and *Italian* Dancers'.[8] 'It was usual for ladies to hold up the volumes of *Pamela* to one another, to shew they had got the book that every one was talking of', said Mrs Barbauld,[9] and a later female admirer noted that 'the person that had not read *Pamela* was disqualified for conversation, of which it was the principal subject for a long time.'[10] Six years after its publication in England it had been translated into French, German, and Italian, and the younger Crébillon wrote from France to Lord Chesterfield that 'Without *Pamela* we should not know what to say or do here'.[11] Its popularity continued for a long time. In 1820 Leigh Hunt drew a picture of the maidservant of his day. Her property includes 'an odd volume of *Pamela*, and perhaps a sixpenny play, such as *George Barnwell* or Mrs Behn's *Oroonoko*'.[12]

Richardson, however, was not satisfied. He was concerned lest his first novel should appear to encourage the idea that 'a reformed rake makes the best husband'. *Clarissa*, his second novel, was written partly to disprove this. It was intended, according to the preface, 'to warn the inconsiderate and thoughtless of the one sex, against the base arts and designs of specious contrivers of the other, and to caution parents against the undue exercise of their natural authority over their children in the great article of marriage.' The actions and conduct of the worthy characters were to exemplify the highest and most important doctrines not only of morality, but of Christianity.

The first part of the novel is concerned with the efforts of Clarissa's family to persuade her to marry a certain Mr Soames, whom she detests. Here Richardson was dealing with a problem relevant to his day, when women were only just beginning to emerge from a position of subservience. Clarissa recognizes the right of her parents to forbid a marriage of which they disapprove. But she opposes their attempts to force her to marry against her will. Clarissa's situation is similar to that of Dorothy Osborne and of many others in real life, though Dorothy's attitude was the more obsequious.[13]

The novel really comes to life from the moment that Clarissa is tricked into putting herself under the protection of Lovelace, a character that Richardson took from a play, *The Fair Penitent*, by Nicholas Rowe. Comparing Lovelace with Lothario in his *Life of Rowe*, Dr Johnson remarked 'it was in the power of Richardson alone to teach us at once esteem and detestation, to make virtuous resentment overpower all the benevolence which wit, elegance, and courage naturally excite; and to lose at last the hero in the villain'. In Richardson's second novel the villain is a much more complex character than Mr B — in *Pamela*, and he is successful in his attempt at seduction. The heroine gains a moral triumph over her disaster instead of a material reward. Many of the situations that occur in *Pamela* are repeated in *Clarissa*: it is in the more subtle manner of treatment that the difference lies.

After quoting a passage from *Clarissa* in which the heroine speaks of 'one half of humanity tormenting the other, and being tormented themselves in tormenting', E. M. Forster compares Richardson and Henry James as two writers who are 'looking at life from the same angle', psychologists sensitive to human suffering who appreciate self-sacrifice and whose work is characterized by 'a sort of tremulous nobility'.[14] Tremulous nobility describes perfectly the impression that Clarissa makes on the reader, and she does so without becoming at all unreal or unduly self-righteous. Her friend Miss Howe strikes this note at the beginning of the novel. It is sustained throughout, and only emphasized by the ignobility of her family, Lovelace, and his appalling associates:

> 'So steady, so uniform in your conduct: so desirous, as you always said, of sliding through life to the end of it unnoted; and, as I may add, not wishing to be observed even for your silent benevolence; sufficiently happy in the noble conscious-ness which attends it: *Rather useful than glaring*, your deserved motto; though now, to your regret, pushed into blaze, as I may say: and yet blamed at home for the fault of others ...'
>
> (I, Letter I, p. 2.)

Lovelace, who 'was always as mischievous as a monkey', is, in a sense, merely a means to bring out the essential nobility of the heroine. He is the conventional stage villain who, as he himself says, 'had been a rogue, had I been a plough-boy'. Yet his description of Clarissa is as rapturous and glowing as Tom Jones's paean to Sophia. He compares himself to Milton's Satan: but he is also an eighteenth-century Leander who can celebrate the beauty of his Hero in prose that almost rivals the Elizabethan richness of Marlowe's poetry:

> Thou hast often heard me launch out in praise of her com-plexion. I never beheld in my life a skin so illustriously fair. The lily and the driven snow it is nonsense to talk of: her lawn and her laces one might indeed compare to those: but what a whited wall would a woman appear to be, who had a com-plexion which would justify such unnatural comparisons? But this lady is all glowing, all charming flesh and blood; yet so clear, that every meandering vein is to be seen, in all the lovely parts of her which custom permits to be visible.
>
> Thou hast heard me also describe the wavy ringlets of her shiny hair, needing neither art nor powder; of itself an orna-ment, defying all other ornaments; wantoning in and about a neck that is beautiful beyond description.
>
> Her head-dress as a Brussels-lace mob, peculiarly adapted to the charming air and turn of her features. A sky-blue riband illustrated that. But, although the weather was somewhat sharp, she had not on either hat or hood. ...

... Her morning-gown was a pale primrose-coloured paduasoy; the cuffs and robings curiously embroidered by the fingers of this ever-charming Arachne, in a running pattern of violets and their leaves; the light in the flowers silver; gold in the leaves. A pair of diamond snaps in her ears. A white handkerchief wrought by the same inimitable fingers, concealed – O Belford! what still more inimitable beauties did it not conceal! – And I saw, all the way we rode, the bounding heart (by its throbbing motions I saw it!) dancing beneath the charming umbrage.

Her ruffles were the same as her mob. Her apron a flowered lawn. Her coat white satin, quilted: blue satin her shoes, braided with the same colour, without lace; for what need has the prettiest foot in the world of ornament? Neat buckles in them: and on her charming arms a pair of black velvet glove-like muffs, or her own invention; for she makes and gives fashion as she pleases. – Her hands velvet of themselves, thus uncovered the freer to be grasped by those of her adorer.

(III, Letter V, pp. 29–30.)

Clarissa's beauty and nobility, thus evoked, are set against the background of Mrs Sinclair, the procuress, the brothel in which she lives, and the house of the sheriff's officer in which she is later arrested for debt and lodged. Mrs Sinclair is described with the same realism as Mrs Jewkes had been in *Pamela*: 'The old dragon straddled up to her, with her arms kimboed again, her eye-brows erect, like the bristles upon a hog's back, and, scowling over her shortened nose, more than half-hid her ferret eyes.' Tormented physically and mentally, subjected to every sort of humiliation and victimization, Clarissa's spirit never breaks. The accompanying abuse that she has to suffer from her family is shown to be as criminal as the physical humiliations inflicted, and to be, in fact, the direct cause of them. Clarissa's greatness is that, while resisting and defending herself to the uttermost, she accepts her fate as just. In cutting herself off from her family, however unjust they are, she cuts herself off from society of the normal kind, but not from God. The situation is a genuinely tragic one.

The agonies and atrocities are relentlessly piled on and culminate in the final physical outrage, after which, for Clarissa, there only remains death. There must, it is suggested, be a world after this to do justice to injured merit and to punish such barbarous perfidy. But this is hinted rather than directly stated. For the reader who has followed the story closely, Clarissa's death comes as a positive relief. The idea of some sort of retribution is merely dramatically suggested in the contrast of the death-scenes of Clarissa and Mrs Sinclair. It is here, in its dramatic presentation of what Christian fortitude and resignation can achieve when the world has done its worst, that this almost completely masochistic novel transcends itself. After all that Clarissa has undergone, Richardson is still able to show, as in *Pamela* he had failed to do, virtue triumphant. Lovelace's description of her on her death-bed, his realization that essentially she is untouched, contains the implicit compliment paid by vice to her nobility; while the reformed accomplice, Belford, gives the last turn of the screw in his account of the end of Mrs Sinclair. After this, the inevitable duel and the death of Lovelace at the hands of Clarissa's single, though ineffective, family supporter, Colonel Morden, appears as a matter of comparatively minor importance, though it does result in the story ending on a note of just retribution.

Richardson's last novel, *Sir Charles Grandison*, was an attempt to present, in contrast to Lovelace, a picture of the ideal gentleman. Though Sir Charles's Italian admirer, Clementina, goes mad, the novel is, generally speaking, lacking in the more melodramatic type of incident. The attempt at the seduction of the heroine, Harriet Byron, by Sir Hargrave Pollexfen, is a very tame affair compared with the activities of Mr B — and Lovelace. Because of the more placid interest in manners and morals, this appears to have been Jane Austen's favourite among the novels.

The characters, divided into men, women, and Italians, are taken almost exclusively from 'high life'. Harriet Byron is the most beautiful woman in England: Clementina, her rival for the hand of the perfect gentleman, is the noblest lady on the Continent. Harriet prefers Clementina to herself. Yet despite this façade, the tone and attitude of the novelist inevitably reflect his middle-class origins. One critic remarked with justice that the description of Grandison Hall sounds like a passage from an auctioneer's catalogue.[15] The characters similarly betray their origin. Harriet Byron, for instance, 'is one of the best economists, and yet one of the finest ladies in the country'. Her life is one of 'orderliness, method, harmony, observance ... ease, dignity, condescension ... she hardly ever was heard to direct twice the same thing to be done or remembered' (V, Letter XX, pp. 140-1). An ideal domestic manager like Pamela, she believes in method and early hours, 'ease without hurry will do anything'. Prudence is as much her characteristic as Pamela's too. She even confesses to be a prude and a Puritan 'in the best senses of those abused words'.

Sir Charles Grandison himself is a quite impossible figure of perfection. Honour and punctilio direct all his actions, and Clementina goes so far as to entreat him to forgive her for preferring God to himself. Not merely the perfect gentleman, he is also the perfect butler. While waiting on the bride and the company at his own wedding feast he makes the waiters look awkward. He is also the embodiment of sentiment, in the best sense, 'Imitating the Divinity, he regards the heart, rather than the head'. A perfect courtier, he disarms two of his enemies, Major O'Hara and Captain Salmonet, but cannot forgive himself for violating the sanctity of his own house. On another occasion, when he refuses to fight his enemies, he can still succeed in extracting admiration from them for his magnanimity. He also possesses the supreme gift of making a compliment to one lady without depreciating the others who are present (for he is, of course, perpetually surrounded by women). As one of them says, 'You are Sir Charles Grandison. Sir, I need not say more.'

A few attempts are made to introduce some human traits into this effigy. He confesses himself that he is naturally choleric, 'subject to sudden gusts of passion', and that he is proud and ambitious. Yet he convinces both the ladies who love him that he is too good for them to accept. He is threatened by another with a poniard, but succeeds in subduing her by his bearing. Even the villain is rescued by Sir Charles late on in the story, and kneels to his deliverer. In Italy, the bishop asserts that if he were one of them he might expect canonization: 'His Holiness Himself would receive you with blessings at the footstool of his throne.' Since, in fact, Sir Charles can put himself in everyone's situation and can forget his own interest so completely, no one can hold out against him. His conduct to his horses, even, is impeccable, for he refuses to dock their tails. Only once is he guilty of trickery. Harriet Byron is persuaded to sign a letter which he has doubled down so that she does not see that she is agreeing to hasten the marriage. But this merely confirms his perfection, since he has forestalled her own wishes. He is, in fact, an example of unbounded charity and universal benevolence to people of all professions, though he is no leveller but believes that rank or degree entitles a man, who is not utterly unworthy, to respect. Amidst all the infection of fashionable vice and folly, his only weaknesses are the few that have been mentioned. But among readers he has not been a universally popular character. Leslie Stephen unkindly described him as a spinner out of indefinite twaddle of a superior kind, and recalled Becky Sharp's famous reflection upon the moral effect of five thousand a year.[16]

Clementina's family, the Porrettas, have also all the English middle-class virtues. They are affectionate to one another, sharing each other's suffering. For as Richardson remarks, 'in Italy, as well as in other countries, there are persons of honour, of goodness, of generosity, and who are above reserve, vindictiveness, jealousy, and those other bad passions by which some mark indiscriminately a whole nation'. Clementina, in particular, has the delicacy which distinguishes the woman of true honour. After all her troubles, she gains glory after her death, for a temple is erected to her in the garden of the Grandisons.

The ideal standards of manners and morals are the same for all the characters. Modesty, good sense, and amiable temper – the Addisonian ideals, in fact – are taken as normal for both sexes, for all ranks of society, in all civilized countries. Wit is reconciled with politeness, and humour restrained by decorum. There is a certain Dr Bartlett, to whom Sir Charles addresses much of his correspondence, and who embodies these standards even more completely than Sir Charles himself. He is described as 'a saint and at the same time a man of true politeness'. Sir Charles recommends his example to Mr Grandison, a reformed rake, who will, he says, be civilized, 'when you can be serious on serious subjects, yet so cheerful in your seriousness, as if it sat easy upon you'. Exactly the same words had been used in *The Tatler* 5. Here a religious work is praised because

> it is written with the Spirit of one who has seen the World enough to under-value it with good Breeding. The Author must certainly be a man of Wisdom as well as Piety, and have spent much Time in the Exercise of both. The real Causes of

Decay of the Interest of Religion are set forth in a clear and lively manner, without unseasonable Passions; and the whole Air of the Book, as to the Language, the Sentiments, and the Reasonings, shews it was written by one whose Virtue sits easy about him, and to whom Vice is thoroughly contemptible. It was said by one of this Company, alluding to that Knowledge of the World the Author seems to have, the Man writes much like a Gentleman, and goes to Heaven with a very good Mien.

Such a work might well have been written by Sir Charles Grandison himself. For he makes it a tacit rule never to begin a journey on Sunday, nor, except when in pursuit of works of mercy or necessity, to travel in time of Divine service. In the absence of a clergyman, he himself says grace at the table, and in church he edifies everybody by his cheerful piety. We can well imagine that both Sir Charles Grandison and Dr Bartlett 'would go to Heaven with a very good Mien'.

It is Richardson's achievement in this novel to have dramatized the ethical and social principles of *The Tatler* and of *The Spectator* so that they could be used by later novelists, such as Fanny Burney and Jane Austen, who had come under other influences, particularly that of Dr Johnson. Jane Austen found the manner and matter of *The Spectator* disgusting to a person of real taste: 'the substance of its papers so often consisting in the statement of improbable circumstances, unnatural characters, and topics of conversation, which no longer concern any one living; and their language too frequently so coarse as to give no very favourable idea of the age that could endure it'.[17] On the other hand, 'every circumstance narrated in *Sir Charles Grandison*, all that was ever said or done in the cedar parlour was familiar to her; and the wedding days of Lady L. and Lady G. were so well remembered as if they had been among living friends'.[18] There is an upstart called Captain Anderson in *Sir Charles Grandison*, who pays court to Harriet Byron's friend, Charlotte Grandison, who might be the model for Willoughby in *Sense and Sensibility* or Wickham in *Pride and Prejudice*. The style of the writing itself, with its subtlety and delicacy of touch, its crispness tending naturally towards epigram, recalls Jane Austen's:

Captain Anderson appeared to me at first a man of sense, as well as an agreeable man in his person and air. He had a lively and easy elocution. He spoke without doubt, and I had therefore the less doubt of his understanding. The man who knows how to say agreeable things to a woman in an agreeable manner has her vanity on his side, since to doubt his veracity would be to question her own merit. When he came to write, my judgement was even still more engaged in his favour than before. But when he thought himself on a safe footing with me, he then lost his handwriting, and his style, and even his orthography.

(II, Letter XXXV, p. 225.)

The theme of the father who is nearly responsible for the ruin of his daughters inevitably reminds the reader of Mr Bennet in *Pride and Prejudice* and of Sir Thomas Bertram in *Mansfield Park*:

Thus had Sir Thomas Grandison with all his pride like to have thrown his daughter, a woman of high character, fine understanding, and an exalted mind, into the arms of a man who had neither fortune nor education, nor yet good sense nor generosity of heart, to countenance his pretensions to such a lady, or her for marrying beneath herself.

(II, Letter XXXVI, p. 267.)

A complete account of the influence of Richardson's novels would require a volume in itself. In England, France, and Germany his works fundamentally altered and shaped the course of the development of fiction. His influence in England was particularly strong on the women writers and readers who patronized the new circulating libraries. In France, Prévost, his translator, said that *Clarissa* had to be softened and watered down to adapt it to the more delicate taste of the French. But Diderot, in his famous *Éloge*, expressed unrestrained admiration: 'O Richardson, Richardson, first of men in my eyes, you shall be my reading at all times! Pursued by pressing needs; if my friend should fall into poverty; if the limitations of my fortune should prevent me from giving fit attention to the education of my children, I will sell my books; but you shall remain on the same shelf as Moses, Euripides, and Sophocles, and I will read you by turns.' Such different writers as Rousseau in *La Nouvelle Héloïse*, and Choderlos de Laclos, the author of *Les Liaisons Dangereuses* (who called *Clarissa* 'un chef d'oeuvre des hommes'), acknowledged their debt. His German translator, Gellert, Professor of Rhetoric at Leipzig, confessed that 'I have formerly wept away some of the most remarkable hours of my life, in a sort of delicious misery, over the seventh volume of *Clarissa* and the fifth of *Grandison*.'[19] The influence on the early Goethe, particularly on *Werther*, is well known.

But perhaps it is only right that the last word on Richardson should be with that discriminating English reader, who, while admiring his power of creating and preserving the consistency of his characters, and whose knowledge of his works was 'probably such as no one is likely again to acquire',[20] could yet still see his faults. In Jane Austen's unfinished novel, *Sanditon*, there is a satirical portrait of a typically enthusiastic admirer of Richardson. Sir Edward Denham had read more sentimental novels than agreed with him: 'his fancy had been early caught by all the impassioned, & most exceptionable parts of Richardson; & such Authors as have since appeared to tread in Richardson's steps, so far as Man's determined pursuit of Woman in defiance of every opposition of feeling and convenience is concerned.' These works had since 'occupied the greater part of his literary hours, & formed his character'. The result of his addiction is shown in the later part of the story. Jane Austen both appreciated Richardson's virtues and was one of his keenest critics. Her mockery was all the more effective because of its delicacy. She owed much to him, but her six slim major novels also contain the final implied comment on his prolix art with its curious mixture of coarseness and distinction.[21]

NOTES

1. See *The Notebooks of Henry James*, ed. F. O. Matthiessen and Kenneth B. Murdock (1947), pp. 11–12.

2. Louis B. Wright: *Middle Class Culture in Elizabethan England* (Chapel Hill, North Carolina, 1935), pp. 476–7.

3. *Pamela*, vol. I, p. 119. The references are to the edition of the complete works with a prefatory note by Austin Dobson and a Life and Introduction by Prof. W. M. Lyon Phelps (London, 1902). In the case of *Pamela*, references are to the volume and page only, since a large proportion of the novel is taken up with her journal. In quotations from *Clarissa* and *Sir Charles Grandison* the number of the letter is also given, for the convenience of readers of other editions.

4. B. W. Downs, *Samuel Richardson* (*The Republic of Letters* Series), p. 112.

5. *Lettre sur Pamela*, quoted by Prof. B. W. Downs, *Samuel Richardson*, p. 101.

6. D. H. Lawrence, *Pornography and Obscenity*. See *Phoenix: The Posthumous Papers of D. H. Lawrence*, ed. with an introduction by Edward D. McDonald (1936), p. 174.

7. Swift, *A Meditation upon a Broom-Stick.*

8. Quoted by F. S. Boas in 'Richardson's Novels and their Influence', in *Essays and Studies of the English Association*, II, p. 46.

9. A. L. Barbauld in *The Life of Richardson* prefaced to *The Correspondence of Samuel Richardson* 1804, p. lviii.

10. Clara Reeve, *The Progress of Romance* (W. Keymer, 1785), I, p. 133.

11. Quoted by C. L. Thomson, *Samuel Richardson. A Biographical and Critical Study* (1900), p. 272.

12. Quoted by M. Phillips and W. S. Tomkinson, *Women's Education in the Eighteenth Century* (1926), p. 162.

13. See *The Letters from Dorothy Osborne to Sir William Temple* (Everyman Library).

14. E. M. Forster, *Aspects of the Novel* (1949), p. 18.

15. C. L. Thomson, *Samuel Richardson. A Biographical and Critical Study* (1900), p. 264.

16. Leslie Stephen, *Hours in a Library*, I, pp. 57 and 73 (new ed., 1909). This excellent essay is by far the best brief introduction to Richardson's novels.

17. From Jane Austen, *Northanger Abbey*, ch. v, final paragraph.

18. J. E. Austen-Leigh, *Memoir of Jane Austen*, ed. R. W. Chapman (1951), p. 89.

19. Quoted by C. L. Thomson, *Samuel Richardson*, p. 285.

20. J. E. Austen-Leigh, *op. cit.*, p. 89.

21. Since writing this essay, two articles have been printed, bearing on the subject of Richardson's novels: 'Clarissa Harlowe and Her Times', by Christopher Hill, *Essays in Criticism*, v (Oct. 1955), and David Daiches's address to the National Book League, published in his *Literary Essays* (1956).

See also Ian Watt, *The Rise of the Novel* (1957).

FIELDING AND SMOLLETT

A. R. HUMPHREYS

Do Fielding and Smollett, with all their reputation as masters of Augustan fiction, still earn their survival as parts of a living 'heritage'? Should the modern reader, besieged by an unmanageable abundance of books, be persuaded to reserve some room for them in his overcrowded attention? Reading them demands not only large stretches of time but also a degree of stamina beyond what mere length in itself would necessitate. Sentence rhythm had in their time not yet acquired for both writer and reader that almost hypnotic flow, that internal stimulating dynamic of self-propulsion, which is common in their great Victorian successors; it still had the strength and in some degree the resistance too of vestigial formality. In Fielding this formality is, as it were, an excellent natural discipline for his abundant vigour of idea – it shows his intellectual awareness of what his creative energy is doing, and it phrases his ideas with aphoristic definition and calculated sequence. The art of the comic writer is evinced here in controlled direction of effort, and even a minor (though delightful) work like the *Voyage to Lisbon* gains a most individual flavour, as a journal of travel, by the ranging and ordering wit. In Smollett the formality is that of firm animated muscular vigour, the native burly idiom of Augustanism. In other words, both novelists exact from the reader a degree (Smollett perhaps the larger) of labour – more so than Scott's easy (though often prolix) expansiveness, than Dickens's vivid hypnotic compulsion, than Trollope's almost excessive consideration for his reader's comfort. It is true that some nineteenth-century novelists deserve a close focus of attention – Jane Austen, Peacock, Emily Brontë, George Eliot, and, indeed, Dickens too – but that is a different thing: they offer significant shades, and details acutely appropriate, the perception of which results in a more discriminating sense of life. The attention needed for Fielding and Smollett is less refined, less a detection of intelligent precisions (though their decisive styles merit continuous observation), than the exercise of mental muscle grappling with a solid body of material expressed with a kind of burly obviousness.

Yet if their styles put up some resistance, both novelists are invitingly wide and hospitable in the survey they make of life, realistically observed and humorously presented: Dryden's praise of Chaucer – that 'we have our forefathers and great-grand-dames all before us' – is apt both in the letter and the spirit. This breadth of life, animated either by Fielding's notable evolution of narrative or Smollett's episodic vehemence, is the originating force of these novels and still, in its comic revelation, the source of their appeal. Fielding's allegiance is to jovial mirth and to a moral sanity which disregards a good deal of convention in favour of goodheartedness; in *Tom Jones* he invokes 'Genius, thou gift of Heaven' as the inspiration of the large comedy of the ages.

> Come, thou that hast inspired thy Aristophanes, thy Lucian, thy Cervantes, thy Rabelais, thy Molière, thy Shakespeare, thy Swift, thy Marivaux, fill my pages with humour; till mankind learn the good nature to laugh only at the follies of others, and the humility to grieve at their own.

Smollett's allegiance is less to such great figures (who, it will be noted, represent on the whole a wealth of intellectual amusement as well as mere comedy of incident) than to the long tradition of miscellaneous incident, devoid of organized plan, whose exemplars were the popular novels of Spain and whose comic spirit was a delight in physical violence and the satiric grotesque. Except (it is a large, an all-important, exception) for his last work, *Humphry Clinker* (1771), Smollett's comedy with its strong element of barbarism has worn worse than Fielding's: as one turns from his usual crowded canvas, impetuous with bustling oddities and almost overbearing with the packed particulars of eighteenth-century life, to the broadly conceived and luminously executed fictional world of Fielding, one perceives at once in the latter a conception of life both more intelligent and more generous.

Enjoyment then is the reward, but not the enjoyment of mere passive reception. Both novelists arouse one to life – Fielding with a broad, controlled comedy of its normal truth, Smollett with such an accentuation of physical realism as bites deeply and perhaps uncomfortably into the consciousness. The enjoyment has not only this active and forceful quality: it is accompanied by knowledge and comprehensiveness also. One is receiving a populous picture of the national life and spirit; the novels are not merely diversions but accurate panoramas of something real, a permanent furnishing of the mind with impressions adequate to the large subject of Hanoverian national life.

This quality has often been remarked, especially in Fielding. A central position has rightly been claimed for him in the landscape of his time. In that masterly guide to intellectual life the *History of English Thought in the Eighteenth Century*, Leslie Stephen, in the full-ness of his knowledge, suggested that 'a complete criticism of the English artistic literature of the eighteenth century would place Fielding at the centre, and measure the completeness of other repre-sentatives pretty much as they recede from or approach to his work'. The procedure, one might suppose, would hardly work if it were a poet who was brought up for trial – Fielding's spirit is essentially that of prose – but as long as the question is concerned with attitudes to life the results might not be unfair. Elsewhere he makes a more extensive judgement:

> His work gives quite a peculiar impression of solidity and reality. Like the work of his friend Hogarth ... we have the conviction that the man has given an absolutely faithful por-trait of all that came within his sphere of vision. He has drawn the men and women of his land so faithfully that we learn more from him of the true character of his contempor-aries than we learn even from a direct observation of the men themselves. An accurate picture of eighteenth-century society may of course be constructed from the memoirs and letters and the various annals of the time. ... But in Fielding's novels we find the work already done to our hands; the essential fact is presented to us in a social picture. ... It is not merely that his portraits are faithful, but that his estimate of the actual forces at work impresses us as absolutely trust-worthy. So far as Fielding sees at all, he sees the real facts, and the important facts.

Repeated readings of Fielding confirm the judgement. Except for Boswell in the *Life of Johnson* there is no other writer who more fairly and comprehensively transports us to Hanoverian England – Horace Walpole, more brilliant, is often showy and sometimes silly. Smollett's 'truth' is not in this way central; not less true than Fielding's to the actual facts of life (there are historical parallels to his coarseness and barbarity), it goes by choice to the odder features of the Hanoverian physiognomy. It corresponds, indeed, to the crude boisterous vigour so frequent in Hanoverian life; it is a selection of physical reality satirically exaggerated. Fielding's is the higher and more philosophical truth which epitomizes the spirit, the ethos, as well as the body, of the time, which deals primarily not in externals but in the nature of man and in an intellectual and moral code.

For a central assessment Fielding was fortunately placed, though mere placing apart from genius would of course be of no avail. Still, given his genius, he had some advantages which compensated for the severe struggles which lie behind (but very little affect) all his work, from the early *Miscellanies* to the valedictory *Voyage to Lisbon*. At one end of the social scale he belonged to the prosperity and culture of the gentry and the well-to-do professionals; at the other he was involved with the poor, struggling on the fringes of Grub Street as hack-playwright, hack-translator, and combative journalist. After 1748, though still poor, he became the most famous of Bow-Street magistrates, immediately concerned with crime and suffering. Travelling on legal journeys between London and the West, over that territory carefully annotated in *Tom Jones*, observing the life of the roads, on intimate terms with the oligarchy, clergy, doctors, actors, writers and lawyers (two hundred legal friends subscribed to the *Miscellanies*), himself country gentleman, hackauthor, propagandist for the Government, magistrate, and social reformer, and illuminating all these activities with a living and humorous sense of classical and modern literature, Fielding seems to focus in himself a large part of the concerns of his generation, and to dominate them with shrewd intelligence and large humanity. His religious position is no less representative than his social; admiring Locke and the great Restoration divines (Captain Booth is redeemed in *Amelia* by reading Isaac Barrow), scorning the Pope and Pretender in the vigorous anti-Stuartry of *Tom Jones* (Books VII, xi, and VIII, ix) and of the anti-Jacobite periodicals *The True Patriot* and *The Jacobite's Journal*, holding with Parson Adams (in his argument with Parson Barnabas; *Joseph Andrews*, Book I, xvii) that God prefers the virtuous heathen to the vicious Christian, Fielding embodies his age in that sensible religion which is discreetly uninquisitive about mystery but is responsibly earnest about conduct and charity. The honest religious trust of Parson Adams, the intelligent full-blooded decency of Dr Harrison in *Amelia*, are the century's central religious attitudes; the greedy vulgarity of Parson Trulliber (*Joseph Andrews*, II, xiv) and the uncharitable pedantry of Captain Blifil (*Tom Jones*, II, v) and Parson Thwackum (*Tom Jones*, III, iii) are as far extravagant on the orthodox side as the intellectual hypocrisy of the Deist philosopher Square (*Tom Jones*, III, iii) is on the heterodox. Again, if Square be taken to represent a second eccentricity – that of unmitigated rationalism – Fielding is equally opposed both to him and to his opposite of fulsome sensibility. Against the unattractive and unnatural postures of stoic virtue on the one hand and the cultivation of emotional indulgence on the other (both fashions in Augustan psychology), he maintains a temperate strength of feeling and a trust in the good-natured impulses of life.

These qualities are evident in *Joseph Andrews* (1742), as sane and attractive a novel as there is. Drawn, as Fielding says, in imitation of Cervantes, its Don Quixote is the unforgettable Parson Adams. Fielding had been under the highly appropriate influence of Cervantes for years; when at twenty he went to Leyden his play *Don Quixote in England* was already sketched, and when he was twenty-seven it appeared as a ballad-opera, with knightly idealist, low-comedy Sancho, comic inn-keeper Guzzle, venal mayor and corporation, and a boisterous squire pointing towards his own Western in *Tom Jones*. Quixote and Adams both live for an ideal, and see the world coloured by it, no matter how experience contradicts them. Adams, like Quixote, is an idealist in his reading; 'knowledge of men', he asserts, 'is only to be learnt from books – Plato and Seneca for that'. He is devoted to Aeschylus, but has never opened the worldly Pope. From the theories of his naturally Christian nature he emerges, under every impulse of a generous combative temper, into the rough and tumble of real life; he is doctrinaire as long as to be so shows a Christian disposition, but as soon as doctrine means narrowness or rigidity he breaks his bonds. At the best he is a Hogarthian figure; it comes naturally to him to be swamped in a basin of hog's blood, butted in the stomach by the hard head of a ruffian, laid low by Parson Trulliber's pig, pummelled with a dirty mop, and assailed by a pack of hounds. Yet not for a moment does he forfeit the affection his warmth of heart compels, or the respect due to his courage.

Of the other persons in the book, Joseph and Fanny are, though unremarkable, a counter in their natural and unintroverted feelings to Richardson's emotional melodrama in *Pamela*: Lady Booby hovers over the action with a kind of glowering life, treated with a ruthlessly funny lack of sympathy; and Squire Booby and Beau Didapper are mere formulae. Those who stick in the mind are rather the grotesques (not extravagantly grotesque, however) like Mrs Slipslop, the inn-keeping Towwouses and the gross Trulliber, and a sketch gallery of minor figures touched off by a characterizing phrase or two each, who populate the book admirably and testify how much invention Fielding has left after he has conceived his major figures and incidents. With few exceptions their hall-mark is that they are 'natural'; if they make themselves ridiculous it is with the ridiculousness of life itself. For the territory Fielding is opening up (and his Preface shows him entirely conscious of his innovations) is that in which both the fanciful idealism of the heroic romance is rejected, on the one side, and the farcical burlesque on the other. Satire is to abound, since the comic novel like the comic drama treats of foibles and affectations, but it is not the novel's major purpose, which is to bring its readers to a healthy and resilient frame of mind through good humour, and that is best found in the recognition of the true comedy that lies around them.

The next important work occurs in the *Miscellanies* (1743): it is Fielding's main incursion into irony, *The Life of the Late Jonathan Wild the Great*. In the significantly distinguished subscription list (including the Prince of Wales, Pitt, Lyttelton, Garrick, Kitty Clive, a liberal sprinkling of the peerage, and a striking number – more than half the subscribers – of Fielding's fellow-lawyers) the most piquant name is that of Sir Robert Walpole, here contributing to a severe dissection of what he, as a representative 'great man', stood for. Fielding revived the story of the historical Wild (executed in 1725, and already an ironic legend celebrated by Defoe, Swift, and Pope, among others) for two ends, the lesser being to undermine the Prime Minister (who fell, however, before the book appeared), the greater to expose corrupt aggrandisement in general. As *Joseph Andrews* simultaneously upholds the accepted structure of society yet brings all men to the equalitarian judgement of morality asserted through humour, so *Jonathan Wild* maintains that structure too, but levels all men by an ironically assumed anti-morality. This needs explaining. What the book does is to assert moral decency by ironically admiring villainy, and moral equalitarianism by showing top and bottom of society moved by the same anti-morality; all power-seekers, in court or gaol, are identical in their treachery. Yet since this admiration and recommendation of villainy is patently ironic, the reader's orthodoxy is fortified; villainy is commended so scornfully that no one could do other than scorn it too. *Joseph Andrews* unifies society across the recognized class-structure by observing those moral values before which men are equal – that is the function of Parson Adams, in his socially low station (his cloth being, in the circumstances of the time, no guarantee of esteem), yet with his moral independence which puts the laws of God before everything. *Jonathan Wild* unifies society, across the conventional antithesis of high and low life, by showing all 'great' men moved by the same immoral principles (*The Beggar's Opera* had done the same thing),[1] and compels the reader to despise them. The book is not faultless; in particular the victimized Mr and Mrs Heartfree are insipid. But though it has some of the weaknesses of propaganda, it goes far beyond mere satire on one man and gains in grandeur both from its panoramic survey of corrupt power and from the mordant strength and control of the ironic and mock-heroic style.[2]

Of *Tom Jones* (1749) one may say, as did Dryden of Chaucer's *Canterbury Tales*, 'here is God's plenty'. The description Fielding applied to *Joseph Andrews*, 'a comic epic poem in prose', is still more applicable here; the scale is larger and the representation of the spirit of the land and age an ampler panorama. Fielding was guided in the art of his fiction by certain critical preconceptions; recognizing himself as 'the founder of a new province of writing', he claimed the liberty 'to make what laws I please therein'. The new province is not that of the prose tale as such, of course, but that of the prose tale so intelligently organized that everything contributes to a pattern and the whole is life intellectually disposed and clarified. Its laws include the discipline of relevance and proportion; they prescribe human nature in its life-like normality to be the subject-matter, and they demand of the author the four-fold equipment of 'genius' (the combination of invention and judgement), knowledge (of history and literature), wide social experience, and generous sympathies.

An epic unfolds a large scene and space of time. *Tom Jones* begins before the hero's birth with an agreeable landscape in the manner of Hanoverian topography and with the benevolent Squire Allworthy's country house (Gothic as a sign of surviving, or reviving, taste). The foundling hero is discovered; the range of characters expands through the Allworthy circle, the village folk, the neighbouring Squire Western with his learned-lady sister and (later) his daughter Sophia, and a miscellaneous company of gamekeepers, parsons, inn-keepers and wives, sergeants and soldiers, doctors and lawyers, beaux and libertines, all moving on a well-plotted stage and all tied in to the texture of this 'heroic, historic, prosaic poem' by a manner of imagery to be discussed later. The characters have the stored traditional force of standard types, together with a new vitality of fresh observation: Parson Supple is the sycophantic chaplain of Restoration comedy; the doctors Fielding always satirizes have their prototypes in Molière; the learned lady reappears as Mrs Western; the pedantic or rascally lawyer and justice, the insolent chambermaid or porter, the irascible hunting squire, the hacks of Grub Street – these are part of the traditional portrait gallery. Fielding's hand in them is distinguished for vitality rather than novelty, but the effect of his working with such accepted moulds is to fill the mind with a social pattern that goes beyond the personal and becomes as it were a distillation of communal consciousness. The best example of his reworking of traditional material is the portrait of Squire Western. In fact, real persons may unwittingly have posed for this; two Tory landowners who came within Fielding's ken, Sir Paulet St John and Carew Hervey Mildmay, have been proposed as originals. But the boorish country squire, tyrannically affectionate to an only daughter, boisterous in the idiom of the stable, derives also from Restoration comedy – for instance, Vanbrugh's Sir Tunbelly Clumsy in *The Relapse* – and Fielding had already adapted him as Squire Badger in *Don Quixote in England*. Fielding's invention seems to work best (as with Parson Adams too) where a general model is in view, but the incarnation of it depends on his own abundant observation of men. Certainly he was no friend to mere derivation; 'Vanbrugh and Congreve copied Nature', he remarks, 'but they who copy them draw as unlike the present age as Hogarth would do if he was to paint a rout or drum,* in the dresses of Titian or of Vandyke. In short, imitation here will not do the business. The picture must be after Nature herself.'³ But equally certainly his work gets a special dimension in being a summation, as it were, of what others had prepared. Epic is not an invention of original material but the interpretation of accepted story so as to base it broadly in national consciousness: Fielding does this in his comic epic.

Yet to say merely that would be misleading: not everything in Fielding sums up tradition. *Tom Jones* is novel in its intelligent control of material, the generosity of its attitudes to life, and most of all in its heroine and hero – the former a courageous, affectionate, and honourable girl who contrasts sharply with Richardson's Pamela, the latter a vigorous, impulsive, fallible, but likeable, young man who contains much of Fielding himself and derives from a fresh knowledge of life. The novel gives a combined impression, then, of tradition still in living contact with social fact, and of original comic genius rendering truly what human nature is.

Amelia (1751) is also, in its own way, representative, though not as a summation of traditional comedy but as an index of the social conscience the eighteenth century was developing⁴: in the same year Fielding published his most important sociological work, *An Enquiry into the Causes of the late Increase of Robbers*, and in 1753 the *Proposal for making an Effectual Provision for the Poor*. The mood is not that of the earlier novels; the criticism is of evils as well as of follies. The substance too is more compact; instead of itinerant comedy we are restricted (except for certain episodes on the Continent) to intrigues on a London stage; the characters are a lord or two, their sycophants, military men and their ladies, justices, attorneys, and, in general, folk living by their wits. As for viewpoint, Fielding is the earnest Christian moralist; his wise counsellor Dr Harrison forcibly denounces duelling, immorality, and corrupt government. The faults of Booth, the hero, are the results of free thought leading to moral irresponsibility and, as we have seen, it is the sermons of Isaac Barrow which redeem him. This grave tone is new in Fielding; he is moved by the corruption of the legal system and of public and private morals, and by the actuality or imminence of poverty. Dr Harrison discusses

* Reception or tea-party.

with a nobleman the state of England (Book XI, ii), which the nobleman asserts to be that of an ageing body in the last stage of decadence. Dr Harrison does not deny the diagnosis and can merely advocate a moral revolution by which national affairs would be put on a footing of common honesty.

The book needs careful reading. There is a certain lengthiness to be discounted and a certain tedium to be admitted: Booth may well appear, as he did to Lady Mary Wortley Montagu, a 'sorry scoundrel', while in fact Fielding intends him as a natural portrait of the young officer, in the straits of half-pay, unsteadied by 'progressive' ideas and a thoughtless disposition, but basically courageous and sound. Amelia's gentle domesticity and the contrast between her frugality and her husband's folly at cards seem designed to touch off a sentimental emotion of pity. Certainly there is less here of the comic novel's healthy emotional control; yet the tenderness of so masculine and intelligent a character as Fielding's is not readily to be condemned as excessive. It is indeed only what a maturing judgement, feeling life touched by disappointment and difficulty, may allow itself. Amelia herself, though her role is on the whole passive, is not insipid; she has gravity, gaiety, resource, and energy, she enjoys society and can find amusement in absurdities, she is unflinchingly devoted without being a patient Griselda, and she is loyal because of her direct and open personality which her whole style of speech reflects. Strength and depth of moral sympathy are the qualities which inspire her portrait, and if Fielding disappoints readers who come to *Amelia* expecting another rubicund comedy he holds the allegiance of those who reflect that this rather saddened sense of goodness in a novel of more careful humanity than before is, despite the book's weaknesses, an experience of notable value.

All this amounts rather to description of the novels, and some inducement to read them, than to criticism. Inspecting them critically one notes (to consider first the comic tales) the lack of an impersonal art; Fielding obtrudes himself upon the reader. The comic technique is active and open rather than subtle and implicit; Fielding takes particular (sometimes excessive) care that no one shall misunderstand him. The explanation lies partly in his nature, partly in the traditional conception of a story as something told by someone to somebody else, and partly also in the obtuse criticism of the time which was (often deliberately) apt to mistake intentions. For reasons which are, then, both sociable and prudential, Fielding's attitude is frankly explanatory.[5] Many of the results are so patent as to be elementary; there is some facetiousness (the only real fault of tone, but at times a troublesome one), some elaborate mock-heroic, and open irony which does the reader's work for him and deprives him of the keener pleasure of detecting the innuendo himself. Yet despite the un-sophisticated method, there can be great pleasure in accepting the invitation into the story, to pass one's own judgements, supply one's own knowledge, and think about human life in general. That writer and reader are frank participants has its advantages.

Moreover, the impression the novels give of large references circumambient to the story arises largely from this interference – from Fielding's digressions and insertions. He keeps the narrative clear (no novelist better) and simultaneously ranges round it con-trolled perspectives of social life and general knowledge. In a short chapter of five pages (IV, vi) Tom's early insensibility to Sophia and attachment to Molly Seagrim are related to a varied range of notions – to fashionable fortune-hunting, the functions of conscience, moral distinctions between man and animals, the lord chancellor as the instrument of justice, the contrast between selfishness and generosity, and a quotation from Congreve. The method sounds pretentious, but it is, in fact, quite natural. The sidelights are organic; the story pro-ceeds, and they are illuminations a well-furnished invention throws relevantly on it. The result is a broad instead of a narrow flow. The effect of the mock-heroics and the anti-heroics, where the lofty manner of heroic romance is turned to trivial objects, is not dissimi-lar. It was a trick the French novelist Scarron had made popular with his *Roman comique* (1651); Congreve tried it at the beginning of *Incognita*, and Fielding practised it with some significant results. Here is a sample from *Tom Jones*:

> Now the little trembling hare, which the dread of all her numerous enemies and chiefly of that cunning, cruel, carniv-orous animal man had confined all the day to her lurking-place, sports wantonly o'er the lawns; now on some hollow tree the owl, shrill chorister of the night, hoots forth notes which might charm the ears of some modern connoisseurs in music; now in the imagination of the half-drunk clown, as he

staggers through the churchyard, or rather charnel-yard, to his home, fear paints the bloody hobgoblin; now thieves and ruffians are awake, and honest watchmen fast asleep; in plain English, it was now midnight.

(Book X, ii.)

That, in a sense, is vulgar; it is certainly crude. But carefully examined it does more than touch off a guffaw; it ties us in to the homespun texture of ordinary Hanoverian life. The mundane similes work in the same way; elderly ladies' virtue is 'like the trained bands, always readiest to go on duty where there is least danger'; dramatic unity of place is settled by the query 'why the audience (provided they travel like electors, without any expense) may not be wafted fifty miles as well as five'; Homer and other ancients are like 'so many wealthy squires from whom we, the poor of Parnassus, claim an immemorial custom of taking whatever we can come at'. This humorous Philistinism sometimes grates, but it performs a subtler service than its crude methods would suggest, by extending the attention from the immediate point of the story into other areas of comedy, without any confusion, spreading the narrative from a limited centre into larger perspectives. Village women gossiping in a chandler's shop are related, in parallel, to men gossiping in barber's shops, and they to Horace and Greek proverbs, and they to the eternal appetite for news (*Tom Jones*, II, iv): the libertine talk of the marching redcoats recalls the saturnalia of the ancients (VII, xi); the Molièrean physicians (II, ix) are the cue for satire on doctors in general. Game-preserving squires are likened to Indian Banians who reverence animal life, with only the difference that 'while they preserve them from other enemies [they] most unmercifully slaughter whole horse-loads themselves' (III, ii). The introductory chapters to each book are deliberate enlargements of the topics they introduce; that to Book IV, which prepares for Sophia's entry, is a staged comic gambit to enlarge the mind's horizon. One's first reaction is perhaps of impatience, but gradually one senses that something indispensable has been created – the sense of a great pattern of daily realities and current reflections spreading around the firm clear central story, references always ready in Fielding's fertile and orderly mind to invoke an extensive context of human comedy and broadening the scope of the novels to an unusual amplitude.

In *Amelia* the effect is different; the range of reference, like the range of scene, is designed not for expansiveness but for thoughtful and analytical concentration. Fielding's wide reading still prompts a good deal of literary quotation, but the mock-heroic panache, the irreverent sallies, and ludicrous similes have gone. Their place is taken by brooding commentary relating to the moral bearing of conduct and social custom. The seriousness is, indeed, little less impressive than the earlier broad comedy; discounting the few sentimentalities as the current fashion for expressing rapture, and a few 'strong' effects from the melodramatic Miss Mathews, we find a style soberly relevant to the close-wrought action. Though less enjoyable than the comedies, *Amelia* deserves admiration for its mental change and growth, and for the success with which its quiet, tempered colouring of style and tone produces a novel of quite individual character.

As there are, in a sense, two Fieldings, so there are also two Smolletts. Modulating from the earlier to the later in Fielding's case, there are his sociological concerns; the transition in Smollett's case is marked by the neglected but not unattractive *Sir Launcelot Greaves* (1760), a Quixote-story instigated by his translation of Cervantes in 1755. As Fielding's later work is darker in tone, so Smollett's, generally speaking, lightens, and the spirit of Cervantes may have something to do with it. Ferocity gives place to benevolence, and *Humphry Clinker* (1771) marks a splendid emergence into good humour.

The first three novels, *Roderick Random* (1748), *Peregrine Pickle* (1751), and *Ferdinand Count Fathom* (1753), have for their heroes adventurers making their way by their wits and fortune. Roderick, a young impecunious Scot seeking his chance in London, gaining some skill in medicine, joining the Navy, and undergoing the atrocious conditions of the Cartagena campaign of 1741, is to that extent at least grounded in Smollett's own life, and his hotheaded pride seems to be that of his author; one can take a considerable though not an unremitting interest in his story. Peregrine is harder of head, haughtier of temper, vengeful, much of a brute, and capable of lies and treachery, though with brief flashes of better qualities meant, unavailingly, to recommend him. Ferdinand is simply a scoundrel, though in one of the most lamentable conclusions to any novel he is permitted to repent, and, indeed, later makes an unexpected reappearance in *Humphry Clinker* as a village doctor and 'a sincere convert to virtue', which shows how purely nominal were most of Smollett's notions of character. What attitude is one to take to these uningratiating personages ?

The answer must be in terms of the tradition to which they belong, that of the Spanish picaro, the rogue whose loosely-strung adventures do not call for characterization save as character prompts his escapades. The preface to *Roderick Random* derives fiction from early legend, through medieval romances to the saving sense of Cervantes, who turned it 'to purposes far more useful and entertaining, by making it assume the sock,* and point out the follies of ordinary life.' But while pointing out the follies of ordinary life Smollett does not approach Cervantes, least of all in these early novels, in his power of awakening sympathy. His immediate model is, in fact, not Cervantes at this stage but Le Sage, whose *Gil Blas* (1715–35) is the biography of an impoverished Spanish soldier's son, educated by his uncle and launched on his travels as a kind of anti-hero moving from master to master through a series of comic disputes, with abundant grimace and gesticulation. Hazlitt, in 1819, said it had, 'next to *Don Quixote*, been more generally read and admired than any other novel'. Defoe had dealt in somewhat the same kind of story, though with a sober and not a satirical intent. The only unity of such novels is in their having one hero, and he exists not necessarily to gain esteem but to act as the centre of the episodes.

One need not, then, expect from the early novels any real focus of sympathy. Roderick to some extent provides one, but really one does not care much about his fate; about Peregrine's or Ferdinand's one cares not at all. Where Richardson invites an emotional participation, and Fielding a friendly cheerful attachment, Smollett fails to involve one in the story save for the limited purpose of watching the action. The eye is exercised in observing grotesque and often fierce incidents and characters; the mind is furnished with a crowded violent sense of existence. This fictional brutality is paralleled in the eighteenth-century's gaols, prisons, hospitals, sports, and naval or military life, and Smollett captures this side of the time better than anyone else. Indeed, to read him after sampling the merely average fiction of the 1750s is to feel a much-heightened admiration for his

---

* Assume the sock, i.e. turn to comedy (from the ancient comic actor's light shoe).

unflinching vitality and manifold invention. But to face this violence one needs a sensibility as tough as Smollett's own; in this world a repartee consists of a punch on the jaw, an argument of a butt in the stomach. Ribs are crushed, teeth kicked out, and skulls cracked with cudgels so that sparks fly from the bone. One simply cannot get involved in a state of affairs where all this is ostensibly normal, even enjoyable. Fortunately, it is not really sadistic; the boneheaded automata who undergo the action are themselves apparently impervious to pain, and the reader soon deduces that he need feel for them no more than they feel for themselves.

This, together with the unpromising heroes, is the main obstacle to one's enjoyment of the early Smollett. The normal sense is affronted, and the response is limited to an elementary interest in action for its own sake regardless of emotional nourishment. On this level, which one can maintain by an act of will more than as spontaneous pleasure, *Roderick Random* at least gives much that is worth having (*Peregrine Pickle*, despite the highly-reputed humours of the eccentric Commodore Trunnion's 'Garrison', is far too long, and not really worth the stamina needed to drive one through it). No one else gives the thousand and one strokes of eighteenth-century practical life better, not even Defoe, who has not Smollett's fierce strength of mind. Stroke after stroke Smollett fills in his sharp outlines, with mordant satire and quarrelsomeness ('generous indignation' he calls it) in the early books, with somewhat precarious tolerance in the later. No part of the subject remains imprecise; his puppets are inhuman, but they are put through decisive manoeuvres. The sentence-rhythms are short and firm, a notable though not always comfortable achievement in prose texture; each of the clear-eyed phrases adds something physical, concrete, graphic. We are aware of Smollett, as we are not of Defoe; his 'vision' is his own pattern of life, and not, as one feels with Defoe, life itself merely using a convenient catalyst to precipitate a train of natural incidents. He shirks little; even in *Humphry Clinker* he relapses at times into medical humour and realistic brutality. But by dealing in such abundance of particular details he creates a fictional world which, though lacking Fielding's large and general truth of human nature, has a forcefully partial truth of its time and place.

A few points may be made about the middle novels – *Ferdinand*

Count Fathom and *Sir Launcelot Greaves*. The former offers itself for comparison with *Jonathan Wild*, and suffers in the process; it lacks the concentration, the trenchant and sardonic power of the earlier book. Instead of Fielding's positive energy and constructive generosity (his strong desire for human decency, under the open and disciplined ironies), Smollett provides a comprehensive guide-book against snares and deceits, and a warning against evil courses. The tone is unengaging and the moral purpose – or at least the moral achievement – superficial. The introduction characteristically argues that men became virtuous by fearing the consequences of vice, that 'for one that is allured to virtue by the contemplation of that peace and happiness which it bestows, a hundred are deterred from the practice of vice by that infamy and punishment to which it is liable'. The morality is cramping and minatory. Yet Sir Walter Scott, whose humanity and generosity were as broad as any man's, while detesting the book's moral tone found it incomparably richer than *Jonathan Wild*, and there is something to be said for that view. Ferdinand's escapades involve us in varied slices of European history and remind us that the eighteenth century was, from Cagliostro downwards, a great age of tricksters. The action moves briskly from one gulling to another; its inventiveness is extensive and some of its scenes are not unexciting, in particular that in chapters twenty and twenty-one where Ferdinand, having lost his way at night in a French forest, to the accompaniment of a storm, is decoyed by an old woman in a solitary house and finds himself in an attic with a bleeding corpse while a gang of thieves is preparing his murder. There is an assault on the nerves of a kind which the later 'novel of terror' was to intensify but which even here is effective enough. This sensationalism is a novelty in Smollett, who has hitherto compelled the reader to watch his menagerie from a distance, and it became famous. For the rest, there is a succession of places and persons, of jargons, fashions, fancies, and trickeries of all sorts, kept perpetually on the brawl. One may well lose interest in Ferdinand's adventures, but the detailed exploration of social life, giving the mid-century's physical actuality more comprehensively, and certainly more forcibly, than even *The Spectator* had done for the days of Queen Anne, can still offer some vivid pages, even if it makes anything but a good novel.

As for *Sir Launcelot Greaves*, there have been few to praise and very few to love it.[6] Its theme is farce; Launcelot, his brain (like Quixote's) turned for love, dons armour, engages a squire (a yokel named Crabshaw), dubs his steed Bronzomarte, and forays across the Hanoverian scene seeking adventures. That this does not make sense is excessively obvious. Yet Launcelot's adventures are easier and pleasanter to follow than Peregrine's or Ferdinand's; he is, by a welcome change, on the side of virtue, endowed with warm heart and good feeling, free from the arrogance of self-assertion. There are passages of feeling (like young Oakley's return to his destitute mother in chapter XII) which are much nearer to Goldsmith than one would ever expect Smollett to get, and others which levitate lamentably in the raptures of sentimentality (but they are not particularly troublesome). Further, there is the interest of a social gospel, which would not in itself either make or mar the literary quality but which in fact warms the novel to a pleasing temper of benevolence. Launcelot is an avenger of wrongs, restores lost sons to mothers, delivers prisoners from corrupt justices, and protects ladies from boorish gallants; his chivalry is civilized and reformatory, and it accords with the social evolution of an increasingly humanitarian age. Punishment falls on those who deserve it and not, as in *Peregrine Pickle*, on anyone a headstrong prankster dislikes. As *Amelia* is buttressed by the social pamphlets, so is *Sir Launcelot Greaves* by Smollett's continuation of the *History of England* (1760–1), which displays the causes of social ills and the due sphere of charity and benevolence. Other pleasures in the book are the pastoral scenes, foreshadowed, with patriotic enthusiasm, in *Ferdinand Count Fathom* when that gentleman first sees Britain (chapter XXVII), but here extended. The picture of Launcelot among his country tenants in the third chapter is a pleasant glimpse of Hanoverian rural life at a time of prosperity. And finally there is some sturdy characterization; Captain Crowe is an acceptable old sea-dog, even given the lunacy of his knight-errantry; Justice Gobble and his wife have their affinities in Fielding but are none the worse for that; Fillet the doctor, Clarke the attorney, Ferret the misanthrope, and Crabshaw the squire are decisively drawn, and there is something new in the foolish, likeable Philip Sycamore and his sycophant Davy Dawdle, who courts him by being quarrelsome. All in all, the novel, with an unexpected generosity of sentiment, a ripe sense of England before the industrial revolution, a bright and vivid opening scene, and a prose-style as clean and direct as even Smollett ever achieved, deserves more than the perfunctory notice it generally gets.

That leaves only *Humphry Clinker* (1771). The hard-edged, two-dimensional grotesques of the early novels, though not absent, sink to the background; the foreground is held by the personal commentary of a varied and comical group – Matthew Bramble, the opinionated and warm-hearted old Welsh squire, his 'proud, stiff, vain, imperious, prying, malicious, greedy and uncharitable' sister Tabitha, Jeremy Melford the brisk Oxonian, his sister Lydia, carefully supplied to yearn for a mysterious adorer and to express an ingenuous pleasure in the life around her; Winifred Jenkins the Welsh maid, and Lismahago the Scots lieutenant. Humphry Clinker, incidentally, makes his first appearance about a quarter of the way through the book and thereafter plays an amusing but subordinate part which one would hardly suppose empowered him to give it its title. Not all of them write the letters of which the book is made up – Smollett's only, and very happy, attempt at the epistolary method – but those who do complement each other and combine in a synoptic picture of persons and places. Besides a sympathetic comedy of human nature of a quality Smollett had never evinced before, there is much that deepens the novel's effect and makes it one of the most understanding works of its age. A ripely comprehensive tour from the western counties and Bath to London, then by the northern road to Harrogate and Scarborough (in their early expansion as watering-places), through Northumberland to Newcastle and Berwick, thence to Edinburgh and Glasgow, and at last, by an intimate and appealing devotion, to the Smollett patrimony in the Vale of Leven and by the shores of Loch Lomond, displays George III's Britain, metropolitan and provincial, in a way to which there is no rival. The scenes, in town and country, are varied and attractive; there is the animation of Bath and London, Edinburgh and Glasgow, and an unusual range of scenic pleasures in England, Wales (Matthew Bramble's account, in his letter of June 8th, of Brambleton Hall in Monmouthshire is almost paradisally delightful), and Scotland (the Loch Lomond scenes are admirable, and forty years before Scott it is refreshing to find the Highlands praised for 'sublimity, silence, and solitude' and the Western Isles for providing 'one of the most ravishing prospects in the whole world'). His health failing in remote Leghorn, Smollett, like Macaulay's exiled Jacobite, recalls these things with a moving (though not explicit) sentiment, and the details are not blurred by distance; the clarity of reminiscence is surprising, and the mental horizon is as well-filled as ever in the earlier novels with real life, though the tone is affectionate and not combative. Here at any rate the reader can live within the scene and accept the invitation now so abundantly offered to a lively and amused participation, and he can admire a prose as vivid as Defoe's without Defoe's formlessness, as natural as Addison's without Addison's primness, as conversational as Richardson's without Richardson's sentimentality, and as bold as Fielding's without Fielding's occasional skittishness. It is a masculine style which lays detail upon detail, not (here at least) too densely or extravagantly but with an assured contribution to a firm and clear effect, a style native to its century yet not in the least mannered or dated.

There is little need now for an extended comparison between the two novelists. That Fielding is the greater is generally conceded. That much of Smollett is hard to get through, and hardly worth the trouble needed to get through it, might be conceded more generally than it is, but he, like any writer, is after all saved by his best, and *Humphry Clinker* would compensate for worse faults than his worst. In both men (in Fielding much less than in Smollett) the novel still lacks much as a form of art – its purpose is, of course, entertainment – though it is already mature enough to be the vehicle, deliberately used, of a personal view of life. The striking thing is less the imperfections of the way in which they practised it than the abundance of idea and observation they both poured into a form whose serious history (in England at least) had been so short. The Augustan age had found its appropriate and particular vehicle, and more than any other writers Fielding and Smollett expressed for a reading public expanding to become coterminous with the nation the practical bustle of purposeful life on its everyday level, enlivened with comedy and stiffened with satire. Their work was popular, strong, and bracing.

NOTES

1. For comment on the function of such works in cutting across the class-structure, see W. Empson, *Some Versions of Pastoral* (1935), p. 199.

2. For analysis of its mock-heroic style, see A. R. Humphreys, 'Fielding's Irony', *R.E.S.*, xviii, 1942, pp.183-196.

3. The comment is quoted by F. W. Bateson, *English Comic Drama, 1700–1750* (1929), p. 117, where it is related to Fielding's plays.

4. See Aurelien Digeon, *The Novels of Fielding* (1925), chapters v and vi.

5. For objections to this lack of impersonality, see F. W. Bateson, *op. cit.*, p. 141.

6. For favourable verdicts, however, see Walter Scott's 'Fielding' and 'Smollett' in *Lives of the English Novelists*, and George Saintsbury's introduction to the Navarre Society edition.

'TRISTRAM SHANDY' AND ITS TRADITION

D. W. JEFFERSON

Tristram Shandy, though a much-loved work, is in many respects misunderstood. It is a pity to have to quarrel with Mr E. M. Forster's engaging description of it:

> There is a charmed stagnation about the whole epic – the more the characters do the less gets done, the less they have to say the more they talk, the harder they think the softer they get, facts have an unholy tendency to unwind and trip up the past instead of begetting the future, as in well-conducted books. ... Obviously a god is hidden in *Tristram Shandy* and his name is Muddle, and some readers cannot accept him.[1]

Tristram Shandy certainly does not satisfy the usual expectations as to how a novel should be organized, but the tendency among critics has been to comment on its structural oddities without first discovering to what literary kind it belongs and what its author was trying to do.[2] Some attempt will be made in this essay to trace its form and pattern. Perfect fidelity to an artistic scheme would be too much to claim for Sterne, but it is important to realize that he had one. The view that *Tristram Shandy* is a muddle is related to a tendency to approach Sterne in the light of his affinities with certain later writers, exponents of the eccentric or the nonsensical. Mr Graham Greene says that 'his whimsicality was inherited by the essayists, by Lamb in particular'.[3] Whatever his relations with the whimsical school – 'whimsicality' is rather a damaging word today – he differs fundamentally from these writers in being also of an older and better school. He belongs to a tradition of wit to which they had no access. It is in relation to this background that we must place *Tristram Shandy*, if we are to appreciate fully its point and structure.

The comic writer is greatly dependent on the quality of the materials – social systems, conventions of behaviour, philosophical or scientific ideas – which his age provides for his powers of distortion and travesty to work upon. The wit of *Tristram Shandy* is very largely of the kind that may be labelled 'learned'; and Sterne's advantage lay in the fact that the learning in which he was saturated offered more scope for witty exploitation than the modern knowledge which has gradually taken its place. For example, the old 'speculative' medicine of medieval tradition – its spirit was not dead when Sterne wrote – provided better opportunities for an uninhibited play of wit and fancy than the materials of modern medical science. Medieval 'science', related to and dominated by metaphysics and theology, was not afraid to offer a rational, complete, and readily intelligible conception of the nature of man, such as a literary artist could play with. Jonson's theory of humours is the obvious example which comes to mind. The points of the system lent themselves to ingenious handling; the habit of free speculation uncurbed by the discipline of modern scientific method was stimulating to a witty imagination; and the technical detail, though sufficiently elaborate, was not, unlike that of modern science, hopelessly beyond the grasp of the average educated person. It was open to any amateur to discuss the influence of radical heat and radical moisture on bodily health. The terms could be manipulated to provide an amusing explanation for any eccentricity of character or behaviour, such as the account in the third section of *The Art of Sinking in Poetry*, of how bad poetry comes to be written:

> Against this I draw an argument from what seems to me an undoubted physical Maxim, That Poetry is a natural and morbid Secretion from the Brain. As I would not suddenly stop a cold in the head, or dry up my neighbour's Issue, I would as little hinder him from necessary writing. . . . I have known a man thoughtful, melancholy, and raving for divers days, who forthwith grew wonderfully easy, lightsome, and cheerful, upon the discharge of the peccant humour, in exceeding purulent metre.

Sterne was immersed in physiological lore; it meant much to his imagination, and though he plays with new ideas as well as old, what is important is that the freedom and familiarity with such writers as Rabelais, Jonson, Donne, and Swift had enjoyed in their witty treatment of learned ideas were not lost to him. Although the crisis of the scientific revolution was passed when Sterne wrote, the traditional habits of thought were still alive – for the comic artist, at least. If Mr Shandy is the last embodiment of what Whitehead refers to as the 'unbridled rationalism' of the later pre-scientific age, he is a very impressive one. It is appropriate that the Shandean philosophy should be stated in physiological terms:

> True Shandeism, think what you will against it, opens the heart and lungs, and like all those affections which partake of its nature, it forces the blood and other vital fluids of the body to run freely through its channels, makes the wheel of life run long and cheerfully round.
>
> (IV, 32.)

The passages in *Tristram Shandy* flavoured by physiological wit are too many to enumerate; and, as we shall see later, Sterne's physiological approach to his subject is part of the secret of the structure of the book.

Almost as important as the materials of medicine are those of law. Here again the subject in its unreformed state compares favourably with its more efficient modern counterpart, when considered from the point of view of the comic artist. The amusing idea of law as a kind of net through which the undeserving, if sufficiently supple, may escape and in which the deserving may be ensnared has less point today than in earlier periods. The old pedantic rigidity of the forms of action has gone, and the reforms of the utilitarians have tended to make the legal system correspond more to what ordinary human nature sees as reasonable and just. *Ubi remedium ibi ius* has become *ubi ius ibi remedium*. Fewer people need to go to law today, which is one reason why legal complications, considered as a pattern in human affairs, play less part in giving shape to works of literature. Under the old regime the legal system, in real life as in literature, was a field for playful invention, some of the fictitious proceedings which were used to manipulate the law, such as those involved in 'barring the entail', having for us the qualities of ingenious farce.[4] The art of the legal quibble is one application of that art of logic-chopping for which the schoolmen were chiefly renowned; and the power to use logic to give a show of plausibility to an absurd or unreasonable argument is, in general, one of the distinguishing marks of the writers in the tradition of wit to which Sterne must be related. Legal quibbles are a common feature in their work. Donne, in 'Woman's Constancy', cynically invents for his mistress a far-fetched excuse, in legal terms, for infidelity. Dryden's Almanzor, confronted with Almahide's betrothal to Boabdelin, seeks for a quasi-legal basis for his own claim to her (*Conquest of Granada*, III). The discussion by the bogus canonist and divine, in Jonson's *Silent Woman*, of the possibilities of a divorce for Morose; the impeachment of Bridlegoose in Rabelais; and the interpretation by the three brothers of their father's will in *A Tale of a Tub*, may also be cited as examples of legal wit. *Tristram Shandy*, of course, is full of it, some examples being based on canon law. The 'petite canulle' joke (I, 20), the 'in nomine patriae' dispute (IV, 29), and the debate as to whether Mr Shandy is of kin to his own child (IV, 29) are admirably entertaining; and Sterne's legal approach to his subject plays its part, along with the medical approach, in giving the novel its theme.

One of the characteristics of the pre-scientific type of learned work was the copious listing of authorities and facts culled from authorities; and this, though it made for intolerable prolixity and tedium, also lent itself to a measure of artistic exploitation. Modern works of science and learning run to lists only for specific utilitarian purposes; the list has lost its rhetorical value; but in books like Burton's *Anatomy of Melancholy* it is a thing of glory, the inventory of a treasure-house. When the facts are numerous, but not too numerous, there is some point in knowing them all, there is a place for the gargantuan appetite of a Burton. Learning of this kind has a personal flavour: it represents individual achievement. Modern learning, with its infinitely greater array of facts and formidable mechanical organization of them, is inevitably more impersonal.

In Burton and other scholars and wits of his school – Sterne is in this tradition – we find two qualities combined; a pedantic thoroughness in the listing of authorities and facts, and a lively grasp of everyday things. The piling on of learned detail does not choke the human interest, while the materials of concrete experience are ordered with a learned thoroughness. In the third book of Rabelais (Ch. 13) where Pantagruel gives advice to Panurge on what to eat and what to abstain from in order to avoid fallacious dreams, we are given the impression that behind the choosing of Panurge's supper lies a vast body of theory on the dietetic properties of all the meats, vegetables, and fruits. Yet accompanying this is a personal knowledge of a particular fruit grown in a particular place. From an almost limitless world of possibilities everything is most studiously hand-picked. A parody of this passage may be quoted from Mr Shandy's letter to Uncle Toby, in which he recommends a suitable diet for a wooer. It is hardly necessary to comment on the solemn absurdity of the advice, which contrasts oddly with the sardonic good sense shown earlier in the letter ('... and thou knowest, dear Toby, that there is no passion so serious as lust'):

> But thou must eat little or no goat's flesh, nor red deer – nor even foal's flesh, by any means; and carefully abstain – that is, as much as thou canst, from peacocks, cranes, coots, didappers, and water-hens. . . .
>
> As for thy drink – I need not tell thee, it must be the infusion of Vervain and the herb Hanea, of which Aelian relates such effects – but if thy stomach palls with it – discontinue it from time to time, taking cucumbers, melons, purslane, water-lilies, woodbine and lettuce, in the stead of them.
>
> (VIII, 34.)

There is a connexion, which needs to be stressed, between the quality of the wit achieved by the writers in this tradition – Rabelais, Jonson, Donne, Swift, Sterne – and the quality of their acquaintance with the learned ideas which they exploited. Their resourcefulness, the abundance of detail at their command, the accuracy with which they parody the solemn enquirer, the superb air of authority which they can assume: these virtues point to a serious intellectual equipment beneath the comic intention. The lack of any comparable equipment in later humorists like Lamb is one of the great differences separating Sterne from writers who are sometimes said to have derived from him. As we move away from the intellectual conditions which Sterne was not too late to profit from, learned wit almost ceases to exist; partly because knowledge becomes too specialized, ceases to be familiar, and develops in ways which do not encourage a play of fancy, and partly because the comic spirit itself seems to have acquired a distaste for such materials.[5]

What Sterne shares with his predecessors is more than a technique for manipulating learned ideas. Learning was closely related to life, and the flexibility of these writers goes beyond the field of abstract ideas to that of attitudes: for example, to religion or sex. The ability to manage the different levels of attitude to these subjects, enjoying a good deal of freedom at the less serious levels, is one of the general virtues of the writers with whom we are concerned here. Modern readers, especially those of puritan or rationalist mentality, often misunderstand them, having lost the idea of a Christian tradition in which so much latitude is possible. Rabelais had moments of tender piety, quickly giving way to ribald gaiety; and it is entirely characteristic that the little company which sits waiting for Tristram Shandy to be born should hear Trim's reading of a sermon as well as Dr Slop's reading of the Ernulphus curse.

Sterne belongs, then, to a tradition of wit unhampered by puritanism, the merit of which lies not only in its freedom but also in its sophistication. The subtle irony with which he handles his own sentimentality, especially in *A Sentimental Journey*, is an excellent example of the latter quality, and the failure on the part of some modern critics[6] to appreciate it is the measure of how far the taste for certain niceties of wit has been lost. As for freedom, this was gradually lost with the encroachment in the eighteenth century of a middle-class spirit in religion and morals.

Another consequence, or aspect, of learning's being close to life is the *concreteness* of so much of the learned wit in Sterne and others of his school. The eloquent description in Rabelais (III, 4) of the members of the body co-operating to make blood shows admirably how well the old physiology lent itself to poetic visualization; and, to take a different type of example, in Swift's account of the Aeolists in the *Tale of a Tub* (VIII) the abstract theory and the concrete embodiment are wedded with appalling effectiveness. The ability of metaphysical poets to use images to convey, or at least to heighten, ideas is well known. *Tristram Shandy* is full of passages in which the learned idea is given a piquant concrete illustration. For example, *à propos* of the Milanese physician's theory concerning 'a very thin, subtle and very fragrant juice' in the cellulae of the occipital parts of the cerebellum, which he affirms to be 'the seat of the reasonable soul', we learn that

> ... the very idea of so noble, so refined, so immaterial and so exalted a being as the *Anima*, or even the *Animus*, taking up her residence, and sitting dabbling, like a tadpole all day long, both winter and summer, in a puddle ... shocked his [Mr Shandy's] imagination. ...
>
> (II, 19.)

This ability to relate the concrete image felicitously to the abstract idea may be traced ultimately – this explanation must necessarily be brief and crude – to a harmony in medieval (that is, pre-Enlightenment) systems of knowledge between things and their meanings, between concrete particulars and the intellectual patterns into which they fit. But this imaginative habit is most conspicuously operative in the period when the old intellectual harmony has been disrupted, but not forgotten, and the poets, the metaphysicals, delight us with an unexpected, fantastic union of images and ideas not conventionally related to each other. It was natural for the medieval imagination to grasp the material world in terms of ordered, schematized patterns of particulars; and this became a feature of literary style which, with modifications, survived in later writers like Jonson and Swift. What was originally a conscientious, conventional schematization became the basis of a formidable rhetorical display, in which extraordinary virtuosity is shown in the marshalling and concentration of the detail.[7] There are passages in Swift – for example, the description of the ludicrous, quasi-ritualistic posturings of the Aeolists – and also in Sterne, where this studied treatment of detail is made to suggest significant and insidious intentions. Much of the art of *Tristram Shandy* lies in this queer ordering of descriptive detail, the motives for which emerge as we examine, in the light of the foregoing pages, the scheme of the novel as a whole.

*　　*　　*

It is one of the good jokes of literature that we reach the third book of *Tristram Shandy* before the hero is born. But not all readers see why the joke is good. The entire structure of the work depends on the fact that the starting-point is not Tristram's birth but his begetting. At the outset (I, 4) Sterne declares his purpose, which is to begin literally *ab ovo*, alluding to Horace's principle, which he proposes to flout, that an epic should *not* begin with 'Leda's egg', that is, with the ancestry and earliest beginnings of the hero.

Between begetting and birth many things may happen, but not such as novelists normally handle. *Tristram Shandy* breaks off before the hero is mature enough to become what in literature is recognized as a character; that is, if we disregard the freakish episodes of Continental travel, quite unrelated to the rest of the work, in book VII.

Of his history we know only what the influences of the pre-natal period and early infancy have done for him. From the point of view of the ordinary novelist very little has happened; but from the point of view of Mr Shandy and the modern psychologist most of the really decisive things have happened. Tristram's character and fortune have been more or less settled by the sequence of events beginning with the unfortunate circumstances of his begetting and culminating in the sash-window tragedy. In this sequence of events lies the pattern of the novel.

We cannot accuse Sterne of not announcing his theme promptly. The first paragraph of the novel is all about the perils which attend one's begetting.

> I wish either my father or my mother, or indeed both of them, as they were in duty both equally bound to it, had minded what they were about when they begot me. ...

He proceeds to elaborate these perils in physiological and psychological terms, with lively imagery. From this introduction we pass to the concrete scene: Mr and Mrs Shandy are about to perform their function. At the critical moment Mr Shandy is interrupted by his wife's question about winding up the clock, and so occurs the first of Tristram's misfortunes. The question, coming at that moment, 'scattered and dispersed the animal spirits, whose business it was to have escorted and gone hand in hand with the HOMUNCULUS, and conducted him safe to the place destined for his reception'.

Tristram's second misfortune takes us into the sphere of legal entanglements. It is because Mr Shandy insists on the terms of his wife's marriage settlement that Tristram is born in the country, not in London; and the result is the tragedy of Tristram's nose. Mr Shandy's theory, reached after much elaborate physiological speculation, is that, 'the excellency of the nose is in a direct arithmetical proportion to the excellency of the wearer's fancy' (III, 38). The flattening of Tristram's nose is therefore a cruel blow to his parental hopes. He falls back on the theory of names, and is again thwarted, by a mistake which causes his child to be given the name which he has condemned as the worst possible. He enquires into the possibility of changing it, and this leads to a great orgy of legal quibbling ending in the decision that the parents have no rights in the matter, not being of kin to their own child! Opportunities continue to present themselves, however, for applying learning to his parental responsibilities. He composes a *Tristrapaedia*, or system of education (V, 16): he interests himself in theories of bodily health (V, 33): *à propos* of putting the child into breeches he makes careful researches into the wardrobe of the ancients (VI, 19). Meanwhile Tristram has encountered further disaster through the fall of a sash-window (V, 17).

The theme of *Tristram Shandy* may be seen in terms of a comic clash between the world of learning and that of human affairs. On the level of theory Mr Shandy makes formidable preparations for his child's welfare, but partly through his own folly or inattention in practical matters, and partly through unlucky accident, his schemes are frustrated. It is Mr Shandy's perverse insistence on legal principle that is responsible for Tristam's being born in the country: he is therefore to blame for the flattened nose. As for the mistake over the name, fortune is cruel in making him just too late to prevent it: the finding and donning of a pair of breeches (IV, 14) cause the fatal delay. The sash-window accident is not his fault directly: it is due to the intemperate zeal of Corporal Trim in the service of Uncle Toby's hobby-horse that 'nothing was well hung in our family', but it is typical of Mr Shandy's character that he should be unaware, in his philosophical absorption, of what is going on in his own house.

A parallel to this theme may be seen in the third book of Rabelais, surely the most wonderful of the five. There is abundant evidence that Sterne knew it well. In each there is a central human problem, for the solving of which an immense body of knowledge is assembled: the question of how to give the infant hero the best start in life, the question of whether Panurge should marry. In each there is unquenchable faith in the validity of learning in its application to life. In each there is a series of phases or episodes in which one form of learning after another is brought to bear on the problem. In each the well-meant efforts are frustrated, in the one case by a mixture of human frailty and the cussedness of things, in the other by perversity in its most pronounced form.

There are other ways in which Sterne's manipulation of learned ideas helps to determine the structure of the novel. Wilbur L. Cross claims that the whole work was organized in terms of Locke's doctrine of association of ideas, and this principle certainly manifests itself very significantly in the behaviour of the characters; for example, when Mrs Shandy inopportunely remembers the clock-winding ritual. It provides a respectable basis for Sterne's favourite habit of digression. It is characteristic of Sterne that what appears at first sight to be wilful untidiness can often be related to some rational theory, though in the later part of *Tristram Shandy* this becomes less and less true.

Sterne had a curious feeling for order which is sometimes accompanied by what would appear to be its opposite, a delight in confusion; but these things are not really opposed. To dwell upon disorder, reducing it to its particulars and bringing out its perversely twisted pattern, involves the introduction of an element of order. The complicated description of how Obadiah tied up Dr Slop's bag of instruments (III, 8) is a good example. This effect may be labelled 'order in disorder', a formula which could be applied to much of Sterne's work. Another manifestation of his sense of order is an insistence on relating happenings to their causes. Causation works in very odd ways in *Tristram Shandy*, curious devices being used for holding the structure of events together, so that one is reminded of some contraption designed by Heath Robinson. Obadiah's entanglement is itself one of the obstacles to Tristram's smooth passage into the world. ('Sport of small accidents, Tristram Shandy! that thou art, and ever will be!') In a delightful passage (V, 6) illustrating the queer mechanisms of family life in the Shandy household, Sterne dwells on the importance of a faulty hinge on the parlour door. Another of his habits is to give a studied precision to descriptions of physical postures in scenes where the composed effect is grotesque rather than dignified. The spotlight is directed in such a way as to heighten the trivial. Mr Shandy, prostrate with grief on hearing of his child's flattened nose (III, 24), Corporal Trim as he takes his stance to read the sermon (II, 17), are notable examples of this type of effect. In another passage Sterne catches Mr Shandy trying to put his left hand into his right-hand coat pocket, and dwells with a connoisseur's finesse on the result (III, 2). Sometimes there is the odd suggestion, or the parody of a suggestion, that the detail is significant, that there is a meaning embodied in the pattern. It seems to be characteristic of the Shandy world that, while the things belonging to order are sabotaged by human muddle, precision and exactness are imposed quite arbitrarily upon the unimportant and incidental.

Uncle Toby's hobby-horse is the most interesting example of Sterne's idiosyncratic ordering of detail, but it is interesting for other reasons as well. It brings us back to learned wit, for military science was a form of learning like any other, and took similar forms to those of Mr Shandy's intellectual interests. It had a relatively clear-cut system, with an ordered grouping of particulars, but with just enough complication to provide a pleasing muddle. It had its lists of learned authorities and a terminology with rhetorical possibilities: *scarp*, *counterscarp*, *glacis*, *covered way*, *half-moon*, and *ravelin*.

In his discourse on hobby-horses (I, 24) Sterne puts forward a theory of characterization, the point of which is that when a man becomes deeply attached to a favourite occupation, his character gradually takes on a shape and colouring derived from the materials belonging to that occupation. There is another side to this process, which Sterne does not mention, though his art illustrates it. If the man's nature is changed by the materials acting upon it, the materials themselves are changed by their association with the man. All organized pursuits or subjects for study may be said to have their abstract, impersonal character – their 'textbook' character, let us say – and also a variable 'human' character imposed upon them by the different sorts of treatment which they receive when human beings have to do with them. The materials of military science, entering so deeply into Uncle Toby's sensibility, take on new shapes in the process.

Uncle Toby's hobby-horse arises, as Sterne explains most fully, out of a difficulty he experiences in making himself clear when he tries to tell the tale of the siege of Namur (II, 1), where he received his wound. Partly because his hearers do not understand the technical terms, and partly because the terrain was somewhat complicated, he gets tied up in his narration, and this (Sterne indulges in some medical speculation here), by irritating him, adversely affects his recovery from the wound. The search for clarity leads Uncle Toby to the study of maps and textbooks. But now he becomes so full of his theme that he has to find other, more elaborate, ways of expressing himself through it, so he builds miniature fortifications on a bowling-green and fights mock battles with field artillery made from leaden gutters, a melted-down pewter shaving-basin, and the weights from sash-windows.

There is a quality about Uncle Toby's hobby-horse which places it on a different imaginative level from other examples in fiction of make-believe and eccentric preoccupation. The difference is one of intensity. Sterne's art manifests itself in the transformation of the concrete objects so that they become completely assimilated to Uncle Toby's all-absorbing idea. A peculiar concentration and control of detail create the spell:

> The corporal, who the night before had resolved in his mind to supply the grand desideratum, of keeping up something like an incessant firing upon the enemy during the heat of the attack, – had no further idea in his fancy at that time, than a contrivance of smoking tobacco against the town, out of one of my uncle Toby's six field-pieces. . . . Upon turning it this way, and that, a little in his mind, he soon began to find out, that by means of his two Turkish tobacco-pipes, with the supplement of three smaller tubes of wash-leather at each of their lower ends, to be tagged by the same number of tin-pipes fitted to the touch-holes, and sealed with clay next the cannon, and then tied hermetically with waxed silk at their several insertions into the Moroccan tube, – he should be able to fire the six field-pieces all together, and with the same ease as to fire one.
>
> (VI, 26.)

Uncle Toby's hobby-horse differs from that of (say) Commodore Trunnion (in *Peregrine Pickle*) or Mr Wemmick (in *Great Expectations*), not only in intensity but in the fact that it refuses to keep within its allotted boundaries. The toys, straying from their places, contribute to the complicated system of traps and obstacles in which the characters, bodily or mentally, are caught. There is the sash-window episode: the drawbridge broken accidentally by Trim is confused with the bridge of Tristram's nose (III, 27): Mr Shandy's mention of a train of ideas makes Uncle Toby think of a train of artillery (III, 18).

The reader of Sterne's novel is usually content to enjoy flavour and atmosphere, to bask in the wanton profusion of human idiosyncrasy, without seeking to understand very much of the kind of mentality presented in the characters or expressed by their creator.

It is an important point in its favour that, even though most of the theme and pattern are missed, its human appeal remains irresistible. But the ways of the Shandy world may be all the better appreciated if we can relate it to the rich and solid tradition of wit behind it.

NOTES

This essay has been adapted from a longer article which appeared in *Essays in Criticism*, I, iii (Oxford, 1951). Thanks are due to the editor, Mr F. W. Bateson, for permission to use this material again. Considerations of space prevent any treatment of *A Sentimental Journey*, to which some attention is given in a general account of Sterne by the present author in the British Council series of booklets, *Writers and their Work*.

1. E. M. Forster, *Aspects of the Novel* (1927), p. 146.

2. But an excellent analysis of Sterne's artistic purpose is found in John Traugott's *Sterne's Philosophical Rhetoric* (California, 1954).

3. From an essay in *From Anne to Victoria*, ed. B. Dobrée (1937), p. 282.

4. Sir Alan Herbert's *Misleading Cases* are a reminder that the legal quibble can still be a source of light entertainment.

5. There are exceptions. Peacock plays with learned materials (in such novels as *Crotchet Castle*) almost as much as Sterne, though the comedy has much less imaginative vitality. Mr Peter Alexander has shown how many of the situations in the *Alice* books provide examples of logical fallacies interesting to the logicians of Lewis Carroll's generation ('Logic and the Humour of Lewis Carroll', in *Proceedings, Leeds Phil. and Lit. Soc., Lit. and Hist. Sect.*, VI, pt. 8, 1951, pp. 551 ff.).

6. But Sir Herbert Read has written admirably on Sterne's sentimentality in *The Sense of Glory* (Cambridge, 1929), p. 140.

7. These effects in Swift are discussed and illustrated more fully in the essay on p. 230.

AUGUSTAN REFLECTIVE POETRY

NORMAN CALLAN

Professor of English, University of London

> Grant me, indulgent Heaven! a rural seat
>   Rather contemptible than great!
> Where, though I taste life's sweets, I still may be
>   Athirst for immortality!
> I would have business; but exempt from strife!
>   A private, but an active life!
> A conscience bold, and punctual to his charge!
>   My stock of health; or patience large!
> Some books I'd have, and some acquaintance too;
>   But very good, and very few!
> Then (if a mortal two such gifts may crave!)
>   From silent life I'd steal into the grave.

To anyone reflecting casually on Augustan poetry it is not perhaps these unassuming verses by Nahum Tate that would come first to mind: rather he would recall as typical of the age such poems as *Hudibras, Absalom and Achitophel, The Rape of the Lock, The Dunciad* – satirical masterpieces, manifesting an exclusive, if disapproving, interest in life as lived in cities. Yet the list would contain exceptions – Gray's *Elegy*, certainly, Thomson's *Seasons*, and perhaps some of Collins's odes. And if this train of thought were pursued it would quickly become evident that the view of Augustan poetry as predominantly satirical is altogether one-sided. In mere quantity the line of poetry which runs from such late-seventeenth-century writers as Charles Cotton through Lady Winchilsea, Pope (before 1717), Thomson, Gray, Collins, Shenstone, and so on to Goldsmith and Cowper is probably preponderant; and if its masterpieces do not seem able to compete with those of satire, this is perhaps because (as Milton found) the depiction of actual evil is more spectacular than that of ideal good. To see in this line (as so many do) a trend which is untypical of the age, or even unrelated to satire, is to miss its significance. In presenting an idealized picture of rural peace (Tate's poem affords an undistinguished but compact example), and using this as the starting-point for reflection, it is clearly the counterpart of satire, and springs from the impulse to comment on human existence which is the mark of all Augustan poetry. To put the point more briefly, there is no great gulf between *The Vanity of Human Wishes* and the *Elegy Written in a Country Churchyard*: and it is no accident that the predominating literary influence of the age is that of the Roman Horace, a poet who excelled both in urban satire and in the poetry of rural meditation.

If at first it seems surprising that an age noted for its urbanity and social sense should devote so much of its energies to the praise of solitude, this is largely because of the way the Augustans have been treated by literary critics and historians, who have mostly taken the line that if Augustan rural solitude is not the rural solitude of the Romantics it is negligible; if it is not negligible, then it is not Augustan. The Romantics themselves fostered the attitude, especially Wordsworth: 'Now it is remarkable', he says in the *Essay Supplementary*, 'that, excepting the *Nocturnal Reverie* of Lady Winchilsea and a passage or two in the *Windsor Forest* of Pope, the poetry intervening between the publication of *Paradise Lost* and *The Seasons* does not contain a single new image of rural nature; and scarcely presents a familiar one from which it can be inferred that the eye of the poet had been steadily fixed upon his object, much less that his feelings had urged him to work upon it in a spirit of genuine imagination. ...' Because he is attempting to create the taste by which his poetry is to be enjoyed, Wordsworth has some justification for these sweeping generalizations: but critically they are misleading, since they are based on assumptions which the Augustans never made. It is comment of this kind which has rendered appreciation of the non-satirical poetry of the period so difficult.

Nor has appreciation been advanced by well-intentioned criticism which, in answer to Wordsworth and Arnold, claims to find in a poet like Matthew Green the dawn of the Romantic movement. 'Green's aim is still self-regarding, but it does not prevent him from entering into the green, liquescent world about him. His senses have thawed, and the genial warmth of the sun-steeped earth has passed through him to his mind and melted its chilly decorum.' From this it would appear that in so far as Green is self-regarding he is a bad poet, but in so far as he is trying to anticipate Keats he is a good one. The fact that it is his self-regarding wit which makes him the peculiar poet that he is has been totally ignored, while the fact that he has a sensitivity to external nature closely akin to that of many of his contemporaries is made to suggest that he has escaped from the conventions of his age. To such wishful thinking a more perceptive critic's verdict on Shenstone provides sufficient answer: '... that Shenstone wrote of his own jasmines and harebells does not prove that he was nearer to Wordsworth than to Horace, or perhaps Virgil. That his friends thought of the Leasowes [Shenstone's elaborately landscaped estate] as Gothic – which it was not – does not ally him with Romance rather than with Reason. That he chose his fashions to suit himself does not remove him from the heart of the eighteenth century. ...'[1] Indeed, when one comes to look closely, it is the pertinacity of critics in decrying the absence of something that was never meant to be there, or in praising the presence of something equally absent that is so surprising. Of no other age has the poetry been so little read for its own sake, or so much for the sake of comparison with other ages.

Tate's poem belongs to what may be called the poetry of rural contentment, a strain descending from antiquity, and appearing in such sixteenth-century lyrics as Dekker's *Sweet Content* and Shakespeare's *Under the Greenwood Tree*. In the two succeeding centuries this strain mingles with that of solitary contemplation, thereby taking in such pieces as Milton's *L'Allegro* and *Il Penseroso*, and Marvell's *Garden*. Here, too, may be included Vaughan's *Retreat* and Traherne's *Solitude*. Thus, in some measure, the poetry to be treated in this chapter derives from a tradition extending far beyond the Augustan period. But within the period the tradition undergoes certain modifications which distinguish the poetry from that which precedes and that which follows; and with the most important of these modifications it would be as well to begin.

The cadences of Tate's poem are those of the seventeenth century: in them may be heard a rather feeble echo of *The Garden* or *The Retreat*. The same is even more true of the much finer poem on a similar theme – Charles Cotton's *The Retirement*,[2] addressed to Izaak Walton:

> Farewell thou busy world, and may
>   We never meet again:

Here can I eat and sleep and pray,
And do more good in one short day
Than he who his whole age outwears
Upon thy most conspicuous theatres,
   Where nought but vice and vanity do reign.

Good God! how sweet are all things here!
How beautiful the fields appear!
How cleanly do we feed and lie!
Lord! what good hours do we keep!
   How quietly we sleep!
What peace! What unanimity!
How innocent from the lewd fashion,
Is all our business, all our conversation.

Oh how happy here's our leisure!
Oh how innocent our pleasure!
Oh ye valleys, oh ye mountains,
Oh ye groves and crystal fountains,
   How I love at liberty
By turn to come and visit ye!

O Solitude, the soul's best friend,
That man acquainted with himself dost make,
And all his Maker's wonders to intend;
   With thee I here converse at will,
   And would be glad to do so still;
For it is thou alone that keep'st the soul awake.

How calm and quiet a delight
   it is alone
To read, and meditate, and write,
By none offended, and offending none;
To walk, ride, sit, or sleep at one's own ease,
And pleasing a man's self, none other to displease!

The conversational rise and fall of this is in sharp contrast to an early
poem by Pope:

Happy the man whose wish and care
   A few paternal acres bound,
Content to breathe his native air
   In his own ground.

Whose herds with milk,whose fields with bread,
    Whose flocks supply him with attire;
Whose trees in summer yield him shade,
    In winter fire.

Blest, who can unconcern'dly find
    Hours, days and years slide soft away,
In health of body, peace of mind,
        Quiet by day.

Sound sleep by night; study and ease
    Together mix'd; sweet recreation;
And innocence which does most please
    With meditation.

Thus let me live, unseen, unknown,
    Thus unlamented let me die,
Steal from the world, and not a stone
    Tell where I lie.

Here the perfect organization of the poem's cadences carries an air of
assurance which is not present in the more hesitant rhythms of its
seventeenth-century counterparts: and this measured emphasis
perhaps forms a line of demarcation between the poetry of the two
centuries. It can be seen, for instance, separating Cotton from Gray:

Beside some water's rushy brink
With me the muse shall sit and think
    (At ease reclin'd in rustic state)
How vain the ardour of the crowd,
How low, how little are the proud,
    How indigent the great!

But such differences, which spring at least to some extent from the
individual temper of the poet, only serve to underline the essential
unity of all these pieces when they are compared with such poems as
The Garden or *The Retreat*. For Marvell and Vaughan 'nature' is a
symbol in whose weaker glories may be spied some glimpses of
eternity – in fact, a mystical symbol. For Cotton or Pope, on the
other hand, if it is a symbol at all, it is a social one, standing for what
is sincere and unpretentious, as opposed to what is affected and
grandiose.

In some degree all the poems from which I have quoted achieve a compromise which is typical of the age. In the earlier part of the seventeenth century, retreat to nature meant retirement from practical business to ideal contemplation: the typical ring of the poetry is other-worldly – 'a green thought in a green shade', 'like stars upon some gloomy grove'. For the Augustans such a retreat meant a turning from ambition to usefulness. Parnell's hermit (in the poem of that name) is not fully equipped for his vocation until he has come out into the world and learned that apparent injustices are all part of God's purpose for mankind. The ring of Tate's poem – like so many of its kind, it derives directly from Horace's second Epode – is markedly practical: he asks for the best of both worlds –

> Where, though I taste life's sweets, I still may be
> Athirst for immortality!

This compromise resolves the old conflict between nature and art: nature is still the antithesis of the artfulness of the courtier and the man of affairs; but she is now 'nature methodiz'd', or perhaps 'nature taught art' – either the useful rural arts of the ploughman and husbandman (as in Pope's poem), or else (a later version, this) the arts of the landscape gardener, as in Shenstone's *Rural Elegance*:

> Whether we fringe the sloping hill
>   Or smooth below the verdant mead;
> Whether we break the falling rill
>   Or through meand'ring mazes lead;
> Or in the horrid bramble's room
> Bid careless groups of roses bloom;
> Or let some shelter'd lake serene
> Reflect flowers, woods, and spires, and brighten
>   all the scene.

When Pope (*Moral Essays*, IV) prophesies the end of Timon's lavish villa, the 'nature' which succeeds it is not that of awe-inspiring desolation, but of the cultivated cornfield:

> Another year shall see the golden ear
> Embrown the slope, and nod on the parterre,
> Deep harvests bury all his pride had plann'd,
> And laughing Ceres reassume the land.

The main strength of Augustan poetry about rural nature lies in its contact with human values. At its best there is nothing trivial or cosy about it. When this contact begins to weaken, the poetry sometimes becomes dilettante and emasculated; but the best of it has a dignity and a detachment which make it both worthy of respect and attractive.

One of the chief reasons for this is its freedom from selfishness. Tate –

> ... would have business, but exempt from strife!
> A private, but an active life –

and John Pomfret, whose poem *The Choice* is another typical Augustan elaboration on Horace's second Epode, makes the point more explicitly:

> I'd have a clear and competent estate,
> Where I might live genteely, but not great:
> As much as I could moderately spend;
> A little more, sometimes, t'oblige a friend.
> Nor should the sons of poverty repine
> Too much at fortune, they should taste of mine. ...

This benevolent note, which echoes through the period in Pope's 'man of Ross' (*Moral Essays*, III) –

> He feeds yon alms-house, neat but void of state,
> Where Age and Want sit smiling at the gate,
> Him portion'd maids, apprentic'd orphans blest,
> The young who labour, and the old who rest –

and in Goldsmith's village parson (*The Deserted Village*, 159 ff.) –

> Pleas'd with their tales, the good man learn'd to glow,
> And quite forgot their vices in their woe;
> Careless their merits or their faults to scan,
> His pity gave ere charity began –

is a reflection of the spirit of the age which saw the beginnings of most of the great philanthropic movements. It rings true, so long as it is not heard with the ear of the twentieth-century welfare state. Philanthropy does not, of course, make poetry; but false sentiment mars it. And it is worth noting that few Augustan poems can be described as sentimental.

To suppose, however, that the Augustan poets never contemplated the more forbidding aspects of nature, or that they were moved only by a field of ripening grain or a hill-side dotted with sheep, would be quite wrong. On the contrary, throughout the period there runs a cult of nature's more awful solemnities, clearly distinguishable in such poems as Parnell's *Night Piece*, Gray's *Bard*, and Collins's *Ode on the Superstitions of the Scottish Highlands*. Some of the best poetry of Thomson's *Seasons* is inspired by the lonelier aspects of Teviotdale, and works such as Dyer's *Ruins of Rome* and Blair's *Grave* are meditations upon scenes of desolation. Some of these lie outside the scope of this chapter, but enough of their characteristics will be found in the poems which do come within our compass to make it clear that the range of sensitiveness was indeed as wide as the famous passage from *The Castle of Indolence* suggests:

> Sometimes the pencil, in cool airy halls
> Bade the gay bloom of vernal landskips rise,
> Or Autumn's varied shades imbrown the walls:
> Now the black tempest strikes the astonish'd eyes;
> Now down the steep the flashing torrent flies;
> The trembling sun now plays o'er ocean blue,
> And now rude mountains frown amid the skies;
> Whate'er Lorrain light touch'd with softening hue,
> Or savage Rosa dash'd, or learned Poussin drew.

Nevertheless, whatever the theme, the Augustan poet was always writing within the social context of his age. Whether the reflections he offers are the minute, practical ones of Green, or the vaster, more nebulous ones of Dyer, they are of a kind which the reader himself will have experienced. He does not aim at shocking his audience into awareness by insisting on his own individuality; he merges himself in the general consciousness of his readers, pointing to what they have in common and ignoring what separates them. This, rather than peculiarities of sensitivity or style, is what separates the Augustan poet from his Romantic successor.

The literary complement of this social awareness is a strong sense of tradition, and a genius for perceiving the relevance of past literature to contemporary themes. The Augustans valued their poetry as much for the literature from which it was derived as for anything novel the writer had to impart. Indeed, the newness of a poem like the *Elegy* or the *Ode to Evening* consists in the subtle relationship which the poet establishes between the experience of the past and that of his own day, creating thereby a sense of timelessness which is 'new' only in the sense that it is unique. In a way, therefore, it is true to say that Augustan poets looked at life through literature. But the description 'literary' which is so often bestowed on them takes no account of the 'literature' in question or of the intensity with which that literature was felt. As a term of critical reproach, 'literary' is useful to describe the kind of writer who takes refuge in the idiom of another age because he wishes to escape from the responsibilities of his own. So far from doing this, the Augustans turned to the poetry of Horace and Virgil – and of Horace in particular – because it seemed supremely significant for their own age, and because it did so well what, in their opinion, poetry ought to do – namely, express in memorable terms the community of ideas and feelings which alone made civilized existence possible. If, in our day, we find the poetry of Donne and Marvell most intensely apposite to our own experience because it stresses individuality of perception, the Augustans felt the poetry of Horace no less strongly because it did exactly the opposite.

The fact that they singled out Horace is, in itself, evidence of more than a merely dilettante intention. He is a poet whose style is essentially the product of his temper – a temper which is balanced, mature and manly. He lacks (or it might be truer to say he avoids) the poignancy of a poet such as Catullus; but this does not mean that he lacks feeling. The pathos of Catullus –

> cum semel nobis brevis occidit lux
> nox est una perpetua dormienda –

is intense because it is personal*: that of Horace –

* Cf. Herrick, *Corinna:*

> So when or you or I are made
> A fable, song, or fleeting shade,
> All love, all liking, all delight
> Lies drowned with us in endless night.

354

pallida mors aequo pulsat pede pauperum tabernas
regumque turres* –

more diffused because more widely applicable. It is this balanced
temper, and the grave, generalized phrasing which flows from it that
the Augustans admired and attempted to reproduce in their own
poetry.

Horace is pre-eminently the poet of general themes. His odes,
apart from those on political subjects, treat of the pleasures of friendship, of rural solitude, the transience of human happiness, the folly of
ambition, and so on – themes which have formed the common
stock of reflection for the ordinary man in every age. These themes
he touches with a remarkable delicacy of language and clarity of
definition, giving to casual rumination the stamp of permanence.
Thus, unlike the Romantic, he is a poet in accord with society, rendering what is potentially poetic in others actually so. He is, in fact,
the best exponent of his own maxim that the poet's task is to handle
a common subject in a personal way.

The key to Horace's odes lies in their perfect decorum: not a
stilted adherence to a critical code, but a delicate adjustment between
language, metrical emphasis, thought, and feeling, which creates in
turn the sense of harmony between poet and reader wherein the
effect of such poetry generally lies. To pin this power of adjustment
down to any particular function of poetic genius is impossible.
Clearly it depends on a special kind of sensitiveness in the poet:
equally it implies lively critical intelligence. Further, it is more likely
to appear in an age in which the reader is willing to be pleased than
in one in which he prefers to be shocked: in fact, an age in which the
reader looks for what he knows in poetry rather than what he does
not know. Above all, it demands on the part of both reader and poet
an understanding of how much personal emotion a poem can bear
without disturbing the balance. All these conditions are best summed
up in the Augustan critical term 'judgement'.

Augustan insistence on proportion allows, it is true, little scope for
that presentation of the unique nature of an emotional experience

---

* Shirley gives the sense, though with different imagery:
    Sceptre and crown must tumble down,
    And in dust be equal made
    With the poor crooked scythe and spade.

which is often so moving in other poetry. But if the range of sensitivity is thus limited in one way, it is extended in another. In Gray's *Elegy* or Horace's poem on the death of Varus (*Odes*, I, 24) the expression of bereavement may be less personally poignant than in Donne's *Nocturnal* or Wordsworth's 'Lucy' poems; but this is because the expression has been framed to imply all such situations, and not simply the poet's own. The poet's sense of loss is held in balance against his awareness of himself as a member of his own audience. And the same attitude enables poetry whose most obvious characteristic is an elegant lightheartedness to include also a strain of genuine sadness. This is the case, for instance, with Horace's 'Quis multa gracilis ...' and with some of Matthew Prior's occasional pieces, whose tone though essentially that of polished irony can yet include an unaffected sadness:

> My bloom of life, my little flower
> Of beauty quickly lost its pride:
> For sever'd from its native bower
> It on thy glowing bosom died.
>
> Yet car'd I not what might presage
> Or with'ring wreath or fleeting youth:
> Love I esteem'd more strong than age,
> And time less innocent than truth.

Largely because of a mistaken division which has been made between light and serious poetry, we have come to notice in poems like these only the elegance, forgetting that elegance can be part of a valid poetic attitude. In both these poems the elegance holds the balance between the 'two ways of looking at things' which are opposed to each other. That the movement of the verse is not dramatic, like the movement of Donne's or Herbert's verse, is true enough; but this again is part of the poet's attitude, for drama necessarily stresses one emotion at the expense of others. Horace's poetry and the poetry of the eighteenth-century Horatian tradition is not dramatic: it is essentially reflective. That is to say, the experiences which it treats are not presented for the sake of their immediate impact, but for the sake of generalized reflections (whether formulated or implied) which flow from a balanced presentation of different emotional states. The remoteness of their presentation is thus intentional. If there is no agony or exaltation in these poems, this is not because the poet does not understand agony or exaltation, but because he is concerned with seeing these states in relation to others.

A good deal of space has been devoted to the poetry of Horace because it is necessary to understand what is at the root of the Augustan tradition of reflective verse. The Augustans modified the Horatian approach to suit their own circumstances, but the habit of observation for the sake of general reflection persists. It is to be seen very clearly in the poetry of Lady Winchilsea, who, partly because of Wordsworth's commendation of the *Nocturnal Reverie*, is sometimes regarded as an exception to the Augustan tradition:

> In such a night when every louder wind
> Is to its distant cavern safe confin'd;
> And only gentle Zephyr fans its wings,
> And lonely Philomel, still waking, sings;
> Or from some tree, fam'd for the owl's delight,
> She, hollowing clear, directs the wand'rer right;
> In such a night, when passing clouds give place,
> Or thinly veil the heaven's mysterious face;
> When in some river overhung with green,
> The waving moon and trembling leaves are seen;
> When freshen'd grass now bears itself upright,
> And makes cool banks to pleasing rest invite,
> Whence springs the woodbine and the bramble-rose,
> And where the sleepy cowslip shelter'd grows;
> Whilst now a paler hue the foxglove takes,
> Yet chequers still with red the dusky brakes,
> When scatter'd glow-worms, but in twilight fine,
> Show trivial beauties watch their hour to shine;
> Whilst Salisbury stands the test of every light,
> In perfect charm and perfect virtue bright;
> When odours, which declin'd repelling day,
> Thro' temp'rate air uninterrupted stray;
> When darken'd groves their softest shadows wear,
> And falling waters we distinctly hear;
> When thro' the gloom more venerable shows
> Some ancient fabric, awful in repose,
> While sunburnt hills their swarthy looks conceal,
> And swelling haycocks thicken up the vale;

When the loos'd horse, now as his pasture leads,
Comes slowly grazing thro' th' adjoining meads,
Whose stealing pace, and lenthen'd shade we fear,
Till torn-up forage in his teeth we hear;
When nibbling sheep at large pursue their food,
And unmolested kine rechew the cud;
When curlews cry beneath the village walls,
And to her straggling brood the partridge calls;
Their short-liv'd jubilee the creatures keep,
Which but endures whilst tyrant man does sleep;
When a sedate content the spirit feels,
And no fierce light disturbs, whilst it reveals,
But silent musings urge the mind to seek
Something too high for syllables to speak;
Till the free soul, to a compos'dness charm'd,
Finding the elements of rage disarm'd,
O'er all below, a solemn quiet grown,
Joys in th' inferior world and thinks it like her own:
In such a night let me abroad remain,
Till morning breaks, and all's confus'd again:
Our cares, our toils, our clamours are renew'd,
Or pleasures, seldom reach'd, again pursued.

The lines about the foxglove and the horse undoubtedly have the kind of sensitivity which characterizes, let us say, the *Ode to a Nightingale*. But this sensitivity is to be found in individual poets of every age: to stress it unduly here is to ignore the pervading tone and intention of the poem, which is that of moral generalization and not the crystallization of a unique experience. The point may be clearer if we set Lady Winchilsea's poem alongside another Augustan 'nocturnal reverie', Parnell's *Night Piece on Death* ...

How deep yon azure dyes the sky
Where orbs of gold unnumber'd lie,
While thro' their ranks in silver pride
The nether crescent seems to glide!
The slumb'ring breeze forgets to breathe,
The lake is smooth and clear beneath,
Where once again the spangl'd show
Descends to meet our eyes below.
The grounds which on the right aspire,
In dimness from the view retire:

> The left presents a place of graves,
> Whose wall the silent water laves.
> That steeple guides thy doubtful sight
> Among the livid gleams of night.
> There pass, with melancholy state,
> By all the solemn heaps of fate,
> And think, as softly-sad you tread,
> Above the venerable dead,
> 'Time was, like thee they life possess'd,
> And time shall be, that thou shalt rest.'

Parnell is the more disciplined poet: the line of his thought moves with more certainty and his work is more obviously composed. Lady Winchilsea is more naïve, and perhaps more physically sensitive than Parnell, with the result that her poem has the effect of greater spontaneity, Parnell's of greater poise. But the temper of the two poems, evident in the firmness with which 'observation' is subordinated to 'reflection', is essentially the same. It springs from the belief that particular reactions can only be given significance in general reflections, and it is this attitude which stamps the whole Augustan tradition.

Within the tradition, as will become increasingly evident, there is scope for great variety. Indeed, it is one of the pleasures of reading this poetry to see the way in which the personalities of different poets emerge. Lady Winchilsea's *Petition for an Absolute Retreat*, for instance, is obviously in the tradition of the poems examined so far, yet it shows evidence of a personality markedly different from Pomfret's or Pope's:

> Give me, Oh indulgent fate!
> Give me yet, before I die,
> A sweet, but absolute retreat,
> 'Mongst paths so lost, and trees so high,
> That the world may ne'er invade,
> Thro' such windings and such shade,
> My unshaken liberty. ...

Lady Winchilsea is an example of a writer of poetry with a strong, lively, and well-stored mind, who is only intermittently a complete poet. At times she can be moving, as in the *Nocturnal Reverie*, or in the opening passages of her elegy for Sir William Twisden:

> But Oh! in vain; things void of sense we call,
> In vain implore the murmuring sound
> Of hollow groans from underneath the ground,
> Or court the loud lament of some steep water's fall;
> On things inanimate we would force
> Some share of our divided grief,
> Whilst Nature (unconcern'd for our relief)
> Pursues her settl'd path, her fixt and steady course. ...

But even in such passages it is the strength of the understanding which makes them impressive. For the most part she holds her reader by the quickness of her intelligence, and it is worth noting that she is able to do so because she is writing within the framework of a tradition where intelligence plays a major part. In any other she might have been a pedestrian versifier; as it is, she is eminently readable.

No poem could better illustrate this point about intelligence than Matthew Green's *The Spleen*, which is in the direct line of Horatian retirement descending from Horace's second Epode and embracing both Pope's 'Happy the man' and Pomfret's *Choice*:

> A farm some twenty miles from town,
> Small, tight, salubrious and my own;
> Two maids; that never saw the town,
> A serving-man not quite a clown,
> A boy to help to tread the mow,
> And drive, while t'other holds the plough;
> A chief, of temper form'd to please,
> Fit to converse, and keep the keys;
> And better to preserve the peace,
> Commission'd by the name of niece;
> With understandings of a size
> To think their master very wise.
> May heaven (it's all I ask for) send
> One genial room to treat a friend,
> Where decent cupboard, little plate,
> Display benevolence, not state. ...

But, once again, it is obvious that we have here quite a different kind of personality from anything we have met so far. This is retorting Horace on Horace, and Pomfret on Pomfret. There are signs of a quick irony which show the writer on guard against the dangers of mere wishfulness always lurking in this kind of writing. His reaction

to the natural scene is sensitive and vivid; but quite unlike that of
Lady Winchilsea:

> And may my humble dwelling stand
> Upon some chosen spot of land:
> A pond before full to the brim,
> Where cows may cool and geese may swim;
> Behind, a green like velvet neat,
> Soft to the eye, and to the feet;
> Where odorous plants in evening fair
> Breathe all around ambrosial air;
> From Eurus, foe to kitchen ground,
> Fenced by a slope with bushes crown'd,
> Fit dwelling for the feather'd throng
> Who pay their quit-rents with a song;
> With op'ning views of hill and dale,
> Which sense and fancy too regale,
> Where the half-cirque, which vision bounds,
> Like amphitheatre surrounds:
> And woods impervious to the breeze,
> Thick phalanx of embodied trees,
> From hills through plains of dusk array
> Extended far, repel the day.
> Here stillness, height, and solemn shade
> Invite, and contemplation aid:
> Here nymphs from hollow oaks relate
> The dark decrees and will of fate,
> And dreams beneath the spreading beech
> Inspire, and docile fancy teach;
> While soft as breezy breath of wind,
> Impulses rustle through the mind. ...

This could almost be used as a catalogue of the external marks of
Augustan reflective poetry – retirement to the 'Horatian' farm, the
Virgilian beech tree as an aid to contemplation, the Horatian allusive-
ness, the 'Roman' vocabulary, and so on. But, as a counterbalance,
there is also a different, almost colloquial vocabulary which, with the
lively verse-movement, seems to mock the solemnities of 'half-
cirque' and 'amphitheatre'. Green is not a satirist: that he feels
directly the attraction of his theme is evident in his *Apology for the
Quakers*:

> O Contemplation! air serene
> From damps of sense and fogs of spleen!
> Pure mount of thought! thrice holy ground,
> Where grace, when waited for, is found. . . .

But he is too subtle and mercurial a poet to be absolutely single-minded; and too honest to pretend to be so. The passage goes on:

> Well-natur'd, happy shade, forgive!
> Like you I think, but cannot live.
> Thy scheme requires the world's contempt,
> That, from dependence life exempt;
> And constitution fram'd so strong,
> This world's worst climate cannot wrong.
> Not such my lot, not Fortune's brat,
> I live by pulling off the hat,
> Compell'd by station every hour
> To bow to images of power;
> And in life's busy scenes immers'd
> See better things, and do the worst.

The few poems Green wrote provide a lively diversion within the Horatian tradition, and leave the reader always wishing he had lived longer and written more.

Yet another example of such variety is to be found in John Dyer.[3] His two poems *Grongar Hill* and *The Country Walk* are instances of what Johnson christened 'local poetry, of which,' he goes on to say, 'the fundamental subject is some particular landscape, to be poetically described, with addition of such embellishments as may be supplied by historical retrospection or incidental meditation'.[4]

To quote in order to demonstrate the common characteristics of Augustan reflective poetry would now be merely repetitive: *Grongar Hill* has all the customary landmarks – the praise of contentment, rural solitude as a stimulus to contemplation, the 'gothic' ruin which inspires sombre thoughts on human greatness, and so on. But unlike Lady Winchilsea and Matthew Green, Dyer's strength does not rest in his reflective powers: it lies in his power to record a visual experience:

> About his chequer'd sides I wind,
> And leave his brooks, and meads behind,
> And groves, and grottos where I lay,
> And vistas shooting beams of day:

> Wider and wider spreads the vale
> As circles in a smooth canal ...
> Still the prospect wider spreads,
> Adds a thousand woods and meads,
> Still it widens, widens still,
> And sinks the newly risen hill. ...

The verse and the manner of description here clearly owe something to *L'Allegro:* but Dyer's eye is the eye of Wordsworth rather than of Milton:

> Where am I, Nature? I descry
> Thy magazine before me lie!
> Temples! – and towns! – and towers! – and woods!
> And hills! – and vales! – and fields! – and floods !
> Crowding before me, edg'd around
> With naked wilds, and barren ground. ...

Yet before hailing these and other lines from *The Country Walk* as one more manifestation of pre-Romanticism, it would be as well to note how Augustan they are. It is not just that Dyer is a lesser poet than Wordsworth and lacks 'a sense of something far more deeply interfused'; his whole attitude is Augustan. 'Nature' is the source of temples and towns, quite as much as of hills and vales. The whole picture is systematically composed, with orderly nature ringed about by the chaos of naked wilds and barren ground. It is a picture to be found repeatedly in Augustan poetry – in Matthew Green's poem on p. 361, for instance, or in Pope's *Windsor Forest*:

> And mid the desert fruitful fields arise,
> That, crown'd with tufted trees and waving corn,
> Like verdant isles the sable waste adorn. ...

Especially it appears in the work of the eighteenth-century landscape gardener. Dyer's individual contribution to the tradition is his peculiar visual awareness – it might almost be called the technique of the expanding prospect – and of this something more will be said below. But his poetry is rooted in the Augustan tradition, and whoever fails to recognize this will miss much of its quality.

So far, an attempt has been made to indicate the general nature of the Augustan tradition of reflective poetry, and to show something of the scope which the tradition afforded for the expression of individual genius. In what remains of the chapter I propose to look in some detail at four poems, namely, Collins's *Ode to Evening*, Thomson's *Castle of Indolence*, Gray's *Elegy Written in a Country Churchyard*, and Shenstone's *Rural Elegance*. Of these, the *Elegy* represents the highest achievement of the Augustan reflective tradition, while each of the others illustrates at least some aspect of the tradition in its most notable form.

Nothing could better illustrate the diversity of effect to be found within the tradition than to read, one after the other, Dyer's *Grongar Hill* and Collins's *Ode to Evening*. In these two pieces, whose material facts and literary sources are much alike, one meets two entirely different kinds of poetic communication. As has already been indicated, Dyer's impulse is to record the effect of what he sees. To avoid misunderstanding it would be as well to stress the word *effect*. *Grongar Hill* is no versified ordnance survey. The reader is always conscious of the poet's eye transmuting visual facts –

> How close and small the hedges lie,
> What streaks of meadow cross the eye –

into an aesthetic experience; and it is in the successful communication of the experience that the value of the poem lies. *Grongar Hill* is, indeed, a very personal poem. Its weakness, as well as its strength, rests in this – that one is continually being reminded of the duality of what is seen and the person seeing it.

With the *Ode to Evening* one is no longer conscious of the poet as an individual, or of some particular scene that is being observed, but only of separately recognizable elements coalescing in Collins's slow modulations to create an unique poem. Superficially the literary elements derive chiefly from Milton. Much of the vocabulary echoes *Lycidas*, and the solitude of

> ... the hut
> That from the mountain's side
> Views wilds and floods ...

is that of *Il Penseroso* rather than of Horace's Sabine farm. But the influence which informs the poem more deeply is that of such odes as the fourth, ninth, and seventeenth of Horace's first book. Particularly the unfolding of the poem, with each stanza drifting into the next, recalls Horatian forms and is quite unlike the sharp transitions of *Il Penseroso* and *L'Allegro*. But the hold which this poem has on the reader lies in the way it gives permanence to a mood; a permanence which is achieved by the poet's power of realizing abstractions. It is in this that Horace and Collins go hand in hand in song. Much nonsense has been written, even by Coleridge, about the Augustan habit of personification, a habit which is closely connected with the Aristotelian maxim that poetry should speak of general truths. While it is of course true that in some Augustan poetry personification offers a poor substitute for imagination, the effectiveness of the practice is completely vindicated by the strength and assurance of the poetry of Gray or Johnson or Goldsmith. With Collins, however, as with Horace, personification is much more than a means of vigorous generalizing: it is a mode of thought and feeling as inherent in his mind as paradox is in the mind of Donne. With him an abstraction at the opening of a poem gradually accumulates (usually through echoes of other poetry) wider and wider implications of feeling, until, at the poem's close, it is realized, not as an intellectual counter, but as the symbol of a state of mind. This process is to be seen at its finest in the *Ode to Simplicity*, in 'How sleep the brave', and, best of all, in the *Ode to Evening*.

Despite its strong literary affinities, to analyse Collins's poetry in terms of such things is dangerous. The echoes of the *Ode to Evening* (like those of Milton's *Comus*) have been so altered by the poet's sensibility that their sources are of little more than historical importance. All that can be said with safety is that the poem is a perfect example of 'imitation', in which literary materials have been absorbed and re-created to suggest at once a continuing tradition and a unique awareness.

By comparison with Collins's poetry, that of Thomson[5] presents fewer difficulties. Collins's mind is inward turning: his poetry, though it never loses touch with human values, has no strong practical bent. Thomson's bent is always social. *The Castle of Indolence*, a poem which uses the *Faerie Queene* stanza, was begun as a private Spenserian joke about the poet's friends. But like others (Gay and Shenstone among them), Thomson became the captive of an enchantment he had set out to deride.

The Augustans were two-minded about Spenser: they tended to regard his vocabulary as material for parody, but at the same time they recognized in him the strain of 'fancy' or 'imagination' which Johnson so well analyses in *Rasselas* and the Life of Collins. The strain of fancy, however, was never exclusively predominant in Augustan poetry at its best. Even in Collins's most 'fanciful' poem, the *Ode on the Superstitions of the Scottish Highlands*, it mingles with a strain of social reflection. Gray's *Bard*, despite its fantastic visioning, is concerned with English history, and it is this concern (as one realizes after long acquaintance with the poem) that holds the work together, giving it the measured progression which Gray's more flamboyant effects at first obscure. In *The Castle of Indolence* the two strains of fancy and social preoccupation are to be seen in their clearest form. The first canto, which describes the enchanted land of Indolence, gives full scope for Thomson's remarkable sensuousness and fantasy:

> And up the hills, on either side, a wood
> Of black'ning pines, ay waving to and fro,
> Sent forth a sleepy horror through the blood;
> And where this valley winded out, below,
> The murmuring main was heard, and scarcely heard, to flow.

> A pleasing land of drowsyhead it was:
> Of dreams that wave before the half-shut eye;
> And gay castles in the clouds that pass,
> For ever flushing round a summer sky ...

It would be difficult to find many parallels to this before *The Lotus Eaters*, and it is perhaps not surprising (though disheartening) that even Thomson's chief editor should say of the poem: 'There is poetry in the first canto; the second is mainly didactic.' Whatever 'didactic' may imply, the second canto, telling of the destruction of the enchanter by the Knight of Industry, forms the essential complement of the first, which, by itself, would be a freak, however delightful. The reader who is looking for surprises will prefer the first canto: the reader who values Augustan poetry for its own sake will sense that a piece of writing such as the one above needs something to complete it:

Nor from his deep retirement banish'd was
The amusing cares of rural industry.
Still, as with graceful change the seasons pass,
New scenes arise, new landskips strike the eye,
And all the enliven'd country beautify:
Gay plains extend where marshes slept before;
O'er recent meads the exulting streamlets fly;
Dark frowning heaths grow bright with Ceres' store;
And woods imbrown the steep, or wave along the shore.

As nearer to his farm you made approach,
He polish'd nature with a finer hand:
Yet on her beauties durst not art encroach;
'Tis art's alone these beauties to expand.
In graceful dance immingl'd, o'er the land
Pan, Pales, Flora and Pomona played ...

Collins and Thomson represent, as it were, the introversive and extraversive poles of the poetic temperament; and it is evidence of the strength and flexibility of the Augustan tradition that it is able to accommodate both without distortion. In Gray's *Elegy*[6] the extremes merge to produce both an epitome and the masterpiece of the tradition. The occasion of the poem may have been the death of a friend, and the pattern may have been the twenty-fourth ode of Horace's first book: yet never do personal sorrow or pedantry intrude. Gray meditates on great general themes – mortality, humility, contentment – and the universality of his themes is reinforced by echoes from earlier literature – Horace, Ovid, Chaucer, Sir Thomas Browne, Milton, Waller all contribute. But the echoes are never verbal copies. Where Horace wrote 'What if you sang a strain more soothing than Thracian Orpheus, would the blood return to the empty face?...', Gray echoes him in such a way that one is aware only of the pressure of great poetry of the past, not of a specific instance:

> Can storied urn, or animated bust,
> Back to its mansion call the fleeting breath?
> Can honour's voice provoke the silent dust,
> Or flattery soothe the dull, cold ear of death?

Similarly, though the vocabulary is classical, words like 'rugged' and 'rude' implying their Latin as well as their more general English sense, the esoteric meaning is there only to strengthen the significance, never to display the poet's scholarship, or startle the reader.

The development of the poem is a movement from landscape images that are the common property of the Augustan tradition to philosophical musings which are no less prevalent; yet in no other poem does meditation flow from image with such naturalness. Gray's poetic temper is so perfectly adapted to this kind of writing that it would almost seem to have been evolved for him. In all his poetry the power of his imagination to endow a local setting with significant forms is evident. The figures which people the landscape of the *Elegy* have their counterpart in the 'idle progeny' of the Eton College ode and the 'insect youth' of the *Ode on the Spring*. In these, however, the effect is perhaps more strained. In the *Elegy* it is not until one looks closely that one realizes how much the strength of the poem owes to the way in which, after a passage of musing, the 'local' element returns, to lead to yet further comment. The effect of the poem is of a series of waves, each growing with almost imperceptible power, then sinking back to the original starting-point.

To isolate characteristics of style and thought is inevitably to falsify the view of this poem; for the triumph of the *Elegy* is the triumph of what I. A. Richards has called 'an exquisitely adjusted tone ... the perfect recognition of the writer's relation to the reader in view of what is being said and their feelings about it'.[7] And to say this is to say that the secret of the poem lies in the age as well as the poet. Only within the Augustan tradition (unless one should include Chaucer's age) could a poet's delicate perception of the contemporary intellectual and emotional atmosphere have found such complete expression.

The *Elegy* marks the culmination of the Augustan reflective tradition: its influence persists, notably in *The Deserted Village*, until the close of the century. But from 1750 onwards the main stream of the tradition – which runs from Shenstone, the landscape artist of the Leasowes and editor of Dodsley's *Collection*, to Cowper – shows a change of temper. Shenstone did not turn his back on Horace:

> From plains and woodlands; from the view
>   Of rural nature's blooming face,
>   Smit by the glare of rank and place,
> To courts the sons of fancy flew ...

> Paternal acres please no more;
> Adieu the simple and sincere delight –
>   Th' habitual scene of hill and dale,
>   The rural herds, the vernal gale,
>   The tangl'd vetch's purple bloom,
>   The fragrance of the bean's perfume,
> Be theirs alone who cultivate the soil,
> And drink the cup of thirst, and eat the bread of toil.

With certain reservations this might have been written by Lady Winchilsea; and it is no more helpful to look for the germs of Romanticism in *Rural Elegance* than in her *Petition for an Absolute Retreat*. Nevertheless, even here a significant shift of emphasis is evident. For Lady Winchilsea, retirement was to afford scope for moral reflection:

> Thus from noise and crowds remov'd,
> Let each moment be improv'd;
> Every object still produce
> Thoughts of pleasure and of use. ...

For the owner of Leasowes it was scope for the expression of sensibility:

> And sure there seem, of human kind
>   Some born to shun the solemn strife;
> Some for amusive tasks design'd,
>   To soothe the certain ills of life;
> Grace its lone vales with many a budding rose,
>   New founts of bliss disclose,
> Call forth refreshing shades, and decorate repose.

By comparison with Lady Winchilsea's tough intellectual fibre there is a languor about this which points to more than a difference between individual poets. It is part of a shift of emphasis which marks all forms of literature in the second half of the century – a shift from moral and social issues towards the cultivation of feeling for its own sake.

'Sensibility' is not, of course, the discovery of the poets of the later eighteenth century; but in the earlier poets it was incidental, in the later ones it is paramount. In Shenstone's Arcadia, moral and social values are of secondary importance to feeling:

Why brand these pleasures with the name
Of soft, unsocial toils, indolence and shame?
Search but the garden, or the wood,
    Let yon admir'd carnation own
Not all was meant for raiment or for food,
    Not all for needful use alone;
There, while the seeds of future blossoms dwell,
'Tis colour'd for the sight, perfum'd to please the smell.

Johnson's most frequently quoted comment on Shenstone is both unkind and untrue. 'Shenstone's pleasure', he says, 'was all in the eye; he valued what he valued merely for its looks; nothing raised his indignation more than to ask if there were fish in his water.' Nevertheless, it puts a finger on an important point.

The qualities of Shenstone's poetry – selective simplicity of language and a sense of appositeness in the use of traditional forms – are essentially Augustan and classical. His classicism, however, is not Chesterfield's rigid subservience to 'the modes'; it is of a kind in which it is possible to be familiar and at ease because not entirely dependent on external standards: and in this Shenstone contributes something to the Augustan tradition of which it was perhaps in need. Yet the gain is offset by a loss. Poetry which has no strong intellectual content is seldom emotionally vigorous. By his preference of 'feeling' to 'understanding' Shenstone paradoxically robs Augustan poetry of much of its robustness. The air of Arcadia is more rarefied, and so more delicate, than that of Grongar Hill. But it is also less fortifying.

NOTES

1. A. R. Humphreys, *William Shenstone*.

2. For an eighteenth-century modification of this kind of poem, see John Gay's *Rural Sports* (*Gay's Poetical Works*, Oxford, 1926).

3. Dyer's *The Fleece* and *The Ruins of Rome* are blank-verse poems in the Augustan 'Georgic' tradition. They are uneven (mainly because of Dyer's uncertain handling of Miltonic blank verse), but they are worth reading for the light they throw on the tradition and for flashes of the 'artist's notebook' quality to be found in *Grongar Hill*. Dyer was at one time a landscape painter.

4. *Lives of the Poets* (Life of Denham). Johnson makes Denham's *Cooper's Hill* (q.v.) the first of this type of poem. See also Samuel Garth's *Poem of Claremont* and Pope's *Windsor Forest*. Nearly all the poems mentioned in this chapter have some 'local' characteristics – especially Gray's *Elegy* and Goldsmith's *Deserted Village*.

5. Thomson's *The Seasons* is the great achievement of the Augustan 'Georgic' tradition. 'Winter', at least, should be read. See also the same poet's *Solitude*.

6. For the growth of this poem, see *The Augustan Reprint Society: Publication No. 31* (1951). This contains the 1751 text and a facsimile of the Eton College MS., as well as a valuable introduction by George Sherburn.

7. *Practical Criticism* (1929), p. 207. See the whole passage, and also the further discussion at pp. 252 f.

OLIVER GOLDSMITH

BORIS FORD

Professor of Education, the University of Sussex

THOUGH Goldsmith (c. 1730–74) himself thought poorly of his chances with posterity, and though he was constantly depressed by the reception he received in his lifetime, he has, in fact, enjoyed a steady popularity from his own day to the present. His success with his contemporaries was not earned without a struggle, for his writings were no more brilliant than his personal appearance or his public manner. Unostentatious as a writer and gauche as a social being, he found himself exclaiming more than once that 'the public will never do me justice; whenever I write anything, they make a point to know nothing about it'. And yet he became a close friend of Dr Johnson and Sir Joshua Reynolds, of Burke and Garrick; and as a member of the Literary Club of nine, which met every Monday night at the Turk's Head in Soho, he was an accepted figure in his own right (Boswell, by contrast, was admitted to the Club long after Goldsmith, and then only at the insistence of Dr Johnson).

In spite of all he said and expected, Goldsmith's main works, when they eventually appeared, were immediately acclaimed: first, *The Traveller* (1764), which Dr Johnson declared the finest poem since Pope; then *The Vicar of Wakefield* (1796), which in five months went into three editions; next, the immediately popular *The Deserted Village* (1770); and finally, his comedy *She Stoops to Conquer* (1773), which he had so long struggled to have performed. These four works earned him a contemporary reputation second only to that of Dr Johnson himself. When he died, it was fitting that Dr Johnson should write the epitaph that was inscribed on a tablet beneath his bust in Westminster Abbey, the first lines of which read:

OF OLIVER GOLDSMITH

A Poet, Naturalist, and Historian
Who left scarce any style of writing untouched,
And touched nothing that he did not adorn;
Of all the passions,
Whether smiles were to be moved or tears,
A powerful yet gentle master;

In genius, sublime, vivid, versatile,
In style, elevated, clear, elegant.*

Since then, Oliver Goldsmith has seldom been out of favour, and his novel has been translated throughout the world. He and his writings survived from an age that was subsequently thought artificial and even superficial, and whose giants of literature have commanded more respect than affection; and they have survived because, perhaps, of the seemingly un-Augustan humanity of nature with which they are imbued. It is significant that the word most commonly used to define Goldsmith's particular quality is 'charm', and this is certainly not a word usually associated with the writings of Swift and Pope, of Dr Johnson and Fielding, or with the art of Hogarth.

Though some of his more renowned anthology-pieces, such as the Lamb-like *A City Night-Piece*, undoubtedly tend to disguise the fact, Goldsmith was essentially an Augustan, and his virtues are those of his age. In his life as a hack who turned his hand from Ancient to Natural History and back again, he was a typical author of the London of his time. Always in debt, always struggling against the clock to put together new work for the press, Goldsmith presents a wretched picture of a considerable native talent squandered on ephemeral work. As he himself wrote in his *Enquiry into the Present State of Polite Learning in Europe*:

> The author, when unpatronized by the Great, has naturally recourse to the bookseller. There cannot be, perhaps, imagined a combination more prejudicial to taste than this. It is the interest of one to allow as little for writing, and of the other to write as much, as possible; accordingly, tedious compilations, and periodical magazines, are the result of their joint endeavours. In these circumstances, the author bids adieu to fame, writes for bread, and for that only. Imagination is seldom called in; he sits down to address the venal muse with the most phlegmatic apathy; and, as we are told of the

* This is a translation, from Crocker's edition of Boswell's Johnson, of the original Latin. In fact Dr Johnson was petitioned, by those who had joined with him to commission the memorial, to re-do the epitaph into English. To which he replied that he 'was willing to modify the sense of the epitaph in any manner that the gentlemen pleased; but he would never consent to disgrace the walls of Westminster Abbey with an English inscription'.

Russians, courts his mistress by falling asleep in her lap. His reputation never spreads in a wider circle than that of the trade, who generally value him, not for the fineness of his compositions, but the quantity he works off in a given time.

For years he was accustomed to a life of hardship and poverty and, above all, of indignity, and this was only aggravated (it was certainly not brought about) by his inability to keep any money in his pockets for longer than a few hours, by his excessive generosity or his weakness for magnificent clothes. The Rev. Thomas Percy, who was later to become celebrated for his 'relics' and ballads, visited Goldsmith at the age of thirty:

> I called on Goldsmith at his lodgings in March, 1759, and found him writing his *Enquiry* in a miserable dirty-looking room, in which there was but one chair; and when, from civility, he resigned it to me, he himself was obliged to sit in the window. While we were conversing together, some one tapped gently at the door, and being desired to come in, a poor ragged little girl, of a very becoming demeanour, entered the room, and dropping a courtesy, said, 'My mamma sends her compliments and begs the favour of you to lend her a chamber-pot full of coals.'

In the end, for all the recognition that came his way, Goldsmith's health collapsed under the strain, and he died miserably and in poverty at the young age of about forty-four.

The wonder is that, though living in an age of harsh satire, his own writings were so free of bitterness – so little 'schooled by continued adversity into a hatred of their kind'; and, moreover, that they maintain so consistent a degree of clarity and elegance, to use Dr Johnson's apt words. Even in *The Vicar of Wakefield*, which is a tale of unending woe if ever there was one, there is no recrimination and the tone is not particularly personal in its pressure. Indeed, the character in that novel most closely modelled on Goldsmith himself is the elder son, George, who introduces his long account of misfortune on the Continent (much of it is autobiographical) with the comment that 'the less kind I found fortune at one time, the more I expected from her another, and being now at the bottom of her wheel, every new revolution might lift, but could not depress me.' Goldsmith too was something of a 'light-hearted vagabond', as he described George; and for all his awkwardness in company, he was liable among friends to be irresponsibly gay, just as, among the needy, he was certain to be irresponsibly generous. Towards the end of his life, a young countryman of his came to him for help and Goldsmith, who was as usual much harassed at that time, gave him work as his amanuensis. Later this M'Donnell wrote: 'I saw him only in his bland and kind moods, with a flow, perhaps an overflow, of the milk of human kindness for all who were in any manner dependent upon him.' When he died, he was mourned not only by his peers, but also, as Washington Irving relates, by 'the lamentation of the old and infirm, and the sobbing of women; poor objects of his charity to whom he had never turned a deaf ear, even when struggling himself with poverty'.[1]

The basis of Goldsmith's distinction as a writer is his straightforward simplicity and the unassuming elegance of his style. These qualities, though they may have come to him easily, were none the less cultivated quite deliberately. His *Enquiry* ends with a clear statement of his beliefs on the nature of good writing:

> As our gentlemen writers have it therefore so much in their power to lead the taste of the times, they may now part with the inflated stile that has for some years been looked upon as fine writing, and which every young writer is now obliged to adopt, if he chuses to be read. They may now dispense with the loaded epithet, and dressing up of trifles with dignity. For to use an obvious instance, it is not those who make the greatest noise with their wares in the streets, that have the most to sell. Let us, instead of writing finely, try to write naturally. Not hunt after lofty expressions to deliver mean ideas; nor be for ever gaping, when we only mean to deliver a whisper.

This could have been written in no other age than Goldsmith's: it has the easy deportment that bespeaks the Augustan virtues. And though it closely accords with Johnson's advice to a budding writer – that he should go through his work and whenever he came on a passage that struck him as uncommonly fine, he should strike it out – yet one feels that Goldsmith followed his own precepts more successfully than his great contemporary. Partly, no doubt, this was due to his own temperament. Moreover, Goldsmith had the advantage, from the stylistic point of view, of not being much given to speculation or deep self-searching, so that he seldom needed to strike a profound any more than a sublime note. He pursued, and most notably in his essays, an even and genial tone that makes him nearly always easy to read, if seldom exciting. For instance:

> Whatever may be the merits of the English in other sciences, they seem peculiarly excellent in the art of healing. There is scarcely a disorder incident to humanity, against which they are not possessed of a most infallible antidote. The professors of other arts confess the inevitable intricacy of things; talk with doubt, and decide with hesitation, but doubting is entirely unknown in medicine; the advertising professors here delight in cases of difficulty; be the disorder never so desperate or radical, you will find numbers in every street, who, by leveling a pill at the part affected, promise a certain cure without loss of time, knowledge of a bedfellow, or hindrance of business.

(It is an irony to reflect that Goldsmith, himself a doctor of sorts, almost certainly hastened his own end by insisting on 'leveling a pill' at his own affected system, a pill of quite the wrong character for his purpose.) This passage, which is chosen pretty well at random from *The Citizen of the World* (1762), is typical of Goldsmith's Grub-Street manner. Its graceful flow is unmistakable. The irony is gentler and less complex than Pope's or Swift's, perhaps because Goldsmith was generally less involved in his subject-matter than they were. But it is an irony related to theirs in that it is founded upon a similar conception of life, reverting to, or at least implying, good sense as the true basis of polite manners and social decorum.

It is this, perhaps, that attracted him so much to Beau Nash and that makes his *Life of Richard Nash* (1762) so sympathetic, albeit so judicious, a study. Partly, of course, Goldsmith was envious of the creator and monarch of fashionable Bath who, though he 'was clumsey, too large and awkward, and his features harsh, strong, and peculiarly irregular; yet even, with these disadvantages, he made love, became an universal admirer of the sex, and was universally admired' – in which one can detect Goldsmith watching himself and wishing for something of the same triumph over a graceless appearance. In fact, however, Goldsmith's lack of brilliance or cleverness made his writings all the more limpid, and his good sense is carried without any flourish of self-importance or self-approbation. The essay which touched lightly on affairs of the day ideally suited his style, and if his writings in this manner are not much read now, that is essentially a tribute to the good journalism that they are: they attempted no more than was appropriate, and Goldsmith would have been the last to suppose that they might be read centuries after they were written. Similarly, his two comedies were successful mainly because of their lack of affectation. If there is nothing much to them as literature, at least they have an abundance of negative virtues.

The Vicar of Wakefield is, without doubt, the work on which Goldsmith's popularity rests. It has been successful from the day of publication until the present – though interestingly enough it lay for two years in the hands of his bookseller and was only brought out after the triumph of his poem *The Traveller:* and Dr Johnson, who had not thought very much of its prospects, observed that sixty guineas was 'no mean price' for Goldsmith to receive for it. The novel's great strength is its quality of stoical resignation. Washington Irving's wholly sympathetic account is probably typical of most people's reactions, when he writes that Goldsmith 'has given them [his scenes and characters] as seen through the medium of his own indulgent eye, and has set them forth with the colourings of his good head and heart.'

But if this prescription was capable of producing great art in the case of Dickens, it was less successful in the case of Goldsmith himself. For it is his very goodness of head and heart that makes it hard to be altogether satisfied with the novel today. Or rather, the goodness portrayed in the Vicar and his family is of too naïve a character; one might almost say that the book suffers for want of the Augustan poise that Goldsmith reveals elsewhere. In the first place, the novel is unusually short, and this has the effect of making its sequence of tumultuous calamities seem rushed and undeveloped. Within a few pages, for instance, the Vicar, who is lodged in jail, learns that one of his daughters has died; then word is brought that his other daughter has been 'carried off by ruffians'; and lastly his son George, whom he had supposed safe with his regiment, is suddenly brought in 'all bloody, wounded, and fettered with the heaviest irons'. This wealth of incident is both underprepared and underdeveloped, and it calls forth only more of the resignation with which the Vicar has met his previous misfortunes. Moreover, on this occasion the Vicar treats the assembled prisoners, who 'loved to hear my counsel', to a lengthy 'exhortation' on the 'equal dealings of providence', a sermon which is tedious by any standards.

This is not, as it may at first appear, a trifling criticism, for the radical weakness of the novel lies in Goldsmith's ambiguous attitude towards the Vicar himself. The novel, to some extent because it is related by the Vicar in the first person, is never able to present the Vicar with the gentle irony that he deserves. The 'exhortation', for example, is tedious but without any suggestion that the reader, let alone Goldsmith, need wonder at tediousness spun out to such a length. Elsewhere, the Vicar reveals an unbearable smugness: on one occasion he finds his daughters dressed for church in what seems to him unbecoming splendour and 'frippery', and he therefore protests strongly, remarking that ' "the nakedness of the indigent world may be cloathed from the trimmings of the vain" '. He continues:

> This remonstrance had the proper effect; they went with great composure, that very instant, to change their dress; and the next day I had the satisfaction of finding my daughters, at their own request, employed in cutting up their trains into Sunday waistcoats for Dick and Bill, the two little ones, and what was still more satisfactory, the gowns seemed improved by this curtailing.

This note of smugness is pervasive, and it is unqualified by any suggestion of implicit criticism. In this respect, the novel is strangely unlike Goldsmith's other writings, which are seldom solemn-faced and decorous – and incidentally this passage is alien to Goldsmith himself, who could never resist decking himself out in fine clothes and never appeared to suffer any pangs of conscience on this account.

The other element in the novel that jars today is its note of romantic artificiality, though in this it is typical enough of its age. Consider, for instance, the passage that describes the Vicar and his family enjoying a picnic:

> On these occasions, our two little ones always read for us, and they were regularly served after we had done. Sometimes, to give a variety to our amusements, the girls sung to the guitar; and while they thus formed a little concert, my wife and I

would stroll down the sloping field, that was embellished
with blue-bells and centaury, talk of our children with rapture, and enjoy the breeze that wafted both health and harmony.

This picture of what the Vicar later calls 'vacant hilarity' is innocent
enough, admittedly; yet it has about it too much of the set-piece, of
the formal group-portrait in costume, where Nature is painted in to
suit the occasion. Though the concert is here described as lending
'*variety*', within a dozen lines we read that 'our young musicians
began their *usual* concert', and this lack of precision blurs the picture
of the reality that Goldsmith clearly intended it to have. Moreover,
the words themselves – 'embellished', 'rapture', 'wafted' – tend to be
cloying, so that though one knows well enough that the confection
is only meant to be simple and innocent, to the palate it tastes
altogether too sweet. Because of this, the Vicar's family remains
two-dimensional. His two daughters are differentiated, to be sure,
but one finds oneself having to turn back to their first introduction
to remind oneself which is which, and then concluding that it does
not matter much anyway. Similarly, when the daughters are ab-
ducted, one notes the horror and sorrow of the Vicar and his wife
without feeling moved to share it. And this is inevitably a blemish,
because detachment, even disinterest, is not at all what Goldsmith
intended, even though one must add, in all fairness, that he did not
intend indulgence either. In *The Vicar of Wakefield*, Goldsmith failed
to work out the appropriate mode for his story, with the result that
the characters are too generalized and they develop with all too little
inner life. Compared with Fielding or Jane Austen, between whom
Goldsmith the novelist seems to stand in an unsuccessful sort of way,
this novel is ultimately a slight, if 'charming', creation.

If this seems an unduly severe judgement, it is one that helps to
define the great assurance and distinction of Goldsmith's major poems,
particularly his *The Deserted Village*, for they succeed where the
novel fails. Early on in the novel, there is a passage that is unusually
apt, though without thrusting itself out of context. After losing their
money, the Vicar and his family move to a simpler and more modest
living, and this new home is introduced thus:

> The place of our retreat was in a little neighbourhood,
> consisting of farmers, who tilled their own grounds, and were

equal strangers to opulence and poverty. As they had almost all the conveniences of life within themselves, they seldom visited towns or cities in search of superfluity. Remote from the polite, they still retained the primaeval simplicity of manners; and frugal by habit, they scarce knew that temperance was a virtue. They wrought with cheerfulness on days of labour; but observed festivals as intervals of idleness and pleasure. They kept up the Christmas carol, sent true love-knots on Valentine morning, eat pancakes on Shrovetide, shewed their wit on the first of April, and religiously cracked nuts on Michaelmas eve. Being apprized of our approach, the whole neighbourhood came out to meet their minister, drest in their finest cloaths, and preceded by a pipe and tabor: A feast also was provided for our reception, at which we sate chearfully down; and what the conversation lacked in wit, was made up in laughter.

The feeling and manner of this description is very close to *The Deserted Village*. It is particularized, and yet the detail does not crystallize into sharp individuality, but rather tends to suggest a generalized reality. The 'they' of this passage, though ostensibly the Vicar's new parishioners, seem mainly to be embodiments of a way of life amidst which he and his family will live. One feels no need to have the 'they' introduced by name, or even to see them as distinct people. And this quality of elegiac generalization is what one finds in *The Deserted Village* and it is what gives the poem a strength that it shares, in many respects, with Gray's great *Elegy*.

Goldsmith was a most assured, if somewhat unimaginative, poet, and it is no wonder that *The Traveller* should have been so well received. It was the first of his works to appear under his own name, and it established him as an author in his own right. Above all, it established him as a great Augustan poet, revealed in the judicious tone, the unruffled movement, the urbane and fluent control of the couplet:

> To men of other minds my fancy flies,
> Embosom'd in the deep where Holland lies,
> Methinks her patient sons before me stand,
> Where the broad ocean leans against the land,
> And, sedulous to stop the coming tide,
> Lift the tall rampire's artificial pride.

Onward methinks, and diligently slow
The firm connected bulwark seems to grow;
Spreads its long arms amidst the watry roar,
Scoops out an empire, and usurps the shore.
While the pent ocean rising o'er the pile,
Sees an amphibious world beneath him smile;
The slow canal, the yellow blossom'd vale,
The willow tufted bank, the gliding sail,
The crowded mart, the cultivated plain,
A new creation rescued from his reign.

This could not be done better, or more exactly. Its imagery, in particular, is so fitting as to draw no attention to itself, and yet it wonderfully conveys the sense of the 'diligently slow', patient creation of the amphibious world of Holland, carved, as it were, out of the sea and yet still part of it, an impression of the 'broad ocean' transformed into the 'slow canal' much as wild nature was being transformed and landscaped in contemporary England.

The theme of *The Deserted Village* is related to some lines towards the end of *The Traveller*, lines which come very close, as does the whole of the later poem, to Goldsmith's sense of being himself an exile:

... Seen opulence, her grandeur to maintain,
Lead stern depopulation in her train,
And over fields where scatter'd hamlets rose,
In barren solitary pomp repose?
Have we not seen at pleasure's lordly call,
The smiling long-frequented village fall?
Beheld the duteous son, the sire decay'd,
The modest matron, and the blushing maid,
Forc'd from their homes, a melancholy train,
To traverse climes beyond the western main;
Where wild Oswego spreads her swamps around,
And Niagara stuns with thund'ring sound?

Goldsmith was a voluntary exile, of course, and he apparently had no overwhelming urge to return to his own village of Lissoy in Ireland, which the diligence of his biographers has identified as the source of the Village in the poem. But this is, on the whole, rather beside the point, for what counts is Goldsmith's *sense* of the idealized village community and of the exile inevitably brought about by the 'barren solitary pomp' (a line of great and measured denunciation). It is this sense that he so powerfully conveys in his elegiac poem, a poem that in many ways continues and completes *The Traveller*, in that the earlier poem relates the poet's wanderings in search of more congenial modes of life and the later poem presents us with the intimate 'long-frequented' world from which he first set out and to which there can be no return because it has fallen into waste and decay.

The poem opens with an evocation of the Village as it once had been, in terms very close, as already suggested, to the description of the Vicar's village. The poet picks out the details in these lines:

> How often have I paused on every charm,
> The sheltered cot, the cultivated farm,
> The never failing brook, the busy mill,
> The decent church that topt the neighbouring hill,
> The hawthorn bush, with seats beneath the shade,
> For talking age and whispering lovers made;
> How oft have I blest the coming day,
> When toil remitting lent its turn to play,
> And all the village train from labour free
> Led up their sports beneath the spreading tree;
> While many a pastime circled in the shade,
> The young contending as the old surveyed;
> And many a gambol frolicked o'er the ground,
> And slights of art and feats of strength went round;
> And still as each repeated pleasure tired,
> Succeeding sports the mirthful band inspired;
> The dancing pair that simply sought renown
> By holding out to tire each other down;
> The swain mistrustless of his smutted face,
> While secret laughter tittered round the place;
> The bashful virgin's side-long looks of love,
> The matron's glance that would those looks reprove:
> These were thy charms, sweet village; sports like these,
> With sweet succession, taught even toil to please;
> These round thy bowers their chearful influence shed,
> These were thy charms – But all these charms are fled.

The adjectives in the first few lines have an effect less of precision than of generalization: if they are exact, it is with the exactness of the familiar rather than, as with Donne, of the previously unperceived. Similarly with the life of the village, 'When toil remitting lent its turn to play': the sports, though detailed indeed, are less the sports of a distinctively individual village (such as Lissoy) than of the *idea* of a village, of an ideally familiar village. If this generalizing tendency of the words seemed to weaken the novel, because there the narrative needed a greater fullness of personal detail, in the poem the same tendency emerges as a strength, because here Goldsmith is not concerned with narrative but with recalling to his readers a common heritage, a scene bred in the bone.

The poem progresses – though, in fact, its total impact is less one of progress than of a picture of past and present perceived all at once – in a series of ebbings and flowings. The village is recalled in its old perfection, and then seen in its present 'shapeless ruin'; recalled again in fresh detail, as 'Remembrance wakens with all her busy train' – a memory above all of sound, of the milk-maid singing, the herd lowing, the gabbling geese, the watchdog's baying voice, the loud laugh, all interleaved with the nightingale's song; and then again banished in the face of today's reality – today when 'the sounds of population fail', when there are 'No cheerful murmurs' but only 'yon widowed, solitary thing', who in her present wretchedness of life is become 'The sad historian of the pensive plain'. The change is felt in the shift from noise to silence, and in the way the movement of the lines slows down to a heavy inertia.

Thus are evoked, like bastions of common virtue and worth from a bygone age, the village preacher and the village schoolmaster and the village inn. Again one notices that the precise details of the scene tend always to evoke a hallowed familiarity; Goldsmith's personal memories of his father and his teacher undoubtedly provided the undercurrent of regret, but he has not left us with individual portraiture. Because of this, the verse is able to move without transition into the lines of general denunciation, in which the poet speaks with a full-dress Augustan weight and poise:

> Yes! let the rich deride, the proud disdain,
> These simple blessings of the lowly train;
> To me more dear, congenial to my heart,
> One native charm, than all the gloss of art;

> Spontaneous joys, where Nature has its play,
> The soul adopts, and owns their first born sway;
> Lightly they frolic o'er the vacant mind,
> Unenvied, unmolested, unconfined.
> But the long pomp, the midnight masquerade,
> With all the freaks of wanton wealth arrayed,
> In these, ere triflers half their wish obtain,
> The toiling pleasure sickens into pain;
> And, even while fashion's brightest arts decoy,
> The heart distrusting asks, if this be joy.

This denunciation, recalling Pope's *Epistle to Boyle* on The Use of Riches, is founded on a conviction that the natural order, which consists of Nature cultivated into fruitfulness by Man, has been despoiled by 'the freaks of wanton wealth':

> The robe that wraps his limbs in silken sloth,
> Has robbed the neighbouring fields of half their growth.

– the word 'sloth' comes suddenly in place of the expected 'cloth', with a hissing, despising force. And the passage ends with the terse epitaph:

> The country blooms – a garden, and a grave.

Goldsmith's verse moves, almost always, at a deceptively even pace. The shifts of tone and emphasis are all but imperceptible, and they seldom startle any more than does the imagery. And yet, within this even tenor, the verse mounts in intensity and sinks back as the poet's vision moves from past to present. Only very occasionally does a single line stand out, like a sudden unassimilable protest, as in the lines where the poet is rejecting the city as a possible refuge for the dispossessed peasantry:

> The dome where Pleasure holds her midnight reign,
> Here, richly deckt, admits the gorgeous train;
> Tumultuous grandeur crowds the blazing square,
> The rattling chariots clash, the torches glare.
> Such scenes like these no troubles e'er annoy!
> Sure these denote one universal joy!
> Are these thy serious thoughts? – Ah, turn thine eyes
> Where the poor houseless shivering female lies.
> She once, perhaps, in village plenty blest,
> Has wept at tales of innocence distrest.

The long-drawn open-vowelled words of the earlier lines, the thick opulence that is conveyed through the sound of 'gorgeous' and 'grandeur', are brought up short in the line 'Where the poor house-less shivering female lies', whose emphatically slow concentration seems to prevent any eye escaping the harsh human tragedy before it. And the 'village plenty' of the following line seems to acquire from the earlier passages of the poem a deep-rooted richness, a harvest richness of life and humanity, that contrasts damningly with the callous opulence of the pleasure dome. But this suddenly vivid detail gives way again to the more generalized picture of the earlier sections of the poem, as the poet sees the 'poor exiles' leaving the village: the 'good old sire', his 'lovely daughter', and her 'fond husband' are not clichés, not lay-figures so much as symbols of a lost order. Indeed, within a few more lines the poet speaks of seeing 'the rural virtues leave the land', the abstract virtues of 'contented toil', 'hospitable care', 'kind connubial tenderness', 'piety', 'steady loyalty', 'faithful love'; and yet, such a felt reality do these abstractions now have in the poem, that the poet is able to imbue them, in a couplet that echoes the earlier rhyme, with a shadowy solidity:

> Downward they move, a melancholy band,
> Pass from the shore, and darken all the strand.

So, by the end, the evoked scene of the village has given way to the virtues it was felt to embody, and 'sweet Poetry' is summoned to

> Teach erring man to spurn the rage of gain;
> Teach him, that states of native strength possest,
> Tho' very poor, may still be very blest.

The moral does not seem out of place, even though it may well seem unnecessary, for the poem has all along revolved implicitly around just such a generalized statement of its theme.

Ultimately *The Deserted Village* represents a triumph of manner, but one has immediately to add that it was a manner that was the product of a settled attitude to life. In other hands, the hands of some of his contemporaries as well as of most of his successors, the theme might easily have been sentimentally done: its nostalgia would in all probability have been overlaid with a thick coating of wistful sentiment. But Goldsmith, for all his weaknesses, was not in the least of a melting disposition, though he was of an intensely sympathetic one. If he wrote nothing of the very first quality and a good deal that was trivial, none the less he comes down to us as one of the central writers of his age, of a geniality and humanity that single him out among his contemporaries. 'Let not his frailties be remembered,' said Dr Johnson, 'he was a very great man.' Though Johnson, one now feels, was exaggerating, one has no doubt that he found in Goldsmith that sterling quality of character that is present so strikingly in his great poem.

NOTE

1. This is quoted by Washington Irving in his *Life of Goldsmith*, a most sympathetic biography to which I am considerably indebted.

WILLIAM COWPER

D. J. ENRIGHT

Professor of English, University of Malaya in Singapore

ALTHOUGH a great deal has been written about Cowper (1731–1800), even in recent years the larger part of it relates either to his life or to the religious and social movements of his time. Detailed studies of his connexion with Evangelicalism and of the part which he played in the various humanitarian activities of the last quarter of the eighteenth century are thus available, but his admirers have made little attempt to justify Cowper the poet as opposed to Cowper the critic of society. Admittedly it is not easy to find much to say about Cowper's poetry itself: for the greater part its virtues are as obvious as its weaknesses. While his work contains something to recommend it both to admirers of Pope and to admirers of Wordsworth, it can arouse neither as much hostility nor as much enthusiasm as both of these writers have done at one time or another. The aim of this essay is to suggest that, uneven as his poetry is, Cowper speaks with an individual, if quiet, voice, and that although he is unlikely to enjoy any future vogue, he has something to offer which will never fall entirely out of fashion or out of date.

Between the self-assured work of the Augustans and the energetic and diverse movements of the Romantic Revival came a period of half-hearted, characterless writing, when the poets, looking backwards and forwards at the same time, drifted on a slow current of change which they could neither govern nor understand. Mr T. S. Eliot's comment on the age is illuminating: 'Instead of working out the proper form for its matter, when it has any ... it merely applies the magniloquence of Milton or the neatness of Pope to matter which is wholly unprepared for it; so that what the writers have to say always appears surprised at the way in which they choose to say it' (see p. 275). On occasion these poets achieved work which, lacking in direction and power, yet wins respect by its honesty and decency. One such monument of 'transition' is Gray's *Elegy Written in a Country Churchyard*, but more of this kind of writing is offered by Cowper than by any of the other poets with whom he is commonly associated.

The poets whom Mr Eliot describes strained their talents in an attempt to achieve effects utterly beyond those talents; when they have the words, the subject seems inadequate, and when they have the subject, the words seem to be the wrong ones. The tedium of reading poets who lie in the trough between two creative waves deters us from seeing tragedy in their efforts to visualize the nature of the wave which should carry them. In this period grandiloquent gestures commonly end in bathos. But bathos, though not absent from Cowper, is comparatively rare; his concern to see that justice was done to God and to man at least gave him something to write about, and when he was writing about nothing in particular a customary modesty prevented his deluding himself. At such moments he would say:

> But no prophetic fires to me belong;
> I play with syllables, and sport in song.

There was always an endearing consciousness of his 'amateur status' as poet about Cowper; it was not a false modesty, but rather a happiness to be of use and a contentment with his limited talent which make him one of the very few poets of his time of whom we do not complain that they should have written either quite differently or not at all. That modesty, together with a confident recognition of the serious nature of his occupation, finds expression in the *Epistle to Lady Austen* –

> I, who scribble rhyme,
> To catch the trifles of the time,
> And tell them truths divine and clear.

He merely 'scribbles rhymes' – yet those rhymes can 'tell truths'. And for a minor poet to be more interested in 'truths' than in 'rhymes' is not unhealthy, for only the major genius can afford to dedicate himself to art.

The 'transitional' nature of Cowper's writing is clearly brought out by *The Sofa* (the first book of *The Task*, 1784). This begins with ninety lines, in an informative and serio-comic style, on the history of seating:

> Thus first necessity invented stools,
> Convenience next suggested elbow-chairs,
> And luxury th' accomplished SOFA last.

After a gently satirical passage on those who sleep when they should be awake, the argument takes a personal turn, remaining humorous still –

> The SOFA suits
> The gouty limb, 'tis true; but gouty limb,
> Though on a SOFA, may I never feel …

The verse then becomes much more personal and the humour drops away:

> For I have lov'd the rural walk through lanes
> Of grassy swarth, close cropt by nibbling sheep …

In a short passage we move from a diluted form of the Augustan-social mode to an anticipation of the Romantic-natural. The rest of the book meanders from topic to topic: description of landscape, the life of the country poor, 'artificial' gardening, the virtues of rural life, Nature preferred to Art, the 'spleen' in cities, an anecdote which reminds us of Wordsworth's Ruth or Margaret, gipsies, the way of life of the 'savage', London, and the preference for a country life.

In the aspect of 'transitional' poet it may be interesting to examine Cowper's attitude towards Pope, the great figure of the last great poetic school, and Milton, the great influence on this 'Transition', who offered something so unlike Pope that imitation of it seemed not merely reaction but progress. Where Pope is concerned, Cowper's feelings are mixed:

> Then Pope, as harmony itself exact,
> In verse well disciplin'd, complete, compact,
> Gave virtue and morality a grace …

No poet (apart from the author of *Don Juan*) will concede so much for a long time to come; we observe that Cowper allows Pope more than social satire – he 'gave virtue and morality a grace'. The passage (which occurs in *Table Talk*) continues thus, however:

> But he (his musical finesse was such,
> So nice his ear, so delicate his touch)
> Made poetry a mere mechanic art;
> And ev'ry warbler has his tune by heart.

Though the criticism is directed against the followers of Pope, the phrase 'mechanic art' looks forward to Matthew Arnold's strictures;

and certainly some of Cowper's letters suggest that he really preferred the verse of Prior. All the same, *Table Talk* is written in heroic couplets, and a comparison with Pope's use of the form indicates less a greater imaginative force or liberty of expression in Cowper than a blurring of point, an absence of dramatic compression and a tendency towards wordiness. Of the difference in tone (should one compare the portrait of Addison in the same passage with Pope's Atticus) we shall say more later.

Cowper's admiration for Milton (whom he undertook to edit in 1791) is wholehearted, and in a letter (31 October 1779) he rushes to defend the poet against Johnson's criticisms. He makes no attempt to excuse the 'childish prattlement of pastoral compositions', it is interesting to note, but picks out for praise in *Lycidas* 'the liveliness of the description, the sweetness of the numbers, the classical spirit of antiquity'. It is, however, the music of *Paradise Lost* – 'like that of a fine organ' – which draws his eloquence.

Cowper's attitude towards a third poet, Homer, is instructive in a different way. In 1793, when he was working on a second edition of his translation of the *Iliad* and *Odyssey*, he wrote *To John Johnson, on his presenting me with an antique bust of Homer*. The opening expresses a decent pride in his work on 'my old fav'rite bard', which suddenly gives way to a grim self-castigating sestet –

> The grief is this, that sunk in Homer's mine
> I lose my precious years, now soon to fail,
> Handling his gold, which, howso'er it shine,
> Proves dross, when balanc'd in the Christian scale

– lines which strike us as the heavy labouring of what for Christians is a self-evident truth. The sonnet ends on a curious note:

> Be wiser thou – like our fore-father DONNE,
> Seek heav'nly wealth, and work for God alone.

We cannot believe that Donne's style of poetry would appeal to Cowper; what weighs with him here – apart from his mother's kinship with Donne – is the fact that the latter became Dean of St Paul's and a famous and powerful preacher. Cowper is more self-consciously Christian than Donne (whose genius was as apt for love-

poetry as for religious); in his attitude towards writing he is closer to
George Herbert. The latter's lines,

> A verse may find him, who a sermon flies,
> And turn delight into a sacrifice,

are echoed by Cowper, for his preoccupation was with Christian
truth, and poetry recommended itself as an acceptable means of con-
veyance. In *The Task* (Book III) he assures us of his concern to drive
his mind 'To its just point – the service of mankind'. The nature of
that service is described more than once; for example, in a letter,
18 February 1781 – 'I am merry that I may decoy people into my
company, and grave that they may be better for it. Now and then I
put on the garb of a philosopher, and take the opportunity that
disguise procures me, to drop a word in favour of religion.'

But if Cowper bears much the same relation to Calvinistic
Methodism as Herbert bears to seventeenth-century Anglicanism,
the fact remains that Methodism and its related movements loom
larger in his work than does Anglicanism in that of Herbert. Occasional similarities of mood – Cowper's

> Perhaps the self-approving haughty world,
> That as she sweeps him with her whistling silks
> Scarce deigns to notice him

reminds us of Herbert's

> Then came brave Glory puffing by
> In silks that whistled, who but he?
> He scarce allow'd me half an eye –

yield to a greater dissimilarity. For while the earlier poet can hardly
be described as an artist for art's sake, yet the question of intellectual
agreement or otherwise raises itself far more frequently with Cowper.
The reason perhaps is that Herbert, quietly assuming fundamental
intellectual consent, presents us with sheer experience, and we have
experienced the poem before the question of agreement can arise.
Cowper, on the other hand, customarily attacks from outside, often
exaggerating the opposition which the reader is likely to put up,
and thus constructing an argument which will find agreement only
where agreement already exists. None the less, that argument is

helped along by simple and telling metaphor, and we can well
believe that Cowper's influence was widespread both in helping the
inarticulate to understand their emotions and in touching off emergent religious feeling. If we postulate a contrast between the poetry
which creates experience and forces it upon the reader and the poetry
which describes and discusses experience, then it is to the latter class
that almost the whole of Cowper's work belongs.

On several occasions Cowper gives a second reason for writing
poetry: 'Amusements are necessary, in a retirement like mine,
especially in such a state of mind as I labour under. The necessity of
amusement makes me sometimes write verses; it has made me a
carpenter, a birdcage maker, a gardener ...' (letter, 6 April 1780).
Discounting his innate modesty and a tendency to apologize for his
authorship, such remarks seem appropriate to the leisurely pace and
comparatively mild emotional drive of much of his verse. His
Miltonics, for instance, are garrulous by comparison with Milton.
At times we suspect that he is deliberately making his 'task' last as
long as possible: compression, economy, and vividness of point
were certainly not virtues at which he aimed. He rarely takes a leap
in his poetical progress, but rather leads the reader by slow and
steady – and too often predictable – steps up to the issue at stake.
The long reflective poem seems his natural medium, and as a representative passage we may take these lines from *The Task* (Book II):

> Oh, popular applause! what heart of man
> Is proof against thy sweet seducing charms?
> The wisest and the best feel urgent need
> Of all their caution in thy gentlest gales;
> But, swell'd into a gust – who then, alas!
> With all his canvass set, and inexpert,
> And therefore heedless, can withstand thy pow'r?

The theme is announced in language which cannot fail to be understood, and to which 'every bosom returns an echo', for the echo has
not ceased sounding since the words were last used. The metaphor of
sail and wind (part of Cowper's recurrent imagery) is then brought
into play, and the antithesis between 'the wisest and the best' and
'inexpert, and ... heedless' is reinforced by the parallel contrast
between 'gentlest gales' and 'gust'. The reader is not made to see

anything in a new light, but Cowper displays his meaning clearly and with little fuss.

Much of his reflective verse is concerned with contemporary abuses – social, political, moral, and religious. The last hundred lines of the first book of *The Task*, where the theme is country versus city, may be instanced. The first twenty-five lines generalize in favour of the former. London, Cowper then says, is

> by taste and wealth proclaim'd
> The fairest capital of all the world,
> By riot and incontinence the worst.

The next twenty-five lines are spent in demonstrating London's 'fairness' – her arts, science, and commerce – while the following twenty-five are allotted to her 'riot and incontinence' – injustice, peculation, deference to fashion instead of to God's laws. This deliberate, carefully balanced picture is followed by twenty-five lines in praise of country life, culminating in the judgement that the folly of sophisticated city dwellers

> Has made, what enemies could ne'er have done,
> Our arch of empire, steadfast but for you,
> A mutilated structure, soon to fall.

The whole passage is extremely readable, but it cannot be said that the situation is clarified by any brilliant image or the point driven home with an intensity that is truly poetic. The consistently easy flow of the verse does not hide the presence of a good deal of padding – tautology as in 'Rank abundance breeds/In gross and pamper'd cities sloth and lust,/And wantonness and gluttonous excess' – which detracts from its impact; the rhythm verges at times on a rather unctuous oratory; the metaphor is largely of a conventional kind, perhaps too decent to deserve the epithet 'cliché' – philosophy's 'eagle eye', 'yon burning disk', 'queen of cities'. On the other hand, Cowper occasionally introduces the aphoristic line which sums up in memorable form the gist of the matter. Two good examples are adjacent in this passage – 'knees and hassocks are well-nigh divorc'd' and the household words, 'God made the country, and man made the town'.

But the prime characteristic of the passage is its generality. The

very largeness and abstractness of 'London' leaves the virtues and
vices ascribed to her rather vague and not particularly convincing.
Cowper is moralizing, not satirizing, and we shall be disappointed if
we look for the type of satirical art achieved by Pope, with its vivid
particularity, its pungency and bite. For Cowper,

> An individual is a sacred mark,
> Not to be pierc'd in play, or in the dark.

He offers nothing comparable to Pope's Sporus or Atticus; we
respect his gentleness as a man, but may wish that, as a poet, he had
felt fewer compunctions. His concern to be scrupulously fair works
rather ambiguously in this sphere. Earlier in the same book of *The
Task*, among descriptions of natural beauties, he has held up to view
the unromantic aspects of country life ('So farewell envy of the
peasant's nest!'), and we incline in the end to feel that Cowper's chief
reason for preferring the country is a negative one – the country is less
dangerous to health and virtue. Great poetry works in ways less
directly just than this, and Cowper's legalistic procedure brings him
near to saying nothing at all, in terms of poetic procedure.

But it is unfair to emphasize the negative aspects of his work and
unsafe to generalize about him, for Cowper's style is rather more
versatile that it at first seems, and his greatest successes are frequently
found in a context of dull conventional versifying. Book II of *The
Task* contains a grim passage on preaching in which ponderous
parentheses and thumping repetition of the magical word ('The
pulpit … The pulpit … I say the pulpit') lead up to a pompous
climax –

> There stands the messenger of truth: there stands
> The legate of the skies!

Its manner is, in fact, of the bullying, 'pulpiteering' type. Yet a little
later comes an excellently dramatic skit on fashionable preachers:

> The things that mount the rostrum with a skip,
> And then skip down again; pronounce a text;
> Cry – hem: and, reading what they never wrote,
> Just fifteen minutes, huddle up their work,
> And with a well-bred whisper close the scene!

Similarly, to take the group of long poems known as the *Moral Satires*, *The Progress of Error* issues in somewhat shrill tones such trite and unconfirmed generalizations as

> Peace follows virtue as its sure reward;
> And pleasure brings as surely in her train
> Remorse, and sorrow, and vindictive pain;

yet we find in *Truth* lively passages, exemplified by the picture of 'sanctimonious pride':

> Yon ancient prude, whose wither'd features show
> She might be young some forty years ago ...
>
> (l. 131 et seq.)

And whereas *Expostulation*, verbosely living up to its title, contains much protracted moralizing – we sympathize with Leslie Stephen's remark that 'Cowper is an instance of a thinker too far apart from the great world to apply the lash effectually' – *Conversation* proves how agile Cowper could be in handling the lesser vices:

> Some men employ their health, an ugly trick,
> In making known how oft they have been sick ....
> They thought they must have died they were so bad –
> Their peevish hearers almost wish they had.
>
> (l. 311 et seq.)

Among his fables, *The Moralizer Corrected* and *The Needless Alarm* are mountains which give birth to mice, while on the other hand *The Retired Cat* demonstrates its 'moral' in a manner altogether charming. And if Cowper sometimes betrays a humourless insensitiveness to words (see the concluding line of *Catherina, The Second Part*) or offers such arrant 'poetic diction' as 'the feather'd tribes domestic' and 'public hives of puerile resort' (i.e. schools), he is nevertheless capable of this fine apostrophizing of an oyster:

> You, shapeless nothing in a dish –
> You that are but almost a fish

while, on a higher level, his vision of the Earthly Paradise Regained in Book VI of *The Task* is suddenly brought alive and made radiant by the brilliant image in which the child, caressing the 'azure neck' of 'the crested worm', receives 'the lambent homage of his arrowy tongue'.

There is no need to dwell long on Cowper as a precursor of romanticism. A certain similarity to Wordsworth is obvious on occasion (e.g. *The Task*, Book I, 'For I have lov'd the rural walk through lanes ...'), but the earlier poet neither rises to the later's direct and powerful vision nor sinks to the insistent cloudy portentousness of which he was capable at times. For sharp and appreciative observation of nature, Cowper is often excellent; but he exclaims against the man who

> views it, and admires; but rests content
> With what he views

and takes extreme care to point out that

> Nature is but a name for an effect,
> Whose cause is God.

The constant acknowledgement of God as the power behind the scenery reminds us that a greater poet, dispensing with such explicit warnings, would have put God *into* the description instead of relegating him to a moralizing footnote.

Happily the greater part of Cowper's work (in which we include his attractive letters) bears little obvious relation to his spiritual torments. The latter may be detected behind the incongruous severity of his diatribe against the workman's pint (*The Task*, Book IV), for instance, or his gloomy misgivings about Handel's popularity (Book VI, 'Man praises man'). Elsewhere his personal anguish emerges in the recurrent image of the storm-tossed sailor or the wrecked ship. To take but a few examples: *Truth* begins thus:

> Man, on the dubious waves of error toss'd,
> His ship half founder'd, and his compass lost ...

The mariner in *The Task*, Book I, in his yearning for 'Nature in her green array', throws himself overboard 'and is seen no more'. In a fairly conventional way shipwreck provides the setting for *Temptation*, one of the Olney Hymns (1779), while something similar, but personally felt, occurs in *To Mr Newton on his return from Ramsgate*:

> I, tempest-toss'd and wreck'd at last,
> Come home to port no more,

and is repeated in *On the Receipt of My Mother's Picture*:

> Always from port withheld, always distress'd –
> Me howling winds drive devious, tempest-toss'd ...

Related imagery is used in *Tirocinium* to describe the plight of a boy handed over to the care of a 'public nursery': 'left upon so wild a beach' and 'adrift upon a rolling sea'. The boy cannot trust to his own moral powers, he needs his father's guidance – just as man needs the direct guidance of God, or Salvation. *Human Frailty* reminds us,

> ... oars alone can ne'er prevail
>   To reach the distant coast,
> The breath of heav'n must swell the sail,
>   Or all the toil is lost.

Thus, in the vicinity of what at first seems a banal metaphor, we find Cowper's most personal poetry – the poetry of one who is convinced of his own damnation. It, and the image, culminate in his last original poem – and his most powerful – *The Castaway*:

> No voice divine the storm allay'd,
>   No light propitious shone;
> When, snatch'd from all effectual aid,
>   We perish'd, each alone:
> But I beneath a rougher sea,
> And whelm'd in deeper gulphs than he.

To sum up, Cowper's original work falls into five groups: the eight *Moral Satires*; the six books of *The Task*; *Tirocinium, or A Review of Schools*; the Olney Hymns; and, lastly, the many miscellaneous shorter poems. While his moral preoccupations naturally drew him to the long reflective poem, it is in the shorter poems that he has preserved the gentler pleasures of his life. The verses on his pets and those of his friends are particularly charming, tender, and unsophisticated without being sentimental – *Epitaph on a Hare*, *The Colubriad*, *On the Death of Mrs Throckmorton's Bullfinch*, and *Epitaph on Fop*, for example. Animals quietened the raw nerve of Calvinism in him, for he did not feel obliged to teach them morality. And when, forgetting, he upbraids his spaniel for killing a bird, Beau's retort is lively and effective –

If killing birds be such a crime,
  (Which I can hardly see)
What think you, Sir, of killing Time
  With verse address'd to me?

The Task would benefit from selective abridgement, but, together
with some of the shorter pieces – *Alexander Selkirk* (with its moving
reference to the 'shocking' tameness of the animals), *Lines written
during a period of insanity, The Poplar field, To Mary, On the Receipt of
My Mother's Picture, On the Loss of the 'Royal George', The Castaway,*
the perennial *John Gilpin* and others – it ensures Cowper's place as
one of the most pleasant and most individual of our minor poets,
one of the few 'transitional' poets whose work is not nullified by
what went before or came after.

JOHNSON

A. R. HUMPHREYS

THANKS mainly, though far from solely, to Boswell, Johnson as a person is the best-known of the Augustans. His fame is that of stalwart character and common sense, opinionative and independent, blunt and dogmatic, holding fast by a robust Tory patriotism. Such a reputation, while neither discreditable nor untrue, is far from an adequate estimate of him, and happily, as the bases of Augustan culture are better understood, the admiration for his written work which the wiser critics and scholars have traditionally felt is spreading. With many readers, it is true, the rational controls and critical cautions of Augustanism are still suspect as being a denial of the full life of man, but the better opinion is gaining ground that the Augustans' vigour and enlightened seriousness achieved, within whatever necessary limitations, a constructive and not merely restrictive civilization such as only sound intelligence, healthy instinct, and a fundamental sense of tradition could accomplish.

Of that civilization Johnson is the strongest representative; to express it was his instinctive and his deliberate aim.[1] A century later Matthew Arnold, equally great as critic and as critical influence, equally the spokesman of classically rooted Christian humanism, was far less favourably placed; he had to speak against the whole trend of his time, for culture had ceased to hold anarchy in check. On the one hand, Johnson's excellence is personal, the excellence of super-lative moral power, and of wit and intellect massive, surprising, sensitive, and subtle: Mrs Thrale's guests once pleasantly compared his mind to an elephant's trunk, 'strong to buffet even the tiger, and pliable to pick up even the pin'. But, on the other hand, it is an excellence also of the time. Culture was quite aware of anarchy, which had so prevailed a century earlier, but it was sure that it could keep anarchy in check, that reason and discipline in faith and morals, good taste and practice in the arts, and social care in matters of daily life were the intended expressions of human nature. These ambiguous terms were defined by the Christian, rational, and humanistic traditions in which Augustanism worked, and they amounted to a thoroughly mature and responsible sense of values.

Johnson was supported (even so vigorous a mind is the better for support) by the strong general ethos of his time, and one of the most significant things about him is his perpetual reference to the open air of public assent. Assertions that 'every reader' likes this or dislikes that, that 'every man' believes this or disbelieves that, are refreshingly abundant – refreshingly not because the postulated unanimity has always worn well (though often it has), but because its attitude is that of frank confident spokesmanship for the ordinary man, though with the important proviso that the ordinary man is assumed to embody sound taste and considered judgement. Johnson's thought has fine, wide publicity; he seeks the truth which (he thinks) all men can know, and he expresses it with a wit which makes it memorable. This truth is not a cynical or tarnished worldly wisdom; it is concerned with the central moral needs of human life, and the generic workings of human nature. It is not peculiar and individual truth, but the truth of a tradition, of which Anglicanism was the presiding faith, the humane arts the exemplars, and human nature within that tradition the norm. Johnson, incidentally, like most Augustan humanists, elevates moral philosophy far above the new fashion for physical science; 'men more frequently require to be reminded than informed', he observes, and whereas information is a function of the growing materialism, reminding is a function of an accepted philosophy, recalling the things needful to the proper conduct of life. The more we know of Augustanism, and of Johnson, the more enviable seems this relationship by which he can refer to the public ('the common sense of readers uncorrupted by literary prejudices') in the most serious matters of life and letters. This is by no means to say that he is a critical demagogue, or eager for general assent in a universal *bonhomie*. The case is precisely the opposite; he does not lower the standards of judgement to those of the average man – he expects the average man to rise to the standards of a large sanity and reason.[2] His sense of responsibility is great – 'I am now writing this', he tells Boswell in a letter, 'and you when you read this are reading, under the Eye of Omnipotence'; he recognizes that responsibility and instinctively bears it, and part of his sense of it is his reference of particular judgements to large grounds of general principle, grounds which are both the bases of his civilization and also personal convictions rooted in his own experience. It is that basis of principle, the belief that truth can be rationally sought and must be expounded plainly, and that men can agree on all important matters, that gives Johnson's thought such amplitude and representative strength.

That amplitude and strength as well as more specifically poetic qualities are prominent in his major poems, *London* (1738) and *The Vanity of Human Wishes* (1749), whose exceptional distinction is the product of strength and subtlety. The words that spring to mind for them – 'monumental', 'grave', 'deliberate', and so on – are insufficient; they recognize weight or volume, but not the verbal vitality which animates what might otherwise be a mere simulacrum of grandeur. Since poetry cannot be interesting without at the very least sounding interesting, it is proper to insist first on the masterly grandiloquence, based partly (though not as a mere decorative trick) on simple sound mechanics like assonance and alliteration –

> While yet my steady Steps no Staff sustains,
> And Life still vig'rous revels in my Veins ...

> Explain their Country's dear-bought Rights away,
> And plead for Pirates in the Face of Day –

and partly on astute variations of rhythm:

> For who would leave, unbrib'd, *Hibernia's* Land,
> Or change the Rocks of *Scotland* for the Strand ?

> O'er Love, o'er Fear, extends his wide Domain,
> Unconquer'd Lord of Pleasure and of Pain.

This recalls Dryden's manner, but there are melodies here both stronger and subtler than Dryden's vigorous tunes, the products of an excellent ear serving an excellent mind and evolving an almost voluptuous interplay of vocables to recommend to the attention not merely the expression's sense but its complex of feelings too:

> Obsequious, artful, voluble and gay ...

> Diffuse the tuneful Lenitives of Pain ...

> The March begins in Military State,
> And Nations on his Eye suspended wait ..

An Age that melts with unperceiv'd Decay,
And glides in modest Innocence away.

The sound is sound not for its own sake, as the imagery is imagery
not for its own sake, but for the sake of the meaning. The collaboration of sound and meaning gives at once one of the full pleasures of
poetry, a sensory organic enrichment of a content in itself interesting.
In such a passage as the following the half-caught alliterations and
assonances, the echoes and onomatopoeia ('snarling Muse', 'brisker
Air', 'silken Courtiers gaze', 'turn the varied Taunt') realize the meaning and, as it were, present it to the mind through the ear:

By Numbers here from Shame or Censure free,
All Crimes are safe, but hated Poverty,
This, only this, the rigid Law pursues,
This, only this, provokes the snarling Muse.
The sober Trader, at a tatter'd Cloak
Wakes from his Dream, and labours for a Joke;
With brisker Air the silken Courtiers gaze,
And turn the varied Taunt a thousand ways.

This vital significance of sound is found too in Johnson's prose,
which is not always credited with phrasing as fine in auditory as in
intellectual quality. In the verse it is important as providing its own
kind of 'body' to themes that in their morality-manner, with generalized categories of idea and example, need as much substantializing
as they can get. The complaint is often heard, indeed, that Johnson's
large meditations on moral themes are too general, too oracular and
insufficiently personal, yet as one comes to know his work it is clearly
the product of a mind both weighty and intelligent which, when it
generalizes (as it often does in writing, though less so in conversation),
does so merely as a broadening of its own experience, and expresses
its ideas with a particularly individual stamp of style.[3] General, then,
the poems are, as public utterance with words as the firm counters
of broad moral points of view; but they have a sweep and comprehension which save the attention from distracting particularities and
are guaranteed not to be vacuous by the full harmony and the flexible
significance of sound.

The guarantee extends further. Johnson's phrasing looks as though
it is the simple elements of meaning – 'hated Poverty', 'rigid Law',

'snarling Muse', 'sober Trader', 'tatter'd Cloak', 'labours for a joke',
or

> Unnumber'd Suppliants croud Preferment's Gate,
> Athirst for Wealth, and burning to be great;
> Delusive Fortune hears th'incessant Call,
> They mount, they shine, evaporate, and fall.

But though simple elements of meaning are here, there is more than
simplicity in them. There is economy, relevance, adequacy. The
epithets are not novel or, at first, striking, but they are something
better; they are in their descriptive definiteness absolutely right. Of
the nouns they accompany one aspect only is to be characterized,
and characterize it they do. They are cogent and precise, and any
impression that Johnson's phrasing disperses on inspection into *mere*
generalization is untenable. The first lines of *The Vanity of Human
Wishes* have been thought vulnerable:

> Let Observation with extensive view
> Survey Mankind, from *China* to *Peru*;
> Remark each anxious Toil, each eager Strife,
> And watch the busy scenes of crouded Life.

Yet these do what is wanted – they open a broad morality-panorama
(the whole poem depends on broad sweeps and general categories –
even its historical figures are there as types and symbols), and they
indicate the required aspect of each word. 'Busy scenes', 'crouded
Life' – like 'Unnumber'd Suppliants', 'Athirst for Wealth, and burning to be great', 'delusive Fortune' and 'incessant Call' – are directly
defined in the one necessary aspect. As for lines like 'Obsequious,
artful, voluble and gay', 'And Sloth effuse her opiate fumes in vain',
or 'They mount, they shine, evaporate, and fall', auditory pleasure
and precise relevant meaning are perfectly united in them: idea,
image, attitude, and moral comment are conveyed simultaneously
by Johnson's clear and subtle undissociated sensibility. Part of their
precision is the fact that words like 'obsequious', 'voluble', 'effuse',
and 'evaporate', though naturalized in English and therefore, unlike
many Augustan Latinisms, easily digested, have a peculiar aptness
arising from their derivation. Johnson was, in fact, keenly aware of
this subtle language-flavour deriving from the complex origins of

English; prefacing the *Dictionary* he says he has aimed at giving both Latin and Teutonic equivalents to improve his readers' awareness of the language.

The poems bring into view both large extents and particular instances, both the generic and the specific, and play the one against the other. The suspicion of vague rhetoric in

> Has Heav'n reserv'd, in pity to the Poor,
> No pathless Waste, or undiscover'd Shore?
> No secret Island in the boundless Main?

is dispelled by the pungency of

> No peaceful Desert yet unclaim'd by *Spain*?

And a famous passage in *The Vanity of Human Wishes* extends its vast remote panorama and then actualizes the theme by a sharp decisive reference:

> But few there are whom Hours like these await,
> Who set unclouded in the Gulphs of Fate.
> From *Lydia's* Monarch should the Search descend,
> By Solon caution'd to regard his End,
> In Life's last Scene what Prodigies surprise,
> Fears of the Brave, and Follies of the Wise:
> From Marlb'rough's Eyes the Streams of Dotage flow,
> And *Swift* expires a Driveller and a Show.

There is harmony in this alternation; the writer uses all his knowledge easily, expanding into large perspectives and also concentrating down to particular persons. The result is so consonant partly because Johnson has found the right mental world for these reflections which are at once moral generalities and particular experience (so particular, indeed, that Johnson burst into tears over the scholar's poverty in *The Vanity of Human Wishes*), and yet so general that such a passage partakes of the nature of parable.[4] This mental world finds a middle ground on which the general and the personal marry, from which the mind easily opens to broad sweeps of idea and as easily focuses to the detail of life. Such a way of putting it is perhaps not very lucid, and a reference to Gray's *Elegy* may help. In that poem the general notion of humble worth and obscure destinies is embodied in the picture of the churchyard tombs, and extends outwards into the pattern of country work and life, ploughing, herding, homecoming, parenthood, and faith. The reader hardly reflects that this is all a *general* theme; the mind is occupied by the churchyard scene, the household (blazing hearth, and children), cockcrow and hunting-horn, the harvesting of crops and the cutting of timber, then (by contrast) the splendour of Church and State which the villagers cannot rival, and then again the humble churchyard. The *Elegy* is a series of images, not an abstraction. Yet its images are not, as it were, particular atoms; the elms and yews symbolize country tradition and peaceful death; the swallow's nest and the housewife's hearth symbolize fruitful life; the cockcrow and the horn, the sickle and plough-ing-teams symbolize active energy. Johnson's praise of the *Elegy* as abounding 'with images which find a mirror in every mind, and with sentiments to which every bosom returns an echo' is a recognition of this representative quality, and though the sentiments of his own longer poems (based on classical satire) by being more sombre are perhaps less universal than Gray's they have a broad acceptable truth of which the images are emblems. In *The Vanity of Human Wishes* the portraits of Wolsey and Charles of Sweden are like this; they do not interest us particularly as persons, but their names touch off the notion of splendour ending in defeat and their descriptions have, in grandiose impetus and volume, both the generality of large ideas and the concreteness of real figures. Wolsey in his 'full-blown Dig-nity', with 'Law in his Voice, and Fortune in his Hand', with the stream of honour flowing at his nod and jealous courtiers ('the Train of State') waiting to desert him, surrounded by the generic symbols of power – 'the Pride of aweful State,/The golden Canopy, the glitt'ring Plate' – is a person embodying a concept, and so is Charles, 'unconquer'd Lord of Pleasure and of Pain', with peace courting his hand, war sounding the trumpet, nations suspended on his glance, and the dramatic ignominy of his fall conveyed by three simple generic images – 'a barren Strand,/A petty Fortress, and a dubious Hand'. One concludes that Johnson felt life strongly as a union of fact and idea, that all life, physical and conceptual, was forcibly real to him. Indeed, thoughts and morality have for him an impressive force which weighs on actual life (his written and spoken aphorisms make almost a physical impact; Mrs Thrale records that 'he was more strongly and more violently affected by the force of

words representing ideas' than anyone she knew). In these rich, resonant, witty, and massive poems Johnson provides more than the
'good sense in good metre' which a contemporary saw in them
(though there is that too): he provides discourses glowing with controlled passion, which steep life in thought and thought in life, and
resound with a grandeur which does not exclude intimacy. *London*
is the more uneven of the two major works, though its best passages
are admirable; *The Vanity of Human Wishes* is among the few very
great Augustan poems.

The shorter poems include the well-phrased *Epitaph upon Claudy
Philips*, brief and deeply moving; the *Prologue at the opening of
Drury Lane Theatre* (1747), so pungent that much of it has become
almost proverbial; and the two quatrain-poems, *A Short Song of
Congratulation* (1780) and *On the Death of Dr Robert Levet* (1782).
Both are in the central Augustan manner – social in substance,
decisive in phrase, mature in vigour, and open-eyed in the light of
common day. The disciplined movement and trochaic tune of the
former were in A. E. Housman's mind as he started *The Shropshire
Lad*, but the character is different – is frank and downright, instead
of poignant and troubling; it is the idiom not of nostalgia and sentiment, but of judgement and audacity. The elegy on Dr Levet is one
of the century's most impressive things – grave, concentrated, and
final. The images are few, conventional, and general – 'hope's
delusive mine', 'sudden blasts', 'misery's darkest caverns'; the vocabulary is plain, with an undertone of Latin usage (words like 'officious'
and 'innocent' have their original, not their modern, sense); the aim
is simply to tell the truth. Nothing calls attention to itself, everything
to its subject: the obscure, brusque, and devoted working doctor is
portrayed decisive phrase by phrase in simple patterns of idea ('sudden
blasts, or slow decline'; 'of ev'ry friendless name the friend'; 'the
pow'r of art, without the show'; 'the busy day, the peaceful night')
so that each item stands in steady relationship to the others. The
voice observes the brief significant lingerings needed for reminiscence ('Yet still he fills affection's eye'), for careful definition
('Obscurely wise, and coarsely kind'), and for earnestness ('And
sure th'Eternal Master found ...'). The only moment that startles is
the almost metaphysical particularity (dramatically justified) of the
last stanza:

> Then with no throbbing fiery pain,
> No cold gradations of decay,
> Death broke at once the vital chain,
> And free'd his soul the nearest way.

No restrictive praise – control, balance, good taste, and the like – is adequate; the tone, as in all Johnson's major work, is exactly right; he serves ends so much greater than himself that blemishes of self-display or superiority are simply not to be found, and the Christian gravity and the strength of his nature display themselves here in charity, integrity, and tenderness.

On 20 March 1750, Johnson emerged, in Boswell's words, 'in the character for which he was eminently fitted – a majestic teacher of moral and religious wisdom'. In other words, he issued the first number of *The Rambler*, a periodical paper to be followed twice weekly for the next two years by 207 successors, of which he wrote all but five. From 1758 to 1760 it was followed, in a lighter tone and brisker style, by the weekly *Idler*, in 103 numbers of which Johnson wrote ninety-one. After a reign of forty years Addison's fashion of essay received not a deliberate but still a real challenge, for Johnson's nature could not be harnessed to the urbane social commentary which *The Spectator* had popularized, and if he fell short of *The Spectator*'s animation he surpassed in grandeur even its more solemn moments, as also those of Berkeley's religious papers in *The Guardian*. If the quality of Addison and Johnson is to be compared, it is reasonable to do so by putting side by side the end of the 26th *Spectator* on the tombs in Westminster Abbey, and the end of the last *Idler*:

> When I look upon the tombs of the great, every emotion of envy dies in me; when I read the epitaphs of the beautiful, every inordinate desire goes out; when I meet with the grief of parents upon a tombstone, my heart melts with compassion; when I see the tomb of the parents themselves, I consider the vanity of grieving for those whom we must quickly follow. When I see kings lying by those who deposed them, when I consider rival wits placed side by side, or the holy men that divided the world with their contests and disputes, I reflect with sorrow and astonishment on the little competitions, factions, and debates of mankind. When I read the several dates of the tombs, I consider that great day

when we shall all of us be contemporaries, and make our appearance together.

(Spectator 26.)

That, in its calculated rise and fall of rhythm, in the careful curve and undulation of each sentence, in its parallelism and symmetry, is an artful masterpiece of construction, but the specious grandeur and profundity with which it treats a severe simple truth are positively distasteful. Put beside its complacency the following, and Johnson's own treatment of a severe simple truth appears immeasurably superior in tone and appropriateness:

> As the last *Idler* is published in that solemn week which the Christian world has always set apart for the examination of the conscience, the review of life, the extinction of earthly desires, and the renovation of holy purposes; I hope that my readers are already disposed to view every incident with seriousness, and improve it with meditation; and that, when they see this series of trifles brought to a conclusion, they will consider that, by outliving the *Idler*, they have passed weeks, months and years which are no longer in their power; that an end must in time be put to everything great, as to everything little; that to life must come its last hour, and to this system of being its last day, the hour at which probation and repentance will be in vain; the day in which every work of the hand, and imagination of the heart, shall be brought to judgement, and an everlasting futurity shall be determined by the past.

Nothing in Johnson's journalism became him like the leaving it, and it may seem unfair to match him at his strongest with Addison who here is not at his best (though he gives signs of thinking he is). Johnson, indeed, would have strongly deprecated any attempt to promote him over his predecessor's head; his *Life of Addison* ends with one of the finest tributes ever paid by one writer to another. Posterity, as Macaulay observes, has come down decisively in Addison's favour and it is Johnson's own aphorism that 'about things on which the public thinks long it commonly attains to think right'. Yet even in his own day there were those who preferred his strength to Addison's smoothness; he himself found Steele 'too thin for an Englishman's taste', and Mrs Thrale formed the impression that really, despite his praise, he felt much the same about Addison.[5] Perhaps it is fairest to conclude, with Arthur Murphy, an early biographer, that 'Addison lends grace and ornament to truth; Johnson gives it force and accuracy'. But for one reader at least, Johnson at his best is so superior to Addison at his best (the 'best's being admittedly in very different kinds of work) as to render insignificant the question whether average Addison is better than average Johnson; average Johnson may be tedious, but the best Johnson adds nobility to life. That *The Rambler*, after a cool initial reception, came by Johnson's death to achieve ten editions in its collected form is a tribute to late Augustan taste.

For while Johnson's immediate incentive was his living ('No man but a blockhead ever wrote except for money'), characteristically he earned it not by coaxing, flattering, or amusing, but by stern concentration on truth. This truth was not the daily realism of life; that, he protests in the 4th *Rambler*, is already 'promiscuously described' in the novel. His theme is 'those parts of nature which are most proper for imitation'; he enlists under the Christian-humanist banner of conduct and faith.[6] He is sometimes too didactic, often too sweeping, and by no means always interesting. But impending always over these venial faults are the virtues of wit and grandeur; ever and anon the morality-subjects are sharpened by aphorism (indeed, typically they begin and end in aphorism, with a masterful survey of the territory in between) raising them into the air of permanent truth, or are deepened by personal contact with the moral realities behind them. As for grandeur, the eighteenth century produced no finer prose than the end of *Rambler* No. 77 on the duties of authors, or No. 185 (Christmas Eve, 1751) on forgiveness, or *Idler* No. 41 on his mother's death, or No. 103 already quoted.

The sense of life as probation stirred Johnson's deepest emotions. The *Prayers and Meditations* he composed for his private use, rich in an earnest Anglican idiom, are full of this theme; so, indeed, is much of his work and not least the periodical-writing. Man he defines as 'a being placed here only for a short time, whose task it is to advance himself to a higher and happier state of existence, by unremitted vigilance of caution and activity of virtue' (*Idler* 43). Periodical essays have seldom been inspired by deeper feelings than these; his sense of his own indolence, arising from intermittent constitutional languor and melancholia, was like a conviction of sin, no more to be dispelled by the counter-evidence of his massive output than the sinner's sense of guilt is dispelled by evidence of his virtues, and he lived under a pressure which none but his intimates knew and which, with ill health, accounted for much of his testiness.

It accounted likewise, however, for his charity and his passion for truth. His judgements on moral problems are movingly wise and tolerant, and as for truthfulness, he imposed on his whole circle, says Boswell, 'perpetual vigilance against the slightest degree of falsehood'. Factual truth was to be told just as it happened; moral truth was to be forwarded both by reiteration of moral principles and by the removal of illusion. In this removal of illusion he may be compared with Swift, but instead of Swift's angry passion in the exposure of human ignominy he dissipates the smoke-screen of distractions which conceal the morality by which one should live. Swift's main intention is, no doubt, constructive and reasonable, but he strips off so much pretension as to leave mankind naked and sore; the process, if just, is the justice of revenge, not of mercy. Johnson's proceedings are different; Mrs Thrale speaks of 'his truly tolerant spirit and Christian charity', and Boswell of his being 'never querulous, never prone to inveigh against the present times'. His sense of moral truth is one which operates on life to help mankind in its basic soundness and its daily struggle: he does not seek to make life seem easier than it is, yet he discountenances those who exact too much of human nature. His sense of human fallibility (his own, in particular) leads him to sympathy, not condemnation; he checks conventional judgements by his own experience and is prepared to defend, for instance, those who rise in the world and forget their friends, those who think better of themselves than circumstances warrant, those who are generous through vanity, and those who write better than they live.

Dryden's phrase on Shakespeare is true of Johnson – 'he is always great, when some great occasion is presented to him'. This is apparent in the periodicals and also in the letters, which deserve more comment than can be offered here (their substance and manner are strikingly interesting),[7] where space allows only the suggestion that nothing better reflects his stature than his letters on bereavements. To James Elphinston on his mother's death, to Mrs Thrale on those of her son and husband, to Bennet Langton on those of his uncle and Thrale and Levet, to Dr Thomas Lawrence on that of his wife, and, above all, to Dr William Dodd on his approaching execution (an epistolary situation of truly appalling difficulty) – in all such cases there can be no rival to the impeccably phrased sympathy and strength with which he calls the survivors back from apathy to life.

Rasselas (1759), which has been called a prose *Vanity of Human Wishes*, is, like the journals and letters, an occasional piece, hurried through to pay his mother's funeral expenses. But like the journals and letters its substance is anything but occasional. To call it the most distinguished English-Oriental moral tale, to compare and contrast it with Voltaire's contemporary *Candide*, is not to touch its essence; its essence is that it is the concentration of Johnson's greatness. Its harmony has the massive and subtle music of the poems; there are modulated melodies – 'Why should not life glide quietly away in the soft reciprocations of protection and reverence ?'; there are orchestrated grandeurs like the compelling dignity of the first sentence, or Imlac's meditation on the Pyramid (chapter xxxii). Its moral quality is a notable triumph for Augustan humanism; since the recipe for happiness proves elusive, it is the practice of virtue that emerges, not at all platitudinously, as the end of life.

Rasselas is a parable, and on that fact depends its method. Its characters are representatives, not individuals; its incidents are diagrams; its imagery, like that of the poems, is of general types, and its illustrations are simple. As Imlac the philosopher observes in a famous dissertation on poetry, 'the business of a poet is to examine not the individual but the species, to remark general properties and large appearances: he does not number the streaks of the tulip'. The tale, though as impressive and important as all but the best of Augustan novels, does not proffer itself as realistic fiction. An inventor devises artificial wings: he drops into a lake. A philosopher preaches stoicism: he is overwhelmed by his daughter's death. A pasha is at the height of prosperity: his Sultan deposes him: the Sultan himself is murdered by his Janissaries. Such events are demonstrative, not realistic. The point is worth making only because unless one consciously resolves to tolerate formal allegory the virtues of *Rasselas* may go unrecognized; a willing suspension of impatience is required for this unrealistic, parabolic narrative, in which the complexities of life are generalized by schematization. Johnson gets simplicity of outline from large propositions which ignore the streaks of the tulip, but by his sacrifice of detail he secures large compensations. Principally he gains clarity of pattern and boldness of mass, and this is appropriate to his needs since his aim as always is to reveal the large outlines of fundamental duty ('As the mind of Dr Johnson was greatly expanded,' remarks Mrs Thrale, 'so his first care was for general, not particular or petty morality'). The simplification is a concentration, not an enfeeblement; distractions are discarded, and the central meaning clarified.

Yet to overstress the general and abstract would be misleading. Like the poems, the tale chooses a middle ground between abstract and concrete, on which morality can be embodied and an impression of real life adequately but not obtrusively maintained. The landscape on which Rasselas meditates (chapter ii) is that of a moralist, not an artist, and it serves to prompt his self-criticism:

> The moon by more than twenty changes admonished me of the flux of life; the stream that rolled before my feet upbraided my inactivity. I sat feasting on intellectual luxury regardless alike of the examples of the earth, and the instructions of the planets.

Yet with its tree-shaded rivers, lake, and fantastic mountains, its playing fish, singing birds, and browsing animals, it is not inadequate in interest. Scenes and places are, for their purposes, sufficiently indicated – the Happy Valley, the Nile, Cairo, the Pyramids, and the desert; the persons, though they talk a *Rambler* idiom, are suitable inhabitants of these representative settings and suitable recipients of moral experience; and the images are easily illustrative:

> Distance has the same effect on the mind as on the eye, and while we glide along the stream of time whatever we leave behind us is always lessening, and that which we approach increasing in magnitude. Do not suffer life to stagnate; it will grow muddy for want of motion; commit yourself again to the current of the world.

Such imagery obeys the harmony of the book; it reveals the meaning with a quiet and satisfactory illumination.

The tone varies between dignity, sombreness, irony, and wit. The dignity and sombreness stress endurance instead of joy, knowledge instead of fancy, honesty instead of illusion; the irony is a simple and strong quality which never (it may be noted) indicates on

Johnson's part any self-congratulation on superior wisdom; the wit generates aphorisms and curiously concentrated (almost 'metaphysical') effects on occasion, like Pekuah's comment on the needlework she did when a prisoner – 'you know that the mind will easily straggle from the fingers, nor will you suspect that captivity and absence from Nekayah could receive solace from silken flowers'. It also, by shrewd analysis and shaping, disciplines and patterns the ragged material of life, for though Johnson did not suppose life to be orderly he did serve a code of letters which elicited unity and definiteness from its confusions, as he did in his social views maintain the ideal of social order. This is his style of mind, evinced in mastery of material and in a firm placing of every detail (even his earliest surviving work, his first letter, already shows it). To illustrate this adequately in a short space is impossible, but it may be seen, for example, in the impeccable organization of the second chapter – 'The discontent of Rasselas in the Happy Valley'. Each item is interrelated with the others, but the effect is not factitious; it is that of a mind creating symmetry and coherence, and improving on what Johnson calls 'mere obvious nature'.

One last point is related to wit and subtlety: it concerns Johnson's handling of commonplaces. They abound in his own writing, and the point of interest is to see him dealing with those of other people, as he does in the tales of two specious philosophers (chapters xviii and xxii) and as, elsewhere, he does with the opinions of the criticasters Dick Minim and Tom Steady (*Idler* 60, 61, 78), of readers who wanted *The Rambler* merely to repeat *The Spectator* (*Rambler* 23), and, most forcibly, of Soame Jenyns, a gentleman-philosopher whose *Free Inquiry into the Nature and Origin of Evil* provoked Johnson to one of the most trenchant of all book reviews. In *Rasselas* the first philosopher is exposed by his remorseless accumulation of clichés and by his desiccated and theoretical manner – 'he shewed ... he compared ... he communicated ... he enumerated ... he exhorted'. The second philosopher is exposed by his failure to define; his axioms – 'to live according to nature' and so on – could come from a *Rambler* individually, but never in this bland abundance unrelieved by the precisions of wit. Johnson knows when generalizations convey and when they avoid a meaning; his own are not intellectual proofs but the warm deductions of experience. He exposes the specious by irony which works sometimes (as with Soame Jenyns) by open assault and sometimes by subtly slanted phrase and by verbiage replacing wit.

The *Journey to the Western Islands of Scotland* (1775), briefer and less lively than Boswell's *Tour to the Hebrides* though it is, and sometimes depreciated because Johnson is supposed not to enjoy scenery sufficiently, nevertheless commands admiration. Along with it should be read the very similar letters to Mrs Thrale from Scotland. Its origin was less in a thirst for Hebridean beauty than in curiosity about 'savage virtues', and the longest section is a dissertation on customs. But the result is broader and deeper than simple sociology. In the first place, as one might expect, Johnson takes to the sublime almost as to his own element – to that height of grandeur and mystery which the vogue of the Bible and Milton, of Longinus and the new aesthetics of Burke[8] was impressing on the Augustan mind (Shakespeare, he once said, surpassed Young as the ocean a tea-kettle, and Corneille as the forest a clipped hedge). Slanes Castle, on its Aberdeenshire cliff, suggests 'all the terrific grandeur of the tempestuous ocean'; he tries to imagine the winter spate at the Falls of Fiers; he finds delight in the loneliness of Glen Moriston; the moonlit sea from Mull to Iona is 'a solemn and pleasing scene', and even a violent storm between Oban and Inverary is praised as 'a nobler concert of rough music of nature than it had ever been my chance to hear before'. History has its own sublimity; he laments the ruins of St Andrews, Aberbrothick, and Elgin, and the meditation on Iona is one of the best things in the book. In the second place, such comments are not the casual embroidery of sentiment. Scenery and history evoke reflections, which come with all Johnson's spacious gravity, on the paradoxical grandeur and weakness of man. Wild landscape, he observes, displays 'one of the great scenes of human existence', and confronts us with the precarious condition of life. No paraphrase does justice to the severe passion with which Johnson enforces this common reflection, but the paragraph towards the end of the 'Anoch' section, beginning 'We were in this place at ease and by choice' and ending 'Yet what are these hillocks to the ridges of Taurus, or these spots of wildness to the deserts of America?' has in full measure his unique impressiveness.

Other sections of this volume treat of criticism, and to discuss critical principles here would be redundant. But to avoid the critical documents altogether would be a sin of omission and a lapse in proportion, for Johnson without the *Preface to the English Dictionary* (1755), the *Preface* to Shakespeare (1765), and the *Lives of the English Poets* (1779–81) would lose considerably in achievement. The first of these, characteristically, is a masterly mixture of general principles and personal experience; intellectually commanding and ingenious amidst all the complications of lexicography, Johnson impresses (as he impressed Boswell) by analytic and comprehensive power. The second, together with the notes on the plays, shows his best power in epitome, the vigour with which he represents the sane and un-idolatrous tradition of Augustan criticism, his conclusive and happy boldness of phrase, and his broad and intimate humanity. To have his say on Shakespeare was for him, as for most critics, a supreme challenge and opportunity, never better taken. As for the *Lives*, 'the biographical part of literature is what I love most,' he told Boswell, who in another connexion observed that 'Johnson loved business, loved to have his wisdom actually operate on real life.' No form could better express his sense of literature as emerging from and reflecting on life than literary biography, already evolved in Walton's *Lives*, Sprat's *Cowley*, Burnet's *Rochester*, and Oldys's *Ralegh*, but still hardly significant as criticism. Johnson's commentaries blossom naturally and pervasively into annotations on life; his subjects are not writers only but men, and his praise of Samuel Butler applies to himself:

> The most valuable parts of his performance are those which retired study and native wit cannot supply. He that merely takes a book from books may be useful, but can scarcely be great. Butler had not suffered life to glide beside him unseen or unobserved. He had watched with great diligence the operations of human nature, and traced the effects of opinion, humour [i.e. disposition], interest, and passion. From such remarks proceeded that great number of sententious distichs which have passed into conversation and are added as pro-verbial axioms to the general stock of practical knowledge.

All Johnson's criticisms, even many of his occasional petulances, are prompted by his sense of truth. This truth is, mainly, the recognizable substance of life, with its normal passions and activities in their due proportions; Shakespeare is praised for allowing love no more preponderance in his plays than it has in life, the metaphysical poets are blamed for their eccentric images and ideas. But behind this quotidian truth is the other, of religion, which allies his criticism with his deepest intuitions and gives it a dimension which other critics seldom approach. This does not appear often; many subjects hardly admit of it. But in the last resort it is there to provide its own scale of judgement. This metaphysical fact, the existence of religious truth guaranteeing a series of moral truths, is Johnson's ultimate authority; its reality for him is the incentive to a certain kind of critical demand – too narrow (we should say) when it requires direct ethical improvement, but bracingly large and generous when it insists on a discipleship not of current vogue or private vision but of life in its permanent and communal reality, held to be recognizable by every man and to be described in terms all recognize as true. The aim of such discipleship, however, is not (it may be repeated) mere realism but a concern for an understanding of life into which enters moral conduct; Johnson's criticism is steeped in the ethos of Christian humanism and it holds, with the astronomer in *Rasselas*, that 'to man is permitted the contemplation of the skies, but the practice of virtue is commanded'.

To speak too much in terms of a general 'ethos', however, is as one-sided as to stress too much the abstract or general in Johnson. That ethos is there, like a sounding-board to give resonance to what he says; one is never far from that other dimension. Still, it is of actual life that Johnson always thinks, and all his thought opens directly into it. 'The highest pleasure the drama can give' lies in the engrossed, uncritical reading of Shakespeare's 'just representations of general nature' (i.e. of life in its broad truth), for 'his drama is the mirror of life'. And this, finally, seems the place for a word about Johnson's idea of literary originality, for the originality that he (like his contemporaries) most valued is that which Shakespeare showed in securing his 'just representations' – that function of the imagination which does not merely 'mirror' life but brings it home to the reader with both novelty and familiarity. Shakespeare does this abundantly; not only the 'practical axioms and domestic wisdom' which Johnson praises in a characteristic but curious phrase, but innumerable other perceptions also are minted from raw experience and added to the stock of recognized truths. Such imagination works not by that 'perverseness of ingenuity' which beset the metaphysical poets but by seeming to remind us, in an improved form, of what we already feel to be true of life. This reminding is Johnson's whole intention in creative as well as critical work; it is concentrated into his comment on a passage he repeatedly praised in Congreve's *Mourning Bride*:

> He who reads these lines enjoys for a moment the power of a poet; he feels what he remembers to have felt before, but he feels it with great increase of sensibility; he recognizes a familiar image, but meets it again amplified and expanded, embellished with beauty and enlarged with majesty.
>
> (*Life of Congreve*)

There is, indeed, nothing unusual in this; most readers of most poetry want recognition-plus-revelation, though at different times the proportions of familiar and novel will differ, and demands for beauty and ennoblement may change, according to the spirit of the time, into those for realism and intensity. The point is that while Johnson's mind naturally encompasses religion and moral philosophy, it is none the less vigorously and variously interested in the daily spectacle of society, and accords the highest praise to writers who best bring to mind the common experience of man.

Johnson was fortunate, in the short run, in that he had an understood code of public taste to express, and, in the long run, in that that code was concerned centrally and intelligently with what the common sense (the conjoined form of those words is far too slight in meaning) of the Christian-humanist tradition indicated to be important about man. An acceptance of duty to God and truth, a discipline of imagination and reason by which eccentricity and whim submit to the large authority of 'things as they are' ('We may take Fancy for a companion', he wrote to Boswell, 'but must follow Reason as our guide'), and a wish to assert human community in serious and intelligent interests, the whole done within a tradition but with striking personal wit and independence – these qualities, exercised through the whole range of mind from vigorously grasped detail to comprehensive sanity about mankind at large, render the criticism (despite its limitations) thoroughly bracing and encouraging. Johnson is a great critic because while he works in a tradition his judgements are not those of tradition merely: they are judgements of tradition from which most of what is superficial has been pruned off by his unsurpassed power of looking at a subject for himself.

No one writing on Johnson can feel happy unless he has set him vividly in the context of his London life, surrounded by friends and acquaintances and reacting to the events of his time. This essay, not being another Boswell's *Life*, has clearly not done that, and may well be accused of having disembodied its subject. To refer the reader to other biographical treatments is, though necessary, no real amends; perhaps, instead, one ought to recall how varied, and how consciously enjoyed, was the Augustans' social world. Not all of it was enjoyable: Johnson's own experience, and the *Life of Savage* (humanly speaking the finest of the *Lives*), are among the abundant evidence that makes that clear. But social enjoyment abounds in Augustan letters, and the zest of Johnson's participation in it is prominent in any portrait of him. Moreover, as Joseph Wood Krutch has put it, the eighteenth century was 'the golden age of the amateur'; the intelligent man might speculate, not indeed on everything (for Augustan orthodoxy was timid about fundamentals, and Johnson himself was infuriated by deists or 'infidels'), but about a wide variety of 'safe' subjects – the classics, the arts, history and current affairs, social life, personalities, the sciences, and so on. Even with John Wilkes, that deplorable Whig, Johnson soon found common ground – 'classical learning, modern literature, wit and humour, and ready repartee' (Boswell's *Life*, III, 79). Common ground there was, in that fortunate Augustan culture of the non-specialist, where the availability of current knowledge enabled and encouraged any intelligent man to pursue an active breadth of interests. The vivacity of Johnson's conversation, Mr Krutch suggests, was partly a safeguard against the onset of depression, but it was partly a sign of his confidence in his company, in the currency of knowledge and ideas – though again with the proviso that fundamentals were not to be shaken. The Augustan unity could not last long, but while it did last it produced a society confident, animated, and coherent, and Johnson, a central figure if ever there was one, was in ideas, personality, and social experience its best embodiment.

NOTES

1. Besides contemporary evidence, such as Boswell's *Life*, and the Piozzi and Murphy reprints in *Johnsonian Miscellanies*, ed. G. B. Hill (London, 1897), see J. W. Krutch, *Samuel Johnson* (London, 1948) and F. R. Leavis's 'Johnson and Augustanism' in *The Common Pursuit* (London, 1952).

2. See F. R. Leavis, *op. cit.*, pp. 97, 103.

3. See Walter Raleigh, *Six Essays on Johnson* (London, 1910).

4. The lines are 135–64. For comment, see *Poems*, ed. D. Nichol Smith and E. L. McAdam (Oxford, 1941), p. 46; and *Johnsonian Miscellanies*, ed. G. B. Hill, I, 180. A similar incident is in Hill, *op. cit.*, I, 284.

5. For contemporary opinion, see Boswell's *Life*, ed. G. B. Hill and L. F. Powell (London, 1934–50), I, 224, and G. B. Hill, *op cit.*, I, 283.

6. See in particular the last *Rambler*, No. 208.

7. See introduction to *Selected Letters of Samuel Johnson*, ed. R. W. Chapman (London, 1925). The letters of condolence referred to are those (to Elphinston) of 25 September 1750; (to Mrs Thrale) of 25 March 1776, and 12 April 1781; (to Langton) of 21 September 1758, and 20 March 1782; (to Lawrence) of 20 January 1780; and (to Dodd) of 26 June 1776.

8. Longinus, *On the Sublime*; and Burke, *The Origin of our Ideas of the Sublime and the Beautiful* (1757).

ARCHITECTURE AND LANDSCAPE

A. R. HUMPHREYS

THE quality of a civilization shows itself best in its arts. This is notably true of the Augustan age, convinced as it was of the ethical-intellectual content of its art-forms: the Renaissance belief that a new philosophical era demanded a new literature and aesthetic was as deep-rooted in England as in Italy or France. This was a deliberate movement in civilization, an allegiance no longer to the medieval but to the humanism of Rome and Italy: the arts which had hitherto subconsciously (though no less effectively) expressed the spirit of their age now did so consciously, and with such success that architecture is the Augustans' mistress-art; in the arts of the whole period there are few experiences comparable in value with the sight of St Paul's, Blenheim, Kedleston, Syon, or the Crescent at Bath.

The arts related themselves not only to aesthetic but also to political, ethical, and educational codes. They had a political bearing because they were held to express the national spirit: as Wren wrote:

> Architecture has its political uses; Public Buildings being the Ornament of a Country; it establishes a Nation, draws People and Commerce; makes the People love their native Country, which Passion is the Original of all great Actions in a Commonwealth.
>
> (*Parentalia, or Memoirs of the* ... *Wrens*, 1750, Tract 1)

A patriot like Defoe could confidently refer the new triumphs of building to the country's growing prosperity. Incidentally, politics had quite a direct bearing on design; the great dining-rooms of the oligarchy, Robert Adam explains in commenting on his scheme at Syon, were meant for those influential dinner-parties in which 'every person of rank' could 'enter with ardour into those discussions to which [politics] give rise'.[1] The great houses were not, as in France, merely country retreats; they were, in the historical circumstances of the age, centres of political manoeuvre. But Augustan architecture had its ethical basis too; its churches have been called the most considerable body of religious art ever produced for a Protestant community up to that time, and its styles, both ecclesiastical and secular, paid homage to an ideal antiquity, to the harmony and order which humanism asserted. Its ideals of balance, lucidity, and controlled power were those that Augustan literature looked to as the standard of human nature.[2] Moreover, as Addison said, though beauty is a quality not objectively 'in' its source but subjectively interpreted from it, the faculty of interpretation is a particular sign of God's beneficence, and a man of a cultured taste, Addison asserts, enjoys not merely dilettante pleasure but the highest qualities of his nature (*Spectator*, 411–13). And finally the arts had their educational bearing because knowledge of them was indispensable to the educated man, nourished not only on classical reading but on connoisseurship at home and preferably on the Grand Tour abroad, where he culti-vated with often obsequious regard Renaissance painting, classical Roman and Italian building (later, Greek and Syrian), and

> ... vases bossed and huge inscriptive stones,
> And intermingling vines and figured nymphs,
> Floras and Chloes of delicious mould.
>
> (DYER: *The Ruins of Rome*)

It is less possible with architecture than with literature to start the period about 1660. Much of Augustan inspiration goes back straight to Inigo Jones (1573–1652), the stormy Welsh genius who collabor-ated and quarrelled with Ben Jonson and who, by a single act of in-novating genius, transplanted from Italy to England the Palladian style.[3] Andrea Palladio (1518–80) was not, like Brunelleschi or Michelangelo, one of the supreme Italian originators; his style is more 'classical' and scholarly. But it is full of grace and power, and it suited the English spirit better than anything more grandiose; with some modification (Inigo Jones, for instance, spaced the details of his façades more widely and so tranquillized them towards that serenity that characterizes English Palladian) it proved the happiest of models. Palladio, says Colen Campbell's *Vitruvius Britannicus* (1715), 'arrived to the *Ne plus ultra* of his art'; and Inigo Jones, in becoming his disciple, also had 'out-done all that went before'. Jones's master-pieces fall between the years 1615 and 1650, and include the Green-wich Queen's House, the Whitehall Banqueting Hall, St Paul's in Covent Garden, and the superb house at Wilton near Salisbury with its double-cube room designed for Van Dyck portraits. Architecture, he said, should be 'solid, proportional according to the rules, masculine and unaffected', and so for nearly two centuries it remained, with the important additions of richness and grace. But besides grander compositions he initiated, in laying out Covent Garden and Lincoln's Inn Fields, that 'terrace' fashion which blossomed into the disciplined order of Augustan streets, squares, and crescents. The Augustans credited his contemporary Peter Mills (c. 1600–70) with having provided London's first regular façade, and having pointed away from Tudor individualism, in designing the adjacent Great Queen Street (c. 1640). However much is said in the following pages of the major churches and country houses, it should never be forgotten that the decent order of modest street architecture, often carefully controlled by by-laws (as with much of London's eighteenth-century development, or Warwick's after the fire of 1694), is, if less spectacular, quite as significant a sign of taste. Not all building was good: not all poets were Popes or all prose-writers Johnsons. But the disciplined craftsmanship which proliferated in capable couplets and orderly sentences made an even greater contribution to English civilization in ordinary domestic architecture and design.

Between Inigo Jones and Wren there were able architects, like Mills already mentioned, who also built the notable Thorpe Hall, near Peterborough,[4] Sir Roger Pratt, architect of Coleshill, Berkshire (burnt down in 1952 and, most regrettably, immediately demolished); and John Webb – 'Inigo Jones's man', Evelyn called him – who oversaw much of his master's work (a fine house by him survives at Lamport in Northamptonshire). But the next great stage is that of Wren (1632–1723), one of those who, with Newton, Boyle, Locke, Milton, Dryden, Purcell, and Grinling Gibbons, remind us that the late seventeenth century, prolifically fertile and imaginative, was among the greatest periods of English genius. His bent was towards science, and his early posts were precocious professorships in astronomy. His architecture is indeed intellectual, though not in a chill or negative sense, intellectual rather as Milton is intellectual, with classical scholarship assimilated in the Renaissance way to original genius, and made to glow into grandeur and beauty by sheer splendour of imagination. Whatever the scale of Wren's work, from moderate parish church or college chapel to palace or cathe-

dral, it always suggests immense and wonderful power, harmoni-
ously informing and enriching its volumes and surfaces. By a
fortunate circumstance Wren was assistant to Sir John Denham, poet
and Surveyor-General of Works, when Denham died in 1669; he
thereby became responsible for designing London's public buildings
after the Great Fire, and his City churches, inventively varied in
adaptation to their awkward sites, are subtly modulated through all

St Paul's Cathedral, London, from the north

stages of their interiors and exteriors up to their crowning obelisks,
lanterns, balls and cones, with a tough reasonableness underlying the
lyric grace which reminds us to which century they belong. These,
with the smaller masterpieces like the Pembroke and Emmanuel
Chapels and Trinity Library at Cambridge, the Sheldonian Theatre
and Trinity Chapel at Oxford, and Morden College at Blackheath,
and with the greater masterpieces at Greenwich Palace, Hampton
Court, Chelsea Hospital, and St Paul's Cathedral, are intellectually
and imaginatively among the richest and strongest of English achievements and make Wren one of the supreme architects of the world.

Greatly as he outshines his contemporaries, six others deserve mention with him, since their combined work marks England's nearest approach to 'baroque' taste – taste expressing not the accuracy and poise of the strict classic but using a classical language to express dramatic energy and emotion in varied outline and ebullient forms.

St Philip's Cathedral, Birmingham

They are William Talman (1650–1720), Nicholas Hawksmoor (1661–1736), Sir John Vanbrugh (1664–1726), Thomas Archer (1668–1743), John James (1672–1746), and James Gibbs (1682–1754). Labels are crude expedients; 'baroque' here means no great formal resemblance between these men but a sharing of imaginative energy

424

which has its counterpart in Restoration literature. Talman, Archer, and James are less important than Hawksmoor, Vanbrugh, and Gibbs. The first of them did some of the City halls after the Fire (the Fishmongers', Haberdashers', Drapers', and Tailors'), but is best remembered for the grandeur of Chatsworth. James's best work is St George's in Hanover Square, with fine bravura in its Corinthian portico and a tower full of spring and vigour. Archer is more interesting than either: he designed St Philip's, Birmingham (the cathedral), and two astonishingly fine London churches in St Paul's, Deptford, and St John's, Westminster. His elevations are strongly modelled and his towers and spires vigorously conceived. St Philip's gratifies the eye with curves vitally related between its portico, its tower walls (which, surprisingly concave, curl outward to buttress-like double pilasters at each corner), and its dome and cupola. St Paul's, Deptford, is a powerful and handsome composition, with bold square nave and a circular tower rising through a semicircular portico; St John's is one of London's most remarkable buildings, conventionally reckoned ungainly but in fact strikingly successful in its command over dramatically interrupted lines, a refreshing and invigorating conception, and, alas, now perhaps to be demolished.

Much greater than these men, however, were Hawksmoor and Vanbrugh, located at the centre of the movement, for Hawksmoor spent thirty years in Wren's office and also worked with Vanbrugh on Castle Howard. The baroque, it has been said, 'intellectualized the picturesque', and the phrase fits both men. Besides the handsome Queen's Library and quadrangle at Oxford (where he also fitted All Souls with its odd Gothic towers), and the boldly fine Easton Neston house in Northamptonshire, Hawksmoor did six remarkable London churches – St Alphege's, Greenwich, where James added the tower; St Annes's, Limehouse, and St George's-in-the-East; St Mary Woolnoth with grandiosely-masonried walls and strange double-peaked front; St George's, Bloomsbury; and Christ Church, Spitalfields, with perhaps the finest feature of all, a west front with columned porch whose barrel-vault and horizontal wings are brilliantly echoed in successive curves and horizontals up the tower and steeple, which soars at last into a virtual Gothic spire. These churches are signalized by their force and emotional daring, which risk ugliness yet save themselves by grandeur. The same thing, more dramatically, is true of

Vanbrugh, playwright-architect, whose work was for two centuries the butt of satire (with, however, some generous eulogies), and is now rightly extolled. The reason is not its habitable convenience; in this respect Blenheim, though perhaps better than often supposed, is unconvincingly organized, and Seaton Delaval strikes one as completely and brazenly preposterous. But Vanbrugh was a modeller rather than a planner, and his successes are not those of domestic efficiency. Castle Howard, in Yorkshire, with a Corinthian order reinforcing the main block beneath a dominating pediment, with a sweep of round-headed but strongly keystoned windows from end to end (the

Castle Howard, Yorkshire

effect has the vitality of multiplied Gothic ogives), with a picturesque enrichment of urn-like finials and chimneys along the skyline, and a theatrical lantern tower and dome dominating everything, is a spectacle of captivating spirit. In Vanbrugh's work, Reynolds perceived, 'there is a greater display of imagination than we shall find perhaps in any other.'[5] The grandeur of the much-visited and well-known Blenheim needs no emphasis: the scale and audacity of its composition are breath-taking: here again Vanbrugh has no British rival. As for Seaton Delaval, if not more astonishing than Blenheim (nothing could be), it is quite as unforgettable. Vanbrugh once referred to 'the tame, sneaking south', and this Northumbrian house seems designed to express the opposite qualities of the north. Along with his other compositions it has the quality of 'movement', which Reynolds defined in him, and later architects like Robert Adam sought successfully to imitate, as the eye is carried back from the forecourt's great projecting wings to the fortress-like and almost castellated main block, with heavy rustication* of its front wall and grouped columns, and superhuman keystones over its arches. Vanbrugh did other buildings elsewhere and his signature is of a severe and generally spectacular grandeur – 'baroque without ornament', it has been called. Here the severity and spectacle are more than merely grand; they are in the highest degree dramatic, and the sight of them is one of the great architectural experiences of life.

As for Gibbs, with less buccaneering energy than Hawksmoor and Vanbrugh and more scholarly training (he had studied in Paris and Rome), he is not inferior in accomplishment, since he fixed a splendid mark on London with St Clement Danes's steeple, St Mary-le-Strand and St Martin-in-the-Fields. Cambridge's Senate House and Fellows' Building at King's, and Oxford's Radcliffe Camera, are not less prominent: at Derby he built All Saints (the cathedral), whose internal open lightness and fluency of curve make it one of the finest of neo-classic churches, and at Ditchley in Oxfordshire he replaced the Earl of Lichfield's antiquated seat by a house of that refined opulence which Lord Burlington and William Kent soon made the century's dominant fashion. In church design he was particularly influential; his *Book of Architecture* (1728) bore fruit in a crop of pseudo-Gibbsian spires, one of the best being on Flitcroft's St Giles-in-the-Fields which, with Hawksmoor's nearby St George's, blossoms delightfully in the architectural desert where Shaftesbury Avenue meets Holborn. Others occur, for instance, in Kent (Mereworth), Worcester (St Nicholas), Wolverhampton (St John), and in the transatlantic colonial style from New England to South Carolina. Gibbs carries on the line of Wren with all the Augustan virtues of a Roman power and richness, and it is hard to think that the classical beauties of Trafalgar Square or the Strand, of Oxford or Cambridge, would not have been diminished if any contemporary other than Wren had been substituted for him.[6]

The phase of taste which brings Augustan domestic building to the height of its splendour is, however, the next, that associated with the man whom Gay calls 'Burlington, belov'd of ev'ry Muse', Pope's friend, and the greatest of patron-connoisseurs. Burlington (1694–1753) gathered round him, in more or less close association, a

* Masonry of large blocks rough-hewn or with channelled or sunken joints.

group who turned from Wren's baroque tradition to the stricter beauties of Palladianism – or, more truly, from what was often (especially in the provinces, and despite the greater architects' example) a rather stolid style of heavy plasterwork, coarse orders, and dark wainscoting, to an ordered opulence.[7] Among Burlington's aides and disciples were most of the best men before Robert Adam – Colen Campbell (d. 1729), the Venetian Giacomo Leoni (1686–1746), Henry Flitcroft ('Burlington Harry', 1697–1769), James Paine (1725–89), and pre-eminently William Kent (1685–1748). Pope put their aims in a couplet –

> Jones and Palladio to themselves restore,
> And be whate'er Vitruvius* was before.

On an illuminating Grand Tour to Italy (1714–15) Burlington drew Palladio's buildings and bought Palladio's sketches. He sponsored Leoni's two magnificent volumes, lavish with text and plates, of *The Architecture of A. Palladio in Four Books* (1715), and also Kent's *Designs of Inigo Jones* (1727), which included some by John Webb and by Burlington and Kent themselves. Among the most handsome of Augustan publications, and historically of great importance, is Colen Campbell's *Vitruvius Britannicus, or the British Architect* (3 vols.: 1715–25), which deplores the ornateness of Italian baroque, holds Palladio and Inigo Jones to be supreme, and still has praises for contemporaries from Wren to Hawksmoor and James. 'Vitruvius Britannicus' was traditionally a soubriquet for Inigo Jones, but Campbell applies it generically to the major English classicists. As one more (not the last) of Burlingtonian volumes there is Robert Castell's splendid *Villas of the Ancients Illustrated* (1728), dedicated to the Earl with a confident tribute:

> When I again reflect that many works of Inigo Jones's and Palladio's had perish'd but for your Love to Architecture, I lay aside my Fears, and the rather as this Work is wholly founded on the Rules of the Ancients, for whom your Lordship has on all Occasions manifested the greatest Regard.

* Marcus Pollio Vitruvius, born about 80 B.C., is noted for his work *De Architectura*, rediscovered in St Gall monastery in the fifteenth century and highly influential throughout the Renaissance.

More now begins to be heard of 'the Ancients'; the Burlingtonians were great revivalists, and set a fashion for archaeological research. The results were of extreme aesthetic importance – Robert Wood brought back the styles of Roman Syria (*The Ruins of Palmyra*, 1753; *The Ruins of Balbec*, 1757), James Stuart and Nicholas Revett's famous *Antiquities of Athens* (1762) launched the severe correctness of a 'Greek' fashion, and Robert Adam proved his scholarship (encouraged to do so, he said, by the welcome given to Wood's volumes) with his *Ruins of the Palace of the Emperor Diocletian at Spalato* (1764). Ultimately the central tradition was dispersed in imitation and eclecticism. Yet we need not anticipate; English Palladian is full of character, and not at all academically decadent. From the 1710s to about 1750 one great building after another rose in a style of rich dignity – Burlington's own Chiswick House, modelled on a Palladian villa, and his York Assembly Rooms, recently restored, with the noble perspective of its Corinthian-columned Egyptian Room glowing with harmonious colour;[8] Leoni's Clandon Park at Guildford, with a fine sense of space and enrichment, Moor Park in Hertfordshire, its loftiness emphasized by Corinthian pilasters and engaged columns rising the whole height of its elevation, and Lyme Hall in Cheshire; Campbell's new front to Burlington House, Piccadilly, and a great house at Wanstead, Essex (since demolished), Houghton in Norfolk, built for Walpole (the interior by Kent), and Stourhead in Wiltshire; Flitcroft's Woburn Abbey in Bedfordshire and Wentworth Woodhouse in Yorkshire; and Kent's Devonshire House in Piccadilly (demolished), Holkham in Norfolk, a notable house in Berkeley Square (No. 44) with a spectacularly-modelled staircase, and the universally familiar Horse Guards. Kent designed or shared in many other buildings, as painter, architect, furniture designer, or, most famously, landscapist (he was the man, in Horace Walpole's phrase, who 'leaped the fence and saw that all Nature was a garden'), and he has consequently been disparaged as a universal dabbler. More properly, a recent (and the only adequate) study of him suggests,[9] he is the strongest candidate for an empty niche between Wren and Reynolds. The spirit of the eighteenth century is in Kent as much as any man; in architecture he has the power of the central tradition and in his 'natural' gardening the confidence of the innovator who thinks himself (in this case rightly) to be moving in a happy direction. His work implies the cultural strength of the oligarchy – wealth, zest, and the disciplined harmony of ordered power. For all its refinements Palladianism is still an idiom of strength; its lordly disposition of mass, its rich decoration, its bold mouldings

44 Berkeley Square, London

and pediments, its commanding Corinthian columns, these inherit the full genius of Augustanism. It steered English architecture clear of the floridity which afflicted the Continent.

As the age of Pope is dominated by Burlington, so, though a shade less completely, is that of Johnson by Robert Adam (1728–92) and his subordinate brother James (1730–94).[10] As the Burlingtonians evolved their style out of baroque but also reacted from it, so the Adams evolved theirs out of the Burlingtonian (their father William was an early and creditable Scots Palladian) but sought greater refinement and a more elegant serenity. The early Georgians' sturdy woodwork, the Palladians' compartmented ceilings and strongly-moulded walls and doorways, gave way before delicate plaster arabesques, silk

Kenwood: Adam Room or Lord Mansfield's Library

damask hangings, and glowing colour. The Palladian fashion of rooms *en suite*, each related to its neighbours, with symmetrical alignments giving vistas and perspectives, Robert Adam carried to perfection, shaping his spaces with coved ceilings or curved apses round which the eye flows with the utmost sense of grace. His masterpieces are such conceptions as the series of rooms which surround the great alabaster-columned hall of Kedleston, or that sequence – entrance hall, anteroom, dining-room, drawing-room, and long gallery, each of exquisite splendour – which he devised at Syon. 'The parade, the convenience, and social pleasures of life', he said, were in his plans 'more strictly attended to in the arrangements and disposition of apartments' than ever before: connoisseurs, he hoped,

> will easily perceive, within these few years, a remarkable improvement in the form, convenience, arrangement, and relief of apartments; a greater movement and variety in the outside composition, and in the decoration of the inside an almost total change.
>
> (*Works in Architecture of Robert and James Adam*, 1778, preface)

And a footnote on 'movement' (for which he admired Vanbrugh) is prophetic:

> *Movement* is meant to express the rise and fall, the advance and recess, with other diversity of form, in the different parts of a building, so as to add greatly to the picturesque of the composition. For the rising and fall, advancing and receding, with the convexity and concavity and other forms of the great parts, have the same effect in architecture that hill and dale, foreground and distance, swelling and sinking, have in landscape; that is, they serve to produce an agreeable and diversified contour that groups and contrasts like a picture.

He clearly looked on his style as a matter not only of elegantly adorning surfaces (he, and more especially his imitators, have been accused of reducing architecture to flat decoration) but of handling masses with a dynamic sense of all three dimensions and producing what might well be called a romantic effect. His terms, perhaps, are misleading; they suggest a painter who has strayed into architecture, a designer of plastic forms rather than of habitable structures, and indeed 'the picturesque' in the romantic sense was not at all beyond him; his numerous 'Gothic' and Piranesian drawings of ruins are evidence, and so, spectacularly, is his astonishing Culzean Castle, that vast crenellated and turreted pile which crowns an Ayrshire cliff and whose exterior vies in romantic feeling with the confronting Firth of Clyde and mountains of Arran. An upheaval in sensibility is not far away. But Adam is far more than a designer of architectural scenery; Culzean itself internally is a fine classical house, with all of Adam's harmony of volume and grace of line, particularly in a circular salon and oval staircase, and like the rest of his work it is the expression by genius of that phase when the early vehemence of Augustan culture had been directed into an admirably ordered civilization. Adam decorated or adapted far more houses than he built; still, in whatever capacity he worked, in places like Shardeloes, Harewood, Kedleston, Osterley, Syon, Kenwood, Nostell Priory, and Mersham-le-Hatch, he and his brilliant executants developed the most exquisite elegances of colour and line that England has to show, displayed in interiors both lavish and refined behind façades of serene distinction.

To touch on the other main names perfunctorily is hardly fair to them; however, it is better than to imply that the whole eighteenth-century achievement was that of a few leaders. In furniture, too, the fame of Chippendale, Sheraton, and Hepplewhite has until recently unjustly obscured the many designers who, in London and the provinces, and indeed across the Irish Sea, worked with excellent invention and taste.[11] The major architects, then, include John Vardy, whose Spencer House presents its quintessentially Palladian façade to Green Park in London; the elder George Dance, with London's Mansion House, and the younger with a formidably severe Newgate Prison (demolished); Sir William Chambers, whose great monument – an unquestioned masterpiece – is Somerset House; and Chambers's pupil James Gandon, whose Dublin Custom House recalls his master. These three last-mentioned were, it has been said, the finest public buildings in Britain since the time of Wren. There are also Lancelot ('Capability') Brown, whom Chambers tartly disliked for carrying off the commission to build Claremont House in Surrey for Clive of India, and who, though principally famous for landscape gardening, was an attractive Palladian;[12] James Paine, who was much in favour before the Adam vogue, and whose great houses at Kedleston and Nostell Priory[13] Adam took over and completed; and James Wyatt, who sprang into fame at twenty-six with the Oxford Street Pantheon (1772) and immediately began to divert fashion from the Adams. The Pantheon, the universal theme of society talk, did not last long, but Wyatt left great classical houses, at Heaton Park near Manchester, Heveningham Hall in Suffolk, and Dodington in Gloucestershire, in a brilliant style, closely resembling yet cooler and chaster than the Adams' – and then turned his tastes with the time and plunged into Gothic.

And finally, there are the sterling architects of the provinces,[14] chief among them the John Woods, father and son, of Bath, who created some of Georgian England's finest compositions in the Palladian terraces of that city – in the North and South Parades, Queen Square, the Circus, Crescent, and Assembly Rooms – and nearby at Prior Park, Titanbarrow, and Belcombe Court. Not far behind comes John Carr of York, engaged on several of the great

Royal Crescent, Bath

country houses, like Harewood, and on town buildings like the handsome Crescent at Buxton. Elsewhere there were Henry Bell of King's Lynn, with his picturesque and Wren-like Custom House there (an object-lesson on how to be delightful on a site about sixty feet square) and perhaps the almost-Continental-baroque Duke's Head; Thomas White of Worcester, who may have worked for Wren and whose Guild Hall and St Nicholas are thoroughly pleasing; and William and John Bastard, who did good street houses and an admirable church in Blandford, Dorset, after a fire in 1731. There were many others – Warwickshire and the Bath-Bristol area were particularly rich in local talent – but to particularize would be to enter too much into detail. What is necessary here is not to investigate the minutiae of architectural history (though, indeed, research into provincial building is paying rewarding dividends of interest) but to stress how the steady and thoughtful evolution of Augustan literature, and its percolation through a more closely united society to every part of the land, were paralleled by the same process in architecture, and accompanied by a similar ability to perform well in visual design, according to the standards of good craftsmanship and accepted models. Even when provincial towns have nothing to show of the first rank, they provide some of the eighteenth-century's most

The Palladian Bridge, Prior Park, Bath

enduring satisfactions in their churches, parsonages, public buildings, and dwelling-houses. The triumphal mansions are, in a way, less significant; having behind them all that money can buy, to some degree they represent a specialized taste. The soundness of Augustan instinct is more reliably shown by those thousands of buildings it produced almost without thinking, for the common purposes of life.

The life span of English neo-classicism is about fifty years longer at each end in architecture than in literature. Its first triumphs are the early ones of Inigo Jones; its last, the great Regency schemes of John

Nash, in Carlton House Terrace and Regent's Park, Sir John Soane's Bank of England, and, indeed, much later buildings in the nineteenth century, like Elmes's St George's Hall in Liverpool. But the story becomes one of multiplying models and dispersed effort, and the spirit anything but Augustan. It is necessary rather to return to the

The Custom House, King's Lynn

eighteenth century to mention two signs of that eclecticism which was to disrupt the settled (though never static) tradition; they are *chinoiserie* and the Gothic. The former[15] arose from the importation, with expanding trade, of Eastern products; it made itself felt first in applied design, particularly of lacquer work, on late seventeenth-century furniture, and thereafter the gay asymmetrical unperspectived decoration of Chinese figures and scenes held its place throughout the eighteenth century, to be amplified in the nineteenth by a rash of pseudo-exotic imitations from all over Asia. Augustan *chinoiserie* is often, though not always, charming; it was simultaneously satirized and cultivated; it produced a crop of eccentric furniture and picturesque latticed bridges and summer-houses; delicately bizarre wall-papers were imported from the Orient and hung in classical mansions like Moor Park and Woburn, or town houses like Mrs Elizabeth Montagu's in Portman Square; the less conservative of aristocrats and gentry indulged their tastes in a 'Chinese' room, as the Duke of Beaufort did at Badminton, the Duke of Bedford at Woburn, and Richard Lord Verney at Claydon. Drawings of Chinese structures and furniture appeared in pattern-books, and Chambers, whose youthful travels in the East enabled him to figure as an expert, produced two remarkable books – *Designs for Chinese Buildings* (1757) and *A Dissertation on Oriental Gardening* (1772) – as well as the Pagoda at Kew. The Chinese were, incidentally, credited by many enthusiasts with sublime virtue, but that is beside the point: their decorative arts would have been quite as influential had they been supposed as iniquitous as other men.

For with Gothic, *chinoiserie* was a glimpse of the strange and unclassical, free from 'the rules of the Ancients', a decorative revelry if not a solid repast. It was the contrasting element of the grotesque in an age of enlightened good sense. Sometimes it was very grotesque, and then it was bad; some eighteenth-century *chinoiserie* furniture is hideous. But sometimes it was only slightly grotesque, and then it provided a kind of English rococo, fanciful and gay. It was a minor mode, until it merged into the larger exoticism of the Romantic Revival; it diversifies the field of Augustan taste most engagingly; and it suggests the puckish readiness of taste to escape from the reasonable into the fantastic.

As for the Gothic,[16] that never quite vanished from favour. Lovers of the past dwelt fondly on the veneration old buildings inspired in them, and indeed the London Society of Antiquaries, extinct for a century, revived in 1717. The popular levels of Augustan taste as reflected in Defoe's *Tour* could still be enthusiastic; indeed, in 1742 the antiquary William Stukeley suggested that Glastonbury should be preserved because of 'that great concourse of strangers that comes to see it'. Men of intelligence like Vanbrugh, Gay, Pope, and Hogarth could admire the Gothic style, though perhaps only half-comprehending it, and provincial builders could still build in it; St Mary's tower at Warwick (1697–1704) has been called the final flourish of English Perpendicular architecture. Gothic was never, therefore, quite submerged. Yet fashionable taste certainly relegated it to a subordinate role, either as a pleasing reminder of outlived barbarism, or as a piquant ingredient in a view. In these dubious guises it broke out as a craze towards the middle of the century: the first sham ruins – those pointed reminders that Augustan taste could be bad – appeared in Lord Bathurst's park near Cirencester about 1733; Kent put up a ruin for Lord Cobham at Stowe (1742), and then did Gothic screens at Gloucester and Beverley; Batty Langley's *Gothic Architecture Improved by Rules and Proportions* (1742) tried to discover from medieval buildings an aesthetic system; Sanderson Miller made his name as a Gothicist with a ruin at Hagley in 1746; and in 1747 Horace Walpole bought Strawberry Hill and set about the battlementing, pinnacling, fenestrating, and cluttering which his letters so rapturously describe. Strawberry Hill is very bad architecture indeed, but it is the most famous portent of an earthquake in taste; Gothic (or, rather, Gothick) was promoted from the recesses of the park to be not only light decoration but the very spirit of a fashionable house. In the later eighteenth century Gothick imitations abound, not all bad; there are some pleasing churches, many charming cottages and villas, and, of course, Culzean.

The connexions of this with literary taste are clear; it is all part of that mixed medievalizing and naturalizing which were soon to transform European aesthetics. But curiously, while the Gothick vogue points towards architectural disaster, its twin-brother of 'natural' gardening was simultaneously producing some of the most delightful and original works of art the English imagination has ever achieved. The evolution of the 'natural' garden, briefly, meant the abandonment of geometrical plans, of straight walks and avenues, of symmetrical terraces, balustrades, and waterworks, in favour of lawns and park-land.[17] Man's control over Nature was exercised not by that dominance which levels hill and valley, regularizes pools and flower-beds, and sets out trees in rows, but by that subtler process which takes advantage of natural features, the slopes of ground, the varying shapes of copses, and the natural flow of water. The stages of transformation at Stowe, for instance, can be followed in successive maps showing the work done in turn by Bridgeman, Kent, and 'Capability' Brown: the geometrical parterre goes first, then by degrees the formal walks focusing on statues and temples, then the canalized stream and the straight-edged lake, until finally (the saplings being given time to grow) the scene extends as at present, with an immense sweep of lawn down to and beyond a 'natural' lake, and screens of trees advancing and receding on either hand to lead the eye easily away – a scene of paradisal serenity. The result is, of course, much better than Nature herself could do – a remark which applies to the whole of pastoral England under its careful regimen of planting and farming, but pre-eminently to estates such as Kent and Brown, and later Humphrey Repton, developed. Subsequently, towards the end of the century, coincidentally with the fuller fervour of Romanticism, opinions were divided; was Nature to be treated in Brown's gentle and placid manner, which might be insipid, or should she be as shaggy and 'picturesque' as possible? But that is really too late a topic for treatment here; its solution, approximately, was to reserve the mild treatment for landscape gardening (fortunately), and to go unkemptly wild in painting or to tour in search of the natural grandeurs of romantic scenery. The vogue of the picturesque enthusiast, like William Gilpin (1724–1804), whose numerous books on the subject[18] are important documents in taste, affected rather landscape at large than in the garden.

To connect Augustan literature and the visual arts is not difficult. In the case of landscape and the Gothic no more need be said here than to stress how strongly, from all quarters, both aesthetic and philosophical, the current set towards the subtler intuitions, the irrational perceptions, a reverence for natural beauty, and a sense of mystery, and of humility before the countryside and the past. Apparently contradicting the intellect's scientific triumphs, there began an aesthetic distrust which dissociated the aesthetic from the rational. But the contradiction was only apparent: the more Nature's processes seemed great, harmonious, and organic, the less right man seemed to have to impose his own discipline upon her, unless he imposed it so discreetly as to make his discipline seem her own work.

But the central Augustan mode is different, for it inherits the authority of the humanist tradition. In all the arts respect was due to the great and acknowledged masters: in literature, neo-classic criticism is founded not on subservience to but at least on admiration for classical precedent; in painting, the two influential critics of the eighteenth century, Jonathan Richardson and Sir Joshua Reynolds,[19] derive the idealizing principles of their art from classical statuary and the Renaissance masters; in architecture, the discipleship is clear. 'The buildings of the Ancients', Robert Adam observes in prefacing *The Ruins of the Palace of the Emperor Diocletian,*

> are in Architecture what the works of Nature are with respect
> to the other Arts; they serve as models which we should
> imitate, and as standards by which we ought to judge.

The closeness of this imitation varied, and as the century advanced the increase in archaeological verisimilitude became a source of weakness. Only as long as architecture maintained a parallel with literature in invigorating its classical devotion with native boldness and invention did the tradition flourish.

To the question why a Mediterranean architecture was so cultivated in (as satirists indefatigably reiterated) an unkind English climate the answer is partly aesthetic; the style was the handsomest English architects had ever seen, and vast porticoes and detached pavilions looked superb, however unsuited they might be to English weather. But more deeply the answer is in terms of the intellectual clarification and social ideals of the day. Augustan styles reflected the great Whig confidence in a 'free', wealthy, and oligarchical society; the lines of classical architecture, palatial or humble, reminded the proprietor that his age had outgrown the obscure chaos of former ages and, with the added advantages of Christian faith and British enterprise, was sharing the cultural light which had shone in Virgil and Horace. Whiggism, with its doctrine of enlightened liberty, had much to do with this spirit. But it was not a Whig monopoly; it belonged to the whole state of society. Augustan literature and art typically find their support in social life; Augustan paintings, instead of rendering a personal vision, fit into Augustan rooms as pieces of furniture to be lived with, part of the décor of that kind of life. As with literature, the public participated ever more widely in art; it bought reproductions; it quarrelled in the press over the style and siting of statues; and from 1768 it had the Royal Academy to flock to. Better than anywhere else society saw its ideals of enlightenment, amenity, progress, classical discipline, and 'polite imagination' expressed in its architecture, and of serene pastoralism realized in its parks.

NOTES

For permission to have the originals of the drawings copied I thank the following: Messrs B. T. Batsford Ltd, for St Paul's Cathedral, from Sacheverell Sitwell's *British Architects and Craftsmen*; Messrs Batsford and the author for St Philip's, Birmingham, from Marcus Whiffen's *Stuart and Georgian Churches*; The Cresset Press Ltd, and *Country Life* for 44 Berkeley Square, from John Summerson's *Georgian London*; *Country Life* for Castle Howard, the Custom House, King's Lynn, and Kenwood, from A. T. Bolton's *Architecture of Robert and James Adam*; the author, the National Buildings Record, Messrs Faber & Faber, and the Director of the Victoria Art Gallery, Bath (owners of the original drawing), for the Royal Crescent, Bath, and the Palladian Bridge, Prior Park, from Walter Ison's *The Georgian Buildings of Bath*.

John Summerson's *Architecture in Britain 1530 to 1830* (Pelican History of Art, 1953) is an invaluable guide to the whole subject.

1. See Christopher Hussey, 'Syon House, Middlesex', in *Country Life*, 1 December 1950.

2. The best analysis of these ideals is in Geoffrey Scott, *The Architecture of Humanism* (London, 1914), chapter 8.

3. On Inigo Jones, Wren, Vanbrugh, Hawksmoor, Gibbs, and Adam, see Sacheverell Sitwell, *British Architects and Craftsmen* (1945).

4. See Howard Colvin, 'The Architect of Thorpe Hall', *Country Life*, 6 June 1952.

5. See Reynolds, *Discourse XIII*.

6. A good many evidences of Gibbs's influence are collected in *Stuart and Georgian Churches outside London*, by Marcus Whiffen (1947).

7. For Burlington's ideals, see Pope, *Epistle to Burlington*, and Christopher Hussey's introduction to *The Work of William Kent*, by Margaret Jourdain (1948).

8. See R. A. Alec-Smith, 'The York Rooms Restored', *Country Life*, 22 June 1951.

9. See Christopher Hussey, *op. cit.*

10. The standard study is A. T. Bolton, *The Architecture of Robert and James Adam* (1922), but *The Age of Adam*, by James Lees-Milne (1947), is more easily available and is highly effective.

11. See R. Edwards and M. Jourdain, *Georgian Cabinet Makers*, 1946.

12. His buildings (and gardens) are well studied in Dorothy Stroud, *Capability Brown* (rev. ed., 1957).

13. For Nostell, see Christopher Hussey, 'Nostell Priory, Yorkshire', in *Country Life*, 16, 23, and 30 May 1952.

14. Marcus Whiffen, *op. cit.*, has much incidental information on provincial

architects ; e.g. White of Worcester, the Bastards, Strachan of Bristol, the Patys of Bristol, the Hiorns and Smiths of Warwick, and the Wings of Leicester. For the Woods, see Bryan Little, *The Building of Bath* (1947), and Gordon Nares, 'Belcombe Court, Wiltshire', in *Country Life*, 22 December 1950. For Henry Bell, see Arthur Oswald, 'King's Lynn, Norfolk, III', in *Country Life*, 20 July 1951; for the Smiths of Warwick, Arthur Oswald, 'Georgian Warwick, I and II', in *Country Life*, 19 and 26 October 1951, and 'Davenport House, Shropshire', in *Country Life*, 27 June and 11 July 1952. For the Woodwards of Chipping Campden, see Howard Colvin, in *Architectural Review*, March 1948, and C. W. Beard and J. A. Piper, 'An Architectural Discovery', in *Country Life*, 9 March 1951. For the Bastards of Blandford, see Arthur Oswald, 'Blandford', in *Old Towns Revisited* (1952), an informative and well-illustrated study of eight country towns.

15. Sir William Chambers's *Designs for Chinese Buildings* (1757) and *Dissertation on Oriental Gardening* (1772) are fascinating but hard to obtain. More available are B. Sprague Allen, *Tides in English Taste* (Harvard, 1937), chapter ix; W. W. Appleton, *A Cycle of Cathay* (New York, 1951); J. Steegman, *The Rule of Taste* (1936); A. O. Lovejoy, 'The Chinese Origin of a Romanticism', in *Essays in the History of Ideas* (Johns Hopkins, 1948); and A. R. Humphreys, 'Lords of Tartary', in *The Cambridge Journal*, III, 1, and *The Augustan World* (1954), chapter vi. There are some interesting pages also in Sacheverell Sitwell, *op. cit.*

16. See B. Sprague Allen, *op. cit.*, chapter xiv, and Lovejoy, *loc. cit.*, also K. Clark, *The Gothic Revival* (rev. ed., 1950).

17. See Horace Walpole, 'Of Modern Gardening', in *Anecdotes of Painting*; Christopher Hussey, *The Picturesque* (1927); H. Repton, *The Theory and Practice of Landscape Gardening* (1805) and *An Enquiry into the Changes of Taste in Landscape* (1806); A. R. Humphreys, *William Shenstone* (1937), Part II; Margaret Jourdain, *op. cit.*, and Dorothy Stroud, *Capability Brown* (1950).

18. See *Observations relative chiefly to ... Cumberland and Westmorland* (1787), *Observations on the River Wye* (1782), *The Highlands of Scotland* (1789), *Remarks on Forest Scenery* (1791), and *Observations on the Western Parts of England* (1798). Also, as satire, W. Combe and T. Rowlandson, *The Tours of Dr Syntax in Search of the Picturesque*.

19. See Richardson, *Theory of Painting* (1715), *The Art of Criticism* (1719), and *The Science of a Connoisseur* (1719): and Reynolds, *Discourses, passim*.

PART
IV

APPENDIX

COMPILED BY C. J. HORNE

FOR FURTHER READING AND REFERENCE

AUTHORS AND WORKS

LIST OF ABBREVIATIONS

E. & S.	Essays and Studies by Members of the English Association	P.Q.	Philological Quarterly
		R.E.S.	Review of English Studies
		S.P.	Studies in Philology
E.L.	Everyman's Library	W.C.	World's Classics
E.L.H.	English Literary History	abr.	abridged
J.E.G.P.	Journal of English and Germanic Philology	b.	born
		c.	circa
M.L.R.	Modern Language Review	d.	died
M.P.	Modern Philology	ed.	edited, edition, editor
O.E.N.	Oxford English Novels	pub.	published
O.S.A.	Oxford Standard Authors	repr.	reprinted
P.M.L.A.	Publications of the Modern Language Association of America	rev.	revised
		trans.	translated
		?	probably, uncertain

Under each author, the aim has been to list first the standard biographies (if any), second standard editions, and third a selection of books and articles for further study. Most of the books with American imprints have also been published in England.

FOR FURTHER READING AND REFERENCE

The Social and Intellectual Setting

Histories: General and Political

Ashley, M. *England in the Seventeenth Century* (Harmondsworth, 1952)

The Cambridge History of the British Empire I (Cambridge, 1929)

Clark, Sir G. N. *The Later Stuarts, 1660–1714* (Oxford, 1934)

Goodwin, A. (ed.) *The American and French Revolutions, 1763–93* (Cambridge, 1965)

Holdsworth, Sir W. S. *A History of English Law* (12 vols., 5th ed., London, 1931)

Horn, D. B. and Ransome, M. *English Historical Documents*, vol. x, *1714–83* (London, 1957)

Keir, Sir D. L. *The Constitutional History of Modern Britain, 1485–1937* (3rd ed., London, 1946)

Lecky, W. E. H. *A History of England in the Eighteenth Century* (rev. ed., 7 vols,. London, 1892)

Lindsay, J. O. (ed.) *The Old Regime, 1713–63* (Cambridge, 1957)

Macaulay, Lord T. B. *History of England from the Accession of James II* (5 vols., 1849–61; cd. T. F. Henderson, 5 vols., w.c., 1931)

Marshall, D. *Eighteenth-Century England* (London, 1962)

Namier, Sir L. B. *England in the Age of the American Revolution* (London, 1930; rev. 1962)

Ogg, D. *England in the Reign of Charles II* (2 vols., Oxford, rev. 1963)

Ogg, D. *England in the Reign of James II and William III* (Oxford, 1955)

Plumb, J. H. *England in the Eighteenth Century* (Pelican, 1950; rev. 1963)

Trevelyan, G. M. *England under Queene Anne* (3 vols., London, 1930–4)

Watson, J. S. *The Reign of George III, 1760–1815* (Oxford, 1960)

Williams, B. *The Whig Supremacy, 1714–1760* (Oxford, 1939; rev. 1962)

Williamson, J. A. *Cook and the Opening of the Pacific* (London, 1946)

Alden, J. R. *The American Revolution, 1775–1783* (London, 1954)

Butterfield, H. *George III, Lord North and the People, 1779–80* (London, 1949)

Feiling, K. G. *A History of the Tory Party, 1640–1714* (Oxford, 1924)

Feiling, K. G. *The Second Tory Party, 1714–1832* (London, 1938)

Namier, Sir L. B. *The Structure of Politics at the Accession of George III* (2 vols., London, 1929; 1957)

Pares, R. *King George III and the Politicians* (Oxford, 1953)

Petrie, Sir C. A. *The Jacobite Movement* (London, 1932; 1948)

Plumb, J. H. *Sir Robert Walpole* (2 vols., London, 1956–60)

Realey, C. B. *The Early Opposition to Sir Robert Walpole, 1720–27* (Lawrence, Kan., 1931)

Rudé, G. *Wilkes and Liberty* (Oxford, 1962)

Trevelyan, G. M. *The English Revolution, 1668–1689* (London, 1938)

Turberville, A. S. *The House of Lords in the 18th Century* (Oxford, 1927)

Walcott, R. *English Politics in the Early 18th Century* (Oxford, 1956)

Williams, E. N. *The Eighteenth-Century Constitution, 1688–1815* (Cambridge, 1960)

THE SOCIAL AND ECONOMIC BACKGROUND

Brown, T. *Amusements Serious and Comical* (1700–1702; ed. A. L. Hayward, London, 1927)

Defoe, D. *The Compleat English Tradesman* (London, 1725–7)

Defoe, D. *An Essay upon Projects* (1697; ed. H. Morley, London, 1889)

Defoe, D. *A Plan of the English Commerce* (1728; Oxford, 1927)

Howard, J. *The State of the Prisons* (1784; ed. K. Ruck, E.L., 1929)

Smith, Adam *The Wealth of Nations* (1776; ed. E. Cannan, 2 vols., London, 1904; in E.L., W.C. and Penguin)

Ward, E. *The London Spy* (1698–1700; ed. A. L. Hayward, London, 1927)

Allen, R. J. *The Clubs of Augustan London* (Cambridge, Mass., 1933)

Allen, R. J. *Life in Eighteenth-Century England* (Boston, 1941)

Ashton, J. *Social Life in the Reign of Queen Anne* (2 vols., London, 1882; 1925)

Ashton, T. S. *An Economic History of England. The Eighteenth Century* (London, 1955)

Ashton, T. S. *The Industrial Revolution* (London, 1948)

Besant, W. *London in the Eighteenth Century* (London, 1902)

Bowden, W. *Industrial Society in England towards the End of the Eighteenth Century* (New York, 1925)

Chancellor, E. B. *The Eighteenth Century in London* (London, 1920)

Clapham, Sir J. H. *The Bank of England* I (Cambridge, 1945)

Clark, Sir G. N. *The Idea of the Industrial Revolution* (Glasgow, 1953)

Clark, Sir G. N. *The Wealth of England from 1496 to 1760* (London, 1946)

Cole, G. D. H. and Postgate, R. *The Common People, 1746–1946* (4th ed., London, 1949)

Collins, A. S. *Authorship in the Days of Johnson* (London, 1928)

Cunnington, C. W. and P. *Handbook of English Costume in the Eighteenth Century* (London, 1957)

Curtler, W. H. R. *The Enclosure and Redistribution of Our Land* (Oxford, 1920)

Darby, H. C. (ed.) *An Historical Geography of England before 1800* (Cambridge, 1936)

Deane, P. *The First Industrial Revolution* (Cambridge, 1965)

Ellis, A. *The Penny Universities. A History of the Coffee-Houses* (London, 1956)

Ernle, Lord [R. E. Prothero] *English Farming, Past and Present* (London, 1912; rev. 1927)

George, M. D. (ed.) *England in Johnson's Day* (London, 1928)

George, M. D. *England in Transition* (London, 1931; Harmondsworth, 1953)

George, M. D. *English Social Life in the Eighteenth Century* (London, 1923)

George, M. D. *London Life in the XVIIIth Century* (London, 1925; rev. 1951; Harmondsworth, 1966)

Habbakuk, H. J. 'English Landownership, 1680–1740', in *Econ. Hist. Review* x (1939–40)

Habbakuk, H. J. 'English Population in the Eighteenth Century', in *Econ. Hist. Review*, 2nd series VI (1953)

Hamilton, H. *The Industrial Revolution in Scotland* (London, 1932)

Hammond, J. L. and B. *The Skilled Labourer, 1760–1832* (London, 1919)

Hammond, J. L. and B. *The Town Labourer, 1760–1832* (London, 1917)

Hammond, J. L. and B. *The Village Labourer, 1760–1832* (London, 1911)

Herbert, A. P. *Mr Gay's London* (London, 1948)

Humphreys, A. R. 'The Rights of Woman in the Age of Reason', in M.L.R. XLI (1946)

Lipson, E. *The Economic History of England* II–III (4th ed., London, 1947)

Mantoux, P. *The Industrial Revolution in the Eighteenth Century* (trans. M. Vernon, London, 1928; rev. 1935)

Marshall, D. *Dr Johnson's London* (New York, 1967)

Marshall, D. *English People in the Eighteenth Century* (London, 1956)

Marshall, D. *The English Poor in the Eighteenth Century* (London, 1926)

Mead, W. E. *The Grand Tour in the Eighteenth Century* (Boston, 1914)

Mingay, G. E. *English Landed Society in the Eighteenth Century* (London and Toronto, 1963)

Nef, J. U. *The Rise of the British Coal Industry* (2 vols., London, 1932)

Notestein, W. *English Folk* (London, 1938)

Patton, J. *The English Village, 1750–1850* (New York, 1919)

Plant, M. *The English Book Trade* (London, 1939)

Quinlan, M. J. *Victorian Prelude, A History of English Manners, 1700–1830* (New York, 1941)

Richardson, Sir A. E. *Georgian England* (London, 1931)

Sutherland, J. R. *Background for Queen Anne* (London, 1939)

Thomson, G. S. *Life in a Noble Household, 1641–1700* (London, 1937)

Thomson, G. S. *The Russells in Bloomsbury, 1669–1771* (London, 1940)

Timbs, J. *Clubs and Club Life in London* (London, 1872)

Traill, H. D. and Mann, J. S. (eds.) *Social England* IV–V (illustrated, London, 1903–4)

Trevelyan, G. M. *Illustrated English Social History* II–III (London, 1950–5; Harmondsworth, 1964)

Turberville, A. S. *English Men and Manners in the Eighteenth Century* (Oxford, 1926)

Turberville, A. S. (ed.) *Johnson's England* (2 vols., Oxford, 1933)

Warner, W. J. *The Wesleyan Movement in the Industrial Revolution* (London, 1930)

Webb, S. and B. *English Local Government* (7 vols., London, 1906–27)

Webb, S. and B. *History of Trade Unionism* (London, rev. 1920)

Whiteley, J. H. *Wesley's England* (London, 1938)

Wordsworth, C. *Social Life at the English Universities in the Eighteenth Century* (Cambridge, 1874)

DIARIES, LETTERS, MEMOIRS, TRAVELS

See under *Authors*: Boswell, Burney, Chesterfield, Cowper, Defoe, Evelyn, Gibbon, Gray, Johnson, Pepys, Swift, Walpole

Aubrey, J. *Brief Lives* ed. A. Clark (2 vols., Oxford, 1898); ed. A. Powell (London, 1949; rev. 1963; Harmondsworth, 1962)

Bayne-Powell, R. *Travellers in Eighteenth Century England* (London, 1951)

Burnet, G. *Bishop Burnet's History of His Own Time* ed. M. J. Routh (7 vols., Oxford, 1823)

Byrom, J. *Private Journals and Literary Remains* ed. R. Parkinson (2 vols., London, 1854–7); *Selections* ed. H. Talon (London, 1950)

Crabbe, G. *Life of the Rev. George Crabbe* (1834; W.C., 1932)

Fiennes, C. *The Journeys of Celia Fiennes* ed. C. Morris (London, 1947)

Fox, G. *The Journal of George Fox* (1694; ed. J. Nickalls, Cambridge, 1952; E.L., 1924)

Hearne, T. *Collections* [Diary, etc., 1705–35], ed. C. E. Doble and H. E. Salter (11 vols., Oxford, 1885–1918)

Hervey, Lord John, *Memoirs of the Reign of King George II* ed. R. Sedgwick (3 vols., London, 1931)

Hickey, W. *Memoirs* ed. A Spencer (4 vols., London, 1913; 1949)

Lewis, W. S. (ed.) *Three Tours through London in the Years 1748, 1776, 1797* (New Haven, 1941)

Montagu, Lady M. W. *Complete Letters*, ed. R. Halsband (3 vols., Oxford, 1965–7); selection in E.L. See Life by R. Halsband (Oxford, 1956)

Moritz, C. P. *Travels in England in 1782* (1795; ed. P. Matheson, London, 1924)

Percy, Thomas (Bishop) *The Percy Letters*, ed. D. Nichol Smith and C. Brooks (Louisiana, 1944 – in progress)

Ryder, Dudley, *Diary, 1715–1716*, ed. W. Matthews (London, 1939)

Smith, D. Nichol (ed.) *Characters from the Histories and Memoirs of the Seventeenth Century* (Oxford, 1918)

Spence, J. *Observations, Anecdotes, etc.* ed. J. M. Osborn (2 vols., Oxford, 1966)

Thrale, Mrs H. L. *Thraliana. The Diary of Mrs Hester Lynch Thrale (later Piozzi), 1776–1809*, ed. K. C. Balderston (2 vols., Oxford, 1942)

Walpole, H. *Memoirs of the Last Ten Years of the Reign of George II* ed. Lord Holland (2 vols., London, 1822, etc.)

Walpole, H. *Memoirs of the Reign of George III* ed. G. F. R. Barker (4 vols., London, 1894)

Wendeborn, G. F. A. *A View of England towards the Close of the Eighteenth Century* (2 vols., London, 1791)

Wesley, J. *Journal*, ed. N. Curnock (8 vols., London, 1909–16; in E.L., 6 vols., 1902)

Wesley, J. *Letters*, ed. J. Telford (8 vols., London, 1931)

Wood, Anthony à, *Life and Times, 1632–95* ed. A Clark (5 vols., Oxford, 1891–1900)

Woodforde, J. *The Diary of a Country Parson, 1758–1802* ed. J. D. Beresford (5 vols., London, 1924–31; abr., W.C., 1935)

Young, A. *The Farmer's Tour Through the East of England* (4 vols., London, 1771)

Young, A. *A Six Months' Tour through the North of England* (4 vols., London, 1770)

Young, A. *A Six Weeks' Tour through the Southern Counties of England and Wales* (London, 1768; 1772)

PHILOSOPHY, RELIGION, AND EDUCATION

See under *Authors*: Berkeley, Burke, Hume, Law, Locke, Shaftesbury
Butler, J. *The Analogy of Religion* (1736; in E.L. and W.C.)
Mandeville, B. *The Fable of the Bees* (1714–29; ed. F. B. Kaye, 2 vols., Oxford, 1924)

Bredvold, L. I. *The Intellectual Milieu of John Dryden* (Ann Arbor, 1934; 1956)

Bredvold, L. I. *The Natural History of Sensibility* (Detroit, 1962)

Bury, J. B. *The Idea of Progress* (London, 1920)

Cassirer, E. *The Philosophy of the Enlightenment* (Princeton, 1951)

Clark, Sir G. N. *The Seventeenth Century* (Oxford, 1929; rev. 1947)

Cragg, G. R. *Reason and Authority in the Eighteenth Century* (Cambridge, 1964)

Fairchild, H. N. *The Noble Savage* (New York, 1928)

Hazard, P. *European Thought in the Eighteenth Century* (London, 1954; Harmondsworth, 1965)

Hearnshaw, F. J. C. (ed.) *The Social and Political Ideas of . . . the Augustan Age* (London, 1928)

Jones, R. F. *Ancients and Moderns. A Study of the Background of the Battle of the Books* (St Louis, Missouri, 1936)

Laski, H. J. *Political Thought in England: Locke to Bentham* (London, 1920)

Lovejoy, A. O. *Essays in the History of Ideas* (Baltimore, 1952)

Lovejoy, A. O. *The Great Chain of Being* (Cambridge, Mass., 1936)

Lovejoy, A. O. *Reflections on Human Nature* (Baltimore, 1961)

MacLean, K. *John Locke and English Literature of the Eighteenth Century* (New Haven, 1936)

Macpherson, C. B. *The Political Theory of Progressive Individualism: Hobbes to Locke* (Oxford, 1962)

Mazzeo, J. A. (ed.) *Reason and the Imagination: Studies in the History of Ideas, 1600–1800* (New York, 1962)

Mossner, E. C. *Bishop Butler and the Age of Reason* (London, 1936)

Price, M. *To the Palace of Wisdom: Studies in Order and Energy from Dryden to Blake* (New York, 1964)

Smith, P. *A History of Modern Culture* II (New York, 1934)

Stephen, Sir L. *History of English Thought in the Eighteenth Century* (2 vols., London, 1876–80)

Willey, B. *The Seventeenth-Century Background* (London, 1934)

Willey, B. *The Eighteenth-Century Background* (London, 1940)

Abbey, C. J. and Overton, J. H. *The English Church in the Eighteenth Century* (2 vols., London, 1878; rev. 1896)

Baumer, F. L. *Religion and the Rise of Scepticism* (New York, 1960)

Clark, H. W. *History of English Nonconformity* II (London, 1911)

Clarke, W. K. L. *Eighteenth Century Piety* (London, 1944)

Coomer, D. *English Dissent under the Early Hanoverians* (London, 1946)

Cragg, G. R. *The Church and the Age of Reason, 1648–1789* (Harmondsworth, repr. 1970)

Cragg, G. R. *From Puritanism to the Age of Reason* (Cambridge, 1950)

Creed, J. M. and Smith, J. S. B. (eds.) *Religious Thought in the Eighteenth Century* (Cambridge, 1934)

Jordan, W. K. *The Development of Religious Toleration in England* IV (London, 1940)

Knox, R. A. *Enthusiasm. A Chapter in the History of Religion* (Oxford, 1950)

Shepherd, T. B. *Methodism and the Literature of the Eighteenth Century* (London, 1940)

Sykes, N. *Church and State in England in the XVIIIth Century* (Cambridge, 1934)

Davis, H. *Stella. A Gentlewoman of the 18th Century* (New York, 1942)

Douglas, D. C. *English Scholars, 1660–1730* (London, 1939; rev. 1951)

Jones, M. G. *The Charity School Movement* (Cambridge, 1938)

Mallet, Sir C. E. *History of the University of Oxford* II–III (London, 1924–7)

Mullinger, J. B. *The University of Cambridge* III (Cambridge, 1911)

Phillips, M. and Tomkinson, W. S. *English Women in Life and Letters* (Oxford, 1926)

Winstanley, D. A. *The University of Cambridge in the Eighteenth Century* (Cambridge, 1922)

Wordsworth, C. *Scholae Academicae. The Studies at English Universities in the Eighteenth Century* (Cambridge, 1877)

SCIENCE

Bennett, J. 'An Aspect of 17th-Century Prose', in R.E.S. XVII (1941)

Burtt, E. A. *The Metaphysical Foundations of Modern Physical Science* (London, 1925)

Bush, D. *Science and English Poetry* (New York, 1950)

Butterfield, H. *The Origins of Modern Science* (London, 1949)

Clark, Sir G. N. *Science and Social Welfare in the Age of Newton* (Oxford, 1937)

Dampier, Sir W. C. *A History of Science and its Relations with Philosophy and Religion* (3rd ed., Cambridge, 1942)

Davie, D. *The Language of Science and the Language of Literature, 1700–1740* (London, 1963)

'Espinasse, M. *Robert Hooke* (London, 1956)

Evans, B. I. *Literature and Science* (London, 1954)

Holmyard, E. J. 'Science, Mathematics, and Astronomy', in *Johnson's England* II (Oxford, 1933)

Jones, R. F. 'The Background of the Attack on Science in the Age of Pope', in *Pope and his Contemporaries*, ed. J. L. Clifford and L. A. Landa (Oxford, 1949)

Jones, R. F. 'Science and English Prose Style', in P.M.L.A. XLV (1930)

MacLean, K. *John Locke and English Literature of the Eighteenth Century* (New Haven, 1936)

Nicolson, M. H. *Science and Imagination* (Ithaca, 1956)

Nicolson, M. H. *Newton Demands the Muse* (Princeton, 1946)

Nicolson, M. H. *A World in the Moon. A Study of the Changing Attitudes towards the Moon.* (Northampton, Mass., 1936)

Raven, C. E. *John Ray, Naturalist* (Cambridge, 1942)

Singer, C. et al. (eds.) *A History of Technology*, III, *From the Renaissance to the Industrial Revolution* (Oxford, 1957)

Sprat, T. *A History of the Royal Society* (London, 1667; ed. J. I. Cope and H. W. Jones, St Louis, Mo., 1958)

Stimson, D. *Scientists and Amateurs. A History of the Royal Society* (London, 1949)

Wheatley, H. B. *The Early History of the Royal Society* (London, 1905)

Whitehead, A. N. *Science and the Modern World* (Cambridge, 1926)

Willey, B. *The Seventeenth-Century Background* (London, 1934)

Willey, B. *The Eighteenth-Century Background* (London, 1940)

Wolf, A. *A History of Science, Technology and Philosophy in the Eighteenth Century* (rev. D. McKie, London, 1952)

ART AND ARCHITECTURE

See under *Authors*: Burke, Hogarth

Campbell, C. *Vitruvius Britannicus; or, the British Architect* (3 vols., London, 1717–25)

Gilpin, W. *Three Essays: on Picturesque Beauty; on Picturesque Travel; and on Sketching Landscape* (London, 1792)

Repton, H. *Observations on the Theory and Practice of Landscape Gardening* (London, 1803)

Reynolds, Sir J. *Discourses* (1769–91; ed. A Dobson, W.C., 1907; ed. R. W. Wark, San Marino, 1959)

Richardson, J. *Essays on the Theory of Painting* (London, 1715; 1725)

Allen, B. S. *Tides in English Taste, 1619–1800* (2 vols., Cambridge, Mass., 1937)

Appleton, W. W. *A Cycle of Cathay. The Chinese Vogue in England* (New York, 1951)

Carritt, E. F. (ed.) *A Calendar of British Taste* (London, 1949)

Clark, Sir K. *The Gothic Revival* (London, 1928; rev. 1950)

Steegman, J. *The Rule of Taste from George I to George IV* (London, 1936)

Esdaile, K. A. *English Church Monuments* (London, 1946)

Esdaile, K. A. *English Monumental Sculpture* (London, 1927)

George, M. D. *English Political Caricature* (2 vols., Oxford, 1959)

Grundy, C. R. *English Art in the Eighteenth Century* (London, 1928)

Klingender, F. D. *Art and the Industrial Revolution* (London, 1947)

Manwaring, E. W. *Italian Landscape in Eighteenth-Century England* (New York, 1925)

Tinker, C. B. *Painter and Poet. Studies in the Literary Relations of English Painting* (Cambridge, Mass., 1938)

Waterhouse, E. K. *Painting in Britain, 1530–1790* (Harmondsworth, 1953)

Waterhouse, E. K. *Reynolds* (London, 1941)

Whinney, M. and Millar, O. *English Art, 1625–1714* (Oxford History of English Art, VIII, Oxford, 1957)

Williams, I. A. *Early English Watercolours* (London, 1952)

Blomfield, Sir R. A. *A History of Renaissance Architecture in England, 1500–1800* (2 vols., London, 1897)

Bolton, A. T. *The Architecture of Robert and James Adam* (2 vols., London, 1922)

Downes, K. *Hawksmoor* (London, 1959)

Gotch, J. A. *The English Home from Charles I to George IV* (London, 1918)

Jourdain, M. *The Work of William Kent* (London, 1948)

Lees-Milne, J. *The Age of Adam* (London, 1947)

Little, B. *The Building of Bath* (London, 1947)

Richardson, Sir A. E. *An Introduction to Georgian Architecture* (London, 1949)

Scott, G. *The Architecture of Humanism* (London, 1914)

Smith, W. H. *Architecture in English Fiction* (New Haven, 1934)

Summerson, J. N. *Architecture in Britain, 1530–1830* (Harmondsworth, 1953)

Summerson, J. N. *Georgian London* (London, 1945)

Summerson, J. N. *Sir Christopher Wren* (London, 1953)

Tipping, H. A. *English Homes*, Periods IV–VI (London, 1921–8)

Whiffen, M. *Stuart and Georgian Churches* (London, 1947)

Clark, H. F. *The English Landscape Garden* (London, 1948)

Hussey, C. *The Picturesque* (London, 1927)

Stroud, D. *Capability Brown* (London, 1950)

Edwards, R. and Jourdain, M. *Georgian Cabinet-Makers* (London, 1944)

Jourdain, M. and Rose, F. *English Furniture. The Georgian Period, 1750–1830* (London, 1953)

Jourdain, M. *English Interior Decoration, 1500–1830* (London, 1950)

PART FOUR

Lenygon, F. *Decoration in England, 1640–1760* (London, rev. 1927)
Lenygon, F. *Furniture in England, 1660–1760* (London, 1920)
MacQuoid, P. *A History of English Furniture* II–IV (London, 1938)

Hadow, Sir W. (ed.) *The Oxford History of Music* III–V (Oxford, 1902–4)
Lonsdale, R. *Dr Charles Burney* (Oxford, 1965)
Scholes, P. A. *The Great Dr Burney* (2 vols., London, 1948)

The Literature

BIBLIOGRAPHIES

Annual Bibliography of English Language and Literature (Cambridge, annually since 1921)
Bateson, F. (ed.) *The Cambridge Bibliography of English Literature* II–V (Cambridge, 1940, 1957)
Crane, R. S., *et al. English Literature, 1660–1800* (4 vols., Princeton, 1950–62. Annually in *P.Q.*)
Dyson, H. V. D. and Butt, J. *Augustans and Romantics, 1689–1830* (London, 1940; rev. 1951)
Horne, C. J. in *The Pelican Guide to English Literature* IV (1957; rev. 1968)
Pinto, V. de S. *The English Renaissance, 1510–1688* (London, 1938; rev. 1951)
Tobin, J. E. *Eighteenth-Century Literature and its Cultural Background* (New York, 1939)
The Year's Work in English Studies (London, annually since 1919)

GENERAL STUDIES

The Age of Johnson, Essays presented to C. B. Tinker (New Haven, 1949)
Beljame, A. *Men of Letters and the English Public, 1660–1744* (Paris, 1881; trans. E. O. Lorimer, ed. N. Dobrée, London, 1948)
Boys, R. C. (ed.) *Studies in the Literature of the Augustan Age* (Ann Arbor, 1952)
Bredvold, L. I. 'The Literature of the Restoration and the Eighteenth Century', in *A History of English Literature* ed. H. Craig (New York, 1950)
Burton, K. M. P. *Restoration Literature* (London, 1958)
Butt, J. *The Augustan Age* (London, 1950)
Camden, C. (ed.) *Restoration and Eighteenth-Century Literature* (Chicago, 1963)
Clifford, J. L. (ed.) *Eighteenth Century English Literature. Modern Essays in Criticism* (New York, 1959)
Clifford, J. L. and Landa, L. A. (eds.) *Pope and his Contemporaries. Essays presented to George Sherburn* (Oxford, 1949)

Dobrée, B. *English Literature in the Early Eighteenth Century, 1700–1740* (Oxford History of English Literature, VII, Oxford, 1959)

Elton, O. *A Survey of English Literature, 1730–1780* (2 vols., London, 1928)

Essays on the Eighteenth Century presented to David Nichol Smith (Oxford, 1945)

Ford, B. (ed.) *The Pelican Guide to English Literature* v (1957; rev. 1968)

Fussell, P. *The Rhetorical World of Augustan Humanism: Ethics and Imagery from Swift to Burke* (Oxford, 1965)

Hilles, F. W. and Bloom, H. (eds.) *From Sensibility to Romanticism* (New York, 1965)

Humphreys, A. R. *The Augustan World* (London, 1954)

Jones, R. F. *et al. The Seventeenth Century* (Stanford, 1951)

Ker, W. P. 'The Eighteenth Century', in *Collected Essays* (London, 1925)

Nichols, J. *Illustrations of the Literary History of the Eighteenth Century* (6 vols., London, 1817–31)

Nichols, L. *Literary Anecdotes of the Eighteenth Century* (9 vols., London, 1812–15)

Phelps, W. L. *The Beginnings of the English Romantic Movement* (Boston, 1893)

Saintsbury, G. *The Peace of the Augustans* (London, 1916; w.c., 1946)

Seventeenth Century Studies Presented to Sir Herbert Grierson (Oxford, 1938)

Sherburn, G. 'The Restoration and Eighteenth Century, 1660–1789', in *A Literary History of England*, ed.. A. C. Baugh (New York, 1948; London, 1950)

Stephen, Sir L. *English Literature and Society in the Eighteenth Century* (London, 1904)

Tillotson, G. *Augustan Studies* (London, 1961)

Tinker, C. B. *The Salon and English Letters* (New York, 1915)

Ward, Sir A. W. and Waller, A. R. (eds.) *The Cambridge History of English Literature* VIII–XI (Cambridge, 1912–14)

Wedgwood, C. V. *Seventeenth Century English Literature* (London, 1950)

Wilson, J. H. *The Court Wits of the Restoration* (Princeton, 1948)

THE LANGUAGE

Adams, E. N. *Old English Scholarship in England, 1566–1800* (New Haven, 1917)

Arthos, J. *The Language of Natural Description in Eighteenth-Century Poetry* (Ann Arbor, 1949)

Baugh, A. C. *A History of the English Language* (New York, 1935)

Dobson, E. J. *English Pronunciation, 1500–1700* (2 vols., Oxford, 1957)

Johnson, S. *Preface to the English Dictionary* (1755; repr. in *Prose and Poetry*, ed. M. Wilson, London, 1950)

Murray, Sir J. A. H. *The Evolution of English Lexicography* (Oxford, 1900)

Serjeantson, M. S. *A History of Foreign Words in English* (London, 1935)

Sledd, J. H. and Gwin, J. K. *Dr Johnson's Dictionary* (Chicago, 1955)

Starnes, W. T. de and Noyes, G. E. *The English Dictionary from Cawdrey to Johnson, 1604–1755* (Chapel Hill, 1946)

Tillotson, G. *Augustan Poetic Diction* (London, 1964)

Tucker, S. I. *Protean Shape: Studies in Eighteenth-Century Vocabulary and Usage* (London, 1967)

Vallins, G. H. *The Wesleys and the English Language* (London, 1957)

Wyld, H. C. *A History of Modern Colloquial English* (3rd ed., Oxford, 1936)

Wyld, H. C. *Studies in English Rhymes* (London, 1923)

POETRY

Aubin, R. A. *Topographical Poetry in Eighteenth-Century England* (New York, 1936)

Beers, H. A. *A History of English Romanticism in the Eighteenth Century* (New York, 1899)

Bond, R. P. *English Burlesque Poetry, 1700–1750* (Cambridge, Mass., 1932)

Brooks, H. F. 'The "Imitation" in English Poetry', in R.E.S. XXV (1949)

Brown, W. C. *The Triumph of Form. A Study of the Later Masters of the Heroic Couplet* (Chapel Hall, 1948)

Bush, D. *Mythology and the Romantic Tradition in English Poetry* (Cambridge, Mass., 1937; New York, 1957)

Bush, D. *Science and English Poetry* (New York, 1950)

Chapin, C. F. *Personification in Eighteenth-Century English Poetry* (New York, 1955)

Courthope, W. J. *A History of English Poetry* III–IV (London, 1903–5)

Davie, D. *Articulate Energy: An Inquiry into the Syntax of English Poetry* (London, 1955)

Davie, D. *Purity of Diction in English Verse* (London, 1952)

Deane, C. V. *Aspects of Eighteenth Century Nature Poetry* (Oxford, 1935)

de Haas, C. E. *Nature and the Country in English Poetry of the First Half of the Eighteenth Century* (Amsterdam, 1928)

Doughty, O. *English Lyric in the Age of Reason* (London, 1922)

Durling, D. L. *Georgic Tradition in English Poetry* (New York, 1935)

Fairchild, H. N. *Religious Trends in English Poetry* I–II (New York, 1939–42)

Goad, C. M. *Horace in the English Literature of the Eighteenth Century* (New Haven, 1918)

Havens, R. D. *The Influence of Milton on English Poetry* (Cambridge, Mass., 1922)

Humphreys, A. R. 'A Classical Education and Eighteenth-Century Poetry', in *Scrutiny* VIII (Cambridge, 1939)

Jack, I. *Augustan Satire, 1660–1750* (Oxford, 1952)

Johnson, S. *Lives of the English Poets* (1779–81; ed. G. B. Hill, 3 vols., Oxford, 1905; in w.c.)

Jones, R. F. 'Eclogue Types in English Poetry of the Eighteenth Century', in J.E.G.P. XXIV (1925)

Leavis, F. R. *Revaluation* (London, 1936; Harmondsworth, 1964)

Lowes, J. L. *Convention and Revolt in Poetry* (Boston, 1919)

Moore, C. A. 'The Return to Nature', in *Backgrounds of English Literature, 1700–1760* (Minneapolis, 1953)

Moore, C. A. 'Shaftesbury and the Ethical Poets in England', in *Backgrounds of English Literature, 1700–1760* (Minneapolis, 1953)

Nitchie, E. *Virgil and the English Poets* (New York, 1919)

Peltz, C. W. 'The Neo-Classic Lyric, 1660–1725', in E.L.H. XI (1944)

Pinto, V. de S. *The Restoration Court Poets* (1965)

Previté-Orton, C. W. *Political Satire in English Poetry* (Cambridge, 1910)

Randolph, M. C. 'The Structural Design of the Formal Verse Satire', in P.Q. XXI (1942)

Reed, A. L. *The Background of Gray's Elegy. A Study in the Taste for Melancholy Poetry, 1700–1751* (New York, 1924)

Shuster, G. N. *The English Ode from Milton to Keats* (New York, 1940)

Smith, D. Nichol, *Some Observations on Eighteenth-Century Poetry* (London, 1937)

Snyder, E. D. *The Celtic Revival in English Literature, 1700–1800* (Cambridge, Mass., 1923)

Spacks, P. M. *The Poetry of Vision* (Cambridge, Mass., 1966)

Stern, B. H. *The Rise of Romantic Hellenism in English Literature, 1732–1786* (Menasha, 1940)

Sutherland, J. R. *A Preface to Eighteenth-Century Poetry* (Oxford, 1948)

Tillotson, G. *Essays in Criticism and Research* (Cambridge, 1942)

Tillotson, G. *Augustan Poetic Diction* (London, 1964)

Van Tieghem, P. *Le Preromantisme* (2 vols., Paris, 1924–30)

Wasserman, E. R. *Elizabethan Poetry in the Eighteenth Century* (Urbana, 1949)

Wedgwood, C. V. *Poetry and Politics under the Stuarts* (Cambridge, 1960)

Williams, G. G. 'The Beginnings of Nature Poetry in the Eighteenth Century', in S.P. XXVII (1930)

THE NOVEL

Alter, R. *Rogue's Progress: Studies in the Picaresque Novel* (Cambridge, Mass., 1964)

Baker, E. A. *The History of the English Novel* III–V (London, 1929–30)

Booth, W. C. *The Rhetoric of Fiction* (Chicago, 1961)

Conant, M. P. *The Oriental Tale in the Eighteenth Century* (New York, 1908)

Foster, J. R. *History of the Pre-Romantic Novel* (New York, 1949)

Gove, P. B. *The Imaginary Voyage in Prose Fiction, 1700–1800* (New York, 1941)

Hazlitt, W. 'On the English Novelists', in *The English Comic Writers* (London, 1819; in E.L. and W.C.)

Kettle, A. *An Introduction to the English Novel* I (London, 1951)

Leavis, F. R. *The Great Tradition* (London, 1948; Harmondsworth, 1962)

Leavis, Q. D. *Fiction and the Reading Public* (London, 1932)

MacCarthy, B. G. *The Later Women Novelists, 1744–1818* (Oxford, 1947)

MacCarthy, B. G. *Women Writers. Their Contribution to the English Novel, 1621–1744* (Oxford, 1944)

McKillop, Alan Dugald, *The Early Masters of English Fiction* (Lawrence, Kansas, 1956)

Morgan, C. E. *The Rise of the Novel of Manners* (New York, 1911)

Scott, Sir W. *Lives of the English Novelists* (London, 1821–4; in W.C.)

Singer, G. F. *The Epistolary Novel* (Philadelphia, 1933)

Spector, R. D. (ed.) *Essays on the Eighteenth-Century Novel* (Bloomington and London, 1965)

Thackeray, W. M. *The English Humorists of the Eighteenth Century* (London, 1853; ed. W. L. Phelps, London, 1913; in E.L.)

Tompkins, J. M. S. *The Popular Novel in England* (London, 1932)

Varma, D. P. *The Gothic Flame: Being the History of the Gothic Novel in England* (London, 1957)

Van Ghent, D. *The English Novel: Form and Function* (New York, 1953)

Watt, I. *The Rise of the Novel: Studies in Defoe, Richardson and Fielding* (London, 1957; Harmondsworth, 1963)

PROSE

Baldwin, E. C. 'The Relation of the Seventeenth-Century Character to the Periodical Essay', in P.M.L.A. XIX (1904)

Bourne, H. R. F. *English Newspapers* (2 vols., London, 1887)

Bond, R. P. (ed.) *Studies in the Early English Periodical* (Chapel Hill, 1957)

Carlson, C. L. *The First Magazine. A History of 'The Gentleman's Magazine'* (Providence, 1938)

Crane, R. S. and Kaye, F. B. *A Census of British Newspapers and Periodicals, 1620–1800* (Chapel Hill, 1927)

Cranfield, G. A. *The Development of the Provincial Newspaper, 1700–1760* (Oxford, 1962)

Drake, N. *Essays, . . . Illustrative of the Tatler, Spectator, and Guardian* (3 vols., London, 1805)

Dyson, A. E. *The Crazy Fabric: Essays in Irony* (London, 1965)

Graham, W. *The Beginnings of English Literary Periodicals* (Oxford, 1926)

Graham, W. *English Literary Periodicals* (New York, 1930)

Hazlitt, W. 'On the Periodical Essayists', in *The English Comic Writers* (London, 1819; in E.L. and W.C.)

Marr, G. S. *The Periodical Essayists of the Eighteenth Century* (London, 1923)

Nangle, B. C. *The Monthly Review (1749–1789)* (Oxford, 1934)

Walker, H. *The English Essay and Essayists* (London, 1915)

Wiles, R. M. *Freshest Advices: Early Provincial Newspapers in England* (Columbus, Ohio, 1965)

Evans, B. 'Dr Johnson's Theory of Biography', in R.E.S. x (1934)

Longaker, M. *English Biography in the Eighteenth Century* (Philadelphia, 1931)

Major, J. C. *The Role of Personal Memoirs in English Biography and Novel* (Philadelphia, 1935)

Pinto, V. de S. (ed.) *English Biography in the Seventeenth Century* (London, 1951)

Shumaker, W. *English Autobiography* (Berkeley and Los Angeles, 1954)

Stauffer, D. A. *The Art of Biography in Eighteenth-Century England* (2 vols., Princeton, 1941)

Stauffer, D. A. *English Biography before 1700* (Cambridge, Mass., 1930)

Hanson, L. W. *Govrnment and the Press, 1695–1763* (Oxford, 1936)

Millar, J. H. *Scottish Prose of the Seventeenth and Eighteenth Centuries* (Glasgow, 1912)

Sutherland, J. R. *On English Prose* (Toronto, 1957)

Sutherland, J. R. 'Some Aspects of Eighteenth-Century Prose', in *Essays on the Eighteenth Century Presented to David Nichol Smith* (Oxford, 1945)

Thomson, J. A. K. *Classical Influences on English Prose* (London, 1956)

DRAMA

Alleman, G. S. *Matrimonial Law and the Materials of Restoration Comedy* (Wallingford, Penn., 1942)

Anthony, R. *The Jeremy Collier Stage Controversy* (Milwaukee, 1937)

Avery, E. L., *et al.* (eds.) *The London Stage, 1600–1800. A Calendar of Plays, etc.* (Carbondale, Ill., 1960 – in progress)

Baker, D. E., Reed, I., and Jones, S. *Biographia Dramatica* (3 vols., London, 1912)

Bateson, F. W. *English Comic Drama, 1700–1750* (Oxford, 1929)

Bernbaum, E. *The Drama of Sensibility* (Boston, 1915)

Boas, F. S. *An Introduction to Eighteenth Century Drama* (Oxford, 1953)

Boswell, E. *The Restoration Court Stage* (Cambridge, Mass., 1932)

Brown, J. R. and Harris, B. (eds.) *Restoration Theatre* (London, 1965)

Chase, L. N. *The English Heroic Play* (New York, 1903)

Cibber, C. *An Apology for the Life of Mr Colley Cibber* (1740; ed. R. W. Lowe, 2 vols., London, 1889; in E.L.)

Deane, C. V. *Dramatic Theory and the Rhymed Heroic Play* (London, 1931)

Dobrée, B. *Restoration Comedy* (Oxford, 1924)

Dobrée, B. *Restoration Tragedy* (Oxford, 1929)

Fujimura, T. H. *The Restoration Comedy of Wit* (Princeton, 1953)

Genest, J. *Some Account of the English Stage from 1660* (10 vols., Bath, 1832)

Gray, C. H. *Theatrical Criticism in London to 1795* (New York, 1931)

Green, C. C. *The Neo-Classic Theory of Tragedy in England during the Eighteenth Century* (Cambridge, Mass., 1934)

Harbage, A. *Cavalier Drama* (New York, 1936)

Hazlitt, W. *The English Comic Writers* London, 1819; in E.L. and W.C.)

Hogan, C. B. *Shakespeare in the Theatre, 1701–1800* (2 vols., Oxford, 1952–57)

Hotson, L. *The Commonwealth and Restoration Stage* (Cambridge, Mass., 1928)

Hughes, L. A. *A Century of English Farce* (Princeton, 1956)

Hunt, J. L. 'Biographical and Critical Notices', in *The Dramatic Works of Wycherley, Congreve, Vanbrugh and Farquhar* (London, 1841)

Knights, L. C. 'Restoration Comedy: The Reality and the Myth', in *Explorations* (London, 1946)

Krutch, J. W. *Comedy and Conscience after the Restoration* (New York, 1924; rev. 1949)

Lamb, C. 'On the Artificial Comedy of the Last Century', in *Essays of Elia* (London, 1821; in E.L. and W.C.)

Langbaine, G. *An Account of the English Dramatic Poets* (Oxford, 1691)

Leech, C. 'Restoration Comedy. The Earlier Phase', in *Essays in Criticism* I (1951)

Leech, C. 'Restoration Tragedy. A Reconstruction', in *Durham Univ. Journal* (1950)

Loftis, J. *Comedy and Society from Congreve to Fielding* (Stanford, 1959)

Loftis, J. *The Politics of Drama in Augustan England* (Oxford, 1963)

Loftis, J. (ed.) *Restoration Drama: Modern Essays in Criticism* (New York, 1966)

Lynch, K. M. *The Social Mode of Restoration Comedy* (New York, 1926)

Macaulay, Lord T. B. 'The Comic Dramatists of the Restoration', in *Critical and Historical Essays* (London, 1843; in E.L.)

MacMillan, D. (ed.) *Catalogue of the Larpent Plays in the Huntingdon Library* (San Marino, Cal., 1939)

MacMillan, D. (ed.) *Drury Lane Calendar, 1747–1776* (Oxford, 1938)

Meredith, G. *An Essay on Comedy* (London, 1877; 1897)

Nicholl, A. *A History of Early Eighteenth Century Drama, 1700–1750* (Cambridge, 1925; rev. 1952)

Nicholl, A. *A History of Late Eighteenth Century Drama, 1750–1800* (Cambridge, 1927; rev. 1952)

Nicoll, A. *A History of Restoration Drama, 1660–1700* (Cambridge, 1923; rev. 1952)

Odell, G. C. D. *Shakespeare from Betterton to Irving* (2 vols., London, 1920)

Palmer, J. *The Comedy of Manners* (London, 1913)

Perry, H. T. E. *The Comic Spirit and Restoration Drama* (New Haven, 1925)

Rosenfeld, S. *Strolling Players and Drama in the Provinces, 1660–1765* (Cambridge, 1939)

Sherbo, A. *English Sentimental Drama* (East Lansing, 1957)

Smith, J. H. *The Gay Couple in Restoration Comedy* (Cambridge, Mass., 1948)

Southern, R. *The Georgian Playhouse* (London, 1948)

Spencer, H. *Shakespeare Improved. The Restoration Versions* (Cambridge, Mass., 1927)

Summers, M. *The Restoration Theatre* (London, 1934)

Sutherland, J. R. 'Shakespeare's Imitators in the Eighteenth Century', in M.L.R. XXVIII (1933)

Wilcox, J. *The Relation of Molière to Restoration Comedy* (New York, 1938)

Wilson, J. H. *The Influence of Beaumont and Fletcher on Restoration Drama* (Columbus, Ohio, 1928)

CRITICISM AND THEORY

Atkins, J. W. H. *English Literary Criticism: 17th and 18th Centuries* (London, 1951)

Bate, W. J. *From Classic to Romantic* (Cambridge, Mass., 1946)

Bate, W. J. 'The Sympathetic Imagination in Eighteenth-Century English Criticism', in E.L.H. XII (1945)

Bentley, G. E. *Shakespeare and Jonson: Their Reputations in the Seventeenth Century Compared* (2 vols., Chicago, 1945)

Bosker, A. *Literary Criticism in the Age of Johnson* (Groningen, 1930; rev. 1954)

Brown, J. E. *The Critical Opinions of Samuel Johnson* (Princeton, 1926)

Brown, S. G. 'Dr Johnson, Poetry, and Imagination', in *Neophilologus* XXIII (1938)

Bullitt, J. and Bate, W. J. 'The Distinctions between Fancy and Imagination in Eighteenth-Century English Criticism', in *Modern Language Notes* LX (1945)

Clark, A. F. B. *Boileau and the French Classical Critics in England, 1660–1830* (Paris, 1925)

Congleton, J. E. 'Theories of Pastoral Poetry in England, 1684–1717', in s.p. XLI (1944)

Crane, R. S. (ed.) *Critics and Criticism, Ancient and Modern* (Chicago, 1952)

Davies, H. S. (ed.) *The Poets and their Critics* (Harmondsworth, 1943)

de Maar, H. G. *A History of Modern English Romanticism* I (London, 1924)

Dennis, J. *The Critical Works*, ed. E. N. Hooker (2 vols., Baltimore, 1939–43)

Draper, J. W. *Eighteenth Century English Aesthetics: A Bibliography* (Heidelberg, 1931)

Dryden, J. *Of Dramatic Poesy and Other Essays*, ed. G. Watson (2 vols., E.L., 1962)

Dryden, J. *Essays*, ed. W. P. Ker (2 vols., Oxford, 1900)

Durham, W. H. (ed.) *Critical Essays of the Eighteenth Century, 1700–1725* (New Haven, 1915)

Elledge, S. (ed.) *Eighteenth Century Critical Essays* (2 vols., Ithaca, 1961)

Empson, W. 'Wit in the *Essay on Criticism*', in *The Structure of Complex Words* (London, 1951)

Russell, P. *The Rhetorical World of Augustan Humanism* (Oxford, 1965)

Gallaway, F. *Reason, Rule, and Revolt in English Classicism* (New York, 1940)

Goad, C. M. *Horace in the English Literature of the Eighteenth Century* (New Haven, 1918)

Green, F. C. *Minuet: A Critical Survey of French and English Literary Ideas in the Eighteenth Century* (London, 1935)

Hagstrum, J. H. *The Sister Arts. The Tradition of Literary Pictorialism and English Poetry from Dryden to Gray* (Chicago, 1958)

Havens, R. D. 'Johnson's Distrust of the Imagination', in E.L.H. X (1943)

Henn, T. R. *Longinus and English Criticism* (Cambridge, 1934)

Herrick, M. T. *The Poetics of Aristotle in England* (New Haven, 1930)

Johnson, S. *Lives of the English Poets* (1779–81; ed. G. B. Hill, 3 vols., Oxford, 1905; in E.L. and W.C.)

Jones, E. D. (ed.) *English Critical Essays* (W.C., 1922)

Leavis, F. R. 'Johnson and Augustanism', in *The Common Pursuit* (London, 1952; Harmondsworth, 1962)

Lovejoy, A. O. 'The Meaning of Romanticism', in *Journey of the History of Ideas* II (1941)

Miller, G. M. *The Historical Point of View in English Literary Criticism from 1570–1770* (Heidelberg, 1913)

Monk, S. H. *The Sublime: A Study of Critical Theories in XVIII-Century England* (New York, 1935)

Needham, H. A. (ed.) *Taste and Criticism in the Eighteenth Century* (London, 1952)

Raleigh, Sir W. (ed.) *Johnson on Shakespeare* (London, 1908)

Robertson, J. G. *Studies in the Genesis of Romantic Theory in the Eighteenth Century* (Cambridge, 1923)

Robinson, H. S. *English Shakespearian Criticism in the Eighteenth Century* (New York, 1932)

Rymer, T. *Critical Works*, ed. C. A. Zimansky (New Haven, 1956)

Saintsbury, G. *A History of English Criticism* (London, 1911)

Smith, D. Nichol (ed.) *Eighteenth Century Essays on Shakespeare* (2nd ed., Oxford, 1963)

Smith, D. Nichol (ed.) *Shakespeare Criticism, 1623–1840* (W.C., 1916)

Smith, D. Nichol *Shakespeare in the Eighteenth Century* (Oxford, 1928)

Smith, L. P. 'Four Romantic Words', in *Words and Idioms* (London, 1943)

Spingarn, J. E. (ed.) *Critical Essays of the Seventeenth Century* II–III (Oxford, 1908–9)

Sutherland, J. R. *English Satire* (Cambridge, 1958)

Swedenberg, H. T. *The Theory of the Epic in England, 1650–1800* (Berkeley, 1944)

Taylor, H. W. *The Idea of Locality in English Criticism of Fiction, 1750–1830* (Chicago, 1936)

Tinker, C. B. *Nature's Simple Plan* (Princeton, 1922)

Trowbridge, H. 'Joseph Warton on the Imagination', in M.P. XXXV (1937)

Warren, A. *Alexander Pope as Critic and Humanist* (Princeton, 1929)

Watkins, W. B. C. *Johnson and English Poetry before 1660* (Princeton, 1936)

Wellek, R. *A History of Modern Criticism* I (London, 1955)

Wellek, R. *The Rise of English Literary History* (Chapel Hill, 1941)

AUTHORS AND WORKS

Collections and Anthologies

The Augustan Reprints (a series of facsimiles, Los Angeles, 1946 – in progress)

George, M. D. (ed.) *England in Johnson's Day* (London, 1928)

Grigson, G. (ed.) *Before the Romantics* (London, 1946)

Grigson, G. (ed.) *The Romantics* (London, 1942)

Anderson, R. (ed.) *The Works of the British Poets* (13 vols., Edinburgh, 1792–5)

Ault, N. (ed.) *Seventeenth Century Lyrics* (London, 1928)

Chalmers, A. (ed.) *The Works of the English Poets* (21 vols., London, 1810)

Crane, R. S. (ed.) *A Collection of English Poems, 1660–1800* (New York, 1932)

Davie, D. *The Late Augustans* (London, 1958)

Dodsley, R. (pub.) *A Collection of Poems* (London, 1748, 1758)

Doughty, O. (ed.) *Forgotten Lyrics of the Eighteenth Century* (London, 1924)

Fausset, H. I'A. (ed.) *Minor Poets of the Eighteenth Century* (E.L., 1930)

Grierson, Sir H. and Bullough, G. (eds.) *The Oxford Book of Seventeenth Century Verse* (Oxford, 1934)

Johnson, S. (ed.) *The Works of the English Poets* (68 vols., London, 1779–81)

Lord, G. de F. and Mengel, E. F. (eds.) *Poems on Affairs of State: Augustan Satirical Verse, 1660–1714* (New Haven and London, 1963 – in progress)

Peacock, W. (ed.) *English Verse: III, Dryden to Wordsworth* (W.C., 1930)

Pinto, V. de S. and Rodway, A. E. (eds.) *The Common Muse. An Anthology of Popular British Ballad Poetry* (London, 1957)

Smith, D. Nichol (ed.) *The Oxford Book of Eighteenth Century Verse* (Oxford, 1926)

Ward, T. H. (ed.) *The English Poets* II–III (London, 1880)

Allott, K. (ed.) *The Pelican Book of English Prose* II–III (Harmondsworth, 1956)

Craik, Sir H. (ed.) *English Prose* III–IV (London, 1894)

Shorter Novels II–III (E.L., 1930)

Ward, A. C. (ed.) *A Miscellany of Tracts and Pamphlets* (W.C., 1927)

Carver, G. (ed.) *Periodical Essays of the Eighteenth Century* (New York, 1930)

Chalmers, A. (ed.) *The British Essayists* (45 vols., London, 1817)

Lynam, R. (ed.) *The British Essayists* (30 vols., London, 1827)

Segar, M. G. (ed.) *Essays from Eighteenth Century Periodicals* (London, 1947)

Bell's British Theatre (21 vols., London, 1776–81; 36 vols., 1791–1802)

Booth, M. R. (ed.) *Eighteenth Century Tragedy* (W.C., 1965)

Cumberland, R. (ed.) *The British Drama* (14 vols., London, 1817)

Dobrée, B. (ed.) *Five Heroic Plays* (W.C., 1960)

Dobrée, B. (ed.) *Five Restoration Tragedies* (W.C., 1928)

Gayley, C. M. and Thaler, A. (eds.) *Representative English Comedies* IV (New York, 1936)

Gosse, Sir E. (ed.) *Restoration Plays* (E.L., 1912; rev. 1932)

Hampden, J. (ed.) *Eighteenth Century Plays* (E.L., 1928)

Hunt, J. L. (ed.) *The Dramatic Works of Wycherley, Congreve, Vanbrugh and Farquhar* (London, 1841)

Inchbald, E. (ed.) *The British Theatre* (25 vols., London, 1808)

MacMillan, D. and Jones, H. M. (eds.) *Plays of the Restoration and Eighteenth Century* (New York, 1931)

Maidment, J. and Logan, W. H. (eds.) *Dramatists of the Restoration* (14 vols., Edinburgh and London, 1872–9)

Nettleton, G. H. and Case, A. E. (eds.) *British Dramatists from Dryden to Sheridan* (Boston, 1939)

Nicoll, A. (ed.) *Lesser English Comedies of the Eighteenth Century* (W.C., 1927)

Sharpe's British Theatre (18 vols., London, 1804)

Stevens, D. H. (ed.) *Types of English Drama, 1660 to 1780* (Boston, 1923)

Taylor, W. D. (ed.) *Eighteenth Century Comedy* (W.C., 1929)

Tupper, F. and J. W. (eds.) *Representative English Drama from Dryden to Sheridan* (New York, 1914; rev. 1934)

Authors

ADDISON, JOSEPH (1672–1719): Essayist, poet and statesman; son of dean of Lichfield; educated Charterhouse (with Steele), Queen's College, Oxford; fellow of Magdalen, 1697–1711; Latin poems attracted Dryden's notice, 1693; toured Europe with pension, preparing for diplomatic service, 1699–1703; celebrated victory of Blenheim in poem, *The Campaign*, 1705; friendship with Swift, Steele, etc.; under-secretary of state, 1706; M.P., 1708–19; to Ireland, chief secretary to

Lord Wharton, 1709; lost office on fall of Whigs, 1711; collaborated with Steele in *Tatler* (1709–11). *The Spectator* (1711–12); great success of tragedy *Cato*, 1713; contributed to *The Guardian* (1713) and new *Spectator* (1714); unsuccessful comedy, *The Drummer*, 1715; again chief secretary for Ireland; political newspaper, *The Freeholder*, 1715–16; a lord commissioner of trade, married Countess of Warwick, 1716; retired with £1500 pension, 1718, estrangement from Steele; buried Westminster Abbey.

Life by L. Aikin (2 vols., London, 1843); P. Smithers (Oxford, 1954)

Works ed. R. Hurd (6 vols., London, 1811; 1854–6; 1883)

Miscellaneous Works in Verse and Prose ed. A. C. Guthkelch (2 vols. London, 1914)

Letters ed. W. Graham (Oxford, 1941)

The Spectator ed. G. G. Smith (8 vols., London, 1897–8; E.L., 1907); ed. D. F. Bond (5 vols., 1965)

The Tatler ed. G. A. Aitken (4 vols., London, 1898–9); selections in E.L.

Essays (selected) ed. J. F. Green (London, 1880, etc.)

See bibliography under *Prose* (p. 458)

    L. A. Elioseff, *The Cultural Milieu of Addison's Literary Criticism* (Austin, 1963)

    S. Johnson, *The Lives of the Poets* (ed. G. B. Hill, vol. II, Oxford, 1905)

    J. Lannering, *Studies in the Prose Style of Joseph Addison* (Uppsala, 1951)

    C. S. Lewis, 'Addison', in *Essays on the Eighteenth Century Presented to David Nichol Smith* (Oxford, 1945)

    Lord (T. B.) Macaulay, 'The Life and Writings of Addison', in *Critical and Historical Essays* II (E.L., 1907)

ARBUTHNOT, JOHN (1667–1735): Physician and wit; b. Scotland; M.D., St Andrews, 1696; taught mathematics in London; F.R.S., 1704; physician to Queen Anne, 1705; close friend of Swift and Pope; supported Tory ministry, 1710–14; political pamphlets, including *The History of John Bull*, 1712; member of Scriblerus Club with Swift, Pope, etc., 1713; contributed largely to *Memoirs of Martimus Scriblerus* (pub. 1741); wrote many progressive medical works; popular for wit, humour, and kind heart.

Life by L. M. Beattie, *John Arbuthnot, Mathematician and Satirist* (Cambridge, Mass., 1935)

Life and Works ed. G. A. Aitken (Oxford, 1892)

History of John Bull ed. H. Teerink (Amsterdam, 1925)

BEHN, MRS APHRA (1640–89): Dramatist and novelist; b. Canterbury or Wye, daughter of (?) John Amis; obscure and probably improper early career; claimed to have lived as child in Surinam, Guiana;

returned to England, 1658; married city merchant, 1664; spy for Charles II in Antwerp, 1666–7, getting information from lover, William Scot; fifteen plays produced, 1670–89, mainly coarse and amatory comedies of contemporary London life; also wrote poems and novels, notable *Oroonoko, or the Royal Slave*, c. 1678, romanticizing her supposed career in Surinam.

Life by V. Sackville-West, *Aphra Behn. The Incomparable Astraea* (London, 1927)
Works ed. M. Summers (6 vols., London, 1915)
Novels ed. E. A. Baker (London, 1913); *Oroonoko* in E.L.
See introductions to eds. of Summers and Baker

BERKELEY, GEORGE (1685–1753): Philosopher; b. Ireland; educated Kilkenny and Trinity College, Dublin; *Essay towards a New Theory of Vision*, 1709; *Principles of Human Knowledge*, 1710; to England, 1713; friendly with Swift, Pope, Steele, Addison; Dean of Derry, 1724; missionary enterprise in America, 1728–32; popular philosophical dialogues, *Alciphron*, 1732; Bishop of Cloyne, 1734; d. Oxford. His philosophical immaterialism opposed to Locke's theory of external, material reality.

Life by A. A. Luce (Edinburgh, 1949)
Works ed. A. A. Luce and T. E. Jessop (9 vols., London, 1948–57)
Select Writings (E.L., 1910)
See G. J. Warnock, *Berkeley* (Harmondsworth, 1953, rev. 1969)

BOSWELL, JAMES (1740–95): Biographer and diarist; b. and educated Edinburgh; son of judge, Lord Auchinleck; studied law at Edinburgh and Glasgow; desired literary fame and acquaintance of the great; visited London, met Dr Johnson, 1763; abandoned law studies at Utrecht, 1764, to make tour of Germany, France, Switzerland, Italy, with variety of amatory escapades; introduced self to Rousseau and Voltaire; visited Corsica, met General Paoli; returned to England, 1766; *Account of Corsica* (1768) achieved European fame; married cousin, 1769; unwillingly practised law in Edinburgh; contributed frequently to newspapers, etc. (essays, *The Hypochondriack*, 1777–83); visited London and Johnson almost annually, 1772–84; led Johnson on tour of Scotland and Hebrides, elected to 'The Club', 1773; sought career in law and politics in London; *Journal of a Tour to the Hebrides*, 1785; settled in London, 1789; *Life of Johnson*, 1791; depression and ill-health in last years; d. London. Mass of manuscript journals discovered in recent years at Fettercairn House and Malahide Castle.

Life by D. B. Wyndham Lewis (London, 1946; 1952); C. B. Tinker (Boston, 1922); F. A. Pottle (London, 1966)

The Private Papers of James Boswell from Malahide Castle ed. G. Scott and F. A. Pottle (18 vols., New York, 1928–34)

Yale Editions of the Private Papers ed. F. A. Pottle *et al.* (London, 1950 – in progress)

Boswell's London Journal, 1762–1763 ed. F. A. Pottle (Harmondsworth, 1966)

Tour to Corsica ed. S. C. Roberts (Cambridge, 1923); ed. M. Bishop (London, 1951)

Tour to The Hebrides ed. R. W. Chapman (Oxford, 1924; London, 1930; ed. L. F. Powell (London, 1950); ed. (from original MS.) F. A. Pottle and C. H. Bennett (New York and London, 1936); in E.L.

Life of Johnson and Journal of a Tour to the Hebrides ed. G. B. Hill (6 vols., Oxford, 1887; rev. and enlarged L. F. Powell, 1934–50)

Life of Johnson, in numerous eds., including E.L. and O.S.A.

Letters ed. C. B. Tinker (2 vols., Oxford, 1924)

See F. Brady, *Boswell's Political Career* (New Haven, 1965)

    B. H. Bronson, 'Boswell's Boswell', in *Johnson Agonistes and Other Essays* (Berkeley and Los Angeles, 1944; Cambridge, 1946)

    F. A. Pottle, *The Literary Career of James Boswell, Esq.* (Oxford, 1929; 1965)

    Sir Walter Raleigh, *Six Essays on Johnson* (Oxford, 1910)

    G. Scott, 'The Making of the Life of Johnson', in *The Private Papers* VI (1929)

    D. A. Stauffer, *The Art of Biography in Eighteenth-Century England* (Princeton, 1941)

BOYLE, HON. ROBERT (1627–91): Natural philosopher and theologian; son of first Earl of Cork; studied in Europe; set up laboratory at Oxford, 1654; industrious experimenter, especially in chemistry; 'Boyle's Law' of gases, 1662; a founder of Royal Society, voluminous writer on science, morality, religion; influence in his day only less than that of Newton.

Life by L. T. More (New York, 1944)
Works ed. T. Birch (5 vols., London, 1744; 6 vols., 1772)
The Sceptical Chemist (1661; E.L., 1911)

BURKE, EDMUND (1729–97): Statesman and political writer; son of Protestant Dublin attorney; educated Trinity College, Dublin, and Middle Temple; frequented society of writers; *A Philosophical Enquiry into the Origin of our Ideas of the Sublime and the Beautiful*, 1757; started *The Annual Register*, 1759; member of 'The Club', 1763; private secretary to prime minister, and M.P., 1765; in speeches and pamphlets opposed attitude of North Ministry towards American colonies; speculations involved him in permanent financial difficulties; championed cause of Ireland and Catholic emancipation; Paymaster of Forces, 1782; joined in impeachment of Warren Hastings, from 1788; denounced French Revolution (*Reflections*, 1790) and broke with Fox and the Whigs; retired with government pension, 1794. Had devoted life to five 'great, just and honourable causes'.

Life by Sir J. Prior (London, 1824, etc.); Lord J. Morley (London, 1879); Sir P. Magnus (London, 1939)

Works ed. W. Willis and F. W. Raffety (6 vols., W.C., 1906–7)

Select Works ed. E. J. Payne (3 vols., Oxford, 1874–8)

The Philosophy of Edmund Burke: A Selection ed. L. I. Bredvold and R. G. Ross (Ann Arbor, 1960)

A Philosophical Enquiry into the Origin of our Ideas of the Sublime and Beautiful, ed. J. T. Boulton (London, 1958)

Correspondence ed. T. W. Copeland (Cambridge and Chicago, 1958 – in progress)

See A. Cobban, *Edmund Burke and the Revolt against the Eighteenth Century* (London, 1929)

　　T. W. Copeland, *Edmund Burke, Six Essays* (London, 1950)

　　W. B. Todd, *A Bibliography of Edmund Burke* (London, 1964)

　　B. T. Wilkins, *The Problems of Burke's Political Philosophy* (Oxford, 1967)

BURNEY, FRANCES, MADAME D'ARBLAY (1752–1840): Novelist and diarist; daughter of Dr Burney, the musician; novels, *Evelina*, 1778, *Cecilia*, 1782; friend of Dr Johnson and protégée of Mrs Thrale; second keeper of robes to Queen Charlotte, 1786–91; married French refugee general, 1793; in France, 1802–12; last part of long life in England. Diaries give account of Johnson's circle and life at Court.

Life by C. Lloyd (London, 1936); J. Hemlow (Oxford, 1958)

Early Diary, 1768–78 ed. A. R. Ellis (2 vols., London, 1889; 1913)

Diary and Letters of Madame d'Arblay, 1778–1840 ed. C. Barrett and A. Dobson (6 vols., London, 1904): selections in E.L.

Evelina ed. Sir F. D. Mackinnon (Oxford, 1930); also in E.L.

See Lord David Cecil, 'Fanny Burney', in *Poets and Story-Tellers* (London, 1949)

BUTLER, SAMUEL (1612–80): Satirist; details of life obscure; son of prosperous Worcestershire yeoman; a censorious child; King's School, Worcester; possibly Gray's Inn; never at university, but greatly learned; in household of Countess of Kent; acquainted with Selden; considered painting as career; clerk to various county magistrates possibly including fanatical Puritan, Sir Samuel Luke; secretary to Earl of Carbery and steward of Ludlow Castle, 1661; *Characters*, 1667–9 (pub. 1759); *Hudibras*, rhymed satire on Puritans, begun before Restoration (three parts, 1662-3-77) delighted Charles II and Royalists; secretary to Duke of Buckingham, whom he probably helped with *The Rehearsal*; pension from King, 1677; died of consumption, though tradition of poverty is exaggerated.

Biographical matter: R. Lamar, 'Du Nouveau sur l'Auteur d'*Hudibras*', in *Revue Anglo-Américaine* I (1924); E. S. de Beer, 'The Later Life of Samuel Butler', in R.E.S. IV (1928)

Works ed. A. R. Waller and R. Lamar (3 vols., Cambridge, 1905-28)
Hudibras ed. J. Wilders (Oxford, 1967)
See D. Gibson, in *Seventeenth Century Studies* ed. R. Shafer (Princeton, 1933)
 I. Jack, *Augustan Satire* (Oxford, 1952)
 R. Quintana, 'Samuel Butler: A Restoration Figure in a Modern Light', in E.L.H. XVIII (1951)

CHATTERTON, THOMAS (1752-70); Poet; posthumous child of poor Bristol schoolmaster; 'the marvellous boy', pub. poems before age of twelve; through muniments of St Mary Redcliffe church became fascinated with Middle Ages; apprenticed to attorney, 1767; fabricated medieval documents and poems of monk Thomas Towley; sent specimens to Dodsley and Walpole; controversy about genuineness; exposed by T. Tyrwhitt; reduced to despair by neglect, poisoned himself in London; 'Rowley' poems pub. 1778, 1782; belated recognition of his poetic genius.

Life by E. H. W. Meyerstein (London, 1930)
Poetical Works ed. W. W. Skeat (2 vols., London, 1871); ed. H. D. Roberts (2 vols., London, 1906)
Rowley Poems ed. M. E. Hare (Oxford, 1911)
See E. H. W. Meyerstein, 'Chatterton: his Significance Today', in *Trans. of Royal Soc. of Literature* XVI (1937)

CHESTERFIELD, PHILIP DORMER STANHOPE, EARL OF (1694-1773): Statesman, wit, letter-writer; distinguished diplomatic and administrative career; ambassador to The Hague, 1728-32; successful Lord Lieutenant of Ireland, 1745-6; contributed to *The World*, 1753-6; generous patron of writers, rebuked by Johnson for neglect of him, 1755; concern for education of illegitimate son (d. 1768), writing to him almost daily; thereafter gave similar attention to godson. A master of manners and worldly wisdom.

Life by S. Shellabarger (London, 1935); W. Connely (London, 1939)
Letters ed. B. Dobrée (6 vols., London, 1932); selections in E.L. and W.C.
See R. Coxon, *Chesterfield and his Critics* (London, 1925)

CHURCHILL, CHARLES (1731-64): Satirist; son of clergyman; educated

Westminster and St John's College, Cambridge; dissipated clergyman; notorious for personal satires, on actors in *The Rosciad* (1761), on Lord Bute and the Scots in *The Prophecy of Famine* (1763); associated with Wilkes, contributing to *The North Briton*; political and social satires against Smollet, Hogarth, Dr Johnson, and Wilkes's adversaries; depicted worst vices of the day, including own, in *The Times*, 1764; d. Boulogne. Wrote in couplets, preferring Dryden to Pope as model.

Life by W. C. Brown (Lawrence, Kansas, 1953)
Poems ed. J. Laver (2 vols., London, 1933); ed. D. Grant (Oxford, 1956)
See E. Blunden, *Votive Tablets* (London, 1931)
    W. C. Brown, *The Triumph of Form* (Chapel Hill, 1948)

CIBBER, COLLEY (1671–1757): Actor and dramatist; son of Danish sculptor; Grantham School; actor, 1690; most important theatrical figure of his time; skilful comedies, *The Careless Husband* (1705) the best; as actor excelled in parts of fops and eccentric characters; controlled theatre in Drury Lane, c. 1710–33; poet laureate, 1730; ridiculed, especially his odes for New Year and King's birthday, by Pope, Swift, Fielding; 'hero' of Pope's revised *Dunciad*, 1743; his *Apology for the Life of Mr Colley Cibber, Comedian* (1740) contains irresistible self-portrait and valuable account of theatre and actors.

Life by F. D. Senior (London, 1928); R. H. Barker (New York, 1939)
Dramatic Works (5 vols., London, 1777)
Apology ed. R. W. Lowe (2 vols., London, 1889); also in E.L.
See F. W. Bateson, *English Comic Drama, 1700–1750* (Oxford, 1929)
    De W. C. Croissant, *Studies in the Work of Colley Cibber* (Kansas City, 1912)

COLLIER, JEREMY (1650–1726): Non-juring clergyman and controversialist; educated Ipswich and Caius College, Cambridge; *A Short View of the Immorality and Profaneness of the English Stage*, 1698, attacking Congreve, Vanbrugh, etc.; kept up attack in further pamphlets, 1699–1708.

A Short View, extracts in *Critical Essays of the Seventeenth Century* III, ed· J. E. Spingarn (Oxford, 1909)
See R. Anthony, *The Jeremy Collier Stage Controversy* (Milwaukee, 1937)
    A. O. Beljame, *Men of Letters and the English Public in the Eighteenth Century* (Paris, 1881; trans. E. O. Lorimer, ed. B. Dobrée, London, 1948)
    J. W. Krutch, *Comedy and Conscience after the Restoration* (New York, 1924)

COLLINS, WILLIAM (1721–59): Poet; b. Chichester, son of hatter;

educated Winchester and Magdalen College, Oxford; *Persian Eclogues*, 1742, while still an undergraduate; *Odes*, 1746, including 'Ode to Evening' and 'How sleep the brave'; *Ode on the Popular Superstitions of the Highlands of Scotland* written 1749; saved from penury by legacy, 1749; suffered from nervous depression, at times insane; d. in sister's house at Chichester.

Life by E. G. Ainsworth (Ithaca, 1937); P. L. Carver (London, 1967)
Poems ed. W. C. Bronson (Boston, 1898); ed. C. Stone (London, 1907; rev. A. L. Poole, 1937); ed. E. Blunden (London, 1929); in *Minor Poets of the Eighteenth Century* (E.L., 1930)
See H. W. Garrod, *Collins* (Oxford, 1928)
    S. Johnson, *Lives of the Poets* (ed. G. B. Hill, vol. III, Oxford, 1905)
    J. W. Mackail, 'Collins, and the English Lyric', in *Studies of English Poets* (London, 1926)
    A. D. McKillop, 'The Romanticism of William Collins', in S.P. XX (1923)
    P. M. Spacks, *The Poetry of Vision* (Cambridge, Mass., 1967)
    A. S. P. Woodhouse, 'Collins and the Creative Imagination', in *Studies in English* (Toronto, 1931)

CONGREVE, WILLIAM (1670–1729): Dramatist; b. Bardsey, Yorkshire; childhood in Ireland, father on military service there; fellow-student to Swift at Kilkenny and Trinity College, Dublin; studied law in London, 1691; pub. verse; novel *Incognita*, 1692; fame with first comedy, *The Old Batchelor*, 1693; *The Double Dealer*, 1694; *Love for Love*, 1695; tragedy, *The Mourning Bride*, 1697; censured by Jeremy Collier; *The Way of the World*, 1700, coolly received; held government sinecures; enjoyed friendship and admiration of Swift, Steele, Pope; intimately attached to Duchess of Marlborough; buried Westminster Abbey.

Life by D. C. Taylor, (Oxford, 1931); J. C. Hodges (New York, 1941)
Works ed. M. Summers (4 vols., London, 1923); ed. B. Dobrée (2 vols., W.C., 1925–8); ed. F. W. Bateson (London, 1930)
Complete Plays ed. H. Davis (London and Chicago, 1967)
Incognita ed. H. F. B. Brett-Smith (Oxford, 1922)
Incognita and *The Way of the World* ed. A. N. Jeffares (London, 1966)
Letters and Documents ed. J. C. Hodges (Ontario and London, 1964)
See under *Drama* (p. 459), studies by Dobrée, Hazlitt, Hunt, Knights, Macaulay, Meredith, Palmer
    V. Woolf, 'Congreve's Comedies', in *The Moment, and Other Essays* (London, 1947)

COWPER, WILLIAM (1731–1800): Poet; b. Great Berkhampstead, son of rector; bullied at boarding school; Westminster School; called to

Bar, 1754; disappointed in love for cousin, temporary insanity; strain of preparing for examinations brought on second attack, with attempted suicide; in retirement with Rev. Unwin at Huntingdon, 1765–7, then with his widow ('My Mary') at Olney; there came under strenuous evangelical influence of Rev. John Newton; *Olney Hymns*, 1779; more peaceful life after Newton's departure for London, though intermittent melancholia; verse satires, suggested by Mrs Unwin, in *Poems*, 1782; humorous ballad, *John Gilpin*, 1782; at prompting of Lady Austen, *The Task*, 1785; trans. Homer; Mrs Unwin d. 1796; stricken in mind and body; tragic lyric, *The Castaway,* 1798. Record of quiet delights of country and his own gentle nature in letters.

> Life by T. Wright (London, 1892; rev. 1921); Lord David Cecil (London, 1929); Maurice J. Quinlan (Minneapolis, 1953); Charles Ryskamp (Cambridge, 1959)
>
> *Works* ed. R. Southey (15 vols., London, 1835–7; 8 vols., 1953–5)
>
> *Poems* ed. J. C. Bailey (London, 1905); ed. H. S. Milford (London, 1905; rev. 1934); selection in E.L.
>
> *Correspondence* ed. T. Wright (5 vols., London, 1904–25); selections in E.L. and W.C.
>
> See L. C. Hartley, *William Cowper, Humanitarian* (Chapel Hill, 1938)
>> R. Huang, *William Cowper: Nature Poet* (London, 1957)
>> N. Nicholson, *William Cowper* (London, 1951)
>> N. Russell, *A Bibliography of William Cowper to 1837* (Oxford, 1963)
>> G. Thomas, *William Cowper and the Eighteenth Century* (London, 1935)

DEFOE, DANIEL (?1660–1731): Journalist and novelist; life of strange and varied adventures, details imperfectly known; wrote more than 400 pieces; b. London, son of dissenting tallow-chandler, James Foe; simple education; travelled on Continent; engaged in Monmouth's rebellion, 1685; joined William III's army, 1688; took up commerce; failed for £17,000; *Essay upon Projects*, 1697; *The True-born Englishman*, 1701; ironic attack on High Church principles, *The Shortest Way with the Dissenters*, 1702; as result fined, pilloried, imprisoned; changed name to Defoe; political and economic *Review*, 1704–13; served cause of Noncomformists and Whigs as secret agent of Godolphin and Harley, largely in Scotland; served Tories, 1710–14; thereafter gave doubtful support to both parties; *Robinson Crusoe*, 1719; other fiction followed, including *Captain Singleton* (1720), *Moll Flanders* (1722), *A Journal of the Plague Year* (1722), *Roxana* (1724); observant traveller, *A Tour thro' the Whole Island of Great Britain*, 1724–7; writing for promotion of English commerce, 1725–31. A shrewd, shifty, ingenious man, much mistrusted and frequently imprisoned; buried Bunhill Fields.

Life by J. R. Sutherland (London, 1937; 1950); J. R. Moore (Chicago, 1958)

Romances and Narratives ed. G. A. Aitken (16 vols., London, 1895)

Novels and Selected Writings (14 vols., Oxford, 1927–8)

Robinson Crusoe; *Captain Singleton*; *Memoirs of a Cavalier*; *Moll Flanders* (all in E.L.); *Colonel Jack* and *Roxana* (in O.E.N., 1965); *Journal of the Plague Year* and *Robinson Crusoe* (Harmondsworth, 1966)

The Review ed. A. W. Secord (22 vols., New York, 1938)

The Best of Defoe's 'Review' ed. W. L. Payne (New York, 1951)

Tour ed. G. D. H. Cole (2 vols., London, 1927; repr. in E.L., 2 vols.)

Letters ed. G. H. Healey (Oxford, 1955)

For extensive list of writings, see C.B.E.L. II, 495–514.

See B. Dobrée, 'Some Aspects of Defoe's Prose', in *Pope and his Contemporaries* ed. J. L. Clifford and L. A. Landa (Oxford, 1949)

P. Dottin, *Daniel De Foe et ses Romans* (3 vols., Paris, 1924; trans., one vol., New York, 1929)

J. R. Moore, *Defoe in the Pillory and Other Studies* (Bloomington, 1939)

M. E. Novak, *Defoe and the Nature of Man* (Oxford, 1963)

M. E. Novak, *Economics and the Fiction of Daniel Defoe* (Los Angeles and Berkeley, 1962)

W. L. Payne, *Mr Review, Daniel Defoe as Author of 'The Review'* (New York, 1947)

A. W. Secord, *Studies in the Narrative Method of Defoe* (Urbana, 1924)

G. A. Starr, *Defoe and Spiritual Autobiography* (Princeton, 1965)

I. Watt, '*Robinson Crusoe* as a Myth', in *Essays in Criticism* I (1950)

V. Woolf, *The Common Reader* I–II (London, 1925–32)

DRYDEN, JOHN (1631–1700): Poet, satirist, dramatist, critic; b. Aldwinkle, Northamptonshire; brought up in Puritan environment; Westminster and Trinity College, Cambridge; served Cromwell's chamberlain; *Heroic Stanzas* on death of Cromwell, 1659; settled in London; celebrated Restoration of Charles II in *Astraea Redux*, 1660; F.R.S., 1662; married Lady Elizabeth Howard, 1663; turned playwright for livelihood, averaging almost a play a year, 1663–81; defined his dramatic principles in prefaces, prologues, essays; *Essay of Dramatic Poesy*, 1667; poem, *Annus Mirabilis*, 1667; poet laureate, 1668; historiographer, 1670; his heroic plays burlesqued by Buckingham (?) in *The Rehearsal*, 1671; blank-verse tragedy, *All for Love*, 1678; political and personal verse satires, *Absalom and Achitophel* (1681–2), *The Medall* (1678–82), *MacFlecknoe* (1682, written 1678); didactic religious poems, *Religio Laici* (1682), *The Hind and the Panther* (1687), the latter after conversion to Roman Catholicism, 1686; lost offices after Revolution, 1688; in old age turned to writing again for a living; plays, odes, translations, with valuable critical prefaces; verse translation of Virgil (1697) said to have earned him £1200; adaptations of Chaucer, Boccaccio, Ovid as *Fables, Ancient and Modern*, 1700, with distinguished preface; *Secular Masque*, hailing a new age, 1700; buried Westminster Abbey.

Life by Sir W. Scott, in Dryden's *Works* I (London, 1808; Edinburgh, 1882); G. Saintsbury (London, 1881); C. E. Ward (Los Angeles and Berkeley, 1961)

See J. M. Osborn, *John Dryden. Some Biographical Facts and Problems* (Gainesville, 1940; rev. 1965)

Works ed. Sir W. Scott (18 vols., London, 1808; rev. G. Saintsbury, Edinburgh, 1882–92); ed. E. N. Hooker, *et al.* (21 vols., Berkeley and Los Angeles, 1956 – in progress)

Poetry, Prose and Plays ed. D. Grant (London, 1952)

Poems ed. G. R. Noyes (Boston, 1908; rev. 1952); ed. J. Kinsley (4 vols. Oxford, 1958; one vol., 1961)

Dramatic Works ed. M. Summers (6 vols., London, 1931–2)

Selected Plays ed. G. Saintsbury (2 vols., London, 1904)

All for Love, in *Restoration Plays* (E.L.) and *Restoration Tragedies* (W.C.)

Essays ed. W. P. Ker (2 vols., Oxford, 1900)

Essay of Dramatic Poesy ed. D. Nichol Smith (London, 1900); ed. J. T. Boulton (London, 1964)

Of Dramatic Poesy and Other Critical Essays ed. G. Watson (2 vols., E.L. 1962)

Translation of Virgil (in W.C.)

Letters ed. C. E. Ward (Durham, N.C., 1942)

Concordance to the Poetical Works, ed. G. Montgomery (California, 1947)

See L. I. Bredvold, *The Intellectual Milieu of John Dryden* (Ann Arbor, 1934; 1956)

    T. S. Eliot, *Homage to John Dryden* (London, 1924)

    T. S. Eliot, *John Dryden. The Poet, the Dramatist, the Critic* (New York, 1932)

    W. Frost, *Dryden and the Art of Translation* (New Haven, 1955)

    A. W. Hoffman, *John Dryden's Imagery* (Gainesville, 1962)

    S. Johnson, *Lives of the Poets* (ed. G. B. Hill, vol. 1, Oxford, 1905)

    A. C. Kirsch, *Dryden's Heroic Drama* (Princeton, 1965)

    F. R. Leavis, *Revaluation*, ch. 1 (London, 1936; Harmondsworth, 1964)

    H. Macdonald, *John Dryden. A Bibliography* (Oxford, 1939)

    Sir W. Raleigh, 'Dryden's Political Satire', in *Some Authors* (Oxford, 1923)

    B. N. Schilling (ed.) *Dryden: A Collection of Critical Essays* (New Jersey, 1963)

    D. Nichol Smith, *John Dryden* (Cambridge, 1950)

    M. Van Doren, *The Poetry of John Dryden* (New York, 1920; London, 1931; rev. 1946)

    A. W. Verrall, *Lectures on Dryden* (Cambridge, 1914)

DYER, JOHN (?1700–1758): Poet and painter; b. Wales, lived most of life there; Westminster School; studied law and, in Italy, painting; became clergyman; *Grongar Hill*, a loco-description poem, 1725 or 6; didactic poems in 'Georgic' tradition. *The Ruins of Rome* (1740), *The Fleece* (1757).

> *Poems* ed. E. Thomas (London, 1903) in *Minor Poets of the Eighteenth Century* (E.L., 1930)
> *Grongar Hill* ed. R. C. Boys (Baltimore, 1941)

ETHEREGE, SIR GEORGE (?1634–?91): Dramatist; of good Berkshire family; brought up in France, travelled, studied law; man of world in London; *The Comical Revenge, or Love in a Tub*, 1664; *She Wou'd if She Cou'd*, 1668; secretary to ambassador in Constantinople, 1668–71; married money and knighted; *The Man of Mode, or Sir Fopling Flutter*, 1676; envoy to Ratisbon, 1685–9; Jacobite exile in France; d. Paris.

> *Plays and Poems* ed. A. W. Verity (London, 1888)
> *Plays* ed. H. F. B. Brett-Smith (2 vols., Oxford, 1927)
> *The Man of Mode*, in *Restoration Plays* (E.L., 1932)
> *Letterbook* ed. S. Rosenfeld (Oxford, 1928)
> *Poems* ed. J. Thorpe (Princeton and London, 1963)
> See B. Dobrée, *Essays in Biography* (London, 1925)
> > B. Dobrée, *Restoration Comedy* (Oxford, 1924)
> > J. Palmer, *The Comedy of Manners* (London, 1913)
> > D. Underwood, *Etherege and the Seventeenth-Century Comedy of Manners* (New Haven, 1957)

EVELYN, JOHN (1620–1706): Virtuoso and diarist; b. Wotton, Sussex; educated Balliol College, Oxford, and Middle Temple; man of means, Royalist; travelled in Europe; settled at Sayes Court, Deptford, 1653, and laid out famous garden; unsuccessfully planned Restoration, 1659; assisted in founding Royal Society; served on public bodies; translations and writings on architecture, engraving, gardening, etc.; removed to Wotton, 1694, where he died. Chiefly remembered for *Diary*, describing travels, leading men and events.

> Life by Lord A. Ponsonby (London, 1933)
> *Miscellaneous Works* ed. W. Upcott (London, 1825)
> *Diary* ed. E. S. de Beer (6 vols., Oxford, 1955; one vol., 1959)
> *The Life of Mrs Godolphin* ed. H. Sampson (London, 1939)
> See W. G. Hiscock, *John Evelyn and his Family Circle* (London, 1956)
> > C. Marburg, *Mr Pepys and Mr Evelyn* (Philadelphia, 1935)

FARQUHAR, GEORGE (1677–1707): Dramatist; b. Londonderry, Ireland, son of clergyman; Trinity College, Dublin, 1694–5; worked

for bookseller; became actor; to London, 1697; *Love and a Bottle*
produced, 1698; *The Constant Couple, or a Trip to the Jubilee,* 1699;
with Army in Holland, 1700; *Sir Harry Wildair,* 1701; *The Inconstant*
and *The Twin Rivals,* 1702; married young lady of pretended fortune,
1703; *The Stage-Coach,* 1704; *The Recruiting Officer,* 1706; *The Beaux'*
Stratagem, 1707; died in poverty. Easy-going, genial character.

Life by W. C. Connely (London, 1949)
Complete Works ed. C. A. Stonehill (2 vols., London, 1930)
Best Plays ed. W. Archer (London, 1906). See Introduction
The Beaux' Stratagem, in *Restoration Plays* (E.L., 1912)
See under *Drama* (p. 459), studies by Boas, Dobrée, Hazlitt, Palmer,
Perry.

FIELDING, HENRY (1707–54): Dramatist, journalist, novelist; b.
Sharpham Park, Somerset, of distinguished legal and military family;
Eton, 1719; studied law, Leyden, c. 1728; struggle for livelihood in
London: wrote plays, 1728–37; managed Little Theatre in Haymarket,
conducting campaign against Walpole till muzzled by Licensing Act
(1737); called to Bar, 1740; periodical *The Champion,* 1739–41; ridiculed
Richardson's *Pamela* with *Joseph Andrew* (1742) and probably *An*
Apology for the Life of Mrs Shamela Andrews (1741); anti-Walpole
Jonathan Wild, 1743; anti-Jacobite periodicals; J.P. for Middlesex,
1748, concerned with poverty and suppression of crime; *Tom Jones,*
1749; *Amelia,* 1751; humanitarian writing in *Covent Garden Journal,*
1752; broken in health, went on voyage to Portugal; d. Lisbon;
Journal of a Voyage to Lisbon, pub. 1755.

Life by W. L. Cross (3 vols., New Haven, 1918); F. Homes Dudden
(2 vols., Oxford, 1952)
Works ed. Sir L. Stephen (10 vols., London, 1882); ed. G. Saintsbury
(12 vols., London, 1893); ed. W. E. Henley (16 vols., New York,
1903); ed. M. Battestin *et al.* (Wesleyan ed., Oxford, 1966 – in pro-
gress)
Novels (10 vols., Oxford, 1926)
Tom Jones; Amelia; Voyage to Lisbon (all in E.L.); *Joseph Andrews; Jonathan*
Wild (in E.L. and W.C.); *Tom Jones* (Harmondsworth, 1966, in English
Library)
Shamela ed. R. B. Johnson (London, 1926); ed. B. W. Downs (Cambridge,
1930); ed. S. W. Baker (Berkeley, 1953); ed. Ian Watt (Los Angeles,
1956)
Covent Garden Journal, ed. G. E. Jensen (2 vols., New Haven, 1915)
See F. W. Bateson, *English Comic Drama, 1700–1750* (Oxford, 1929)
M. C. Battestin, *The Moral Basis of Fielding's Art: A Study of 'Joseph*
Andrews' (Middletown, Conn., 1959)

A. Digeon, *Les Romans de Fielding* (Paris, 1923; trans. London, 1925)

I. Ehrenpreis, *Fielding: 'Tom Jones'* (London, 1964)

W. Empson, '*Tom Jones*', in *Kenyon Review*, XX (1958), 217–49

W. Hazlitt, *The English Comic Writers* (London, 1819; in E.L. and W.C.)

A. R. Humphreys, 'Fielding's Irony', in R.E.S. XVIII (1942)

W. R. Irwin, *The Making of 'Jonathan Wild'* (New York, 1941)

M. Johnson, *Fielding's Art of Fiction* (Philadelphia, 1961)

A Kettle, *An Introduction to the English Novel* I (London, 1951)

R. Paulson (ed.) *Fielding: A Collection of Critical Essays* (New Jersey, 1962)

G. Sherburn, 'Fielding's *Amelia*: an Interpretation', in E.L.H. III (1936)

G. Sherburn, 'Fielding's Social Outlook', P.Q. XXXV (1956)

Sir L. Stephen, *Hours in a Library* III (London, 1879)

A Wright, *Henry Fielding: Mask and Feast* (London and Berkeley, 1965)

GAY, JOHN (1685–1732): Poet and dramatist; b. Barnstaple; apprenticed to London mercer; *Wine*, 1708, poem against water-drinkers; *Present State of Wit*, 1711; secretary to Duchess of Monmouth, 1712–14; serious and burlesque pastorals, *Rural Sports* (1713), *The Shepherd's Week* (1714); satirical farce, *What d'ye Call It*, 1715; mock heroic *Trivia, or the Art of Walking the Streets of London*, 1716; minor public employments, patronage of various nobles, friendship of Pope and Swift; unable to fend for himself, was cared for by Duke and Duchess of Queensberry; popularity of *Fables* (1727, 1738); *The Beggar's Opera*, 1728; sequel *Polly* banned on political grounds, 1729.

Life by W. H. Irving (Durham, N.C., 1940); P. M. Spacks (New York, 1965)

Poetical Works (and major plays) ed. G. C. Faber (London, 1926)

Plays (2 vols., London, 1923)

The Beggar's Opera ed. O. Doughty (London, 1923); ed. F. W. Bateson (London, 1934)

Letters ed. C. F. Burgess (Oxford, 1966)

See S. M. Armens, *John Gay, Social Critic* (New York, 1954)

 A. Forsgren, *John Gay, Poet 'of a Lower Order'. Comments on his Rural Poems and Other Early Writings* (Stockholm, 1964)

 F. Kidson, *The Beggar's Opera. Its Predecessors and Successors* (Cambridge, 1922)

 W. E. Schultz, *Gay's 'Beggar's Opera'*, etc. (New Haven, 1923)

GIBBON, EDWARD (1737–94): Historian; b. Putney, of good family; 'unprofitable' education at Westminster and Magdalen College, Oxford; owed precocious erudition to 'invincible love of reading'; turned Roman Catholic, 1753; under Calvanist pastor at Lausanne,

1753–8, abandoned Romanism; fluent in French; forced to break off engagement to Swiss girl; captain in Hampshire militia, 1761–3; in Rome formed plan of writing history of its decline, 1764; settled in London, 1772, proceeded with historical studies; M.P. and minor offices, 1774–83; first vol. of *History of the Decline and Fall of the Roman Empire*, 1776; replied to protests against his attitude to Christianity; vols. II–III, 1781; retired to Lausanne, 1783; completed *History*, 1778; returned to England, 1793, lived with Earl of Sheffield; buried Fletching, Sussex.

Life by D. M. Low (London, 1937)

Decline and Fall of the Roman Empire ed. J. B. Bury (7 vols., London, rev. 1926–9); in E.L. (6 vols., 1910), W.C. (7 vols., 1903–4); abr. (Harmondsworth 1964)

Miscellaneous Works ed. Lord Sheffield (5 vols., London, 1814)

Autobiographies ed. J. Murray (London, 1896), in E.L. and W.C.

Letters ed. J. E. Norton (3 vols., New York, 1956)

See E. Blunden, *Edward Gibbon and his Age* (Bristol, 1935)

H. L. Bond, *The Literary Art of Edward Gibbon* (Oxford, 1960)

E. Clodd, *Gibbon and Christianity* (London, 1916)

M. Joyce, *Edward Gibbon* (London, 1953)

G. M. Young, *Gibbon* (London, 1932)

GOLDSMITH, OLIVER (1730–74): Journalist, essayist, poet, novelist, dramatist; son of Irish clergyman; educated Trinity College, Dublin; studied medicine at Edinburgh, Leyden; piped and sang his way through Europe, 1755–6; returned destitute, failed as physician and teacher, became hack-writer of reviews, biographies, etc.; *Enquiry into the Present State of Polite Learning*, 1759; met Dr Johnson, 1761; member of 'The Club'; *Chinese Letters* (*The Citizen of the World*), 1760–2; *The Vicar of Wakefield*, 1762 (pub. 1766); *The Traveller*, 1764; removed from Islington to the Temple; *The Good-natur'd Man* at Covent Garden, 1768, after being rejected by Garrick; *She Stoops to Conquer* immensely successful, 1773; *The Deserted Village*, 1770; *Retaliation*, 1774; buried in Temple Church. Wrote and translated great diversity of works for booksellers; a man often foolish, always in debt, but generous, tender-hearted, and loved by all.

Life by Sir J. Prior (2 vols., London, 1837); J. Forster (London, 1848; 2 vols., 1954); A Dobson (London, 1888); R. M. Wardle (Lawrence, 1957)

Works ed. P. Cunningham (4 vols., London, 1854); ed. A Friedman (5 vols., Oxford, 1966)

Poems; Essays; Vicar of Wakefield; Plays (in E.L., O.S.A., W.C.)

The Vicar of Wakefield ed. O. Doughty (London, 1928)

Collected Letters ed. K. C. Balderston (Cambridge, 1928)

Selected Works ed. R. Garnett (London, 1950)

See W. F. Gallaway, 'The Sentimentalism of Goldsmith', in *P.M.L.A.* XLVIII (1933)

    M. Emslie, *Goldsmith: 'The Vicar of Wakefield'* (London, 1963)

    R. Quintana, 'Goldsmith's Achievement as a Dramatist', in *Univ. of Toronto Quarterly* XXXIV (1965)

    H. J. Smith, *Oliver Goldsmith's 'The Citizen of the World'* (New Haven, 1926)

GRAY, THOMAS (1716–71): Poet and scholar; b. London, son of broker; at Eton formed 'quadrumvirate' with Horace Walpole, West, and Ashton; Peterhouse, Cambridge, 1734–8; travelled in France and Italy with Walpole, 1739–41, quarrelled, and returned alone; resided at Peterhouse, studying law; *Odes* and *Sonnet on the Death of West*, 1742; friendship with Walpole renewed, 1745; *Elegy in a Country Churchyard* completed, 1750; removed to Pembroke College, 1756, as result of undergraduate prank; *The Progress of Poesy* (1754) and *The Bard* printed by Walpole, 1757; declined laureateship, 1757; settled in London to read at British Museum, 1759–61; imitations of Icelandic and Celtic verse; professor of history and modern languages at Cambridge, 1768; interested in botany; visited Scottish Highlands, 1765; tour of Lake District, 1769, described in journal; buried at Stoke Poges, Buckinghamshire, the village usually associated with the *Elegy*.

Life by R. Martin (Toulouse, London, 1934); R. W. Ketton-Cremer (Cambridge, 1955)

Works ed. Sir E. Gosse (4 vols., London, 1884; rev. 1902–6)

Complete Poems ed. H. W. Starr and J. R. Hendrickson (Oxford, 1966)

English Poems ed. C. D. Tovey (Cambridge, 1898; rev. 1904); ed. A. L. Poole (Oxford, 1917; rev. L. Whibley, 1937)

Correspondence ed. P. Toynbee and L. Whibley (3 vols., Oxford, 1935)

Poems and Letters ed. J. Drinkwater (E.L., 1912)

Selected Letters ed. J. Beresford (W.C., 1925)

See M. Arnold, *Essays in Criticism. Second Series* (London, 1888)

    Lord D. Cecil, 'The Poetry of Thomas Gray' in *Poets and Story-Tellers* (London, 1949)

    S. Johnson, *Lives of the Poets* (ed. G. B. Hill, vol. III, Oxford, 1905)

    W. P. Jones, *Thomas Gray, Scholar* (Cambridge, Mass., 1937)

    F. R. Leavis, *Revaluation* (London, 1936)

    R. Martin, *Essai sur Thomas Gray* (Paris, London, 1934)

    C. S. Northup, *A Bibliography of Thomas Gray* (New Haven, 1917)

    C. E. Norton, *The Poet Gray as a Naturalist* (Boston, 1903)

    A. L. Reed, *The Background of Gray's Elegy* (New York, 1924)

    H. W. Starr, *Gray as a Literary Critic* (Philadelphia, 1941)

AUTHORS AND WORKS

G. Tillotson, 'Gray the Scholar-Poet' in *Essays in Christian and Research* (Cambridge, 1942)

GREEN, MATTHEW (1696–1737): Poet; remembered solely for his poem *The Spleen* (1737), admired by Pope and Gray.

Poems, in *Minor Poets of the Eighteenth Century* (E.L., 1930)
The Spleen ed. W. H. Williams (London, 1936)

HOGARTH, WILLIAM (1697–1764): Painter and engraver; b. London; apprenticed to silversmith and engraver; set up independently as engraver, c. 1720; began attending Thornhill's art school, c. 1724; illustrations to *Hudibras*, 1726; married Jane Thornhill, 1729; painted 'conversation pieces', 1728–9; 'A Harlot's Progress' (first of the 'pictur'd Morals'), 1732; 'A Rake's Progress', 1735, 'Hogarth's Act' protecting engravers' copyright, 1735; letter on sham 'Old Masters', 1737; 'The Four Stages of Cruelty', 1738; 'Marriage à la Mode', 1745; 'Beer Street' and 'Gin Lane', 1751; pub. *The Analysis of Beauty*, 1753; 'The Election' series, 1754–66; serjeant-painter, 1757; quarrel with Wilkes and Churchill, 1762–3; d. at Leicester Fields, London. Attacked connoisseurs for neglect of native talent; excelled as sincere pictorial satirist, depicting both tragic and humorous scenes.

Life by A. Dobson (London, 1879; rev. 1898)
The Analysis of Beauty ed. J. Burke (Oxford, 1955)
See F. Antal, *Hogarth and his Place in European Art* (London, 1962)
    M. Ayrton (ed.) *Hogarth's Drawings* (London, 1948)
    R. B. Beckett, *William Hogarth* (London, 1949)
    W. Hazlitt, *The English Comic Writers* (London, 1819; in E.L. and W.C.)
    F. D. Klingender, *Hogarth and English Caricature* (London, 1944)
    C. Lamb, 'On the Genius and Character of Hogarth' (1811), in *Works*, ed. E. V. Lucas 1 (London, 1903)
    R. E. Moore, *Hogarth's Literary Relationships* (Minneapolis, 1948)
    R. Paulson, *Hogarth's Graphic Works* (2 vols., New Haven, 1965)
    P. Quennell, *Hogarth's Progress* (London, 1955)

HUME, DAVID (1711–76): Philosopher and historian; b. Edinburgh; Edinburgh University; in France, 1734–7; *Treatise of Human Nature*, 1739–40; in Europe, 1745–8; *Enquiry concerning Human Understanding*, 1748; *Enquiry concerning the Principles of Morals*, 1751; clerical opposition; *Political Discourses* (1752) extended fame to Europe; Keeper of Advocates' Library, Edinburgh, 1752–7; leader in Edinburgh intellectual life; *History of Great Britain*, 1754–61; secretary of British Embassy in Paris, 1763–6; brought Rousseau back to England and quarrelled; under-secretary of state, 1767–8; retired to Edinburgh; *Dialogues concerning Natural Religion*, pub. 1779. Logical scepticism in religion and philosophy; demonstrated in his life that virtue is not dependent upon religion.

Life by J. Y. T. Greig (London, 1931); E. C. Mossner (Edinburgh, 1954)
Philosophical Works ed. T. H. Green and T. H. Grose (4 vols., London, 1874–5)
Essential Works ed. R. Cohen (New York, 1965)
Treatise of Human Nature ed. L. A. Selby-Bigge (Oxford, 1941); in E.L.
Letters ed. J. Y. T. Greig (2 vols., Oxford, 1932)
See E. C. Mossner, *The Forgotten Hume* (New York, 1943)
    N. K. Smith, *The Philosophy of David Hume* (London, 1941)
    J. B. Stewart, *The Moral and Political Philosophy of David Hume* (New York, 1963)
    B. Willey, *The Eighteenth-Century Background* (London, 1940)

JOHNSON, SAMUEL (1709–84)· Lexicographer, critic, poet, essayist; son of Lichfield bookseller; ailing childhood, Pembroke College, Oxford, 1728; left after four terms because of poverty; intermittent country-schoolmastering; married much older widow, 1735; to London, 1737, with pupil, Garrick; contributed to *The Gentleman's Magazine* parliamentary reports, etc.; adaptation of Juvenal's satire, *London*, 1738; *Life of Savage* (1744), record of friendship shared in poverty; preparing ed. of Shakespeare and dictionary; *The Vanity of Human Wishes* and production of tragedy *Irene* by Garrick, 1749; *The Rambler* twice weekly, 1750–2; wife died, 1752; contributed to *The Adventurer*, 1753–4; fame with *Dictionary of the English Language*, 1755, after rejecting Lord Chesterfield's belated offer of patronage; *The Idler* weekly, 1758–60; *Rasselas*, Abyssinian moral tale, 1759; government pension, 1762, brought leisure for company and conversation; met Boswell, 1763, and the Thrales, 1764, with whom he often stayed at Streatham; founded 'The Club', 1764; ed. of Shakespeare, 1765; series of Tory pamphlets in 1770s; journey to Highlands and Skye with Boswell, 1773, recorded in *Journey to the Western Islands of Scotland* (1775) and in Boswell's *Tour* (1785); at request of London booksellers, 1777, wrote *Lives of the Poets* (1779–81); buried Westminster Abbey, after quarter-century of almost undisputed literary predominance.

Life by J. Boswell (2 vols., London, 1791; ed. G. B. Hill, 6 vols., Oxford, 1887; rev. L. F. Powell, 1934–50; in E.L. and O.S.A.); J. W. Krutch (New York, 1944; London, 1948); J. L. Clifford (London, 1955)

Works ed. A. Murphy (12 vols., London, 1792, etc.); (11 vols., Oxford, 1825); ed. H. W. Liebert *et al.* (New Haven, 1958 – in progress)

Prose and Poetry (selected) ed. R. W. Chapman (Oxford, 1922); ed. M. Wilson (London, 1950)

Poems ed. D. Nicol Smith and E. L. McAdam (Oxford, 1941)

Rasselas ed. R. W. Chapman (Oxford, 1927); in E.L.

Johnson on Shakespeare (selections) ed. Sir W. Raleigh (London, 1908)

Journey to the Western Islands ed. R. W. Chapman (Oxford, 1924)

Lives of the Poets ed. G. B. Hill (3 vols., Oxford, 1905; in E.L. and W.C.)

The Critical Opinions of Johnson ed. J. E. Brown (Princeton, 1926)

Johnsonian Miscellanies ed. G. B. Hill (2 vols., Oxford, 1897)

Letters ed. R. W. Chapman (3 vols., Oxford, 1952; selections in W.C.)

See J. C. Bailey, *Dr Johnson and his Circle* (London, 1913; rev. L. F. Powell, 1944)

 W. J. Bate, *The Achievement of Samuel Johnson* (New York, 1955)

 B. H. Bronson, *Johnson Agonistes* (Berkeley, 1944; Cambridge, 1946)

 R. W. Chapman, *Johnsonian and Other Essays* (Oxford, 1953)

 W. P. Courtney and D. Nichol Smith, *A Bibliography of Samuel Johnson* (Oxford, 1915)

 D. J. Greene, *The Politics of Samuel Johnson* (New Haven, 1960)

 D. J. Greene (ed.) *Samuel Johnson: A Collection of Critical Essays* (New Jersey, 1965)

 J. H. Hagstrum, *Samuel Johnson's Literary Criticism* (Minneapolis, 1952)

 F. W. Hilles (ed.) *New Light on Dr Johnson* (New Haven, 1960)

 P. H. Houston, *Dr Johnson. A Study in Eighteenth-Century Humanism* (Cambridge, Mass., 1923)

 Johnson, Boswell and their Circle. Essays Presented to L. F. Powell (Oxford, 1965)

 F. R. Leavis, in *The Common Pursuit* (London, 1952; Harmondsworth, 1962)

 Sir W. Raleigh, *Six Essays on Johnson* (Oxford, 1910)

 S. C. Roberts, *Doctor Johnson* (London, 1935)

 R. B. Voitle, *Samuel Johnson the Moralist* (Cambridge, Mass., 1961)

 W. B. C. Watkins, *Johnson and English Poetry before 1660* (Princeton, 1936)

 M. Whaba (ed.) *Johnsonian Studies, including a Bibliography, 1950–60* (Cairo, 1962)

 W. K. Wimsatt, *The Prose Style of Samuel Johnson* (New Haven, 1941)

LAW, WILLIAM (1686–1761): Theologian; b. King's Cliffe, near Stamford; fellow of Emmanuel College, Cambridge, 1711; refused oaths to George I; controversies with latitudinarians and deists; *A Serious Call to a Devout and Holy Life* (1728), manual of Christian behaviour, inspired the Wesleys; tutor in Gibbon family, 1728–40; centre of small spiritual community at King's Cliffe from 1740.

Life by J. H. Overton (London, 1881)

Works ed. G. B. Morgan (9 vols., Brockenhurst, 1892–3)

A Serious Call ed. J. H. Overton (London, 1898); ed. C. Bigg (London, 1899); in E.L.

Selected Mystical Writings ed. W. L. and S. H. Hobhouse (London, 1938)

See H. Talon, *William Law: A Study in Literary Craftsmanship* (London, 1948)

LOCKE, JOHN (1632–1704): Philosopher; b. Somerset; educated Winchester, Christ Church, Oxford; lecturer on rhetoric and moral philosophy at Oxford; physician in house of Earl of Shaftesbury, 1667; *Essay concerning Toleration*, 1667; F.R.S., 1668; various official posts; in France, 1675–9; resided in Oxford, expelled for supposed complicity in Shaftesbury's plots, 1684; lived in Holland; restored to public offices by William III; *Essays concerning Human Understanding*, 1690; *Treatise of Government*, 1609; *On Education*, 1693; *Reasonableness of Christianity*, 1695. The great empirical rationalist of modern philosophy.

Life by H. R. Fox Bourne (2 vols., London, 1876); M. Cranston (London, 1957)

Educational Writings ed. J. W. Adamson (Cambridge, 1912; rev. 1922)

Essay concerning Human Understanding ed. A. S. Pringle-Pattison (Oxford, 1924); abr. in E.L.

Two Treatises of Government ed. W. F. Carpenter (E.L., 1924)

See R. I. Aaron, *John Locke* (London, 1937)

S. Alexander, *Locke* (London, 1908)

J. W. Gough, *John Locke's Political Philosophy* (Oxford, 1950)

K. MacLean, *John Locke and English Literature of the Eighteenth Century* (New Haven, 1936)

D. J. O'Connor, *John Locke* (Pelican, 1952)

E. L. Tuveson, *The Imagination as a Means of Grace. Locke and the Aesthetics of Romanticism* (Berkeley, 1960)

B. Willey, *The Seventeenth-Century Background* (London, 1934)

MACKENZIE, HENRY (1745–1831): Novelist; b. and educated Edinburgh, a leader in its political, legal, literary life; novels of 'sensibility', *The Man of Feeling* (1771, a 'bosom favourite' of Burns), *The Man of the World* (1773), *Julia de Roubigné* (1777); also four plays; periodicals, *The Mirror* (1779–80) and *The Lounger* (1785–7); interested in German literature. Dubbed by Scott the 'Northern Addison'.

Life by H. W. Thompson, *A Scottish Man of Feeling* (Oxford, 1931)

Works (8 vols., Edinburgh, 1808)

The Man of Feeling ed. B. Vickers (London, 1967)

MACPHERSON, JAMES (1736–96): 'Translator' of Gaelic poems;

b. Scottish Highlands, son of farmer; Aberdeen and Edinburgh Universities; schoolteacher; *Fragments of Ancient Poetry ... translated from the Gaelic or Erse Language*, 1760; followed up success with 'translations' of Gaelic poet Ossian, *Fingal* (1762), *Temora* (1763), largely his own invention; gratified current hunger throughout Europe for primitive national poetry; authenticity challenged by Dr Johnson and others; political posts in America and London; buried Westminster Abbey.

> Life by T. B. Saunders (London, 1894)
> *The Works of Ossian* ed. W. Sharp (Edinburgh, 1896); ed. O. L. Jiriczek (3 vols., Heidelberg, 1940)
> See J. S. Smart, *James Macpherson* (London, 1905)
>   E. D. Snyder, *The Celtic Revival in English Literature* (Cambridge, Mass., 1923)
>   P. Van Tieghem, *Le Préromantisme* II (Paris, 1930)

NEWTON, SIR ISAAC (1642–1727): Mathematician and natural philosopher; b. Woolsthorpe, Lincs.; Grantham School; fellow of Trinity College, Cambridge; made numerous advances in mathematics and conceived idea of universal gravitation, 1665–6; F.R.S., 1672; laws of motion and theory of gravitation expounded in *Philosophiae Naturalis Principia Mathematica*, 1687; president of Royal Society, 1703–27; theories of light and colour in *Opticks*, 1704; quarrel with Leibniz over priority of invention of 'method of fluxions'; master of Mint, 1699; knighted, 1705; also wrote on theology and biblical chronology; buried Westminster Abbey.

> Life by Sir D. Brewster (2 vols., Edinburgh, 1855; 1860); L. T. More (New York, 1934); E. N. da C. Andrade (London, 1950)
> *Correspondence* ed. H. W. Turnbull (3 vols., Cambridge, 1959–61)
> See M. H. Nicolson, *Newton Demands the Muse* (Princeton, 1946)

OLDHAM, JOHN (1653–83): Poet and satirist; son of Gloucestershire dissenting minister; educated Tetbury and St Edmund Hall, Oxford; usher and private tutor, 1676–81; 'set up for a wit' in London, 1681; wrote amorous verse, pindaric odes, imitations of classical and French writers; chiefly remembered for ironical *Satyr against Vertue* (1679) and political *Satyrs upon the Jesuits* (1681); *Poems and Translations*, 1683; eulogized by Waller and Dryden.

> *Poetical Works* ed. R. Bell (London, 1854); ed. B. Dobrée (London, 1960)
> See H. F. Brooks, 'A Bibliography of John Oldham', with biographical and critical introduction, in *Oxford Bibliographical Soc. Proc.* V (1936)

OTWAY, THOMAS (1652–85): Dramatist; b. Sussex; Winchester and Christ Church, Oxford; failed as actor; unrequited passion for Mrs Barry, the actress; success of rhymed heroic tragedy, *Don Carlos*, 1676; with army in Holland, 1678; adaptations of Racine and Molière and mediocre comedies; added sentimental pathos to heroic manner in blank verse tragedies, *The Orphan* (1680), and *Venice Preserv'd* (1682), both frequently revived on stage; dissipated life, died destitute.

Life by R. G. Ham, *Otway and Lee* (New Haven, 1931)
Works ed. J. C. Ghosh (2 vols., Oxford, 1932)
Best Plays ed. R. Noel (London, 1888)
Venice Preserved in *Restoration Plays* (E.L.) and *Restoration Tragedies* (W.C.)
See B. Dobrée, *Restoration Tragedy* (Oxford, 1929)
   S. Johnson, *Lives of the Poets* (ed. G. B. Hill, vol. I, Oxford, 1905)

PEPYS, SAMUEL (1633–1703): Diarist and public servant; son of London tailor from Huntingdonshire; St Paul's School, Trinity Hall and Magdalene College, Cambridge; love-match with French girl, Elizabeth St Michel, 1655; served relative, Edward Montagu (Earl of Sandwich), with whom brought Charles II from Holland, 1660; energetic official and reformer of abuses as Clerk of Acts in Navy Office, etc.; lover of wine, women, music, theatre, books, business, and money; record in cipher of private life and public events, 1660–9, in *Diary*; Secretary to Admiralty, 1672; imprisoned in Tower during Popish Plot, 1679; voyage to Tangier, 1683; president of Royal Society, 1684; again Secretary to Admiralty, 1684; deprived of office after Revolution, 1689; retirement at Clapham.

Life by A. Bryant (3 vols., Cambridge, 1933–8)
Diary ed. H. B. Wheatley (10 vols., London, 1893–9); in E.L.
Private Correspondence, etc. ed. J. R. Tanner (2 vols., London, 1926)
Further Correspondence ed. J. R. Tanner (London, 1929)
Letters and Second Diary ed. R. G. Howarth (London, 1932)
The Letters of Samuel Pepys and his Family Circle ed. H. T. Heath (Oxford, 1955)
See C. Marburg, *Mr Pepys and Mr Evelyn* (Philadelphia, 1925)
   Lord A. Ponsonby, *Samuel Pepys* (London, 1928)
   J. R. Tanner, *Mr Pepys. An Introduction to the Diary* (London, 1925)
   J. H. Wilson, *The Private Life of Mr Pepys* (New York, 1959)

POPE, ALEXANDER (1688–1744): Poet; b. London, son of Roman Catholic linen-draper; precocious child, health ruined by early illness; lived in Windsor Forest, 1700–16; debarred by religion from universities; introduced by Wycherley to London life, c. 1704; already

polished poet in *Pastorals*, 1709 (written earlier); quarrel with Ambrose
Philips; *Essay on Criticism* (1711) brought him into Addison's circle;
Rape of the Lock, 1712 (enlarged, 1714); political allusions in *Windsor
Forest* (1713) appealed to Tories; lifelong friendship with Swift;
breach with Addison, 1715; *Poems*, 1717; moved to Twickenham,
1719; friendship with Lady Mary Wortley Montagu and Martha
Blount; fortune and fame with verse translations, *Iliad* (1715-20),
Odyssey (1725-6); attacked for religion and incompetence in Greek;
ed. of Shakespeare, attacked by Theobald, 1725; turned to ethical
poems and satires; *The Dunciad*, with Theobald as mock hero, 1728
(enlarged, 1729; recast, 1742, Cibber replacing Theobald as 'hero';
complete, four books, 1743); *An Essay on Man*, 1732-4; four *Moral
Essays*, 1731-5, on false taste, on avarice, on characters of men and
women; *Imitations of Horace*, 1733-8, satirizing social follies, political
corruption, with defence of own life and art; pub. private correspondence by devious methods, 1735-42; buried Twickenham.

Life by G. Sherburn, *The Early Career of Alexander Pope* (Oxford, 1934)
Works ed. W. Elwin and W. J. Courthope (10 vols., London, 1871-89)
Poems (Twickenham Ed.) ed. J. Butt, *et al.* (10 vols., London, 1939-67;
    1 vol. 1963)
Poetical Works ed. H. Davis (London, 1966)
Prose Works ed. N. Ault (vol. 1 only, *Earlier Works, 1711-20*, Oxford 1936)
Correspondence ed. G. Sherburn (5 vols., Oxford, 1956; selections in w.c.)
See L. I. Bredvold, 'The Gloom of the Tory Satirists', in *Pope and his
    Contemporaries* ed. J. L. Clifford and L. A. Landa (Oxford, 1949)
    R. A. Brower, *Alexander Pope: The Poetry of Allusion* (Oxford, 1959)
    J. Butt, 'The Inspiration of Pope's Poetry', in *Essays on the Eighteenth
    Century Presented to David Nichol Smith* (Oxford, 1945)
    P. Dixon, *The World of Pope's Satires* (London, 1968)
    R. H. Griffith, *Alexander Pope: A Bibliography* (Austin, Texas, 1922-7)
    S. Johnson, *Lives of the Poets* (vol. III, Oxford, 1905)
    D. Knight, *Pope and the Heroic Tradition* (New Haven, 1951)
    G. W. Knight, *Laureate of Peace: On the Genius of Alexander Pope*
    (London, 1954)
    F. R. Leavis, *Revaluation* (London, 1936; Harmondsworth, 1964)
    M. Mack (ed.) *Essential Articles for the Study of Alexander Pope*
    (Hamden, Conn., 1964; London, 1965)
    M. Mack, 'The Muse of Satire', in *Yale Review* XLI (1951)
    M. Mack. 'On Reading Pope', in *College English* VII (1946)
    M. Mack, ' "Wit and Poetry and Pope" ': Some Observations on his
    Imagery', in *Pope and his Contemporaries* (as above: L. I. Bredvold)
    R. P. Parkin, *The Poetic Workmanship of Alexander Pope* (Minneapolis,
    1955)
    R. W. Rogers, *The Major Satires of Alexander Pope* (Urbana, 1955)
    R. K. Root, *The Poetical Career of Alexander Pope* (Princeton, 1938)

G. Sherburn, 'Pope at Work', in *Essays on the Eighteenth Century* (as above, J. Butt)

E. Sitwell, *Alexander Pope* (London, 1930)

Sir L. Stephen, *Pope* (London, 1880)

G. Tillotson. *On the Poetry of Pope* (Oxford, 1938; 1950)

G. Tillotson, *Pope and Human Nature* (Oxford, 1958)

A. Warren, *Alexander Pope as Critic and Humanist* (Princeton, 1929)

A. L. Williams, *Pope's Dunciad: A Study of Its Meaning* (Methuen, 1955)

PRIOR, MATTHEW (1664–1721): Poet and diplomatist; b. Wimbourne, son of joiner; Westminster and St John's College, Cambridge, under patronage of Earl of Dorset; wrote verses, Latin and English, from boyhood, Spenser his favourite poet; with Montagu burlesqued Dryden's *Hind and the Panther*, 1687; diplomat in Holland and France; as secret agent in Paris, 1711, negotiated Treaty of Utrecht for Tories; imprisoned by Whigs, 1715–16; magnificent subscription ed. of *Poems*, 1718; with proceeds and £4000 from Lord Harley purchased Down Hall, Essex; noted for epigrams, familiar, occasional, and narrative verse; also wrote long philosophical poems; buried Westminster Abbey.

Life by F. Bickley (London, 1914); L. G. W. Legg (Cambridge, 1921); C. K. Eves (New York, 1939)

Literary Works ed. H. B. Wright and M. K. Spears (2 vols., Oxford, 1959)

Selected Poems ed. A Dobson (London, 1889); ed. F. Bickley (London, 1923)

See O. Doughty, 'The Poet of the "Familiar Style" ', in *English Studies* VII (1925)

RAY, JOHN (1627–1705): Naturalist; b. Essex, son of blacksmith; educated Braintree and Trinity College, Cambridge; met group of eager young scientists; influenced by Cambridge Platonists; during illness began study of plants; travelled extensively in Great Britain recording flora and fauna, 1658–62, and in Europe, 1663–6, visiting leading scientists; F.R.S., 1667; began scientific classiffcation of species; the founder of modern biological science; wrote also on dialects, proverbs, religion.

Life by C. E. Raven (Cambridge, 1942)

See B. Willey, *The Eighteenth-Century Background* (London, 1940)

RICHARDSON, SAMUEL (1689–1761): Printer and novelist: b. Derbyshire, son of joiner; little education; apprenticed to London printer, whose daughter he married; set up printing business; compiled manual of letter-writing for uneducated people, with directions 'how to think

and act justly and prudently in the common Concerns of Human Life',
1741; led to epistolary novels, *Pamela* (1740–1), *Clarissa Harlowe* (1747–
8); European fame; *Sir Charles Grandison* (1753–4); made many feminine
friendships.

> Life by A. L. Barnauld (London, 1804); A. D. McKillop (Chapel Hill,
> 1936)
> *Works* ed. Sir L. Stephen (12 vols., London, 1883–4)
> *Novels* ed. A. Dobson and W. L. Phelps (19 vols., London, 1902); (19
> vols., Oxford, 1930)
> *Pamela*; *Clarissa* (in E.L.)
> *Selected Letters of Samuel Richardson*, ed. John Carroll (Oxford, 1964)
> *Familiar Letters, etc.* (1741; ed. B. W. Downs, London, 1928)
> See E. Birkhead, 'Sentiment and Sensibility in the Eighteenth-Century
> Novel', in E. & S. XI (1925)
>> F. S. Boas, 'Richardson's Novels and their Influence', in E. & S. II
>> (1911)
>> R. F. Brissenden, *Samuel Richardson* (London, 1958)
>> P. Dottin, *Samuel Richardson, Imprimeur de Londres* (Paris, 1931)
>> B. W. Downs, *Samuel Richardson* (London, 1928)
>> A. Kettle, *An Introduction to the English Novel* I (London, 1951)
>> B. Kriessman, *Pamela-Shamela: A Study of the Criticisms, Burlesques,
>> Parodies and Adaptations of Richardson's 'Pamela'* (Lincoln, Nebraska,
>> 1960)
>> F. R. Leavis, *The Great Tradition* (London, 1948)
>> A. D. McKillop, *The Early Masters of English Fiction* (Kansas, 1956)
>> A. D. McKillop, 'Epistolary Technique in Richardson's Novels',
>> *Rice Institute Pamphlet* XXXVIII (1951)
>> A. D. McKillop, *Samuel Richardson: Printer and Novelist* (North
>> Carolina, 1936)
>> V. S. Pritchett, 'Clarissa', in *The Living Novel* (London, 1949)
>> B. L. Reid, 'Justice to Pamela', *The Hudson Review*, IX, No. 4 (1957)
>> W. M. Sale, 'From *Pamela* to *Clarissa*', in *The Age of Johnson* (New
>> Haven, 1959)
>> Sir L. Stephen, *Hours in a Library* I (London, 1874; 1909)
>> D. Van Ghent, 'Clarissa Harlowe', in *The English Novel, Form and
>> Function* (New York, 1935)
>> I. Watt, *The Rise of the Novel* (London, 1957)
>> *Critical Remarks on Sir Charles Grandison, Clarissa and Pamela, by a
>> Lover of Virtue* (1754; reproduced in *Augustan Reprints*, Los Angeles,
>> 1950)

ROCHESTER, JOHN WILMOT, EARL OF (1647–80): Poet, wit, satirist,
courtier, libertine; b. Ditchley, Oxfordshire; succeeded to earldom,
1658; educated Burford, Wadham College, Oxford; travelled on
Continent, 1661–5; studied at Padua; at Court, 1665; fought in war
against Dutch, 1665–6; favourite of Charles II, by whom frequently

banished from Court and pardoned; most notorious of group of noble rakes; Paris, 1669; patron of poets, including Dryden; *Satyr against Mankind*, c. 1675–6; wrote amorous lyrics; conversations with Burnet, 1679–80; seriously ill, 'conversion', public recantation, June, 1680; d. Woodstock.

Life by V. de S. Pinto, *Enthusiast in Wit* (London, 1935; rev. 1962)
Collected Works ed. J. Hayward (London, 1926)
Poems ed. V. de S. Pinto (London, 1953; rev. 1964)
Poems on Several Occasions ed. J. Thorpe (Princeton, 1950)
The Rochester–Savile Letters, 1671–1680 ed. J. H. Wilson (Columbus, Ohio, 1941)
See S. F. Crocker, 'Rochester's *Satire against Mankind*', in *West Virginia Univ. Studies* III (1937)
F. R. Leavis, *Revaluation* (London, 1936; Harmondsworth, 1964)
K. B. Murdock, ' "A Very Profane Wit" ', in *The Sun at Noon* (New York, 1939)
J. Prinz, *John Wilmot, Earl of Rochester* (Leipzig, 1927)
C. Williams, *Rochester* (London, 1935)
J. H. Wilson, *The Court Wits of the Restoration* (Princeton, 1948)

SHADWELL, THOMAS (?1642–92): Dramatist and poet; b. Norfolk; educated Bury St Edmunds, Caius College, Cambridge, Middle Temple; travelled abroad; after 1668 produced dramatic pieces almost yearly, pictures of contemporary manners in tradition of Jonson's comedy of humours; feud with Dryden from 1682 and ridiculed by him in *MacFlecknoe* and *The Medall*; superseded Dryden as poet laureate and historiographer after the Revolution.

Life by A. S. Borgman (New York, 1928)
Complete Works ed. M. Summers (5 vols., London, 1927)
Best Plays ed. G. Saintsbury (London, 1903)
See B. Dobrée, *Restoration Comedy* (Oxford, 1924)
C. Lloyd, 'Shadwell and the Virtuosi', in P.M.L.A. XLIV (1929)

SHAFTESBURY, ANTHONY ASHLEY COOPER, THIRD EARL OF (1671–1713): Moral philosopher; pupil of Locke, whose philosophy he rejected; Winchester School; travelled in Europe; M.P., 1695–8; earldom, 1699; abandoned public life because of ill-health; *Characteristicks of Men, Manners, Opinions, Times*, 3 vols., 1711; d. Naples. Deist, Platonist, churchman; 'optimistic' philosophy, that man is naturally virtuous, the 'Moral Sentiment'.

Life by R. L. Brett (London, 1951)
Characteristics ed. J. M. Robertson (2 vols., London, 1900)

See W. E. Alderman, 'Shaftesbury and the Doctrine of Benevolence in the Eighteenth Century', in *Trans. Wisconsin Academy* XXVI (1931)

W. E. Alderman, 'Shaftesbury and the Doctrine of Moral Sense in the Eighteenth Century', in P.M.L.A. XLVI (1931)

C. A. Moore, 'Shaftesbury and the Ethical Poets in England, 1700–1760', in *Backgrounds of English Literature, 1700–1760* (Minneapolis, 1953)

V. de S. Pinto. *The Restoration Court Poets* (1965)

C. Vieth, *Attribution in Restoration Poetry* (1963)

B. Willey, *The Eighteenth-Century Background* (London, 1940)

SHENSTONE, WILLIAM (1714–63): Poet; contemporary of Samuel Johnson at Pembroke College, Oxford; laid out estate, Leasowes, according to newer modes of gardening; Spenserian imitation. *The Schoolmistress* (1737–42–8) and *Pastoral Ballad* (1755), continuing tradition of descriptive poetry; also wrote elegies, odes, songs, ballads, essays, and lively letters.

Life by M. Williams (Birmingham, 1935); A. R. Humphreys (Cambridge, 1937)

Poetical Works ed. G. Gilfillan (Edinburgh, 1854)

Letters ed. M. Williams (Oxford, 1939); ed. D. Mallam (Minneapolis, 1939)

See C. E. de Haas, *Nature and the Country in English Poetry* (Amsterdam, 1928)

SHERIDAN, RICHARD BRINSLEY (1751–1816): Dramatist and orator; son of actor-elocutionist; educated Harrow; moved to Bath; escorted beautiful singer, Elizabeth Linley, to France, fought two duels with her persecutor and married her, 1773; *The Rivals, St Patrick's Day, The Duenna* produced, 1775; acquired Garrick's share in Drury Lane Theatre, 1776; *A Trip to Scarborough* and *The School for Scandal* produced there, 1777; burlesque farce, *The Critic*, 1779; M.P., and government offices, 1780–1812; celebrated speeches impeaching Warren Hastings, 1787–8; confidential adviser to Prince of Wales; debts and brain disease in last years. A man of brilliant wit and charm, of gaiety and gallantry; splendid public funeral.

Life by W. Sichel (2 vols., London, 1909); R. C. Rhodes (Oxford, 1933)

Plays and Poems ed. R. C. Rhodes (3 vols., Oxford, 1928)

Plays ed. A. W. Pollard (London, 1900); also in E.L., O.S.A., and W.C.

The Letters ed. C. Price (3 vols., Oxford, 1966)

See J. Dulck, *Les Comédies de R. B. Sheridan: Étude Littéraire* (Paris, 1962)

T. H. Sadler, *The Political Career of Sheridan* (Oxford, 1912)

SMART, CHRISTOPHER (1722–71): Poet; Durham School and Cambridge; fellow of Pembroke Hall, 1740–9; convivial alehouse companion; journalist, wit, satirist in London; debts and religious mania; in madhouse, 1757–63; belated recognition of masterpiece, *A Song to David* (1763); *Jubilate Agno* composed during madness, which it imaginatively documents.

Life by E. G. Ainsworth and C. E. Noyes (Columbia, Mo., 1943)

Collected Poems ed. N. Callan (2 vols., London, 1949)

Rejoice in the Lamb ed. W. F. Stead (London, 1939)

A Song to David ed. E. Blunden (London, 1924); ed. P. Searle (London, 1924); facsimile (Oxford, 1926); ed. J. B. Broadbent (London, 1960)

See C. Devlin, *Poor Kit Smart* (London, 1961)

    A. Rodway, *The Romantic Conflict* (London, 1963)

    P. M. Spacks, *The Poetry of Vision* (Cambridge, Mass., 1966)

SMITH, ADAM (1723–90): Political economist; b. Kirkcaldy; Glasgow University; Balliol College, Oxford; professor of logic, Glasgow, 1751, of moral philosophy, 1752; friend of Hume; *Theory of the Moral Sentiments*, 1759; visited France, met Voltaire, 1764; studious retirement at Kirkcaldy, 1767; originated scientific study of economics with *An Enquiry into the Nature and Causes of the Wealth of Nations*, 1776; member of Johnson's Literary Club.

Life by J. Rae (London, 1895)

The Wealth of Nations ed. E. Cannan (2 vols., London, 1904; 1920) also in E.L. and W.C.

See Sir A. Gray, *Adam Smith* (London, 1948)

    W. R. Scott, *Adam Smith as Student and Professor* (Glasgow, 1937)

SMOLLETT, TOBIAS GEORGE (1721–71): Surgeon, journalist, and novelist; b. Dumbartonshire, of good family; studied medicine at Glasgow University; to London, 1739 (see *Roderick Random*); naval surgeon during warfare in West Indies, 1740–4 (see *Roderick Random*); London surgeon, 1744; *Roderick Random* (anon.) and trans. *Gil Blas*, 1748; *Peregrine Pickle*, 1751; *Ferdinand Count Fathom*, 1753; trans. *Don Quixote*, 1755; *Sir Launcelot Greaves*, 1760–2, in instalments; ed. *Critical Review*, 1756–63; popular *History of England*, 1757; fined, imprisoned for libel, 1759; ed. pro-government *The Briton*, 1762–3; from 1763 travelled widely in search of health; *Travels through France and Italy*, 1766; to Italy, 1769; *Humphry Clinker*, 1771; d. Leghorn.

Life by L. L. Martz, *The Later Career* (New Haven, 1942); G. M. Kahrl (Chicago, 1945); L. M. Knapp (Princeton, 1949)

Works ed. W. E. Henley and T. Seccombe (12 vols., London, 1899–1901);
  ed. G. Saintsbury (12 vols., London, 1895, etc.)
Novels (11 vols., Oxford, 1925–6)
Roderick Random (E.L.; W.C.); *Peregrine Pickle* (E.L.; O.E.N.); *Humphry
  Clinker* (E.L.; W.C.; Harmondsworth, English Library, 1967; O.E.N.);
  Travels (W.C.)
Letters ed. E. S. Noyes (Cambridge, Mass., 1926); ed. F. Cordasco (Madrid,
  1949)
See H. S. Buck, *Smollett as Poet* (New Haven, 1927)
  H. S. Buck, *A Study in Smollett* (New Haven, 1925)
  W. Hazlitt, *The English Comic Writers* (London, 1819; in E.L. and
  W.C.)
  C. E. Jones, *Smollett Studies* (Los Angeles, 1942)

STEELE, SIR RICHARD (1672–1729): Essayist, dramatist, and politician;
b. Dublin; Charterhouse (with Addison) and Merton College, Oxford;
captain in Life Guards; dissipated living but wrote edifying treatise,
The Christian Hero, 1701; comedies produced, *The Funeral* (1701)
The Lying Lover (1703), *The Tender Husband* (1705); official gazetteer,
1707; second wife, Mary Scurlock ('dear Prue'); heavy drinking and
debts; *The Tatler*, 1709–11; lost gazetteership, 1710; *The Spectator*,
with Addison, 1711–12; *The Guardian*, attacked by Tories, 1713;
Whig M.P., 1713; pamphlets against Swift and government; *The
Englishman*, 1713–14; expelled from parliament, 1714; new appoint-
ments under Hanoverians, and knighted, 1715; quarrelled with
Addison, 1718; last comedy, *The Conscious Lovers*, 1722; driven from
London by debts; d. Carmarthen.

Life by G. A. Aitken (2 vols., London, 1889); C. Winton, *The Early
  Career of Richard Steele* (Baltimore, 1964)
Dramatic Works ed. G. A. Aitken (London, 1894; Mermaid ed., 1903)
The Christian Hero ed. R. Blanchard (Oxford, 1932)
The Tatler ed. G. A. Aitken (4 vols., London, 1898–9); selections in E.L.
The Spectator ed. G. G. Smith (8 vols., London, 1897–8; E.L., 1907); ed.
  D. F. Bond (5 vols., Oxford, 1965)
The Englishman ed. R. Blanchard (Oxford, 1955)
Periodical Journalism, 1714–16 ed. R. Blanchard (Oxford, 1959)
Tracts and Pamphlets ed. R. Blanchard (Baltimore, 1944)
Correspondence ed. R. Blanchard (Oxford, 1941)
Selected Essays ed. L. E. Steele (London, 1902)
See bibliography under *Prose* (p. 458)
    F. W. Bateson, *English Comic Drama, 1700–1750* (Oxford, 1929)
    B. Dobrée, *Variety of Ways* (Oxford, 1932)
    W. Hazlitt, *The English Comic Writers* (London, 1819; in E.L. and W.C.)

STERNE, LAURENCE (1713–68): Novelist and clergyman; b. Clonmel, Ireland, son of poor lieutenant; school near Halifax; cared for by uncle; Jesus College, Cambridge; ordained, 1737; vicar of Sutton-in-the-Forest, 1738; prebend of York Minster, 1741; married, 1741; first two vols. of *Tristram Shandy* (1760) denounced on moral and literary grounds; later vols., 1761–7; visited London, 1760, great social success; *Sermons of Mr Yorick*, 1760; because of ill-health travelled abroad, 1762–4, 1765–6; fell in love with Mrs Draper, 1767 (*Journal to Eliza*); separation from wife; *A Sentimental Journey through France and Italy*, 1768; d. London, in debt but not poverty-stricken.

> Life by W. L. Cross (New York, 1909; rev., 2 vols., New Haven, 1925; 1929); T. Yoseloff (New York, 1945)
>
> *Works* ed. G. Saintsbury (6 vols., London, 1894); ed. W. L. Cross (12 vols., New York, 1904); (7 vols., Oxford, 1926–7)
>
> *Tristram Shandy*; *A Sentimental Journey* (in E.L., W.C., Penguin)
>
> *Tristram Shandy* ed. I. Watt (Boston, 1965)
>
> *Letters* ed. L. P. Curtis (Oxford, 1934)
>
> *Selected Works* ed. D. Grant (London, 1950)
>
> See L. P. Curtis, *The Politicks of Laurence Sterne* (Oxford, 1929)
>> E. N. Dilworth, *The Unsentimental Journey of Laurence Sterne* (New York, 1948)
>>
>> H. Fluchère, *Laurence Sterne, From Tristram to Yorick* (London, 1965)
>>
>> L. Hartley, *Laurence Sterne in the Twentieth Century* (Chapel Hill, 1966)
>>
>> D. W. Jefferson, '*Tristram Shandy* and the Tradition of Learned Wit', in *Essays in Criticism* I (1951)
>>
>> Sir H. Read, *The Sense of Glory* (Cambridge, 1929)
>>
>> Sir L. Stephen, *Hours in a Library* III (London, 1892)
>>
>> J. Traugott, *Tristram Shandy's World* (Berkeley, Los Angeles, 1954)
>>
>> V. Woolf, 'The "Sentimental Journey"', in *The Common Reader*, Second Series (London, 1932)

SWIFT, JONATHAN (1667–1745): Satirist; b. Dublin, posthumous child of English parents; Kilkenny School, Trinity College, Dublin; entered household of Sir William Temple, 1689, where he educated Esther Johnson ('Stella'), then a small child; prebend of Kilroot, near Belfast, 1695; returned to Temple at Moor Park, 1696; defended Temple against Bentley and Wotton in *The Battle of the Books*, pub. with *A Tale of a Tub*, 1704; after Temple's death (1699), returned to Ireland; vicar of Laracor, etc., established Stella in Dublin; protracted visits to England during 1701–14; sought benefits for Irish clergy; friend of Addison, Arbuthnot, Steele, Pope; religious pamphlets and humorous pieces, *Miscellanies*, 1711; losing faith in Whigs on ecclesiastical issues, turned to Harley (Lord Oxford) and St John (Bolingbroke); political influence as Tory propagandist, *The Examiner* (1710–11), *The Conduct of the Allies* (1711), against prolongation of war with France; record of daily life in *Journal to Stella*; met Esther Vanhomrigh ('Vanessa'); dean of St Patrick's, Dublin, 1713; on fall of Tories, returned to 'exile' in Ireland, 1714; began to write on behalf of oppressed Irish, 1720; *Drapier's Letters* against 'Wood's Halfpence', 1724; national hero of Irish; Vanessa died, 1723; *Gulliver's Travels* (1721–5) pub. 1726, during visit to England; death of Stella, 1728; *Miscellanies*, 1727–8; attacked Irish bishops and Presbyterians, 1732; increasing ill-health and loss of memory, 1738; unsound in mind, 1742–5; buried St Patrick's.

Life by J. Forster (London, 1875); Sir H. Craik (2 vols., London, 1894); J. Ehrenpreis (3 vols., London and Camb., Mass., 1962 – in progress)

Prose Work ed. T. Scott (12 vols., London, 1897–1908); ed. H. Davis (14 vols., Oxford, 1939–67)

Poems ed. Sir H. Williams (3 vols., Oxford, 1937; rev. 1958); ed. J. Howell (2 vols., London, 1958)

Correspondence ed. Sir H. Williams (5 vols., Oxford, 1963–5)

Journal to Stella ed. Sir H. Williams (2 vols., Oxford, 1948)

A Tale of a Tub and The Battle of the Books, etc. ed. A. C. Guthkelch and D. Nichol Smith (Oxford, 1920; rev. 1958)

The Drapier's Letters ed. H. Davis (Oxford, 1935)

Gulliver's Travels and Selected Writings ed. J. Hayward (London, 1934)

Selected Prose Works ed. J. Hayward (London, 1949)

Swift on his Age. Selected Prose and Verse ed. C. J. Horne (London, 1953)

See C. A. Beaumont, *Swift's Classical Rhetoric* (Athens, Georgia, 1961)

    A. E. Case, *Four Essays on 'Gulliver's Travels'* (Princeton, 1945)

    H. Davis, *Jonathan Swift: Essays on his Satire and Other Studies* (New York, 1964)

    I. Ehrenpreis, *The Personality of Swift* (London, 1958)

    O. W. Ferguson, *Jonathan Swift and Ireland* (Urbana, 1962)

    Sir C. H. Firth, 'The Political Significance of *Gulliver's Travels*' in *Essays, Historical and Literary* (Oxford, 1938)

    M. P. Foster (ed.) *A Casebook on Gulliver among the Houyhnhnms* (New York, 1961)

    P. Harth, *Swift and Anglican Rationalism* (Chicago, 1961)

    L. A. Landa, *Swift and the Church of Ireland* (Oxford, 1954)

    F. R. Leavis, 'The Irony of Swift', in *The Common Pursuit* (London, 1952; Harmondsworth, 1962)

    R. Paulson, *Theme and Structure in Swift's 'Tale of a Tub'* (New Haven, 1960)

    R. Quintana, *The Mind and Art of Jonathan Swift* (London, 1936; 1953)

    R. Quintana, *Swift, An Introduction* (London, 1955)

    E. W. Rosenheim, *Swift and the Satirist's Art* (Chicago, 1963)

M. K. Starkman, *Swift's Satire on Learning in 'A Tale of a Tub'* (Princeton, 1950)

H. Teerink, *A Bibliography of the Writings of Jonathan Swift* (The Hague, 1937; 2nd. ed., rev. A. H. Scouten, Philadelphia, 1963)

E. Tuveson (ed.) *Swift: A Collection of Critical Essays* (New Jersey, 1964)

M. Voigt, *Swift and the Twentieth Century* (Detroit, 1964)

K. Williams, *Jonathan Swift and the Age of Compromise* (Lawrence, 1958)

TEMPLE, SIR WILLIAM (1628–99): Statesman and author; b. London; Emmanuel College, Cambridge; travelled abroad; met Dorothy Osborne, whom he married, 1655, after opposition of her Royalist family; in Ireland; diplomatic missions; declined political office; retired, 1681; frequently visited at Moor Park by William III; employed Swift as secretary; wrote memoirs of diplomatic missions and essays on government, gardening, etc.; *Of Ancient and Modern Learning* (1690) set going in England Ancients *v.* Moderns controversy.

Life by C. Marburg (New Haven, 1932); H. E. Woodbridge (New York, 1940)

Works (4 vols., Edinburgh, 1814)

Early Essays and Romances ed. G. C. Moore Smith (Oxford, 1930)

Essays on Ancient and Modern Learning and on Poetry ed. J. E. Spingarn (Oxford, 1909)

Five Miscellaneous Essays ed. S. H. Monk (Ann Arbor, 1963)

See Lord (T. B.) Macaulay, *Critical and Historical Essays* I (E.L., 1907)

THOMSON, JAMES (1700–48): Poet; b. Ednam, son of Scottish minister; Edinburgh University; abandoned theological training and moved to London, 1725; private tutor; *The Seasons*, 1726–30, reflecting interest in nature, science, theology; acquaintance of Arbuthnot, Gay, Pope; travelled in France and Italy as tutor to son of Lord Chancellor; *Liberty*, 1734–6; five tragedies; from 1736 lived retired at Richmond on pension, continually revising *The Seasons*; probably contributed 'Rule Britannia' to masque, *Alfred*, 1740; Spenserian allegory on his way of life, *The Castle of Indolence*, 1748; buried Richmond.

Life by L. Morel (Paris, 1895); G. C. Macaulay (London, 1908); D. Grant (London, 1951)

Works ed. Lord Lyttleton (4 vols., London, 1750, etc.)

Poetical Works ed. J. L. Robertson (London, 1908)

The Castle of Indolence and other Poems ed. A. D. McKillop (Lawrence, Kansas, 1961)

The Seasons ed. O. Zippel (Berlin, 1908)

Letters and Documents ed. A. D. McKillop (Lawrence, Kansas, 1958)

See books on eighteenth-century nature poetry, under *Poetry* (pp. 456–7)
R. Cohen, *The Art of Discrimination* (London, 1964)
S. Johnson, *Lives of the Poets* (ed. G. B. Hill, vol. III, Oxford, 1905)
J. W. Mackail, *Studies of English Poets* (London, 1926)
A. D. McKillop, *The Background of Thomson's 'Seasons'* (Minneapolis, 1942)
D. Nichol Smith, *Some Observations on Eighteenth-Century Poetry* (Oxford, 1937)
P. M. Spacks, *The Varied God* (Berkeley and Los Angeles, 1959)

VANBRUGH, SIR JOHN (1664–1726): Dramatist and architect; son of London tradesman, grandson of refugee Flemish merchant; studied architecture in France, 1683–5; entered army, 1686; imprisoned in France, 1690–92; *The Relapse*, 1696; *The Provok'd Wife*, 1697; comptroller of board of works, 1702–12, 1715; manager of Haymarket Theatre, 1705–7; designed Castle Howard, Blenheim Palace, Haymarket Theatre, etc.; knighted, 1714; among other plays, mostly from the French, were *The Country House* (1703), *The Confederacy* (1705), *The Provok'd Husband* (completed by Cibber, 1728).

Life by G. H. Lovegrove (London, 1902)
Complete Works ed. B. Dobrée and G. Webb (4 vols., London, 1927–8)
Best Plays ed. A. E. H. Swaen (London, 1896)
The Provoked Wife, in *Restoration Plays* (E.L., 1912)
See under *Drama* (pp. 459–61), studies by Boas, Dobrée, Palmer, Perry.
  B. Dobrée, *Essays in Biography* (Oxford, 1925)
  P. Mueschke and J. Fleisher, 'A Re-Valuation of Vanbrugh', in P.M.L.A. XLIX (1934)
  L. Whistler, *Sir John Vanbrugh, Architect and Dramatist* (London, 1938)

WALPOLE, HORACE, EARL OF ORFORD (1717–97): Author and collector; youngest son of Sir Robert Walpole; Eton and King's College, Cambridge; grand tour of France and Italy with Gray (*q.v.*), 1739–41; M.P., 1741–67; turned Strawberry Hill, Twickenham, into 'a little Gothic castle' and set up printing-press; wrote on noble authors, painting, engraving; 'Gothic romance', *The Castle of Otranto*, 1764; kept up lively, gossiping correspondence with friends, giving entertaining record of the age; 'the best informed gossip of his century'; succeeded to earldom, 1791.

Life by R. W. Ketton-Cremer (London, 1940; rev. 1964)
Letters ed. Mrs P. Toynbee (19 vols., Oxford, 1903–5, 1918–25); selections in E.L.
Correspondence ed. W. S. Lewis (New Haven, 1937 – in progress)
The Castle of Otranto ed. W. S. Lewis (London, 1964); also in E.L.
See I. W. U. Chase, *Horace Walpole, Gardenist* (Princeton, 1943)

W. S. Lewis, *Horace Walpole* (New York and London, 1961)
D. M. Stuart, *Horace Walpole* (London, 1927)

WARTON, JOSEPH (1722–1800): Critic and poet; educated Winchester, Oriel College, Oxford; clergyman; notably unsuccessful headmaster of Winchester, 1766–93; friend of poet Collins; *Odes*, 1744, 1746, avoiding didacticism and showing feeling for nature; *Essay on the Genius and Writing of Mr Pope*, 1756–82, admiring him but condemning imitators; friend of Johnson and circle; edited Pope, 1797.

Life by J. Wooll (London, 1806)
The Three Wartons. A Choice of their Verse ed. E. Partridge (London, 1927)
See W. L. Macdonald, *Pope and his Critics* (London, 1951)
   H. Trowbridge, 'Joseph Warton on the Imagination', in M.P.
   XXXV (1937)

WARTON, THOMAS (1728–90): Critic and poet; Trinity College, Oxford; *Pleasures of Melancholy*, 1747; ed. collections of verse and classical texts; *Observations on the Faery Queen* (1754) the first adequate criticism of Spenser; professor of poetry, Oxford, 1757–67; pioneer *History of English Poetry*, 1774–81; professor of ancient history, Oxford, 1785–90; poet laureate, 1785–90; ed. Milton's early poems, 1785; wrote humorous verse, sonnets, and poems inspired by antiquarian interests; friend of Dr Johnson.

Life by C. Rinaker (Urbana, 1916)
Poems ed. R. Mant (2 vols., Oxford, 1802)
The Three Wartons. A Choice of Verse ed. E. Partridge (London, 1927)
See W. P. Ker, *Collected Essays* I (London, 1925)
   D. Nichol Smith, 'Warton's History of English Poetry', in *Proc. of British Academy* (1929)
   R. Wellek, *The Rise of English Literary History* (Chapel Hill, 1941)

WINCHILSEA, ANNE FINCH, COUNTESS OF (1661–1720): Poet; née Kingsmill, ancient Hampshire family; maid of honour at Court, 1683–4; withdrew on marriage to Heneage Finch, later Earl of Winchilsea; Eastwell Park, Kent, from 1689; *Miscellany Poems by a Lady*, 1713; other poems remained in MS.; friend of Pope and Rowe; her *Nocturnal Reverie* noticed by Wordsworth for its new images of rural nature.

Poems ed. M. Reynolds (Chicago, 1903); also in *Minor Poets of the Eighteenth Century* (E.L., 1930)
See R. A. Brower, 'Lady Winchilsea and the Poetic Tradition of the Seventeenth Century', in S.P. XLII (1945)

H. S. Hughes, 'Lady Winchilsea and her Friends', in *London Mercury* XIX (1929)

J. M. Murry, 'Anne Finch', in *New Adelphi* I (1927)

WYCHERLEY, WILLIAM (1640?–1716): Dramatist; b. Clive, near Shrewsbury; became Roman Catholic in France; Inner Temple and Queen's College, Oxford; *Love in a Wood*, 1671; favoured by king's mistress, Duchess of Cleveland; *The Gentleman Dancing-Master*, 1672; commission in army, 1672; *The Country Wife*, 1672 or 3; *The Plain Dealer*, 1674; secret marriage to Countess of Drogheda displeased Charles II; imprisoned for debt; *Miscellany Poems* (1704) led to friendship with young Pope, who corrected his later verses and quarrelled; remarried just before death.

Life by C. Perromat (Paris, 1921); W. Connely (New York, 1930)
Complete Works ed. M. Summers (4 vols., London, 1924; 1965)
Complete Plays ed. G. Weales (New York, 1966)
Plays ed. W. C. Ward (London, 1888)
The Country Wife in *Restoration Plays* (E.L., 1912)
See under *Drama* (pp. 459–61), studies by Dobrée, Hazlitt, Hunt, Macaulay, Palmer, Perry.
    R. A. Zimbardo, *Wycherley's Drama* (New Haven, 1965)

YOUNG, EDWARD (1683–1765): Poet; b. Upham, near Winchester, son of clergyman; Winchester School; fellow of All Souls, Oxford; entered London literary circles; tragedies, 1719–21; satires, *The Universal Passion* (1725–8), much admired until outclassed by Pope; rector of Welwyn, 1730; failed to get expected bishopric; married daughter of Earl of Lichfield, 1731; her death inspired the 'pious gloom' of *The Complaint, or Night-Thoughts on Life, Death, and Immortality* (1742–5), which gained European fame; *Conjectures on Original Composition*, 1759.

Life by H. C. Shelley (London, 1914)
Complete Works ed. J. Doran (2 vols., London, 1854)
Poetical Works ed. J. Mitford (2 vols., London, 1830, etc.)
Conjectures on Original Composition ed. F. J. Morley (Manchester, 1918)
See I. St J. Bliss, 'Young's *Night-Thoughts* in Relation to Contemporary Christian Apologetics', in P.M.L.A. XLIX (1934)
    H. H. Clark, 'The Romanticism of Edward Young', in *Trans. Wisconsin Academy* XXIV (1929)
    J. W. Mackail, *Studies of English Poets* (London, 1926)
    W. Thomas, *Le Poète Edward Young* (Paris, 1901)

INDEX